Dan A. Pirtle

W9-BEP-466

Donald Finkel

THE ULTIMATE GUIDE

San Francisco

THE ULTIMATE GUIDE

San Francisco

RANDOLPH DELEHANTY

Drawings by William Walters
Bird's-eye views by John Tomlinson

Chronicle Books
San Francisco

Copyright © 1989 by Randolph Delehanty.
All rights reserved. No part of this book may
be reproduced in any form without written
permission from the publisher.

Printed in the United States of America.

Library of Congress
Cataloging-in-Publication Data

Delehanty, Randolph.
    San Francisco: the ultimate guide /
        Randolph Delehanty.
            p.   cm.
    Includes index.
    ISBN 0-87701-529-5
    1 San Francisco (Calif.)–Guide-books.
        I. Title.
    F869.S33D43 1989
    917.94'6'0453–dc20   89-33137
                                              CIP

Editing: Deborah Stone
Book and cover design:
    Seventeenth Street Studios
Composition: Another Point

10 9 8 7 6 5 4 3 2 1

Chronicle Books
275 Fifth Street
San Francisco, California
94103

for my grandmother
Carlota Urruela de Larrondo
1894–1981
who opened my mind to history

Contents

ACKNOWLEDGMENTS ix

SAN FRANCISCO STATISTICS xi

USING THIS GUIDE xii

PRELIMINARIES 1

TOUR ONE

Union Square 26

TOUR TWO

The Financial District 44

TOUR THREE

Chinatown 77

TOUR FOUR

To The Wharf 105

TOUR FIVE

Russian Hill 134

TOUR SIX

Nob Hill 149

TOUR SEVEN

Eastern Pacific Heights 172

TOUR EIGHT

Japantown to Cathedral Hill 192

TOUR NINE
*Mission Dolores
and the Mission District*   212

TOUR TEN
The Castro and Noe Valley   229

TOUR ELEVEN
The Haight-Ashbury   241

TOUR TWELVE
*Golden Gate Park
to Lands End*   257

TOUR THIRTEEN
*The Presidio and
Along the Golden Gate*   276

TOUR FOURTEEN
Day Trips   291

INDEX   329

Acknowledgments

Many who visit San Francisco come back to live. It happened to me. I first visited San Francisco with my parents in 1962 upon graduation from high school. I chose San Francisco as my home in 1970. I have never tired of her expressive people and her changing skies. My most heartfelt acknowledgment is to the city among whose people it is my good fortune to live and work.

My rewards have always come from those members of the public, readers, students, clients, editors, and friends—not mutually exclusive categories—who have asked me good questions and found ways to be supportive of my work. I am especially appreciative of the support my work has received from Mr. and Mrs. Albert J. Moorman and Peter M. Hirsch.

William Walters' drawings record with great precision, I think, the architectural character of San Francisco. They are from a portfolio of his drawings available from William Walters, Architectural Consulting, 1101 De Haro Street, San Francisco, CA 94107. The fine bird's-eye views of the Financial District, Chinatown, Nob Hill, and Russian Hill were field-compiled and hand-drawn by John Tomlinson and show San Francisco in the spring of 1989. For information on the four bird's-eye views in this book contact John Tomlinson, P.O. Box 8714, Portland, OR 97207.

This guide owes much to many other diligent investigators. My Union Square and Financial District chapters are built on the solid research of Michael R. Corbett's *Splendid Survivors* (1979), the benchmark architectural inventory of the downtown prepared by Charles Hall Page & Associates for The Foundation for San Francisco's Architectural Heritage. I am indebted to John Thomas Johnston for information on Union Square shops. Ralph A. Mead and the San Francisco Department of City Planning's *Jackson Square* (1971) is the primary source for the Jackson Square Historic District. Roger Olmsted and T. H. Watkins' *Here Today: San Francisco's Architectural Heritage* (1968), Sally B. Woodbridge and John M. Woodbridge's *Architecture San Francisco* (1982), and David Gebhard and others' *The Guide to Architecture in San Francisco and Northern California* (1985) are essential. My general view of American urban development owes much to Jon C. Teaford's *The Unheralded Triumph: City Government in America, 1870–1900* (1984). Peter R. Decker's *Fortunes and Failures: White-Collar Mobility in Nineteenth-Century San Francisco* (1978), and Terence T. McDonald's *The Parameters of Urban Fiscal Policy: Socioeconomic Change and Political Culture in San Francisco, 1860–1906* (1986) are modern historical scholarship's two great gifts to San Francisco's self-understanding. For the postindustrial city, John H. Mollenkopf's *The Contested City* (1983), and Chester Hartman's *The Transformation of San Francisco* (1984), are the places to start. Architect and historian Philip P. Choy generously made available to me the San Francisco Landmark Preservation Advisory Board's case report on the Chinatown historic district. Architectural historian Anne Bloomfield's work on Russian Hill is fundamental. I learned much from Mr. Seizo Oka at the CFB–Japanese American History Room of the Japanese Cultural & Community Center of Northern California. Judith Lynch and the Stanford Research Institute published the first important architectural research on the Mission District in 1974. Christopher H. Nelson and Gary A. Goss' "The Haight: History and Architecture" in the April, 1987 *Heritage Newsletter* of The Foundation for San Francisco's Architectural Heritage is basic. Charles Perry's "From Eternity to Here: What a Long Strange Trip It's Been," and the rest of the February 26, 1976 issue of *Rolling Stone*, captures the hippie flowering. Raymond H. Clary's multi-volume *The Making of Golden Gate Park* (1980 and 1987) is richly informative. Mark L. Brack and James P. Delgado and the National Park Service, Western Region's *Presidio of San Francisco National Historic Landmark District* (1985) is exemplary of the high standards of the National Park Service. I have also benefited from other U.S. Department of the Interior, National Park Service studies conducted for the Golden Gate National Recreation Area. Loren Partridge's work on John Galen Howard and the University of California, and Paul V. Turner's *The Founders and the Architects: The Design of Stanford University* (1976), are important. The California Coastal Commission's *California Coastal Resource Guide* (1987) is the essential guide to the scenic California coast. No commodius glove compartment should be without James D. Hart's practical *A Companion to California* (1986), an encyclopedia of topographical, historical, biographical, and general information and the "user's manual" to the Golden State.

For maps and copies of specialized studies published over the past eighteen years I wish to thank the San Francisco Department of City Planning. For their many years of courteous assistance I wish to thank the staffs of the San Francisco Archives at the San Francisco Public Library, the Science, Technology & Government Documents Collection at the San Francisco Public Library, the California Historical Society Library, and the Mechanics Institute Library, all in San Francisco, and the Bancroft Library at the University of California, Berkeley, and the California State Library in Sacramento.

San Francisco Statistics

Latitude 37°46'11" North, longitude 122°27'53" West at the Planetarium in Golden Gate Park. Land area about 45 square miles. Altitude ranges from sea level to 938' (at Mount Davidson). Mean annual temperature is 56.4° F; the mean temperature of the coldest month, January, is 50° F and of the warmest month, September, 61.5° F. Average annual rainfall is 21.85 inches. Incorporated April 15, 1850. City limits were set in 1856 and remain unchanged. Current City Charter in effect since 1932. San Francisco is California's only combined city and county. Municipal government is by a mayor and eleven-member Board of Supervisors elected at large. Population in 1988: 741,300. Population of the nine-county San Francisco Bay Area: 5,793,551. Estimated gross regional product of the Bay Area: $112 billion in 1985, the fourth largest market in the United States.

Using This Guide

Welcome, traveler, to the beautiful and hospitable city of Saint Francis. Nature has favored us with an incomparable setting of water, mountains, and hourly changing atmospheres. History has showered us with gold and silver and silicon and all the peoples of mankind.

The chief object of this guide is to enable the traveler to employ his or her time and money to the best advantage. It breaks the city into neighborhoods or districts with practical suggestions on parking, transit, cafés, restaurants, shopping, bars, and sometimes entertainment, at the beginning of each section. It is best to scan this first, especially for the optimal times to visit.

What makes this guide distinctive is that *it is built from the inside out.* Most of the walks here are organized around the often-almost-hidden minimuseums and key historic and modern interiors open to the public that tell parts of San Francisco's rich history in bright bits and pieces. The hours and best times to see these places are noted. With these interiors as starting points or goals, this guide plots the path that best reveals the social and architectural layers of each neighborhood or district.

Tours usually begin and end at points served by public transit, and often near parking garages. Budgeting garage fees into your travel plans makes for an easier trip. Using transit and/or taxis solves the parking problem entirely and precludes worrying about your car. Public telephones at bars and restaurants and radio-dispatched taxis make it very easy to dart around San Francisco and to see a lot, even in only one or two days. Some tours end at or include vantage points with panoramas of the city and its magnificent setting. Many of the paths traced through the separate districts in this guide have continuations, and many tours links together either directly or through easy transit hops.

What is distinctive about the *physical* San Francisco—her streets, blocks, bay windows, colors, landscapes and views—and what is distinctive about the many histories of the *people* of San Francisco are sought here. The goal is to read San Francisco's architecture and people the way a detective would read the scene of a crime, that is, to look not only *at* a place but *through* it to visualize the people whose lives it was and is. For you should take great care in San Francisco to be distracted by her people. (Not all that difficult.) They have created, and sustain, a most distinctive city.

The errors that are inevitable in a book such as this should be called to my attention in care of Chronicle Books, Drawer RD, 275 Fifth Street, San Francisco, CA 94103. Bibliographies are also available. I thank in advance all who help me improve subsequent editions of this guide to make it as practical and accurate as possible.

KEY MAP

SAN FRANCISCO BAY

The Embarcadero

The Financial District

2

Portsmouth Square

Montgomery

North Beach

Telegraph Hill

Chinatown

3

Columbus Avenue

Moscone Convention Center

1

Union Square

4a

Fisherman's Wharf

Aquatic Park

Fort Mason Center

4b

5

Russian Hill

6

Nob Hill

Van Ness Avenue

Marina Green

Lombard St

Lafayette Park

7

Eastern Pacific Heights

8

Japantown

Mission Dolores Park

9

The Mission District

Dolores Street

Alta Plaza

California Street

Market Street

Alamo Square

Geary Blvd

10

The Castro and Noe Valley

Twin Peaks

THE GOLDEN GATE

Lincoln Boulevard

Presidio of San Francisco

13

Along the Golden Gate

Buena Vista Park

The Haight-Ashbury

11

Eastern Golden Gate Park

Lands End

Lincoln Park

Cliff House/Seal Rocks

GOLDEN GATE PARK

12

Western Golden Gate Park

The Great Highway

Ocean Beach

PACIFIC OCEAN

N W E S

credit: San Francisco Department of City Planning

Preliminaries

Best Times to Visit

Spring and fall are generally considered the best seasons to visit San Francisco. The weather is fine and the main attractions are not crowded. Summer, of course, is the peak season and you should have advance reservations, especially for motels. Summer is also San Francisco's foggiest time of year, though the mist usually burns off by 10 A.M. It is generally cooler here in summer than most visitors expect. But fogs that quickly come and go are one of the special characteristics of this particular spot on the planet.

Winter—December, January, and February—is the riskiest but perhaps most beautiful season to visit. Between (usually) quite brief rainstorms are days of sapphire blue skies with clouds that look like baroque paintings, only alive and moving. The rains also wake the vegetation, making San Francisco's winter the equivalent of spring. (We like to be unusual.) In December the grass-covered California hills turn emerald green in a twinkling. Wild flowers blossom. Temperatures are cool, 60° F or so, but rarely really cold (below 40° F).

Because city hotel rates are often greatly reduced on weekends, and because rural attractions like the Napa Valley and coastal highway are least crowded on weekdays, you should stay in the city on weekends and see the countryside on weekdays. Sometimes rural hotels and inns have special mid-week rates.

Weekly patterns are conventional: Friday is the busiest "going out" night, and Saturday the next busiest. The finest French restaurants are closed on Sundays. Museums are closed on Mondays and Tuesdays.

The traveler should work around the two daily rush hours: 8 to 10 A.M. and 4 to 6 P.M. If you can avoid it, there is no reason to be driving during those hours when drivers are impatient with those not on automatic pilot. Buses are best between 10 A.M. and 2 or 3 P.M., when they become flooded with voluble schoolchildren. Normality returns about 4 P.M.; rush hour is at 5 P.M.

The best way to experience San Francisco's many districts is with a stimulating coffee at a local café about 10 A.M.—San Francisco wakes up slowly. A morning and noontime's walking around, lunch in a local restaurant after the rush at about 2 P.M., browsing in the shops on the local shopping strip in the afternoon, and then dinner in a different neighborhood entirely on the other side of town (*via* taxi, not automobile) is the best way to skip around compact San Francisco.

If you are here during the summer and want to ride the cable cars, as you will, do so early in the morning, say 8 A.M., then go off to do something else. This will save you long waits in lines in often unpleasant places.

Few San Francisco public attractions require advance reservations. In the Bay Area only Alcatraz, Filoli, Tao House, and soon probably Muir Woods require advance reservations. The famous restaurants also do, and you should phone well ahead of time in those cases. Usually, however, you can phone in your restaurant reservation in the morning for a table that evening.

San Francisco is not a twenty-four-hour town. Her restaurants keep civil, but not late, hours. Many stop seating patrons about 10 or 10:30 P.M. But San Francisco is probably the best city in the nation for evening strolls or dawn jogging. Both are safe in San Francisco. The top of Nob Hill makes a fine and level evening constitutional, as does window-shopping and people-watching on posh Union Street. The view of the inky Bay from Telegraph Hill is impressive at night. Fisherman's Wharf and Chinatown's Grant Avenue are alive with lights and tourists in the evenings. A few spots such as North Beach's Broadway, the west end of Haight Street, and Eleventh Street south of Market attract nightclubbers from about 11 P.M. to bar-closing time at 2 A.M. Aquatic Park and the beach in front of the bleachers behind the Maritime Museum across from Ghirardelli Square might be the most beautiful place to stroll and sit at night, with the dark Bay edged with light spread out before you and the Japanesque profile of Mt. Tamalpais like an ink wash in the distance.

Maps and Information

San Francisco Visitors' Map. Visitor Information Center, Hallidie Plaza, Market and Powell streets. Take escalator to lower level, near Powell and Market cable car turntable. Provides a useful free map that shows the downtown, cable car lines, and the Forty-Nine-Mile Scenic Drive. Call (415) 391-2000 for information. Foreign language recording also available: English, 391-2001, French, 391-2122, German, 391-2004, Spanish, 391-2122, Japanese, 391-2101.

The San Francisco Book, an informative minimagazine, is available for $1 from The San Francisco Convention & Visitors Bureau, P.O. Box 6977, San Francisco, CA 94101. Allow three weeks for delivery.

California State Automobile Association Maps 150 Van Ness Avenue, at Hayes Street, near the Civic Center.

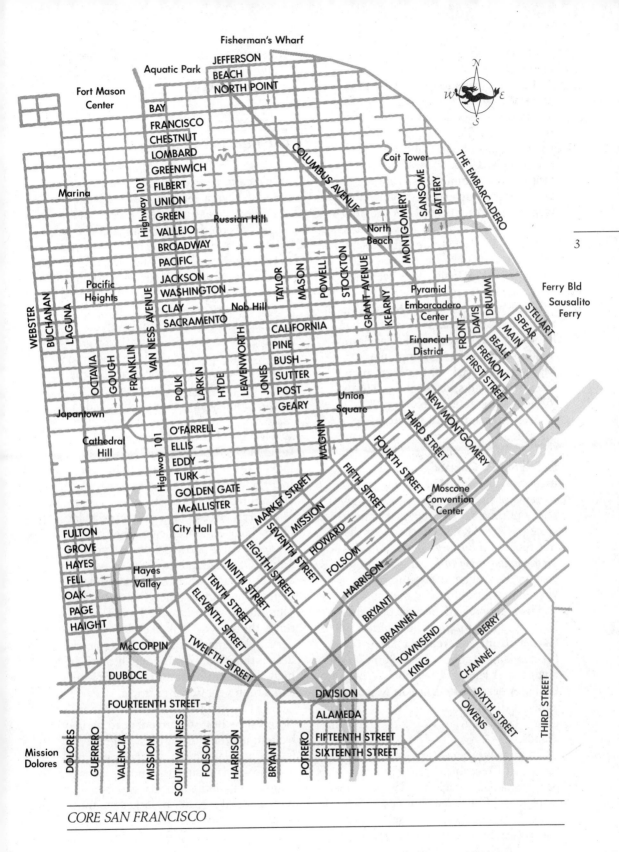

CORE SAN FRANCISCO

Lobby level office open Monday–Friday 8:30 A.M.–5 P.M.; 565-2711.

The best maps for drivers are those published by the AAA with a complete and impressive selection. If you are a member, a stop here will secure both the standard map of San Francisco and the San Francisco Tour Map. If you plan to visit the wine country, ask for the Sonoma and Napa county maps; if you plan to see Monterey, ask for the Tour Map of Monterey Peninsula. (Standard maps and Tour Maps are not the same thing.) Parking tickets can be paid at a window here as well. Maps available to AAA members only.

The Municipal Railway **Muni Map** of all public transit lines is for sale in some bookstores and at the Cable Car Barn and Powerhouse at Washington and Mason streets. Ask for the Muni map (shows city parks) or call 673-MUNI (673-6864) for assistance.

A **Regional Transit Guide/Map** is published by the Metropolitan Transportation Commission, Metro Center, 101 Eighth Street, Oakland, CA 94607. This map shows the interconnecting transit systems of the entire Bay Area and gives phone numbers for all regional transit systems. At BART stations ask for the free *BART and Buses: A Guide to Public Transportation from BART.* It is useful for visiting the Oakland Museum or the University of California, Berkeley.

The National Park Service publishes a handsome free **map of the Golden Gate National Recreation Area**. Try the excellent Maritime Book Store on the Hyde Street Pier at Fisherman's Wharf or GGNRA headquarters at Fort Mason (enter at the Franklin Street gate). Useful for the Presidio, Marin County, and Muir Woods.

Thomas Brothers Maps, 550 Jackson Street, off Columbus Avenue in North Beach; 981-7520. Publishes detailed street maps for all California counties. It is a fine general map store; also sells reproductions of historic views and maps.

Rand McNally Map Store, 595 Market Street at Second; 777-3131. Sells maps of the world, heavens, California, and San Francisco as well as computer graphics.

Climate and Clothing

While palm trees do grow here, San Francisco is not semitropical; its average daytime temperature is 59° F year-round. The city is on the shifting edge of the bright skies to the south and the gloomy gray skies to the north. The daily changes in temperature are usually only within about 10° F, yet the daily changes in atmospheric effects can be dramatic. The fogs have a transforming effect, turning the city and the Bay into a *grisaille* world. Spring is the best season to observe the fog's fantastic forms. Sometimes fog pours over Twin Peaks, or the Marin County approach to the Golden Gate Bridge, like a white, slow-motion waterfall. Other times, at night, the wind blows the fog around so that it looks like falling snow in July. In summer the fog usually burns off by 10 A.M. and returns about 3:30 P.M.

San Francisco enjoys the cleanest skies of any large American city. The constant westerly winds blow pollution across the Bay to Oakland and the South Bay. One can *see* in San Francisco, a phenomenon increasingly rare in cities. Sunsets are often memorable over the Pacific. At times the sea will look like burnished silver and the spacious cloud effects beggar description. The coloring when there are high clouds can be startling, bright pink and lemon yellow, for example.

The "layered look" of a sweater and jacket is the best way to adapt to variable temperatures. Even in the summer, it is cool here late in the day. Men will find medium-weight suits the most practical; women will find a light dress or suit with a warm sweater or jacket the most comfortable. Summer clothes are rarely useful here, except during the brief Indian Summer in September. Dressing

4

The Golden Gate

Marina

The Presidio

Downtown
(see page 10)

San Francisco Bay

Pacific Heights

Presidio
Heights

Japantown

Sea Cliff

Richmond

Western Addition

South of Market

Golden Gate Park

5

Haight-Ashbury

Duboce/Castro

N

Sunset
Heights

Mission

Potrero

W E

Sunset

Twin
Peaks

Noe

S

Forest Hill

Diamond
Heights

Bernal
Heights

Parkside

Mt. Davidson

Glen
Park

St. Francis Wood

Balboa

Bay View

Pacific Ocean

Lake Merced

Outer
Mission

Excelsior

Hunters
Point

Ingleside/
Ocean View

Visitation Valley

Crocker Amazon

NEIGHBORHOODS OF SAN FRANCISCO

as if the city were a tropical cruise ship will signal to everyone that you are a tourist, and that you will be chilly come late afternoon. If you dress for fall, you'll be comfortable year round. Sensible walking shoes are recommended. Sunglasses are not an affectation in California; the light is quite strong here.

Expenses and Tipping

The Convention & Visitors Bureau estimates that conventioneers spend about $160 a day, other travelers about $130. A savvy cabbie estimates typical spending at about $200 a day per person, $400 a day for a couple. Of course, it can be done for much less.

Conventional tips are 15 to 20 percent for taxis and restaurants. Allow 20 percent for waiter service at bars. Bellhops expect $1 minimum, or 75¢ per bag. Desk clerks and elevator operators are not tipped, but doormen expect a minimum of $1 at arrival and a tip when summoning a taxi. Chambermaids should be tipped $2.00 per night; leave the money in an envelope marked "For the Maid."

Foreign Exchange

San Francisco Airport

Citibank and Bank of America branches in the International Terminal are open for foreign currency exchange from 7 A.M. to 11 P.M. daily. The airport has longer hours than downtown exchanges.

Downtown San Francisco

Major Financial District banks are open Monday to Friday, 10 A.M. until 3 P.M.

Deak International, 100 Grant at Geary Street; (415) 362-3452. Monday–Friday, 9 A.M. to 5 P.M.

Foreign Exchange, Ltd., 415 Stockton Street, near Sutter; (415) 397-4700. Monday–Friday, 8:30 A.M. to 5 P.M.; Saturday, 9 A.M. to 1:30 P.M.

Macy's at Union Square will exchange foreign currency for purchases at the Cashier's Office, open all store hours.

American Express

237 Post Street, between Stockton and Geary, off Union Square, (415) 981-5533. Currency exchange; has automatic teller.

Automatic Tellers near Union Square

Bank of America, 400 Post Street near Powell, across from the Hotel St. Francis.

Wells Fargo Bank, 2 Grant Avenue at Market.

Citicorp Savings, 590 Market Street, north side between Montgomery and Sansome streets.

Transportation

Airport to City

San Francisco International Airport

Airport information: (415) 761-0800. With three linked terminals in a horse shoe around a central parking structure, SFO serves many foreign airlines and is a regional hub for Pan Am, United, and US Air airlines. A Beniamino Bufano statue entitled "Peace" in the road median at the entrance to the airport is decorated with mosaic faces of all races. The upper level of the loop roadway is for departures, the ground level for arrivals. The best times to arrive or depart are between 6 A.M. and 11 A.M. and 8 P.M. and 9 P.M. Peak congestion is between 12 and 3 P.M. A **free shuttle bus** circles the upper level. You can walk from one end of the airport to the other in fifteen or twenty minutes.

SFO has all the usual airport services, plus often imaginative art exhibits. The Bank of America and Citibank branches in the International Terminal have the longest hours for currency exchange, longer than anyplace downtown. Clearing Customs and Immigration at the International Terminal takes from thirty minutes to an hour, sometimes longer at peak periods. Barber and shower facilities are available during business hours. Downtown San Francisco is a twenty-minute, eleven-mile drive north on the Bayshore Freeway, Highway 101.

SuperShuttle's seven-passenger vans will take you to your door anywhere in the city for $8; call (415) 558-8500 for information.

The **Airporter** bus leaves every fifteen minutes for Downtown and Fisherman's Wharf hotels; the cost is about $6.

The **SamTrans** 7B bus links the airport with the Transbay Terminal in San Francisco but makes many stops along the way.

The **BART subway** does not serve the airport.

Metropolitan Oakland International Airport

Airport information: (415) 577-4015. Equally convenient is this smaller airport across the San Francisco–Oakland Bay Bridge. Outside rush hours, it is a twenty-five minute ride to downtown San Francisco. There is an AirBART shuttle to the Coliseum BART subway station (BART stops running at midnight).

Taxis

The carless traveler should plan on spending money on taxis. While rates are high, the distances are generally short and so costs remain reasonable. Taxi fare from the airport to downtown San Francisco is about $25.

Public telephones and radio-dispatched taxis make it easy to dart around the city, even when time is limited. And taxis eliminate the parking problems altogether—no small benefit. Ask the driver to take slower, scenic streets. This will add little to the fare and show you the city's most attractive streets.

De Soto—(415) 673-1414

Luxor–(415) 282-4141

Veteran's—(415) 552-1300

Yellow—(415) 626-2345

To the San Franciscan, one of the distinctive musics of the city is the sound of the taxi dispatcher calling the paired names of San Francisco addresses: "Larkin and Cal, Forty-six and Wawona, Hyde and Filbert, Broadway and Diviz, Sutter and Polk, Sixteenth and Sanchez." Each is a flash card of people and places.

Automobile

SOME DRIVING TIPS

If you are driving up the coast from Los Angeles to San Francisco, turn off Highway 1 onto Highway 17 at Soquel (near Santa Cruz) and then take Interstate 280 up the center of the San Mateo Peninsula. The rolling, golden, oak-dotted hills here are a magnificently Californian landscape. The Junipero Serra Freeway, one of the last freeways designed by Caltrans District 4 Engineers, is one of the most beautiful freeways in California. Its soaring concrete overpasses on their sculpted pedestals make art out of roadbuilding.

Once over the city line, take the San Jose Avenue exit from I-280 and follow San Jose Avenue to palm-lined Dolores Street. San Jose Avenue follows *El Camino Real*, the King's Highway, which linked Baja and Alta California's presidios and missions, and which followed earlier Native American and animal trails. Bright, clean, residential Dolores Street, with its central strip of mature palms and its roller-coaster profile, is a splendid entrance to San Francisco. Mission Dolores, at Dolores and Sixteenth is an appropriate first stop.

Cable cars always have the right of way. Do not tailgate them. According to the California Traffic Code, pedestrians always have the right of way, even when they are wrong. You may make right-hand turns at red lights after slowing and yielding right of way to pedestrians.

PARKING

The Traffic Code requires that cars parked on grades block their wheels against the curb by "toeing" the front tire when headed downhill, or "heeling" it parked uphill. You can be ticketed for unsafe parking. In addition, you should set the emergency brake and leave the car set in gear or in park.

San Francisco has several different

colored curbs each with its own restrictions.

White—Passenger loading zone, short stops permitted.

Green—Ten-minute parking limit.

Yellow—Half-hour loading zone for vehicles with commercial plates; parking allowed after 6 P.M.

Red—No stopping, standing, or parking.

Blue—Parking for the physically disabled.

Towaway Zones—You may be towed from any illegal spot. This is most frequent when some streets switch to no parking to provide extra lanes for morning and afternoon rush hours. Read parking signs posted on each block for this restriction. S.F.P.D.'s towed vehicle information is at 553-1235.

Ferries

Commuter ferries are least crowded and most enjoyable midday, between the morning and evening rush hours, roughly between 10 A.M. and 3 P.M.

Angel Island
Pier 41, in Fisherman's Wharf area. For schedule and fares phone (415) 546-2815.

Larkspur
Behind Ferry Building at foot of Market and California streets. For schedule and fares phone (415) 332-6600. The Larkspur ferry is almost exclusively used by commuters and terminates at a space-frame terminal and a large parking lot. Larkspur Landing, the nearby shopping center, serves mostly local shoppers.

Sausalito
Ferry Building, foot of Market Street. For schedule and fares, call Golden Gate Ferry, (415) 332-6600.

Tiburon
Pier 41, Fisherman's Wharf. For schedule and fares phone (415) 546-2815. The Tiburon ferry docks right next to

Guaymas (435-6300), a Californian-Mexican restaurant with a modern, airy design. The town of Tiburon consists of a one-block-long overrestored Main Street that does not feel real, even though it is.

Cable Cars

The best way to experience the cable cars, especially during the busy summer season and weekends, is to get up very early and to travel much of the 4.4-mile system back and forth between 6 A.M., when the cables start up, and about 8:30 A.M., when the morning rush begins. (When the Powell-Mason and Powell-Hyde lines to Fisherman's Wharf are packed, it is often possible to ride the less-used California Street cable line.)

Adults should secure a $6 all-day transit pass good until midnight on all cable cars and all the rest of the municipal transit system. Passes are sold by ticket machines that take $1 and $5 bills; these are at the ends of all the lines and at the California and Powell transfer point on Nob Hill. There are no ticket machines at the Powerhouse. Special children's all-day passes are not available, but you may buy them adult passes. If you use the transit system to get around, it will be amply worth the expense.

Rainy, blustery days, all bundled up in a raincoat and hat are the best times to ride the cable cars. They return then to their old mix of local hill-dwellers and hardy visitors. It goes without saying that the cable cars are most enjoyable and historically evocative when not jam-packed with people. Vistas and sensations differ from different seats, so vary where you sit—on the outside, on the inside, in front, in back. It's hard to pick out where the cable car is most itself—perhaps climbing the seemingly perpendicular Hyde Street grades between Bay and Chestnut, or the California car stopped athwart Grant Avenue on a quiet, foggy night when Chinatown's

Grant Avenue with its glowing neon feels like a Dashiell Hammett mystery locale.

Cable Car Powerhouse and Museum
1201 Mason Street, northwest corner of Washington
Open daily 10 A.M. to 5 P.M.; April to October 10 A.M. to 6 P.M.; closed Thanksgiving, Christmas, and New Year's Day; free. The museum has the best souvenir stand of cable car memorabilia and books.
Cable car fares are liable to change but tickets can be bought on the cable cars or at machines located at the end of each line and at the California and Powell transfer point (but not at the Cable Car Powerhouse). The all-day transit pass is recommended.

"One of the principal developments of mechanical genius in San Francisco," wrote C. P. Heininger in his guide to San Francisco in 1889, "is the extensive and perfect system of cable street railways, of which the Clay street line was the pioneer. The system is unique, and a triumph of inventive genius and engineering skill, of which San Francisco has just cause to be proud." The surviving fragment of San Francisco's once-extensive cable line network is a living monument to nineteenth-century American mechanical and promotional genius.

Cable cars were first developed in San Francisco in the late 1870s. The plain brick powerhouse on the northwest corner of Washington and Mason, on the border between Chinatown and Russian Hill, powers the four endless, or looped, cables that run under sixty-nine blocks of San Francisco's streets (California, Powell, Hyde, and Mason) propelling the three remaining cable car lines. There are twenty-six of the green, single-end cable cars on the Powell-Hyde and the Powell-Mason lines, and eleven of the larger, red, double-ended cable cars on the California Street cable line. Most of the Powell-Hyde and Powell-Mason cable cars date from 1887 to 1891; the California

Street cable cars were built in 1906 through 1914, after the fire. The maximum number of cars with passengers on all 4.4 miles of track at one time is twenty-six. Today, the Powell-Mason and Powell-Hyde lines carry forty-one thousand passengers a day.

Like many inventions, the cable car has more than one "inventor." In both Europe and America, men were seeking better passenger transit systems for growing cities. Andrew Smith Hallidie, popularly considered the "inventor" of the cable car in 1873, is more accurately described as the first successful *developer* of a cable car line.

Andrew Smith was born in London in 1836 and apprenticed as a mechanic. He adopted the surname Hallidie in honor of his uncle, Sir Andrew Hallidie, an English physician. With his father, a wire rope manufacturer, he came to California in 1852. He began designing wire-rope haulage systems for gold mines. In 1857 he established a small factory in North Beach to manufacture wire rope (cables with manila hemp cores with steel wire wrapped around them). In 1867 he patented a system of gripping and ungripping ore buckets on an endless overhead cable. After 1869, he attempted to organize the financing to build a cable line up California Street on the east escarpment of Nob Hill. Construction costs seem to have been less on Clay Street two blocks north, however, and some Clay Street property owners were willing to invest in Hallidie's enterprise. The Clay Street Hill Railroad had its trial run on August 1, 1873. With Hallidie at the controls, the tiny car went down Clay from Jones to Kearny, and then back up. Hallidie formed the Traction Railway Company in 1875, hired the best legal talent, and attempted, with much success for a while, to patent all the important aspects of cable traction and to force other cable car lines to pay his company a royalty based on their mileage.

At their peak, San Francisco had eight cable car lines operating over 112 miles

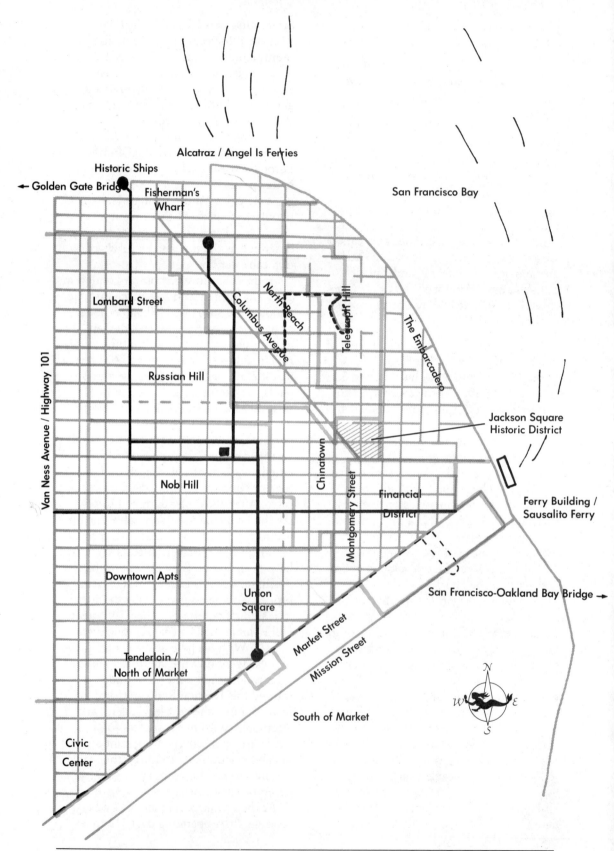

Alcatraz / Angel Is Ferries

Historic Ships

← Golden Gate Bridge

San Francisco Bay

Fisherman's Wharf

Lombard Street

North Beach

Columbus Avenue

Telegraph Hill

The Embarcadero

Van Ness Avenue / Highway 101

Russian Hill

Jackson Square Historic District

Chinatown

Nob Hill

Montgomery Street

Financial District

Ferry Building / Sausalito Ferry

Downtown Apts

San Francisco–Oakland Bay Bridge →

Union Square

Market Street

Tenderloin / North of Market

Mission Street

South of Market

Civic Center

N
W E
S

CABLE CAR SYSTEM (39 Coit bus heavy dashed line. Market Street Historic Trolleys dashed line.)

of track directly employing some 1,500 men.

The cable car brought the power of the stationary steam engine out onto the street where it could be used to propel cars and passengers in a more hygienic and more dependable way than existing horse-car technology. (Cars pulled along tracks by horses polluted with animal wastes. And they could not be used on steep hills.) Despite their expensive construction and high operating costs, cable car lines were the state-of-the-art for the six years between 1882 to 1888, peaking in 1889. They were rapidly made obsolete by the development of the superior, cheaper electric streetcar which emerged in both Germany and America in the late 1880s.

Because there were no traffic signals, in 1882 the city required all cable cars to carry bells or gongs and to ring them as they crossed intersections. (Cable car bell-ringing has developed into a local art form. Every summer a bell-ringing contest at Union Square pits conductors and gripmen against each other for the prize. Each contestant has one minute to impress the judges with their rhythm, flair, and musicality. Contact the Convention and Visitors Bureau for the date of the contest.)

Cable car systems have many drawbacks. They are costly to construct with expensive underground conduit in addition to tracks, they are mechanically complex and prone to breakdowns, and they are expensive to operate because they require two-man crews. Also, cable cars cannot pass one another on the same track; lost time cannot be made up; and one stoppage anywhere on a line shuts down the entire line. As if all this were not enough, cable car systems are prodigious energy wasters. Some 4 percent of the energy generated is used to move the cars and their passengers, and some 60 to 80 percent is used moving the cable.

Increasingly after 1893, cable car lines were replaced with more efficient electric streetcars. After the earthquake in 1906, traction companies replaced cable with electric where they could, keeping cable operations on only the steepest slopes: Nob Hill, Russian Hill, Pacific Heights, and the Castro hill. The Castro Street cable line was converted to buses in 1941, and the scenic Washington-Jackson cable line in Pacific Heights was shut down in 1956, preceded by a brass band playing dirges. Today only Nob and Russian hills are served by cable lines.

Upon municipalization of many cable car lines after 1944, cost-conscious city government announced plans to replace all the cable lines with buses. In 1947 a Citizen's Committee to Save the Cable Cars was formed by Frieda Klussman to raise public consciousness about the value of the unique cable car lines to the city. Eventually, a truncated system was preserved, and in 1964 the existing system was placed on the National Register of Historic Places, making this the nation's first moving landmark.

The entire cable car system was rebuilt between 1982 and 1984, mostly with federal public transportation grants plus local corporate and individual contributions. New tracks and underground conduit were constructed, and the Powerhouse and Car Barn reconstructed.

Chin and Hensolt Engineers, Inc., with Ernest Born, consulting architect, took the fragile, red brick Ferry and Cliff House Railways Powerhouse hastily built in 1909, stabilized the four brick walls, scooped out the building's interior, built new foundations under the old brick walls and a new steel frame and concrete structure within the old four walls, then bonded the brick walls to the new, much stronger steel and concrete building. What you see is an entirely new, seismic-resistant building carefully tailored to fit within the old garment.

On entering the Powerhouse at its corner entrance, turn left and walk down the staircase to see the sheaves, the underground wheels playing out the four cables underneath the intersection at

Washington and Mason streets. This unique viewing room was added in the reconstruction of 1984. Climb back upstairs to the viewing platform that lets you look down onto the great spinning wheels that power and regulate the cables, keeping them taut and smooth-running. The spinning white wheels power the looped cables. The electric engines themselves are quite compact and are mounted near the wheels. A few explanatory plaques mounted on the handrail explain the cables and their fig-ure-eight loops.

The small old cable car on the pedestal near the head of the stairway is venerable Car No. 8 of the Clay Street Hill Railroad. It made the first trip with Hallidie at the controls in 1873. The relic survives because it was lent to Baltimore for an exhibition in 1905, and thus escaped the earthquake and fire of 1906. In 1907, when Baltimore suffered a great fire, the car was presumed lost. It was discovered in a Baltimore junkyard in 1959 and rescued. The other two cars in the museum are from the Sutter Street Railway and date from 1876. They have open cars, "dummies," that contained the grip, linked to closed passenger cars with no grip of their own. Scale models in the museum trace the rich, continuing history of public transportation in San Francisco.

The cables are kept moving at a speed of 9.5 miles per hour under the surface of the streets and make a throaty humming sound. Cables last from about 110 days on the Powell-Mason line to 300 days on the California Street line. To operate a cable car, the gripman in the center of the cable car operates a lever, or grip, that reaches through a slot in the street and grasps or lets go of the cable moving in its underground conduit. To stop a cable car, the grip lets go of the cable, then a second person applies the wheel brakes and track brakes, wooden blocks that scrape the rails. The grip and brake-man communicate through bell signals.

The interior of the great machinery

room where the cables are propelled has an immensely strong, unadorned, gray-painted steel I-beam supported roof. It is like being under a bridge, not inside a building. The steel is this strong because the cable cars themselves are all stored at night on the upper level. The Power-house and Car Barn is on a slope with a one-story drop at the two ends of the lot, a most characteristic San Francisco hill lot which permits vehicular access to more than one level of a building.

THE CALIFORNIA STREET CABLE LINE

The California Street Cable Railroad Company was the third cable line in the city and was organized in 1876 by railroad millionaires Leland Stanford and Mark Hopkins, who wanted to build atop Nob Hill, and other local magnates. It was one of the most luxurious cable lines ever built, with the best equipment and largest cars. Its double-ended cars weigh six tons and carry thirty-four passengers. This "California" type car subsequently served as a model for the first electric streetcars. The California cable line opened in 1878 and ran up wide California Street from the edge of the banking district at Kearny out to Fillmore Street in nineteen minutes. It served the Nob Hill palaces and opened up the Western Addition to Victorian house building. The California Street line does not have turntables since its cars are double-ended and need only a switch-back at the ends of the tracks.

THE POWELL-MASON CABLE LINE

The Powell-Mason cable line was designed by engineer Howard C. Holmes, built by the Ferries & Cliff House Railroad Company, and put in service in 1888. To power it, the Power-house (reconstructed in 1909 and 1984) was built on Mason Street, between Jackson and Washington. Because the original lines went both east-west and north-south (only a fragment of the system survives), the cables feed out of the southeastern corner of the Powerhouse at Mason and Washington and circle the block to the east bounded by Mason, Powell, Washington, and Jackson streets. Navigating this block is called going "around the horn" in cable car lingo. Cars from the Powell-Mason line survived the Fire of 1906 because they were stored outside the burned district in the cable car barn at Sacramento and Walnut. Some of the 1887–1891 vintage cars continue in use today.

THE POWELL-HYDE CABLE LINE

The present Powell-Hyde line was originally part of the California Street Cable Railroad and opened as an extension of that line in 1891. The Hyde line was built to link Russian Hill with downtown shopping via a crosstown cable line. The Hyde Street line also terminated a block from the Hyde Street Pier and the Sausalito and Tiburon ferries. It was the last cable line built in San Francisco. Its 3.5 miles of track traverse the steepest slope, Hyde Street between Bay and Chestnut, with a 20.67 percent grade. It also enjoys the most spectacular panoramic views of the Golden Gate and mountainous Marin County.

Public Transit

San Francisco has a smorgasbord of public transportation systems, of which cable cars are only the most famous. If you are a normally car-driving person, San Francisco's many lines, selectively used, let you see a city based on public transit. Drivers and operators know the system well and can guide you: they will call out stops if you request them to. With a $6 daily transit pass, you will not fumble with fares. And you can, if you want, really see a lot of the city inexpensively. Muni maps can be bought at many bookstores and at the Cable Car Barn and Powerhouse at Washington and

Mason streets. You will need exact fare since Muni drivers do not make change. When you board, ask for a transfer. Muni has a generous transfer policy; transfers are good for two uses in *any direction*, until the last time shown, about 90 minutes. You can also call 673-MUNI (673-6864) to ask for assistance planning your route.

Hotels

San Francisco is justly famous for her hotels and has a complete spectrum of accommodations from the most luxurious to the spartan. In this she is unusual for an American city. You can come back to San Francisco many times and stay in an entirely different kind of hotel in a completely different part of the city. San Francisco has everything from commanding suites with panoramas of the Bay Area, to cozy, plant-embowered bed and breakfasts.

The average hotel rate in 1988 was about $95 per night per person. Luxury hotels such as The Portman have suites up to $400 to $550. Fisherman's Wharf's midrise motels are the most popular; the lowest rates there are about $75. Nob Hill's hotels are the costliest, with minimum rates about $100.

The older, midsize downtown hotels along Post and Sutter streets, north of Union Square, are recommended for carless travelers and are a good value. You can economize on your room and splurge on good restaurants and theater tickets if you choose to stay in this area. (Plan to garage your car if you stay downtown.)

Today, business travelers comprise about half the hotel customers in San Francisco. On weekends, when corporate travelers are home, many luxury hotels cut their rates to about half to lure weekenders. So always ask about weekend specials.

The 11 percent city hotel room tax on

your final bill is the gentle "squeeze" San Franciscans extract for your enjoying yourself here. In 1987 this tax brought in about $5.5 million, which was used to help support the Convention and Visitors Bureau, dance companies, theaters, musical performances in the parks, parades, museums, the symphony, and all the things that make this a rewarding city to visit or live in. Some one-hundred-and-twenty arts and cultural organizations get part of their funding, and the important imprimatur of civic approval, from the Hotel Tax Fund.

The San Francisco Convention & Visitors Bureau publishes a free *San Francisco Lodging Guide*. Write them at P.O. Box 6977, San Francisco, CA 94101.

Major Hotels

A brief listing of major hotels has been included below. Entries with asterisks are mentioned in greater detail as they fit into the city's historical and architectural tapestry.

NOB HILL

The Fairmont Hotel and Tower, Mason and California, San Francisco 94108; (415) 772-5000.*

The Huntington Hotel, 1075 California, San Francisco 94108; (415) 474-5400. A hotel that prides itself on personal attention and remembering its guests.*

Mark Hopkins Inter-Continental Hotel, 1 Nob Hill Circle, San Francisco 94108, at California and Mason; (415) 392-3434.*

The Stanford Court, 905 California, San Francisco 94108; (415) 989-3500. A favorite with business travelers.*

FINANCIAL DISTRICT

Hyatt-Regency, 5 Embarcadero Center, San Francisco 94111, foot of California; (415) 788-1234. Inside this 1973 design

by John Portman and Associates is a seventeen-story interior space enlivened by light-studded glass elevators.*

Holiday Inn Financial District, 750 Kearny, San Francisco, 94108; (415) 433-6600.

The Mandarin Oriental, 222 Sansome, San Francisco 94104-2792, at California; (415) 885-0999. The top eleven stories of Interstate Center at 345 California; twin towers in the sky with regional panoramas; glass "skybridges"; north views best. Opened in 1987; expensive.

Park Hyatt Hotel, 333 Battery, San Francisco, 94111; (415) 392-1234.

UNION SQUARE / DOWNTOWN

The Four Seasons–Clift Hotel, Geary and Taylor, San Francisco 94102; (415) 775-4700. Hotel men regard The Clift as one of the top hotels in the country. The elegant Redwood Lounge of 1935 was restored in 1977.

Hyatt Union Square, 345 Stockton, San Francisco 94102, at Post, on Union Square; (415) 398-1234.*

Nikko Hotel, San Francisco, 222 Mason Street, San Francisco 94102, at O'Farrell; (415) 394-1111.

The Portman San Francisco, 500 Post, San Francisco 94102, at Mason; (415) 771-8600. Opened in 1988.*

Ramada Renaissance Hotel, 55 Cyril Magnin, San Francisco 94102, at Ellis and Fifth Street North; (415) 392-8000.

San Francisco Hilton & Towers, 333 O'Farrell, San Francisco 94102, at Mason; (415) 771-1400. Recently expanded to a full block; now one of the largest hotels on the West Coast.

Sir Francis Drake Hotel, 432 Powell, San Francisco 94102, at Sutter; (415) 392-7755. Designed by Weeks and Day in 1928; one of the best designs from the stylish 1920s.*

The Westin St. Francis Hotel and Tower,

Powell and Geary, San Francisco 94102, on Union Square; (415) 397-7000.*

Marriott Hotel, Fourth and Mission streets, San Francisco 94103; (415) 896-1600.

Meridien San Francisco, 50 Third Street, San Francisco 94103, near Market; (415) 974-6400. Chef Alain Chapel, a Michelin three-star chef, oversees the acclaimed Pierre Restaurant; call (415) 974-6400 for reservations.

Sheraton-Palace Hotel, New Montgomery and Market streets, San Francisco 94105; (415) 392-8600.* Note: The Palace is closed for renovation through 1989 and part of 1990.

JAPANTOWN

Miyako Hotel, 1625 Post Street, at Laguna, San Francisco 94115; (415) 922-3200. A fourteen-story hotel in the east end of the 1968 Japan Center. Hotel suites have sunken tile baths and contemporary Japanese styling.

Best Western Kyoto Inn, 1800 Sutter at Buchanan, San Francisco, CA 94115; (415) 921-4000.

Boutique Hotels

The newest wave in hotels are so-called "boutique" hotels, mostly clustered near Union Square. These once-faded Edwardian hotels with good locations have been renovated into stylish lodgings with pampering service and blend the best of old and new.

The Bedford Hotel, 761 Post Street, San Francisco 94102, between Jones and Leavenworth; (415) 673-6040.

Campton Place Hotel, 340 Stockton, San Francisco 94198, at Campton Place

between Post and Sutter; (415) 781-5555. An expensive, well-appointed hotel with the Campton Place Restaurant, one of the best new restaurants and bars; call (415) 781-5155 for restaurant reservations.

The Cartwright Hotel, 524 Sutter Street, San Francisco 94102, at Powell; (415) 421-2865. Filled with antiques and fresh flowers.

The Castro Hotel, 560 Castro Street, San Francisco 94114; (415) 621-6222.

Diva Hotel, 440 Geary Boulevard, San Francisco 94102, near Taylor; (415) 885-0200.

Galleria Park Hotel, 191 Sutter Street, San Francisco 94104, at Kearny, next to Crocker Galleria; (415) 781-3060. Located between the Financial District and Union Square, close to Chinatown.

Hotel Regis, 490 Geary Boulevard, San Francisco 94102, at Taylor; (415) 928-7900. Designed by Righetti and Headman in 1912, this fine Edwardian hotel is distinguished by shallow squared bay windows. Superbly transformed with a fine restaurant and cocktail lounge.

Hotel Union Square, 114 Powell Street, San Francisco 94102, between O'Farrell and Ellis; (415) 434-4560.

The Hotel Vintage Court, 650 Bush Street, San Francisco 94102, near Powell; (415) 392-4666. The renowned Masa's Restaurant is located here; call (415) 989-7154 for reservations.

Inn at the Opera, 333 Fulton Street, San Francisco 94102, at Franklin; (415) 863-8400.

The Inn at Union Square, 440 Post Street, San Francisco 94102, near Powell; (415) 397-3510. The rejuvenation of a 1907 residential hotel designed by George A. Applegarth. Swaine Adeney is in the ground floor.

Juliana Hotel, 590 Bush Street, San Francisco 94108, at Stockton; (415) 392-2540.

15

A delight. Near, but not in, Union Square and Chinatown. Palm Restaurant of San Francisco, a branch of the New York steak-and-lobster house, is next door; call (415) 981-1222 for reservations.

Kensington Park, 450 Post Street, San Francisco 94102, between Powell and Mason; (415) 788-6400. This is the fine 1924 Elks Club by Meyer and Johnson, with some decoration by Anthony Heinsbergen.

The Majestic Hotel, 1500 Sutter Street, at Gough, San Francisco 94109, near Japantown; (415) 441-1100. A posh 1902 hotel resplendantly restored and lavishly furnished with antiques. Stanley Eichelbaum's Majestic Café serves California cuisine with an emphasis on old San Francisco dishes; call (415) 776-6400 for reservations.

Orchard Hotel, 562 Sutter Street, San Francisco 94102, between Powell and Mason; (415) 433-4434.

Petite Auberge, 863 Bush Street, San Francisco 94108, near Mason; (415) 928-6000. A delightful twenty-six-room French-style country inn downtown.

Savoy Hotel, 580 Geary Boulevard, San Francisco 94102, between Taylor and Jones; (415) 441-2700.

Villa Florence Hotel, 225 Powell Street, San Francisco 94102, at O'Farrell; (415) 397-7700. On the Powell cable car line.

The York Hotel, 940 Sutter Street, San Francisco 94109, between Leavenworth and Hyde; (415) 885-6800. The sophisticated Plush Room Cabaret showcases fine entertainers in one of the city's most agreeable showrooms; call (415) 885-6800 for information.

Bed & Breakfast Inns / Small Historic Hotels

Many of San Francisco's bed-and-breakfast inns and small, revived historic hotels are in Victorian and Edwardian buildings and let you live, for a moment, in old San Francisco. They also bring you closer to San Francisco's congenial neighborhoods, for all are outside the downtown. Bed and breakfasts in San Francisco tend to be pricey but memorable. A few are covered as architectural sites elsewhere in this guide.

PACIFIC HEIGHTS

Hermitage House, 2224 Sacramento Street, San Francisco 94115, between Laguna and Buchanan; (415) 921-5515. An elegant inn in a 1902 Pacific Heights townhouse.

Jackson Court, 2198 Jackson Street, San Francisco 94115, at Buchanan; (415) 929-7670. An elegant old stone building of 1900 tastefully furnished with antiques in 1982 in a fine, quiet location.

The Mansion Hotel, 2220 Sacramento Street, San Francisco 94115, between Laguna and Buchanan; (415) 929-9444. A theatrically enlivened Queen Anne house of 1887 compatibly expanded in 1917.

The Monte Cristo Hotel, 600 Presidio, San Francisco 94115, corner of Pine; (415) 931-1875. An 1875 hotel with a colorful past refurbished in 1980. Close to Presidio Heights.

The Queen Anne Hotel, 1590 Sutter Street, San Francisco 94109, at Octavia, near Japantown; (415) 441-2828. A gabled and bay-windowed Queen Anne hotel with corner turret built in 1890 and restored in 1981.

UNION STREET AREA

Kavanaugh's Bed & Breakfast Inn, 4 Charlton Court, San Francisco 94123, off Union between Laguna and Buchanan; (415) 921-9784. Two cozy cottages in a mews; restaurants and shopping around the corner.

16

The Sherman House, 2160 Green Street, San Francisco 94123, near Fillmore, in tony Cow Hollow; (415) 563-3600. Built in 1876 with a three-story Music Room added in 1901. Restored in 1984 and furnished in antiques.

Stewart-Grinsell House, 2963 Laguna Street, San Francisco 94123, between Union and Filbert; (415) 346-0424. In an 1880s Stick Style house.

Union Street Inn, 2229 Union Street, San Francisco 94123, near Fillmore; (415) 346-0424. An Edwardian built in the 1900s and attractively adapted in 1979.

NOB HILL

The Nob Hill Inn, 1000 Pine Street, San Francisco 94109; (415) 673-6080. This fine 1907 bay-windowed Edwardian building was luxuriously converted into a small hotel in 1982. Staying here, the traveler experiences the post-fire building type so important to the real San Francisco, and the tasteful period restorations that have been so characteristic of the city in the last twenty years.*

ALAMO SQUARE

Alamo Square Inn, 719 Scott Street, San Francisco 94117, at Fulton; (415) 931-7101. An 1895 Queen Anne with a grand staircase furnished in Victorian and oriental decor.

The Langtry, 637 Steiner Street, San Francisco 94117, between Hayes and Fell, near Alamo Square; (415) 863-0538. An 1894 Queen Anne house adapted as a hotel in 1986. A favorite with women travelers.

HAIGHT ASHBURY–BUENA VISTA

The Red Victorian, 1665 Haight Street, San Francisco 94117; (415) 864-1978. Upstairs on Haight Street between Clayton and Belvedere; an Edwardian hotel revived

with themed "hippie" rooms such as the Peacock Suite.

The Spencer House, 1080 Haight Street, San Francisco 94117; (415) 626-9205. A very fine Queen Anne house of 1895 on the corner of Haight and Baker, facing Buena Vista Park. Fine original interiors.*

The Spreckels Mansion, 737 Buena Vista West, San Francisco 94117; (415) 861-3008. An imposing 1898 Classic Revival house facing Buena Vista Park on a block with sweeping views. Perhaps too gleefully painted, but has some fine art glass.*

Stanyan Park Hotel, 750 Stanyan Street, San Francisco 94117, at Waller, facing Golden Gate Park; (415) 751-1000. A three-story, bay-windowed Edwardian hotel of 1904 attractively restored and improved in 1983. Good if you want to jog in Golden Gate Park in the early morning.*

Victorian Inn on the Park, 301 Lyon Street, San Francisco 94117, corner Fell and the Golden Gate Park Panhandle; (415) 931-1830. A corner Queen Anne built in 1897 and opened as a hotel in 1982.

THE CASTRO / UPPER MARKET

Albion House, 135 Gough Street, San Francisco 94102, near Market; (415) 621-0896. A post-earthquake hotel once popular with musicians in the sixties, now comfortably refurbished.

Inn on Castro, 321 Castro Street, San Francisco 94111, north side of Market; (415) 861-0321. A bay-windowed Edwardian.

24 Henry Street, San Francisco 94114, near Castro and Sixteenth; (415) 864-5686. No breakfast; five rooms. An 1887 Victorian adapted as a guest house.

The Willows Bed and Breakfast, 710 Fourteenth Street, San Francisco 94117, near Market and Church Muni Metro stop;

(415) 431-4770. A 1900s twelve-room inn upstairs.

THE MISSION DISTRICT

The Inn San Francisco, 943 South Van Ness Avenue, San Francisco 94114, near Twenty-first Street; (415) 641-0188. An 1872 mansion attractively adapted as a fifteen-room bed and breakfast.

NORTH BEACH

The Washington Square Inn, 1660 Stockton Street, San Francisco 94133, at Filbert facing Washington Square; (415) 981-4220. An intimate two-story, bay-windowed Edwardian hotel now tastefully furnished with antiques. Shared and private baths. Some corner rooms. Perfectly located for sightseeing, dining, and for walking around at night.

San Remo Hotel, 2237 Mason Street, San Francisco 94133, near Chestnut, in North Beach; (415) 776-8688. A few flat blocks from Fisherman's Wharf is this restored three-story, typical 1906 Edwardian hotel. The San Remo Café and Bar on the first floor is a perfect evocation of turn-of-the-century San Francisco and serves Northern Italian cuisine and seafood; call (415) 673-9090 for reservations.

Small Downtown Hotels

Between penance and luxury there ought to be well-located, clean, inexpensive hotels. San Francisco has a good selection of these hotels as well.

The Andrews Hotel, 624 Post Street, San Francisco 94109, near Taylor; (415) 563-6877.

Atherton Hotel, 685 Ellis Street, San Francisco 94109, near Larkin; (415) 474-5720. Mixed gay and straight patronage; has a cozy lounge.

Beresford Arms Hotel, 701 Post Street, San Francisco 94102, near Jones; (415) 673-2600.

Beresford Hotel, 635 Sutter Street, San Francisco 94102, near Mason; (415) 673-9900. Small, comfortable rooms.

Canterbury Hotel & Whitehall Inn, 750 Sutter Street, San Francisco 94109, near Taylor; (415) 474-6464. Comfortably furnished and with a pub lounge.

Carlton Hotel, 1075 Sutter Street, San Francisco 94109, near Larkin; (415) 673-0242.

El Drisco Hotel, 2901 Pacific Avenue, San Francisco 94115, at Broderick; (415) 346-2880. Secluded in Pacific Heights; serves meals.

The Gaylord Hotel, 620 Jones Street, San Francisco 94102, near Geary; (415) 673-8445.

Hotel Californian, 405 Taylor Street, San Francisco 94102, at O'Farrell; (415) 885-2500. Close to the Geary Street theaters.

Hotel King George, 334 Mason Street, San Francisco 94102, near Geary; (415) 781-5050. A favorite with European visitors. Excellent location for public transit.

Hotel Mark Twain, 345 Taylor Street, San Francisco 94102, near Ellis; (415) 673-2332.

Lombard Hotel, 1015 Geary Boulevard, San Francisco 94109, near Polk; (415) 673-5232.

Raphael Hotel, 386 Geary Boulevard, San Francisco 94102, at Mason, behind the St. Francis; (415) 986-2000. Many Californians stay here when they come to San Francisco.

Budget Hotels

Adelaide Inn, 5 Adelaide Place, San Francisco 94102, an alley off Taylor between Geary and Post; (415) 441-2261. Well located. European students stretching their money stay here.

Basque Hotel & Restaurant, 15 Romolo Place, San Francisco 94133; (415) 788-9404. On a steep alley off Broadway, immediately east of Columbus in North Beach. Simple rooms, shared baths.

Beverly-Plaza Hotel, 334 Grant Avenue, San Francisco 94108, at Bush; (415) 781-3566. Between Union Square and Chinatown, near the Financial District.

Grant Plaza Hotel, 465 Grant Avenue, at Pine, San Francisco 94108; (415) 434-3883. Located in Chinatown in a 1921 concrete building built for the Shanghai Low Company. Interesting stained-glass windows on the top floor.

Hotel El Dorado, 150 Ninth Street, San Francisco 94103, off Market near City Hall and Opera; (415) 552-4660. Self-service laundry.

Leland Hotel, 1315 Polk Street, San Francisco 94109, at Bush; (415) 441-5141.

Obrero Hotel and Basque Restaurant, 1208 Stockton Street, San Francisco 94133, between Pacific and Broadway in Chinatown, upstairs; (415) 989-3960. Well-located for sightseeing, also near North Beach. Pension with breakfast and family-style dinners; simple rooms; shared baths.

Oxford Hotel, Mason at Market Street, San Francisco 94102; (415) 775-4600. In the Tenderloin. A fine 1911 hotel designed by William H. Weeks.

Pensione Hotel San Francisco, 1668 Market Street, San Francisco 94102, two blocks west of Van Ness; (415) 864-1271. Near the Castro, well-located for transit; the Pensione Caffè is downstairs.

Motels

The most popular listing of motels is the *AAA TourBook* for California and Nevada. The boldface type there is pur-

chased and is not a quality distinction. The annual *Mobil Travel Guide* is another good listing. This list of motels is not comprehensive.

FISHERMAN'S WHARF

The modern motels in Fisherman's Wharf are the favorites of families traveling during school vacations. They enjoy the highest occupancy rates in the city. Be sure to book ahead if you plan to stay here. All have parking.

Howard Johnson's Motor Lodge and The Anchorage Shopping Center, 580 Beach Street, San Francisco 94133, at Leavenworth; (415) 775-3800. A combination motel and shopping center with a small court. Well located.

Holiday Inn at Fisherman's Wharf, 1300 Columbus Avenue, San Francisco 94133-1397, at North Point; (415) 771-9000. Two buildings, some rooms have views of the Bay; Charley's Restaurant and Lounge has entertainment nightly.

Ramada Hotel–Fisherman's Wharf, 590 Bay Street, San Francisco 94133 at Jones; (415) 885-4700. A 230-room motel with The Conch Pearl Restaurant and Pecan's Lounge.

San Francisco Marriott–Fisherman's Wharf Hotel, 1250 Columbus Avenue, San Francisco 94133 at Bay; (415) 775-7555. Wellington's Restaurant located here also has a cocktail lounge.

Sheraton at Fisherman's Wharf, 2500 MasSan Francisco 94133, at North Point; (415) 362-5500. One of the newest motels, it has four small landscaped courts. Shannon's Lounge has entertainment nightly.

Travelodge-at-the-Wharf Motor Hotel, 250 Beach Street, San Francisco 94133, at Mason; (415) 392-6700.

Wharf Inn Motel, 2601 Mason Street, San Francisco 94133, at Beach (415) 673-7411.

LOMBARD STREET

San Francisco's motel row is along Lombard Street, Highway 101, from Van Ness Avenue to the Golden Gate Bridge; more than thirty motels cluster here. As a blur of colored lights at night it is a very Californian street.

Motel Capri, 2015 Greenwich Street, San Francisco 94123, at Buchanan; (415) 346-4667. A quiet, modern 1950s motel one block south of Lombard.

Star Motel, 1727 Lombard Street, San Francisco 94123; (415) 346-8250. Simple, with a classic neon sign.

VAN NESS AVENUE

Van Ness Avenue and Market Street are the widest streets in San Francisco. About a dozen motels cluster on Van Ness and almost as many along Market Street.

Cathedral Hill Hotel, 1101 Van Ness Avenue, San Francisco 94109, at Geary; (415) 776-8200.

Holiday Inn–Golden Gateway, 1500 Van Ness Avenue, San Francisco 94109, at Pine; (415) 441-4000. A stucco cereal box tower with excellent views east toward Nob Hill. Located near the end of the California Street cable car line.

Holiday Lodge, 1901 Van Ness Avenue, San Francisco 94109, at Washington; (415) 776-4469. Some suites with kitchenettes. A classic piece of good California motel design using wood, sandstone, and plantings to create a soft, modern environment. Good place to stay for evening strolls in Pacific Heights.

Van Ness Motel, 2850 Van Ness Avenue, San Francisco 94109, at Chestnut; (415) 776-3220. Basic; moderate rates.

CHINATOWN

Royal Pacific Motor Inn, 661 Broadway, near Stockton, San Francisco; (415) 781-6661. A typical contemporary American motel with rooms you have slept in before (was it Newark, Delaware?). Its freestanding sign is so bad it's good.

SOUTH OF MARKET

San Francisco's budget motels are right off the freeway ramps in the South of Market district. This is the utilitarian, unfashionable, but not unsafe side of town. Because San Francisco is so compact, you are still only a hop from all the major attractions.

Best Western-Civic Center Motor Inn, 364 Ninth Street, San Francisco 94103, near Harrison; (415) 621-2826. Not in the Civic Center.

National 9 Inn, 385 Ninth Street, San Francisco 94103; (415) 431-5131. At Ninth Street exit off Highway 101, near Harrison.

RICHMOND / OCEAN BEACH

Seal Rock Inn, 545 Point Lobos Avenue, at Forty-eighth Avenue, San Francisco 94121; (415) 752-8000. At the end of Geary Boulevard near the Cliff House, this "escape" motel is great for nature lovers; some rooms have a view of the ocean. The Ocean Beach and rugged Lands End with its panorama of the Golden Gate is a short walk away.

Hostels

SAN FRANCISCO

San Francisco International Hostel, Building 240, Fort Mason, San Francisco 94123; (415) 771-7277. Near the foot of Van Ness, at Bay. Well located near Aquatic Park and Fisherman's Wharf. Open for registration from 7 A.M. to 2 P.M. and from 4:30 P.M. to midnight. From the airport take SamTrans 7B bus to the TransBay Terminal in San Francisco. There take a Muni *northbound* 42 Downtown Loop "Gold Arrow" bus to Van Ness and Bay; follow the hostel signs.

YMCA of San Francisco, 166 The Embarcadero, San Francisco 94105; (415) 392-2197. A block south of the foot of Market Street; BART/Muni Metro Embarcadero Station. Clean and popular.

NORTH COAST

There are several hostels along the scenic, rugged coast near San Francisco. Some are in former lighthouses; the Point Reyes Hostel is in a former ranchhouse surrounded by fields. Splendid, hilly, seacoast hiking. For a free list of California hostels and membership information send a S.A.S.E. to American Youth Hostels, 425 Divisadero Street #306, San Francisco 94117, at Oak Street; (415) 863-1444. Hostels are not limited to the young and are open to all ages. Members and nonmembers may stay here. A safe way for single travelers to find companion-explorers.

Residence Clubs

These clubs offer rooms with shared baths and meals and are useful for those planning longer stays and for job-hunters.

Baker Acres, 2201 Baker Street, San Francisco 94115, near Jackson; (415) 921-3088. Shared baths; meals optional; in Pacific Heights.

Kenmore Residential Club, 1570 Sutter Street, San Francisco 94109, near Gough; (415) 776-5815.

Monroe Residence Club, 1870 Sacramento Street, San Francisco 94115, near Franklin; (415) 474-6200. Shared baths; well located in Eastern Pacific Heights apartment district.

Recreational Vehicles / Campgrounds

There are no campgrounds within the San Francisco city limits.

The San Francisco Recreational Vehicle Park, 250 King Street, San Francisco 94107; (415) 986-8730. Off the Fourth Street exit of Interstate 80, on the block bounded by Third and Fourth, Townsend and King streets, across the street from the CalTrain Depot. (Rail buffs should note that commuter trains operate from here to San Jose.)

Restaurants, Cafés, and Bars

This book is only incidentally a guide to San Francisco's more than four thousand restaurants and numberless bars, far too many to discuss individually. Several restaurant guides are available to help you pick and choose among the multitude. The Yellow Pages also lists many of San Francisco's restaurants by cuisine.

California—the Bay Area and Los Angeles' Westside in particular—seems to be making up for two hundred years of bad food by going through an accelerated evolutionary process of culinary development. The best general influence on contemporary San Francisco cooking is that of Asia and its low-meat, steamed, and stir-fried foods. Today "California cuisine" has emerged as a health-conscious style of cooking and of food-as-art presentation. The universally acclaimed temple to gastronomy today is Jeremiah Tower's Stars Restaurant; (861-7827), located at 555 Golden Gate Avenue, between Van Ness Avenue and Polk Street, near the Civic Center.

The spirit of the western saloon is alive and kicking in San Francisco, and always will be. In the Victorian city, there was a saloon on virtually every corner. Historian A. M. Schlesinger wrote that in 1890 San Francisco had more saloons relative to its population than any other American city. Private sanctums, sophisticated *boîtes*, middle-class lounges, single bars, sports bars, working-class taverns, black joints, ethnic havens, gay rendezvous, mixed places—San Francisco's bars and taverns have always been the city dweller's democratic "clubs." It is how Americans relax and compete at the same time. San Francisco bars are liveliest on Fridays and Saturdays after about 11:30 P.M.; all bars close at the early hour of 2 A.M.

SOME NEW CLUBS

South of Market, colloquially known as SOMA, is where you'll find the city's newest hot spots. In the daytime, Eleventh Street, between Folsom and Harrison streets is a light industrial zone. By night it blossoms into an entertainment district, most active Friday and Saturday nights between 11 P.M. and 2 A.M.

Ace Café, 1539 Folsom Street, between Eleventh and Twelfth; 621-4752. Monday–Friday; lunch, 11:30 A.M. to 3 P.M.; dinner, 6 P.M. to 1:30 A.M.; Saturday lunch, Sunday brunch. Painfully up-to-date interior; active late, inexpensive.

The DNA Lounge, 375 Eleventh Street, near Harrison; 626-1409. Open after hours, without alcohol, until 4 A.M. A large, two-level rock club.

Hamburger Mary's, 1582 Folsom Street, near Twelfth, 626-9516; Funky; almost a survivor from the hippie days; inexpensive.

Manora's Thai Restaurant, 1600 Folsom Street, at Twelfth; 861-6224. Moderate.

Norfolk Alley, between Folsom and Harrison, Eleventh and Twelfth, near The Ace Café. Has the best graffiti in town, but the spray can art is not as spontaneous as it looks; it's done from sketchbooks.

Paradise Lounge, 1501 Folsom Street, at Eleventh; 861-6906. A bar and small lounge featuring local talent.

Rings Fine Seasonal Cuisine, 1131 Folsom,

between Seventh and Eighth; 621-2111. Contemporary California cooking; moderate.

Slim's Nightclub, 333 Eleventh Street, near Folsom; 225-0333. Boz Scagg's fine blues, r&b, jazz, and rock club. The best choice here.

Soma Caffè, 1601 Howard, at Twelfth; 861-5012. A most relaxed and welcoming place.

Southside, 1190 Folsom, near Ninth; 431-3332. White tablecloths; the most uptown of these very downtown clubs.

The Stud, 399 Ninth, at Harrison; ;863-6623. Alive, young and gay since 1969; active dance bar even on weekday nights.

Taxi Café, 374 Eleventh near Harrison; 558-8294. Lunch till 3 P.M., dinner till 11 P.M.; moderate. Serves "new American cuisine" in an airy, minimal interior.

Museums

San Francisco has no encyclopedic museums of art or natural history, but many specialized museums, some of which are jewels, are spread out over the city. Several tours are built around these historical treasure houses. Asterisked entries are covered in greater detail in the appropriate chapter. The Oakland Museum, the Museum of California, is outstanding. *See Tour 14.*

Art Museums

Asian Art Museum/Avery Brundage Collection. *See entry for M. H. de Young Memorial Museum.**

California Palace of the Legion of Honor, Lincoln Park, 750-3600. Wednesday–Sunday, 10 A.M.–5 P.M.; fee. Large Rodin collection, including "The Shades" across the parking lot from the museum. The black granite Japan-America Peace monument faces the Golden Gate.*

M. H. de Young Memorial Museum, Music Concourse, Golden Gate Park; 750-3600. Wednesday–Sunday, 10 A.M.–5 P.M.; fee. The city's most diversified art museum also includes the Asian Art Museum, located next door. The Mr. & Mrs. John D. Rockefeller 3rd collection of American art, over a hundred fine works, was donated in 1979. Avery Brundage Collection and Asian Art Museum, 668-8921.*

San Francisco Museum of Modern Art, Van Ness Avenue at McAllister, in the Civic Center; 863-8800. Daily except Monday; fee, free Tuesdays. In a French Baroque building of 1932 designed by Brown and Landsburg; museum interior by Robinson and Mills, 1972. Changing exhibits, excellent photography galleries and a fine permanent collection.

San Francisco Art Institute, 800 Chestnut between Jones and Leavenworth, two blocks west of Columbus on Russian Hill; 771-7020. Tuesday–Saturday, 10 A.M.–5 P.M.; free. Shows in the Emmanuel Walter Gallery and student exhibitions. Not always open.*

Stanford University Art Museum, Museum Way, Stanford campus, Stanford; 497-3469. Tuesday–Friday, 10 A.M.–4:45 P.M., Saturday–Sunday, 1–4:45 P.M.; closed Monday and during August. See Tour 14.

The University Art Museum, Bancroft Way, between Bowditch and College, Berkeley; 642-1207. Eleven galleries; some Asian art; notable Hans Hoffmann collection; small fee. The Museum also houses the agreeable theater of the Pacific Film Archives (642-1412) which screens interesting films almost every evening. See Tour 14.

Historical and House Museums

African-American Historical and Cultural Society, Fort Mason, Building C; 441-0640. Tuesday–Saturday, 12–5 P.M.; free.

Alcatraz Island. See Tour 14.*

Bank of California, Museum of the Money of the American West. See Tour 2.*

Cable Car Museum and Powerhouse. See Transportation.*

California Crafts Museum, 900 North Point, in Ghirardelli Square; 771-1919. Daily, 10 A.M.–6 P.M.

California Historical Society, Whittier Mansion. See Tour 7.*

Chinese Historical Society of America. See Tour 3.*

Craft & Folk Art Museum of San Francisco, Fort Mason, Building A, first floor, next to Greens Restaurant; 775-0990. Tuesday–Sunday, 12–5 P.M.

Haas-Lilienthal House, See Tour 7.

Jewish Community Museum, 121 Steuart Street, near the foot of Mission Street; 543-8880. Daily 10 A.M.–4 P.M., closed Saturdays and Jewish and national holidays; usually free.

Judah L. Magnes Museum, Western Jewish History Center, 2911 Russell Street, Berkeley, near Claremont Hotel; 849-2710. Sunday–Friday, 10 A.M.–4 P.M., closed Saturday and Jewish and national holidays; small fee. Jewish ritual artifacts from all ages and places; materials on the Jewish communities in California and the western United States; changing art and history exhibits.

Joseph D. Randall Junior Museum, 199 Museum Way, near Buena Vista Park area; 863-1399. For children, Tuesday-Saturday, 10–5; free.

Mission Dolores Museum. See Tour 9.

Museum of Russian Culture, 2450 Sutter, between Divisadero and Broderick; 921-4082. Wednesday and Saturday, 11 A.M.–3 P.M.

North Beach Museum. *See Tour 4.*

Octagon House, 2645 Gough at Union; 441-7512. Second and fourth Thursday and the second Sunday of each month, from 12–3; free. An 1861 octogonal house furnished by the Colonial Dames of America.

Old Mint Museum, Fifth and Mission streets; 974-0788. Monday–Friday, 10 A.M.–4 P.M.; free. "The Granite Lady" was built in 1874 and minted silver dollars and gold coins until 1937. In 1973 it opened as a U.S. Treasury Department museum with gold nuggets, coins, exhibits on minting and Victoriana. Grand landmark with lackluster, perfunctory exhibits.

Pacific Heritage Museum, Bank of Canton of California. *See Tour 2.**

San Francisco Archives for the Performing Arts, War Memorial Opera House; 431-0717. Monday–Friday, 10 A.M.-5 P.M.; phone first.

San Francisco Fire Department Museum, 665 Presidio between Pine and Bush; 861-8000. Thursday–Sunday, 1–5 P.M.; free. Antique equipment and memorabilia of the city's great fires.

San Francisco History Room and Archives, Public Library, Civic Center, third floor; 558-3949. Tuesday, Thursday–Saturday, 10 A.M.–6 P.M., Wednesday 1–6 P.M.; Free. Showcases San Franciscana. Also conducts City Guide Walks; call 558-3981 for information.

San Francisco Presidio Museum, *See Tour 13.**

Society of California Pioneers, 456 McAllister, across from City Hall; 861-5278. Monday–Friday, 10 A.M.–4 P.M.; free. California history before 1869; has best collection of Victorian silver.

Sutro Library, 480 Winston Drive, near Nineteenth Avenue and Stonestown; 731-4477. Monday 10 A.M.–9 P.M., Tuesday–Saturday, 10 A.M.–5 P.M.; free. San Francisco photographs and other materials collected by Mayor Adolph Sutro, changing exhibits.

Telecommunication Museum. *See Tour 2B.**

Treasure Island Museum, Treasure Island, Building 1; 765-6182. Daily, 10 A.M.–3:30 P.M. Navy, Marine Corps, Coast Guard museum.

Wells Fargo Bank History Room. *See Tour 2A.*

Maritime Museum and Historic Ships

Hyde Street Pier historic ships. *See Tour 4B.**

S.S. Jeremiah O'Brien, National Liberty Ship Memorial, Fort Mason, Pier 3 East; 441-3101. *See Tour 4B.**

U.S.S. Pampanito Submarine, Pier 45, at Fisherman's Wharf; 929-0202. *See Tour 4B.**

Balclutha, 1886 square-rigger, Hyde Street Pier, near Fisherman's Wharf. *See Tour 4B.**

National Maritime Museum/Golden Gate National Recreation Area; 556-8177. *See Tour 4B.**

Scientific Museums and Zoo

California Academy of Sciences, Music Concourse, Golden Gate Park: Aquarium, 750-7145; Planetarium, 750-7141; small fee. Exhibits on natural history, an aquarium, and a planetarium.*

Exploratorium, Marina Boulevard and Lyon, behind Palace of Fine Arts; 563-3200. Open Wednesday–Friday, 1–5 P.M.; Wednesday evenings 7:30–9:30

P.M., Saturday–Sunday, 12–5 P.M.; small fee. This science museum has interactive exhibits on light and color, sound and music, motion, electricity and other natural phenomena with emphasis on human perception and how our senses work.

San Francisco Zoo, Sloat Boulevard and Forty-Sixth Avenue, in the far southeastern corner of the city; 661-4844. Daily, 10 A.M.–5 P.M., $4.

Lawrence Hall of Science, Centennial Drive, in the hills above the University of California campus in Berkeley; 642-5132. Monday–Friday 10 A.M.–4:30 P.M., Saturday, 10–5 P.M., Sunday, 12–5 P.M.; small fee. Astronomy, computer, and biology activities, also a planetarium.*

The Lowie Museum of Anthropology, University of California, Berkeley, Bancroft Way at College Avenue; 643-7648. Monday–Tuesday, Thursday–Friday, 10–4:30, Saturday–Sunday, 12–4:30 P.M.; closed Wednesday and holidays; small fee. Changing exhibits from an outstanding anthropological collection. *See Tour 14.*

Miscellaneous Museums

Carousel Museum, 655 Beach at Hyde, in Fisherman's Wharf; 928-0550.

Chevron's World of Oil Museum, 555 Market between First and Second; 894-6697; free.

Guinness Museum of World Records, 235 Jefferson, in Fisherman's Wharf; 771-9890; fee.

Musée Mechanique, 1090 Point Lobos Avenue, in the Cliff House; 386-1170; fee.

The Museum of Conceptual Art, 693 Mission at Third; 495-3193.

Museum of Modern Mythology, 693 Mission near Third; 546-0202. Founded

in 1982; changing exhibits such as "100% Polyester: Shirts of Art from the Palette of Science."

Ripley's Believe It Or Not Museum, 175 Jefferson near Taylor, in Fisherman's Wharf; 771-6188. Daily, 10 A.M.–10 P.M., Saturday and Sunday to midnight; fee.

San Francisco International Toy Center and Museum, 1005 Market Street, between Sixth and Seventh; 864-1169.

Tattoo Art Museum, 30 Seventh, off Market; 864-9798.

Wax Museum at Fisherman's Wharf, 145 Jefferson between Mason and Taylor; 885-4975; fee.

25

Union Square

EMPORIUM OF THE WEST

What This Tour Covers

Union Square:
San Francisco's Civic Stage

SAN FRANCISCO'S SPECIALTY STORES

I. Magnin
Neiman-Marcus / City of Paris Rotunda
Wright's 140 Maiden Lane
Saks Fifth Avenue
Macy's California
Emporium-Capwell
Nordstrom / San Francisco Centre
Marshall's / Old Hale Brothers

UNION SQUARE THEATERS

Geary Theater
Curran Theater

South of Market

MOSCONE CONVENTION CENTER

Clothing Factory Outlets

Contemporary Galleries

CONTINUATION

Esprit Factory Outlet

Best Times To Do This Tour

About 10 A.M. to noon on weekdays is generally the least crowded time to shop, both at department stores and individual shops. Saturdays are the busiest times around Union Square. Some factory outlets are only open on Saturdays, though not the ones listed here.

Parking

The glory of the Union Square shopping area is that it is a pedestrian zone. Garaging your car will cost about $13 for a full day from 10 A.M. to midnight. The twelve-level municipal Sutter/Stockton Garage one block northeast of Union Square is *the* garage; enter from Bush headed east. The private Downtown Center Garage at Mason/O'Farrell, a block to the southeast of the Square, is well-located for evening theater-going. The city garage underneath the Square itself, entered from Geary headed west, is central. Other garages are shown on the map.

Near Market Street, a massive Fifth and Mission city parking garage serves Nordstrom, The Emporium, and other Market Street stores.

Restaurants, Cafés, and Bars

UNION SQUARE AREA

Lascaux Bar and Rotisserie, 248 Sutter between Grant and Kearny, in basement; 391-1555: moderately expensive. Wonderfully named for a restaurant in a basement, Lascaux is brilliantly decorated with motifs taken from some of mankind's oldest art of about 14,000 B.C. Designed by Pat Kuleto, it serves "European country food." (Did the French have restaurants even then?)

Campton Place Bar and Restaurant, 340 Stockton in Campton Place Hotel, a half-block northeast of Union Square; 781-5155; very expensive. A fine, new and stylish bar and restaurant serving American food. Excellent breakfasts. The correct place to loiter, offering porthole glimpses of Union Square.

Janot's, 44 Campton Place, off block of Stockton between Post and Sutter; 392-5373; moderately expensive. A fine place for lunch with a calm, modern interior.

Ed's, 137 Kearny between Geary and Post, next to Sherman-Clay; inexpensive. The downtown worker's favorite hole-in-the-wall luncheonette for meatloaf sandwiches and chocolate milkshakes.

CLUBLAND RESTAURANTS

Fleur de Lys, 777 Sutter Street near Jones; 673-7779: expensive. Fine French cuisine well presented in a comfortable setting.

Donatello, 501 Post Street at Mason, in Pacific Plaza Hotel; 441-7182; expensive. Excellent Northern Italian cuisine nicely presented; no lunch.

Masa's, 648 Bush between Powell and Stockton; 989-7154; very expensive. No lunch. Closed Sunday and Monday, reservations essential. Fine French *haute cuisine* well presented.

Trader Vic's, 20 Cosmoy near Post and Taylor, 776-2232; expensive.

La Quiche, 550 Taylor between Post and Geary; 441-2711; inexpensive. Closed Sunday. Excellent quiche and crepes.

Mason Street Wine Bar, 342 Mason Street at Geary; 391-3454. Open seven days a week, 11 A.M. to 1 A.M.; piano music nightly. A wide selection of wine by the glass from California and Europe, nonalcoholic "wines," beers, Italian sodas, and juices.

Oz, at the top of the 1972 Tower of the Hotel St. Francis, Powell and Geary; 397-7000. Open 5 to 6:30 P.M. cocktail hour. The fastest exterior elevators in the

Copyright 1989 William Walters

An art glass dome made by the United Art Glass Co. in 1908 caps the belle époque rotunda of Bakewell and Brown's lost City of Paris department store reconstructed within Johnson/Burgee's 1982 Neiman-Marcus at Stockton and Geary, at the southeast corner of Union Square. The Latin motto is that of Paris: "It floats and never sinks."

city give a quick view of Union Square; acrophobes beware.

The Starlight Roof, in the Sir Francis Drake Hotel, twenty-one stories above the intersection of Powell and Sutter; 392-7755. Closed Sunday. Sophisticated dancing nightly. The festive electric sign and revolving neon star atop the hotel are visible from Union Square and add the perfect touch of glamour and unreality to the downtown at night.

SOUTH OF MARKET / MOSCONE CENTER

Max's Diner, 311 Third off Folsom, catercorner from the back of Moscone Center; 546-6297; inexpensive. Recreates the all-American diner with juke box selectors mounted on the counter and in the booths.

Entertainment

STBS (pronounced "stubs"), Stockton Street near Geary, on the edge of Union Square itself; 433-7827. Open 12–7:30 P.M.; closed Sunday and Monday. This small pavilion sells half-price, cash-only, in-person unsold tickets for day of performance events; also sells full-price tickets in advance as a BASS outlet.

Hotel St. Francis Theater Ticket Agency, Powell and Geary. Call 362-3500.

City Box Office, 141 Kearny at Sutter in Sherman-Clay music store. Monday–Friday, 10 A.M.–4 P.M.: 392-4400.

Downtown Center Box Office, 325 Mason in Downtown Center. Call 392-7469.

Ticketron, 325 Mason. Serves all California; charge by phone: 392-7469.

Shopping

San Francisco Health Food Store, 333 Sutter, near Grant, 392-8477. Open from 9:15 A.M. to 5 P.M.; Saturday till 1 P.M. The best California dried fruits; juice bar.

Morrow's Nut House, 111 Geary between Stockton and Grant; 362-7969.

The Candy Jar, 210 Grant near Maiden Lane; 391-5508. Makes its own chocolate truffles. The highest quality at a fair price.

John Walker & Co., Wines and Spirits, 175 Sutter near Kearny; 986-6836.

Malm Luggage, 222 Grant between Post and Sutter; 392-0417. Carries all major lines.

Louis Vuitton, 317 Sutter between Stockton and Grant; 391-6200.

Gucci, 200 Stockton at Geary; 772-2522.

Mark Cross, 170 Post between Grant and Kearny; 391-7770.

Hermes, 1 Union Square, Stockton at Geary; 986-6184. Much like the store in Paris; this is downtown San Francisco's new classic.

Swaine Adeney Brigg and Sons, Ltd., 434 Post near Powell; 781-4949. This deeply recessed shop front was designed in 1924 for John Howell's rare book shop. Inside are fine umbrellas, walking sticks, riding tack, dressage, shotguns, and cashmere sweaters.

JEWELRY

Tiffany & Co., 252 Grant Avenue near Sutter; 781-7000.

Cartier Jewelers, 213 Post between Stockton and Grant; 397-3180.

Shreve & Co., 201 Grant at Post; 421-2600. A historic Western silversmith that made many of the impossibly ornamented presentation pieces popular in the Victorian era out of Nevada silver.

J. M. Lang Antiques, 323 Sutter between Stockton and Grant; 982-2213. A treasure-trove of antique jewelry, objects of art, silver, ivory, amber, Russian Imperial things.

Robert R. Johnson, Inc., 353 Geary between Powell and Mason; 421-9701. Coins and estate jewelry.

Note: Those interested in silver should see the pieces at the Society of California Pioneers museum at 456 McAllister, 861-5278.

LINEN

Kris Kelly, 174 Geary, downstairs; 986-8822. Fine linen and hand-embellished tablecloths and bed linen. Designed by Media Five of Costa Mesa; one of the very best contemporary "stages" for fine merchandise.

Scheuer Linens, 318 Stockton between Post and Sutter; 392-2813. Fine table linens, sheets, and towels, also French and Italian sheets.

COOKWARE

Williams-Sonoma, 150 Post between Grant and Kearny; 362-5904.

FABRIC

Britex Fabrics, 146 Geary between Stockton and Grant; 393-2910. Four floors of fabrics from around the world, multilingual staff.

Pierre Deux Original Fabrics, 532 Sutter between Powell and Mason; 788-6380. Fine French fabrics.

City of Shanghai, 519 Grant between Pine and California; 982-5520. A large selection of fine silks; custom tailoring.

CLOTHING

Jessica McClintock Boutique, 353 Sutter between Stockton and Grant; 397-0987. Beautiful clothes behind a post-modern façade that makes a theatrical contrast between plate glass and a stage-set stone wall.

Laura Ashley, 253 Post between Stockton and Grant; 788-0190.

Obiko, 794 Sutter near Jones; 775-2882. Clothes as art; fine hand-woven textiles and contemporary designs.

The Forgotten Woman, 550 Sutter between Powell and Mason; 788-1452. High fashion for large sizes.

Comme Des Garçons, 70 Geary near Grant; 362-6400. Tokyo designer Rei Kawakubo's striking minimalist interior and art-furniture sets off her advanced clothing for men and women.

Polo–Ralph Lauren Shop, 90 Post at Kearny, near Crocker Galleria; 567-7656.

Banana Republic, 224 Grant above Post; 788-3087. This chain was founded in San Francisco.

Hound, Gentlemen's Clothiers, 111 Sutter near Montgomery; 989-0429. In Schultz and Weaver's fine Hunter-Dulin Building of 1926. Socks, tweed jackets; perhaps the best men's store in San Francisco.

A. Sulka & Co., 188 Post near Grant; 362-3450. There are only four A. Sulka & Co. shops in the world; shirts, ties, silk underwear.

Billy Blue, 73 Geary near Grant; 781-2111. Men's clothing.

Brooks Brothers, 201 Post at Grant; 397-4500. A large branch of this men's clothing store.

Cable Car Clothiers–Robert Kirk Ltd., 1 Grant near Market; 397-4740.

Bullock & Jones, 340 Post facing Union Square; 392-4243.

Burberrys, 225 Post between Stockton and Grant; 392-2200

Scotch House–Sweaters from Scotland, Ltd., 187 Post near Grant; 391-1264. Located in basement.

Eddie Bauer, 220 Post between Stockton and Grant; 986-7600.

Kaplan's Surplus & Sporting Goods, 1055 Market between Sixth and Seventh streets; 863-3486. Owned by The Gap, Kaplan's is stocked in depth and is a museum of classic American work, athletic, military and casual clothing. Also carries practical items a traveler might need in its camping department.

TOBACCO AND PIPES

Alfred Dunhill of London, Inc., 290 Post at Stockton; 781-3368.

Jim Mate's Pipe Shop, 575 Geary between Taylor and Jones; 775-6634.

BOOKSHOPS

Charlotte Newbegin's Bookshop, 8 Tillman Place, near Grant and Sutter; 392-4668. Small and inviting; fine selection; good for children's books.

Cookbook Corner, 620 Sutter, between Mason and Taylor; 673-6281. Includes local and early cookbooks.

B. Dalton Bookseller, 200 Kearny at Sutter; 956-2850.

Doubleday Book Shop, 265 Sutter between Grant and Kearny; 989-3420.

A Clean Well-Lighted Place for Books, 601 Van Ness at Opera Plaza; 441-6670.

Hunter's Bargain Bookstore, 151 Powell between Ellis and O'Farrell; 397-5955. Good for remaindered books.

Argonaut Book Shop, 786-792 Sutter near Jones; 474-9067. Californiana, Western Americana, a few African masks.

Yerba Buena Books, 882 Bush between Mason and Taylor; 474-2788.

Eastern Newsstand, 3 Embarcadero, Sacramento between Davis and Drumm; 982-4425. Best downtown newsstand; has the *International Herald-Tribune* daily.

Jeremy Norman & Co., 442 Post; 781-6402. A cozy den of rare books, including medicine and life sciences.

John Scopazzi, Bookseller, 278 Post, suite 305; 362-5708. Art, literature, maps.

Bernard M. Rosenthal, Inc., 251 Post; 982-2219. Medieval books and manuscripts.

Brick Row Book Shop, 278 Post, sixth floor; 398-0414. English and American literature, first editions.

Randall & Windall, 68 Post, third floor. Literature, travel, medicine.

TOYS

F.A.O. Schwartz Fifth Avenue, 48 Stockton at O'Farrell; 391-0100. Two floors of toys.

Art Galleries

The John Pence Gallery, 750 Post between Taylor and Jones; 441-1138.

John Berggruen Gallery, 228 Grant Avenue between Post and Sutter, upstairs/elevator; 781-4629.

Erika Meyerovich, 231 Grant Avenue between Post and Sutter, upstairs/elevator; 421-9997.

Fuller-Goldeen, 228 Grant between Post and Sutter, upstairs/elevator; 982-6177.

Stephen Wirtz Gallery, 345 Sutter between Stockton and Grant, upstairs; 433-6879.

Pasquale Iannetti, 522 Sutter near Powell; 433-2771. Original prints and drawings from the sixteenth century to the present.

Circle Gallery, 140 Maiden Lane, off Stockton (originally V. C. Morris Store); 989-2100. Superb Frank Lloyd Wright 1949 interior with gentle spiral ramp, some original Wright furniture, indifferent art.

Academy of Art College Gallery, 625-27 Sutter between Mason and Taylor streets; 765-4234. Behind a splashy, Spanish Colonial Revival façade of 1921 is this storefront gallery which mounts work by students and occasionally faculty.

ANTIQUES

Therien & Co., Inc., 534 Sutter between Powell and Mason; 956-8850. Period antique furniture and decorations.

Ed Hardy, Inc., Antiques, 750 Post between Jones and Leavenworth; 771-6644.

ASIAN ANTIQUES

Orientations, 34 Maiden Lane, off Stockton; 981-3972. Three compact levels of very fine Asian art; see the precious things in the basement vault.

Gump's, 250 Post between Stockton

and Grant; 982-1616. The Jade Room is on the third floor toward the front.

Far East Fine Arts, Inc., 518 Sutter near Powell, third floor; 421-0932.

Restrooms

The Ladies Lounge on the fifth floor of I. Magnin at Geary and Stockton is spacious and immaculate and has chairs where you may rest. Basic men's facilities are located on the ground floor of the Hotel St. Francis on Powell and Geary. They are all the way in the back, beyond the Tower addition's new lobby and its restaurants.

Introduction:
Emporium of the West

Fashion is, as Ambrose Bierce defined it, "A despot whom the wise ridicule and obey." In San Francisco, the seat of fashion is Union Square. San Francisco's Union Square area is one of the three best shopping districts in the nation, behind New York's and Chicago's, doing about $1 billion in sales in 1986. Great shops *say* something; and Union Square shops have a lot to say.

Because the entire district, with the exception of the new specialty department stores and parking garages, was designed during the peak of the streetcar era, and because people until recently would climb stairs or take elevators to second and upper floors, Union Square's shopping configuration is layered with uses; jewelers, furriers, hair salons, tailors and dressmakers, for example, are found over women's dress and shoe stores. To really savor Union Square, you must go upstairs inside buildings, to the second floor at least. Try the upstairs art and photography galleries in the 1905–07 Shreve Building at Post and Grant.

A highrise boom of the 1970s doubled

the amount of office space in the downtown and was followed by a boom in hotel building and the opening of three new upscale specialty stores in Union Square. Saks Fifth Avenue opened on the northwest corner of Union Square in 1981; Neiman-Marcus on the southeast corner in 1982; and in 1988 a spectacular new Nordstrom opened next to The Emporium on Market Street near the Powell Street cable car turntable. San Francisco's shopping district is like a fine old chassis fitted with a powerful new engine.

The recent history of Union Square is not surprising: with the revitalized city, rents have gone up to levels that only well-capitalized chain stores can afford. The individual, perfectionist shop is losing ground. On the positive side, these powerhouse specialty stores energize the luxury shopping district. Specialty store advertising draws shoppers past all the other shops and services surrounding Union Square. Post and Sutter streets still offer individual, one of a kind quality shops with fabrics, clothing, jewelry, fine books, and art.

Union Square:
San Francisco's Civic Stage

Union Square derives its name from pro-Union rallies held here in the 1860s on the eve of the Civil War. It is the center stage of the city's life, much more so than the misnamed Civic Center. Built into the west side of the center of Union Square is a little-noticed concrete platform/stage. The imposing façade of the Hotel St. Francis serves as its pleated back curtain. Here public receptions are staged and occasional protests erupt.

Of all the protests staged here, the memory of one always brings a smile. In August 1958, North Beach's beatniks, tired of being the objects of visitors' curiosity, marched—if that's the word— from North Beach, across Union Square, into the major department stores and hotels. Called "The Squaresville Tour," a hundred beats in Bermuda shorts and beards, or black slacks and sandals, followed a bongo drum player and brandished signs that read: "Hi Squares! The citizens of North Beach are on tour!" After amazing the bourgeoisie, the beats fell back to Upper Grant Avenue.

Union Square itself, the park, is something of a vacuum. Its benches are mostly left to the poor who sit and watch the whirlpool of Fashion swirling by. The park is flooded at lunchtime with office workers eating their lunch and socializing. Designed for hard use and occasional large crowds, it is also the landscaped roof of a five-level underground parking structure built in 1942 and designed by Timothy Pfleuger. It was the first, and still the best, of several such garages under downtown parks. In its early days the Union Square garage offered valet parking and shoppers could have their car call for them at nearby stores.

In the center of the park is the ninety-foot-tall **Dewey Monument** commemorating Admiral Dewey's victory over the Spanish navy at Manila Bay in 1898 during the Spanish-American War. This granite Corinthian column was designed by Newton Tharp, capped by a bronze of Victory bearing a trident and a wreath by sculptor Robert Aitken. The imperial monument was built by public subscription and dedicated by Theodore Roosevelt in 1903 at the peak of the Edwardian era. It did not topple in the 1906 earthquake.

Union Square and Geary Street together are the chief rift in the complex fault zones of San Francisco's social stratification. To the north is wealth and privacy, to the south and east are the poor, out Geary Street to the west is the middle class. In ten blocks, from California south downhill to Market, Mason Street slices through all the layers in the American class system from uppercrust to underclass.

The key players in the pageant of style here are the early morning wave of shoppers, particularly the wealthy matrons in chic suits wearing massive, sculpted jewelry. The famous white-gloved San Francisco old ladies are early shoppers, too. Both are in some quiet place by lunchtime when the second, younger wave of office worker shoppers fills the sidewalks and floods the department stores. After school come bands of teenagers; after 5 P.M., office workers do their shopping, perhaps staying downtown for dinner with a friend and a show.

Space for what became Union Square was reserved as one of only two new open spaces in Jasper O'Farrell's fateful city plan of 1847. Between Nob Hill and Market Street, Union Square became the focus for the elite Protestant churches and the principal Jewish synagogue. Calvary Presbyterian, the First Unitarian, and Trinity Episcopal churches faced the Square. Elite congregations occupied the sites of the Hotel St. Francis and Saks. Temple Emanu-El was a block up at 450 Sutter Street, and the First Congregational Church was, and is, a block west at Post and Mason. Elite private clubs also settled on the corners of the Square on Post Street, including the predecessors of the Pacific-Union Club and the Concordia and Argonaut clubs. The First Congregational Church, organized in San Francisco in 1849, moved to Post and Mason in 1879. It was the only one to stay; all the others migrated west with their congregations later in the nineteenth century to cluster along the axis of fashionable Van Ness Avenue and Franklin Street (see Tour 7).

Sutter Street leading west from the Square was a fashionable residential street in the Victorian period. Unlike Bush, Sutter had no alleys cutting up its prestige block fronts. It had immediate access to all the services of the center of the city without crossing through any industrial zones or intervening slums. As happened everywhere in nineteenth-century cities, high-class retail pursued

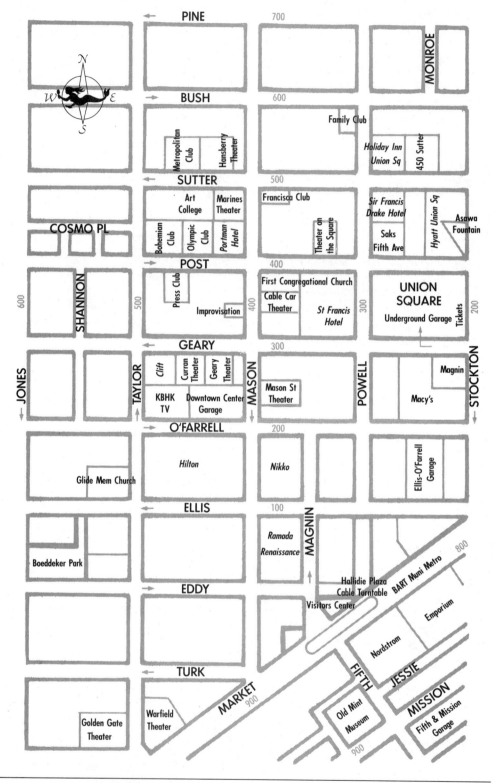

UNION SQUARE AREA AND SOUTH OF MARKET

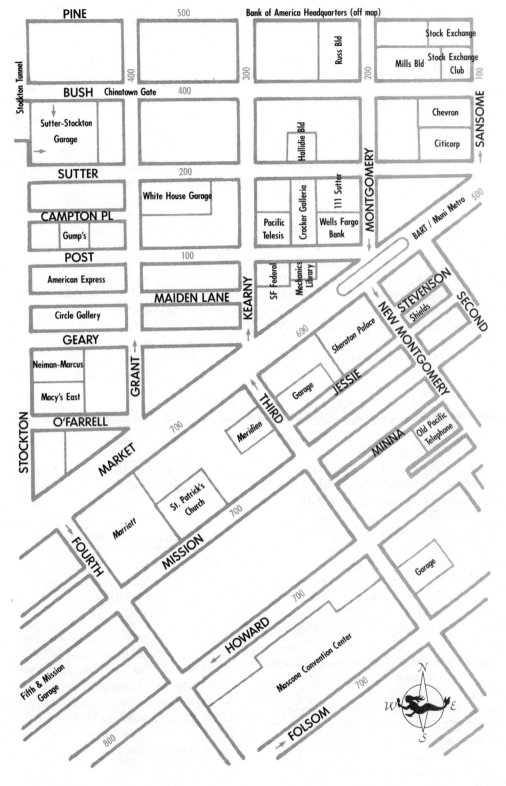

UNION SQUARE

fashion and "invaded" aristocratic streets. In Manhattan it was Fifth Avenue that changed; in San Francisco, Sutter Street. As the rich were attracted to better, newer, and more fashionable houses further west in Pacific Heights, business occupied leased-out, adapted houses along Sutter.

The next big change was the construction of the Hotel St. Francis on the west side of the Square in 1904–1908. Developed by the Crocker family, and designed by Bliss and Faville, this great, modern hotel skyscraper shifted the nature of the Square from churches and clubs to commerce. As originally built, the hotel occupied only the Powell and Geary corner and was expanded to reach across the entire block front. (The compatible tower with its giant "cornice" and exterior elevators was added in 1972 and designed by William Pereira Associates.)

The Spring Valley Water Company, William Bourn's great monopoly, built the City of Paris department store across the Square in 1896 where Neiman-Marcus now stands. When rebuilt by Bakewell and Brown in 1908, that store introduced the new commercial Union Square's great architectural treat: the great Rotunda. Here the city's fanciest Christmas tree delighted generations of San Francisco children being initiated into the "seasons" of shopping.

When the earthquake and fire destroyed the downtown in 1906, steel-frame buildings like the Hotel St. Francis and the City of Paris were rebuilt using the original frames. When lot owners rebuilt near Union Square after 1906, the city's very best architects were called on to design the new stores. If you look up here—hard as that is with all the things to see at eye-level—you will see a very handsome city, the city of the City Beautiful movement of the 1890s and early 1900s. Classical embellishments such as Corinthian pilasters, egg and dart moldings, sculpted brackets, and a whole dictionary of architectural

decorations make this district a great ensemble of American Edwardian city design. Each architect did something interesting with the design of the upstairs windows. There are treasures for those who look carefully.

The façade of **311–19 Grant Avenue** above Sutter, for example, is an example of unnoticed genius. This, the Abrahamsen Building, whose architect is unknown, is a reinforced concrete building that intelligently understands its fate. The composition of the windows of the top three stories floats forever separate above ground floor shops whose façades are destined to change. It uses the Chicago window, a large window flanked by two narrow ones, in a pattern that rises to the level of art.

Another real sleeper is the Bemiss Building at **266–70 Sutter** near Grant. This 1908, five-story building, whose architect is also unknown, was apparently designed using the largest standard size sheet of plate glass available. The windows are set in an almost skeletal façade. Here is one of the furthest developments in the efforts by San Francisco architects to get more natural light into their buildings.

San Francisco's Specialty Stores

I. Magnin & Co.
233 Geary Street, southwest corner of Stockton Street; 362-2100
1946, Pfleuger and Pfleuger

The oldest San Francisco specialty store is I. Magnin, founded in 1876. Its white marble-clad building at the southwest corner of Geary and Stockton has been a symbol of San Francisco sophistication since its redesign by Pfleuger and Pfleuger in 1946. Under this smart, modern skin is a prefire 1905 steel frame. The store's two great moments are the silver-foiled Cosmetic Hall on the main floor, and the Lalique-chandeliered third floor. The chandeliers look like glass plumes and are immensely festive. Out the window are the palms in Union Square.

These two spaces are among the best 1940s interiors in the city. Look carefully at the Cosmetic Hall and its low-relief silver foil ceiling, Lalique lights, and lotus-motif showcases. The clock is original.

Neiman-Marcus / City of Paris Rotunda
150 Stockton Street, southeast corner of Geary; 362-3900
1982, Johnson/Burgee

On the prime southeast corner of Geary and Stockton, facing Union Square, is the harlequin-patterned, reddish Italian granite-clad Neiman-Marcus designed by Philip Johnson and John Burgee which opened in 1983. Within its round glass and aluminum corner is the superb rotunda preserved from Bakewell and Brown's rebuilt City of Paris department store of 1908. Enter the rotunda and look up at the pale-colored art glass dome depicting a sailing ship—the emblem of the city of Paris—and the motto, *fluctuat nec mercitur*, "I float and do not sink." This four-story rotunda with its elaborate plaster decorations is one of the finest bits of *belle époque* design in the city—lavish, beautiful, festive. Its predominant colors are white and pale gold, a most sophisticated combination.

At the fourth level is **The Rotunda Restaurant** (call 367-4777 for reservations; lunch only; expensive) from which piano music sometimes wafts. Some tables have a clear view of the square across the street. The booths are comfortable. Good but less pricy is the **Fresh Market Restaurant** on Neiman's third floor.

The interior of the new store is not much; there are some postmodern columns on the second level of the store at the entrances of the men's and women's areas, but that's about it. The skylit crystal display room on the top floor offers a view of the tops of the city's old and new buildings.

Neiman-Marcus has one of the best large men's stores in San Francisco.

Circle Gallery / V. C. Morris
140 Maiden Lane, between Stockton and Kearny
1949, Frank Lloyd Wright

Halfway down Maiden Lane at number 140 is the outstanding V. C. Morris shop, now the Circle Gallery, which was designed by Frank Lloyd Wright in 1949, completely transforming a 1911 structure. This is one of the greatest architectural works in San Francisco. The façade and even the sidewalk were originally designed by Wright to work light into the architecture. Indirect lights are placed in the brickwork borders of the façade. White plastic lights with a key design border the bottom of the façade. Now cemented over, the three-quarters circle in the sidewalk in front of the entrance had lights under a thick slab of glass. The building was designed to lure the walker at night with its enticing lighting. Even when closed, the shop could be penetrated by walking into the glass-roofed entrance vestibule and looking up. (The acceptably designed metal gate is a recent, unwelcome addition.) The original handsome Wrightian lettering is still visible, reading V. C. Morris. The red square tile placed in the lower left-hand corner of the façade bears Wright's signature.

Inside, a gently curved ramp rises weightlessly toward the skylighted ceiling. Some of Wright's original circle-motif walnut furniture survives among store fixtures. As a crystal and china shop, this was a perfect marriage of purpose and design. The round shapes of the dishes and glasses were repeated subtly in every detail of the building, from the semicircular entrance to the round stools to sit on, to the translucent ceiling with its circles.

Saks Fifth Avenue

384 Post Street, northwest corner of
Powell; 986-4300
1981, Hellmuth, Obata & Kassabaum

On the northwest corner of the
Square, at Post and Powell, is the round-
cornered Saks Fifth Avenue store of 1981
designed by Hellmuth, Obata & Kassabaum. For a contemporary department
store, its exterior fits in relatively well
with its context—it has windows and
some modulation of its blank walls and
is an appropriate color. Its top floor
curved bay is occupied by The Restaurant at Saks (call 986-4758; open for
lunch and tea; no dinner). Some tables
here look down on Union Square and
across to the Hotel St. Francis. Saks has a
disappointing central area crisscrossed by
escalators going up five levels. A plain
skylight caps the space. It is instructive
to compare this space with the City of
Paris rotunda: the Edwardians did it
better.

Saks has some of the best clothes
shopping in the city for both women
and men.

Macy's California

101 Stockton Street, at northwest corner
of O'Farrell; 954-6000.
1928, 1948, Lewis Hobart; 1968, brick
façade on Geary Street

Fronting on Geary, Stockton, and
O'Farrell streets, Macy's California is
hardly ever looked at, which is understandable. It is an *ad hoc* building formed
out of an old one, the O'Connor-Moffatt
department store whose Gothic façade
of 1928–1948 faces Stockton and O'Farrell streets, and two intrusive 1968 brick-
faced additions facing Geary Street and
Union Square. It does, however, have a
useful public clock, an increasingly rare
service.

Macy's California revitalized retailing
in San Francisco in the 1970s, earning a
reputation for an entertaining shopping
environment. It does $200 million in

sales a year and is strongest in fashion,
home furnishings, and electronics.

Macy's has expanded across Stockton
Street into Macy's East, the blank-
fronted former Liberty House store built
in 1974. Men's clothing is downstairs and
a black and spacey electronics department occupies the entire top floor.

Emporium-Capwell

835-65 Market Street, at foot of Powell;
764-2222
1896, 1908, Albert Pissis
and Joseph Moore

Built in 1896, The Emporium on Market Street has a grand, classical façade, a
spacious rotunda, but a lackluster interior. The introduction of the restaurant
on a platform in the rotunda was a good
idea poorly executed. The huge building
was built for the Parrott Estate and
designed by Albert Pissis and Joseph
Moore. It was rebuilt with a steel frame
behind its original sandstone and brick
façade in 1908. The California Supreme
Court once occupied the third floor.

Nordstrom / San Francisco Centre

870 Market Street, southeast corner of
Fifth; 243-8500
1988, Whistler-Patri; Robinson, Mills &
Williams, and Stephen Guest,
project designer

Opened in 1988, Nordstrom's spectacular new store was designed by
Whistler-Patri with Robinson, Mills &
Williams and Stephen Guest as project
designers. It occupies the top four levels
of San Francisco Centre, a ten-level vertical shopping mall with some one
hundred other shops. The stately gray
granite façade relates to the great architectural row of which it is a part without parodying its Neoclassical neighbors.
The top of the building is stepped back
to allow more sunlight into Hallidie
Plaza across Market Street. The building's atrium is capped by a large glass-
and-steel dome that opens when the
weather is good. Three pairs of wide,
curved escalators designed by Mitsubi-

shi, the first of their kind in the United States, link the first four levels of the complex (there are conventional escalators and elevators on the higher floors). A three-screen cinema is tucked in the basement.

Like older great department stores, San Francisco Centre is directly linked to BART, Muni Metro, and its neighbor, The Emporium. The complex's most dramatic feature is not visible to the public: two special 60-foot-long elevators that lift 60,000 pound trucks from the street to the upper floors to deliver merchandise.

Marshall's / Old Hale Brothers
901–19 Market Street, southwest corner of Fifth
1912, Reid Brothers

Across Fifth Street from Nordstrom is the handsome classical block of the former Hale Brothers Department Store of 1912 designed by the Reid Brothers. Between its giant columns are modified Chicago windows. It originally had a columned court on its roof open to the sky. The building has been adapted for stores and offices.

Union Square Theaters

Old theaters seem to hold in themselves something of all the emotions and pleasures that have saturated them over the years. A transporting piece of theater in a fine old theater has a satisfaction few things in life can equal. The ornate Geary Theater of 1909 and the Curran Theater of 1922 next door, on the 400 block of Geary between Mason and Taylor streets, are two of the finest-for-their-purpose buildings in San Francisco. They, along with the War Memorial Opera House of 1932, make a night at the theater feel like a night at the theater.

Geary Theater
415 Geary Street
1909, Bliss and Faville

The Geary opened as the Columbia Theater and was designed by Bliss and Faville. It is built of reinforced concrete and finished inside with Utah Caen stone and Tennessee marble. Its façade is notable for its polychrome terra cotta columns of fruits and garlands. The legends "Comedy" and "Tragedy" adorn opposite sides of the doorway. It is the home of the American Conservatory Theater.

Curran Theater
445 Geary Street
1922, Alfred Henry Jacobs

The elegant Curran Theater was built by Homer Curran and designed by Alfred Henry Jacobs in 1922. It is also of reinforced concrete with a fine ornamented façade, mansard roof, and fine marquee. Its metal sidewalk sign frames are notable.

Cable Car Theater
430 Mason near Geary, downstairs next to Regency III
771-6900

Lorraine Hansberry Theater
620 Sutter, near Mason, in Sheehan Hotel
474-8842

Golden Gate Theater
42 Golden Gate Avenue, northwest corner Taylor at Market
473-3800

Improvisation
401 Mason near Geary, downstairs
441-7787

Marine's Memorial Theater
609 Sutter at Mason
771-6900

Mason Street Theater
340 Mason near Geary, upstairs
981-0371

Theater on the Square
450 Post near Mason
433-9500

Warfield Theater
982 Market, northeast corner Taylor
775-7722

Clubland

The blocks of Post and Sutter to the northwest of Union Square, where Nob Hill begins to rise steeply, are the heart of San Francisco's Clubland. There are fourteen private clubs in San Francisco, some of which have erected monumental, if discreet, buildings for their clubhouses. Most are in a modified Renaissance palazzo style. Some city clubs also own country retreats: golf links, farms, and redwood groves. All the city clubs provide dining rooms, bars, lounges, and libraries; some clubs are organized around in-club theatricals. A quick tour of part of Union Square's Clubland would begin at the corner of Powell and Bush at The Family Club.

The Family Club
545 Powell Street, at Bush Street
1909, C. A. Meussdorffer

The Family Club, a men's club, dates from 1902. The club's motto is "Keep Young," and its emblem is the stork. Its purpose is fellowship and the staging of entertainments performed exclusively by its members. The club has a country refuge in Woodside, The Family Farm. The city clubhouse is an elegant building designed in 1909 by C. A. Meussdorffer in the Renaissance palazzo mode and fitted onto a steep Nob Hill corner lot with a dramatic wedge-shaped base. Here is a classic San Francisco hill lot whose steep grade encourages the design of a building with its services accessibly tucked underneath it. It's the *base* of such buildings that makes them uniquely San Franciscan. A row of handsome arched windows marches around the corner to provide a well-lighted interior. It is a jewel of understated Edwardian elite design.

Tessie Wall's Townhouse
535 Powell Street
1911, C. A. Meussdorffer

Immediately downhill from The Family Club is Harcourt's Gallery in a Second Empire townhouse built in 1911 and also designed by C. A. Meussdorffer. It is notable as the only surviving structure downtown built as a single-family residence. It was bought by Frank Daroux, the Republican boss of the Tenderloin's vice, for his bride Tessie Wall, a madam. Despite the centrally located real estate, Tessie shot Frank dead.

The Francisca Club
595 Sutter Street, at Mason
1919, E. E. Young

The Francisca Club, on another prime corner, is a women's club housed in a sedate three-story Federal palazzo. It was designed by E. E. Young in 1919 and is built of fine red brick accented by white trim. Its domestic front door, painted in gleaming white enamel with white-shiny brass, is one of the most beautiful in the city, an icon of Anglo-American aristocratic design.

The Metropolitan Club
640 Sutter Street,
between Mason and Taylor
1916, Bliss and Faville; 1922, expanded

The Metropolitan Club, a women's club, is one of the finest club buildings in the city. It was designed and expanded by Bliss and Faville in 1916 and 1922. It originally housed the Women's Athletic Club. It is a brick and terra cotta-clad Renaissance palazzo with a colonnaded loggia. Two large escutcheons bear an intertwined W, A, and C.

The Portman San Francisco Hotel
500 Post (at the corner of Mason)
1987, John Portman

On land owned by the adjoining

Olympic Club stands the posh Portman San Francisco Hotel designed and managed by Atlanta architect-developer John Portman and his five sons and daughter. It opened in 1987 and features luxurious high-tech business conference facilities.

Like Portman's own house outside Atlanta, the design motif here is a semi-circular arch with a notch where the keystone would be. The windows have this shape, as do many of the elements inside the building. The Portman is designed around the automobile and features a drive-in area that cuts across the corner site. You must take the elevators to the third floor to see the grand lobby-atrium. The hotel has 348 rooms arranged around this sixteen-story open space. You may have a drink here or in the lounge on the top floor. The centerpiece sculpture of four dancing bronze figures is by Elbert Weinberg.

The Olympic Club
524 Post Street,
between Mason and Taylor
1912, Paff and Baur; 1906 pool pavilion
by Henry Schultz

The light sandstone base of the Olympic Club's Renaissance palazzo catches the eye in this brick-clad district. It also has a notable top story faced in fine, elaborate terra cotta ornamentation and a sheet metal cornice. One of the best club buildings in the nation, it was designed in 1912 by Paff and Baur, who won a competition staged by the club. Sandwiched between the club and the new Portman Hotel is the low swimming pool pavilion designed by Henry Schultz right after the earthquake of 1906. The pool inside is surrounded by a two-story colonnade capped by a glass roof, one of the most opulent interiors in the city. For many years this pool had its own pipe all the way out to the ocean to provide it with fresh seawater. The Doric-columned entrance to the clubhouse is designed after that of the Palazzo Massimi in Rome. The marble statues of athletes in the vestibule date

from 1912–1913 and are by Haig Patigian. To the right is the boxer Damoxenus, and to the left, the athlete Kreugas.

The all-male Olympic Club has its roots in the German elaboration of gymnastics and the organization of German-American *turn vereins* in the mid-nineteenth century. Twenty-three charter members held their first meeting at the socially elite Lafayette Hook and Ladder Company in 1860.

The Bohemian Club
625 Taylor Street, corner of Post
1934, Lewis Hobart

Next door to the Olympic Club, the Bohemian Club stands out for its mantle of green ivy over its red brick. It is a building built after the fire and completely remodeled in 1934 by Lewis Hobart in a discreetly classical Moderne style. The basement of the sloping site contains a large theater. The club dedicatedly maintains the only boxwood hedge downtown. With the vines and the hedges, the clubhouse seems to want to make its own forest on a city corner. On the Taylor Street side is a fine bronze *bas-relief* of Bret Harte characters sculpted by J. J. Mora in 1919. Around the corner on Post Street is the building's bronze cornerstone with the club's emblem—the owl—and motto, "Weaving spiders come not here." It bears the dates 1872, 1909, and 1933. The bronze plaque was designed by Haig Patigian and is one of the finest, if smallest, sculptures in the city, a gift to the observant walker.

The Bohemian Club was organized in 1872 by newspapermen, writers, and artists, hence its name. In a process of social gentrification, it evolved into a businessmen's club with a slant toward the arts. The club stages year-round entertainments in its theater in the base of this building and owns the 2,700-acre Bohemian Grove on the Russian River north of the city, the site of summer encampments and theatricals.

With 2,300 members, all male, the

Bohemian Club attracts attention for the great number of business and political movers and shakers who enjoy its hospitality. Perhaps the club's golden age was the early 1900s when it counted among its members Ambrose Bierce, Jack London, Frank Norris, Sinclair Lewis, and photographer Arnold Genthe. In the post-1906 period many of the city's best architects and fine artists, club members, designed and embellished the modern Edwardian city we enjoy today. The Bohemian Club's collection of art work by members includes the best collection of bronzes, paintings, and fine books created in turn-of-the-century San Francisco.

The Commonwealth Club of California
Call (415) 543-3353 for information about Friday speeches. These speeches are also broadcast live on KQED-FM, 88.5, at 12:30 P.M. Or write 595 Market Street, San Francisco 94105.

Organized in 1903, the Commonwealth Club of California has its roots in the reform movement of early Progressive California. Its Friday lunches with speakers are San Francisco's principal platform for policy statements by major public figures. It is characteristic of how well-organized—and how small—San Francisco is that there should be but one "bully pulpit" in town. The club has 23,500 members and is open to those who subscribe to its purposes: the investigation and discussion of problems affecting the welfare of the Commonwealth of California.

South of Market

Moscone Convention Center
747 Howard Street, between Third and Fourth streets. Moscone Convention Center event information, 974-4065; offices, 974-4000
1981, Hellmuth, Obata and Kassabaum

Moscone Convention Center opened in 1981. Designed by Hellmuth, Obata and Kassabaum, with T. Y. Lin, engineer, the white steel space-frame entrance pavilion caps enticingly designed escalators and stairs that cascade down to the underground exhibit hall. The hall has 300,000 square feet of space and is the size of six football fields. In 1990–1992, the center's size will be doubled with rooftop meeting space and an underground addition designed by Gensler & Associates, with Daniel, Mann, Johnson and Mendenhall. Gardens and pavilions are planned on the roofs of both halls. There will be a theater designed by James Stewart Polsheck and gardens designed by Mitchell/Giurgola; Maki and Associates of Tokyo will design a visual arts center. Swiss architect Mario Botta will design the new San Francisco Museum of Modern Art to be built on Third Street, between Mission and Howard, near Moscone.

Moscone Center hosts about 10 percent of San Francisco's conventions. (The rest meet in the large convention hotels, of which there are many.) Conventions began in the 1870s when railroad excursion tickets were sold to fraternal organizations. The first big conventions were the Mason's, the Odd Fellows, the Improved Order of Redmen, the Knights of Pythias, and all that panoply of small town and big city fraternal and Civil War veterans' organizations so important in late nineteenth-century America. Great parades up Market Street were the high points of these gatherings. Showy costumes and brass bands, flags, regalia and horses, carriages and floats passed between temporary plaster classical columns and bunting-draped streets. Some Market Street façades had lightbulbs worked into their ornamentation so that they could be turned on for evening parades.

Today, of course, conventions are usually business, labor, or professional meetings. They are, like the old Improved Order of Redmen conclaves, also intensely political; officers are elected or installed; politicking and palaver and deals flourish. The American genius for voluntary organizations thrives in these associations. They satisfy the political animal in Americans perhaps more than the political parties themselves.

CLOTHING FACTORY OUTLETS

Clustered in these south of Market blocks, roughly between Second and Fifth streets and Folsom and Townsend streets, are a number of clothing factory outlets. The **Van Heusen Outlet**, 601 Mission Street at Second, sells men's and women's shirts. **Six Sixty Center**, 660 Third Street at Brannan, is a cluster of factory outlets open Monday–Saturday 10 A.M.–5:30 P.M. At **275 Brannan Street**, near Second Street, is a cluster of factory outlets. On Bluxome Street between Fifth and Sixth streets, you will find **C. P. Shades' outlet** (777-5552) selling their usually high-priced sportswear at very reasonable prices: Also located in this alley are the **Banana Republic Outlet** (777-0250) and the **Rainbeau Factory Store** (777-5629). The diligent bargain-seeker will be rewarded with many discoveries; some outlets also sell a detailed map of area outlets.

CONTEMPORARY GALLERIES

871 Folsom near Fifth, one very long block west of Moscone Center, is a small but important cluster of contemporary art galleries all located in the same building. **871 Fine Arts** (543-5155), at 871 Folsom near Fifth, is a ground-floor gallery and book shop that stocks a comprehensive collection of catalogs on contemporary artists and exhibitions. **Don Soker Gallery** (974-6489), 871 Folsom on the second floor, displays fine contemporary art. **Crown Point Press** (974-6273), 871 Folsom on the third floor, is where many of the nation's premier artists have their lithographs and prints made; a wide selection of superb work.

South of the South of Market district,

on its former railyards, the Santa Fe Pacific Realty Corporation is planning the single largest construction project in San Francisco's history, Mission Bay a 300-acre complex of offices, light industrial space, housing, and parks.

Continuation

Located farther south of South of Market, in the industrial district off Third Street, is the **Esprit Factory Outlet** (957-2500) at Sixteenth and Illinois streets. The 22 Fillmore electric trolley and the 15 Third Street bus stop a block from the outlet. This clothing supermarket with its abundance of choices is techindustrial in image and the future now in mood. The Esprit Factory Outlet was designed in 1984 by Esprit's Bruce Slesinger and is one of *the* pieces of contemporary San Francisco environmental design worth examination. The store, the restaurant, and the heavy-duty poured concrete walls around the parking lot invite inspection. Although the handsome parking lot walls are too strong for their purpose, they manipulate the high building technology of today for effect. The heavy disco beat controls the mood and space inside the store. The clothing racks look like movie studio staging with their heavy aluminum pipes on industrial casters. Special stagelike lights spotlight the clothes. Behind the building, **Caffe Esprit** (777-5558), open Monday–Saturday from 11 A.M.–3 P.M., sells salads and pizzas.

43

The Financial District

DOMINANT INSTITUTIONS IN THE
POSTINDUSTRIAL CITY

What These Tours Cover

Tour 2A: The Jackson Square Historic District and The Financial District

[1] 700 Block of Montgomery Street: 1850s Survivors

[2] 400 Block of Jackson Street: Victorian Commercial Architecture / Antique Row

THE FINANCIAL DISTRICT

[3] Columbus Avenue / The Old Transamerica Flatiron / The Transamerica Pyramid / Observation Room / The Bank of San Francisco

[4] The Bank of Canton of California / Pacific Heritage Museum / Commercial Street

[5] 456 Montgomery Street

[6] Wells Fargo Bank History Room / Wells Fargo Bank Headquarters

[7] The Bank of California / Museum of the Money of the American West / California Street: Historic Divide

[8] Union Bank

[9] First Interstate Center / Mandarin Hotel / Tadich Grill

[10] Merchant's Exchange / Grain Exchange Hall / Coulter Marine Paintings

[11] Security Pacific Bank / Kohl Building

[12] Bank of America / History Exhibit / Carnelian Room / Panorama

CONTINUATION

Embarcadero Center / Hyatt Regency Hotel / The Royal Exchange / Old Federal Reserve Bank / Embarcadero Center West

Tour 2B: Skyscraper Sampler

[13] Russ Building

[14] Mills Building and Tower

[15] Chevron / Standard Oil of California Headquarters

[16] One Bush / Old Crown-Zellerbach Building

[17] Shell Building

[18] 130 Bush Street

[19] Shaklee Terraces

[20] 388 Market Street Flatiron / Market Street: Main Stem and Great Divide

[21] Citicorp Center

[22] Hunter-Dulin Building

[23] Former French Bank

[24] The Hallidie Building

[25] Crocker Galleria / Pacific Telesis Tower

[26] Mechanics' Institute Library

[27] New Montgomery Street / Sheraton Palace Hotel

[28] Sharon Building / House of Shields

[29] Pacific Telephone and Telegraph Company / Telecommunication Museum

Preliminaries

Best Times To Do This Tour

Bank hours are Monday to Friday, 10 A.M. to 3 P.M. and that is when you should explore the Financial District. Noontime is people-watching time; Transamerica's Redwood Park or the steps around the BART subway station near Montgomery and Market are good spots to sit. If you lunch at Tadich Grill about 3 P.M., you will not have to wait to be seated (they take no reservations) and the restaurant will be calm and relaxing. After 3 P.M. the Carnelian Room cocktail lounge is open atop the Bank of America. The view from here at sunset and afterglow is the best in the city. If you visit the downtown at midday, you can take the California cable car to Drumm Street, cross The Embarcadero to the Ferry Building, and take the Golden Gate Ferry to Sausalito for dinner. This lets you view the city skyline reflected in the water and from across the San Francisco Bay.

The Financial District is, of course, ruthlessly governed by time and bureaucratic etiquette. All this seriousness finds its only tribal release on the last business day of the year when office workers throw desk calendar pages to the winds and make confetti out of the preceding year. For several days the sidewalks downtown are a mosaic of random, provocative dates, black for business, red for holidays. It seems such a carefree, unbusinesslike thing to do, to throw away one's calendar with its record of the year's work. And so it would be if office workers actually threw *their* calendars out the window. But they don't; when you inspect the pages, all are blank. These are extra calendars stowed away for just this ritual of release. So even this "spontaneity" is calculated—cost control managers point to the expense of sweeping up the mess. Humans understand the urge.

Parking

The city's Portsmouth Square Garage at Kearny and Clay is the least expensive. There is another city garage at St. Mary's Square; enter from Kearny north of Pine, across from the Bank of America. On Saturdays parking is free in Embarcadero Center with a validated purchase; on Sundays it is plain free.

Transportation

The California cable line plunging downhill from Powell Street and Nob Hill is the most dramatic way to enter the Financial District. There is also a stark, white-tiled BART subway station at Montgomery and Market streets.

Restaurants, Bars, and Cafes

The Financial District has coffee shops, not relaxed cafés. **Caffe Roma** on Columbus near Vallejo in North Beach is a fine retreat well out of the Financial District. The recommended restaurant is the Buich brothers' historic, high-standard **Tadich Grill** (391-2373), 240 California Street between Battery and Front. It is the oldest restaurant in California. Charcoal-broiled seafood, fresh California vegetables, and rice pudding are the specialties. Reservations are not taken. **Jack's Restaurant** (421-7355, 986-9854), 615 Sacramento Street above Montgomery, opened in 1864 and serves French/Continental cuisine in a historic 1907 restaurant building with private rooms upstairs. Some say regulars are treated better than visitors. **Ernie's** (397-5969), 847 Montgomery near Pacific in the Jackson Square Historic District, serves pricey *nouvelle cuisine* in a plush Victorian environment. **Bix Restaurant and Lounge** (433-6300), 56 Gold Street in the Jackson Square Historic District, is a stylish new restaurant in a grandly converted old brick warehouse. For its mon-

Copyright 1989 William Walters

The Bank of California, at the center of the banking district, fuses Bliss & Faville's 1908 Corinthian temple with Anshen and Allen's 1967 fluted highrise.

umental old wood bar with pillars and arches, the 1912 **House of Shields**, 39 New Montgomery across from the Palace Hotel, is worth a drink.

One of the best high-toned Financial District bars is the **Royal Exchange**, 301 Sacramento Street at Front across from One Embarcadero Center. Here good-looking people in good-looking clothes talk the local *patois*: percentages. Downtown's many bars are liveliest weekdays from about 5 to 7 P.M.; they really hop on Friday. The cocktail lounge with the best view is the **Carnelian Room** atop the Bank of America, open to the public after 3 P.M., a good place to conclude your exploration.

Shopping

Sutter Street between the Financial District and Union Square has several fine men's clothing stores. *See Tour 1.*

The fine **antique shops** along Jackson Street between Montgomery and Sansome, in the Jackson Square Historic District, are jewels. Fine English and French antiques are agreeably displayed in Victorian brick buildings along a tree-lined block. (Dress up; unlike most of San Francisco, you will be judged by what you wear here.) At any one of the shops you can ask for a copy of the Jackson Square Art and Antique Dealers Association brochure/map. These are also fine blocks for an evening's stroll. The closed shops leave their lights burning; the effect is quite domestic. Montgomery Gallery, 824 Montgomery near Pacific, often shows fine regional paintings from the nineteenth and early twentieth centuries. Here you can see some of the western landscapes and Indian and cowboy scenes long popular with San Francisco collectors.

Introduction: Dominant Institutions in the Postindustrial City

San Francisco has been called the "instant city" because of its phenomenal development from a sleepy backwater port of less than a thousand to a booming city of 20,000 after the Gold Rush of 1849. As the major American seaport on the West Coast (which quickly overtook older Portland, Oregon), San Francisco attracted Navy and Army headquarters, federal offices, shipping companies, banks, importers, manufacturers, preachers, lawyers, doctors, architects, engineers, photographers, actors, restaurateurs, journalists and writers, prostitutes and all the other specially skilled people needed to make a city.

The Victorian city that developed between the global sealanes and the transcontinental railroad became the cultural center for the entire Pacific Slope. A jerky series of building booms and busts resulted in a chaotic jumble of old and new buildings. Without zoning, the untrammeled controlling force was the price of lots, which was set by a combination of accessibility, notions of prestige, and demand.

The growing city soon abandoned its early center at Portsmouth Square and migrated onto bayfill east of Montgomery Street. Banks, then as now, were the institutions that determined the geographical heart of the Financial District. When William Ralston's then-dominant Bank of California built a Renaissance Revival marble palace at California and Sansome in 1866, it determined where prestige would focus. Despite its prominence in the city's layout, Market Street never rivaled California Street as *the* prime address. Luxury retail also moved south from Portsmouth Square to settle along lower Kearny Street in the 1860s and 1870s, later shifting westward to Union Square in the early 1900s.

The booming Victorian city was an

eclectic mixture of architectural styles. The sober Greek Revival of the post-Gold Rush days, still visible in traces in the Jackson Square Historic District, was soon superseded by much fancier stucco-covered brick and timber buildings in the Italianate, Eastlake, Renaissance Revival, Gothic Revival, and mansarded Second Empire styles.

From within this brick city a new kind of building erupted in the 1890s: the iron and steel frame, brick-clad skyscraper. The first was the Chronicle Building at Market and Kearny built in 1889 for the San Francisco *Chronicle* and designed by the Chicago firm of Burnham and Root. (The building survives at 690 Market under the banal veneer of an unfortunate 1962 modernization. Its restoration would be a key addition to the city's architectural heritage.) Today the best remaining example of this first wave of steel-frame construction is the Mills Building at 220 Montgomery at Bush, built in 1891 in the Romanesque Revival style and designed by Burnham and Root. In 1902 Charles Keeler described these new buildings: "A gratifying feature of the work is the simplicity of design followed in nearly every instance. Costly materials and the most perfect of modern workmanship, combined with good proportions on broad lines, are bound to make the new San Francisco an eminently satisfying city architecturally." What he saw as simplicity in 1902, we call "ornamented" today.

The new skyscrapers of the 1890s and turn of the century made possible the vertical expansion of the downtown. They were served by the streetcar system that focused commuter flows in the city and made downtown lots all the more central and valuable. In 1904, the Society for the Improvement and Adornment of San Francisco was formed by the city's business elite under the leadership of banker and former reform mayor, James D. Phelan. This private group invited Daniel Burnham and Edward Bennett to come to San Francisco to

"blue sky" a modern plan for the city. In 1905 the grandiose Burnham Plan was published, which called for carving a system of Parisian boulevards diagonally across the city's built-up gridiron of streets. The plan also called for a new, monumental civic center, and vast parks in the undeveloped southwestern section of the city reaching from Twin Peaks to the sea. It was far too gargantuan a plan to ever be implemented and lacked any suggestion as to just how private property owners were to be compensated for parting with their land to accommodate the grand boulevards.

When the earthquake struck in 1906, the city was in the midst of a great building boom. There were about two dozen steel-frame buildings then in the Financial District and along Market Street. While all were gutted by the fire that broke out after the earthquake, their steel frames survived and most were reconstructed and stand today. The old brick Victorian buildings, on the other hand, became irreparable shells. Between 1906 and about 1909, San Francisco was an "instant city" for a second time. The Burnham Plan was ignored in the rush to rebuild. While most of the buildings were destroyed, the patterns of lot ownership and relative prestige were not. A proposal to widen Montgomery Street was thwarted by a single property owner who refused to shave the necessary square feet from his prime lot. By the summer of 1907, six thousand buildings had been completed and three thousand others were under construction. Part of the capital for this boom was money paid out by insurance companies. (This substantial payout depended on a fortunate court decision that held that it was not the earthquake but the subsequent fire that destroyed the city and that fire insurance policies had to be honored.)

Because the city rebuilt all at once, the result was an up-to-date Edwardian city of a remarkable architectural coherence. The steel-frame skyscrapers of the immediate prefire years set the standards for the rebuilding. Unlike the very earliest tall buildings which were clad in brick or stone, the postfire steel-frame buildings were clad in lighter terra cotta tiles, most in a pleasing off-white, softly light-reflecting color.

A second smaller, but architecturally creative, building boom hit San Francisco in the mid-1920s. This time taller skyscrapers with set-back towers appeared, changing the city's skyline. For the first time, the skyscraper was made to appear to soar upward. Miller and Pfleuger's 450 Sutter Street medical office building of 1929 was the last structure built during this boom, which was ended by the Stock Market Crash of the same year. There was to be little major building downtown until the late 1960s.

In the 1960s investors, city planners, and architects declared war on the traditional city fabric and in a great wave of development—the first of two massive urban renewals—built either isolated towers in "plazas," or put parking garages on the ground level as podiums for large buildings placed atop them. Such city busting designs gave the choice ground level to automobiles and relegated pedestrians to elevated walkways connecting the arid rooftop plazas. Highrise design hit rock bottom about 1960 with Albert F. Roller and John Carl Warnecke's new Federal Office Building in the Civic Center. Here the "tower in a plaza" becomes utterly soul-crushing, an Orwellian, alienating monolith sterilizing an entire wind-swept block.

Fortunately, in the design of Embarcadero Center with its half-dozen highrises, in the second phase of Urban Renewal design that began about 1970, ground level was returned to the pedestrian and parking was moved underground, where it belongs in the cosmic scheme. All the city's richest corporations, especially the banks and insurance companies, commissioned grand architectural works culminating in the dark red granite Bank of America World Headquarters of 1969 and the slim, white Transamerica Pyramid of 1971. When Crocker Bank built its sleek pink granite headquarters in 1982 on the Montgomery, Kearny, Post, Sutter block, the last of the big hometown corporations built its palatial new tower, this time with a glass-roofed shopping arcade enlarging and enriching the walker's domain.

Because of the configuration of its recent growth, the "energy" of the office core has "imploded" rather than dissipated as has happened in most American downtowns since the 1950s. The traditional center is still central in San Francisco, and that is the key to the Financial District's attractiveness.

Large new buildings north of Market Street have had to be ingenious to fit into the prime historic blocks. Imaginative construction and preservation projects are making the Financial District ever more complex and "layered." When New York's Citicorp built its fine new tower at One Sansome, it converted the bank temple on the corner of its plot into the glass-roofed entrance court for a new tower. At 345 California Street, California Center, at one of the choicest locations in San Francisco, a brilliant "shoehorn" job was pulled off by Skidmore, Owings and Merrill in 1986. Here four corner office buildings important to the fabric of the traditional Financial District were preserved and a new tower built in the center of the block with elegantly designed sidewalk-level concourses threaded through the block to the tower.

Partial preservation of historic buildings in new projects has a mixed record in San Francisco. The fault has not been in the saving of the old fragments but in the insipidity of many of the new designs. The scale of artifacts saved has jumped from the half-dozen granite walrus heads salvaged from the Alaska-Commercial Building by First California Bank in 1977 to the forty-ton fragment of the richly ornamented cornice of the

Holbrook Building handsomely mounted inside a restaurant in the base of the Citicorp Center highrise in 1984. But when these bits and pieces of the old city are appropriately handled, they add much to the new Financial District, educating people about the value of ornament on buildings and making people more aware of their architectural environment.

The city-changing building boom from 1965 to 1985 added a million square feet of office space a year, doubling the total amount of office space in San Francisco to 38 million square feet. While the big banks built the showpieces, most of this growth was financed by insurance companies seeking large, secure investments. Since the mid-1980s, the very finest Financial District architecture has been commissioned by foreign investors willing to spend top dollar to erect premium buildings. By 1986 about 30 percent of San Francisco's Financial District office buildings were foreign-owned. The crest of this latest wave of investment are California Center at 345 California Street built by Norland Properties owned by an American insurance company and Middle Eastern investors, and 388 Market, the sleek red granite-clad flatiron building at Market and Pine, built by Honorway Investments and Hong Kong investors.

Such phenomenal growth made continued commercial development *the* hot political issue. The office boom stoked the housing-price boom that quintupled residential real estate values between 1973 and 1976. Tax assessments on a typical home in the city zoomed up 582 percent during the 1970s. Growth in jobs continues to outpace the production of housing both in the city and in the Bay Area as a whole. Widespread choice of independent single living has meant a declining number of people in each unit of housing and therefore a growing need for more units.

It is the *imbalance* between housing and office growth, rather than office growth itself, that is the region's major challenge. San Francisco has led the nation in requiring new office developers to contribute towards the construction of affordable housing, public transit, new open space, and child care programs to mitigate, as the word has it, the impact that office construction has on the rest of the city. Increasingly, other cities are following San Francisco's lead.

Despite what it looks like in the magazine ads, not all San Franciscans are rich. A majority are renters. The rapid escalation in rents precipitated the move to establish rent control in 1979, and to reduce the rate of downtown expansion to 475,000 square feet a year (the equivalent of one twenty-five story highrise) in 1986. Establishing a quota for new office construction is precedent-setting. An ultimate political-economic question is at stake here: How can commercial and housing growth achieve balance? Why cannot America produce middle- and lower-income housing? Who is a city for?

The best thing that has happened in downtown San Francisco over the past decade is the now general recognition of the high architectural quality of almost all of it and of the necessity of conserving and adding to it rather than detracting from it. The real works of art, such as the Pacific Telephone Headquarters at 140 New Montgomery, are today recognized by their owners for what they are. Pacific Telephone's six-year-long restoration of its 1925 terra cotta-clad Moderne masterpiece is the kind of corporate commitment to the downtown that has created, and that sustains, what is undoubtedly the most pleasant, and though costly, most efficient office core in the United States.

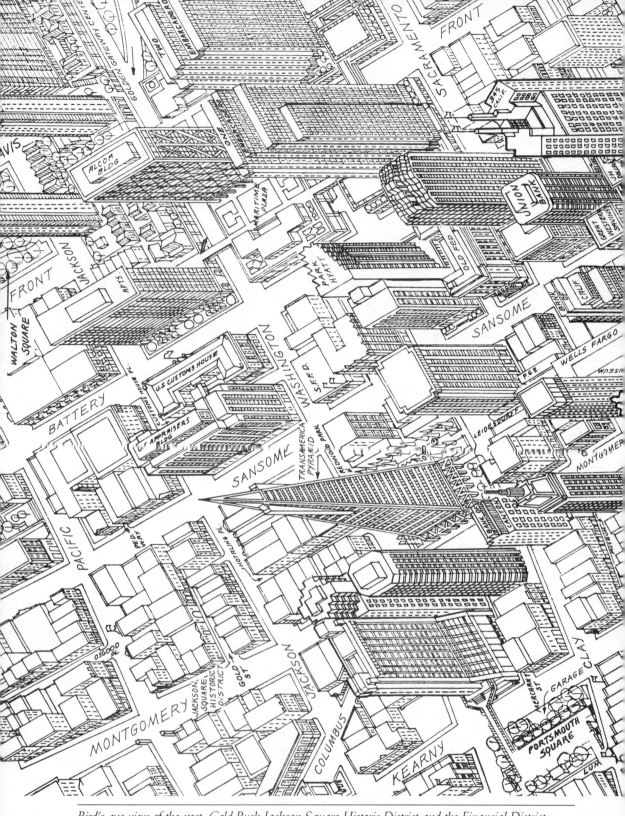

Bird's-eye view of the post–Gold Rush Jackson Square Historic District and the Financial District from the Transamerica Pyramid to Market Street.

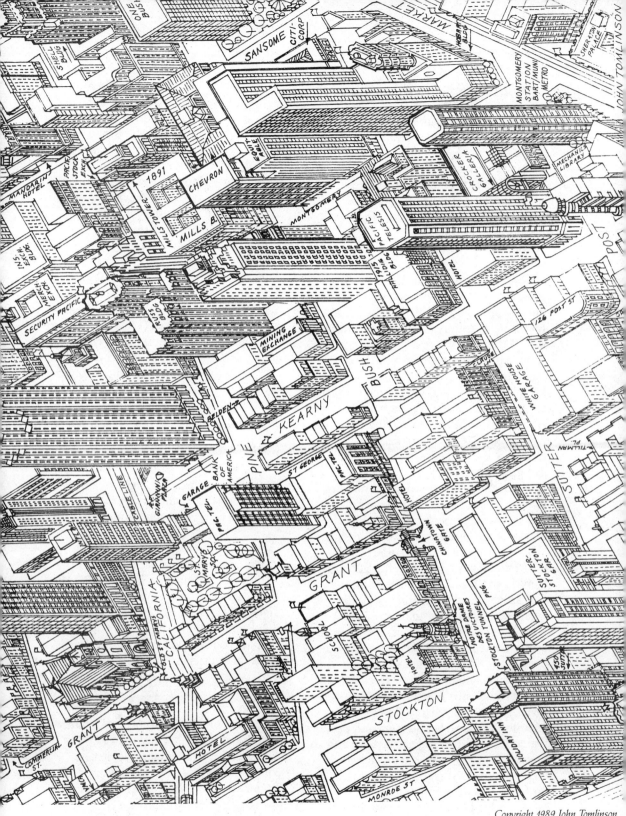

Copyright 1989 John Tomlinson

Tour 2A

The Jackson Square Historic District

The Jackson Square Historic District was established in 1971 and consists of approximately four-and-a-half blocks bounded by Washington, Columbus, Pacific, and Sansome streets. It preserves what survives of the post-Gold Rush commercial district. It is San Francisco's first historic district.

Montgomery Street was the original shoreline of the port of Yerba Buena. In the boom that followed the discovery of gold, the young city of San Francisco quickly filled in the cove to make space for piers, warehouses, shops, and offices. Part of this fill consisted of abandoned ships which still underlie some of the buildings. Balance Street, a short alley between Jackson and Gold streets, is said to be named after a ship buried there when the instant city expanded into the Bay. Immediately west of the docks, these blocks attracted shops, professional and governmental offices, banks, consulates, assembly halls, and small manufacturing operations. Among the distinguished early San Franciscans who had offices or businesses here were General William Tecumseh Sherman; Colonel Jonathan Stevenson; James King of William; Faxon Dean Atherton; Domingo Ghirardelli; Anson Hotaling; and mayors Charles Brenham and Ephraim Burr.

As San Francisco grew, its commercial center shifted south. Like a receding tide, prestigious users left the area behind. These quickly old buildings then were rented out to small factories, wholesalers, liquor and tobacco dealers, cigar factories, and later on printing and paper warehouses. When the earthquake and fire struck in 1906, the buildings here were freak survivors. But because the area was no longer prime real estate, owners expediently patched-up their buildings but did not significantly alter or modernize them. Pacific Street attracted dance halls, saloons, boarding houses, and prostitutes' "cribs"—earning that part of the district the nickname Barbary Coast, after the pirate-infested stretch of the North African coast.

The Depression of the 1930s weakened the fringe industrial uses that had settled here, and some artists and writers were attracted to the low-rent district. (Today a display case in the lobby of the Washington Montgomery Tower recounts the history of this 1930s bohemia.) By the 1940s, some buildings on these historic blocks stood vacant. Fortunately, the district was spared wholesale demolition for parking lots, the fate of many Victorian commercial areas near American downtowns. (The historic Montgomery Block, however, was demolished for parking.) In the early 1950s, interior decorators and the wholesale furnishings industry discovered the area and began restoring and improving these intimate blocks with appropriate signage and street trees. After them came architects looking for inexpensive space adjacent to clients downtown. It was the decorator trade that coined the name "Jackson Square," after the concentration of vintage structures along the 400 block of Jackson Street.

Eventually, restaurants, clubs, and advertising and law offices displaced the decorators who then went on to pioneer the preservation and conversion of the larger red brick warehouses at the base of Telegraph Hill in the 1960s, before skipping south to the former warehouses in the Showplace Square area in the 1970s where the decorator and furnishings industries cluster today. Today a few retail shops in Jackson Square, including the outstanding William Stout Architectural Books at 804 Montgomery and a cluster of fine art and antique dealers along Jackson Street, retain the district's connection with decoration and design.

The oldest row of post-Gold Rush survivors is along the east side of the 700 block of Montgomery, between Washington and Jackson. On the **northeast corner of Montgomery and Washington streets** is the elegant former Columbus Savings Bank built in 1905, a fine Beaux Arts building with a rounded corner and Ionic engaged columns designed by Meyer and O'Brien. It is faced with gray-green Colusa sandstone. Next door, at **708 Montgomery Street**, is the Canessa Building, built right after the 1906 fire. It has a white glazed brick façade and four round windows along its top. It was once the home of the Black Cat Bar, one of San Francisco's most famous—or infamous—bohemian rendezvous. Owner Sol Stoumen described his patrons as "merely members of the bohemian intelligentsia who gather at the Black Cat to discuss art and semantics, in the best San Francisco tradition." The Black Cat was famous for its out-of-the-closet Halloween costume parties and for police harassment. It closed on Halloween 1963.

At **722 Montgomery Street** is the Belli Building built in 1851 by Henry W. Halleck, an engineer who devised a novel foundation for brick buildings built on landfill, consisting of a redwood "raft" eight feet thick. The building's first recorded tenant was Langerman's tobacco warehouse. It was later converted into the Melodeon Theater and presented, among others, singer Lotta Crabtree. Later tenants included commission merchants, an auctioneer, a Turkish bath, and, in the 1880s, a medical establishment specializing in hydrotherapy. In 1958 lawyer Melvin Belli bought the old building and gussied it up New Orleans style. The original stucco was stripped to reveal the brickwork and an antique French post box was attached to the façade. The colorful Belli has decorated the first floor front office with mementos of his career.

Number **728–30 Montgomery Street**, the Belli Annex, originally the Genella Building, is a three-story, Italianate brick and timber structure erected in 1853–54 on the foundation of an 1849 building. This site is the birthplace of Freemasonry in California; Lodge No. 1 met here on October 17, 1849, right after the Gold Rush. Later its upstairs hall was used by the Odd Fellows.

A plaque affixed to the old Transamerica flatiron across the street records that on that site the first Jewish religious service in San Francisco was held on Yom Kippur (5610), September 26, 1849.

Number **732 Montgomery Street** is the *Golden Era* Building, built about 1852 on the foundations of an 1849 structure destroyed in the fire of 1851. The cast-iron pilasters on its façade are dated 1892 and are a later addition, the pilasters on the rear of the building facing Hotaling Place are dated 1857. *The Golden Era*, an early literary weekly that published work by Mark Twain and Bret Harte, was edited here. On the corner stands a larger building built in 1965 with blank red brick panels in a modern style that once housed the Playboy Club. Its façades were recently redesigned to blend better with the historic district.

400 BLOCK OF JACKSON STREET:
VICTORIAN COMMERCIAL
ARCHITECTURE / ANTIQUE ROW [2]

The block of Jackson Street between Montgomery and Sansome streets, the heart of the Jackson Square Historic District, is interesting because it shows the shift from the plainer commercial architecture of the 1850s to the fancier styles of the 1860s. The north side of the block is dominated by 1850s buildings, the south side by more elaborate buildings of a decade later. Today this block harbors a cluster of the finest antique shops in the city.

On the northeast corner at **804**

55

Montgomery Street is the two-story base of the originally three-story Bank of Lucas, Turner and Co. built in 1853–1854. This St. Louis-based bank was briefly headed by William Tecumseh Sherman, who resigned his army commission in 1853 to come to California. The building's first-floor façade is covered in rusticated granite; its brick walls originally were stuccoed, scored, and painted to imitate stone. Later it was the home of the Sacramento Rail Road, the West's first railroad. After the earthquake and fire of 1906, its top floor was removed. Much later the building housed the West Coast office of the National Trust for Historic Preservation and also the first home of the Foundation for San Francisco's Architectural Heritage. Today **William Stout's Architectural Books**, San Francisco's best architectural bookstore, is on the ground floor.

At **472 Jackson Street** is the old French consulate known as the Solari Building West. It was constructed between 1850–1852 and is, architecturally, perhaps the most important post-Gold Rush building in the district. Its severe brick and timber architecture and its original second-floor cast iron shutters make it much like the Wells Fargo Express offices built in the Gold Country. The building backs up on Gold Street where its brick construction and granite still can be inspected. While other buildings in the district are more eye-catching, this one in its purity of design better displays the typical commercial designs built by Yankee merchants.

Next door is **470 Jackson Street**, the Solari Building East, or Larco's Building, built in 1852 by Nicholas Larco, a prominent Italian-American businessman. At different times it housed the French, Spanish, and Chilean consulates, along with the offices of the Italian Benevolent Society and *La Parola*, an Italian language newspaper. Domingo Ghirardelli briefly had an office here. Number **440–44 Jackson Street** was built in 1891 as a

stable for the horses that drew the cars along part of the Presidio and Ferries Railroad. Its second floor was removed in 1907 and the façade remodeled in 1955. The Yeon Building at **432 Jackson Street** at the corner of Balance Street is one of the handsomest on the block. It was built after the 1906 earthquake and fire on the foundations of the Tremont Hotel of 1855. It is distinguished by an arcade of five arches along its first floor.

The two-story in-fill building at **408 Jackson Street** was built in 1953 as the district was reviving. It demonstrates how modern designs, when sensitively handled, can add to historic districts without being mock antique. The last building in the row, on the corner of Jackson and Sansome, is the Grogan-Lent-Atherton Building at **400 Jackson Street**. It was built in 1859 and rebuilt after severe damage in 1906. In its early days it was home to numerous real estate, mining, and stock brokers, including Faxon Dean Atherton.

The south side of Jackson is lined with more ornate Italianate commercial buildings from the 1860s. They are the rare surviving companions to the city's many rows of Italianate houses. Next to the parking lot at Sansome and Jackson is number **407 Jackson Street**, a three-story building constructed in 1860 and used by the Ghirardelli Company as an annex for the manufacture of chocolate. Number **415–31 Jackson Street** was built in 1853 and two years later became the first Ghirardelli chocolate manufactory. (In 1894 the Ghirardelli operation moved to the Old Pioneer Woolen Mill at what is now Ghirardelli Square.) **Number 441** was built in 1861 over the hulls of two ships abandoned during the Gold Rush. Its cast iron pilasters are ornamented with *caducei*, the staff with entwined serpents that is both the emblem of Mercury, the god of commerce, and the medical profession.

The next three buildings flanking Hotaling Place, numbers **445, 451, and 463–73 Jackson Street** were all at one time part of Anson Parsons Hotaling's liquor, trading, and real estate business. These substantial masonry buildings replaced simpler frame buildings. Hittell's guidebook of 1888 noted that,

year by year the wooden buildings that form the landmarks of earlier days are being crowded out by substantial brick and iron edifices.... The leading business blocks are built up of brick, with the front on the ground floor of iron, which allows nearly all the width to be occupied for windows and doors. The architecture is elegant and varied. The ceilings are high; the glass is large plate.

Two-story **number 445** was built about 1860 and was originally the Tremont Stables. It has its original cast iron shutters on the ground floor and elaborate frames around its second-floor windows. The most elaborate building in the row is **451 Jackson** erected in 1866 in the Italianate style. It is built of brick covered in scored stucco painted to look like stone, with exaggerated quoins at its corners to give the illusion of masonry construction. Its ground floor has cast iron pilasters and cast-iron shutters; its upper floors have windows with alternating arched and triangular pediments over the windows, hallmarks of the Italianate style, the first of the fancy Victorian styles popular in San Francisco. Here Hotaling housed his collection of books and paintings. The building escaped the fire of 1906, leading one wit to pen the jingle,

If as they say God spanked the town for being over frisky,
Why did he burn the churches down and spare Hotaling's whiskey?

Across the alley is **463–73, the Hotaling Annex**, built about 1860 and also decorated in the Italianate style. In the 1930s, this building was the headquarters of the Federal Artists and Writers projects and later housed artists' studios when this was part of San Francisco's bohemia. The row ends with a much larger building from 1965 origi-

nally in a starkly modern style which has been "historicized" to better fit with its context.

Contrasting the Hotaling buildings with number **472 Jackson Street** across the street neatly sums up the evolution from the plain brick structures of the immediate post-Gold Rush days to the ornate buildings characteristic of the Victorian era. Commercial buildings became ever more decorated and drenched with ornament. Montgomery and Market streets were lined with them by the late 1880s. All were lost in 1906, leaving a gap in the architectural history of the city between these survivors of the mid-1860s and the reconstructed office blocks of the 1890s.

To see High Victorian commercial architecture in the Bay Area you must go to the 400 block of downtown Oakland's Ninth Street, between Broadway and Washington. There one block survives as a monument to High Victorian commercial architecture in the Bay Area.

The Financial District

COLUMBUS AVENUE / THE OLD
TRANSAMERICA FLATIRON [3]

Return to Montgomery Street and the intersection of Columbus, Montgomery, and Washington streets. Columbus Avenue, originally Montgomery Avenue, was cut across the city's grid in 1873. This highly visible intersection, the "hinge" between the Financial District and North Beach, attracted a cluster of fine Edwardian banks, three of which survive. The capstone is the white terra cotta-clad **Old Transamerica Building** built in 1909 for the Banco Populare Italiano Operaia Fugazi, which was organized right after the earthquake and fire. It was originally designed by Field and Kohlberg as a two-story building. In 1916 a third story with a now-lost cupola was designed by Italo Zanolini. The circular porticoed entrance at the corner is the focal point of the design. In 1928 the Fugazi Bank was merged into A. P. Giannini's Bank of Italy (which later became the Bank of America) and this building continued as a branch bank until 1931. In 1938 the building became the headquarters of Giannini's holding company, Transamerica Corporation, organized in 1928. The landmark flatiron remained the Transamerica headquarters until the completion of the Pyramid across the intersection.

The Transamerica Pyramid & Observation Room [3]
600 Montgomery, at Washington
1972, William Pereira and Associates
Observation Room on 27th floor open
Monday to Friday, 9 A.M.–4 P.M., free.

The slim, white, 853-foot tall Transamerica Pyramid is the tallest office building (Sutro Television Tower is the tallest structure) in San Francisco and is the signature building on San Francisco's contemporary skyline. It was designed by Los Angeles architect William Pereira and Associates, begun in 1970, and completed in 1972. The forty-eight story structure is capped by a hollow, 212-foot spire lighted from within, probably the largest architectural ornament of our time. Its prominent site cost $8 million, and the building itself $35 million. Changing art exhibits are presented in the lobby; an observatory on its twenty-seventh floor is open free during business hours. Immediately east of the Pyramid is Redwood Park, a gated oasis designed by Tom Galli landscaped with eighty redwoods from the Santa Cruz mountains, making the complex a man-made mountain with its own transplanted forest at its foot.

The Pyramid was initially designed to be fifty-five stories and one thousand feet tall but was down-sized after vigorous protests. It was the brainchild of then-chairman John R. Beckett, who wished to give the hard-to-visualize conglomerate a memorable corporate image. In this he succeeded.

The Pyramid pops into view in the most unexpected places throughout the city. It is especially dramatic when lighted on winter nights when it serves as the city's giant Christmas tree. From across the Bay, its graceful form counterbalances the flat-topped mass of the city's new highrises and makes the San Francisco skyline memorable. The Pyramid stands on the northern edge of the highrise district on the city's original shoreline, and will never be obscured by other highrises to the north.

The Pyramid has a slope angle of five degrees. Its curtain wall consists of three thousand quartz aggregate concrete panels weighing three-and-a-half tons each. Its windows are on pivots so that they can be washed from inside the building. The largest floor, the fifth, is 149 feet on each side with 22,000 square feet; the smallest floor, the forty-eighth, is only 45 feet square. The "wings" on the two sides of the building house eighteen elevators on the east side, and emergency stairs and a smoke tower on the west side. The building has an advanced life-safety and fire protection system linked to an underground command post. Its foundation is a concrete and steel block nine feet thick weighing more than 30,000 tons at the bottom of a 52-foot-deep excavation. Some fifty firms, mostly law and banking, along with Transamerica's own headquarters, occupy the building. More than 1,500 people work here.

Transamerica was founded by A. P. Giannini in 1928 as a bank holding company. In the 1950s, it divested itself of its bank stock and in the 1960s it evolved into the archetypical corporate conglomerate. At one time it and its subsidiaries sold insurance, made loans, developed snapshots, moved furniture, flew airplanes, rented cars, manufactured turbines, leased containers, and distributed movies. Insurance, however, was long its major business and the corporation has restructured itself as a financial services

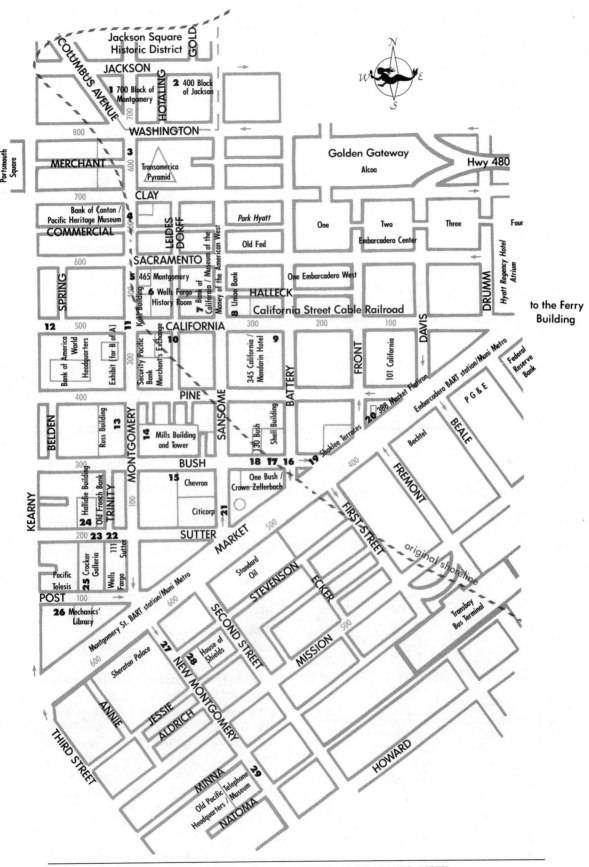

THE FINANCIAL DISTRICT FROM THE BANK OF AMERICA TO NEW
MONTGOMERY STREET

and insurance company. By 1985 it had assets of $13.75 billion.

The Pyramid stands on the historic site of the Montgomery Block, San Francisco's first prestige office building. Designed by engineer Henry W. Halleck in 1853, the four-story brick building sat on a "raft" of redwood logs buried in the mud. The Montgomery Block also housed the U.S. Army Corps of Engineers, the city's first law library, the Adams Express Company's bullion vaults, the offices of the Pacific and Atlantic Railroad, and two early newspapers, the *Alta California* and the *Daily Herald*, among other tenants. Its Bank Exchange Saloon was a celebrated meeting place and dispensed its famous Pisco punch. Mark Twain is said to have met the fireman Tom Sawyer in the basement steam baths here.

When the business district shifted south, the Montgomery Block became the favorite location for low-rent artists' studios. Ambrose Bierce, Frank Norris, Joaquin Miller, Gelett Burgess, George Sterling, and many other writers and artists had rooms here. The rugged building with its rich historic and artistic associations survived the earthquake and fire of 1906 only to be demolished for a parking lot in 1959.

The Bank of San Francisco [3]
552 Montgomery, at Clay
1908, Shea and Lofquist

Facing the Pyramid on the southeast corner of Clay is the nine-story Bank of San Francisco with its opulent banking hall. The building was built in 1908 to designs by Shea and Lofquist as the headquarters of A. P. Giannini's Bank of Italy. It is a prime example of Beaux Arts architecture. It has a rusticated granite base and terra cotta-cladding on its upper stories. The rich marble and decorative plaster banking hall has fine bronze fittings including elaborate old tellers' cages from the days when bank security was bars, not cameras.

The Bank of Canton of California / Pacific Heritage Museum [4]
555 Montgomery Street
1984, Skidmore, Owings and Merrill

Across Montgomery Street is the dusty Texas pink granite-clad headquarters of the Bank of Canton of California completed in 1984 and designed by Skidmore, Owings and Merrill. This seventeen-story bank headquarters is a strong, smooth, rectangular block capped by a three-step pyramidal mechanical penthouse ornamented with small gold-leafed plaques. The large, clear glass windows have narrow, muted red frames. Inside is a large contemporary banking hall behind geometric metal grills recalling the historic banking temples of the Financial District. The subtly gold-accented hall has a coffered ceiling and a large, four-paneled geometric mural in tan, beige, and rust. The elevator lobby is a high, white octagonal drum with a shallow dome that produces an echo when a person speaks from the bull's eye marked out in the colored granite paving. The building is a suave contemporary interpretation of traditional San Francisco bank buildings of great sophistication. The Bank of Canton of California has been located on this block since the 1930s. Its Chinatown branch is in the historic Chinese Telephone Exchange pagoda of 1909 (*see Tour 3*).

Around the corner at 608 Commercial Street is the Bank of Canton's superb **Pacific Heritage Museum** in the restored U.S. Subtreasury building of 1875. Originally designed as a four-story brick building by Treasury architect William Appleton Potter, the building was gutted in 1906 and reconstructed as a one-story structure. It stands on the site of the first U.S. Branch Mint, which was established in 1854 in the wake of the Gold Rush. When the new Bank of Canton was built, the landmark Subtreasury was elegantly restored and converted into the Pacific Heritage Museum by Page, Anderson and Turnbull.

This gem of a museum houses changing exhibits on the artistic, cultural, and economic links across the Pacific. Pale, calm colors and plush, light carpeting make this museum a downtown oasis. In addition to its fascinating exhibits, the museum has a permanent display on the history of the Subtreasury with a cutaway section through the old structure, architectural plans, and historic photographs. In the basement is the brick vault and the guard's walk, a narrow corridor around the bullion vault. The museum is open Monday–Friday, 11 A.M.–4 P.M.; free.

COMMERCIAL STREET [4]

Narrow Commercial Street was not part of the original plan of the city and was cut through in July 1850, from the Central Wharf to Grant Avenue. It was lined with substantial New York-like brick buildings and quickly became an important business and banking center. Look west, uphill, to see Chinatown and one of the city's last brick-paved streets. To the east is the tower of A. Page Brown's **Union Ferry Depot** of 1895–1903. The light-colored highrises that bracket the now toylike tower are part of **Embarcadero Center**, a complex of highrises that includes the Hyatt Regency Hotel designed in 1970 by Atlanta architect John Portman and Associates. Pedestrian concourses between the towers continue the line of Commercial Street to the Sausalito Ferry.

Visible one building east of Montgomery, at **569 Commercial Street**, is the monumental façade of the old Pacific Gas & Electric Station J, built in 1914 to the designs of Frederick H. Meyer, with a large cartouche over its entrance. The substation was converted first into a nightclub and more recently into offices.

456 Montgomery Street [5]
1983, Roger Owen Boyer and Associates

On the southeast corner of Montgomery and Sacramento streets is 456 Montgomery, a twenty-four story highrise perched atop two small historic bank temples. This highrise was designed by Roger Owen Boyer and Associates in 1983 and is one of several examples of partial, or façade, preservation in the new Financial District. The small granite building at the corner with Tuscan columns was built for the Italian-American Bank in 1908 to designs by Howard and Galloway (John Galen Howard was the architect of the fine Beaux Arts buildings at the University of California, Berkeley, including the monumental campanile). The old bank was a steel-frame and concrete building with monolithic granite columns. The other small bank on the other side of 456 Montgomery was the Anton Borel Bank and was designed in 1908 by Albert Pissis, one of the most important San Francisco architects at the turn of the century. It, too, has monolithic granite columns, these in the Corinthian order.

The modern highrise is notable for its column-free interiors: the walls of the new structure are load-bearing. While the preservation of the old banks was a good idea, and the modern silver tower is competent, the entrance between the historic banks is clumsy and unsatisfactory.

Wells Fargo Bank History Room [6]
420 Montgomery Street
The museum is open weekdays
9 A.M.–5 P.M.

Not more than ten feet from its original location is the entrance to the **Wells Fargo Bank History Room**, an adjunct to the bank headquarters around the corner on California Street. This fascinating museum recounts the history of the California Gold Rush which made San Francisco a great city. The centerpiece of the History Room is a fine red-

61

and-yellow stagecoach made in Concord, New Hampshire. Exhibits and maps explain the discovery of gold and Wells Fargo's role as an express company that carried the treasure from the Sierra foothills to the instant metropolis on the Bay, and from there back East. Gold nuggets, gold dust, strongboxes, and other mementos fill the showcases here. Upstairs, in the museum's mezzanine, is a reproduction of a stagecoach that you may sit in while listening to a tape of a nineteenth-century English traveler's description of just how uncomfortable stagecoach travel was.

Wells Fargo Bank Headquarters [6]
464 California Street
1959, Ashley, Keyser, and Runge

Wells Fargo is the oldest bank in the West. Today it is the third largest bank in California, famous for its hard-driving management. On March 18, 1852, upstate New Yorkers Henry Wells and William George Fargo and their associates met in New York City to form a joint stock association "for the purpose of carrying on [an] Express and Exchange business [between] the City of New York and San Francisco [and] other Cities and Towns in California." Wells, Fargo & Co. began its banking and express business on July 13, 1852 on Montgomery Street, a few feet from the museum. By 1855 Wells Fargo had fifty-five offices and was the major express company in California; by 1890 it had 2,600 agencies nationwide.

In 1905 the express business in New York was severed from the banking business in San Francisco. In that same year, Bavarian-born Isaias W. Hellman merged Wells Fargo Bank with his Nevada National Bank. Hellman had come to America at sixteen to work as a clerk in his cousin's dry-goods business in the small village of Los Angeles. In the 1860s he posted a sign in a corner of the store that read, "I. W. Hellman, Banker." In 1870 he made a fortunate marriage to Esther Neugass, the daughter of a New

York and London banking family related to the Lehmans. He moved to San Francisco and bought silver baron James G. Fair's Nevada Bank. He merged Wells Fargo with his Union Trust Company in 1923. Hellman held interests in some fifteen California banks, Los Angeles and San Francisco street railways, and Southern California real estate. In 1901, during the heyday of the trusts, he obtained control of the California wine industry.

When the earthquake devastated the city in 1906, Hellman checked his deposits in eastern banks and announced to the press, "It will only take one-third of the Hellman resources to pay off the depositers of the Wells Fargo Nevada Bank and the Union Trust Company. The Hellman surplus will be $30 million. Every dollar of this will be used for the rebuilding of San Francisco." I. W. Hellman died in harness at seventy-seven. One of his favorite mottos was, "Work is a very necessary and good habit."

In 1960 Wells Fargo Bank took over the American Trust Company and moved its headquarters to the unspectacular gray granite **464 California Street**, built in 1959 by Ashley, Keyser, and Runge for American Trust. In 1986, Wells Fargo Bank nearly doubled in size when it bought the Crocker Bank from the British Midland Bank making Wells Fargo the number three bank in California and the tenth largest bank in the nation by 1987 with $44.2 billion in assets.

The Bank of California / Museum of the Money of the American West [7]
400 California Street
1907, Bliss and Faville; 1967, Anshen and Allen, highrise

Walk through the Wells Fargo headquarters to emerge on the 400 block of California, the historic epicenter of California banking. Across narrow Leidesdorff Street is the glass base of the modern highrise adjoining the classical banking temple of the Bank of California. Founded in 1864, the Bank of California very early had branches in Oregon and Washington, making it the first West Coast bank. When the then-dominant bank built at the corner of California and Sansome in 1866, it determined the heart of the banking district.

This was D. O. Mills and William Ralston's bank. Ralston was the financier behind many of California's earliest industrial enterprises including San Francisco's first woolen mill, first iron mill, first dry dock, the enormous Palace Hotel, the San Francisco Sugar Refinery, the New Montgomery Street extension, the Sherman Island reclamation in the Delta, and the vast California Theater. He was California's first great empire builder. His more cautious partner, William Sharon wrote:

In building the Palace Hotel he wanted to get some oak planks for it and he bought a ranch for a very large sum of money and never used a plank for it.... I said to him, "If you are going to buy a factory for a nail, a ranch for a plank, and a manufactory to build furniture, where is this thing going to end?"

Alas, it ended one day when the bank was examined and found seriously over-extended. That afternoon Ralston went for his customary swim off Aquatic Park and drowned. His funeral was the biggest social event in the city.

The bank survived Ralston's swim. In 1907 it commissioned Bliss and Faville to design a grand Corinthian temple built of steel and granite. It is the grandest banking temple in a city noted for its banking temples and was modeled on McKim, Mead, and White's long-lost Knickerbocker Trust Building in New York City. It is surrounded on three sides by great windows and Corinthian columns. Inside is a great banking hall with sixty-foot-high ceilings. Soft-colored Tennessee marble lines an interior capped by a magnificent coffered ceiling. Arthur Putnam carved the mountain lions that guard the vault.

In the basement of the imposing temple is a jewel of a collection known as the **Museum of the Money of the American West**. Displayed here among other precious items are examples of "necessity coinage," privately struck gold coins that circulated before the establishment of a United States Mint in San Francisco. The historic $50 octagonal gold slug of 1851 and smaller octagonal gold coins are on display as well as the extraordinarily beautiful Saint-Gaudens double eagle $20 gold coin and special coins minted for the Panama-Pacific International Exposition of 1915 with the Bohemian Club's owl on the reverse. One section of the museum is devoted to Nevada's Comstock silver lode which the Bank of California helped finance. The museum is open Monday–Thursday, 10 A.M.–3:30 P.M., 5 P.M. on Friday.

In 1967 Anshen and Allen designed the compatible highrise that adjoins the temple and that houses the bank's offices. The tower's concrete panels echo the fluting of the granite columns. The roof of the bank became an outdoor garden entered from the highrise (see illustration). It is one of the best marriages of new and old architecture in San Francisco. Today the historic Bank of California, after long being controlled by the French Rothschilds, is owned by Tokyo's Mitsubishi Bank.

CALIFORNIA STREET:
HISTORIC DIVIDE [7]

California Street was laid out wider than the other downtown streets north of Market and cuts back from the foot of Market Street near the Ferry Building, through the Financial District, and straight up Nob Hill out west to Pacific Heights. Historically, it was always a prestigious address, both downtown and at its western, residential end. Its cable car line had the largest, most luxurious cars and all along this line elaborate houses were constructed. West of Franklin Street, California still has many large often overlooked Victorian houses.

Union Bank [8]
370 California Street, northeast
corner of Sansome
1977, Skidmore, Owings, and Merrill

Across Sansome from the Bank of
California is the headquarters of the
Union Bank designed by Skidmore,
Owings and Merrill in 1977. The large
glassed openings and columnlike elements of the design seek to relate the
modern building to the Corinthian temple it faces. At the side entrance between
the tower and its California Street neighbor is a row of granite walrus heads
saved from the historic Alaska Commercial Building that once graced this corner.
A plaque here, in a finely carved white
marble frame also salvaged from that old
landmark, tells something of the Alaska
Commercial Building's history.

The Union Bank has its roots in the
agency of the Yokohama Specie Bank
opened in San Francisco in 1886. By 1988
Union Bank was the sixth largest bank
in California. It is owned by the Bank of
Tokyo, Ltd. Japanese banks have recently
supplanted British banks as the major
foreign owners of California banks. By
that year five of the eleven largest banks
in the state were Japanese-owned. (By
1986, eight of the world's ten largest
banks were Japanese.) San Francisco, in
the nineteenth century a gateway for
British capital seeking investment in the
resource-rich American West, has
become ever more closely linked with
Japan in this century.

First Interstate Center /
Mandarin Hotel [9]
345 California Street
1987, Skidmore, Owings and Merrill

Cross California Street to the midblock entrance of the First Interstate
Center, designed by Skidmore, Owings
and Merrill and completed in 1987.
Flanking the entrance to the new tower
are the J. Harold Dollar Building of 1920
and the Robert Dollar Building of 1919.
First Interstate Center's flag-capped, dia-
mond-shaped towers rise forty-seven
stories from the middle of this prime
block. At 724 feet it is the third-tallest
office building in San Francisco and cost
$225 million.

The building preserves the four corner
vintage office buildings. A T-shaped
pedestrian concourse with retail shops
linkiides of the block threads
through the building, which has thirty-
one floors of office space and an eleven-
story luxury hotel in twin towers. Twin
booms fly large flags.

This complex project is worth looking
at from several angles. Its lobby is simple
but elegant and paneled in African
mahogany. The T-shaped pedestrian
concourse is lavishly clad in gray gran-
ites from Sweden and Sardinia, deep red
Swedish granite, polished black African
granite, and gray and pink mottled granite from India. It is lighted by the finest
new light fixtures in the city. The tower
itself is clad in both dark and light gray
granite, which mask the building's bulk.
Tho building usoo darli coloro at ito baoo
and lighter colors at its top to relate to its
two very different contexts, the street-
scape and the skyline. The modernistic
booms surmounting the towers are illuminated at night. The building adds a
new accent to the city's skyline without
mimicking forms from the past. The
Mandarin Oriental hotel occupies the
top eleven floors with the glass "skybridges" between the two towers.

Tadich Grill [9]
240 California Street (between Battery
and Front)
Closed Saturday–Sunday; 391-2373;
moderate.

The two-story, green terra cotta-clad
façade of Tadich Grill was built in 1909
and attributed to Crim and Scott. Behind
a plate glass window with gold lettering
is an agreeably plain interior unchanged
since the 1920s. There is a counter as
well as tables and booths. The Buich
brothers' Tadich Grill is the oldest restaurant in California and is deservedly

64

popular. It serves charcoal-broiled meats and fresh seafood, including a memorable *cioppino*. They do not take reservations and close early. The best time to eat here is about 3 P.M., after lunch and before dinner.

Merchant's Exchange Building / Grain Exchange Hall / Coulter Marine Paintings [10]
465 California Street, corner of Leidesdorff
1903, Willis Polk

The Merchant's Exchange Building is one of the most important prototypical office buildings in San Francisco. It was designed by Willis Polk, the local architect of the Chicago firm of D. H. Burnham and Co., in 1903 and reconstructed after the earthquake and fire of 1906. It contains some of the finest public art in San Francisco. (While she once had her offices in this building, there is no solid evidence that Julia Morgan designed the post-fire hall.) Today, among other tenants, the Merchant's Exchange Building houses the San Francisco Chamber of Commerce, the Merchant's Exchange Club in its basement, and the Commercial Club on its top floors.

Pass through the twin-columned entrance into the marble lobby with its elaborate elevator doors and fine ship models. A skylight here reveals a large light court. At the end of the lobby is the entrance to the great **Grain Exchange Hall**, today the Financial District branch of First Interstate Bank. This room was originally the center of commercial life on the West Coast. News of ship arrivals was transmitted from the belvedere on the roof to the merchants in the exchange hall. Here complete information was kept on every Pacific Coast ship from start to finish of every voyage. Shippers, ship owners, ship chandlers, warehousemen, exporters, and importers gathered here to do business. This great space was considered the "Forum of San Francisco." On April 29, 1910, $4 million was raised in two hours in a mass meeting held here to launch the great Panama-Pacific International Exposition of 1915.

In plan, the Grain Exchange Hall is like the porch of a temple. Looking through the entrance there are four giant columns, and beyond them a series of large oil paintings by marine painter William A. Coulter and one by Nils Hagerup. Coulter was born in Ireland in 1849 to a seafaring family. He went to sea as a cabin boy and then as an able-bodied seaman. He later studied art in Europe and was an illustrator for the San Francisco *Call*. He devoted much of his art to the history of maritime shipping in Northern California and this post-1909 group of paintings, which tells the history of this historic seaport, is his masterpiece.

Port Costa, by Coulter. A view through the Silver Gate where the American and Sacramento rivers enter San Francisco Bay. Sailing vessels ride at anchor while a hay scow and two barges towed by a stern-wheeler head for San Francisco. The agricultural riches of California's great Central Valley flowed down these river routes to the *entrepôt* of San Francisco on their way to world markets.

Honolulu Harbor, by Coulter. The stepping stone between San Francisco and Asia, and a major focus of San Francisco investment was preboom Honolulu, shown here, a small seaport at the base of towering green volcanoes. Pristine Waikiki Beach and Diamond Head are seen to the right. A Matson steamship loaded with island sugar steams toward the viewer and San Francisco. An outrigger canoe returns from fishing back to Oahu.

Arrived, All Well, by Coulter. Shows the sailing ship *W. F. Babcock* of the Dollar Line (note the flag with its dollar sign) being towed into the harbor as the sun pierces the late-afternoon fog. Small ships dot the harbor. On the horizon, red-brick Fort Point guards the entrance to the Bay; Telegraph Hill with its Gothic castle appears to the far left.

Full and By, by Coulter. The wonderfully named ship *Dashing Wave* cuts through a blue sea with rain squalls to the right and dappled clouds above. She is passing Tatash Light carrying a cargo of redwood lumber destined for San Francisco. North Coast redwood and Oregon pine and fir were used to build San Francisco's elaborate Victorian houses.

War Time, by Coulter. Shows the launching of the freighter *Cotati* at the Hunter's Point shipyards in the southeast corner of San Francisco. The other vessels riding at anchor sport geometrical World War I camouflage patterns, while an early airplane flies overhead.

Northwest Passage, 1903–06, by Nils Hagerup. Depicts the tiny one-masted schooner-rigged sloop *Gjoa* commanded by Danish captain Roald Amundsen, the first vessel to make the long-sought-after Northwest Passage from the Atlantic to Pacific. The fearless ship with its seven sailors plunges through Arctic swells off a bleak coast. Amundsen discovered the Passage and determined the location of the magnetic north pole on his three-year expedition. Today the historic ship is at Norway's National Maritime Museum after sitting for many years beached near the ocean end of Golden Gate Park.

Security Pacific Bank [11]
300 Montgomery Street
1922, George Kelham; 1941, L. J. Hendy, addition

At the southeast and northeast corners of California and Montgomery stand two important architectural works, today's Security Pacific Bank next door to the Merchants Exchange, and the ornate Kohl Building across California Street.

The Security Pacific Bank's grand banking hall is modeled on a Roman basilica, originally not a church type but a large meeting hall used for law and public administration. Plaster bulls and bears decorate the hall's frieze. The columns here have been given a *scagliola* finish in imitation of veined marble. This hall and the original building were designed by George Kelham in 1922 for the American National Bank. In 1941 this became the headquarters of the Bank of America and the building's exterior was remodeled and an addition was added on the Pine Street end designed by the Capital Co., L. J. Hendy, architect. The fine Moderne lobby at 300 Montgomery dates from this period. The remodeled building presents Ionic colonnades on three sides.

The Security Pacific National Bank, headquartered in Los Angeles, was founded in 1871. By 1988 it was the second-largest bank in California, and the seventh-largest in the nation, with more than $72 billion in assets.

Kohl Building [11]
400 Montgomery Street
1901, Percy and Polk; 1907, Willis Polk, reconstruction

Across California Street is the historic Kohl Building, on the northeast corner of Montgomery Street, originally the Alvinza Hayward Building. It was designed by Percy and Polk in 1901 in an H shape. While its base has been remodeled several times, the upper stories and elaborate cornice survive from the original design. It was an early "fireproof" steel-frame structure and survived the earthquake and fire of 1906 with no fire damage above the fourth floor, making it a unique survivor. It was reconstructed by Willis Polk in 1907. Its brick curtain walls are clad in greenish Colusa sandstone. The rich cornice and giant order at the upper stories are fine examples of Edwardian design.

Bank of America / History Exhibit / Carnelian Room Panorama [12]
555 California Street
1968, Wurster, Bernardi and Emmons; Skidmore, Owings and Merrill

The dominant building on the city's skyline, and still the dominant financial institution in California, is the Bank of America World Headquarters, which occupies the full block between California and Pine, Montgomery and Kearny streets. Rising up fifty-two stories or 779 feet, and containing 1.8 million square feet of prime office space, the dark red granite-clad tower was designed in 1968 by Wurster, Bernardi and Emmons; Skidmore, Owings and Merrill, with Pietro Belluschi as design consultant. It was completed in 1970–1971. In 1985 the landmark highrise was bought by San Francisco real estate magnate Walter H. Shorenstein for $660 million, the highest price ever paid for one building in this country. By 1987 he was reported to own 12 million square feet of office space in San Francisco, Houston, Kansas City, Los Angeles, and other American cities, and to manage roughly 30 percent of the commercial real estate in San Francisco's Financial District.

The Bank of America world headquarters—despite its disruptive dark color so at odds with the rest of this light-reflecting city—is one of the most magnificent tall buildings of our time. Along with the Transamerica Pyramid (also erected by a Giannini-founded corporation) and St. Mary's Roman Catholic Cathedral, it is one of the great architectural monuments of the boom that transformed San Francisco in the go-go 1970s. Rising abruptly from its granite-paved plaza, the huge building has zig-zag façades of two-sided bay windows which do not look particularly large from outside but which are very large from within. (This sawtooth façade is curiously like the 1937 Art Deco concrete abutments that anchor the suspension cables of the Golden Gate Bridge.) While regular along its base and midsection, these bays are irregular at the top of the tower, giving the building a subtly animated profile within its simple box shape. The tower is most dramatic from the narrow passage on Montgomery Street between the lowrise, freestanding banking hall and the preserved California Commercial Union Building of 1921 at the corner of Montgomery and Pine. From this compressed space the tower seems to soar in splendid isolation like the superb sculpture it is. The building is sheathed in 3.5-inch-thick slabs of mirror-polished carnelian granite from South Dakota. Late in the day, under certain light foggy atmospheres, when the sun's rays strike the prismlike façades at low angles, the polished granite and glass reflects the light in beams that seem to emanate from within the building. The looming structure is then transformed into a gleaming crystal in a moving, diaphanous atmosphere. At sunset, it becomes a glittering shaft of gold rising out of the white cubist cityscape.

On the California Street side of the tower is the **A. P. Giannini Plaza** with a plush auditorium underneath it. Standing in the plaza is the sleek, black Swedish granite sculpture executed by Masayuki Nagare entitled "Transcendence." (San Franciscans have dubbed it "the banker's heart.") Over time, greenery and benches have been introduced here, softening the single-minded monumentality of this granite-paved plaza.

The mezzanine level of the banking hall on the corner of California and Montgomery houses an exhibit on the history of the bank and a collection of old office machines. Among these artifacts is a Boston-made gold scale from the 1850s with four wood columns and an arch—itself a monumental architectural work. In glass cases along the edge of the mezzanine are historic photos tracing the history of the institution from its foundation.

A. P. Giannini was born in 1870, the son of a Genoa-born, San Jose hotel owner who died when the boy was very young. His mother then married Lorenzo Scatena, a produce wholesaler who moved the family to San Francisco. Here A. P. went into his stepfather's business and became a partner at nineteen. He proved to be a whiz with numbers and with people. In 1892, at twenty-two, he married Clorinda Cuneo.

In 1904 with Antonio Chichizola and others, he founded his own bank serving, at first, Italian-Americans. Soon it began to court other immigrant groups, such as the Portuguese and Chinese, that established WASP banks disdained. By serving the "little fellow," a great bank was built.

By 1921 it was the largest bank in the West; and in 1930 it shed its immigrant beginnings and proudly rechristened itself the Bank of America (using the name of a New York City bank established in 1812 which Giannini had acquired in 1928). The new Bank of America became a key instrument in financing the municipalities, ranches, and industries of the state.

After this tour exploring the heart of the banking district, from the Gold Rush survivors of the Jackson Square Historic District to the opulent steel-frame towers of the present, it is appropriate to end with an elevator ride to the top of Bank of America's tower. After 3 P.M., the Bankers Club atop the commanding Bank of America is open to the public as the **Carnelian Room**, (433-7500), a cocktail lounge and restaurant. It has the finest views in the city, especially memorable at sunset.

580 California Street, northeast corner of Kearny [12]
1983, Philip Johnson and John Burgee

The much ballyhooed postmodernist Philip Johnson has not been a Good Thing for San Francisco. His harlequin-pattern Neiman-Marcus store, the cutesy gazebo in front of cylindrical 101 California Street, and the faceless statues here that look like the Grim Reaper are all pure kitsch. Office towers should be serious works of up-to-date architecture, not frivolous pastry decoration such as this.

The hideous statues by Muriel Castanis that crown this 23-story office building were not an auspicious return of ornament to downtown buildings. This postmodern confection has an acceptable and practical arcaded entrance most appropriate on this windy corner, detailed like good 1920s design. The wall treatment, with its very slightly bowed out windows and light-colored granite facing, is acceptable, even if it misunderstands the architectural patterns of San Francisco's Financial District. But the pseudomansard glass roof with its weak cresting and ominous statuary is just rampant bad taste.

Continuation

Continue Tour 2A by walking down California Street to Battery for an exploration of the Embarcadero complex, which includes an array of shops, boutiques, restaurants, and cafés.

EMBARCADERO CENTER

Approximately five blocks from Battery Street to the Embarcadero, between Sacramento and Clay, with an L-shaped extension to California and Market streets.
1971–1981, John C. Portman, Jr. and Associates

One Embarcadero Center
45 stories, Battery and Sacramento streets

Two Embarcadero Center
35 stories, Front and Sacramento streets

Three Embarcadero Center
35 stories, Davis and Sacramento streets

Four Embarcadero Center
45 stories, Drumm Street at the foot of Sacramento

Embarcadero Center, recently expanded, today consists of six office towers, two major hotels, and some 175 retail shops, boutiques, restaurants, cafés, and galleries. It is virtually a satellite city,

68

perhaps the best of its kind. San Francisco was fortunate that when urban renewal moved downtown it had the large, obsolete, architecturally undistinguished, lowrise produce and wharfside warehouse district to condemn and expand into.

Two very different phases of urban renewal design are displayed here and across Clay Street. The first, cruder phase north of Clay Street, designed between 1959 and 1964 produced the dark, x-braced Alcoa Building and the banal concrete highrise boxes of Golden Gateway, both set atop massive, unrelieved parking podiums. Skidmore, Owings, and Merrill's Alcoa Building was deliberately set to block the view corridors of Front and Merchant streets. There is a very fine Henry Moore sculpture, "Knife Edge Figure," in the unpeopled sculpture garden on the sunny west side of the Alcoa Building.

The second wave of urban renewal learned from the city-busting mistakes of the first. In John C. Portman, Jr. and Associates' Embarcadero Center, parking was put underground where it belongs and the sidewalk level of the complex's podiums were designed to draw in pedestrians. The old line of Commercial Street was carried through the four-block megaparcel of assembled blocks as an internal walkway. Three levels of restaurants, shops, and terraces linked by pedestrian bridges over intervening streets and garnished with a collection of modern sculpture serve as the base for four thin, slablike towers. Louise Nevelson's thirty-four-ton Corten steel **"Sky Tree"** at Three Embarcadero Center facing Sacramento Street, between Davis and Drumm, is probably the best piece.

The site plan set the office towers along the north edge of the parcel, putting the three-level podiums with their terraces atop them on the sunny side of the site. In section the towers look like slightly splayed playing cards. This gives each floor from ten to fourteen corner offices rather than the usual four. The general styling of Embarcadero Center's towers with their accentuated thinness and vertical striped effect is reminiscent of Rockefeller Center in New York, still the finest of modern in-city megadevelopments. One Embarcadero Center, the westernmost tower of Embarcadero Center, between Battery and Front streets, is set slightly off the axial arrangement of the three other towers, a bit like the former RCA Building in New York. All four towers line up with their skinny side to the city, thereby disturbing the fewest views from residential Russian Hill to the west. In every way these big buildings did everything they could, including adopting a light color, to fit into the city while introducing the radically larger scale of contemporary redevelopment.

Hyatt Regency Hotel / Five Embarcadero Center
1973, foot of California Street at Drumm

The splashiest space in Embarcadero Center is the **Hyatt Regency Hotel's** seventeen-story atrium. This modern space is quite active with cafés, bars, and people. The sculpture is "Eclipse," by Charles O. Perry. (The Embarcadero BART and Muni Metro stations are right outside the hotel.)

The Royal Exchange
301 Sacramento Street, at Front
1911, Righetti & Headman; 1972, Ron Kaufman, restoration

The Royal Exchange, across the street from One Embarcadero Center, is a large, stylish, welcoming Financial District watering hole. The bar fills the ground floor of a 1911 Edwardian commercial building designed as a warehouse by Righetti and Headman. In 1972 developer Ron Kaufman reinforced the building with exposed interior steel bracing (painted yellow and visible through the upstairs windows) and converted the building to offices with the new-old Royal Exchange perfectly fitted into the handsome original cast-iron and plate-glass Edwardian storefront.

Old Federal Reserve Bank
400 Sansome Street, at Sacramento
1924, George Kelham; 1988, Kaplan, McLaughlin & Diaz, restoration/adaption

Embarcadero Center West
255 Battery Street, at Sacramento
1988, John C. Portman, Jr. and Associates

Park Hyatt Hotel
333 Battery Street, at Clay
1988, John C. Portman, Jr. and Associates

Embarcadero Center has been a success and has expanded to the west, where it has bought, restored, and redesigned the starchy old Federal Reserve Bank designed by George Kelham in 1924. Two new buildings, Embarcadero Center West, a thirty-three-story tower with a whittled top, and the twenty-four-story Park Hyatt Hotel, were built to either side of the neoclassical Old Fed in 1988. The new buildings are also by John C. Portman, Jr. and Associates, with Kaplan, McLaughlin and Diaz as associate architect for the restoration work on the Old Fed. These new elements of Embarcadero Center remain three separate blocks within the old city grid, not assembled, multi-block mega-parcels. The latest wave of city building has come back to appreciate the basic city pattern it once did everything to erase.

In a fine piece of city mending that is the hallmark of the best present-day projects, the old Federal Reserve Bank, once the sharp edge of the Financial District with its giant portico facing Sansome Street to the west and its utilitarian armored car entrance facing Battery Street and the Produce District to the east, has been "turned around" and transformed into a link between Embarcadero Center and the banking core through the addition a second giant portico to the eastern, Battery Street, side of the building. Inside, the three-story banking hall and the banking

lobby with its Jules Guerin mural has been refurbished as a great public space with a swank restaurant.

Tour 2B

A Skyscraper Sampler

San Francisco's compact downtown is a choice sampler of skyscraper architecture, one of America's most distinctive inventions. Historically, after New York and the "Windy City," it had the third largest concentration of tall buildings in the country. This second tour highlights some of the most interesting of these steel-frame structures from the Bank of America and across Market Street to the Palace Hotel and the Moderne Pacific Telephone skyscraper at 140 New Montgomery Street.

The Russ Building [13]
235 Montgomery Street between Pine and Bush
1927, George Kelham
Gothic Revival

Long the tallest skyscraper in the West, the thirty-one story Russ Building has lost none of its beauty. The building's tower is a grace note on the horizon, and the east, or back, side of the building facing Nob Hill is nicely detailed. The bronze elevator indicator with its moving lights is informative and artistic, one of the downtown's best kinetic sculptures.

The Mills Building and Tower [14]
220 Montgomery, at Bush
1891, Burnham and Root, Chicago School office block; 1908, Burnham & Co./Willis Polk, reconstruction; 1914 and 1918, Willis Polk, Bush Street additions; 1931, Lewis Hobart, tower addition

This historic and handsome office block is built around a central light court. On its Bush Street side is a compatible series of additions, culminating in the first tower addition to a San Francisco landmark, Lewis Hobart's fine twenty-two-story Mills Tower. The building is worth careful scrutiny for its superior exterior finish. Above its two-story white Inyo marble base, large, plain, yellowish-buff brick areas set off intricate terra cotta decoration.

This monument was built by Darius Ogden Mills, founder of the first bank in the West and later of the Bank of California. It long housed the downtown municipal law library and was the center of legal activity in the city. Later, insurance companies were prominent tenants. The Sierra Club was incorporated in an office here in 1892 when this was a brand-new building. In 1898 Paul Elder's bookshop and publishing house was located here during the artistic high-point of book publishing in the West.

Chevron / Standard Oil of California Headquarters [15]
225 Bush Street, at Sansome
1922, George Kelham; 1948, Harry Thomsen, addition
Florentine palazzo

There was a fascination with Italian Renaissance design in the United States in the 1910s and 1920s. The gardens of the elite, public libraries, campuses, and some office buildings dressed themselves in suave Italian style. This very fine, reticent but luxurious design is modeled after York and Sawyer's winning competition design for the Federal Reserve Bank of New York. In 1948, as Aramco was developing Saudi Arabia, Harry Thomsen designed an identical wing that made the L-shaped building a U-shape. The "back" of the building facing Market Street has a fine stairtower. The top of the building, with its corbelled cornice, attic, and red tile roof recalls Renaissance Florentine city palaces.

This is the second Standard Oil Company building in San Francisco; the energy giant has built several newer towers on Market Street. But the chairman's office remains here. Note the oil derrick on the Renaissance cartouche over the main entrance on Bush Street. Chevron, as it is known today, is the richest corporation headquartered in San Francisco with revenues of $26 billion in 1987, more than double those of second-place Bank of America. It recently passed Pacific Gas & Electric to post the highest net income, just over $1 billion dollars in 1987.

One Bush / Old Crown-Zellerbach Building [16]
1 Bush Street, at Battery
1959, Hertzka and Knowles; Skidmore, Owings and Merrill; plaza by Lawrence Halprin & Associates
Tower in a plaza

A very fine work of architecture but a disastrous piece of urban design, the high-quality Crown-Zellerbach Building, now an official city landmark, first introduced the "tower in a plaza" idea to the new San Francisco that emerged about 1960. Admired by many and put in a class with Lever House in New York City by some, this rectangular tower on a full triangular block brought Le Corbusier's Ville Contemporain of 1922 and Ville Radieuse of 1935 from fantasy illustration to urban actuality. The idea was to completely break away from the city as it had evolved and to stand apart in a new form consisting of towers standing in large open spaces with lower building and complex traffic routes between. What was actually banished in this Puritan vision was the continuous ribbon of commerce and sidewalk-life-producing activities that had always crowded their way down busy downtown streets. Arranged like two contrasting pieces of sculpture in a shallow granite bowl, the green glass rectangular tower "converses" with the low, round building set like a flat, folded steel chrysanthemum in the southwest corner. The artfully paved sunken plaza with its fine stainless steel wall fountain has no chairs or benches. Blocks of a city developed as freestanding islands sterilize the urban environment.

Shell Building [17]
100 Bush Street, at Battery
1929, George Kelham
Moderne skyscraper

The Shell Building both knits with the surrounding buildings of the city and soars in a graceful, artistic tower from its corner site. Clad in sepia-glazed terra cotta with blue-green cast concrete spandrels, the building is designed to emphasize its verticality. Moderne dishlike ornaments floodlit at night cap the tower. Abstracted shell designs are worked into the ornament. This urbane tower follows the model of Eliel Saarinen's Chicago Tribune Tower Competition entry (which won second-place and was never built).

130 Bush Street [18]
1910, MacDonald and Applegarth
Gothic Revival skyscraper

This twenty-foot wide, eleven-story, bay-windowed, Gothic Revival skyscraper clad in intricate, cream-glazed terra cotta is one of San Francisco's three narrowest skyscrapers and looks like a hinge between its two large neighbors. Bay windows are exceedingly rare in the post-1906 Financial District.

Shaklee Terraces [19]
444 Market Street, between Bush and Front
1982, Skidmore, Owings and Merrill

The undulating, silvery aluminum-clad Shaklee Terraces relates creatively to Market Street's diagonal, though not successfully to its 1908 neighbor. The top of the tower is a series of set-back, glassed-in terraces with trees looking out over San Francisco Bay. It is one of the few contemporary towers to use its top in this way; mechanical equipment monopolizes the top of most highrises.

388 Market Street, between Front and Pine [20]
1986, Skidmore, Owings and Merrill
1980s Flatiron

This is the jewel of late 1980s highrise construction in San Francisco, and the magnificent flagship of the flotilla of flat-iron buildings on the north side of Market Street. The sophisticated, luxuriously understated design fuses a wedge and a cylinder in a teardrop-shaped building rounded at both ends. The subtly faceted, cylindrical Front Street end echoes the shape of Philip Johnson and John Burgee's colossal, cylindrical 101 California Street tower across Pine Street. Number 388 Market is clad in polished deep red granite mounted on precast concrete panels. Its flat and curved clear glass windows are set in narrow aquamarine metal frames. The building is a layer cake of uses: underground parking for 120 cars; a two-story retail base with a pass-through from Pine to Market Street; sixteen floors of offices; mechanical equipment floors; and six floors containing one- and two-bedroom condominiums on top. (Number 388 Market was granted permission for additional floors because of the incorporation of housing.) A shallow dome on the roof masks cooling equipment; this is a building designed to be attractive when looked down upon from its taller neighbors. It was built by Honorway Investment Corporation of Hong Kong.

MARKET STREET: MAIN STEM AND GREAT DIVIDE [20]

1847, Jasper O'Farrell; 1971–1978, beautification project by Mario Ciampi, Lawrence Halprin and Associates, John Carl Warnecke and Associates

Market Street was laid out by Irish-born civil engineer Jasper O'Farrell in 1847 and aligned not to the existing city grid to its north which it cuts across at a 36 degree angle, but to Twin Peaks, its visual terminus. Why O'Farrell did this he never explained; its effect has been to make traffic connections across Market Street difficult and to divide the city into the prestigious middle- and upper-class north and the industrial and working-class south.

The railroad interests organized the Market Street Cable Railway which opened in 1883 and which eventually ran lines up Market and out Valencia and Castro streets south of Market, and up Market and out west on McAllister, Hayes, and Haight streets through the Western Addition to Golden Gate Park. The narrow cable conduit slot down Market Street became, figuratively, the social dividing line in San Francisco society as "South of the Slot" increasingly became a working-class "other city."

Later the municipality itself built a competing transit line down Market Street and for many years four sets of tracks busy with streetcars made crossing Market Street and boarding streetcars risky business. Department stores came to mid-Market Street in the 1890s and some bank headquarters between 1900 and 1920. After the fire of 1906 and into the 1920s, Market Street between Golden Gate and Van Ness avenues became the street for movie palaces. The 120-foot-wide street was described in the WPA guide of 1940 as a "streamlined array of neon signs, movie-theater marquees, neat awnings, and gleaming window glass...." Below Montgomery Street, Market Street was a much quieter zone of railroad and steamship companies, nautical supplies, and transient hotels.

When the Muni Metro/BART subway was built under Market Street in the early 1970s, the sidewalks and pocket plazas along Market were redesigned by Mario Ciampi, Lawrence Halprin and Associates, and John Carl Warnecke and Associates with a $24.5 million bond issue approved in 1968. Unfortunately, it is a graceless design, even through granite was lavishly used. The only positive note was the replication of the 1917 "Path of Gold" streetlights with their three elegant lamps designed by Willis Polk, Arthur Putnam, and Leo Lentelli, the handsomest street furniture San Francisco has ever seen. The bas-relief panels at their base are entitled "The Wining of the West" and are Putnam's work.

Citicorp Center [21]
1 Sansome Street, at Sutter and Market 1910, Albert Pissis, London Paris Bank; 1921, George Kelham, bank temple expansion; 1984, William Pereira and Associates, highrise and bank temple adaptation; 1915, A. Stirling Calder "Star Figure" statue

Enter the cold but impressive white marble-faced forecourt to the fine 1984 tower built within the granite shell of the Beaux Arts London Paris Bank of 1910. A pricy café here lets you enjoy the splendid isolation money can provide. The statue presiding over the space is one with much meaning for San Francisco. It is A. Stirling Calder's "Star Figure" sculpted for the great Panama-Pacific International Exposition of 1915. A woman in clinging drapery stands lightly on a globe with her hands held over her head in a diamond pattern framing a rayed, starry headdress.

The tower designed by Pereira is sleek and clean. Its light, rounded corners and the windowlike openings at its top create a design that is both assertive and contextural. The wraparound corner windows exploit the best view edges of tall buildings. Despite its large horizontal windows, the building wall seems predominantly a light-reflecting white. As office space, what is remarkable about the building is that it is a "smart building"; that is, it incorporates into its operation an "electronic nervous system" that can offer tenants computer services that enhance the technological reach of small, well-capitalized offices or branch offices.

The construction of the new tower involved the retention of the fine exterior of the 1910–1921 bank temple and the saving of a forty-ton section of the richly decorated cornice of MacDonald and Applegarth's fine 1912 Holbrook Building that once occupied the tower's site. That impressive architectural fragment makes a dramatic sculpture/memento mounted on the back wall of the restaurant tucked into the base of the tower.

Citicorp is the largest bank in the United States and is headquartered in New York City in a distinctive 1977 slant-topped tower. It had assets of $183.4 billion in 1988. Citicorp Center in San Francisco is owned by Citicorp and Dai-ichi Mutual Life Insurance Company, Japan's second largest insurance company.

Hunter-Dulin Building [22]
111 Sutter Street, at Montgomery
1926, Schultze and Weaver
Romanesque/châteauesque skyscraper

A stately castle in the air whose copper-trimmed top is now enjoyed mostly from the plain tall buildings that surround it

Former French Bank Building [23]
110 Sutter Street, at Trinity
1902, Hemenway and Miller; 1907/1913, E. A. Bozio, complete remodel and addition
Beaux Arts skyscraper

Opulent, assured, very beautiful.

Hallidie Building [24]
130-50 Sutter Street
1917, Willis Polk; 1979, Kaplan, McLaughlin and Diaz, restoration and compatible ground floor
World's first glass curtain wall

The Hallidie Building is the centerpiece of one of the most beautiful blocks in downtown San Francisco. It was built as an investment property by the Regents of the University of California, and named after a fellow Regent, the developer of the cable car, Andrew Hallidie.

From an architectural-historical point of view, this is the single most important

building in San Francisco. Its metal and glass curtain wall is hung a foot beyond the reinforced concrete structure. (The term "curtain wall" refers to the fact that the façade does not help support the building but rather is hung in front of the building like a protective curtain.) Here Willis Polk used metal and glass in a way that reveals the protective nature of the modern wall. Framing this bold "frontless" building are graceful Regency-inspired fire escapes and a heavy-looking (but actually light) sheet metal Venetian Gothic cornice capped by a white flagpole.

In 1979, Kaplan, McLaughlin and Diaz designed the restrained, close-to-original post office and bank shopfronts that make an appropriate metal and plate glass base for the building. Glass is what this building is about; it is in its way San Francisco's most important "window."

Crocker Galleria / Pacific Telesis Tower [25]
1 Montgomery Street between Sutter and Post, Montgomery and Kearny
1908, Willis Polk, bank at Montgomery and Post; 1982, Skidmore, Owings and Merrill, tower, galleria, and rooftop park over corner bank

The corner bank was designed for the First National Bank in 1908 and expanded in 1921 to create one of the most opulent banking halls in the city. When Crocker Bank redeveloped the block, it preserved the sumptuous banking hall and demolished the ten-story office tower above it, replacing it with a rooftop park. Utilitarian Lick Place became the site of a three-level, glass-roofed galleria of shops. **Japonesque**, a shop of modern Japanese art on the third level of the Crocker Galleria, is outstanding. At the corner of Post and Kearny, a pink granite-clad, thirty-eight-story tower was built which has since been renamed Pacific Telesis Tower. This classic, chamfered highrise's granite sheathing is both polished and rough-finished, creating a subtle checkerboard pattern. The tower reflects the lights and atmospheres of the city in ever-changing ways. Circolo Restaurant and Champagneria (362-0404), at 161 Sutter right next to Crocker Galleria, serves moderately expensive Italian cuisine. The murals in the bar come from the Old Poodle Dog, a famous San Francisco restaurant. Some window tables offer a view of the Hallidie Building across Sutter Street.

Mechanics Institute Library [26]
57-65 Post Street
1909, Albert Pissis

This fine Beaux Arts building houses a subscription library formed by the merger in 1906 of the Mechanics' Institute Library founded in 1854 and the Mercantile Library Association founded in 1852. Both collections, alas, were destroyed in the great fire. The second and third floors house the library assembled since then.

In the lobby of the building is a fine 1909 painting by Arthur F. Mathews, "The Arts," which depicts the Muses inspiring workers erecting a grand dome much like that of the later Panama-Pacific International Exposition. At the back of the lobby, behind a metal grill door, is one of the finest staircases in San Francisco, a spiral of iron and marble.

NEW MONTGOMERY STREET [27]

New Montgomery Street was the first attempt to pull San Francisco's downtown across Market Street. It was a privately cut-through street on land owned by Asbury Harpending and William Ralston, using $2 million of the Bank of California's money. Ralston built the great Palace Hotel in 1875 on the southwest corner of Market and New Montgomery, putting the hotel's entrance on his own New Montgomery Street. (The new Palace Hotel built in 1909 preserved that pattern.) "New" Montgomery Street was intended to extend prestigious Montgomery Street, the city's principal

business street, across Market Street, but only recently has the prime office district office district expanded south of Market Street.

Sheraton-Palace Hotel [27]
Market Street at New Montgomery
1909, Trowbridge and Livingston; 1915-1925, additions, George Kelham; 1989, refurbishing, Skidmore, Owings & Merrill

Constructed on the site of the historic Palace Hotel built by William Ralston and opened in 1875, the new Palace Hotel of 1909's most famous amenity is the splendid glass-roofed Garden Court, one of the finest Beaux Arts spaces in the nation. Also worth seeing in the hotel is the Pied Piper Room with fine mahogany paneling and an enamel-like Maxfield Parrish mural of the Piper and his followers.

The Palace Hotel and the fine ten-story Monadnock Building to the north designed in 1906 by Meyer and O'Brien conform to the height limits on Market Street briefly set by the city between the summer of 1906 and April of 1907. That Paris-inspired law limited building heights to one-and-one-half times the width of the streets they faced, an almost always agreeable height. In the pressure to rebuild after the fire, this regulation was done away with.

Sharon Building / House of Shields [28]
39-63 New Montgomery Street
1912, George Kelham

This nine-story Beaux Arts office building has on the ground floor the original Webster Cigars and The House of Shields, an unchanged Edwardian bar and restaurant redolent of the turn-of-the-century city's strictly masculine downtown. A high ceiling, imposing fine wood bar, booths and upstairs tables, and decorative light fixtures of draped women holding stalks of light bulbs make this a fly-in-amber Edwardian interior, the real thing.

Pacific Telephone and Telegraph Company / Telecommunication Museum [29]

140 New Montgomery Street
1925, Miller and Pfleuger, A. A. Cantin
Moderne skyscraper

Built as the headquarters of PT&T, this F-shaped office tower was once the largest corporate office building on the West Coast and long stood in splendid isolation south of Market Street. Clad in light gray terra cotta, the soaring design culminates in flowerlike ornaments, stern eagles, and an exclamatory flagpole. (Originally it was capped by a light whose color forecast the weather.) A painstaking six-year restoration recently brought this masterpiece back to perfect condition. The lobby, with its bronze doorway, black marble, and intricate plaster ceiling with pheasants and Chinese cloud patterns, is a knockout.

A small Telecommunication Museum has recently been opened off the lobby. Open Monday to Friday, 9 A.M. to 3 P.M.; free. The Telephone Pioneers of America, a service group of Pacific Bell employees, runs the small museum.

Chinatown

A TALE OF THREE CITIES

What This Tour Covers

[1] Portsmouth Square / Site of the Mexican Plaza / Financial District Holiday Inn / Chinese Culture Foundation Gallery / Portsmouth Square Garage / Buddha's Universal Church

[2] 700 Block of Washington Street / Old Chinese Telephone Exchange / Bank of Canton

[3] Grant Avenue / Calle de la Fundación

[4] Citicorp Savings

[5] Wentworth Street to Adler Place: Victorian Vice

[6] Grant Avenue from Jackson Street to Broadway

[7] Mural of San Francisco Scenes

[8] 700 Block of Jackson Street / Jewelry District

[9] Ross Alley

[10] Spofford Street

[11] Stockton Street Past and Present
[12] Kong Chow Temple / U.S. Post Office

[13] The Chinese Six Companies / Chinese Central High School / Kuo Ming Tang Headquarters

[14] Stockton Street Tunnel

[15] First Presbyterian Church

[16] Chinese Methodist Episcopal Church / Chinese American Citizens Alliance

[17] Waverly Place Associations and Temples Cluster

[18]Grant Avenue from Clay to California / Site of William Richardson's Trading Post of 1835

[19] Commercial Street / Chinese Historical Society of America Museum

[20] 700 and 800 Blocks of Sacramento Street

[21] Old St. Mary's Roman Catholic Church and Rectory / St. Mary's Square / Statute of Sun Yat-Sen

[22] Sing Chong and Sing Fat Buildings

[23] Grant Avenue to Bush Street Chinatown Gate

[24] 500 Block of Bush Street: Memories of the French Pioneers

Locke, California

Preliminaries

Best Times To Do This Tour

Chinatown's peak time is Saturday, from 10 A.M. to 3 P.M. Everything in Chinatown is going full blast then, especially food shopping. Chinatown is one of the parts of San Francisco open latest into the night. It is safe to use the alleyways in Chinatown, and it is a necessity to use them to see behind Chinatown's façade. The hours that both the Chinese Historical Society of America Museum and the Tin How or Norras temples are open (Tuesday to Saturday, 1 to 5 P.M.) are the best time for the explorer. To the knowledgeable San Franciscan there is no bad or boring time to Chinatown, for new discoveries pop up on every single exploration.

The noisy, festive, debt-settling Chinese (Lunar) New Year usually occurs in February, just when the quince in California's great Central Valley is budding. The most beautiful morning of the year in Chinatown is when the first quince arrives and you see elderly men bearing the leafless branches with the pearly pink buds to their rooms. For information on the Chinese New Year Parade write to the Chinese Chamber of Commerce, 730 Sacramento, 94108, 982-3000.

For Chinatown's district and family associations and tongs lucky-numbered "Double Ten," the tenth day of the tenth month, October 10th, is when every important building breaks out its flags and turns on the electric lights that outline it.

Walks

The Chinese Culture Foundation offers several walks. The Chinese Heritage Walk is on Saturday at 2 P.M., the Chinese Culinary Walk and Luncheon is weekdays at 11 A.M. Call

Copyright 1989 William Walters

The Ying On Labor and Merchant Benevolent Association at 745 Grant Avenue, near Clay, was built right after the earthquake and fire in 1906 for A. B. Ware and remodeled with an elaborate chinoiserie façade in 1920.

the Chinese Culture Foundation at 986-1822 to make reservations.

Parking

It is not easy to find street parking in Chinatown. Avoid unnecessary frustration by garaging your car. If the Portsmouth Square garage is full, there is another strategically placed city garage at Sutter and Stockton between Union Square and Chinatown, and another one in nearby North Beach over the police station at 766 Vallejo, between Stockton and Powell. On bustling Saturdays there is free parking in the Embarcadero Center garages with a minimum validated purchase in the center; on Sundays and holidays parking is free in Embarcadero Center. From there it is an easy three-block walk up narrow Commercial Street to Portsmouth Square and the heart of Chinatown.

Transportation

For the bus traveler, the key transit line is the 30 Stockton electric trolley bus, which links Chinatown with Union Square to the south and with Aquatic Park and Fisherman's Wharf to the north. The California Street cable car line bisects Chinatown. It is one of San Francisco's special moments when the twin Chinese roof pagodas pop up at California and Grant on the east slope of Nob Hill. The place to ride is an outside bench facing north when the car stops athwart Grant Avenue. The vista opens before you like a door. Grant Avenue, San Francisco's first street, is a minicanyon stage set alive with Chinese signs and festive architectural trumpery mostly from between 1909 and 1929.

Restaurants

It is not easy to find outstanding restaurants in Chinatown. The hole-in-the-wall **Hunan Restaurant** (788-2234) at 853 Kearny near Jackson serves hot, peppery northern Chinese cuisine. This is where chef and cookbook writer Henry Chung started in 1973; go at an off hour to avoid waiting, though you will probably find the line entertaining, if lines entertain you. It's a great corner to stand at to see the racial swirl of San Franciscans. A larger branch, also called Hunan Restaurant (956-7727) is at 924 Sansome off Broadway.

For its historic decor, not for its bland, humdrum cooking, the **Far East Cafe** at 631 Grant near California, 982-3245, is worth eating at.

The large **Hong Kong Tea House** (391-6365) at 835 Pacific Avenue west of Stockton is famous for its variety of *dim sum*; another is the **Hang Ah Tea Room** (982-5686) at 1 Pagoda Place/Hang Ah Alley, facing the midblock Chinese Playground near Sacramento and Stockton. They operate from 9 A.M. to 3 P.M.

Japanese restaurants have historically been sprinkled in and near Chinatown. Right outside the Chinatown Gate, along Bush Street and Kearny, there are several.

Shopping

Gump's is the oldest Asian art dealer in the city. It's located at 250 Post Street, near Union Square. Along Grant Avenue, the first two blocks closest to Union Square between Bush and California have the higher quality furniture and ceramics. Trinket heaven extends from there all the way to the Wharf. **Guillermina** (982-6152) at 771 Sacramento has Chinese and Japanese furniture and arts. The **Lun On Shop**, in back of the gallery, dates from 1908 and makes fine, custom-made bamboo and woven shades.

Clarion Music Center (391-1317) at 816 Sacramento near Waverly Place, in the basement, carries gongs, cymbals, drums, and traditional Chinese stringed instruments. Posters here announce Chinese musical recitals and programs by the Chinese Orchestra of San Francisco.

Eastwind Books & Arts (781-3331) at 1435A Stockton near Columbus, in the basement level of the Eureka Savings Building, has the best and widest selection of books in both English and Chinese. They also sell calligraphic brushes and ink stones. The latest English-language books on Asian-American themes are here. Progressive Chinese books are at **China Books and Periodicals** (282-2994) 2929 Twenty-fourth Street in the Mission District. *See Tour 9.*

Introduction: A Tale of Three Cities

Chinatown is old and Chinatown is new. It is not a jumble or a chaos; it is a pattern of changing patterns. If one listens with the ears of an historian over a century and a quarter, the happiest sounds today are the squeals of Chinatown's many children in the lively school playgrounds. Chinatown has never had so many children with such bright prospects.

Today Chinatown is best understood as the complex overlay of three "cities": the old Chinese ghetto-become-neighborhood with its 20,000 residents, half of them elderly, who live on San Francisco's oldest blocks almost in the shadow of the Financial District's highrises; the cultural "capital city" for the Bay Area's affluent, assimilated Chinese-Americans who descend on it on Saturdays; and a special shopping district for non-Chinese San Franciscans and a visitor-pleasing tourist attraction. Today Chinatown is the second densest neighborhood in the

nation with 160 people per acre, second only to New York City's Chinatown. Three-quarters of its residents are foreign-born; the comparable citywide proportion is 28 percent. The median household income here is about $10,000, half the median income of the city as a whole.

The population history of Chinatown has been a dramatic J-shaped curve. From the Gold Rush through the 1870s a large migration of mostly single male laborers came to San Francisco and the American West, as well as to Canada and Peru. With the Chinese Exclusion Act of 1882, the nation's first racially restrictive immigration measure, the Chinese-American population aged without replacing itself and San Francisco's Chinese population fell from 26,000 in 1881 to 11,000 at its nadir in 1920. There were vacant storefronts on Chinatown's side streets in the 1920s, hard as that is to imagine today. In 1943, during World War II when the U.S. allied with China against Japan, the Chinese Exclusion Act was repealed by Congress, though war in the Pacific and a very small quota of 105 Chinese a year kept migration low.

The first migration streams from China to San Francisco were overwhelmingly men from four regional dialect groupings within Guangtung Province in southern China. A series of disastrous floods in the Pearl River Delta downriver from Canton propelled a virtual diaspora of Cantonese dialect-speaking people all around the Pacific Basin. These are the *huagiao*, the Overseas Chinese. Historians estimate that some 2.5 million emigrated from China between 1840 and 1900. Between 1852 and 1882, many mostly male Chinese laborers and a few merchants and labor brokers came to San Francisco.

"Mayflower" migrants from the three districts of Nomhai, Punji, and Shunteh,

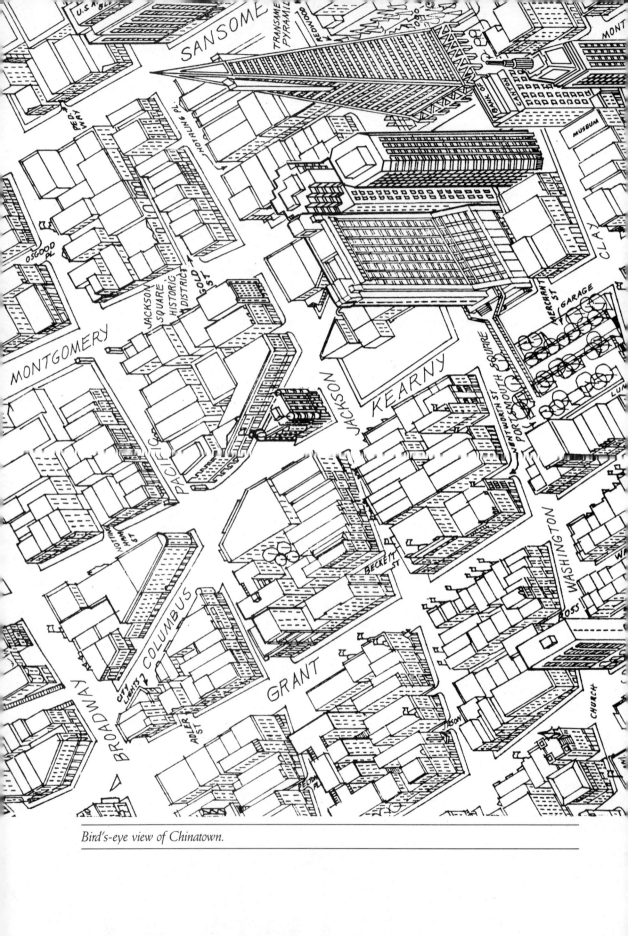

Bird's-eye view of Chinatown.

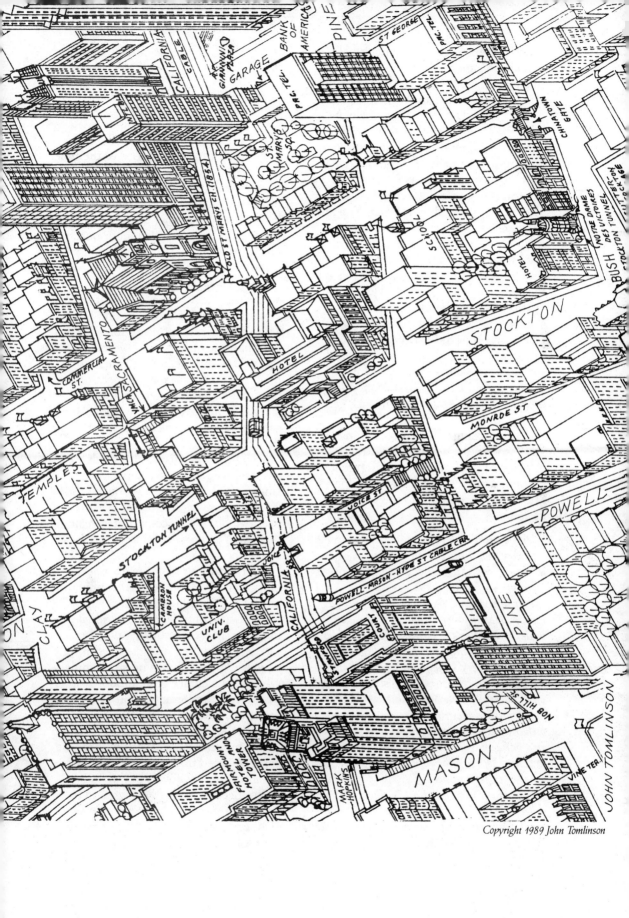

Copyright 1989 John Tomlinson

wealthy commercial and agricultural districts near Canton, dominated. In 1851 they organized as the Canton Company, also known as the Sam Yup Association, or the "Three Districts." The organizers were well-wired merchants who dominated the economic life of the expatriate community. Peasant migrants also came from less advanced areas further from Canton speaking a different dialect. They felt oppressed by the Sam Yup and organized as the Sze Yup or "Four Districts" in the same polarizing year. In 1852 migrants from Heungshan, Tsengshing, and Tungkun organized as the Young Yo Company. Hakka speakers from Xin'an withdrew from the Young Yo Company to form the Sun On Company, later the Yan Wo Company.

Just as within the larger American society where different immigrant groups carved out different economic niches—Italian-Americans in truck gardening, or Greek-Americans in coffee shops, for example—so too the tongs and associations within Chinatown established (and fought over) different economic turfs. In 1984, historian John Kuo Wei Tchen sketched the general pattern:

> A hierarchy of businesses developed along economic and district-of-origin lines. Wealthier Sanyi tended to control the larger, commercially successful companies, such as export-import firms. Nanhai District people monopolized the men's clothing and tailoring trade, in addition to butcher shops. Neighboring Shunde District folk controlled the overalls and workers' clothing factories. Chinese hailing from the Zhongshan District, the second largest population of Chinese in California, controlled the fish businesses and fruit-orchard work, and predominated in the women's garment, shirt, and underwear sewing factories. The Siyi, or Four District people, by far the largest and poorest group of Chinese, controlled the low end of the business pecking order in occupations such as laundries, small retail shops, and restaurants. Up until World War II, class affiliations within Tangrenbu [Chinatown] were largely predetermined by district of origin.

Most important associations were controlled by Chinatown's tiny merchant elite. These merchants profited as the intermediaries between labor-starved large American corporations of the nineteenth-century West (railroads, land reclamation companies, commercial farms, mines, and early factories) and the limitless reliable labor pool of China. Most Chinese immigrants were poor but healthy and motivated young men who came to America for a brief time to better their chances back home. They came across the Pacific on the "credit-ticket" system. Under it Cantonese and Hong Kong merchants lent peasant sojourners their passage of forty to fifty dollars. On this side of the ocean, San Francisco merchants oversaw the payment of the principal and the interest on the loans and also contracted out the laborer in gangs to American employers. When they contracted the labor, San Francisco's Chinese merchants also made exclusive arrangement to sell supplies to the small armies of Chinese workers working all over the arid, frontier West. To oversimplify a very complicated reality, the Sam Yup grew rich brokering the labor of the Sze Yup.

All the various Chinatown associations were small empires worth fighting over. They levied dues and exercised other social controls over individual immigrants. Most eventually owned real estate, if only their headquarters in Chinatown, and it was no small thing who got the choice ground-floor store. Much more important, some of these associations had the power to grant or deny the exit permits granted by the steamship companies. The fee for these permits varied from a couple of dollars to ten or twenty dollars in the mid-1880s. Because the early migration to California was of sojourners, men who planned to go back home to marry and have a family, this was an important "tax power." (This exit permit system continued until 1949 when passage to China ceased.)

Cutting across the so-called "nonvoluntary associations" based on family or birthplace were often equally nonvoluntary "voluntary associations" called tongs, which were workers' and merchants' guilds with labyrinthine and competing interests. There were legitimate tongs and criminal tongs. Some ran Chinatown's protection rackets, gambling, loan-sharking, and prostitution.

During the height of anti-Chinese hysteria in California in the early 1880s, Chinatown's mutually suspicious key associations formed an umbrella association. "Uniting" the most important of the district associations in what became known as the Chinese Six Companies—officially the Consolidated Chinese Benevolent Association—in 1882 (incorporated in the State of California in 1901) made that organization the cockpit for personal and group political, economic, and social contention.

Romantic old Chinatown, then, was a tense place. When tensions ran high violence erupted within California's Chinatowns. This violence came from within, between rival Chinese groups inside the ghettos. The domination of the Sam Yup grew more resented over time as Chinese immigrants became more Americanized. The dean of contemporary historians of Chinatown, engineer and writer Him Mark Lai wrote in 1987 that:

During the nineteenth century and early twentieth century, when tong wars erupted frequently and Chinatown was a jungle where the strong preyed on the weak and unprotected, many larger clan associations organized into two branches. One, administered by the elders, had jurisdiction over affairs affecting the entire clan, while the other acted as the clan association's defense unit against outside threats to members' interests. In many respects this latter was akin to a secret society in behavior.

Inside the Chinese Six Companies (which actually numbered seven, and briefly eight), there was intense conflict. Once again, the smaller associations like the Sam Yup, Young Wo, and Kong Chow, which had a greater proportion of wealthy merchants, dominated. The system was an oligarchy run by intermarried merchant families. This rankled the members of the populous Ning Yung Association, the one with the largest membership whose exit permits accounted for about half the Six Companies' income. In 1928 the Ning Yung Association temporarily withdrew from the Six Companies and withheld its contributions.

In 1930 the Six Companies rewrote its bylaws to apportion the fifty-five seats on its board according to the number of registered members in 1926. This gave the Ning Yung one less member than half the board and reduced the Sam Yup, Young Wo, and Kong Chow to a total of thirteen board seats among them. The new arrangement also set the president's term at two months to be rotated every other term between the Ning Yung and all the others. The American notion of representation based on population, not status or wealth, became the method for apportioning power inside the Six Companies.

As Chinese immigration dwindled, and as individual assimilation took place—and it does in America—parochial clan and regional attachments weakened. With the republican revolution in China in 1911, San Francisco's Chinese men cut off their queues, ancient symbols of Manchu domination. In the 1920s traditional Chinese dress disappeared in favor of western, if uniformly dark and somber, garb. Dating and personal choice in marriage partners gradually replaced family-arranged unions. After 1933 tong warfare faded away. While the Chinese were, practically speaking, segregated within Chinatown until the late 1940s, some assimilation nonetheless took place. The post-World War II era saw the economic and social advance of Chinese-Americans. The nullification of California's antimiscegenation law in 1948 and the striking down of racially restrictive covenants in the sale of California real estate in the same year emancipated Chinese-Americans and other Asian-Americans. Chinese-Americans made impressive gains in income and status and surpassed the median national income level in 1960. In 1949, when the Nationalist government retreated to Taiwan, an influx of Mandarin-speaking professionals and wealthy merchants fled Red China to San Francisco.

In 1965 the Civil Rights Act was passed and the United States began to break through the psychological and legal barriers of its historic racial antipathies and to put a positive spin on its reality as a multiracial society. In the same year immigration quotas were reconfigured to reflect a multiracial reality and to permit more Asian immigration. From 105 a year, quotas for Chinese grew to 20,000 per year by 1970. By that time, 56 percent of Chinese-Americans were in white-collar occupations.

Since the late 1970s, more and more Chinese from Vietnam, along with other Southeast Asian peoples, have arrived in San Francisco. Many have side-stepped Chinatown. This latest wave found rents cheaper in the Tenderloin than in high-priced old Chinatown and they have formed a new, loosely sprinkled Vietnamese Chinatown southwest of Union Square. By 1970, 52 percent of all San Franciscans of Chinese ancestry were foreign-born. The new immigration laws favor migrants with skills and/or capital and the recent migration includes many highly skilled people with education. This wave is Americanizing and suburbanizing faster than all its predecessors.

Chinatown's uniquely dense associational history is spelled out across the façades of its principal buildings. Originally a makeshift adaptation and overcrowding of the ramshackle "discarded"

buildings of Mexican Yerba Buena and early American San Francisco of 1840–1860, the quarter was owned by white landlords. Of 153 pieces of property in Chinatown in 1873, only ten were Chinese-owned. All the rest were leased from Franco-Americans, Italian-Americans, and German-Americans. In 1904, of 316 parcels, only twenty-five were Chinese-American in ownership.

Early Chinatown saw little "Chinese architecture" but it did see a distinctly Chinese way of decorating and treating buildings. Big red paper lanterns were hung from balconies and cornices, sign boards were affixed, posters appeared plastered to walls, and a Chinese "look" was given to old Italianate buildings.

Ramshackle old Chinatown was completely wiped away by the fire of 1906. When the district was rebuilt by non-Chinese absentee landowners between 1906 and about 1929, a newer, cleaner— if still extraordinarily dense—early twentieth-century city of remarkable consistency emerged. These new buildings conformed to better municipal building laws that required brick or concrete construction in the "congested district." The resulting Edwardian buildings are the stuff of today's Chinatown.

Over time two things happened. Chinese-Americans, particularly associations, bought their lots and buildings, and plain brick buildings of the 1906–1915 period were enriched to varying degrees with chinoiserie, especially the upper floors where associational meeting halls and a few temples were located. Periods of building or remodeling are recorded in the dates on their parapets.

While European architecture indulged in chinoiserie in the late eighteenth century and sporadically in the late nineteenth century, the post-earthquake and fire chinoiserie in San Francisco was something essentially local and new. There were no Chinese-American architects during this period and San Francisco's established "Anglo" architects turned their hands to stage-set Chinese remodels and encrustations of varying degrees of elaborateness.

The twin gateway pagoda-capped buildings at California and Grant of 1909 and the old Pacific Telephone Exchange of the same year set the architectural standards for others to follow all the way (almost) to the present. In the 1909–1929 era, building outlines and features such as balconies and pagoda cornices were studded with lightbulbs that could be turned on for festive occasions. San Francisco's Beaux Arts-trained or -influenced architects were adaptable designers, and they collectively left a remarkable legacy of "San Francisco Chinese" architecture. The thing to look for in Chinatown is the Edwardian city under the overlays of chinoiserie. Those who look above the shopfronts will see tight rows of expressive façades set like masks on a high shelf. Connoisseurs will observe changes in the chinoiserie itself, particularly the introduction of zappy neon trimming in the late 1940s.

In the early 1970s more serious Chinese-style designs were built, now by Chinese-American architects, including Clayton Lee's Bush Street Gate, Ed Sue's Citicorp Savings at 845 Grant, and the new Kong Chow Temple.

In the late 1980s some Chinatown buildings, both new and remodeled, introduced super modern stainless steel façades, which, alas, in this climate are not stainless. Relentlessly blatant shopfronts are also spreading in Chinatown with completely open fronts, harshly overlighted, exposed interiors, and industrial roll-down steel doors. Vintage 1906–1929 shopfronts disappear every month before this hideous and apparently unstoppable new trend. These open-front shops are modeled on Beirut or Hong Kong, with their paranoid roll-down steel doors, rather than on San Francisco, and increasingly deaden the streets at night. Remodelings in Chinatown are so drastic that the observer must constantly be checking his or her old favorites and intensely enjoying

them. For they only *seem* lost in time. Chinatown ought to be a landmark San Francisco Historic District but is still not one. Restoration, rather than the latest radical modernization, has not yet come to Chinatown.

PORTSMOUTH SQUARE/SITE OF THE MEXICAN PLAZA [1]

Chinatown's Portsmouth Square is the forgotten seed of this great city. Few realize when they park in its banal 1960 underground garage that this was San Francisco's historic center. Here Mexican governor José Figueroa of Alta California authorized *alcalde* Francisco de Haro to engage Swiss ship captain and engineer Jean Jacques Vioget to plat out a town in 1839. This was done to regularize and shape the spontaneous settlement sprouting around sandy-bottomed Yerba Buena Cove, where four years earlier William A. Richardson, an English trader married into a Mexican land-owning family, had built a trading post.

Jean Jacques Vioget laid out a checkerboard settlement with a central plaza facing the public beach where goods were landed. His layout accommodated the two already-existing groups of buildings: a string of half-a-dozen one-story adobes along what is now Grant Avenue, and a cluster of Yankee frame buildings on the shoreline at what is now Clay Street between Montgomery and Kearny. The area Vioget laid out is today bounded by Pacific Avenue to the north, Sacramento Street to the south, Grant Avenue to the west, and Montgomery Street to the east. The small block sizes and narrow street widths are still characteristic of today's Chinatown.

Inexplicably, Vioget did not make right-angled blocks, but rather blocks 2.5 degrees off square, forming trapezoids. (This peculiarity was later corrected.) Each of Vioget's blocks was divided into six lots. The central plaza—now Portsmouth Square—was never a full block. Vioget built himself a house at the southeast corner of the plaza, on the corner lot at Kearny and Clay. The town's only official map, inscribed with lot holders, was hung behind the bar of a plaza saloon.

When war broke out between the United States and Mexico in 1846 over the annexation of Texas, the U.S. Navy swiftly occupied Alta California. On July 9, 1846 Navy captain John B. Montgomery of the war sloop *U.S.S. Portsmouth* raised the Stars and Stripes in the plaza of Yerba Buena and took possession of the port. He appointed one of his officers, Washington A. Bartlett, as the first United States *alcalde*.

The peace treaty with Mexico that ceded the vast Southwest to the United States was signed on February 2, 1848. Days before, on January 4, gold was discovered by John Marshall at Coloma in the foothills of the Sierras. It was in Portsmouth Square on May 12, 1849 that Samuel Brannan, editor of the *California Star*, the town's first newspaper, announced the discovery of gold. When President Polk formally announced the discovery to Congress in Washington, the famous California Gold Rush began. With the Gold Rush stampede, the flyspeck port exploded. Landfill quickly spread out into the shallow cove and on it the new American city developed. (see Tours 2A and 2B).

Holiday Inn Financial District / Chinese Culture Foundation Gallery [1]
750 Kearny Street
1971, Clement Chin, John Warnecke and Associates

The downtown side of Portsmouth Square faces Kearny Street, one of the first streets to be widened in San Francisco in a process that continues very slowly but steadily. The unattractive Holiday Inn was an Urban Renewal project exempt from the City Planning Commission's design review procedure and was built on former public land, the site of the old police headquarters and courts building. The hotel's unfortunate

pedestrian bridge, which intrudes on a public park is both useless and ugly.

On the third floor of the Holiday Inn is the Chinese Culture Foundation Gallery, which hosts changing exhibitions of Chinese-American and Chinese art.

Except for the egregious Holiday Inn and the intrusive Empress of China Restaurant, built in 1966, the buildings embracing Portsmouth Square preserve the scale of the nineteenth-century city. Almost all date from the period of rebuilding in 1906–1909, after the earthquake and fire.

Lost on the upper level of the terraced park is the **Robert Louis Stevenson Monument** designed by Bruce Porter and sculptor George Piper and dedicated in 1897. This handsome, if neglected, monument consists of a fine granite base capped by Piper's bronze model of the galleon *Hispaniola* from Stevenson's *Treasure Island*. The shaft is inscribed with excerpts from his "Christmas Sermon." Its lengthy inscription is worth contemplating

Portsmouth Square Garage [1]
Under Portsmouth Square
1960, Royston, Hanamoto and Mayes

Beginning in 1942, San Francisco excavated its few downtown parks to build underground parking garages. Portsmouth Square was hit in 1960 and the unfortunate decision and design now seem irreversible. (North Beach's Washington Square was to be next, but escaped.) Even admitting the usefulness of parking, it is hard to find much to admire in the garage *or* park designs. The park is used, of course; Chinatown would use the space if it were just blacktop, for it has all too few parks. Old Chinese-American men in particular enjoy the park and gather there to chat and play checkers. Some young mothers bring their children to the sand box area along the Kearny Street edge of the park.

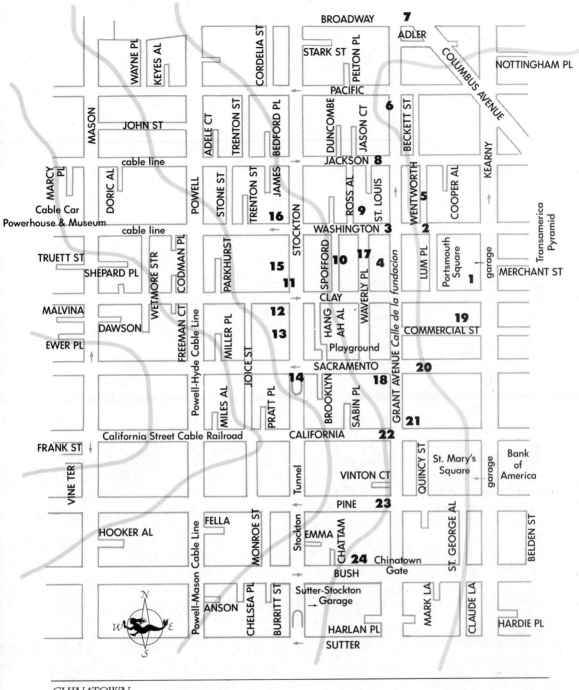

BROADWAY

7

ADLER

NOTTINGHAM PL

COLUMBUS AVENUE

WAYNE PL
KEYES AL
CORDELIA ST
STARK ST
PELTON PL

MASON
JOHN ST
ADELE CT
TRENTON ST
BEDFORD PL
PACIFIC
DUNCOMBE
JASON CT
6
BECKETT ST
KEARNY

cable line
DORIC AL
POWELL
STONE ST
TRENTON ST
JAMES
JACKSON **8**
WENTWORTH
COOPER AL

MARCY PL
Cable Car
Powerhouse & Museum
TRENTON ST
16
ROSS AL
ST. LOUIS
5
Transamerica Pyramid

cable line
STOCKTON
WASHINGTON **3**
9
2
LUM PL
garage
MERCHANT ST

TRUETT ST
WETMORE STR
CODMAN PL
PARKHURST
15
SPOFFORD
10
17
4
Portsmouth Square **1**

SHEPARD PL
11
Calle de la fundación

MALVINA
FREEMAN CT
MILLER PL
12
CLAY
HANG AH AL
WAVERLY PL
COMMERCIAL ST **19**

DAWSON
Powell-Hyde Cable Line
13
Playground
GRANT AVENUE
20

EWER PL
JOICE ST
SACRAMENTO
18

14
MILES AL
PRATT PL
BROOKLYN
SABIN PL
21

California Street Cable Railroad
CALIFORNIA
22

FRANK ST
Tunnel
VINTON CT
QUINCY ST
St. Mary's Square
garage
Bank of America

VINE TER
Stockton
PINE **23**
ST. GEORGE AL
BELDEN ST

HOOKER AL
FELLA
MONROE ST
EMMA
CHATTAM

Powell-Mason Cable Line
24 Chinatown Gate
MARK LA
CLAUDE LA

ANSON
CHELSEA PL
BURRITT ST
BUSH
HARDIE PL

N
W E
S
Sutter-Stockton Garage
HARLAN PL
SUTTER

CHINATOWN

Buddha's Universal Church [1]
720 Washington Street
1952, Campbell & Wong

Tours of the temple are given Sundays between 1 and 3 P.M.

This modern white temple was designed by Campbell & Wong in 1952. While an International Style building, it has a recessed penthouse with a meeting room just like traditional Chinatown association buildings. The teak-trimmed entrance is simple and pleasing. The foyer has a brass wall screen of Buddha seated under the *bodhi* tree.

700 BLOCK OF WASHINGTON STREET [2]

At **733 Washington**, just up from the park, is the Mow Fung Company, an original shopfront dating from 1912 and designed by William H. Crim, Jr. Here, seemingly lost in time, is a bit of old Chinatown unchanged, an Edwardian shopfront with Chinese lettering. Such antique shopfronts are an endangered species in Chinatown. In fact, perhaps by the time you read this guide, this historic business will be gone.

At **737-39 Washington**, the old Arata Hotel, now the Silver Restaurant, is a 1906 building radically remodeled and given a stainless steel cladding that is quickly discoloring. Chinatown is about a generation behind the rest of San Francisco in understanding the value of its vintage architecture. What happens here to commercial buildings used to happen to Victorian houses all over the city.

Old Chinese Telephone Exchange / Bank of Canton [2]
743 Washington Street
1909, C. W. Burkett, engineer

Pressed between two neighbors is one of Chinatown's most delightful concoctions, the old Pacific Telephone and Telegraph Company's Chinatown Exchange built in 1909. It is one of the most "Chinese" of Chinatown's buildings and epitomizes the efforts to make rebuilt Chinatown an "Oriental city." This was probably the only telephone exchange in the United States operated in a foreign language. Its originally male operators were required to be proficient in English and five Chinese dialects: the Som Yup, Say Yup, Geung Son, Gow Gong, and Aw Duck dialects. Since there is no Chinese alphabet, the Chinese telephone directory was arranged by streets. The street with the most subscribers came first and that with the least last. The earliest male operators lived in quarters on the building's second floor; later operators were female and lived in their own homes. The Bank of Canton has carefully preserved this very important building, and its interior has been converted for the bank.

Grant Avenue / Calle de la Fundacion [3]

The tourist boom of the mid-1920s induced the Chinese Chamber of Commerce to urge the creation of unique street lamps for Grant Avenue. These fine ornamental standards were the result. Designed by W. D'Arcy Ryan, they are as fine as the "Path of Gold" light standards on Market Street and the fine lamps along Post Street downtown. Two dragons uphold the lanternlike lamps. On the southeast corner of Washington and Grant is the **Sang Wo Company building** of 1907 designed by Charles M. Rousseau. At some point, perhaps, in the 1940s, its corner was clad in black and orange tiles in a striking pattern. Tile was used because it has a hard surface and could withstand the removal of the wall posters traditional in this part of the city.

Citicorp Savings [4]
845 Grant Street
1970, Ed Sue

Up Grant Avenue is Chinese-American architect Ed Sue's Citicorp Savings of 1970. In that decade several important Chinese-style buildings were built in

Chinatown as the district enjoyed a burst of business prosperity. This bank with its well-proportioned gatelike façade is perhaps the best of its period. The gold-glazed roof tiles and guardian lions came from Hong Kong and Taiwan.

WENTWORTH STREET TO ADLER PLACE: VICTORIAN VICE [5]

While most tourists simply pour down Grant Avenue in a straight line from Bush to Broadway, the explorer must thread through Chinatown's many side streets and narrow alleyways to get behind the tourist façade and experience the residents' district. The alleys in Chinatown are safe by day or night. Even in 1888 Hittell's guidebook noted that, "Ladies unaccompanied by gentlemen can venture into Chinatown in the daytime with entire safety, and in the evening are in as little danger as in some streets of the city occupied exclusively by white inhabitants." Because they attract fewer tourists, alleyways tend to be much plainer than Grant Avenue and preserve more of the feel of Chinese Chinatown. They are part of the first of Chinatown's three "cities," that of the 20,000 residents and workers of the district. Wentworth Street, the alley between Washington and Jackson east of Grant, is a typical example.

In nineteenth-century American cities, alleyways inside blocks were often lined with working-class housing, while middle-class houses were built facing the wider main streets. Chinatown and the South of Market districts preserve this old pattern. Ghettos then, as now, often also harbored the city's vice, especially gambling and prostitution, and in Chinatown, the infamous opium dens.

Despite the popular image of Victorian society as straight-laced, San Francisco and most other American cities had well-known red-light districts. In San Francisco in the late 1880s, the alleys inside the blocks near Pacific and Grant harbored many of San Francisco's brothels. Most catered to white prostitution, but some served Chinatown's overwhelmingly male population. In 1909 the Police Commission decided on a policy of strict segregation and contained most prostitution in a zone from Sacramento to Broadway and from Kearny to Stockton. This created a joint-tenancy between Chinatown and the brothels. The city Board of Health conducted periodic medical examinations and even issued the "working girls" identification cards. Eventually pressure from some church groups led the city to abandon this system of regulated toleration. It was not until the purification campaigns of the Progressive era and America's entry into World War I in 1917 that prostitution was driven underground. Of course prostitution did not evaporate, it simple dispersed to other areas, in particular to what today is called the Tenderloin west of Union Square.

Quant Sang Chong & Co.
32 Wentworth Street

It is in Chinatown's byways that some of its oldest businesses survive. The old façade of Quant Sant Chong & Co. is such a spot. Here the window displays exotic imports such as sharks' fins.

GRANT AVENUE FROM JACKSON STREET TO BROADWAY [6]

The northern end of Grant Avenue below Broadway has several poultry and fish vendors who cater to the Chinatown market. These blocks are alive with shoppers early in the morning; later in the day tourists fill the sidewalks. Grant Avenue was called Dupont Street in the early days but had its name changed to honor the general and president during the first decade of this century, when merchants and reformers sought to "clean up" the image of this part of the city. Some elderly Chinese-Americans still refer to the street as "Dupont Gai."

In the pre-1948 days of racially restrictive covenants in the sale of real estate, Chinatown was tightly circumscribed. Major streets like Kearny and Broadway were "white," while Chinatown began several lots inside these lines. As happened in New York City, Little Italy and Chinatown both located in the oldest parts of the city right next to each other. In San Francisco, wide Broadway was the dividing line between the two. Teenage toughs enforced these sharp social divisions and beat up those who strayed from their turf. But Italian-Americans assimilated faster than Chinese immigrants and second- and third-generation San Franciscans of Italian ancestry moved into the Marina in the 1920s and out to truck gardens in the southern districts of the city, slowly draining North Beach of its Italian flavor. Chinatown, in contrast, was reinvigorated after 1965 by a new wave of immigration, and Chinese-Americans began buying property in North Beach and along Broadway. Today both sides of Broadway are Chinese in character.

Across Broadway is a recent addition to Chinatown, the **Emperor Herbal Restaurant** (433-3765) at 626 Grant Avenue. It is the first herbal restaurant in the United States and features "dieto-therapeutic" meals.

Mural of San Francisco Scenes [7]
Broadway and Columbus

On the northwest corner of Broadway and Columbus is a four-story Edwardian building with large murals showing San Francisco scenes and musicians painted by Bill Weber and Tony Klaas in 1987.

Chinese Historical Society of America Museum
650 Commercial Street
Open Tuesday–Saturday 1–5 P.M., free; 391-1188

As this guide went to press the Chinese Historical Society of America

Museum relocated from Adler Place to 650 Commercial Street, near Montgomery, a couple of doors from the Pacific Heritage Museum. This small and agreeable museum displays the mementos, work tools, artifacts, and photographs of the Chinese pioneers in California. A fine series of photo panels explains the migration of the Chinese and the evolution of Chinese-American culture in America.

Near the entrance is an old lacquered wood Taoist altar from Napa carved in 1889. It is decorated with crimson bunting and orange gold-flecked paper banners. Suspended from the ceiling is a Chinese-style sampan made of redwood about 1900. In the basement are a shrimp-cleaning machine and a wheelbarrow made of wood and wire. Some fine old green, gold, and black carved wood signs are hung at the head of the basement stairs. Linger here and you get a feeling for the work and endurance of the early Chinese migrants, and a better appreciation of the history of this part of San Francisco. The Chinese Historical Society of America presents lectures and publishes a journal on Chinese-American history; other interesting books on Chinese-American history are for sale here as well.

700 BLOCK OF JACKSON STREET / JEWELRY DISTRICT [8]

Return south down Grant to Jackson and walk uphill half a block, turning left into Ross Alley. In this vicinity was Li Po-Tai's alley, named after Chinatown's most successful nineteenth-century herbalist who amassed considerable real estate inside Chinatown. Li Po-Tai and his assistants were said to see from 150 to 300 patients a day; in his clientele were such notables as Leland Stanford and Mark Hopkins. Rumor put his income at $75,000 a year.

When Chinese did buy real estate, they had to pay a premium for it. In

1873 the *Real Estate Circular* reported that a lot on Jackson Street had been sold to Chung Hoon Hoy *et al.* for $9,000, which worked out to nearly $500 per front foot. As the editor noted, "When Chinamen either lease or purchase property here they are always made to pay a very high price." The *Circular* also noted that Chung had borrowed $5,000 from the Odd Fellows' Bank to build on the lot and that this was "the first instance, in our recollection, of a Chinaman borrowing from a savings bank."

Today nearly all of Chinatown is owned by Chinese-Americans, but this is a relatively recent development.

At either end of Ross Alley are clusters of small jewelry stores catering to the Chinese-American market. With prosperity for Chinese-Americans and with the influx of traditionalistic new Chinese immigrants to San Francisco, there has been a boom in jewelry shops. Today there are more than fifty jewelry stores in Chinatown alone. Some of these businesses have been established by jewelers with links to Hong Kong's booming trade in precious metals. Comparison shoppers can find here perhaps the best souvenirs of their visit to San Francisco, though prices are not low. The Chinese market prefers a yellower gold than the American market; jade of course, has always been coveted here. Fine spinach-green and pale lavender jade pendants entice the window-shopper. Some gold objects in red cases and frames are meant not for wearing but for display and are presented at anniversaries and other family occasions.

ROSS ALLEY [9]

Long neglected by the city, Chinatown's alleys have been repaved and improved since 1980. The formation of the Ross Alley Improvement Association (a most San Franciscan tradition, these neighborhood improvement associations) has brought municipal investment even here. At **23 Ross Alley** is the Golden Gate Fortune Cookie Company. A few storefront garment factories also operate here. At **14 Ross Alley** is the Sam Bo Trading Company with a most modern yellow-and-red plastic sign and an old Edwardian door with an oval glass insert. Inside is a universe of Chinese religious goods: statues, banners, lanterns, hangings, plaques, scrolls, small shrines, and Buddhas. This is where Chinese-American shopkeepers themselves shop for the small shrines with the red electric vigil lights often seen in Chinese shops. At the Washington Street end of the alley is another cluster of jewelry shops. Cross Washington and enter Spofford Street, another narrow alley.

SPOFFORD STREET [10]

Spofford is another alleyway, perhaps not scenic but of real historic interest. The clacking of *mah jong* tiles is sometimes heard here. Halfway up the alley at **36 Spofford Street** is a small red door with old gold lettering on its glass pane reading "Chinese Free Mason" with a compass and square insignia and "CTK" in place of the usual Masonic "G." It is the headquarters of the Chee Kung Tong, housed in a 1907 building designed by Charles M. Rousseau. This secret society was organized about 1853 and incorporated in 1879. In 1904 Dr. Sun Yat Sen stayed here and utilized the society's newspaper, *The Chinese Free Press,* as his political platform for some six years. From here Chinese-American support was generated for the overthrow of the Manchus in China. When the revolution erupted in China on October 10, 1911, this building became the American outpost from which government notes were sold. On November 5, 1911, nearly all the associations in Chinatown hauled down the triangular yellow standard of the Manchu dynasty with its dragon and hoisted the modern red, white and blue flag of the new Republic of China. This remains the flag of Nationalist China

(Taiwan) and is the flag that still flies from Chinatown's many flagpoles on festive occasions.

At **33 Spofford Street**, attached to a 1907 building designed by the O'Brien Brothers, is the signboard of the Chinese Laundry Association. Laundry work was one of the economic niches that Chinese immigrants carved out for themselves in the hostile climate of nineteenth-century San Francisco. In 1888 some three thousand Chinese laundrymen were at work in the city. The laundrymen's tong sought to protect the Chinese from discriminatory municipal taxation and to regularize competition. The tong set rules specifying the minimum number of shopfronts between laundries and also arbitrated disputes within the industry.

Spofford was the scene of several violent confrontations between warring criminal tongs in the 1900s. The formation of the General Peace Association in 1913 and the dwindling of the population of Chinatown in the 1920s led to the diminution of tong warfare. The last outburst was in 1933 during the depths of the Great Depression.

At the end of Spofford, on the west side, on the St. Mary's Playground wall, are four fine **murals** painted by Aratani in 1986 depicting Chinatown residents shopping.

STOCKTON STREET PAST AND PRESENT [11]

Wide Stockton Street is not as scenic as narrow Grant Avenue, but it has an important past and a lively present. Today Stockton is the location of several of the most important cultural and political institutions serving the Bay Area's large Chinese-American population. It is the "capital city," the second of Chinatown's three "cities." Stockton is also the premier shopping street for Chinese culinary needs.

Few know that Stockton Street was San Francisco's first fashionable address. As the haughty, blue-and-gold-bound

Social Manual of San Francisco explained in 1884,

In spite of the prevailing lack of repose [San Francisco high] society began to show signs of combined effort in 1852. Its first attempt of importance was on Stockton Street north of Washington where some dwellings and a few scattering churches going to ruin still show traces of ancient grandeur.

But "le Boulevard Stockton" very quickly lost its cachet as the city grew and fashion jumped to Rincon Hill, South of Market.

Kong Chow Temple / U.S. Post Office [12]
Stockton and Clay streets
1977, Ed Sue
Temple open from 9 A.M.–4 P.M. daily

On the southwest corner of Stockton and Clay is the tan-colored Kong Chow Temple designed by Ed Sue. An elevator in the building lobby takes you to the temple on the top floor. Note the huge antique bronze urn with dragon handles. Chinese pioneers from the Kong Chow district, one of the Chinese Six Companies, established their first San Francisco temple in 1857. The patron deity here is Kuan Ti who presides over the seventeen gods and goddesses of the temple. Many of the furnishings are antique and worth examination. By shaking the canisters with their divination sticks until one falls out, devotees determine the most auspicious days for business dealings and travels. In a small room behind the altar ancestor tablets are ranged in racks in memory of the dead. From the temple's balcony there is a good view down Stockton to the Bay. Visible to the north up Stockton are the masts of the *Balclutha* of 1886, the *C.A. Thayer*, built in 1895, and wooded Angel Island. The post office on the ground floor houses some fine old gilded Chinese signs from the old post office that faced Portsmouth Square.

The Chinese Six Companies [13]

843 Stockton Street
1908–1909 Cuthbertson and Mahoney
Main Hall open 2–5 P.M. on weekdays

Up Stockton toward the tunnel is this exuberant building housing the most famous association in Chinatown, the association of district associations formally known as the Chinese Consolidated Benevolent Association but popularly known as the Chinese Six Companies. This elaborate building was constructed in part with forty thousand taels of silver ($20,000) in relief funds sent to Chinatown by the imperial court after the earthquake of 1906. The money was not used for that purpose but rather for the construction of this Chinese school building with its ground-floor meeting hall. The building is alive with color: yellow, bright green, Chinese red, and sky blue. Two pairs of stone guardian lions flank the entrance with its freestanding, green tile-roofed gateway ornamented with dragons, birds, and fish. The main doors are painted Chinese red, the luckiest color. Climb the stairs and enter the raised porch. The building's façade is an interesting juxtaposition of straightforward, utilitarian elements such as pillars and fire escapes, overlaid with bright colors and rich ornament. The sky-blue glazed tile is especially attractive.

The building's main hall is laid out like a courtroom with a rail and swinging gates separating the public vestibule from the room itself. A stained-glass and gilded wood screen with a central niche covers the back wall. The old tile floor has a ruglike design. Three long central tables are set in the middle of the room and fine rosewood Chinese armchairs are ranged around its four sides. Art Deco lamps are suspended from the unfortunately modernized ceiling. Small American and Nationalist Chinese flags on streamers crisscross the room. It is a space with a severely formal presence and is worth a peek. In its early years the Six Companies wielded much power both within Chinatown and among the Chinese-Americans across the United States. Disputes between associations were arbitrated here. The association also served to witness contracts and property sales. In the late nineteenth century, the Chinese elite managed to establish a kind of cultural extraterritoriality by winning unofficial recognition from the white civic elite.

Chinese Central High School [13]

827–29 Stockton Street
1914; 1970, Stephen Lee, entrance
pavilion and roof

A few doors up Stockton is "Victory Hall," the home of the Chinese Central High School. The two-story school was built as the Chinese Christian Institute in 1914. In 1970, a one-story entrance pavilion with a green-tile pagoda roof designed by Stephen Lee was added. The ancestor of this school was the Ta Ching Shu Yuan organized in 1884; its trustees were the Chinese Six Companies. Chinese-American parents interested in preserving Chinese language and culture have long supported after-hours schools for their children.

Kuo Ming Tang Headquarters [13]

830–48 Stockton Street
1915, D. J. Patterson

Facing the elaborate Six Companies across Stockton is the nondescript Kuo Ming Tang Headquarters, a three-story building built in 1915 and remodeled in 1932. The round blue shields with the white sun are the party's emblem. This political party has its roots in Dr. Sun Yat-Sen's republican movement of the early twentieth century, which triumphed in 1911. Later it became the party of Generalissimo Chiang Kai Shek whose Nationalist regime retreated to Taiwan in 1949. The KMT publishes the *Young China Daily* from 49-51 Hang Ah Alley behind this building.

Stockton Street Tunnel [14]
1914, Michael M. O'Shaughnessy

Visible south up Stockton is the "triumphal arch" entrance to the Stockton Street Tunnel designed by City Engineer Michael M. O'Shaughnessy in 1914. It was one of the urban improvements spurred by the Panama-Pacific International Exposition of 1915. It shows how handsome the City Beautiful municipal improvements under long-time Mayor James Rolph were.

First Presbyterian Church [15]
925 Stockton Street
1907, H. Starbuck
Sunday morning services in Mandarin at 9 A.M., English at 10:45 A.M., and Cantonese at noon

Protestant churches conducted several missions in Chinatown to Christianize and Americanize its inhabitants. The Presbyterian Board of Foreign Missions founded a church in San Francisco in 1853 and built a church on this site in 1857. This Classical Revival church with Ionic pilasters, portico, and pediment was designed by H. Starbuck and erected the year after the earthquake. It is a rare design in Chinatown today and of great importance to the history of the post-fire quarter.

Chinese Methodist Episcopal Church [16]
1001-11 Stockton Street at Washington
1910, Henry H. Meyers

On the northwest corner of Stockton and Washington is the cross-and-pagoda-capped Chinese Methodist Episcopal Church designed by noted architect Henry H. Meyers in 1910. Missionary work among the Chinese in San Francisco was an extension of the strenuous efforts American Protestant churches made in nineteenth-century China. This congregation was organized in 1868 by Reverend Otis Gibson following his return from ten years of missionary work there; Gibson was a vigorous defender of the Chinese in their darkest days of persecution. This post-earthquake building originally housed a chapel, a school, and an orphanage for young Chinese girls rescued from prostitution.

Chinese American Citizens Alliance [16]
1044 Stockton Street
1920, Charles E. J. Rodgers

On the opposite side of Stockton, midblock, is the four-story Chinese American Citizens Alliance building built in 1920 and designed by Charles E. J. Rodgers. It is a thoroughly American design typical of the rebuilt city. This building houses the first civil rights organization founded by Chinese-Americans, organized as the Native Sons of the Golden State in 1895. It assumed its present name in 1915. The organization battled successfully in the courts to protect the rights of native-born Americans of Chinese ancestry. In 1898, in the landmark case of the *United States v. Wong*, the Supreme Court affirmed citizenship by right of birth in the United States regardless of race. The organization of the CACA marked the emergence of Chinese-Americans into the larger society outside the Chinatown ghetto. Inside this building is a framed copy of the 1946 law that repealed the Chinese Exclusion Act of 1882, and the pen used to sign it. The CACA was active in the effort to secure Chinatown's first playground in 1925.

WAVERLY PLACE ASSOCIATIONS AND TEMPLES CLUSTER [17]

Two-block-long Waverly Place is perhaps Chinatown's most interesting pocket and is worth careful examination. It houses two of Chinatown's most interesting temples. Before this area became part of Chinatown it was called Pike Street, named by Dr. Augustus J. Bowie in honor of his wife's Maryland family. In the late nineteenth century it was lined with brothels, but these were replaced by a string of Chinese association buildings after the catastrophe of 1906. To see the buildings here to their best advantage, walk down the east side of narrow Waverly Place.

Hip Sen Tong / Universal Cafe
824–26 Washington Street
1910, O'Brien Brothers; 1960, Stephen Lee

A 1910 Edwardian building with a 1960 remodel by Stephen Lee with a pagoda cornice.

Chan, Woo, Yuen Family Association
834–40 Washington Street
1909, Walter K. Yurston; 1920, A. A. Cantin

This elaborate façade looks down Waverly and defines one end of the street. It was built in 1909 for Goong Quon Cheong, described as a "Chinese capitalist." In 1920 the building passed to the Oak Tin Benevolent Association which raised the ceiling on the top floor and commissioned A. A. Cantin to design an exuberant metal canopy, balconies, penthouse, and cornice with the date "1920" inscribed on it. The façade uses tile, marble, and glazed brick and is an outstanding example of San Francisco chinoiserie.

Golden Dragon Restaurant
823–33 Washington Street, corner of Waverly
1906, architect unknown

On the corner is a plain post-fire brick building which has had its cornice removed and its ground floor covered in green ceramic tile. To complete its "improvement," gold-colored anodized aluminum windows have been inserted.

Commercial / Residential Building
151–55 Waverly Place
1906, architect unknown

This building was also built immediately after the earthquake and shows how plain Edwardian Chinatown was.

Its brick façade has been stuccoed, scored, and painted to look like stone. The ground floor has two shopfronts, one still original and one modernized.

Wong Gow Building
143–47 Waverly Place
1906, Emil Guenther

Above its modern backlit plastic sign is a handsome pale yellow brick Edwardian façade with a fine dark green fire escape and dark green window sash. The gold leaf characters on the second-story windows are striking. The pale yellow, dark green, and gold color scheme present classic old Chinatown at its best.

Yick Keung Benevolent Association / Hop Sing Tong
137–41 Waverly Place
1909, W. J. Cuthbertson

Above the modern black granite facing of the ground floor with its bronze lettering and sun design is a brick façade painted a bright shade of sherbet green. The railings of the three balconies/fire escape have a vaguely Chinese design. The octagonal mirrors affixed to the railings are intended to confuse any evil spirits wanting to invade the premises. The building is capped with a pagoda cornice and a flagpole. Under the cornice is a green marble tablet with gold Chinese characters. Among the building's occupants is the Sinocast radio and television studio.

Yee Fung Toy Family Association
131 Waverly Place
1908, Hamilton Murdock

This four-story association building was built with cast iron columns and girders and sports a light yellow brick façade. Its original windows are effectively painted with dark green frames and red sash and doors. The top floor meeting room has an open loggia with a pagoda cornice and flagpole. Its interior was described in the April 1908 *Architect and Engineer*:

Solid walnut doors, with iron thresholds, lead into the large assembly room [on the top floor], which has an oak floor, decorative skylight screen, and is resplendent with imported carvings, screens, hangings, draperies, altar stand, furniture, vases, etc. Off this room is a committee room of equal splendor.

Sometime in the 1940s, probably, the entrance was decorated with fine green and maroon ceramic tile and a pagoda hood.

Tin How Temple / Sue Hing Benevolent Association
123–29 Waverly Place
1911, O'Brien Brothers
Temple hours 10 A.M.–5 P.M. and 7–9 P.M. daily; donation requested

The top floor of this building contains what is probably Chinatown's most evocative room: the Tin How Temple.

The building is a classic example of the multiuse "layer-cake" of Chinatown: There is a shop on the ground floor, association offices on the second and third floors, and the temple on the top floor. The building was designed by the prolific O'Brien Brothers in 1911, though its ground floor has been remodeled with unattractive 1960s dark tiles imprisoning two old Corinthian pilaster capitals. The light yellow brick façade has two open loggias, one on the third and the other on the top floor. Sandwiched between these is the plain-jane second floor. The loggias have composite columns and marble door surrounds with black characters emblazoned on them. The loggias and balconies are painted a brilliant yellow with red trim. Attached to the balconies are modern plastic signs reading "Tin How Temple." The top two floors are also outlined with lightbulbs. Everything that could happen to a Chinatown building can be found on this one.

Visitors may climb the narrow stairs to see the Tin How Temple, founded in 1852 and dedicated to Tien Hon, the Goddess of Heaven. Sailors, travelers, fishermen, wandering minstrels, actors, and prostitutes look to her for protection. She is the protectress of the sojourner and has long been an appropriate presence in this immigrants' colony. The temple houses antique fragments from other Chinese temples destroyed when the Chinese were driven out of remote towns in Northern California in the 1880s. Pious families donate the tins of vegetable oil used to keep the temple lights burning. Oranges are a favored offering because they are a pun on the Chinese word for "wealth," similarly, the word for tangerines sounds like "luck" in Chinese. Nineteenth-century San Franciscans called these temples "joss houses" after the pidgin English term for God derived from the Portuguese *Dios*.

Ching Chong Dong Building
117–19 Waverly Place
1907, J. E. Freeman

The euphonious Ching Chong Dong Building is a handsome Edwardian red brick structure with yellow brick bands across its façade and over its windows. The cheap plastic lettering clashes with the historic façade; gilded wooden letters would be appropriate here. For many years the *Chinese Times* was housed here and posted the day's paper in the ground floor windows for all to read.

Norras Temple / Lee Family Association
109–11 Waverly Place
1907, J. E. Freeman
Temple hours from 9 A.M.–4 P.M. daily; donation requested

Above the altered ground floor is a very fine façade of yellow brick with white terra cotta trim enframing the windows and running in bands across the width of the building. (The third-floor Norras Temple has inexplicably painted its terra cotta seafoam green.) The building boasts its original windows, and fine metal brackets and railings on its balconies. It has a coffered cornice with a Baroque parapet and a white flagpole. On the third floor is the

Norras Buddhist temple with an altar with gold-colored Buddhas surrounded by incense, flowers, and offerings. Trance-inducing tapes are played here of gongs, bells, and drums.

Gee Family Association
101–05 Waverly Place
1907, Jules Lambla; 1948, Uguste Ortion

On the corner of Waverly and Clay is this three-story stuccoed building painted a light lime green. It is most notable for its neon-trimmed entrance canopy and pagoda cornice.

Eng Family Benevolent Association
53–65 Waverly Place, corner of Clay
1907, architects unknown; 1948, remodel

On the southwest corner of Waverly and Clay is the bay-windowed Eng Family Benevolent Association, a 1907 building remodeled in 1948. It is handsomely painted in pink, ivory, green, red, and yellow (which looks better than it reads). There are very few bay-windowed buildings in Chinatown; this one has corner bays with neon-trimmed pagoda tops, an architectural amalgam uniquely San Franciscan. The loggia, pagoda cornice, and "Mission" parapet were decorated in 1948 and faced in pink and maroon tile. Should that not be festive enough, everything is trimmed in neon. This is the best late 1940s chinoiserie in San Francisco.

Ning Yung Benevolent Association
41–45 Waverly Place
1907, T. H. Skinner

This building originally housed the Chinese Merchants Association. It has a red brick façade trimmed with white brick and cast iron ground floor pilasters. It is most notable for its fine sheet metal balustrade-parapet with a large cartouche bearing the legend "07." The ground floor and second floor aluminum sash windows are weak and disrupt the original design.

Wong Family Benevolent Association
37–39 Waverly Place
1911, F. H. Howard, builder

Above the remodeled ground floor with its odd juxtaposition of carnelian granite and pale aqua-green tile is a fine façade of white glazed brick with three balconies and an emphatic parapet. The parapet boasts three large white stars and a flagpole. Again, the modern dark aluminum windows detract from the design.

Bing Kong Tong / Chinese Masonic Temple
29–35 Waverly Place
1911, O'Brien Brothers

Here, too, the new ground floor of cheap stucco and weak aluminum windows clashes with the fine original architecture above. This is the Chinese Masonic Temple, as is evident by the neon compass insignia suspended in the loggia. The façade's yellow brickwork is set in raised bands. The lunettes on the third floor are inset with streaked art glass. The top floor loggia has what might be called Chinese-Doric columns and a fine pagoda cornice in green, yellow, and red. But, oh, the shopfront!

First Chinese Baptist Church
1–15 Waverly Place, at Sacramento
1908, G. H. Moore; 1931, George E. Burlingame

This emphatic red clinker brick church, with offices above, serves a Baptist congregation organized in 1880 in rented rooms on Portsmouth Square. The church moved to this site in 1888; the American Baptist Home Mission Society of New York built this building two years after the earthquake. In 1931 a compatible third floor was added and in 1980 the chapel was remodeled and a contemporary stained-glass window facing Sacramento Street was commissioned.

After examining each of Waverly Place's buildings individually, look back to see this landmark row as a whole. The east side is lined with plain post-earthquake buildings, only one of which has any chinoiserie. Some of these buildings still have their old wood and glass shopfronts painted the traditional green.

Chinatown YMCA
855 Sacramento Street
1925, Meyer & Johnson

The Waverly Street landmark row is concluded by the gate of the Chinatown YMCA of 1925 designed by Meyer & Johnson. This concrete building has been described as Chinese Classical in style and has fine ornamental touches including Chinese style terra cotta decorations around its entrance. The walls of the playground have been covered with **murals by Victor Q. Fan** depicting Chinese pioneers, Pacific Island peoples, and Asian-Americans as modern scientists and professionals shown against the San Francisco skyline.

GRANT AVENUE FROM CLAY TO CALIFORNIA / SITE OF WILLIAM RICHARDSON'S TRADING POST OF 1835 [18]

This middle section of Grant Avenue is the heart of tourist Chinatown, an industry that employs neighborhood residents in its kitchens and stockrooms and Chinese-American small businessmen from other parts of the city. Its restaurants are not particularly outstanding and its shops run to trinkets and souvenirs made in Taiwan. Wicker fingerlocks, T-shirts, and switchblade pocket combs are among the innumerable "novelties" sold here. **The Wok Shop** at 804 Grant sells Chinese cooking equipment and cookbooks and will ship your purchases. This part of Grant is lively until late at night.

At **747–49 Grant** in the Ying On Merchant and Labor Association is an elaborate building built for A. B. Ware in 1906 and made "Chinese" in 1920. On the northeast corner of Clay at **801–07**

Grant Avenue is the Soo Yuen Benevolent Association, built as a roominghouse for Charles Hirsch in 1906 by Salfield and Kohlberg. Its elaborate chinoiserie was added between 1919 and 1922 by Albert Schroepfer and Edward G. Bolles. The old-fashioned metal canopy over the sidewalk preserves an old western pattern lost nearly everywhere else in the city. On its Clay Street side is a red-board-covered sidewalk stall, an example of the intensive use of every inch of space in crowded Chinatown.

The Dick-Young Apartments at **823 Grant Avenue** were built for the Adams Investment Co. in 1907 and designed by W. D. Woodruff. This building is ordinary by Chinatown standards; however, its site is considered the approximate location of William Richardson's adobe trading post erected in 1835, the first building on Yerba Buena Cove and the birthplace of the settlement that became the city of San Francisco. A rarely spotted plaque records this curious fact.

COMMERCIAL STREET [19]

Commercial and nearby Merchant streets, as their names if not their buildings record, were among Gold Rush San Francisco's prestige business addresses. The block of Commercial below Grant is still paved in red brick, one of the last such streets in the city. The distant flat part of Commercial was originally Long Wharf, a two-thousand-foot-long wharf built out into Yerba Buena Cove. Commercial and Merchant streets were privately developed and were originally lined with brick commercial buildings. By the 1870s many of the buildings were occupied by Chinese shoe, slipper, and cigar factories, and laundries: Chinatown's own "industrial district." Until 1908 the Chinese Six Companies was on this street.

After 1906 the street was rebuilt and partially occupied by brothels. The two-story French Baroque Dubois Building at **746–48 Commercial Street**, designed by Righetti & Kuhl, may have been built as a "fancy house." Number **681–83 Commercial Street**, the Anna Giselman Building, designed by William Curlett and Son in 1908, is intact and shows just how handsome San Francisco's ordinary post-fire buildings are. At 650 Commercial, downstairs, is the Chinese Historical Society of America Museum (see page 92).

At 608 Commercial Street is the **Pacific Heritage Museum** on the site of the West's first mint. The museum mounts changing exhibitions on the broad theme of the history of the economic, cultural, and artistic interchanges across the Pacific. Inside you can see the old vaults and a display on the history of the building as well as first-rate changing exhibits often featuring very fine Asian art and fascinating historic artifacts. It is one of the finest specialized museums in California. (For more information, see entry for Bank of Canton of California/Pacific Heritage Museum in Tour 2A.)

700 AND 800 BLOCKS OF SACRAMENTO STREET [20]

The 700 block of Sacramento, between Grant and Kearny, was the first block where Chinese immigrants were able to rent rooms and establish a toe-hold in San Francisco. In the nineteenth century it was known as "Tong Yen Gai," or Street of the Chinese. Today it still boasts both the Chinese Chamber of Commerce and the Nam Kue Chinese School. First Sacramento, then Dupont (now Grant), then Jackson between Kearny and Stockton became Chinese. Unlike all of San Francisco's other ethnic enclaves, Chinatown has never moved, only grown.

One of the most interesting buildings here, however, is not Chinese. On the southeast corner of Grant and Sacramento, at **654–70 Grant Avenue**, is the three-story Edwardian hotel with interesting window surrounds designed by Stone, Smith in 1907 for A. P. Giannini and S. Scatena. Giannini was the founder of the Bank of Italy, later the Bank of America. It is one of the handsomest buildings of its type in the city. Catercorner to it is the **Lowry Estate Building** of 1906 with a Bank of America branch in its modernized ground floor. On its second floor, entered from Sacramento Street, is the **Gold Mountain Sagely Monastery** recently established by the Dharma Realm Buddhist Association. While not historic or especially attractive, the monastery conducts Buddhist ceremonies; Monday to Friday at 6:30 P.M. and Saturdays and Sundays at 12:30 P.M.

At **728–30 Sacramento Street**, is the Chinese Chamber of Commerce designed in 1912 by R. J. Patcha and elaborated in 1925 by J. E. Freeman. While not particularly impressive, it does have a loggia and pagoda cornice and is of historic significance since the formation of this organization in 1908 signified the healing of the deep rifts inside Chinatown between the Sam Yup and the Sze Yup. Across the street, at **755–65 Sacramento**, is the Nam Kue School with its front courtyard, an extravagant gesture in dense Chinatown. This after-hours Chinese language school was founded by merchants from the Fook Yum Tong, some of Chinatown's wealthiest men. The building was designed by Charles E. J. Rodgers in 1925 and opened with a staff of four teachers from Pekin University. It is a unique design in Chinatown.

From the 600 block of Grant, on the east side, there is a fine view of the landmark pagoda-capped buildings at Grant and California. At **631 Grant Avenue** is the Far East Restaurant, established in 1920, and the Chinatown restaurant with the most evocative "old Chinatown" interior, if a bland tourist cuisine. The exterior gives no hint of the high-ceilinged interior with its dark wood wainscotting and curtained private booths in the back. Most remarkable are the old electric chandeliers of phantasmagoric ornateness. The murals on the walls are banal except for the one that depicts the Chinese Pavilion at the Panama-Pacific International Exposition of 1915. This was one of the first authentically Chinese buildings in San Francisco.

California and Grant, where the cable car bisects Chinatown on its way from the Financial District to Nob Hill, is one of the spots every visitor will remember and every San Franciscan treasures. Here hills, cable cars, and architecture seem to say "San Francisco" to everyone. East meets West in the architectural counterpoint between the red brick Gothic Revival tower of old St. Mary's Roman Catholic Church and the twin Chinese pagoda-capped buildings on Grant.

Old St. Mary's Roman Catholic Church and Rectory [21]
600 California Street, at Grant, 1854; 1907–1909, Craine and England; 1969, Welsh & Carey; 1964, Skidmore, Owings & Merrill rectory

St. Mary's itself tells part of San Francisco's unique history, for its brick is said to have "come around the Horn" and its granite base is said to be from China. Old St. Mary's was the first Roman Catholic cathedral on the Pacific Coast and was dedicated by 1854 by Archbishop Joseph Sadoc Alemany. It was built on land donated by pioneer banker John Sullivan, whose wife lies buried in its crypt. The Irish-dominated Catholic church, unlike the Protestant churches, did little missionary work among the Chinese in Chinatown. This did not change until 1903. In 1894 a new St. Mary's was built on fashionable Van Ness Avenue and this became a Paulist church. The church was gutted in the 1906 fire and rebuilt, expanded in 1929, burned again in 1969, and rebuilt a second time. (Its interior is not noteworthy.) Under its clock is the stern inscription: "Son Observe the Time and Fly from Evil." This message was placed here to face the brothels that once stood across the street in what is today St. Mary's Square. The church's most American

touch is something no one "sees": the black steel tower atop the brick tower with its large gold cross outlined with light bulbs. The handsome rectory on the California Street side with its courtyard was designed by Skidmore, Owings and Merrill in 1964.

St. Mary's Square [21]
1955, John Jay Gould; 1960, landscape by Eckbo, Roysten and Williams

Statue of Sun Yat-Sen [21]
St. Mary's Square
1938, Beniamino Bufano

Across California Street from Old St. Mary's is this tucked-away city park with its fine statue of Sun Yat-Sen. Today the park is the landscaped roof of a city parking garage designed by John Jay Gould and built in 1955. Its landscaped roof was designed by Eckbo, Royston and Williams in 1960 and is a good example of streamlined landscape design from that period. There is a fine view of the Bank of America tower from here. Standing in the square is a statue of Sun Yat-Sen (1866–1925) by Beniamino Bufano commissioned by the New Deal's Works Progress Administration and placed here in 1938. The streamlined statue is made of stainless steel and pink granite and is a fine example of the public art of the period. Facing it across the square is a fine Chinese-style open work bronze screen commemorating "Americans of Chinese ancestry who gave their lives for America in World Wars I and II."

Agitation for a park to replace the brothels clustered here was begun by Fr. M. Otis in 1895; the park was purchased by the city in 1906 after the earthquake. Unfortunately, the construction of a dark gray slab of a building by the Pacific Telephone Company in 1967 south of the park robs it of sunlight. The wall-like building is a monument to the atrocious city planning of the 1960s. Such a light-blocking structure would not gain city approval today.

Sing Chong Building ("Trade Mark") [22]

601-25 Grant Avenue, northwest corner of California
1907–08, T. Patterson Ross and A. W. Burgren

Sing Fat Building

555-97 Grant Avenue, southwest corner of California
1907–08, T. Patterson Ross and A. W. Burgren

In 1905 John Partridge organized the U.S. Improvement and Investment Company whose stated purpose was to buy up Chinatown and relocate its residents to distant Hunters Point. He claimed that by widening Grant Avenue and expelling the Chinese, the value of the real estate here could be increased from $6 million to $25 to $30 million. Nothing came of this early private "urban renewal" scheme. Instead, when Chinatown burned in 1906, the ideas of Chinese-American merchant Look Tin Eli prevailed. It was his dream to rebuild Chinatown as an "Oriental City" with Chinese-style architecture. The San Francisco Real Estate Board endorsed the notion and recommended that the overwhelmingly white property owners of Chinatown "have their buildings rebuilt with fronts of Oriental and artistic appearance." The twin buildings at the highly visible intersection of California and Grant were among the first to display the new style. The *Architect and Engineer* wrote in 1908 that,

To [architect T. Patterson] Ross and [engineer A. W.] Burgren more than any other architectural firm in San Francisco must be credited the responsibility for the radical changes that have been followed in the style and construction of buildings in the Oriental district. Where previously the rigid lines of cheap occidental building construction had provided perpendicular walls, now the fantasy of the Far East has been borrowed and in the Chinatown of today the pagoda style quite generally predominates.

GRANT AVENUE TO THE BUSH STREET CHINATOWN GATE [23]

The block of Grant between California and Pine is lined on both sides with fine Edwardian buildings with surprisingly little chinoiserie. On the northeast corner of Grant and Pine at **500 Grant** is one of the few bay-windowed buildings in Chinatown. It was built in 1910. Adjoining it is **506–10 Grant**, the Tai Chong Company Building, designed by Righetti and Kuhl in 1907. The narrow building has fine brickwork on its upper stories and an old shopfront and intact shop interior on the ground floor. While slightly altered, the shopfront retains the handsome design of post-fire Chinatown tourist shops.

The view down Pine Street is terminated by the handsome pair of the old Matson Building and the Pacific Gas & Electric headquarters. The **Matson Building** on the left, capped by an open tower, was designed by Bliss and Faville in 1921. It was the former headquarters of the Matson Shipping Lines and once housed the mainland offices of Hawaii's Big Five corporations. The old **Pacific Gas & Electric** headquarters on the right was designed by Bakewell and Brown in 1925. It is distinguished by a giant order capped with urns on its upper floors. (PG&E built a modern tower behind it on Mission Street in 1971.) Both buildings are clad in terra cotta and are handsome examples of dignified 1920s corporate architecture.

On the southeast corner of Grant and Pine is **450–64 Grant Avenue**, the old Peking Bazaar with its fine corner pagoda tower. This building was designed by Sidney B. and Noble Newson, successors to an important Victorian architectural firm in California. Built in 1921, its upper floors retain their fine design, while the ground floor was indifferently remodeled recently and the old shop interior, alas, lost.

The downhill block between Pine and Bush has several of Chinatown's better shops and is terminated by the elaborate Bush Street Gate. At **445 Grant Avenue**, midblock, is the KHC Plaza, though, fortunately, there is no "plaza" here. It is the unfortunate fusion of the façade of the old Shanghai Low Nightclub of 1922, designed by the O'Brien Brothers, with a brutally ugly 1985 six-story addition behind. There is no excuse for the block-like balconies and the general bleakness of this intrusive building.

Chinatown Gate
Grant Avenue and Bush Street
1970, Clayton Lee

At Grant and Bush stands the Chinatown Gate designed by Clayton Lee in 1970. The green-tile-capped gate with its triple portals makes a monumental announcement to Chinatown's elaborate Grant Avenue to the north.

The building painted light green on the northeast corner of Grant and Bush at **400 Grant** was built as the Friedman Hotel and Mandarin Cafe in 1913 in a French Baroque style. In 1924 Ashley & Evers designed its Chinese-style top with a small pagoda tower.

500 BLOCK OF BUSH STREET: MEMORIES OF THE FRENCH PIONEERS [24]

In the 1850s this general area was favored by French immigrants to California and was nicknamed Frenchmen's Hill. The Goethe Institute at **530 Bush** with its German library and English- and German-language cultural programs occupies part of a fine 1916 utility substation built by W. Garden Mitchell in 1916 and converted in 1982 by Storek & Storek. Next door is the Chancery of the French Consulate at **540 Bush**, in a modern solar-conscious building designed by Storek & Storek in 1979.

The only souvenir of the early French settlement is the twin-towered church of **Notre Dame des Victoires** at **566 Bush Street** built in 1913 and designed by Louis Brochoud after a church in Lyon. It was San Francisco's French national Roman Catholic church and was established in 1856. It has a fine 1915 organ and conducts sung masses in French on Sundays at 10:30 A.M. The treasure in the church is a sixteenth-century Flemish tapestry of Christ at the Mount of Olives.

If you descend the stairs at Bush and Stockton to the Stockton Tunnel, you will connect with the 30 Stockton electric trolley bus, which goes south to Union Square, Market Street, and continues south across Market Street to Moscone Convention Center.

Going north the 30 Stockton line passes across Broadway into North Beach and goes to Fisherman's Wharf, Aquatic Park, and Fort Mason/GGNRA before continuing west through the Marina District's civilized Chestnut Street. The line ends at Broderick and North Point streets, one block from a 1962 concrete replica of Bernard Maybeck's romantic "temporary" Palace of Fine Arts of 1915.

LOCKE, CALIFORNIA

If you want to go farther afield, consider visiting Locke, California. A small Delta town on the Sacramento River northeast of San Francisco, Locke was built about 1915 for the Chinese laborers who raised the levees, built the railroads, and planted crops. Locke consists of a narrow main street lined with plain, two-story balconied buildings like an old western mining town. It is of historical and architectural interest as the last rural Chinatown in California and is listed on the National Register of Historic Places. Take scenic Highway 160 along the river to Walnut Grove, cross the bridge to Highway E 13 north.

To The Wharf

NORTH BEACH, TELEGRAPH HILL,
AND FISHERMAN'S WHARF

What These Tours Cover

Tour 4A: North Beach and Telegraph Hill

Columbus Avenue from the Transamerica Pyramid to Broadway

Columbus Tower

The Broadway Entertainment Strip

City Lights Bookstore

LITTLE ITALY CLASSICS WEST OF COLUMBUS AVENUE

Molinari's Delicatessen

Victoria Pastry Co.

Panelli Bros. Delicatessen

North Beach Museum / Eureka Federal Savings

A. Cavalli & Co.

The Bank of America

Fugazi Hall / Casa Coloniale Italiana

LITTLE ITALY CLASSICS EAST OF COLUMBUS AVENUE

St. Francis of Assisi Roman Catholic Church

Columbus Cutlery

Postermat

Biordi Art Imports

Figoni Hardware

Panama Canal Ravioli Factory

Italian French Baking Co. of San Francisco

[1] Washington Square: The Ideal Park

[2] Sts. Peter and Paul Roman Catholic Church

TELEGRAPH HILL

[3] Old Telegraph Hill Dwellers Association Clinic /North Beach Alleys

[4] Upper Grant Avenue Shops and Café Strip

[5] To Coit Tower / Coit Tower / Panorama and WPA Murals

[6] Greenwich Steps / Julius Castle Restaurant

[7] Malloch Apartment Building

[8] Filbert Steps / Napier Lane

[9] Levi Strauss & Co. Headquarters / Levi's Plaza

Tour 4B: Fisherman's Wharf

[1] Taylor Street Wharf and Restaurant Row

[2] U.S.S. *Pampanito* / Pier 45

[3] Jefferson Street Amusement Zone

[4] Pier 39

[5] The Historic Fishing Fleet

[6] Hyde Street Pier / Historic Ships

[7] The Cannery

[8] Haslett Warehouse

[9] Victorian Park / Hyde Street Cable Car Turntable

[10] National Maritime Museum / Aquatic Park Casino / Municipal Pier / Aquatic Park

[11] Ghirardelli Square

[12] Fort Mason Center ("Fort Culture") / Golden Gate National Recreation Area (GGNRA) Headquarters

[13] Golden Gate Promenade to Fort Point

Preliminaries

Best Times To Do This Tour

Very early in the morning, from 4 A.M. to 9 A.M., the Wharf is a fish distribution center with fish arriving by ship and truck to be sold and shipped. Almost no one else comes to watch the action.

Each October at the time of the celebration of the Madonna del Lume and the blessing of the fishing fleet, the Wharf holds a weekend Festa Italiana with food, music, entertainment and fireworks. Phone 673-3782 for dates and information.

Parking

In North Beach there is a city parking garage tucked away over the police station on Powell at Vallejo. Telegraph Hill has very little parking. Not surprisingly, parking is not always easy in Fisherman's Wharf. The best unmetered parking is at the foot of Van Ness Avenue at the far west edge of the Wharf, near Ghirardelli Square. Other unmetered zones with no time restrictions are on the blocks east of Powell and north of Bay streets. You can find fee parking lots on Jefferson between Taylor and Powell. The Pier 39 Garage on Beach between Powell and Stockton has the highest rates and highest occupancy (because signs point cars that way). The Anchorage Garage at Jones between Jefferson and Beach has 700 spaces. There are also 300 spaces under Ghirardelli Square; enter from Beach or Larkin streets.

Transportation

Most visitors take the cable cars to the Wharf (see section on cable cars for suggestions). *The Powell-Hyde line is much*

Copyright 1989 William Walters

The oldest, most graceful, wooden boats in San Francisco's fishing fleet are given the most visible berths, those facing the 200 block of Jefferson Street, between Taylor and Jones.

more scenic than the Powell-Mason. Scrutinize the cars' signs, for otherwise they are identical. Alternative transit routes include the 30 Stockton electric trolley from Union Square and the 19 Polk bus. The 39 Coit bus links Washington Square in North Beach with Coit Tower on Telegraph Hill and then the Wharf. *Within* the Wharf the 19 Polk runs west on Jefferson to Ghirardelli Square, and east on Beach. There is "owl service" from midnight to 6 A.M. on the 15 Third bus on North Point, between Taylor and Powell, to Market Street downtown.

Restaurants, Cafés, and Bars

North Beach and Berkeley have more good cafes than any other American settlements. North Beach's *caffès*—Italian, not French—are frequented by natives, newcomers, and visitors. Each has its own particular personality and clientele. You are sure to find one just right for you. Every San Francisco neighborhood now has its own cafe(s), but North Beach's were first and are still probably the most fun. People read, page through the want ads, write, and chat. At the Caffè Trieste and others, tables are shared when the place fills up. It's a natural way to meet the locals.

Caffè Roma, 414 Columbus near Vallejo. Open Sunday–Thursday, 7 A.M. to midnight, Friday–Saturday until 1 A.M. In the 1920s this was an Italian bakery. The then owner had J. G. Giribone paint scenes of *putti* engaged in confectionary making on the walls and ceiling. Mercury with his bag of gold shares the ceiling with a blond goddess and *putti* scattering sweets from the painted skies. When Sergio Azzollini opened the Caffè Roma, he restored the delightful artwork. Window seats here are great people-watching spots. The caffè serves breakfast, and pizza, pasta, and salads and is perhaps the best for visitors who want to taste North Beach today; an airy, welcoming place.

Caffè Trieste, 708 Vallejo at Grant; 392-6739. Open Sunday–Thursday, 7 A.M.–10:30 P.M., Friday–Saturday until 12:30 A.M. Opened in 1956, the Trieste is a San Francisco institution. Every Saturday from noon to 2 P.M. there is Italian singing and spontaneous entertainment. The jukebox features operatic favorites. Next door, the Trieste roasts and sells its own coffees.

The Savoy-Tivoli, 1434 Grant between Green and Union. Open daily, 2:30 P.M.–2 A.M. This an open-fronted café has a restaurant inside; good *capuccino*; lively and noisy on weekends.

Mario's Bohemian Cigar Store, 566 Columbus at Union, facing Washington Square. Open Tuesday–Saturday, 10 A.M.–1 A.M., Monday until midnight. Excellent *capuccino* and a non-yuppie ambience. Meatball sandwiches and *fritatta*; a local crowd.

FISHERMAN'S WHARF RESTAURANTS

Scoma's Fisherman's Wharf, Pier 47 at the foot of Jones on Jefferson; 771-4383.

Castagnola's Restaurant, 286 Jefferson; 776-5015.

Alioto's Restaurant, #8 Fisherman's Wharf (on Taylor); 673-0183. Established in 1925.

A. Sabella's Restaurant, 2766 Taylor at Jefferson; 771-6775.

Fisherman's Grotto, #9 Fisherman's Wharf (on Taylor); 673-7025.

Tarantino's Restaurant, 206 Jefferson; 775-5600.

Franciscan Restaurant, Pier 43 1/2 on The Embarcadero; 362-7733.

Sabella & La Torre, 2809 Taylor near Jefferson; 673-2824.

Pompei's Grotto, 340 Jefferson; 776-9265.

Tokyo Sukiyaki, 225 Jefferson at Taylor; 775-9030. Sashimi, sushi, and seafood.

108

Introduction: North Beach, Telegraph Hill, and Fisherman's Wharf

Tucked in the sunny, wind-sheltered valley between Telegraph and Russian hills, North Beach is one of San Francisco's oldest neighborhoods. It has seen many changes. Originally and briefly a fashionable part of town, it lost its appeal for the middle class as newer districts were made accessible by the cable cars. Shortly after fashion abandoned the area, it became the city's Latin Quarter with a mixed population of working-class Chilean, Peruvian, French, Spanish, Mexican, Basque, and Portuguese immigrants. Jammed between the docks and the downtown, the area became increasingly industrial when bayfill expanded the district north of Bay Street, obliterating sandy North Beach. (Today North Beach has no beach.) Railyards and factories including the Del Monte cannery and the Ghirardelli chocolate factory located here and employed many Italian-American immigrants.

The first Italian colony located in the poor, congested blocks south of Broadway along Pacific, Jackson, Washington, and Clay streets, in what is today's Jackson Square Historic District. The cutting through of Columbus Avenue in 1873 displaced part of this population and propelled it north of Broadway to Upper Grant Avenue and the western slope of Telegraph Hill. The Yankees, Germans, and Irish who had previously occupied these blocks drifted away, the non-Italian migrations diminished, and the Italian presence grew stronger, turning the Latin Quarter into Little Italy. St. Francis of Assisi church at Vallejo off Columbus became the religious center of this colony. While there were but 5,000 Italian-Americans in San Francisco in 1890, by 1939 some 60,000 packed into North Beach. In 1931 there were five Italian-language newspapers in North Beach. Unlike the East Coast's Italian migration,

San Francisco's Italian immigrants were predominantly northerners from Genoa, Liguria, Turin, Lombardy, Milan, and Piedmont.

California was promoted as the "American Italy" and many city residents began to move out of the congested city to farm the land. Italian-Americans established truck gardens, vineyards, and orchards all over California. Santa Rosa in Sonoma County, for example, and the nearby Napa Valley, became noticeably Italian-American. Italian truck gardens were familiar sights in the outlying undeveloped parts of San Francisco itself in what is now the Civic Center, Mission, Ingleside, and Bayview districts. Italian-Americans captured the fishing industry, driving out the Chinese who were relegated to marginal shrimping operations. Others founded export-import companies, opened restaurants, or began food processing businesses. Scavenging (garbage collection) also became a money-making Italian-American monopoly in San Francisco.

The Italian-Americans did not stay trapped in the ghetto. During the prosperity of the 1920s many moved up and out; after World War II mobility accelerated. It was partly because the neighborhood was "decongesting" that the beats found low rents here in the 1950s. Proximity to downtown also drew many young office workers to North Beach's convenient apartments and flats. Today the Italian heritage is evident in a few venerable institutions, restaurants, old businesses, and social groups such as *Il Cenacolo*, but it no longer dominates the neighborhood. Instead, booming Chinatown has spilled over across Broadway and moved up Stockton into North Beach.

BOHEMIAN SAN FRANCISCO

The unbohemian *Oxford English Dictionary* defines the bohemian as

the gipsy of society; one who either cuts him-

self off, or is by his habits cut off, from society for which he is otherwise fitted; especially an artist, literary man, or actor, who leads a free, vagabond, or irregular life, not being particular as to the society he frequents, and despising conventionalities generally. (Used with considerable latitude with or without reference to morals.)

Bohemians first appeared in Paris in the mid-1840s. Since the gypsies in France were traditionally from Bohemia (today part of Czechoslovakia), the Parisian press dubbed them "bohemians." Novelist Henry Murger defined Bohemia as an imaginary region "bordered in the North by hope, work and gaiety, on the South by necessity and courage, [and] on the West and East by slander and the hospital."

San Francisco had a milquetoast bohemia of literary dabblers and lightweight poets in the 1890s. This bohemia lived on then-inexpensive Russian Hill and slummed in cafés and bars near Pacific Street and the waterfront. The architect Willis Polk was a member of *les jeunes* ("the young"), as this coterie styled itself. Frank Norris, the well-born, Harvard-educated naturalistic novelist, was the only important writer to emerge from this genteel bohemia.

Another bohemia took root on Telegraph Hill in the 1920s in a cluster of shacks on the east side of the hill. In the depressed 1930s, left-wing radicals found North Beach one of their low-rent havens. Protest songs flowered; some painters took the social crisis of the time as their theme. The painters who worked with Ralph Stackpole on the 1934 murals in Coit Tower created a major American monument of the period. Although no important literature came out of this era of political and class struggle, the visual arts flowered vividly.

The San Francisco bohemia that was most significant, however, was that of the beats of the mid-1950s. These gypsies from bourgeois postatomic America introduced sexual and racial variety in their freefloating subculture, and drugs too. Cool jazz was its music, black was its basic color, red wine and caffeine were its drugs of choice. San Francisco's North Beach emerged as one of three poles around which this movement drifted. New York's Greenwich Village and Los Angeles' Venice Beach, all faded areas with low rents that sprouted jazz clubs, were the other two beat magnets. Besides breaking America's race line—a contribution of immense social importance—this movement's prophetic monument is Allen Ginsberg's poem "Howl," an apocalyptic vision of the madness of atomic warfare. A famous municipal obscenity trial of 1957 cleared the book—and gave it great publicity. (The trial provoked the classic newspaper headline: "THE COPS DON'T ALLOW NO RENAISSANCE HERE.")

Amazingly, poet Lawrence Ferlinghetti's City Lights Books at Columbus and Broadway, and the funky Vesuvio Cafe across the alley, survive from the beat days. The beatnik bohemia of the mid-1950s existed in the corners and cracks of the ethnically mixed lower-middle-class North Beach apartment district. Beatniks evolved a distinctive "look": beards and berets for the men, and black toreador pants and tops for "chicks." They created an argot—hip talk—which owed much to black jazz musicians. It was a night-creature culture based on staying up late. This bohemia had its painters, but it's the poets who have lasted. It was never a mob scene like the later hippie wave in the Haight-Ashbury. There were always only a few beats, and they were scattered, much like the punks today.

Today, San Francisco's bohemia is scattered, linked together by clunker automobiles, beat-up motorcycles, and redundant delivery trucks. The North Mission area, a gray zone between the South of Market and the Inner Mission, is its "center." Rock music is its chief art, though there is some painting and sculpture as well. Videos, alas, seem to have erased the written word. Its events are announced by severely black-and-white photocopied posters taped to utility poles in the North Mission, near the South of Market rock clubs on Eleventh Street, and along upper Haight Street.

There also is a vaguer, looser (more sanitary and healthy) "bohemia," a bohemia of the heart we might call it, and it is an important part of the character of this city. San Franciscans revel in human variety and are a bit more open to people of different persuasions. The working definition of a well-adjusted San Franciscan is that he or she is a bohemian at heart.

Tour 4A: North Beach and Telegraph Hill

COLUMBUS AVENUE FROM THE TRANSAMERICA PYRAMID TO BROADWAY

Originally named Montgomery Avenue, and retroactively cut across the existing grid of streets and houses in 1872–1873, Columbus Avenue is one of the very few concessions San Francisco's street plan has made to the city's undulating topography. Renamed Columbus Avenue in recognition of the large Italian-American colony in North Beach and along the industrial North Waterfront, the wide street is visually anchored by the Transamerica Pyramid at its south end and by Mt. Tamalpais in Marin County across the Bay. The walk up the gentle rise of Columbus to Broadway passes between the Jackson Square Historic District to the east and Chinatown immediately west.

This entire quadrant of the city burned to the ground in 1906. It had been the Victorian city's slum district. As North Beach quickly rebuilt between 1906 and about 1915, it built with new, more stringent, building codes. The even scale and coherent pattern of North Beach is due to these then-advanced

codes. Mostly three to four stories high, the flats, apartments, hotels, and shops that were built then almost all survive.

Columbus Avenue is San Francisco's greatest Edwardian boulevard, though few see it as such. The most interesting post-1906 buildings were built on the many triangular lots along prestigious Columbus Avenue. Each one of these buildings is unique. This is a rewarding street to walk along, all the way to The Cannery near Fisherman's Wharf.

Columbus Tower
906 Kearny Street, at Columbus
1905–1907, Salfield and Kohlberg

North on Kearny, at the diagonal of Columbus Avenue, rises the cupola of the flatiron Columbus Tower designed by Salfield and Kohlberg before the earthquake and finished after it. It is a landmark building clad in gleaming white tile and sporting fine green, copper-clad bay windows. It has long been a favorite building in San Francisco. Its top floor housed turn-of-the-century political boss Abe Ruef's thriving real estate brokerage business after his release from San Quentin prison. Movie producer Francis Ford Coppola bought and restored the building in the 1970s. A new six-story building designed by William Podesto and Associates was built behind Columbus Tower in 1988.

THE BROADWAY ENTERTAINMENT STRIP

Broadway, wider than most San Francisco streets, was the principal street to the passenger docks in San Francisco's earliest years. Like long-distance bus terminals now, such areas attracted transients, low-life bars, and cheap hotels. A block south of Broadway "Terrific" Pacific Street thrived with dives and whorehouses, later to be romanticized as the "old Barbary Coast." This red-light district was shut down in February, 1917 when the United States entered World War I. The construction of the Broadway Tunnel under Russian Hill in 1952 and of

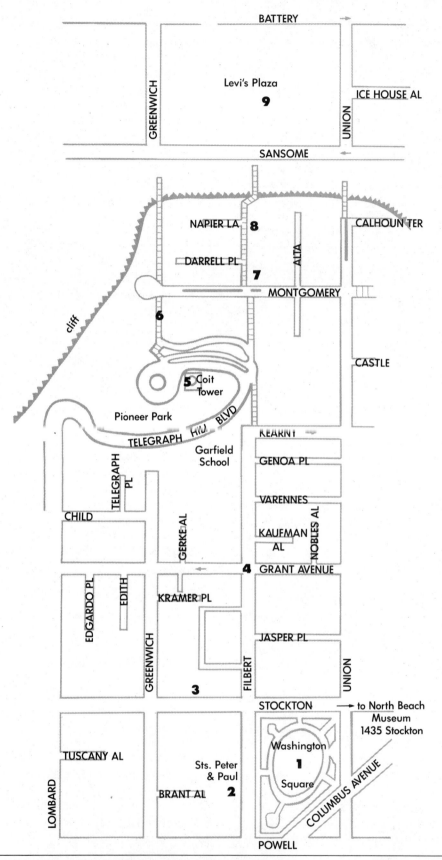

NORTH BEACH TO TELEGRAPH HILL AND COIT TOWER

the Embarcadero Freeway in 1962, which dumps all its traffic onto Broadway, made Broadway accessible from all over the Bay Area and sparked a boom in nightclubs and restaurants. In a city under continual gentrification, Broadway seems to be perversely sliding backwards. The topless club craze that took off in 1964 and that lasted until the early 1970s is long over. Video porn seems to have found a niche in the blocks downhill from Broadway, appropriately enough backing up on Pacific.

One or two good jazz clubs have always hung on here. **The Jazz Workshop** (398-9700) at 473 Broadway near Kearny is today's best venue. After a seventeen-year hiatus, Mike White has brought back what is probably *the* most historic jazz nightspot in San Francisco. The **Finocchio Club** (982-9388) at 506 Broadway, at Kearny, upstairs, offers male actresses in a polished and fun revue.

Skull-decorated speed metal fans, rockers, and punkers in black leather and silver studs mob **The Stone** (391-8282) at 412 Broadway near Montgomery and other rock clubs at the freeway end of the strip. Nearby is **Broadway's Rock**, a shop selling rock star iconography and regalia. **Goldfield's Original Tattoo Studios** is an artistic reminder of the long-gone waterfront. Broadway is in one of its eternal transitions. Theater districts are like that, going dark between acts.

City Lights Bookstore
261 Columbus, below Broadway
Open daily 10 A.M.–11:30 P.M., Friday and Saturday until 12:30 A.M.; 362-8193.

Poet Lawrence Ferlinghetti opened City Lights in 1953, one of the earliest paperback bookstores anywhere. As he recently reminisced, "We opened up the pocketbook shop to pay the rent on this literary magazine we were doing. The magazine folded but the bookstore kept going. We stayed open to midnight. Just couldn't get the door closed." The shop

was named after Charlie Chaplin's film and its image of "the little man against the cold cruel world." This landmark bookstore occupies the ground floor and basement, where there are chairs for browsers. It has books, avant-garde magazines, and a definitive selection of little magazines. City Lights is also a publishing house with a distinguished series of pocket poetry books including "Howl," among many other titles. Ferlinghetti, poet Gary Snyder, Ginsberg, and Gregory Corso were among the original beats. The store and publishing house thrive.

Vesuvio Café (362-3370) at 255 Columbus near Broadway opened in the 1940s across narrow Adler Place. It is the only other surviving beat haunt. It is located in the ground floor and mezzanine of the old Cavalli Italian-American bookstore, an erudite pressed-tin landmark of the post-fire rebuilding. This is perhaps San Francisco's most elaborate sheet-metal façade. Inside, the bar has a magpie decor. The front tables are a good place for people watching.

LITTLE ITALY CLASSICS WEST OF COLUMBUS AVENUE

Broadway west of Columbus is now fully absorbed into Chinatown, but a cluster of old Italian-American shops, and one key venerable landmark, Fugazi Hall, survive in the blocks near Vallejo and Stockton.

Molinari's Delicatessen
373 Columbus Avenue, at Vallejo; 421-2337

The real thing, with a transporting, caloric aroma, Molinari's manufactures its own *ravioli* and *tagliarini*, and makes its own fine salami. San Francisco's uniquely mild climate is ideal for the curing of Italian dry salami; traditional makers cure their pungent pork and bulk meat sausages for forty-five days.

113

Victoria Pastry Co.
1362 Stockton Street, corner of Vallejo
Open Monday–Saturday 7 A.M.–6 P.M.;
Sunday, 8 A.M.–5 P.M.; 781-2015

Established in 1914, this is San Francisco's best Italian bakery and specializes in *gâteau St. Honoré*, and *zuccotto*, a Tuscan sponge cake filled with surprises; also rum cakes, *cannoli*, and *panettone*.

Panelli Bros. Delicatessen
1419 Stockton, near Vallejo; 421-2541.
Excellent made-to-order sandwiches; good for picnic fixings for travelers on a budget.

North Beach Museum / Eureka Federal Savings
1435 Stockton Street, near Columbus
Open Monday–Thursday, 9 A.M.–4 P.M.; Friday 9 A.M.–5 P.M.; Saturday 10 A.M.–12:30 P.M.; closed Sunday and holidays; free.

The Art Deco Cavalli Building was unattractively altered for the bank and the insertion of basement-level shops, including the excellent Eastwind Books and Arts (*see Tour 3*). Inside the bank on the mezzanine is a fine small museum devoted to the history of North Beach. In changing exhibits, it recounts the story of the Italian-American community and of Chinese-American North Beach as well. This intimate museum is filled with old photographs that evoke old Little Italy and the many other cultural currents that have swirled through these historic blocks.

A. Cavalli & Co.
1441 Stockton Street, between Vallejo and Green

This newsstand and simple sundries shop was established in 1880 and once occupied the fine building where Vesuvio Café is today. The latest Italian soccer scores are posted here, and Italian newspapers and magazines are available.

The Bank of America
1455 Stockton Street, at Columbus

This one-story Art Deco corner bank shows how artistically the architects of the 1940s manipulated reinforced concrete. The upper part of the building has faces worked into its decoration. It is a fine period piece and was designed by Capital Co. in 1947. The locally founded bank was especially proud of the branches it built in North Beach. Another elegant branch, now a Carl's Jr. fast-food place, stands on the gore lot at Broadway and Columbus.

Fugazi Hall / Casa Coloniale Italiana
678 Green Street, between Columbus and Powell
1912, Italo Zanolini
Theater offers ongoing performances of "Beach Blanket Babylon"; call 421-4222 for ticket information.

Most of the important ethnic groups in San Francisco in the nineteenth and early twentieth centuries built at least one community meeting hall. In North Beach, John F. Fugazi, a banker and the founder of the Transamerica Company and an eventual partner of A. P. Giannini, gave his community this splendid building in 1912. It was designed by Italo Zanolini and has a rich buff brick façade decorated with elaborate terra cotta ornament and crowned by a central niche with a bust. The façade looks like the frontispiece of an old volume. It is very Old World in flavor and seems to burst with pride in Italian culture. The theater inside is now host to the long-running musical show, "Beach Blanket Babylon," a fun evening of zaniness. Fugazi Hall has a *trompe l'oeil*-decorated basement banquet hall and offices upstairs for several Italian-American philanthropic and cultural organizations. It is the major secular landmark of San Francisco's large Italian-American community, now, of course, integrated into every aspect of city life. Go upstairs and ask to see the historical display.

St. Francis of Assisi
Roman Catholic Church
610 Vallejo, off Columbus

This Franciscan church was established on June 12, 1849 and was the first Roman Catholic parish in California after the Spanish missions. Bishop Joseph Sadoc Alemany, the Bishop of Monterey, resided here from 1850 to 1854, before Old St. Mary's Cathedral was completed on California Street. The present light-painted Gothic Revival church was built in 1860. It was gutted by the 1906 fire and was rebuilt shortly thereafter within the original brick walls. It was one of the early focal points of the Italian colony. Today this is a Chinese-American parish.

Columbus Cutlery (362-1342), at 358 Columbus Avenue, near Vallejo is owned by Pietro and Ottilia Malattia. Their tiny shop sells, sharpens, and repairs all kinds of scissors, shears, razors, clippers, and knives. If they don't have it, it isn't made.

Postermat, 401 Columbus at the corner of Vallejo with an Annex at 435 Columbus, sells perception-altering posters by such artists as Rick Griffin, Wes Wilson, Stanley Mouse, Alton Kelley, and Victor Moscoso. They were created to promote mid-1960s rock shows at the Fillmore Auditorium, Avalon Ballroom, and The Family Dog.

Biordi Art Imports (392-8096), at 412 Columbus Avenue near Vallejo sells hand-painted Italian dinnerware and ceramics and gourmet cookware. Gianfranco Savio's shop is the best in its line; and they will ship.

Figoni Hardware at 1351 Grant is an old-fashioned hardware store with a vintage enameled-metal-and-neon Sherwin-Williams paint "Cover the Earth" sign. Inside are wooden floors and shelves stacked with small boxes. Good for Italian kitchen implements and basic glassware.

Panama Canal Ravioli Factory (421-1952), at 1358 Grant near Green was established in 1915; they make excellent ravioli, noodles, and sauce.

R. Iacopi & Co. Meat Market and Deli (421-0757), 1462 Grant at Union, was established in 1910 and makes Sicilian, Calabrese, and Tuscan-style sausages; also *tortas* of many different kinds.

Italian French Baking Co. of San Francisco (421-3796), 1501 Grant at Union, makes excellent breads and *panettone*.

WASHINGTON SQUARE:
THE IDEAL PARK **[1]**

Placid, green Washington Square surrounded by its pale, light-reflecting buildings, with the twin spires of Sts. Peter and Paul floating over it, is one of the finest parks in the United States. Washington Square's current landscape design dates from 1955 and is both simple and agreeable. A light screen of varied trees surrounds the square while a large sunny lawn spreads out at its center. The square is the lowest depression between Telegraph and Russian hills. It was reserved as a park by Jasper O'Farrell in 1847 and never saw serious attempts at private encroachment, something highly unusual for a nineteenth-century San Francisco park. Pressure to convert the park into playing fields was relieved by the creation of the North Beach Playground one block north in 1910. (The movement to put parking garages under downtown parks came as far as Washington Square and then was fortunately stopped.)

On the Columbus Avenue side of Washington Square is the bronze statue by Haig Patigian in honor of the city's volunteer firemen, erected in 1933 with part of Lillie Hitchcock Coit's bequest. The statue of Benjamin Franklin in the center of the park was the gift of H. D. Cogswell in 1879. Cogswell was a prosperous dentist and active prohibitionist. The long-dry taps at the base of the monument are inscribed "Cal Seltzer," "Vichy," and "Congress," though they provided only ordinary tap water.

The **Fior d'Italia Restaurant** (986-1886), 601 Union, on the south side of the square is the oldest Italian restaurant in San Francisco. It was founded in 1881 and is favored by North Beach's Italian-American establishment.

Stockton Street, bordering the park, was an early fashionable residential address, the "Pacific Heights" of a much smaller city. Washington Square was then only an open lot with a low board fence around it and a flagpole dead-center. When Columbus Avenue was cut through, clipping off the southwestern corner of the park, the park was landscaped with irrigated lawns and sheltering rows of densely planted conifers like Christmas trees. A new flagpole and fence were erected and a small keeper's kiosk built at Columbus and Union near today's bus stop. In the 1860s, Washington Square was the only island of green that city dwellers could easily walk to.

What is best about Washington Square today is the generally peaceful mood of all the very different kinds of people who use it almost round the clock. It is what a park is supposed to be, a piece of sky and grass and momentary release from the urban world. The plan of the park is fine in its unpretentiousness and in its openness to sunlight. Retired men sit on the benches facing Union Street; Chinese-American families take their tots to the sandbox play area in the northwest corner of the park; and passersby sit on the benches facing the lawn on the path parallel to Stockton Street. Young people like spots on the central lawn. Washington Square is filled with human life of all ages and conditions.

Sts. Peter and Paul Roman Catholic Church [2]
666 Filbert Street
1922, Charles Fantoni

The twin spires of Sts. Peter and Paul

Roman Catholic Church, illuminated at night, float over the north side of the square. It was designed in 1922 by Charles Fantoni in the Romanesque style and was two decades in construction. Sts. Peter and Paul was San Francisco's Italian-language parish and is served by the Salesians of St. John Bosco whose special mission is the instruction of boys from the poor and laboring classes. At its dedication in 1924 this church was hailed as "a monument which glorifies God, and reflects honor upon our City, our colony and our far away Italy." The stately church is also a manifestation of the prosperity San Francisco's Italian-American colony achieved, principally through cornering wholesale fish and produce markets.

This church is known as "the Church of the Fishermen" and has inside it a painting of "La Madre del Lume," Our Lady of Light, the patroness of Porticello. Processions depart from here for the annual blessing of the fishing fleet early each October.

This steel-frame and concrete building is actually two buildings in one: a large church with a grammar school wrapped around its "nave." The inscription that runs across the façade is from the opening line of Dante's *Paradise*, "The glory of Him who moves everything penetrates through the universe, and is resplendent in one part more and in another less." The interior is quintessentially Italian in its saint-crowded feeling. Even when empty the church seems full of people because of all the statues and images. It is as gregarious as Italian-American culture itself. The altar is an impressive extravaganza, a heavenly city of sumptuous marble spires and life-size angels.

TELEGRAPH HILL

Old Telegraph Hill Dwellers Association Clinic [3]
1736 Stockton, near Filbert
1907, Bernard Maybeck

This is an important building in the history of San Francisco for it represents the beginning of the movement to create voluntary grassroots neighborhood associations, today a fundamental way in which politically active San Franciscans are organized. Architecturally, the building is interesting for its distinguished early pedigree as a 1907 design by Bernard Maybeck, much expanded and altered by perhaps a dozen architects since then. In imagery rustic or Swiss, its small courtyard with its one tree achieves a sense of separation from the city streets. Today converted to private offices, it is a good reminder of the great flexibility and adaptability of frame buildings.

The building opened as a settlement house clinic founded by two upper-class San Francisco women, Alice Griffith and Elizabeth Ashe. The center fought overcrowding in the slums, vaccinated children, ran baby clinics, and cared for the sick during three major flu epidemics. It called for better sanitation and health conditions in the crowded tenements of the immigrant newcomers, for conditions were bad in the tenements of the poor. Little Italy disappeared when life got better and its people moved up and out.

NORTH BEACH ALLEYS

The flats and apartments in North Beach's narrow alleys were forbidden to have bay windows by the city's fire code. Today many of these buildings house working-class Chinese-American families. In the rebuilding after the fire in 1906, the very old city pattern of building working-class housing along alleys inside blocks and middle-class housing on the wider streets at the periphery of blocks was preserved. Multiclass blocks are something later real estate trends almost obliterated. Until quite recently, it was always thought an advance to segregate classes in order to create homogeneous tracts. Survivals such as this of an older, multiclass city form are instructive.

UPPER GRANT AVENUE SHOP AND CAFÉ STRIP [4]

Grant Avenue from Broadway to Greenwich is perhaps the most interesting inexpensive shopping/browsing street in San Francisco both for visitors and residents. In form, it is the classic Edwardian city of three-story, bay-windowed frame buildings with shops along the ground floor and apartments and hotels above. The uniform architecture creates a narrow street with "corrugated" sides of bay windows. A strong and even cornice line "holds" the sky and defines the visual edge of the minicanyon. The sidewalks are narrow and the shops all of the same general small size, creating an environment that is intimate, like a village. Some vintage shopfronts survive here with their tile work, long an Italian-American specialty in the building trades.

Faded here and there, not swank, Upper Grant's shops are great hunting grounds for unusual items. The relatively low-rent storefronts strung out continuously along both sides of narrow Upper Grant are a changing mix of old-time Italian-American businesses (just a few are left), antique stores and interesting offbeat shops, new Chinese-American stores, storefront offices and garment shops, and services such as dry cleaners catering to Telegraph Hill and North Beach residents. A light sprinkling of contemporary clothes shops and art galleries enlivens this *potpourri*.

Travelers who need postcards should check out **Quantity Postcards** at 1441 Grant with its twenty thousand old and new postcards. **Grant Antiques** at 1415 Grant is also good hunting. **The Saloon** at Grant and Fresno Alley, right above the diagonal of Columbus, looks and smells just like its name and presents some of the best Bay Area rock and jazz music. Up Grant at 1353 is the **Lost &**

Found Saloon, a bit of a dive but also a place where the music cooks; they serve up live blues and rock with no cover charge. This was once the famous Coffee Gallery, a beat haven.

TO COIT TOWER [5]

The stairs at the head of Filbert Street are the most direct path up steep Telegraph Hill. Walk along the shoulder of Telegraph Hill Boulevard to Coit Tower. The alternative is the convenient and scenic 39 Coit bus, which runs every twenty minutes and stops at Union near Columbus, on the south edge of Washington Square, or along Stockton between Filbert and Lombard. Sit on the driver's side for the best view as the bus climbs Lombard and swings onto curvy Telegraph Hill Boulevard. The pale stucco apartments, flats, and houses of Telegraph Hill are neat and tidy, light-reflecting facets of this cubist cityscape. Sudden views of the blue Bay and its distant shores make this short ride memorable. Now a posh enclave, Telegraph Hill was once solidly working class with Irish-American dock-workers on its east face and Italian-American fishermen on its north face all living in modest cottages.

Where Telegraph Hill Boulevard swings in a loop at the head of Lombard is a granite monument with a bronze plaque dedicated to Guglielmo Marconi, the inventor of wireless telegraphy. The memorial was placed here by public subscription in 1938 shortly after the inventor's death. Immediately behind it, at **275 Telegraph Hill Boulevard**, is architect Gardner Dailey's own house designed in 1942. This elegant modern stucco design blends in so well with its neighbors that few notice it. Dailey was one of the Bay Area's greatest designers and in this subtle building he masterfully utilized the views from the site and incorporated roof terraces into the original design. Striving to be rigorously pure and modern, he eschewed adding bay windows. His widow, however, ended up adding one to the back of the house.

Coit Tower / Panorama and WPA Murals [5]
Telegraph Hill
1933, Arthur Brown, Jr.; 1934, WPA murals, various artists
Tower and murals open 10 A.M.–5 P.M. daily.

Coit Tower stands atop Telegraph Hill surrounded by the green trees of Pioneer Park, one of the oldest parks in the city. Originally a barren hilltop, this 295-foot hill got its name from a semaphore built here in 1850 to advise merchants in the port of the approach of ships. It functioned for only three-and-a-half years before an electric telegraph station was built on Point Lobos, at the entrance to the Golden Gate, which bypassed the primitive semaphore. During Gold Rush days, the residents of the then-remote port thronged the summit of the hill to watch the arrival of the Pacific Mail steamer with its letters and news from home. In 1876 a group of civic-minded businessmen, perhaps wanting to celebrate in some tangible way the nation's centennial, purchased four lots at the top of the hill for $12,000 and donated them to the city to create Pioneer Park; later purchases by the city considerably expanded the park.

Lillie Hitchcock Coit, a pioneer San Franciscan, was brought to San Francisco as a child in 1851. She developed a life-long fascination with fires and firemen. As a young girl, she was made an honorary member of the Knickerbocker No. 5 Fire Company. A southern sympathizer during the Civil War, Coit spent the war years first in the South and then in Paris. Eventually she returned to San Francisco and when she died in 1929 she left $100,000 to the City of San Francisco "to be expended in an appropriate manner for the purpose of adding to the beauty of the city which I have always loved."

The Coit Advisory Committee used the funds to erect the statue to the volunteer firemen that stands in Washington Square and to construct an observation tower atop Telegraph Hill. Arthur Brown Jr., the architect of the City Hall, was commissioned to design the 210-foot-tall reinforced concrete tower which was completed in 1933. In form, the tower is a giant fluted column with an arcaded observatory at its top. So that it would appear vertical to the human eye, the tower is slightly tapered and is eighteen inches smaller in diameter at its top than its base. In style, Coit Tower might be called "stripped classical." Over the entrance is a high relief plaque by sculptor Robert Howard showing the phoenix rising from its ashes, San Francisco's emblem adopted after the devastating fires of the 1850s which repeatedly destroyed the Gold Rush city.

An elevator carries the visitor to a landing from which thirty-seven steps lead to the open loggia at the top of the tower with its splendid view. The panorama here embraces the entire north Bay from the Golden Gate in the west to the Contra Costa hills on the east. The construction of a tall apartment building on the north side of the hilltop led to the first height limits in San Francisco in 1931 "so that skyscrapers would not interfere with the view from or detract from the beauty of the Coit Memorial." (In 1963 a forty-foot, or four-story, height limit was imposed on all the north waterfront to prevent a Miami Beach-like wall of bayfront highrises from destroying the views from the rest of the city.)

It was originally intended to put a restaurant or an exhibit hall in the ground floor of the tower but neither came to pass. Instead, in 1934 San Francisco artist Bernard Zakheim contacted Dr. Walter Heil, a San Franciscan then serving in President Roosevelt's New Deal, urging that the interior of the tower be embellished as a relief project for local artists. Heil, head of the Public Works of Art Project (PWAP), liked this idea and the result was the first relief work project for artists sponsored by the federal government. Twenty-five master artists and nineteen assistants were commissioned to cover the interior with frescoes depicting the working life of California. All received the monthly salary of $94. The work was accomplished in eight-and-a-half months and produced one of the most important pieces of public art in California.

Though the Coit Tower frescoes are unified in narrative conception, each section was done by different hands and a few vary markedly in style. Some panels are straightforwardly documentary, while others are militantly political. The frescoes are well worth careful examination.

American Eagle, artist unknown. Enter the tower and look over the inner archway leading to the elevators. A pair of penetrating eyes surrounded by clouds, lightning, rain, the sun, and the moon stare at the viewer like the eyes of God the Creator in a Byzantine apse. An American eagle adorns the arch itself. Step to the left and follow the frescoes in a clockwise direction.

Animal Force and Machine Force, Ray Boynton. This panel flanks the doorway on both sides of the inner north wall. On the left is the ancient source of power, human and animal muscle. The fishermen pulling their heavy nets from the sea repeat an ancient fresco theme. In a small niche a young boy reads the dedication book for Coit Tower. To the right of the doorway a modern hydroelectric dam harnesses elemental forces for the modern world's work.

California Industry: Timber and Dairying, Gordon Langdon. On the outer wall, in the northeast corner, is Langdon's depiction of a sawmill processing redwood trees into milled lumber. Look carefully in the mill to find the primitive worker's graffito on a pillar, a wry reference to the roots of art.

Farmer and Cowboy, Clifford Wright. Flanking the east window are Wright's figures holding implements of their trade. The two figures represent the classic struggle in the West between the rancher's desire for open ranges and the farmer's need for fenced-in fields.

California, Maxine Albro. Across the inner east wall is Maxine Albro's synthesis of California agricultural scenes. From left to right are wheat farming (California's first important crop and the basis of much of the wealth of Victorian San Francisco), flower-raising, and viticulture and winemaking.

Department Store, Frede Vidar. On the outer wall, in the left southeast corner, is Vidar's panel showing a soda fountain, a wine shop, and a department store with clerks and customers. Fear and foreboding of the coming world war permeate the soda fountain. One woman hides behind another as if afraid of a photographer. In the background a woman reads a newspaper with headlines of Hitler and of the destruction of Diego Rivera's controversial murals in New York's Rockefeller Center.

Banking, George Harris. On the outer wall, in the right southeast corner, is Harris' fresco showing lawyers reading in a law library, armed guards protecting a bank vault, and the interior of the Grain Exchange Board. The downward sloping line on the graph in the Grain Exchange tells the story of the Great Depression.

Stockbroker and Scientist, Mallette Dean. Flanking the south window are two figures with symbolic tools of their professions. The man who creates intellectual capital—the scientist or inventor—and the man who makes ideas economic realities—the investor or businessman—frame the window looking down on the skyscrapers of the Financial District. A light switch on the wall is incorporated into the scientist's observatory.

City Life, Victor Arnatoff. On the inner south wall is Arnatoff's great vision of San Francisco in the 1930s. This complex scene is the apex of the cycle and shows various parts of the city as they looked in the 1930s. A newsstand occupies the center of the composition. The man with the hat at the right staring at the viewer is Ralph Stackpole. A car crash has taken place in front of the Stock Exchange. A holdup is in progress as the indifferent city crowd hurries by. The city's varied people is the theme: silk-hatted capitalists and sailors, laborers and shoppers, policemen and thieves all animate the city streets. Hovering over all this activity is a stock exchange ticker and quotations. Note the three newspapers that surround the prosperous-looking businessman in the brown homburg. He is reading the New York stock tables while a woman's legs peek out from the paper clutched under his arm. He stands on a cheap tabloid depicting a gangster slaying.

Library, Bernard B. Zakheim. On the outer wall, in the left southwest corner, is Bernard B. Zakheim's controversial depiction of workers reading in the library's periodical room. Most of the newspapers are Communist and socialist periodicals whose headlines record the political and social crises of the day. The most prominent figure is reaching for Marx's *Capital*. A happy hedonist among these politically passionate readers relishes a girlie paper.

News Gathering, Suzanne Scheuer. On the outer wall, in the right southwest corner, is Suzanne Scheuer's fresco showing the editorial office, linotyping, composing, printing, and selling of the *San Francisco Chronicle*. A reporter with his back to the viewer hands his story in to his editor. The frame around the small window shows the printing of the separate colors for the Sunday comics. A newsboy stands to the left with the finished product. On the windowsill is a copy of the *Chronicle* with the headline, ARTISTS FINISH COIT TOWER MURALS.

Surveyor and Steelworker, Clifford Wright. On the outer wall flanking the west window are Clifford Wright's two figures representing mental and physical labor.

Industries of California, Ralph Stackpole. On the inner west wall is Stackpole's large fresco depicting in realistic detail California industries from canning to steel to chemicals. Diego Rivera's influence on the artists is strongest here. The NRA blue eagles on the sacks refer to the New Deal's attempt to organize the devastated American economy.

Railroad and Shipping, William Hesthal. On the outer wall in the northwest corner is William Hesthal's pairing of land and sea transport.

California Industrial Scenes, John Langley Howard. On the outer north wall is John Langley Howard's fresco showing construction, oil drilling, mining, and panning for gold. Striking black and white miners mass menacingly before the viewer. A poor migrant family with its battered car is camped out in the open, panning for gold in California's worked-over streambeds. They are the object of the curiosity of the idle rich who have come in their yellow limousine. The hungry mongrel and the pampered poodle eye each other, summing up the conflict. Looming over the squalid migrants' camp is a modern hydroelectric dam and a sleek streamlined train.

Social Revolution, John Langley Howard. Over the inner lintel of the door leading outside is the little-noticed conclusion to the cycle. In the cramped space over the door, a vast wheatfield moves under a stormy, lightning-streaked sky. The wheatfield below is ablaze; out of the flames rises the clenched fist of social revolution.

To the left of the front door is a scrap of paper with a quip from President Franklin Roosevelt on his return from a fishing expedition, "I'm a tough guy. I learned a lot from the barracudas and the sharks."

The Coit Tower murals were completed just as San Francisco entered one of its most acute crises. A longshoremen's strike that July turned into a four-day general strike after police killed two union members. Politics and paint became an explosive combination when rumors began circulating about the "subversive" frescoes. The city's Art Commission ordered a hammer and sickle removed from one fresco and then decided to close the tower

until tempers in the city cooled. The Artists' Union picketed the locked monument. Finally, in October, the frescoes were opened to the public. Rarely has public art so touched the nerves of San Francisco the way these murals did during the polarized year of 1934.

Of related interest, San Francisco's second important WPA fresco cycle was painted in 1936–1937 by Lucian Labaudt and is located in the Beach Chalet at the far western end of Golden Gate Park, facing the Ocean Beach (*See Tour 12*). Those murals depict play and recreation, complementing these on work and industry.

GREENWICH STEPS [6]

Leave Coit Tower, turn right, and cross the road to the light pole; here you will find the head of Greenwich Steps, a right-of-way too steep to pave. The hidden stairs are embowered in greenery and give access to secluded houses and apartments. In the nineteenth and early twentieth centuries, the east face of the hill was inhabited by Irish-American dockworkers who labored on the bustling piers below. In 1888 one woman described how hard it was to locate a particular shanty in this jumble:

It requires some physical exertion to mount a Telegraph Hill stairway, but that is nothing in comparison with the mental effort necessary in finding one's way after reaching the top. We jump a ditch that serves as an open channel for sewage, make a detour around a pile of tomato cans, bring up in a blind alley that purports to be a street leading directly to the house we seek, try a path that ends abruptly on the edge of the cliff, and narrowly escape a landslide that goes careening down the bluff, and which has lost its precarious hold just a moment too soon to give us a free toboggan ride....

Small local grocery stores catered to the isolated hillside residents. Goat trails webbed the steep slopes. There were many empty lots on the hill then, and the cheap real estate within hiking distance of the cafés and bars along Pacific and Broadway drew a small band of artists to the hill. Where Greenwich meets Montgomery, Harry Lafler, an artist and newspaperman who also sold real estate, built a fenced cluster of five cottages known as The Compound. It became a gathering place for writers such as local poet George Sterling. The isolation, splendid views, and good weather began to attract others to the hill.

In 1931 Montgomery Street was graded, split into two levels, and paved. The construction of Coit Tower gave the hill a new image and new houses and apartments began to pop up here and there. Better garbage service and landscaping also spruced up the hill. By 1939 some quite artistic buildings were constructed and the hill tipped toward those with "the longing for bohemia ... whose income permits them to be comfortably daring." The same observer noted that the once working-class hill "is well on the way to becoming smart." Telegraph Hill was one of the first areas in San Francisco to undergo what today is called "gentrification." While only a few shingled shacks remain today, the explorer can find here and there evidence of the hill's early days. In 1986 the Telegraph Hill Historic District was established to preserve the surviving small-scale hill cottages.

Julius Castle Restaurant [6]
1541 Montgomery Street
1921, Louis Mastropasqua
Lunch 11:30 A.M.–3 P.M., dinner 5:30 P.M.–11 P.M.; expensive; 362-3042.

At the head of Montgomery is crenellated Julius Castle, a restaurant with a splendid view built in 1921 and designed by Louis Mastropasqua, a gifted Italian-American architect and cartoonist for *La Vita Italiana*. In the 1920s a turntable in front of the restaurant was the only practical way to turn autos around on the narrow street. (Today the restaurant has valet parking.) Walk up the lower side of Montgomery. The retaining wall

here has been heavily planted and gives the illusion of a park.

Malloch Apartment Building [7]
1360 Montgomery Street
1936, Irving Goldstine

On the corner of Montgomery and Filbert streets is one of San Francisco's Art Deco treasures, a four-story apartment house built in 1936 and remodeled in 1939 by Irving W. Goldstine. Bogart and Bacall's "Dark Passage" was filmed with this Moderne building in the background. Large *sgraffito* panels decorate the building. Facing Montgomery is a stevedore holding a globe with the Bay Bridge and Coit Tower visible at his feet. Above him are three Manila Clippers, the earliest air link across the Pacific, inaugurated in 1936. At the other end of the façade is a Spanish conquistador. On the Filbert Street side is a panel with a female figure representing California with a rainbow and a map of the state. A sun sets in a zigzag landscape. The entrance is decorated with an etched glass window with the obligatory leaping gazelle. Streamlined corners, glass blocks, and a railing along the top of the building make this a quintessential piece of Moderne design.

FILBERT STEPS [8]

Filbert Steps and Napier Lane, lined with simple Victorian cottages and embowered in gardens, is one of San Francisco's most-loved enclaves. Another street right-of-way too steep to pave, Filbert is made accessible by wooden stairs. The perpendicular gardens here, filled with flowers and carpeted with Baby Tears, are a labor of love for Filbert Steps residents, who continue the efforts begun by Grace Marchant many years ago. The modest cottages, lush plantings, and sweeping views of the Bay, all so close to the downtown's skyscrapers, sum up the best of San Francisco.

At **228 Filbert Street** is a Gothic Revival cottage built in 1873 by an Englishman from Jersey in the stevedore business. It replaced an earlier shanty. Further down the steps, at **224 Filbert** at the corner of Napier Lane, is an 1863 cottage thoroughly restored and improved in 1978. This simple vernacular cottage is one of the oldest on the hill and gives a taste of the first wave of building here. Before its restoration by architect-owner Robert J. Fogel it was in a decrepit state; today it charms all who see it. On the opposite corner of Filbert Steps and Napier Lane is **222 Filbert**, a simple frame building that once housed Michael Thornton's grocery store and "blind pig," an unlicensed saloon. Legend has it that some of the cottages here were used to "shanghai" sailors. "To shanghai" was a verb coined in early San Francisco.

NAPIER LANE [8]

Napier Lane, originally Napier Alley, is a short boardwalk, one of the last in the city, lined with cottages and modest apartment buildings. Pots of flowers bloom here all year long, and sleek cats patrol their intricate territories. Number **10 Napier Lane** is a one-story, Italianate house built in 1875. Number **21 Napier Lane** was built in 1885 and is typical of the working-class housing that once predominated on the hill. Its precipitous exterior staircase creates interesting patterns. The gaps between the Napier Lane cottages permit glimpses of the gardens, porches, and roof decks that spill down the eastern face of the hill.

At the bottom of Filbert is a cliff-clinging concrete staircase built in 1972 to replace the rickety wooden staircase that once gave access to Sansome Street and the piers down below. The stairs traverse a former quarry. Rock excavated from Telegraph Hill was used to fill behind the city's seawall to make space for the warehouses that backed up the once-busy piers. In 1878 a heavy rainstorm uncovered traces of gold near the Filbert Steps and a brief flurry of gold

fever struck the hill. While the "gold rush" turned out to be brief, the quarrying of rock was long profitable and was not stopped until several houses at the edge of the excavation slid down into the pit. Today aromatic wild anise, red valerian, and yellow and orange nasturtium cling to the rocks. Visible from here is the roof of the four-story **H. G. Walters Warehouse** with a Moderne-style house, garden, and guesthouse perched on its roof.

The red brick former warehouse district at the foot of Telegraph Hill, between Sansome and The Embarcadero, is one of the oldest sections of San Francisco. Buried under its landfill are Gold Rush ships abandoned when their crews took off for the mines. The brig *Palmyra* lies buried underground near the Levi's Plaza fountain here. Three blocks from here, on Front flanking Vallejo, are the twin Gibb Warehouses built in the 1850s, among the oldest buildings in the city. The district has seen dramatic change since the 1960s. When shipping moved across the Bay to the Port of Oakland's modern container cargo facilities, the solidly built warehouses here were converted first into furniture showrooms and architects' and designers' offices, and then as real estate values continued to escalate, into offices. All the former warehouses and factories that line the waterfront in an arc from Broadway to Ghirardelli Square have been converted to new uses in the postindustrial city.

Levi Strauss & Co. Headquarters / Levi's Plaza [9]
1155 Battery Street
1982, Hellmuth, Obata & Kassabaum with Howard Friedman and Gensler & Associates; 1982, Lawrence Halprin and Omi-Lang, landscape architects

Cross Sansome and enter landscape architect Lawrence Halprin's handsome park at the heart of Levi's Plaza, the corporate headquarters of Levi Strauss & Co. An attractive fountain here hewn out of a rough chunk of granite is a good place to rest. The lowrise, five-building complex was designed by Hellmuth, Obata & Kassabaum with Howard Friedman and Gensler & Associates in 1982. It is designed to blend with both the old warehouse district of which it is a part and the cubist jumble of Telegraph Hill's houses behind it. Levi's Plaza also incorporates the fine old **Italian Swiss Colony wine warehouse** at the corner of Battery and Greenwich designed by Hemenway & Miller in 1903.

124   Levi Strauss & Co. is one of San Francisco's best-known firms. Their products have carried San Francisco's initials on their copper rivets around the world. The company has its roots in a clothing import business begun in 1850 by David Stern. Stern invited his brother-in-law, Bavarian-born Levi Strauss to join him in 1853 and Levi Strauss & Co. was born. In 1871 Jacob W. Davis, a Reno, Nevada saddlebag maker who purchased duck twill from Levi Strauss, secured the seams of heavy work pants with copper saddlebag rivets. The next year Davis and Levi Strauss applied for a patent for an "improvement in fastening pocket-openings" which was granted the following year. The company began the manufacture of denim overalls that were sold throughout the west. Today Levi Strauss is one of the world's largest apparel manufacturers, with about a fifth of the denim jeans market.

Levi Strauss also offers tours by appointment of its factory and design center at 250 Valencia, in the Mission District, between Duboce and Fourteenth, on Wednesdays at 10:30 A.M.; reservations must be made in advance at 565-9159. The one-and-a-half hour tour includes a BBC documentary on the company, a museum of memorabilia on the famous jeans, and a look at the design department.

At Sansome and Greenwich in Levi's Plaza is a branch of **Il Fornaio**, (986-0100), a very fine Italian bakery and restaurant. **The Fog City Diner** (982-2000) is located across the street from the plaza

at 1300 Battery in a chrome and neon evocation of a traditional diner designed by Pat Kuleto in 1985.

The 42 Downtown Red Arrow Loop bus runs north up Sansome Street and The Embarcadero to Columbus and North Point, one block from The Cannery and Fisherman's Wharf. On Battery Street the 42 Downtown Gold Arrow Loop runs south to Battery and California in the Financial District and the California Cable Car line.

Tour 4B: Fisherman's Wharf

San Francisco's northern waterfront, from Fisherman's Wharf to Fort Mason, is one of the glories of this city, for it offers something for everyone, from bustling carnival crowds to quiet pierheads and bluffs with some of the most beautiful views of San Francisco Bay's ever-shifting colors and moods.

Fisherman's Wharf is San Francisco's single most popular visitor destination and attracts some 11 to 12 million people a year. Though it began to draw a few visitors in the late nineteenth century who came to watch the fishermen repairing their nets and working on their boats in this then-industrial district, today's booming recreation district is actually little more than thirty years old and is more contemporary than historic. Fisherman's Wharf is much more complex than most people think, though everyone notices the difference between the happy honky tonk at one end and the spacious green parks at the other.

In 1853 Harry Meiggs built a long wharf near the foot of present-day Powell Street. Shipbuilders were active here in the 1860s along the sandy North Beach (now approximately Bay Street). With the construction of the Great Seawall, North Point Cove was quickly filled in. All the flat blocks from Bay Street north are landfill that soon obliterated the northern beach. With the filling of the cove, lumber yards, warehouses, a woolen mill, chemical works, a gas lighting plant, and the Selby Lead and Smelting works located here. Later the California Fruit Canners Association and the Ghirardelli Chocolate Company built large factories on the Northern Waterfront. Piers and railyards completed the industrial zone.

In 1900 the fishing fleet was moved from the foot of Union Street, near present-day Levi's Plaza, to the foot of Taylor Street where a remnant survives today. Fish Alley, across Jefferson Street from The Cannery, between Taylor and Hyde, survives today like a fossil embedded in the bustling restaurant, retail, and hotel district.

The big change to the district began in the 1960s as tourism boomed while industrial maritime activities dwindled. The opening of Cost Plus Imports in 1958, the adaptation of the old Ghirardelli Chocolate factory to a major shopping complex in 1968, the rebuilding in 1968 of the 1907 California Fruit Canners Association red brick cannery as The Cannery, a restaurant and shopping complex, and in 1978 the development of Pier 39 transformed the Wharf.

TAYLOR STREET WHARF AND
RESTAURANT ROW [1]

The center of attraction at Fisherman's Wharf is the row of fish stalls, outdoor crab pots, and waterfront restaurants at Taylor and Jefferson streets. Many of these restaurants look down on the fishing fleet and across the wide Bay. Walkaway crab cocktails seem to have been first promoted by Tomaso Castagnola in 1916. He got the idea from the stand-up chowder stands that once served the fishermen and market workers who had to eat on the run as they sold their perishable catch in the early morning. An arcade of fish stalls lines a block of Taylor and part of Jefferson Street. The special treat here is sweet Dungeness crab trapped in pots outside

the Golden Gate. The traditional way for a San Franciscan to greet New Year's Day is with cracked crab and California white wine. Other seafood specialties served in the restaurants here are king and silver salmon; sea bass; ling, rock, and black cod; sand dabs, rex, and petrale sole; mackerel; ocean perch; halibut; abalone; and squid. Tiny flavorful shrimp and Olympia oysters from Washington State are also prized. A local dish much favored is *cioppino*, a shellfish and seafood stew flavored with tomatoes and white wine.

Many of the restaurants along this strip bear the names of locally prominent Italian-American families who have moved over the generations from fishing to restaurants. Many are open until midnight and offer validated parking. Most post their menus at their entrance. Ask for a window table. There are more than a hundred eating places. A partial list appears in the restaurant section at the front of this tour.

Two of San Francisco's best seafood restaurants are not located at the Wharf. **Scott's Seafood Grill & Bar** (563-8988), one of the best in San Francisco, is located at 2400 Lombard on the corner of Scott. And the **Hayes Street Grill** (863-5545) at 324 Hayes Street, known for its impeccably fresh fish, is located near the Civic Center.

U.S.S. *Pampanito* / U.S. Navy Vessels Pier 45 [2]
Open daily, 9 A.M.–9 P.M.; $3 for adults, $2 for children; 929-0202.

Pier 45, at the foot of Taylor on The Embarcadero, is one of the last vestiges of the working wharf and still serves the fishermen and fish brokers who crowd it early in the morning. Four large sheds and public parking occupy the big pier. You should walk to its end for an open view of the Bay. On the pier's east side the *U.S.S. Pampanito* is moored, a *Balao*-class submarine built in 1943 at Portsmouth Naval Shipyard, New Hampshire. She operated at a depth of 600 feet,

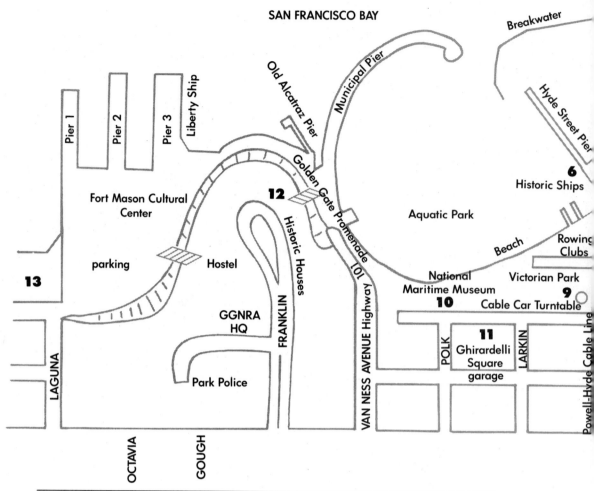

SAN FRANCISCO BAY

Breakwater

Pier 1

Pier 2

Pier 3

Liberty Ship

Old Alcatraz Pier

Municipal Pier

Hyde Street Pier

6
Historic Ships

Golden Gate Promenade

Fort Mason Cultural Center

12

Aquatic Park

Beach

Rowing Clubs

Historic Houses

parking

Hostel

13

101

National Maritime Museum

Victorian Park

9

FRANKLIN

GGNRA HQ

10

Cable Car Turntable

VAN NESS AVENUE Highway

POLK

11

Ghirardelli Square garage

LARKIN

Powell–Hyde Cable Line

Park Police

LAGUNA

OCTAVIA

GOUGH

FISHERMAN'S WHARF AND FORT MASON

made six patrols, and sank five Japanese ships. Operated by the National Maritime Museum Association and opened to the public in 1982, there are exhibits onboard and a self-guided audio tour.

Pier 45 is also a favored berth for visiting U.S. Navy vessels (open to the public between 1 and 4 P.M. on Saturday and Sundays; free).

JEFFERSON STREET AMUSEMENT ZONE [3]

Jefferson Street is Fisherman's Wharf's amusement strip lined with high-volume T-shirt and souvenir shops and wax museums. The block from Taylor to Mason is the epicenter of all this

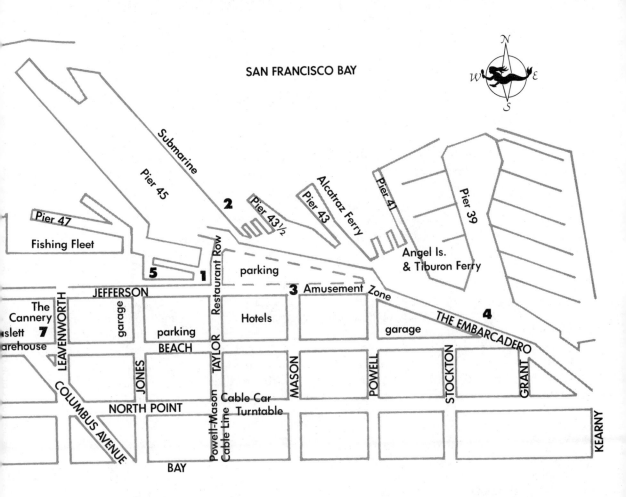

SAN FRANCISCO BAY

Submarine

Pier 45

Pier 47

Fishing Fleet

2

Pier 43½

Alcatraz Ferry

Pier 43

Pier 41

Pier 39

Angel Is.
& Tiburon Ferry

5   1

Restaurant Row

parking

JEFFERSON

3   Amusement   Zone

The
Cannery
slett   7
arehouse

garage

LEAVENWORTH

parking

Hotels

THE EMBARCADERO

garage

4

BEACH

JONES

TAYLOR

MASON

POWELL

STOCKTON

GRANT

NORTH POINT

Cable Car
Turntable

Powell-Mason
Cable Line

COLUMBUS AVENUE

KEARNY

BAY

activity. Jefferson has a populist mix of
attractions, especially for young people,
that makes it a magnet for vacationing
families. During peak summer periods,
an estimated three thousand people per
hour stroll by here, making Jefferson one
of the most heavily traveled pedestrian
corridors in the city. Street performers
are drawn by the milling crowds. Entre-
preneurial young boys stand on milk

crates holding poses which they change
intermittently with mechanical
precision.

Pier 39 [4]
1978, Walker and Moody

At the east end of the Jefferson Street
strip is Pier 39, a shop and restaurant
complex designed in 1978 by Walker and
Moody surrounded by a large marina

filled with white sailboats with blue canvas covers. Modern Pier 39 is built over a 1905 pier on Port Commission property under a sixty-year lease. Its design features an enticing central walkway designed to draw the stroller down its length and past shops built out of recycled lumber from the old pier shed. It *does* seem stranded on the wrong coast. Pier 39's best feature is its perimeter walkway with sweeping views of the Bay and of Telegraph Hill with the downtown highrises popping up over it.

THE HISTORIC FISHING FLEET [5]

San Francisco's historic fishing fleet ties up at the piers between Taylor and Hyde, north of Jefferson Street. The area is most active very early in the morning. By about 10 A.M. the catch has been sold and the fishermen and brokers are on their way home. Of the approximately 140 vessels berthed here, only 80 are licensed fishing boats and only about half of those are active year round; twenty-five years ago, the Wharf had some 300 fishing boats. While the Wharf still lands about 20 million pounds of fish, possibly five to ten times that amount comes in by truck to supply the Bay Area's restaurants and fish markets.

Helen Throop Purdy described old Fisherman's Wharf in 1912:

If the fleet is out, you will find some of the fishermen left behind to mend their nets, festooning them along the wharf to dry, or busy about their boats—always picturesque—their love of color displayed in bright shirts, in red and blue Tams, or in their gay little boats, painted rainbow colors, bright blue, yellow, green or striped. And if you happen upon just the right time to see the fleet, the sight is unforgettable—dozens of these bright boats with their tawny, three-cornered sails like a flock of great, yellow butterflies as they glide over the water.

The Italian fishermen recreated in America their traditional vessels, the *felucca*, a narrow, fast, lateen-rigged ship with an ancient Mediterranean lineage. Over time, a new kind of fishing boat evolved in Northern California known as the "Monterey clipper" with a graceful, curved bow. Look carefully at the row of small fishing boats given "front row" berths facing Jefferson, between Taylor and Jones. They are the heirlooms of the old fleet, industrial antiques worth preserving.

While very few visitors perambulate it, the Port Commission has made every effort to open the edge of the Wharf to pedestrians. You may walk all along the edge of the water up and down the wooden wharfs. Sleek seals (who eat only seafood, not bread) glide in and out among the boats. Seagulls and cormorants fish here too. The small wood fisherman's chapel at the end of Pier 49 has one stained-glass window, over the door so that it is seen on exiting. It depicts a steering wheel.

HYDE STREET PIER/HISTORIC SHIPS [6]

The Hyde Street Pier at the foot of Hyde, near the cable car turntable, is one of San Francisco's most historically evocative places. The **Maritime Book Store** (775-2665) at the entrance to the pier has an outstanding selection of books and posters associated with ships and the sea and regional guides. You may also obtain the National Park Service's excellent free map of the Golden Gate National Recreation Area here, which is useful if you wish to explore the Presidio or see the redwoods in Muir Woods National Monument across the Golden Gate.

The Hyde Street Pier was built to serve the Sausalito and Berkeley ferries, which ceased operating after the Golden Gate Bridge was built. (Today the Sausalito ferry departs from the Ferry Building at the foot of Market Street; (*see Tour 14*). Eventually the pier became the mooring for a fleet of five historic ships, three of which visitors may board. These historic ships recall the days when San Francisco Bay was an animated scene of sail and steam, and ships both great and small crowded the West Coast's most important port. Scattered along the pier are other exhibits including an ark, a flat-bottomed barge with a cottage built atop it, used as a floating summer house, and the Victorian office of Tubbs Cordage furnished as it was a hundred years ago.

Tied up here is the sidewheel ferry *Eureka*, built in 1890 and once the world's largest passenger ferry. The white-painted *Eureka* was powered by a four-story steam engine and today carries a fleet of historic automobiles and trucks. Nearby is the **C. A. Thayer**, a wood-hull, three-masted schooner built in 1895 to carry lumber from the Pacific Northwest to booming San Francisco. Also tied up here is the hay-scow **Alma**, launched in 1891, a flat-bottomed, shallow-draft workhorse used to carry hay and lumber around the Bay. The ocean-going steam tug **Hercules**, appropriately named, towed sailing ships out to sea. The **Wapama** is a 1915 steam schooner that carried both cargo and passengers.

The steel-hulled, three-masted, square-rigged sailing ship **Balclutha** launched in Glasgow, Scotland in 1886 was named for the ancient Gaelic word for the site of Dumbarton, Scotland, the home of Robert McMillan, her original owner. She made her maiden voyage around Cape Horn to San Francisco and served in the deepwater trade carrying wine and spirits from London, hardware from Antwerp, and coal from Wales. Returning to Europe she carried California wheat. She is a typical British merchant ship of the late Victorian era. After 1899 she flew the Hawaiian flag and transported lumber from Puget Sound to Australia, returning with coal for the locomotives of the Southern Pacific Railroad. From 1902 until 1930, she engaged in the Alaska salmon trade carrying cannery supplies and up to three hundred men north for the fishing season. In 1906 she was renamed *The Star of Alaska*; she made her final voyage for the Alaska Packers Association in 1930, the last

square-rigger in the salmon trade. From 1933 to 1952, she was gaudily painted and used as a showboat; eventually she was laid up on the Sausalito mud flats. In 1954, before she could be sold for scrap, she was purchased by the San Francisco Maritime Museum, which restored her original name and undertook a complete rehabilitation of the historic ship. The local shipping industry and eighteen labor unions participated in the year-long project. She opened as a part of the museum in 1955 painted in her original colors.

The Cannery [7]
2801 Leavenworth, between Beach and Jefferson Streets
1907, William M. Mooser, Sr.; 1968, Joseph Esherick Associates

Illusion is one of architecture's methods. In the rebuilt Cannery, the illusion is that this is an old industrial structure adapted in an *ad hoc* way for shops and restaurants. Its visitor-pleasing courtyards and internal mazes give the sense of unplanned reworkings over time. In reality, however, The Cannery, the brainchild of San Franciscan Leonard V. Martin, is an entirely new reinforced concrete building constructed in 1968 and designed by Joseph Esherick and Associates. It is neatly inserted within the four brick walls of architect William M. Mooser, Sr.'s, California Fruit Canners Association cannery built in 1907.

Escalators take the browser up three levels to an open-air maze of shops, where there are good views of the Bay from the top of the added third floor. On the ground floor is the **Chart House Bar and Restaurant** (474-3476), whose comfortable living-room-like lounge is a part of William Randolph Hearst's artistic plunder. The fine Jacobean oak paneling, mantles, and fancy plaster ceiling from the Long Gallery of Albyns Hall, a 1609 English manor house.

Haslett Warehouse [8]
Hyde Street, between Beach and Jefferson streets
1907–1909, William M. Mooser, Sr.

Across from what was originally the railroad spur that served the peach cannery is the red brick Haslett Warehouse, originally the other half of the cannery complex. Its monumental brick wall faces Victorian Park on Hyde Street. The solid warehouse was built in three stages between 1907 and 1909 and was also designed by William M. Mooser, Sr.

The Haslett Warehouse has been publicly owned since 1963, when it was purchased by the Maritime Museum. Today it is a part of the Golden Gate National Recreation Area. It is the perfect location for a combination National Maritime Museum facing the cable car turntable at Hyde and Beach.

Victorian Park / Hyde Street Cable Car Turntable [9]
Hyde Street, at Beach
1960, Thomas D. Church

The Hyde Street cable car line is the most scenic of the three surviving lines. It ends at a turntable in Victorian Park.

The park was designed by Thomas D. Church in 1960 with a formal arrangement of a double row of benches facing each other and a central flower bed. The landscaping of the 5.6-acre park is kept low so as not to block the sweeping view of the Bay. The **Buena Vista Café** at Beach and Hyde (474-5044), facing the park, is a fine bay-windowed Edwardian commercial-residential building of about 1910. The café is reputed to be the place where Irish Coffee was first served. (Caffeine, alcohol, and butterfat; is there anything more?) This is a fine place for an early morning breakfast; open at 9 A.M. Monday–Friday, and 8 A.M. Saturday and Sunday.

National Maritime Museum / Aquatic Park Casino [10]
Beach Street, at foot of Polk
1939, William M. Mooser, Jr.

Open daily except Monday; free; 556-2904.

At the west end of Victorian Park is the white, streamlined Aquatic Park Casino built in 1939 by the WPA and designed by William M. Mooser, Jr. Since 1951 it has been the home of the Maritime Museum, now part of the GGNRA. The Casino, one of the great Streamline Moderne designs in the West, was designed in imitation of a luxury liner. The rectangular, three-level reinforced structure has semicircular ends. Each level is stepped back giving the appearance of a ship's decks. Porthole windows, steel railings, and cowl ventilators complete the nautical theme.

The building is flanked by bleachers, two streamlined towers intended for public address systems, and two restrooms set far apart. The entire site was landscaped to match the building and a man-made beach was created facing Aquatic Park where there was once a railroad trestle and a polluted bayshore. The complex was designed to accommodate five thousand bathers daily, but the water is too cold and few come. (You will, however, spot some cold-blooded swimmers here from the nearby rowing clubs.) The building is enlivened with WPA art works. Sargent Johnson carved the greenish slate decorations around the entrance and Hilaire Hiler painted the vivid murals depicting undersea life in the lobby.

The Casino was closed for many years until the Maritime Museum was established by Karl Kortum in 1951. The nautical building is filled with ship models, artifacts, and old paintings and photographs which bring alive San Francisco's history as a seaport.

MUNICIPAL PIER/AQUATIC PARK [10]

The construction of the curved, 1,850-foot-long Municipal Pier in Aquatic Park between 1929 and 1934 and the addition of the Casino together make one of the finest waterfront parks in any American city.

Ghirardelli Square [11]

900 North Point Street
1864, architect unknown; 1893–1916,
William M. Mooser, Sr.; 1962–1968,
Wurster, Bernardi and Emmons; John
Matthias; Lawrence Halprin and
Associates

Ghirardelli Square is a San Francisco
landmark in several senses. Its handsome old red brick factory buildings are
an architectural landmark; its fine old
electric sign is a visual landmark; and its
conversion into shops and restaurants
was an economic landmark in the evolution of the postindustrial city. Visitors
are sure to enjoy strolling, shopping in its
sixty quality shops, and dining in one of
its dozen restaurants serving an international array of cuisines.

Domingo Ghirardelli, born in Rapallo,
Italy, came to Gold Rush San Francisco
in 1850 *via* Peru and began the manufacture of chocolate in a shop now in the
Jackson Square Historic District. His
sons expanded the business and in 1893
purchased this then-remote block with
the 1864 Pioneer Woolen Mill, one of the
oldest factories in the West. Around that
old building, placed at an eccentric angle
because it was oriented to the original
shoreline, not the city's street grid, Domingo's sons began the construction of a
model factory. Architect William
Mooser, Sr., father of the designer of the
Aquatic Park Casino, designed the crenellated complex in stages between 1893
and 1916. The buildings were constructed of brick and timber with cast
stone trim. Eventually the buildings
ringed the block, leaving a central lawn
where workers ate lunch when the
weather permitted. The last building in
the complex was the Clock Tower office
building on the corner of North Point
and Larkin, whose ornament was modeled on that of the château at Blois. Its
vestibule has a mosaic of an eagle, the
Ghirardelli trademark, and antique mill-
stones from the old chocolate works
downtown. The great electric sign reading "Ghirardelli" capped the factory in
1926 and is visible to ships entering the
Bay.

Advances in technology made the old
plant obsolete and a modern chocolate
plant was built across the Bay. For a
while it seemed that the historic factory
would be replaced by highrise apartments. William M. Roth, a civic-minded
San Franciscan and heir to the Matson
shipping fortune, bought the block to
prevent its demolition and then cast
about for a new use for it. He decided to
create a shop and restaurant complex. He
added an underground garage, completed the ring of red brick buildings
with new ones designed by Wurster, Bernardi, and Emmons, and created a series
of landscaped terraces designed by Lawrence Halprin and Associates. John Matthias designed the small red-brick
pavilion buildings with the fanciful roofs
in the center of the complex. Thus Ghirardelli Square is a fusion of new *and* old
buildings, not simply the adaptation of
existing structures. The use of two
designers, not just one, avoided the
monotony so prevalent in large new
developments—an innovation later
developers have followed.

To create a focal point for the Square,
sculptor Ruth Asawa was commissioned
to design "Andrea" in 1968, the refresh-
ing fountain of nursing mermaids surrounded by water, lily pads, tortoises,
and dancing frogs. Bill Roth wanted to
preserve even the aroma of the old chocolate works, and while that wasn't possible, some of the old German machinery
was saved and installed in the ground
floor of the Clock Tower building behind
the Ghirardelli Ice Cream Parlor. Built
into the wall are three cacao-bean roas-
ters, belt-driven chocolate mills, giant
mixers, and conching machines.

The most interesting interior in Ghirardelli Square is that of the superb **Mandarin Restaurant** (673-8812), located on
the top floor of the old Woolen Mill. The
old brick-and-timber interior was
retained and enhanced with tile floors

131

and filled with fine Chinese art. For a sweeping overview of the Square and all Fisherman's Wharf, take the elevator or climb to the top of the glass-enclosed stairs of the Chocolate Building in the southwest corner of the Square, near the Gaylord India Restaurant.

Across Larkin from the elegant Ghirardelli Clock Tower is the late-1960s timber **Greenpeace Shop**. The shop and small gallery document the activities of this activist environmentalist group. A few doors down is **872-80 North Point Street**. Behind the Dutch door is a narrow passageway leading to a surprising hidden garden surrounded by art and rug galleries and designers' studios. This lush courtyard is one of the best examples of Northern California's infatuation with plants. Vine-draped decks, porches, and staircases surround what was originally just another back yard, but which here has been transformed into a jungle of greenery with a soothing, trickling fountain. Tucked away here is the **North Point Gallery** (open Tuesday–Saturday, 10 A.M.–6 P.M.), a virtual museum of nineteenth-century California landscape painting, with examples of grand mountain scenery and views of California a century ago. The art shown in this intimate gallery is one of the best windows into the history of the West.

Fort Mason Center ("Fort Culture") / Golden Gate National Recreation Area (GGNRA) Headquarters [12]
GGNRA information, 556-0560

At the foot of Van Ness Avenue, near the entrance to the Municipal Pier, is a narrow stairway that climbs the bluff of Fort Mason, today the headquarters of the Golden Gate National Recreation Area, established in 1972. (There are automobile entrances to Fort Mason at Bay and Franklin streets and another at Laguna and Beach streets that leads to a parking lot.) On this bluff, with its spectacular views of the Bay, Spanish soldiers from the Presidio built a small battery in 1797 which they christened *Batería San*

José. In 1850, Black Point, as the Yankees called it, perhaps because of the dark laurel that grew here, was one of the three important U.S. Army reservations created within San Francisco by President Millard Fillmore. The Army did not immediately occupy the point, so squatters built houses here. In 1863 the squatters were removed and the commanding site was terraced for batteries as part of the system of harbor defenses. Recent archaeological excavations have uncovered part of these Civil War-era batteries. (Eventually, a Rodman cannon from the Smithsonian Institution will be mounted here.) Fort Mason became the headquarters of the commanding general of the U.S. Army in the West during the Indian wars in the interior.

The three large Victorian houses on the wooded bluff, built between 1855 and 1863, are still officers' housing. A cluster of seven Victorian enlisted men's houses built between 1864 and 1891 survives on the west, or inland, side of Franklin Street. Nearby McDowell Hall, built in 1877 as the commandant's residence, is today an Officers Club. The name *Fort Mason* was adopted in 1882 in honor of Colonel Mason, the military governor of California from 1847 to 1849.

In-harbor fortifications were soon obsolete, though Fort Mason remained an administrative and logistical center as the Quartermaster's Depot. Three substantial piers were constructed in 1912, and large warehouses behind them three years later. All were connected with the port's Belt Line Railroad by a tunnel under the bluff. The post saw its peak activity during World War II as a point of embarkation for 1.6 million soldiers who passed through here on their way to Pacific Theater. Today, at Pier 3 East, the Liberty Ship **S.S. *Jeremiah O'Brien*** is moored, the last unaltered Liberty Ship of the 2,751 launched between 1941 and 1945. She serves as a memorial to the men of the U.S. Merchant Marine. Open daily from 9 A.M.–3 P.M.; $2 adults, $3 children, $5 family; 441-3101.

The military was the only institution with the foresight and the power to make public reservations in the Bay Area in 1850. Vast stretches of shoreline including the scenic Marin Headlands and islands such as Alcatraz were reserved for harbor fortifications and slowly developed and landscaped over a century of occupation. But changes in technology and high costs made these in-city installations redundant. Proposals were floated by developers to build on these waterfront sites, but local environmental groups saw these magnificent properties as part of the national heritage and as potential parks for the Bay Area's five million residents and millions of visitors.

The late San Francisco Congressman Philip Burton, one of the most powerful men in Congress and a staunch environmentalist, enthusiastically supported the idea and made this his local monument. Congressman Burton forced the creation of the GGNRA in 1972, which was assembled from a core of historic military lands and buildings no longer needed for defense. Today, the GGNRA is considered one of the nation's most popular national parks. The 1902 hospital in the center of the post is today GGNRA headquarters; the information center stocks maps and brochures; call 556-0560 for information.

To insulate the new urban national park from politics, the independent, nonprofit Fort Mason Foundation was formed to manage the facilities. The Fort Mason Center opened in 1977 and sponsors fairs, festivals, and exhibits. The piers and warehouses at Fort Mason became home to more than fifty nonprofit visual and performing arts, cultural, and environmental organizations. This book can only lead you to this Ali Baba's cave of culture. **The Magic Theater**, 441-8822, is just one of the many treats here. For information write to the Golden Gate National Park Association, Fort Mason, Building 204, SF 94123-1308, or call 556-0693 for information.

One of Fort Mason's most popular features in the San Francisco Zen Center's **Greens restaurant** (771-6222) in Building A, a gourmet vegetarian restaurant with a splendid view of the Golden Gate. Open for lunch daily; dinner Tuesday–Sunday; reservations advised. Also located here is the **Tassajara Bread Bakery**, with baked goods, soups, and sandwiches.

GOLDEN GATE PROMENADE
TO FORT POINT [13]

From the Hyde Street Pier to Fort Point near the Golden Gate Bridge is the 3.5-mile footpath of the Golden Gate Promenade along the scenic, breezy northern shore of San Francisco. The path is especially popular with joggers. It passes through Aquatic Park, Fort Mason, the marina in Gashouse Cove, flat Marina Green, the St. Francis Yacht Club, Crissy Field, the old Coast Guard station in the Presidio, and then along the granite seawall to historic Fort Point begun in 1853 and completed in 1861. Looming above the fort is the south tower of the Golden Gate Bridge (*see Tour 13*).

Russian Hill

URBAN CLIFF DWELLERS

What These Tours Cover

Tour 5A: Russian Hill's Summit and Shingle Cluster

[1] Hyde and Union: Edwardwian Commercial Crossroad

[2] Union and Leavenworth: Post-Fire Apartments

[3] 1101 Green Street

[4] 1000 Block of Green Street

[5] The Summit Apartments

[6] Macondray Lane

[7] Vallejo Street Improvements

[8] Russian Hill Place

[9] The Hermitage

[10] Williams-Polk House

[11] Florence Street Pueblo Revival Group

[12] 1000 Block of Broadway

Tour 5B: Russian Hill's Northern Spur and Lombard Street's Crooked Block

[A] Marine View Apartments

[B] 1100 Block of Filbert / Steepest Paved Street

[C] Alice Marble Tennis Courts / Greenwich Street Stub

[D] Crooked Block / 1000 Block of Lombard

[E] The San Fransciso Art Institute

Preliminaries

Best Way To See Russian Hill

Russian Hill is a quiet residential island in the sky overlooking the historic core of San Francisco. The best way to see it is slowly, on foot, step by step. Large tour buses are barred from its steep streets and it is unlikely that drivers will enjoy negotiating the hill's sharp grades and surprise dead-ends.

With more cable car trackage than any other part of San Francisco, you can combine cable car rides and walks.

Pick almost any route zigzagging across the hill's two summits, looking back frequently as you walk for retrospective views. Climb the landscaped staircases where street grades become too steep for anything but stairs. Pay attention to the abstract patterns created by wooden backstairs and glassed-in sunporches on the backs of so many buildings. Note the penthouses added here and there to exploit the panoramic views and how rooms and bay windows "lean" toward distant views. Peek over, but do not open, garden gates to glimpse down the unexpected front gardens that survive here and there on the hill. Take the time to let the sweeping views from the steep intersections seep in. Above all, do not rush. The hill will open itself only if given time.

Russian Hill is worth a second, evening, stroll once you've become familiar with it in daylight. The views of the downtown's lit-up glass highrises—with the slim Transamerica Pyramid standing away from the mass and the inky blue-black Bay with its necklace of twinkling orange lights and great illuminated suspension bridges—seem all the more brilliant from the dark, abrupt streets of Russian Hill. Russian Hill is safe to walk about in at night, though the sidewalks will seem deserted. The view from the roof deck of the modern addition to the San Francisco Art Institute at 800 Chestnut, at Jones, is splendid. Two blocks downhill, at Columbus and Bay, at the edge of the Fisherman's Wharf district, is **Tower Records**, open until midnight seven days a week, and stocked with the city's largest selection of recordings.

Parking

Russian Hill is best approached by cable car or taxi to its summit. Do not expect to find a parking space here because there aren't any; parking is limited to two hours between 8 A.M. and 9 P.M. for those without neighborhood residential parking stickers.

Transportation

The 41 Union electric trolley-bus links Russian Hill with North Beach, Chinatown, and then the Financial District and Embarcadero Center. Going west, the 41 Union line passes between the north slope of posh Pacific Heights and the well-to-do Marina District and serves the lively restaurant and shopping district along Union Street.

Restaurants, Cafés, and Bars

There are a few restaurants sprinkled on Russian Hill, particularly down Hyde from Union Street. They generally serve a neighborhood clientele.

Le Petit Café, 2164 Larkin, at Green is a neighborhood oasis. Monday–Saturday, 7:30 A.M.–10 P.M.; Sunday 8:30 A.M.–3 P.M.

Introduction: Urban Cliff Dwellers

Russian Hill appears as a name on U.S. Coast Survey maps as early as 1859. The Russian Hill Neighbors Association defines the neighborhood as the thirty-four blocks bounded by Taylor, Pacific, Polk, and Francisco streets. The hill merges with Nob Hill to the south at Pacific Avenue. Its summit is at Vallejo Street between Taylor and Jones, with an elevation of 294 feet. To the northwest, at Hyde and Lombard, is the hill's northwest spur with dramatic views of the north Bay and the Golden Gate.

In 1850 minister Bayard Taylor describe a San Francisco winter seen from undeveloped Russian Hill: "When the floating gauze of mist had cleared off the water, the sky was without a cloud for the remainder of the day, and of a fresh, tender blue, which was exquisite relief to the pale green of the hills." Taylor took to climbing the hill "just in the rear of the town" from where the harbor, the strait into San Pablo Bay, the Golden Gate, and the horizon of the Pacific could be seen.

On the top of the hill are the graves of several Russians, who came out in the service of the Russian [fur trapping] company, each *surmounted with a black cross, bearing an inscription in their language. All this ground, however, has been surveyed, staked into lots, and sold, and at the same rate of growth the city will not be long in climbing the hill and disturbing the rest of the Muscovites.*

Years ago, excavations for retaining walls near Jones and Vallejo uncovered some unidentified graves that might have been those of the "Muscovites."

Jasper O'Farrell's rigid gridiron of blocks was projected over the abrupt hill creating some streets too steep to pave, which end in stairways. (The steepest paved street in San Francisco is on the downtown side of Russian Hill, the 1100 block of Filbert between Leavenworth and Hyde streets.) Old photographs show sturdy, well-maintained fences guarding Russian Hill's unbuilt lots from the encroachment of squatters. No public reservations for open land or parks were provided for in the city survey of Russian Hill; the city has had to buy sites over time for public needs. Ina Coolbrith Park at Taylor and Vallejo streets was bought by the city in 1858 for a school site; a schoolhouse stood there from 1864 to 1877. The green summit block bounded by Hyde, Larkin, Greenwich, and Lombard, today the Alice Marble Tennis Courts, was a reservoir property of the private Spring Valley Water Company acquired by the municipality in 1930.

Houses were built all around the hill before development crept up its slopes. Not until the first transit line ascended the hill in 1880, the Presidio & Ferries Railroad's cable line on Union Street, did the summit of the hill become popular as a place to live. The cable line on Mason Street was not built by the Ferries and Cliff House Railway until 1888. The dramatic north-south Hyde Street cable line that descends to Victorian Park opened as an extension of the California Street Cable Railroad as late as 1891.

Russian Hill's initial population was not as wealthy as that on Nob Hill's

Copyright 1989 William Walters

WILLIAM
WALTERS

Marine View Apartments, at the southeast corner of Hyde and Filbert Streets, was built in 1912 to designs by Edward E. Young. This bay-windowed Edwardian apartment building shows how the Victorian neighborhoods burned in 1906 were rebuilt with more, if smaller, apartments and flats.

summit, or later in Pacific Heights. Houses much like those built anywhere else in the Victorian city popped up on its slopes. A few houses had large gardens and fine views of the growing city and the crowded harbor below.

A unique cluster of buildings and gardens accumulated on the summit block bounded by Taylor, Broadway, Jones, and Vallejo streets. At the head of the street, where a handsome concrete balustrade and cliff-edge park are today, the Rev. Joseph Worcester built a one-story redwood and shingle cottage in 1890 that looked down on the city. Worcester was a Swedenborgian minister from Massachusetts with a mystic love of nature. His deliberately simple cottage with its exposed wood introduced a new aesthetic and philosophy to over-decorated Victorian San Francisco. Influ-

enced by the Arts and Crafts Movement, some houses and interiors such as Worcester's strove to look "natural." His influential cottage was demolished for a highrise that was never built. (The fine Church of the New Jerusalem that he commissioned from A. Page Brown in 1895 is perfectly preserved at 2107 Lyon, at Washington Street, in Pacific Heights.)

The Marshall houses and the Worcester cottage were joined by other brown-shingled houses and flats built over the years by Horatio P. Livermore, who owned much of the block at the Vallejo summit. Livermore and other Russian Hill dwellers commissioned some of San Francisco's best designers to build artistic houses here, set behind gardens under what grew to become tall trees.

But the block or two of Russian Hill featured here and in architectural histories (and only partially visible from the sidewalk) are not really the most important phase of Russian Hill's development. It is the post-1906 rebuilding that is the stuff of contemporary Russian Hill. And it is too easily overlooked, for extraordinary buildings do not make a city; the texture of its "ordinary ones," the buildings most people live in and use, count most. In place of the large single-family houses that had covered most of the slopes of Nob and Russian hills, apartment houses serving many singles and couples living near the office and retail jobs downtown were built between 1906 and the 1920s. This was the golden age for the Russian Hill of today. Most of these buildings were two to four stories high. Later there was a small eruption of isolated 1920s "Spanish" and 1930s Art Deco concrete highrises. In the 1960s and 1970s much larger and more disruptive residential highrises were built, until a forty-foot height limit was imposed in 1974.

Pre-1974 city planning permitted tall buildings on the tops of hills to "define" them and to preserve views from the slopes. Along Green Street on the summit of Russian Hill, and Jones Street atop Nob Hill, very large highrises sprouted. They are the last of their kind to be built, for masses of such buildings threatened to overwhelm the neighborhood. Russian Hill residents and property owners, better educated than most and familiar with the power of city zoning, pressured the city to impose a reasonable height limit that would allow for intensive multiunit development without turning the hill into canyons of skyscrapers. Russian Hill's active citizens spearheaded the conservation of San Francisco's neighborhoods and traditional housing stock through height limits.

Tour 5A: Russian Hill's Summit and Shingle Cluster

HYDE AND UNION: EDWARDIAN COMMERCIAL CROSSROAD [1]

The surviving Hyde Street cable line was built in 1891 as an extension of the California Street Cable Railroad. It was built to link Russian Hill residents with the Union Square retail district, not to serve Fisherman's Wharf and Aquatic Park, its current pole of attraction. Because this cable line was built so late and cut a crosstown path over the older east-west cable lines, the Hyde Street grip, the man who operates the lever that holds or releases the moving cable, had to drop his cable more than any other gripman. Where transit lines crossed, as at Hyde and Union, corner buildings (allowed to cover 100 percent of their lot—inside lots had to leave back yards) were built with commercial uses on their ground floors and affordable apartments on their second, third, or fourth floors. At Hyde and Union this pattern survives.

The commercial establishments clustered here, from laundries to ice cream places to restaurants and shops, serve a local clientele. Today the Union and Hyde intersection is insulated by congestion. San Franciscans do not drive here because there is no place to park; tourists pass through it on the packed cable cars without daring to get off. Thus locals have this intersection to themselves, more or less.

To literary historian Don Herron, **29 Russell Place**, a gabled cottage on a sidestreet near Hyde and Union, is "one of the most important literary sites in post–World War II America." It was here, in 1952, in Neal and Carolyn Cassady's attic study, that Jack Kerouac drafted three of his major works, *On The Road*, *Visions of Cody*, and *Doctor Sax*. (Carolyn Cassady described this *ménage à trois* in her 1976 memoir *Heart Beat*.)

These reconstruction-era buildings of two to four stories are the basic fabric of Russian Hill. The even rhythm of their bays pulls all the buildings together. The row of three-story, bay-windowed flats that step up from the southeast corner of Union and Leavenworth are a classic example of how fine post-1906 reconstruction was. These are outstanding blocks of great regional architecture. Rising from the summit a block away is a tall, bleak concrete highrise from the boom of the 1960s.

The intersection of Union and Leavenworth should be carefully "danced." Look down all the corners of the intersection from the sidewalk. (Pedestrians have the right of way at these crosswalks, but some drivers do not know this, or do not obey it. Be careful.) The views here are exceptional and give you a taste of why apartments on Russian Hill are sought after. To the north down Leavenworth is Alcatraz and wooded, pyramidal Angel Island State Park behind it. To the east is the summit of Telegraph Hill with Coit Tower, the statue of Christopher Columbus, and Esherick, Homsey, Dodge & Davis' buff-colored Garfield Grammar School at the head of Filbert Street. The city has historically placed parks on hilltops, and schools near parks, if possible. Here the classic pattern of San Francisco's white and green development is displayed dramatically.

1101 Green Street [3]
1930, H. C. Baumann

At the southwest corner of Leavenworth and Green rises the white shaft of 1101 Green, a twenty-story reinforced concrete apartment building designed by the prolific H. C. Baumann and completed in 1930. The elegant tower has a heavily ornamented neo-Churrigueresque entrance and lobby on the high corner. Shallow bay windows project from the skyscraper. Its rooftop utility penthouse is styled to complete the building's profile. Generous wall space, painted a light-reflecting white, makes even such a huge building blend with the city like one crystal longer than the others in a cluster. The garage entrance is minimalized in the design, tucked downhill, and covered with an opaque (not a see-through) door. In every way the design of this building is superior to the residential highrises that came after it in the 1960s and 1970s.

Down Green to the west is **1111-33 Green**, a complex of Tudor-gabled apartments built atop a high retaining wall. The walls here show how drastically the hill was graded.

1000 BLOCK OF GREEN STREET [4]

The 1000 block of Green Street between Leavenworth and Jones has at its heart a cluster of eleven setback houses, flats, and apartments with fenced front gardens, each building in a different architectural style. Street trees further the garden enclave feeling. The structures are set like small treasures between the great bookends of the flanking concrete highrises. The sudden contrast in the scale of buildings here makes this a very American space; a place developed by individuals each with varied, clashing imaginations.

Standing in the shadow of its concrete highrise neighbor, the Tudor Revival former Engine House No. 31 at **1088 Green Street** was built in 1908 and designed by City Architect Newton J. Tharp. It was deactivated in 1952 and bought by philanthropist Louise S. Davies in 1958. She restored it and permits the Russian Hill Neighbors and the St. Andrews Society to use it for meetings. In 1978 she donated it to the National Trust for Historic Preservation.

The most curious building on the block is the **Feusier Octagon House** at 1067 Green Street built about 1859 and given an added story and a mansard roof

139

Bird's-eye view of the summit of Russian Hill.

Copyright 1989 John Tomlinson

with a cupola in the 1870s or early 1880s by produce merchant Louis Feusier. It has a high basement and is built out of an early concretelike material. Its form follows that suggested by phrenologist Orson S. Fowler in his *A Home for All*, a book touting octagonal houses as healthier to live in. (Another frame octagonal house at 2645 Gough, near Union Street's shops, has been preserved by the Colonial Dames of America; open to the public on the first Sunday and the second and fourth Thursdays of each month, from 1 P.M. to 4 P.M.; free; 441-7512.)

Next door, **1055 Green Street** was built about 1866 and then completely reworked by Julia Morgan in 1915 for importer and merchant David Atkins. Morgan transformed a simple Italianate house into a stucco Beaux Arts villa with its entrance recessed under the *piano nobile* with its arcade of windows. The house sits in a large garden. The garage visible down the driveway echoes the façade.

The O'Brien House at **1045 Green Street** to the east was built about 1867 in the Italianate style and remodeled with brown shingles and a cupola in the Craftsman style. It looks like it was originally a firehouse, but it was always a dwelling. The house was bought by John O'Brien, an employment and real estate agent in 1875. His son, a postman, Charles W. O'Brien, added the shingles and the turret between 1910 and 1916. A side bay window was added later.

At **1039-43 Green Street**, behind a vintage iron fence, is a three-story, three-flat Italianate building with an unusual exterior staircase. It was built in 1885 and designed by the often showier Newsom Brothers, Samuel and Joseph Cather. Hidden behind and above its ivy-covered garage is **1011 Green Street**, best seen from across the street. This interesting house was designed by Ernest Coxhead around 1905. It creates privacy for itself with its garage and marked setback. Its brown shingles are

elegantly complemented with black-painted trim. An iron bracket braces its brick chimney.

At **1030 Green Street**, across the street and behind a brick wall and a green hedge, is a fine Pueblo Revival house designed in 1913 by Oscar Haupt. This two-story stucco residence has a square turret and a recessed side entrance with a Tuscan arcade. **1040 Green Street** was built in 1912 to designs by Llewellyn B. Dutton. It combines Colonial Revival features with a Mission Revival-style stucco exterior. The detached garage was added in 1953.

The jewel of the block is **1050 Green Street**, the George A. Bos Apartments, designed by Lewis P. Hobart in 1913. This five-story, Classical Revival stuccoed apartment building is one of the most elegant small buildings in San Francisco. Hobart studied at the École des Beaux Arts in Paris between 1901 and 1903. Here he brought a Parisian feel to a San Francisco apartment house. Its black wrought-iron front door is beautiful at night when lighted from behind. The simple garden, with its formal *allée* of rose "trees," is startlingly effective in creating an aristocratic air. The building backs up on Macondray Lane at the summit's edge and enjoys fine views to the north.

The Summit Apartments [5]
999 Green Street
1965, Claude Oakland & Associates

Looming up at the southeast corner of Jones Street is this 1965 residential high-rise designed by Claude Oakland & Associates and built for Joseph Eichler, the builder of much of the middle-class stucco housing in the Sunset District in the 1940s and 1950s. Eichler reserved a two-story penthouse atop the spectacularly placed tower for himself. In the 1960s, high-art buildings strove, and succeeded, in setting themselves apart from their urban context. The Summit Apartments is a sculpted piece of futuristic design, quite successful if contemplated in the abstract. It stands on its corner and presents a vast, blank, multistoried parking structure to the neighborhood.

The highrise's design was so ambitious that it created a space with a fine view but no use. Atop the garage is a dead "park space" underneath the tower visible from the stairs at the end of Russian Hill Place. The design of the glass tower—if glass towers are appropriate in San Francisco, an arguable proposition—is very well done. The tower has the air of a moment perhaps best called "Brasilia Modern." Beyond the Summit Apartments, a rocky outcropping pinches Green Street. In the *cul-de-sac* at the end of this block of Green, there are box-seat views of the downtown.

MACONDRAY LANE [6]

Between Jones and Taylor streets, below Green Street, is Macondray Lane, a landscaped pedestrian lane that ends in steep stairs lined with mostly ordinary but pleasing houses, flats, and apartments. Four of its buildings survived the 1906 fire, and almost all the rest were built in the next three years during the reconstruction boom.

The Taylor Street end of Macondray was the furthest westward extent of Italian-American North Beach about the turn of the century. Many who lived here were natives of Genoa. Local painter Giuseppe Cadenasso, Genoa-born, who rose from a waiter to head of the Mills College art department, was the artistic luminary among early residents. Today Macondray Lane has a varied white-collar population. The lane's geography, if not its population, has been memorialized in Armistead Maupin's slice-of-gay-life *Tales of the City* as "Barbary Lane."

At the corner of Macondray Lane and Jones is **1950 Jones Street**, an apartment building built in 1907–1908 by contractor Otto A. Craemer. The typical Edwardian shape is clothed in natural brown shingles, making a deliberately

Russian Hill building. The building has polygonal bay windows at its corners and bay windows along its two sides. It steps down the Jones Street slope such that the second floor of the uphill half connects with the third floor of the downhill section. The building has a recessed entry capped by a great curving broken pediment.

At **68 Macondray Lane** is Charles Bovine's house, built in 1908 and designed by Louis Mastropasqua. Bovine came from Italy in 1884 and became a maker of cut glass and curved glass for curved bay windows such as the one on his own house. The house has been converted into several apartments and has lost the small square stained-glass windows that flanked the bay window on the upper floors.

Vallejo Street Improvements [7]
1915, Willis Polk & Company

At Jones and Vallejo streets are the elegant concrete retaining wall, automobile ramps, and sidewalks of the Vallejo Street improvements designed by Willis Polk & Company in 1915. These high-style improvements were paid for not by the city but by the adjoining property owners, organized by Horatio P. Livermore, who owned several lots here and who built the buildings flanking the ramps. To the north are the four townhouses on Russian Hill Place designed by Willis Polk. To the south are **1085 Vallejo, 1740**, and **1742 Jones Street**, three houses designed by Charles W. McCall in 1915. This block of Vallejo is narrow and passes between high embankments leading to a balustraded turnaround. Steps embowered in greenery zigzag down the eastern escarpment of the hill to Taylor Street.

RUSSIAN HILL PLACE [8]

Off this summit block of Vallejo are privately built Russian Hill Place and Florence Street, two quiet *cul-de-sacs* sheltering sophisticated architecture.

Norman Livermore engaged Willis Polk to design the row of four Mediterranean villas along **Russian Hill Place** backing up on Jones Street in 1915. In 1926 the Livermores deeded brick-paved Russian Hill Place to the city as a public right of way. Russian Hill Place ends in a short staircase with a view through the bottom of the Summit Apartments.

The Hermitage [9]
1020 Vallejo Street
1982, Esherick, Homsey, Dodge & Davis

Though the Livermore family began to sell its properties on Russian Hill in the 1950s, subsequent owners have been careful to preserve the buildings and gardens here and to change them minimally. The last Livermore family development was Putnam Livermore's construction of the contexturalist, brown-shingled Hermitage at 1020 Vallejo designed by Esherick, Homsey, Dodge & Davis and built in 1980–1982. This four-story, seven-unit condominium building adopts as its ornament the square-section urns of Willis Polk's 1915 balustrade. It sits on the edge of the cliff and looks down on the city. This was the site of Joseph Worcester's shingled cottage with its simple redwood interiors which introduced the Craftsman aesthetic to Russian Hill and San Francisco. The view from the balustraded turnaround here is splendid.

Williams-Polk House [10]
1013-19 Vallejo Street
1892, Polk & Polk

Near the head of the Vallejo Street staircase, behind a fence and embowered in trees, is the brown-shingled Williams-Polk House. It is one of Russian Hill's distinctive cliff-dwellings. This duplex was built in 1892 by Mrs. Virgil Williams and designed by Polk & Polk. Dora Norton Williams was the widow of painter and teacher Virgil Williams, one of the founders of the School of Design, now the San Francisco Art Institute. Mrs. Williams lived in the western half

of the house, Polk in the eastern half. This twin-gabled house was Polk's first "rustic" design. Bands of simple, white-painted casement windows stretch across the two stories of the building at a uniform height concealing a three-foot difference in the floor levels in the two separate units. From the Vallejo stairs, two stories and an attic with a windowed gable are visible; the back of the building, which faces a panoramic view of the downtown, has six stories and is a loose piling of rooms with balconies and terraces looking like a random accumulation of hillside shacks. (A good distant view of this brown shingle jumble can be had from the northeast corner of Taylor and Jackson streets.) Its interior used natural unvarnished redwood and is cabinlike and homey. California architectural historians revere this building, though to the layman it may not look all that special.

In 1918 Edward A. Morphy recounted the possibly apocryphal story that architect Willis Polk and artist Emil Carlsen, while rambling the hill one night, came across an unoccupied house owned by Horatio P. Livermore. The next morning Polk went to Livermore's office on Sansome Street and secured the house rent-free in exchange for Polk's fixing it up. Polk did. As Morphy put it, "there upon ensued the famous 'roseleaf parties' that lent a new and wholly original distinction to Russian Hill and proved a lodestone to the artists and scribblers and other geniuses of sorts...." This coterie of artists, writers, and singers of the day slummed in the "Terrific Pacific" Street bars down the hill.

Mrs. Livermore, who lived in the East Bay on a large estate, heard about "the fashionable eminence the erstwhile despised Livermore house on Russian Hill had acquired. She came and was enchanted. Mrs. Livermore went to her husband and told him that his house on Russian Hill was the loveliest place in San Francisco and that she had got to live in it at once. Wherefore Willis Polk,

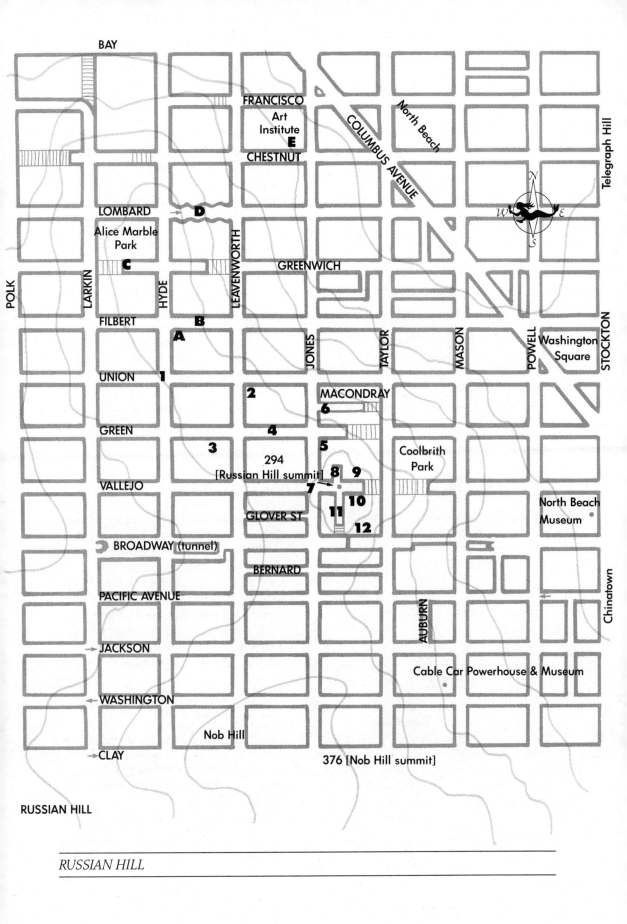

BAY

FRANCISCO
Art
Institute
E
CHESTNUT

COLUMBUS AVENUE

North Beach

Telegraph Hill

LOMBARD
D

Alice Marble
Park

C

GREENWICH

POLK

LARKIN

HYDE

LEAVENWORTH

JONES

TAYLOR

MASON

POWELL

STOCKTON

Washington
Square

FILBERT
B
A

UNION **1**

2

MACONDRAY
6

GREEN

4

3

5

Coolbrith
Park

294
[Russian Hill summit] **8** **9**

VALLEJO

7

10

GLOVER ST

11

North Beach
Museum

12

BROADWAY (tunnel)

BERNARD

Chinatown

PACIFIC AVENUE

AUBURN

JACKSON

WASHINGTON

Cable Car Powerhouse & Museum

Nob Hill

CLAY

376 [Nob Hill summit]

RUSSIAN HILL

RUSSIAN HILL

having no lease, had to get out." This was perhaps the first time artists gentrified a neighborhood in San Francisco.

FLORENCE STREET PUEBLO
REVIVAL GROUP [11]

Starting in 1913, Horatio P. Livermore began the construction of a row of stucco Pueblo Revival style houses along one-block-long **Florence Street**, between Vallejo and Broadway. They form a remarkable stucco cluster, a quiet *cul-de-sac* garnished with meticulous landscaping.

The interesting cubic Pueblo Revival design at **1071 Vallejo Street**, southwest corner of Florence, was designed in 1912 by Charles F. Whittlesey for Norman Livermore. It is a U-shaped, two-flat building with an entrance court facing Florence Street. The building has a bold, manipulated design. In 1947 it lost its rough pebble dash stucco to a smoother finish. In 1913 Whittlesey designed **37 Florence Street** for the same client. This stucco design has a fine door and entry window and a graceful curve worked into the design of its second story window. The carefully trained landscaping in front of these houses is meticulously kept.

Across the street and behind a wall is the Livermore house built in 1857 and much enlarged and enhanced over time. The brown-shingled house originally had its address on Vallejo but is today **40 Florence Street**.

1000 BLOCK OF BROADWAY [12]

Florence Street ends in a steep staircase leading down to Broadway; the view of the downtown's highrises is fine from here. Most of Broadway's traffic passes under the hill in a tunnel built in 1952; up here, it is a dead-end street. Cross Broadway at the retaining wall to the opposite side of the street to look back north. The sidewalk here is so steep it is partly stepped. The high concrete retaining wall built in the early 1890s when Broadway was graded served as a buffer for the summit block when the fire swept much of the city in 1906.

Clearly visible and surrounded by trees and greenery is **1020 Broadway**, a superb brown-shingled Craftsman house designed by Albert Farr in 1909 for Ethel Parker Roeder. It was built with another house, **1629 Taylor**, around the corner, for a brother and sister who had grown up in their grandparents' house on the corner lot; that house was demolished for a large garden when the Farr houses were finished. Because it is so visible from across Broadway, this house is worth studying. It is very modern, a real break from Victorian design.

Behind the noble old oak tree to the left is **1032 Broadway**, the Atkinson House, built in 1853, added to about 1860, and remodeled about 1893 by Willis Polk. It is an E-shaped Italianate house with long, narrow windows and bracketed gables built around an ancient oak and set in a fine garden designed by Bruce Porter in 1894. The Atkinson House is the oldest and most intact house on Vallejo summit. At some point it was stuccoed without losing its ornamentation. Catherine Atkinson, the original owner's daughter, conducted something of a salon here in the 1890s; here her cousin Gelett Burgess and the rest of *Les Jeunes* discussed art and gossiped. The roomy old house was later converted into a private school and is today occupied by law offices.

Tour 5B: Russian Hill's Northern Spur and Lombard Street's Crooked Block

Marine View Apartments [A]
2054 Hyde Street, southeast corner of Filbert
1912, Edward E. Young

The fine four-story, round bay-windowed Edwardian Marine View Apartments stands on a fine light yellowish brick veneer base. Its three-quarter circle corner bay windows on the upper floor maximize the dramatic views up and down the steep streets by permitting the residents to step "outside" the envelope of the building. The great cylinder of corner bays makes the building turn its corner most satisfactorily. Curved bays are mixed with slant-sided bays to animate the façade. A welcoming vestibule with a fine beveled glass door and a wood-paneled lobby show the great care Edwardian architects took in the transition from the sidewalk to the apartments.

1100 BLOCK OF FILBERT STREET / STEEPEST PAVED STREET [B]

This precipitous block of Filbert Street has a grade of 31.5 percent and is the steepest paved street in San Francisco. Its sidewalks become shallow steps.

ALICE MARBLE TENNIS COURTS/ GREENWICH STREET STUB [C]

The block of Green bounded by Hyde, Larkin, Lombard, and Greenwich streets was the site of a Spring Valley Water Company reservoir and became municipal property when the city bought the water company in 1930. It has been planted with cypress and other wind-resistant trees and provides the summit of the hill with its largest park. For the walker, the special experience here is walking into the stub end of Greenwich Street, at Hyde, along the south edge of the park, turning around, and walking back to Hyde. As you return east, up the slight hump in the road, Coit Tower atop Telegraph Hill seems to grow up out of the ground. The hilltop-to-hilltop view is remarkable.

The summit blocks of Hyde are lined with large apartment buildings built before the imposition of height limits.

The slim **View Tower at 2238 Hyde Street**, between Greenwich and Lombard streets, is a sixteen-story, bay-windowed steel-frame sliver built in 1927 on a standard house lot. It rises out of the middle of its block like a mathematical model of maximum floor-area ratio. Such a building could not be built today.

Crooked Block/1000 Block of Lombard [D]

The 1000 block of Lombard Street, between Hyde and Leavenworth, is nicknamed "the crookedest street in the world." It has eight switchbacks in its one-block descent. A little-used cobbled street with a 27 percent grade until 1922, the corkscrew design was installed by the city as a way of making the street accessible to automobiles. Carl Henry, the founder of the Owl Drug Co., who owned lots on the block, was the first to propose the design. City engineer Clyde Healy designed the road with a 16 percent grade. The municipality paid for the grading and the paving and the lot owners facing the block paid for the fancier-than-usual brick steps and plantings and agreed to pay for the garden maintenance. The street achieved its purpose of making the lots accessible, thus increasing their value.

The crookedest street suffers from overpopularity. Because it *is*, as an advertisement could for once say honestly, "a unique driving experience," it attracts far too much traffic. It has turned out to be a mistake to promote a major tourist attraction in the middle of a residential area. And in this case the impact is on the *opposite* slope of the hill where summer traffic backs up on Lombard, while cars overheat and frequently catch fire. Because the street is a public way maintained by public funds, there is principled objection to closing it or restricting its use. Scenic it is, sensible it is not.

When looking at the street, be sure to look at the buildings that define it as well. Most are stucco flats and apartments with clean, modern lines built since the 1940s. While none is outstanding individually, as a group they make a distinctive block that can only be San Franciscan.

Rarely noticed across the street from the head of the crooked block is the palatial bulk of **1100 Lombard Street**, northwest corner of Hyde, Willis Polk's Fannie Osborne Stevenson house of 1900. Much added onto and adapted over time, this rambling house was built for Robert Louis Stevenson's widow. Remembering Italy, California architects looked to the Mediterranean in their stucco buildings at the turn of the century.

The San Francisco Art Institute [E]
800 Chestnut Street, at Jones
1926, Bakewell and Brown; 1969, Paffard Keatinge Clay, addition
Gallery information: 441-2787

One institution clinging to the side of the hill at Chestnut and Jones continues to draw artists and art students to Russian Hill. The San Francisco Art Institute is well worth seeing and makes a perfect conclusion to an exploration of the hill. The school's very fine concrete "monastery" with a tower was built in 1926 by Bakewell and Brown. A high wall sets off the school from the street. Inside an intimate courtyard hangs student work, often of real interest. A modern concrete addition in 1969 by Paffard Keatinge Clay has a rooftop deck with a superb view.

The San Francisco Art Institute was established in 1871; in 1893 Edward F. Searles gave it the gingerbread castle of the Mark Hopkins House atop Nob Hill where the Mark Hopkins Hotel stands today. (This was the first time a great San Francisco house was given to a philanthropic purpose.) In the 1906 fire, that house was destroyed and the school built a temporary frame building on the site. It then sold the corner to the builder of the Mark Hopkins Hotel, taking the money to buy a lot and erect the new school on Russian Hill. Here master San

Francisco architects Bakewell & Brown designed the working art school of studio spaces, a library, offices, and galleries around a courtyard and a tower. The result is one of the finest Spanish Colonial Revival style buildings in San Francisco. There is a 1931 Diego Rivera mural in the Rivera Gallery showing the artist (with his ample backside to the viewer) painting a mural in honor of the American workman.

The Art Institute presents art exhibits in its two galleries. The utility pole in front of the entrance to the Art Institute is a good place to check for flyers announcing events that can't afford to advertise. The roof deck of the 1969 addition is the perfect place to rest and look out over the city and the Bay.

Nob Hill

THE ENDURING IMPRINT OF THE RAILROAD AND SILVER BARONS

What This Tour Covers

[1] California and Powell Cable Car Transfer Point / View of San Francisco-Oakland Bay Bridge

[2] University Club

[3] The Stanford Court Hotel / Site of Stanford Mansion

[4] The Mark Hopkins Hotel / Site of the Hopkins Mansion

[5] Mason Street Townhouse Row / Morsehead Apartments / 1021 California Street

[6] Pacific-Union Club / Flood Mansion

[7] The Fairmont Hotel and Tower

[8] View from Sacramento and Mason Streets

[9] 1100 Block of Sacramento Street (1150 Sacramento Street / The Nob Hill Community Apartments / 1172 Sacramento Street / 1190 Sacramento Street)

[10] Huntington Park / Site of the Colton Mansion

[11] Huntington Hotel

[12] California Masonic Memorial Temple / Masonic Museum

[13] Grace Episcopal Cathedral and Close / Site of the Crocker Mansions

[14] 1100 Block of Taylor Street

[15] 1200 Block of Taylor Street / Site of First Cable Car Line

[16] 75 Pleasant Street

[17] 1200 Block of Sacramento Street / Chambord Apartments

[18] Nob Hill Summit

[19] Sacramento Street / Western Slope of Nob Hill / Leroy Place and Golden Court / Leavenworth and Sacramento Streets

[20] Coronado Apartments

[21] Polk Street

150

Preliminaries

Best Times To Do This Tour

Grace Cathedral is open 7 A.M.–6 P.M., Saturdays 8 A.M.–6 P.M. Free tours of the cathedral are given Monday to Friday, 1–3 P.M., Saturday, 11:30 A.M.–1:30 P.M., Sunday, 12:15–2 P.M. A magnificent Holy Eucharist and choral service is celebrated Sundays at 11 A.M. with a coffee hour afterwards that permits you to mingle with San Franciscans. Evening prayer is offered daily in the Chapel of Grace at 5:15 P.M. with a choral service, Evensong, on Thursdays. Carillon recitals are at 3 P.M. on Sunday and 5 P.M. Wednesday and Friday; fine concerts are held frequently. Call 776-6611 for information.

The ideal way to begin this walk is with breakfast at the **Big Four Restaurant and Bar** in the Huntington Hotel at California at Taylor streets (7–9:30 A.M. weekdays; brunch weekends from 9 A.M.–3 P.M.; 771-1140). The Big Four is a virtual museum of railroad and silver baron memorabilia.

Parking

City-owned St. Mary's Square Garage, Kearny between Pine and California, is the least expensive; hop the California cable car three steep blocks uphill to Powell. The Fairmont Garage is at Powell, near California, where this tour begins. The Crocker Garage is on California, between Mason and Taylor at the crest of the hill; there is also a garage under the Masonic Auditorium at California and Taylor across the street from Grace Cathedral.

Transportation

All cable lines cross at Powell and California. The 1 California electric trolley

Copyright 1989 William Walters

View of Huntington Park, donated in 1915, and previously the site of the Colton, later Huntington, Mansion that burned in 1906. To the north is the 1100 block of Sacramento Street with residential highrises and a two-story Edwardian building remodeled in 1968 by Ted Moulton as a French-style townhouse.

goes up Sacramento Street to Powell from the Financial District and continues up to the crest of the hill and down to Polk Street.

Restaurants, Cafés, and Bars

The **Vienna Coffee House** in the Hotel Mark Hopkins makes its own breakfast pastries. Cocktails at the **Top of the Mark** (392-3434), entrance on California Street, is a local tradition; open 4 P.M. to 2 A.M.; Sunday buffet, 11 A.M.–3 P.M. **L'Etoile** (771-1529) in the Huntington Hotel, is a most sophisticated watering hole and a fine French restaurant. **Vanessi's** Italian restaurant (771-2422) at California and Jones is less pricey and good. **Le Club** (771-5400) in the Clay-Jones at Clay and Jones streets, serves fine French cuisine. One of San Francisco's institutions is the **Venetian Room** (772-5163) at the Fairmont, a supper club opened in 1947 featuring famous entertainers in an intimate setting. The **Cirque Bar** (772-5101) in the Fairmont with its Art Deco circus murals opened in 1934 and has recently been restored.

Polk Street, at the western foot of the hill, has many moderately-priced restaurants and one lunch-time jewel, **Swan Oyster Depot** (673-1101), serving the best cold seafood and hot clam chowder in San Francisco at its old marble counter; a tradition since 1907. **Victor's Daughter's Restaurant** (885-1660) at 1411 Polk, near Pine, serves some of the best pizza and calzone in the city and feels very real. The **Hunan Shaolin** (771-6888), 1150 Polk near Sutter, is good for peppery Hunan cooking.

Introduction: The Enduring Imprint of the Railroad and Silver Barons

In a city of hills, Nob Hill is the most famous. It rises 338 feet above sea level and looms over the Financial District the way a baron's castle looks down on a village. It is one of the few places in San Francisco that is a part of every American's mental geography.

Three waves of development have swept over this steep hill. The first saw the construction of ordinary frame houses on the sandy, hard-to-climb hill. Before the cable car, the rich preferred level streets.

Nob Hill, then known as the California Street hill, was sprinkled with modest houses on small lots, one of which was to attain a curious fame. There were some early fancy houses on the hill: in the late 1850s, William Walton, a wealthy merchant, built a grand house at Taylor and Washington streets, William T. Coleman of Vigilante fame built what contemporaries described as a Roman villa in a walled garden, and Senator George Hearst, father of the mining and publishing magnate, built a "Spanish" palace of white stucco on the hill.

The invention of the cable car in 1871—and the emergence of great railroad and silver mining fortunes—led to a second wave of building on the hill. Andrew Hallidie's invention conquered the steep hills and made their summits choice real estate rather than hard-of-access backwaters. In 1876 the city granted a franchise to the California Street Cable Railroad and service began in 1878. Among the early investors in the line was Leland Stanford of the Central (later Southern) Pacific Railroad. *The San Francisco Real Estate Circular* predicted in 1876 that:

> *The wire-cable mode of propelling street cars being susceptible of use on the very steepest of hills, where horses could not possibly*

be used, will prove ultimately to be one of the most valuable aids to increase of San Francisco real estate values ever devised. Much of the most beautiful real estate in this county is situated on the highest hills.... It will ... in future, be possible to have a residence on the steepest side-hills, commanding panoramic views, and still be in a place that will be quickly, easily, and cheaply accessible.

Leland Stanford bought up all the parcels on the block bounded by California, Powell, Pine, and Mason streets, kept the downtown-facing half of the block for himself, and sold the uphill half to his partner Mark Hopkins. Together they built the formidable granite retaining wall on the Powell, Pine, and Mason streets sides of the block with Sierra granite from the railroad's quarry at Rocklin. (The granite retaining walls, along with the reconstructed Flood Mansion, are all that remain of the grand Nob Hill houses.) The third member of the railroad's Big Four, Charles Crocker, bought up all but one elusive lot on the block bounded by California, Taylor, Sacramento, and Jones streets. The existing buildings were demolished and in their place rose some of the grandest houses in the West.

Robert Louis Stevenson described the summit of Nob Hill in 1882:

The great net of straight thoroughfares lying at right angles, east and west and north and south, over the shoulders of Nob Hill, the Hill of palaces, must certainly be counted the best part of San Francisco. It is there that the millionaires are gathered together vying with each other in display. From thence, looking down over the business wards of the city, we can descry a building with a little belfry, and that is the Stock Exchange, the heart of San Francisco: a great pump we might call it, continually pumping up the savings of the lower quarters to the pockets of the millionaires on the Hill.

It was sometime in the 1870s that the hill got its famous name. "Nob" is a contraction of the plain English word *knob*

meaning an isolated rounded hill or mountain. It is one of those simple, matter-of-fact, almost brutal mining era names that dot the West. The sandy hill became the epicenter of wealth in nineteenth-century California. The railroad and silver barons stamped the hill with its indelible cachet which has survived earthquake, fire, shifting real estate patterns, and even the income tax.

Nob Hill's mansions were not destined to be occupied for long, nor did they prove to be very happy places. Mark Hopkins died in his railroad car in Arizona before occupying the fantasy his wife hallucinated. "Bonanza Jim" Fair's marriage shattered before he got to build his house. Charles Crocker's domain was spoiled by one man who would not sell him his lot with its modest house. (Crocker proceeded to build a thirty-foot-high spite fence around three sides of hold-out Nicholas Yung's house.) Senator Stanford lost his only son. A bitter lawsuit brought by Mrs. Colton exposed the systematic political corruption on which the railroad millions were based.

Nor did contemporary San Franciscans react with awe to the architectural excesses that crowned the hill and lorded over the city. *The Real Estate Circular* branded them "all gingerbread, ignorance, and bad taste" and protested that all such structures did was "bury capital."

What the moralists decried the earthquake and fire of 1906 wiped away.

In the third wave of building, the many Victorian houses on the slopes of the hill were quickly replaced by income-producing apartment houses built on the 25-foot by 100-foot house lots. They are nearly all frame and incorporate bay windows that project out over the sidewalks, making the apartments seem larger from within and giving the hilly blockfronts a corrugated profile. They blanket the slopes of the hill and, along with contiguous Russian Hill and North Beach, create one of the most coherent Edwardian districts in the nation. These buildings have always housed moderate-income people, singles and couples mostly, who work downtown.

The big parcels on the summit, sites of the lost mirages, were slower to rebuild. The Fairmont Hotel opened a year to the day after the catastrophe, and the brownstone Flood mansion was soon remodeled for the Pacific-Union Club. The Crocker family donated its block to the Episcopal church. But it was not until the mid-1920s that large hotels, many originally residential hotels, were erected on the commanding hill. The Episcopal cathedral was begun in the 1920s, but only partially completed.

A burst of highrise construction in the 1960s saw tall buildings sprout along the Jones Street spine, along with the completion of Grace Cathedral. The historic image of the hill began to shine more brightly. There were no height limits on the hill before 1968, and after that date the height limits were extremely generous. The threat that highrises would blanket the slopes of thell as the summit led the neighborhood to organize to push for the reduction of height limits in two steps in 1979 and 1986. A new six-story height limit now preserves the even-scale, moderate-income slopes and will prevent over-congestion of the summit.

Nob Hill's highrises today house the well-to-do and luxury hotels, while the apartment buildings on the slopes house people of decidedly modest income. Today, about half the population of the hill as a whole is Chinese-American, and Chinese-Americans own perhaps 80 percent of the apartment buildings on the north and west slopes of the hill. The famous hill is today a lively, varied, and very San Franciscan neighborhood accommodating many races, classes, and cultures.

CALIFORNIA AND POWELL CABLE CAR TRANSFER POINT [1]

The intersection of California and Powell streets is one of the natural gathering spots for visitors to San Francisco. It is here that the three surviving cable car lines intersect and transfers are made. It is worth carefully crossing this lofty intersection and looking down from each corner. Visible at the foot of California Street is the red brick bulk of the 1916 former Southern Pacific railroad headquarters designed by Bliss and Faville. The Southern Pacific railroad's predecessor was the western section of the first transcontinental railroad, the utility that made the United States a continental market. It was the dominant corporation in nineteenth-century California and much of the arid West. This was the railroad, steamship, and real estate company controlled by the Big Four: Charles Crocker, Leland Stanford, Collis P. Huntington, and Mark Hopkins.

VIEW OF SAN FRANCISCO–OAKLAND BAY BRIDGE [1]

Beyond the old SP building rises one of the piers of the streamlined Bay Bridge, which was carefully placed to terminate the vista down the California Street hill. This is one of San Francisco's too-few protected view corridors. Begun in 1933, during the depth of the Depression, the great bridge was built by the State of California and financed by the New Deal Reconstruction Finance Corporation. Its gifted designers were Charles H. Purcell, chief engineer; Charles E. Andrew, bridge engineer; and Glenn B. Woodruff, design engineer. It was completed in November 1936 for $70 million.

The two elegant suspension bridges, each a 2,310-foot span, are joined in the middle of the channel by a man-made concrete pier "island" that extends 220 feet into the Bay. The four great steel piers of the suspension bridges have great X-braces that create an overlapping

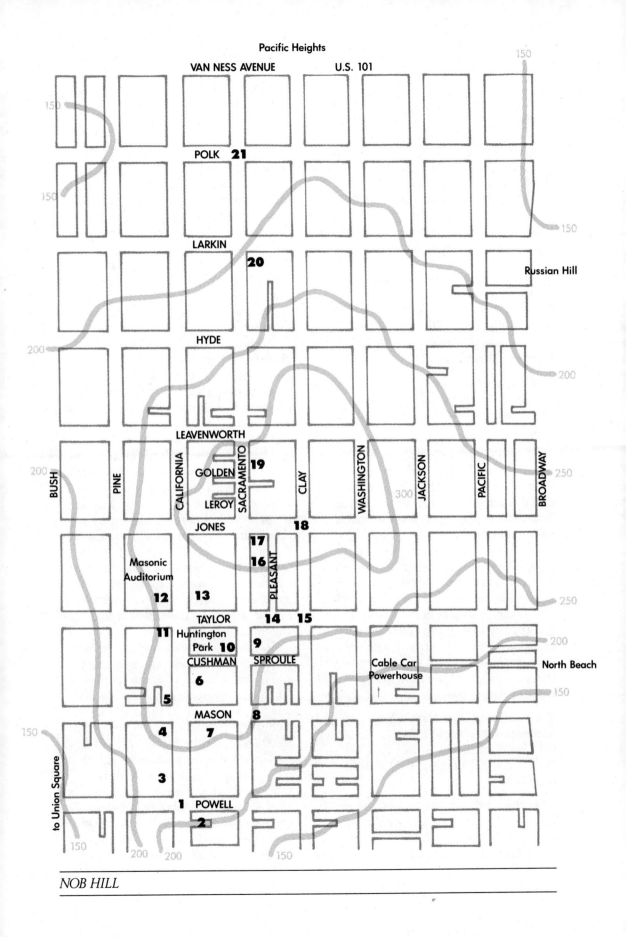

Pacific Heights

VAN NESS AVENUE   U.S. 101

150

150

POLK **21**

150

LARKIN

20

Russian Hill

HYDE

200

200

LEAVENWORTH

200
BUSH
PINE
CALIFORNIA
GOLDEN
LEROY
SACRAMENTO
JONES
19
CLAY
WASHINGTON
JACKSON
300
PACIFIC
BROADWAY
250

18

17

16

PLEASANT

250

Masonic
Auditorium
12   **13**

TAYLOR   **14**   **15**

11 Huntington
Park **10**   **9**

SPROULE

Cable Car
Powerhouse

North Beach

200

CUSHMAN

6

5

150

MASON   **8**

4   **7**

150

to Union Square

3

1 POWELL

2

150

200   200

150

NOB HILL

diamond pattern as you pass under and through them.

While the Golden Gate Bridge is the great crowd pleaser in the Bay Area and is virtually the symbol of San Francisco, the San Francisco-Oakland Bay Bridge's twin silver suspension spans are the connoisseur's bridge. Steel bridges, especially the works of the 1930s, are the great artistic monuments of a mobile people. There is something at once stripped-down and basic and yet graceful, thoughtful, and pure about the design of the four piers of the San Francisco-Oakland Bay Bridge. It persuades us that it is steel in as strong, economical, and elegant a disposition as possible. Every rivet counts. The beauty of the Bay Bridge is the always persuasive beauty of simplicity.

University Club [2]
800 Powell Street, at California
1912, Bliss and Faville

On the northeast corner of California and Powell stood Stanford's opulent stables. In 1912 Bliss and Faville designed the red brick University Club, a men's club designed in the style of a Florentine Renaissance city palace. It is a dignified, reticent design, favored by many of the men's clubs built in San Francisco after 1906.

Visible at the foot of Powell are the three masts of the *Balclutha* (*see Tour 4B*). This is the one street in the twentieth-century city that shows the tall masted sailing ships that once terminated the view down so many of San Francisco's streets. Standing in the now-quiet Bay is wooded Angel Island.

The Stanford Court Hotel / Site of Stanford Mansion [3]
905 California Street
1911, Creighton Withers; 1972, Curtis and Davis

At the southwest corner of California and Powell, with glass-enclosed conservatories added, is the solid-looking Stanford Court Hotel built in 1911 to designs

by Creighton Withers and completely reconstructed inside in 1972 by Curtis and Davis when the former apartment house was converted into one of the city's finest hotels. The great dark granite wall along Powell Street is all that remains of the Stanford mansion that once rose here.

Leland Stanford was born in Watervliet, New York in 1824 and practiced law in Wisconsin before moving to California in 1852 to join his five brothers in a retail grocery store. He moved to Sacramento, the state capital, and helped organize the Republican party there. He was elected governor in 1862 and supported the Union cause and railroad interests.

With four other Sacramento merchants Stanford launched the Central Pacific Railroad, for which he became the public spokesman. In Washington, the transcontinental railroad was pushed as a war measure with a generous congressional subsidy of ten square miles of federal land for every mile of track laid. In 1864 the railroad's promoters had a bill passed that defined mountains by soil composition, not elevation, because subsidies were higher for rail-laying over mountains. As Oscar Lewis wrote in *The Big Four*, "Any group who could move the base of the Sierra Nevadas twenty-five miles westward into the center of the [Central] valley and could net a half-million dollars by the exploit would bear watching."

Stanford took to his millions with enthusiasm. His horse-breeding ranch and country house, now the campus of Stanford University, consisted of 7,200 acres of the finest land in California. His vineyard in Tehama County embraced 55,000 acres on the Sacramento River; his Gridley Ranch spread over 21,000 acres in Butte County. He lived the sobriquet "railroad baron" to the hilt. In 1876, with his redoubtable wife Jane, he commissioned C. S. Bugbee to design his Nob Hill mansion, a brown-painted Italianate pile that he had Eadweard Muybridge photograph inside and out. One of Stanford's enemies labeled it "a modern furniture drama."

The Stanford's doted on their only child, Leland Stanford, Jr. He was privately tutored and extensively traveled. He began a boy's hoard of rare and wondrous things: interesting stones, miniature steam engines, crystals, an inquisitive boy's magpie collection of wonderful curiosities. It became a small private museum.

Then, at fifteen, young Leland died in Florence while on a European tour with his parents. The Stanfords decided to endow a university in the boy's memory. Today, in a remarkable room at the University Museum at Stanford University in Palo Alto south of San Francisco, you can see some of the things that a young boy collected in his parents' Nob Hill mansion and that his compulsive mother saved (see Tour 14). That that childlike curiosity, that most marvelous of capacities, should be the genesis of a now world-renowned seat of learning is happy indeed.

The excellent Provençal-California restaurant, **Fournou's Ovens** (989-1910), entered from California Street, is designed as an amphitheater oriented toward seven functioning ovens.

The Mark Hopkins Hotel / Site of the Hopkins Mansion [4]
999 California Street, at Mason
1925, Weeks and Day

Up the hill from the Stanford Court Hotel, at the southeast corner of California and Mason, is the famous Mark Hopkins Hotel designed by Weeks and Day. This commanding location was the site of the ornate Mark Hopkins mansion. All that remains of it are the granite retaining walls, including a stone turret with an iron finial on the Pine Street side, that capped a stable. The redwood Stick style Hopkins Mansion was the most ostentatious of all the Victorian houses built in California—no small claim. It was a monument not to

the plain-living, vegetarian Mark Hopkins, who liked to cultivate his own garden, but to his splashy wife, Mary.

Mark Hopkins was another upstate New Yorker who came West with the Gold Rush. With Collis P. Huntington, he ran a hardware business in Sacramento serving the miners in the hills. He was one of the early investors in the Central Pacific Railroad and served as its treasurer. He moved to San Francisco, where he was content to live in a relatively simple frame house. But his cousin-wife Mary had grander ideas. She had a passion for possessions and eventually accumulated great houses in New York City, Massachusetts, and Block Island, along with the architectural mirage on Nob Hill. The California Street castle was a phantasmagoria of turrets, gables, pinnacles, and chimneys with a great Gothic-style glass conservatory on its Mason Street side. One wit claimed that if all the gingerbread was chopped off "there would be no house left." When Mark Hopkins died in 1878, his widow married Edward T. Searles, a young interior decorator she met when building her Great Barrington château. After his wife's death, Searles donated the house to the University of California for use by the San Francisco Art Institute. It made a splendid bonfire in 1906. Afterwards the Art Institute built a temporary school here before selling the property and moving to Russian Hill (see Tour 5).

Weeks and Day designed the lofty Mark Hopkins Hotel for Comstock mining engineer George D. Smith in 1925. It is a twenty-story, steel-frame, buff brick and terra cotta-clad building notable for the urbane way that it defines the southeast corner of the summit of the hill. Its brick-paved plaza and ornamental terra cotta entrance pillars with their great lamps make a welcoming gesture to arriving guests. The tall central tower and its two wings are accented with Gothic Revival ornament, an appropriate if unconscious recall of the lost Hopkins

Bird's-eye view of the summit of Nob Hill.

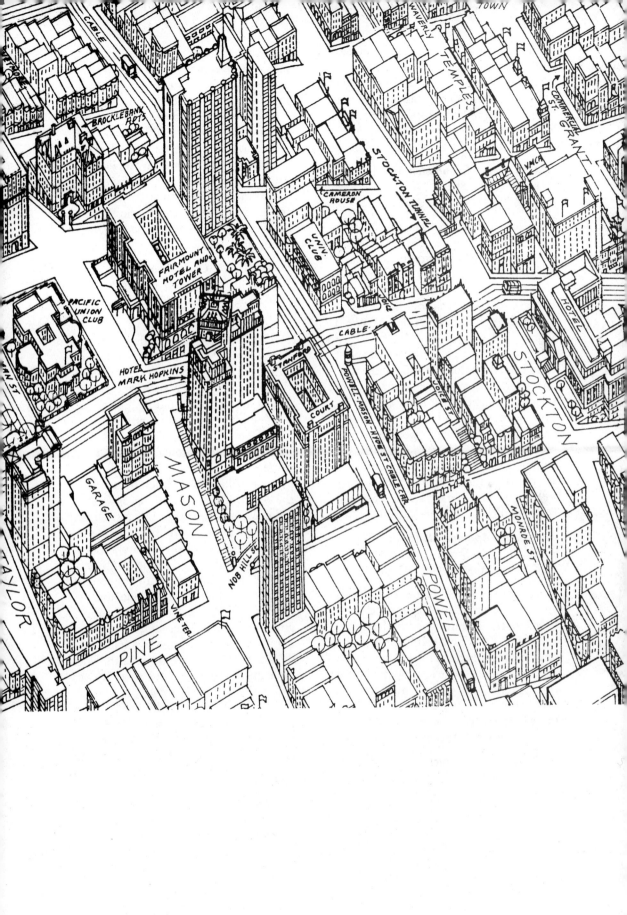

extravaganza. It was built as a residential hotel but has since become one for travelers. In 1936 Timothy Pflueger designed the hotel's rooftop cocktail lounge, the famous **Top of the Mark** (since remodeled inside and out with an intrusive, if understandable, band of windows).

Mason Street Townhouse Row [5]
831–49 Mason Street
1917, Willis Polk

Visible from this corner, on the opposite side of Mason, are 831, 837, 843, and 849 Mason Street, an urbane row of townhouses designed by the ubiquitous Willis Polk in 1917. The elegant detailing of these four identical row houses is typical of the period before the First World War.

Across Pine Street, on the southwest corner of Mason, is **900–08 Pine**, a characteristic, bay-windowed apartment building designed in 1915 by the prolific firm of Rousseau and Rousseau, designers of many of the city's postfire apartment buildings. The vista down Mason, cutting through the raffish Tenderloin at the bottom of the hill, is terminated by the diagonal of Market Street. Beyond is Potrero Hill.

Morsehead Apartments [5]
1001 California Street
1915, Houghton Sawyer

On the southwest corner of California and Mason stands the elegant Morsehead Apartments designed by Houghton Sawyer in 1915. This French-style, six-story building is one of the handsomest in San Francisco. The shallow bays at its corners reflect the oval rooms within. Its lobby is ornamented with statuary and mosaic work. A sophisticated discotheque, **Alexis**, is tucked into its corner.

1021 California Street [5]
1911, George Schasty

Next door is a discreet three-story townhouse that steps down the hill to a five-story rear. It was designed in 1911 by New Yorker George Schasty for Her-

bert Law, the patent-medicine millionaire who eventually owned the Fairmont across the street. The diminutive building was once described as standing "like a quiet, well-dressed child among grownups." It was highly unusual in the rebuilding after 1906 for single-family dwellings to be built on Nob Hill. The fire and earthquake propelled wealthy San Franciscans westward away from the core and out to Pacific and Presidio heights and south down the San Mateo Peninsula.

Pacific-Union Club / Flood Mansion [6]
1000 California Street, at Mason
1886, Augustus Laver; 1912, Willis Polk; 1934, George Kelham

The dark Connecticut brownstone Pacific-Union Club is social San Francisco's ultimate bastion. This gentleman's club occupies the reconstructed Flood Mansion originally built in 1886 and designed by Augustus Laver for James Clair Flood. Flood was born in 1826 of Irish immigrant parents in New York and came to California in 1849. With his partner William S. O'Brien he opened the Auction Lunch, a saloon on Commercial Street near the Financial District. There the two men rubbed shoulders with mining stock manipulators they soon outmanipulated in the frantic stock market. They ended controlling mines in Nevada's Comstock silver lode and formed the famous Consolidated Virginia mine. Soon after quitting tending bar, they had an income of a half-million dollars a month. With his wealth, Flood built this impressive stone mansion atop Nob Hill and a great estate in Menlo Park on the San Mateo Peninsula.

Perhaps because of the rage for brownstone in his native New York, Flood commissioned Augustus Laver to build his mansion of that material. Laver, an Englishman trained in London, migrated to Canada and with two partners won the competition for the new Parliament Building in Ottawa. He also designed the Roman Catholic Cathedral in Montreal. In the mid-1860s, he moved to New York City, where with another partner he won the competition for the new capitol at Albany. In 1870 he moved once again, this time to San Francisco. Here he won the competition for the grand new City Hall begun in 1878 and lost in the 1906 cataclysm. He also secured the commission for both Flood's country and city houses.

The Flood Mansion is one of the great landmarks of San Francisco. It was the only Nob Hill palace built of stone, not wood, and its gutted shell survived once the flames of 1906 had passed over the hill. The building is in the Italianate style, a style introduced in London's Pall Mall men's clubs. The Flood Mansion is important because it epitomizes the style adapted for the Victorian city's ubiquitous redwood-built row houses. You will see the same window design in redwood in the surviving Victorian districts in the city. The now-green bronze fence and the side gates off the main stairs show Laver's more fanciful side. This is the finest Victorian metalwork in San Francisco (matched only by the later Beaux Arts metal work inside the 1915 City Hall.) It was said that Flood employed one man full-time just to polish his $30,000 fence.

When the fire swept the hill, the Floods departed for Pacific Heights (see Tour 7) where two more Flood Mansions were subsequently built, both in light colors. The half-block site with its gutted ruins was purchased by the Pacific-Union Club. A $900,000 bond issue floated among the 450 members of the club financed the acquisition. Substantial remodeling was undertaken by architect Willis Polk, a club member. The first thought was to pull down the walls, but Polk preferred to preserve them and to modify the structure. The tower was lowered and two spreading wings added to the building, giving it more restful proportions. Windows inserted at the third story increased the building by one story. The lighter-colored balustrade at

the top is sheet metal, not stone. Inside, Polk designed club rooms as opulent as any back East. In the basement, on the Mason Street side, he inserted a Minoan-columned plunge with an electrically illuminated stained-glass ceiling that ranks among the most astounding—and inaccessible—rooms in San Francisco.

The Pacific-Union Club was incorporated in 1881 as a consolidation of the Pacific Club founded in 1852, and the Union Club founded in 1854, and is considered the most exclusive men's club in the West. When members die, the club's flag is flown half-staff from the tower.

The Fairmont Hotel and Tower [7]
950 Mason Street, between California and Sacramento
1902–07, Reid Brothers; 1962, Mario Gaidano (tower)

The grand Fairmont Hotel and Tower occupies the block assembled by another Nevada silver baron, James Graham Fair. Born in County Tyrone, Ireland in 1831, Fair migrated to Illinois before joining the Gold Rush in 1849. From a successful quartz mining operation, Fair moved to Nevada silver, where, in association with Flood, Mackay, and O'Brien he helped develop the Comstock lode with its fifty-foot vein of silver, thus earning the nickname "Bonanza Jim." Like many other mining magnates, Fair invested heavily in San Francisco real estate and reputedly owned sixty acres of downtown and South of Market property which he barely maintained. Fair had himself elected senator by the Nevada legislature and held that seat from 1881 to 1887. His marriage shattered in 1883 before he built his city mansion.

Fair's daughter, Theresa Alice (Tessie) decided to build a grand hotel on the Nob Hill block, the first hotel on the hill. She commissioned James and Merritt Reid to design a steel-frame, terra cotta-clad Beaux Arts monument. Construction began in 1902, but building proceeded slowly on the 600-room hotel and it consumed more money than Tessie anticipated. In 1906 Herbert and Hartland Law, patent-medicine millionaires, bought the unfinished building in exchange for the Rialto and Crossley Buildings on New Montgomery Street.

Before the hotel opened, while crates of furniture sat inside it, the earthquake struck on April 18, 1906. When the subsequent fire claimed the City Hall on Portsmouth Square, the mayor and the emergency Committee of Fifty repaired to the unfinished hotel. In its ballroom Brigadier General Frederick Funston, commandant at the Presidio, announced his plans to dynamite firebreaks across the city to stop the fire from consuming the western districts. At dawn on April 19th, the fire advanced up the hill destroying all the great mansions and gutting the unfinished hotel. Gertrude Atherton described the scene,

I forgot the doomed city as I gazed at the Fairmont, a tremendous volume of white smoke pouring from where its roof had been, every window a shimmering sheet of gold; not a flame, not a spark shot forth. The Fairmont will never be as demonic in its beauty again.

The Laws engaged Julia Morgan to restore the ruined hotel. A garden terrace was built on the Powell Street side of the hotel with a view of the rebuilding city below. Working feverishly, the great hostelry was completed and opened one year to the day after the earthquake, on April 18, 1907. The elite Merchants' Association held a grand dinner in the ornate dining room that consumed 600 pounds of turtles, 13,000 oysters, and $5,000 worth of wine and champagne.

In 1927 financier John S. Drumm of the American Trust Company built an opulent three-bedroom penthouse designed by Arthur Upham Pope atop the hotel. Its circular library had a ceiling painted with the constellation of the night sky; its game room was tiled like a Persian pleasure dome. When Prohibition ended, the Fairmont engaged Timothy Pfleuger to design an Art Deco cocktail lounge off the lobby. It is decorated with murals on the theme of the circus painted by Esther, Margaret, and Helen Bruton against a gold-leaf background.

During World War II, the Fairmont and the other great hotels in the city were taken over by the military and their staffs unionized. The hotel's greatest hour came after the war when San Francisco's War Memorial Opera House was chosen as the place where the United Nations charter was signed. Secretary of State Stettinius headed the United States delegation and occupied the Fairmont's penthouse. Stettinius, the USSR's Molotov, the United Kingdom's Eden, and China's Soong, representatives of another Big Four, conferred there.

In 1945 Benjamin H. Swig and a partner bought a controlling interest in the grand hotel and began renovating it. Dorothy Draper was commissioned to redecorate the lobby in 1947. In the same year the famous **Venetian Room** opened, a legendary San Francisco supper-club featuring name entertainers (772-5163). In 1961 a modern twenty-two story tower with 252 rooms was added to the hotel.

To tour the hotel, enter by the main entrance. The grand lobby is now a period piece of late 1940s *luxe*. Its patterned carpet with swirling leaves makes one a bit giddy. The columns here are covered in a golden marble. Follow the corridor to the left. Off this corridor is the Main Ballroom, originally the Main Dining Room, with its wedding-cake plaster work. It is a great *belle époque* interior. On the corridor walls is an extensive, if depressing, collection of photographs of Nob Hill after the fire. Farther down, the corridor jogs to the left; in the corner is a splendid watercolor rendering of the Reid Brothers' original design, a fine work of art itself. At the end of the corridor are plain gold-colored elevator doors leading to the Crown Room atop the Tower. Take this agreeably slow glass-walled elevator up and then back down. San Francisco's Financial District highrises seem to grow up out of the ground as you ascend. The panorama is breathtaking.

The **Fairmont Hotel Pharmacy**, 801 Powell at California, at the cable car transfer point, has a good selection of books, maps, and postcards of San Francisco. Come back out through the lobby to Mason Street and its intersection with steep Sacramento Street.

VIEW FROM SACRAMENTO
AND MASON STREETS [8]

The intersection of Mason and Sacramento streets offers dramatic views. Down the slope of Mason to the north is the red brick Cable Car Powerhouse with its bottle-shaped chimney. In the distance is Russian Hill with its dark shingled houses. The white church with the twin towers is Nuestra Señora de Guadalupe, built in 1906–1912, the first reinforced concrete church in the city. It marks the spot of the Gold Rush-era Latin Quarter where many Chileans and Peruvians lived.

The corner building at **1000 Mason Street** with the brick-paved court and the curiously small windows is the Brocklebank Apartments designed by Weeks and Day and completed in 1926. Like the Mark Hopkins Hotel by the same architects, it graciously defines one corner of the hill's summit. It was the pride and joy of Mrs. M. V. B. Mac-Adam, who set out to build an apartment house "which would be a credit to San Francisco and myself." She oversaw every step of its design and erection; the architects must have had great patience. During the boom of the 1920s, she sank her entire fortune into this project. To furnish its 277 rooms, she sold off an apartment house on Sutter Street and forty-six "sand lots" out on the beach. Most unhappily, her $1 million loan was foreclosed during the dark days of the Great Depression. Even the furnishings in her own apartment were threatened. As she wrote years later in her sad memoir, "Added tears are futile: so, with

outward calm I passed through the door which closed upon my little world wherein I had lived in supposed security." The Brocklebank's entrance pillars and lamps are especially handsome.

1083 Clay Street
1986, Donald MacDonald

A detour for those interested in contemporary San Francisco architecture lies down the steep slope of Mason Street and around the corner downhill at 1083 Clay Street. Best seen from across the street, this dense, eleven-unit building was designed by Donald MacDonald and built in 1986. It takes the traditional San Francisco bay window in new directions. Like agitated waves, the curved bays break across the upper four stories of the white stucco building. A dramatic, if quite steep, staircase slices up from the sidewalk to a small lobby that leads to a patio in the rear. The top story has a recessed roof deck, a relatively new departure in San Francisco building that makes a great deal of sense in this hilly city.

1100 BLOCK OF SACRAMENTO STREET [9]

1150 Sacramento Street
1987, Rony Rolnizky

West on Sacramento Street, on a long-empty lot once occupied by the Sproul Mansion at the corner of Sacramento Street and Sproul Lane, is the latest luxury building to rise on Nob Hill. It was the first building built on the summit of the hill under the new sixty-five foot height limit. Designed by Rony Rolnizky and completed in 1989, it contains forty-five condominiums and has a fanciful parapet echoing the general shape of the nearby Park Lane.

The Nob Hill Community Apartments
1170 Sacramento Street
1958, architect unknown

Across Sproul Lane rises this tall condominium tower built before height limits were imposed on the hill. A driveway circles through the ground-floor level of the tower. Along its west side is a sliver of a garden.

1172 Sacramento Street
1908; 1968, Ted Moulton

This bijou townhouse is one of the most-noted confections on Nob Hill. It is best appreciated from Huntington Park across the street. Its façade is ornamented with mahogany pillars and fancy cast-iron grilles over plate-glass French windows. From across the street the illusionist effect of the converging lines on its mansard roof are quite effective. Like the lost Nob Hill Victorian palaces, its roof is trimmed with cast-iron cresting. It is actually an extensively reworked postfire, two-flat building constructed about 1908. In 1968 it was remodeled by Ted Moulton for Edward T. Haas. Not the sort of building architects admire, it is more a stage set than architecture. It can best be described as a High Decorator 1960s version of an eighteenth-century French *hôtel particulier*.

1190 Sacramento Street
1954, Angus McSweeney

Next door, on the northeast corner of Sacramento and Taylor, is a striking pink-and-black International Style twelve-story highrise designed with a slight flavor of Miami Beach by Angus McSweeney in 1954. It is a fine example of a not-much-appreciated period of building in San Francisco.

Huntington Park / Site of the Colton Mansion [10]
California Street, at Taylor
1915

Huntington Park is one of San Francisco's landscape jewels and is an agreeable island of peace and sunlight that serves as the public center to this private hill. It was the site of the David Colton mansion built in 1872. The white-painted, Renaissance-style mansion was unique

among the millionaires' palaces in that it was the only one that showed any architectural restraint. Its low granite retaining walls survive to define the park.

David Colton was born in Maine and came to California in 1850. He made his first fortune from the Amador gold mine and became a leader in California Democratic politics. He was a vice president of the Southern Pacific Railroad and was derisively branded by the newspapers the one-half of the "Big Four and a Half." When he died in 1878, his widow became embroiled in nineteenth-century California's most notorious lawsuit when the surviving Big Four contested the estate. At the sensational trial, Mrs. Colton entered into evidence a series of six hundred letters from Colton to Collis P. Huntington detailing how the railroad had bought elections, bribed congressmen, and ruled the political destiny of the Golden State. The trial revealed the corruption on which the Nob Hill palaces were built. A bitter but victorious Mrs. Colton left San Francisco in the 1880s.

Strangely enough, Collis P. Huntington bought the Colton mansion in 1892. It stood until 1906. After the fire, the lot stood empty until 1915, when Huntington's widow donated the half-block parcel for a city park stipulating that it be named in honor of her first husband.

The park was most likely designed by John McLaren. Its simple design is curiously like that of a great house. Axial paths divide the park into four quadrants. At the center is a copy of the Tartarughe Fountain of 1581 erected by Pope Alexander VII in Rome's historic ghetto. The front quadrants of the park, where parlors would be located in a great house, are occupied by formal lawns, one with a small bronze sculpture of children entitled "Dancing Sprites." The rear quadrants of the park are occupied by the children's playground just the way children's rooms were placed in the back of Victorian houses. It is a most agreeable design for a park and was retained when a public-private partnership restored the park under the leadership of the Nob Hill Association in 1984. One very Nob Hill touch is the pillared and red-tile-roofed toolshed, which looks like a small temple.

Huntington Hotel [11]
1075 California, at Taylor
1924, Weeks and Day

Across California Street is the unostentatious Huntington Hotel, one of the very finest in San Francisco. Built in 1924 and designed by Weeks and Day as a residential hotel, the Huntington stands on the site of Mrs. Tobin's pre-1906 residence. The clublike **Big Four Bar and Restaurant** (771-1140) at the corner of Taylor Street is a virtual museum of nineteenth-century Nob Hill and well worth dressing up to savor. The atmospheric interior was designed by Sid Del Leach in 1976. Also in the hotel, the fine **L'Etoile Restaurant** (771-1529) is one of the best French restaurants in San Francisco and provides the hotel's room service. The Huntington's green-liveried doorman's shrill, hollow whistle calling for taxis is a familiar sound on the hill.

California Masonic Memorial Temple / Masonic Museum [12]
1111 California Street
1958, Albert F. Roller
Masonic Museum open daily
10 A.M. –3 P.M.

The slick, white Vermont marble-clad California Masonic Memorial Temple and Auditorium stands on the southwest corner of California and Taylor streets. It was designed by Albert F. Roller and was dedicated in 1958. On its façade is a *bas-relief* depicting four figures representing the four branches of the armed services. Adjoining them is a frieze of fourteen figures engaged in a tug-of-war between the forces of good and evil.

A terrace at the Taylor Street side of the Temple gives a view of the city below. Sheltered by the entrance portico are two twenty-three-foot high marble pillars, one supporting a globe and the other the heavens. They are supposed to represent the twin pillars of the porch of the Temple of Solomon. Inside the lobby is a huge historical window executed by Emile Norman and Brooks Clement in 1957. The central figure represents a Mason with his ceremonial apron. Above him is the Masonic All-Seeing Eye. A brochure available in the lobby explains some of the window's symbolism. The window consists of a sandwich of Plexiglas holding thousands of bits of stained glass, metal, parchment, felt, linen, silk, foliage, agates, shells, and, along the bottom of the design, gravel and soil from California's fifty-eight counties and the Islands of Hawaii.

The second floor of the Temple houses the Masonic Museum. A terrace here lets you look down on the postfire apartment houses that line Pine Street below. The top floor of the Temple houses the offices of the Grand Lodge and the Grand Master. The heart of the building is a 3,165-seat auditorium and concert hall used for musical programs and Masonic ceremonies. Architecturally, this is a good example of stripped classical 1950s design, perhaps the dullest period for formal (as opposed to zappy commercial) design in California's architectural development.

This corner was the site of the A. N. Towne Residence, a Colonial Revival house built in 1891. Its marble portal survived the catastrophe of 1906 and was the subject of a famous photograph framing the city's ruins entitled "The Portals of the Past." The portal was saved and moved to Golden Gate Park's Lloyd Lake where it serves as one of only two memorials to the great earthquake and fire (*see Tour 12*). (The other memorial is the depressing late-WPA mural in the former Rincon Annex Post Office at 99 Mission Street, south of Market Street.)

165

**Grace Episcopal Cathedral and Close /
Site of the Crocker Mansions** [13]
Cathedral: 1925–1928, Lewis P. Hobart
with Ralph Adams Cram, 1961–1964,
Weihe, Frick, and Krause with W. Fox;
Cathedral House: 1935, Lewis P. Hobart;
Diocesan House: 1935, Lewis P. Hobart;
Cathedral School for Boys, 1966:
Rockrise and Watson

Grace Cathedral is the seat of the
Episcopal bishop of California whose
dioceses originally embraced the entire
state but which today consists of the San
Francisco Bay Area. The cathedral and
its grounds occupy the block assembled
by another of the Big Four, Charles
Crocker. Crocker was yet another
upstate New Yorker who came to California by way of Indiana seeking gold in
1850. He opened a store in Sacramento,
joined three other local merchants, and
supervised the construction of the Central Pacific Railroad. He commissioned
Arthur Brown to design a great Second
Empire-style house here in 1877 where
the nave of the cathedral stands today.
He gave the uphill half of the block to
his banker son William H. Crocker who
built a Queen Anne-style mansion in
1888. When the Crocker houses were
lost in the 1906 fire, the family donated
the block to the Episcopal church.

Grace Cathedral was essentially built
in two stages to designs by École des
Beaux Arts-trained Lewis P. Hobart. The
building was finally completed and con-
secrated in 1964. Hobart modeled his
church on thirteenth-century French
Gothic designs, chiefly Notre Dame in
Paris. The cathedral is 329 feet long and
162 feet wide at the transepts; its two
towers rise 174 feet. The gilded cross
atop the spire is 247 feet above street
level. The cathedral faces west, instead
of the traditional east, in order to face
Huntington Park and downtown. While
antique in image, it is modern in construction. The danger of earthquakes led
to the use of concrete and steel rather
than stone.

Enter the cathedral through the door
under the Children's Tower at Taylor and
California. The modern baptismal font
was designed by Hans and Norman
Grag in 1964.

Walk down the center aisle towards
the altar. The altar, also designed in 1964,
is made of blocks of California granite
with a California redwood tabletop.
Richly embroidered frontals often drape
the altar. The flanking candlesticks of
bronze, steel, and gold are symbolic of
San Francisco's motto: "Gold in peace,
steel in war."

Particularly beautiful are the needle-
point kneelers designed by Mona Spoor
and made by the women of the diocese.
They show California wildflowers and
the coats of arms of California's Episcopal dioceses.

Beyond the sanctuary and its high
altar is the choir with its Gothic-style
stalls.

The Grace Cathedral Choir of men
and boys was founded in 1913 and sings
every Sunday and Thursday. The eagle-
topped oak choir lectern was carved by
Gutzon Borglum in 1908.

The central windows in the apse
were designed by Charles Jay Connick in
1931 and show Christ the Light of the
World (left), and Christ the Good Shepherd with a lamb (right). The sixty-
seven stained-glass windows in the
cathedral are mostly from two periods.
The traditional leaded windows are
mostly the work of Connick and were
executed in the 1930s; the modern windows are made of faceted, or chipped,
glass set in concrete. Turning away from
the altar, the Cathedral's most splendid
window can be seen, the twenty-five-
foot wide rose window made at the
Gabriel Loire studios near Chartres,
France. Designed in 1964, it makes vivid
St. Francis of Assisi's mystical thirteenth-
century "Canticle of the Sun." At the
center of this wheel of light is Brother
Sun. Circling the sun clockwise are the
Chi Rho, the first two letters of the
Greek title *Christ*, then come air, stars,

and Sister Moon (top), fruits and flowers of Sister Earth (right), Sister Death (right center), Sister Water (bottom), Brother Fire (lower left), and Brother Wind with two birds (upper left).

Ranged along the blind arcade of the south aisle wall (California Street side) are a series of wax tempera and gold leaf murals by John H. DeRosen executed in 1950, including one showing St. Francis receiving St. Clare on a starry night. The later murals closer to the entrance are by Antonio Sotomayor and were completed in 1983 in acrylic on canvas. On a wall opposite the California Street entrance and up a few steps is a rare late-Romanesque Catalan crucifix carved about 1260.

Nearby is the Chapel of Grace, a gift of the Crocker family and the first part of the cathedral to be completed. The chapel is closed except for services (open at 5:15 P.M.) and is protected by a fine wrought-iron grille made by one of America's greatest metal craftsmen, Samuel Yellin, in 1931. The chapel altar is French and dates from 1430. Above it hangs a three-paneled, Flemish oak reredos made for Hambye Abbey in France about 1490.

The stained-glass windows of Grace Cathedral depict moderns as well as ancient saints. The "Human Endeavor" series of faceted Loire windows incorporates in its designs Albert Einstein (with his famous formula $E = mc^2$), astronaut John Glenn, Supreme Court Justice Thurgood Marshall, medical reformer William H. Welch, social worker Jane Addams, poet Robert Frost (born in San Francisco in 1874), plant man Luther Burbank, President Franklin Delano Roosevelt, architect Frank Lloyd Wright, labor leader John L. Lewis, industrialist Henry Ford, and philosopher and educator John Dewey. These windows are located in the clerestory (upper) section of the nave toward the front towers.

Exit from the door under the Singing Tower, so called because it houses a carillon of forty-four bronze bells cast in Croydon, England, in 1938. The largest bell weighs six tons and rings the hour.

Outside the cathedral, in the central east portal, hang copies of Lorenzo Ghiberti's bronze doors to the Baptistry in Florence.

The gift shop in the basement of the cathedral, entered under the stairs at Taylor and California, sells a complete guide to this treasury of religious art. Across a small courtyard is Cathedral House, where coffee is served after the 11 A.M. Sunday service. It was built in 1912 as the Church Divinity School of the Pacific and faced in white Utah limestone. Next to it, on Taylor Street, is the Diocesan House, also by Hobart, built in 1935. At the northwest corner of Sacramento and Jones is the Cathedral School for Boys designed by Rockrise and Watson in 1966. It is a congenial modern work with a small entrance court and utilizes its roof for a playground.

On a less Christian note, east of these gates, between the two palm trees facing Sacramento Street, was the cottage that Nicholas Yung refused to sell to Crocker. Furious, Crocker built an infamous thirty-foot-high spite fence around three sides of Yung's property. In 1877 Denis Kearney, the fiery leader of the Workingmen's party, led a mass protest against Crocker's fence. Vigilantes chased and clubbed the protestors back down the hill to the flats. Not until 1904, after Yung's death, were Crocker's heirs able to buy the lot and assimilate the holdout parcel.

1100 BLOCK OF TAYLOR STREET [14]

The two flat blocks of Taylor Street north of Huntington Park, between Sacramento and Washington, are lined with an interesting array of post-1906 apartment buildings more ornamented and with more individuality, than the standard post-fire buildings that blanket the slopes of Nob Hill. The apartment building on the **northwest corner of Taylor and Sacramento streets** was the site of

Senator George Hearst's house and has recently sprouted a modern penthouse. At **1135–41 Taylor**, at the corner of Pleasant, is an elegant shingled building with several units designed in 1908 for artist Emil Pissis by Bakewell and Brown. Its side elevation is interesting and fuses formality with seeming randomness.

Across Taylor Street is **1153–57 Taylor**, a three-story frame building with an urbane design by Martens and Coffey built in 1906. It has a garage and entryway on the street level, a beautiful window centered at the second story, a large bay window on the third story, and a glass windscreen along the top sheltering a roof deck. It epitomizes how "citywise" postfire architecture got in San Francisco. The design is practical, elegant, individual, and fits perfectly into its block front. Would that contemporary architects could handle garages as suavely.

1200 BLOCK OF TAYLOR STREET / SITE OF FIRST CABLE CAR LINE [15]

On the southeast corner of Taylor and Clay is a corner grocery store typical of the patterns of the old prezoning city. From here you can look down steep Clay Street with its 17 percent grade to the soaring, 853-foot-high Transamerica Pyramid. On this slope Andrew S. Hallidie built the world's first cable car line, the Clay Street Hill Railroad. Partially financed by Clay Street property owners, the primitive cable car (preserved in the Washington and Mason Powerhouse and Museum) made its first trip on August 1, 1873 with Hallidie himself at the controls. The line ran from Kearny Street to Van Ness Avenue and in three years was carrying 150,000 nickel-paying passengers per month. Cable cars ran every three minutes during the evening rush; the one-mile-long trip took eleven minutes. The line was discontinued in 1891, but not before a bottle of champagne was broken over the last grip.

At **1224–32 Taylor Street** is a decidedly French-style apartment house designed by Austin Whittlesey in 1914. It is a fine work and deserves better treatment than it is getting. At **1234 Taylor Street** is a modern condominium designed by Kurtzman and Kodama in 1980. The use of unpainted wood is an impractical affectation in San Francisco's damp climate and already this building looks stained and dreary. On the southwest corner of Taylor and Washington, at **1255–57 Taylor Street**, is a naive, if exuberant, building designed by Falch and Knoll in 1915. Its giant columns and clumsy balconies are eye-catching.

At this point you may either walk downhill or return to Taylor and Sacramento streets, climb one steep block, and then descend the west slope of Nob Hill toward Polk Street to see more of the post-1906, Edwardian city.

75 Pleasant Street [16]
1983, Charles Pfister and Richard M. Brayton

Up Pleasant Street, almost at Jones, is **75 Pleasant Street**, a post-modern townhouse completed in 1983 and designed by Charles Pfister and Richard M. Brayton. It makes an interesting contrast with 1153-57 Taylor and with the two typical Edwardian buildings that frame it. Its exaggerated rusticated base and the round-arched top play on themes garnered from its neighbors. The large circular window over the entrance is set on pivots. The design manages to be monumental on a constricted lot.

1200 BLOCK OF SACRAMENTO STREET [17]

The steep north side of the 1200 block of Sacramento Street, the sunny side of the street facing Grace Cathedral, has attracted a handsome row of apartment buildings. Halfway up the block, best seen from across the street, are **1230 and 1242 Sacramento Street**, two Parisian-style buildings by Arthur Laib built in 1916. Facing the cathedral modeled on Notre Dame, this is as close as San Francisco comes to its pretentious early-twentieth-century claim to being "the Paris of the West." Number **1230 Sacramento Street** is marked by three French windows with semicircular balconies and ornamental iron railings at the second floor. It has a marble-lined vestibule and wrought iron and plate glass doors. Number **1242 Sacramento Street** has rounded bay windows with a highly ornamented railing that masks the fire escape. Three round-headed French windows with balconies mark the second floor. Red tiles incongruously fringe the roof line.

The Chambord Apartments [17]
1298 Sacramento Street, at Taylor
1921, James F. Dunn

At the top of the street is the Chambord Apartments built in 1921 and designed by James F. Dunn. Like the Morsehead Apartments across from the Mark Hopkins Hotel, this elegant building features oval living rooms stacked at the corners. Their shape is expressed in the billowing corner bays. As originally designed, each floor had two units, each consisting of the oval living room, a bedroom with a bay window, a dining room, a kitchen, and a bath. All the rooms branched off an elevator foyer. Though small, the apartments were designed for formal entertaining and provided an opulent standard for single living.

The top floor was originally a single C-shaped unit arranged around an open court. In 1926, when Herbert E. Law bought the building, this floor was altered and an undistinguished sixth-floor penthouse was added.

NOB HILL SUMMIT [18]

The intersection of Clay and Jones streets is the highest point on Nob Hill at 338 feet above sea level. The Clay-Jones at **1250 Jones Street**, one of the earliest residential highrises in San Francisco, is still one of the best designed. It is a slender, Art Deco shaft capped by a radio tower, a very modern touch. Its garage entrance is unobtrusively tucked around the corner on Clay. The building was converted into condominiums in 1973. Inside is **Le Club** (771-5400), a swank restaurant with mildly Art Deco decor.

Diagonally across the intersection of Clay and Jones at **1333 Jones Street** is the block-long, highrise Comstock Apartments built in 1960 by Hammarkerg and Herman. The Comstock presents a sterile face to its sidewalk with a parking podium barely relieved by a parsleylike fringe of green hedges. During the 1960s and 1970s, many buildings were erected in San Francisco which paid no attention to their urban context and which gave undue prominence to parking needs.

SACRAMENTO STREET / WESTERN SLOPE OF NOB HILL [19]

The bay-windowed, post-1906 apartments that march down the slopes of Nob Hill are among San Francisco's most important and least appreciated buildings. They are, as a matter of fact, almost invisible to San Franciscans, being so coherent as a group that most only notice the exceptions. Constructed between 1906 and about 1915, these Edwardian buildings are not quite old enough to be considered antique and so are merely old. Like Victorian houses in the 1950s, many owners "renovate" and "improve" them rather than restore them. The fact that they were well built and are still highly serviceable, but not at all fashionable, is the main force that preserves them.

Since 1979, rent control has prevented speculation in these buildings. Limited street parking and general lack of garages (these close-to-downtown areas were built during the heyday of public transit and before middle-class city dwellers owned automobiles) has discouraged more affluent renters from favoring this area. These "disadvantages" work to keep these apartments relatively affordable.

The buildings owe their configuration—the rhythm of their bay windows and back yards that create open spaces for light and air—to "tenement laws" agitated for by public health advocates. The coherence of this district is also a result of the fraternity of architects in Edwardian San Francisco, who largely agreed on how to build within the city-mandated building envelope. The aim of these designers was to create individual designs within a formula and to work out plans that were efficient but had style.

LEROY PLACE AND GOLDEN COURT [19]

Halfway down the 1300 block of Sacramento, on the south side, are two hidden *cul-de-sacs*. **Leroy Place** is lined with "popsicle" trees. At 14–16 Leroy Place is a very fine, four-story, two-unit condominium designed by Hudd and Miller and completed in 1987. It is a suave design with a unique treatment of the traditional bay-windowed façade— the epitome of contextural design. In a few years most people will think it has always been here. It is notable for its imaginative and attractive garage entrance. This is probably the best solution to this key design problem in the contemporary city. A few steps down Sacramento is **Golden Court**, whose architecture is ordinary but whose fuchsia plantings are delightful.

LEAVENWORTH AND SACRAMENTO STREETS [19]

At the northeast corner of Leavenworth and Sacramento streets at **1202–06 Leavenworth Street** is a multi-unit, brown-shingled, vine-covered building built in 1911 by Charles McCall. Its Leavenworth Street entrance with per-

golas is a good example of the relaxed feeling created by many buildings from what architectural historians call the First Bay Regional Tradition, which flourished between the 1890s and the 1920s. The northside Berkeley hills are the best place to see this rustic style

Across the street is the surprisingly long façade of **1201–19 Leavenworth**, a Classic Revival Edwardian building built by James F. Dunn, architect of the Chambord, in 1908–1909. Unlike most post-fire apartment houses, it does not have bay windows. Though not fancy, it is a good design and shows how classy even ordinary post-fire buildings often were. This was a great period for frame construction, America's vernacular building material and method. On the southwest corner of Sacramento, **1155 Leavenworth Street** was mystery writer Dashiell Hammett's home. Here he finished *The Maltese Falcon* and began *The Glass Key*, the best book on San Francisco in the corrupt, booming 1920s. Hammett listed himself at this address for the first time in the city directory as a "writer."

At **1151–55 Sacramento Street** between Leavenworth and Hyde stands a unique design, a postfire building with an Art Nouveau flavor. Note the treatment of the spade-shaped entrance arch and the swooping cornice, best seen from across the street. The two bays are of different shapes and are linked by a false balcony. It is a one-of-a-kind design. A garage was inserted in the base in 1988. Art Nouveau designs appeared only rarely in San Francisco, and then mostly in shop and restaurant interiors which have long since been remodeled.

Coronado Apartments [20]
1500 Sacramento Street
1911, architect unknown

A block-and-a-half down Sacramento on the northeast corner of Larkin stands the assertive **Coronado Apartments**, built in 1911. This large, U-shaped apartment building is one of the flowers of

Edwardian design in San Francisco and employs its rounded bay windows to great effect. It piles five stories of housing with forty-five units atop a buff-colored brick-veneer base. The light color helps mask the building's bulk. It is notable for beveled-glass doors that sparkle invitingly when you pass them at night and the lobby's art glass ceiling. This landmark-quality building anchors its corner with great assurance.

Larkin Street is one of the "seams" in San Francisco's street plan. The blocks east of Larkin—today's downtown— were laid out by Jasper O'Farrell in 1847 while those west of Larkin and as far as Divisadero were laid out in 1855 as the expanding city's first "Western Addition."

POLK STREET [21]

At the base of Nob Hill and parallel to once-aristocratic Van Ness Avenue is **Polk Street**, one of San Francisco's many lively commercial strips that developed along old street-car lines. The 19 Polk bus runs south to City Hall and the Civic Center, and north to Ghirardelli Square, Fort Mason, and Fisherman's Wharf. In the Victorian era, Polk Street catered to the carriage trade atop Nob Hill and along Van Ness. South of California Street, Polk attracted many German-Americans who called the artery "Polkstrasse." Today the only sign of that era in the street's history is the monumental **California Hall**, originally the German National Community Hall, designed by Frederick H. Meyer and built in 1912. This splendid German Renaissance Revival building at Polk and Turk with its elaborate terra cotta façade was the finest ethnic hall in San Francisco, befitting the progressive, successful, rapidly assimilated German-American community. Today it houses the **California Culinary Academy**; call 771-3500 for lunch or dinner reservations.

Frank Norris's naturalistic novel, *McTeague: A Story of San Francisco*, pub-

lished in 1899, was set on Polk Street. McTeague hung his giant gold tooth from his second floor dental parlor at Polk and California and watched the crowds below:

Evening began: and one by one a multitude of lights, from the demonaic glare of the druggists' windows to the dazzling blue-whiteness of the electric globes, grew thick from street corner to street corner.... Now there was no thought but for amusement. The cable cars were loaded with theatergoers—men in high hats and young girls in furred opera cloaks. On the sidewalks were groups and couples—the plumbers' apprentices, the girls of the ribbon counters, the little families that lived on the second stories over their shops, the dressmakers, the small doctors, the harness makers—all the various inhabitants of the street were abroad, strolling idly from shop window to shop window, taking the air after the day's work.

Polk Street is still animated, though after the fire of 1906 and the loss of the great mansions, the carriage trade drifted to other streets. The nondescript former Hotel Wently at **1214 Polk Street** at the corner of Sutter was a nest of Beats in the late 1950s. Today Polk Street is characterized by inexpensive restaurants, ultratrendy clothing shops, and a sprinkling of gay bars. Its south end abuts the Tenderloin and is somewhat raffish, especially at night.

The street's architectural "sleeper" is the façade of Miller and Pfleuger's **Royal Theater**, an Art Deco sheet metal delight designed in 1925 but inexplicably neglected. At **1326 Polk Street**, between Pine and Bush, is the street's treasure, a landmark-quality, one-story commercial building housing **Freed, Teller, and Freed's** coffee, tea, and spice emporium. Its interior is a delight, a museum of legal addictions and their paraphernalia. **Fields Book Store** at 1419 Polk Street between California and Pine is an island of calm and specializes in metaphysical books.

Eastern Pacific Heights

VICTORIAN AND EDWARDIAN
LANDMARKS

What This Tour Covers

[1] Van Ness Avenue / Highway 101 /
1700 California Street

[2] California and Franklin Victorian and
Edwardian Mansion Group (Edward
Coleman House / Lilienthal-Pratt House /
Wormser-Coleman House / Bransten
House)

[3] First Church of Christ, Scientist /
Franklin Street Apartment Buildings

[4] Lafayette Park

[5] Spreckels Mansion

[6] Washington Street Houses and
Phelan Mansion / The Mary Phelan
Mansion / Washington Tower

[7] Beaux Arts Apartment Buildings

[8] Gough Street Victorians

[9] Clay Street Modern Flats

[10] Golden Gate Spiritualist Church

[11] Haas-Lilienthal House Museum / The Foundation for San Francisco's Architectural Heritage

[12] Greenlee Terrace Apartments

[13] Matson-Roth Houses / West German Consulate

[14] 2000 Block of Jackson Street

[15] Whittier Mansion Museum / California Historical Society / Ottilie R. Schubert Hall

[16] 2535 Laguna Street

[17] 2000 Broadway / 2040 Broadway

[18] The Hamlin School / James Leary Flood Mansion

[19] Bourn Mansion

[20] Sacred Heart Schools / James Leary Flood Mansion / Convent of the Sacred Heart School / Joseph Donohoe Grant Mansion / School of the Sacred Heart / Andrew Hammond Mansion / Stuart Hall School for Boys

[21] View of the Palace of Fine Arts and the Golden Gate

Preliminaries

Best Times To Do This Tour

The Haas-Lilienthal House is open on Wednesday and Sunday from 12:30 P.M. to 4:30 P.M. The Whittier Mansion is open Wednesday, Saturday, and Sunday from 1 P.M. to 4:30 P.M.

Parking

Garages under the Wells Fargo Bank branch at Van Ness, enter from California heading east; 1700 California Street, at Van Ness, enter from California heading west; paid lot behind B of A, Sacramento between Polk and Van Ness. You can return near here by public transit.

Transportation

For public transit to starting point, catch the California Street cable car to its western terminus at Van Ness Avenue, or take the California trolley-bus to Sacramento and Franklin. The 83 Pacific runs west on Jackson (stopping in front of the California Historical Society at Laguna) and east on Washington, passing the Spreckels Mansion.

At end of tour, the 22 Fillmore trolley-bus goes north (downhill) to Union Street or south to Sacramento Street. A transfer east on the 1 California trolley-bus on Sacramento Street will take you to Van Ness Avenue, or downtown to Chinatown and the Financial District.

Restaurants, Cafés, and Bars

At the end of this tour, an easy walk downhill takes you to Union Street with its many fine shops, restaurants and bars. Try the Balboa Cafe (922-4592), at 3199 Fillmore, off Union, an Edwardian gem. Or you can walk south on Fillmore to an array of Upper Fillmore shops and restaurants. The 22 Fillmore trolly-bus runs up and down Fillmore.

Introduction: Victorian and Edwardian Landmarks

Pacific Heights is sharply defined and embraces the blocks in the Western Addition bounded by California Street on the south, Van Ness Avenue on the east, Green Street to the north, and Presidio Avenue on the west. It divides into two parts at Fillmore Street where the 22 Fillmore trolley-bus runs. Eastern Pacific Heights, closest to the downtown and the oldest half, saw most of its Victorian mansions replaced with swank apartment houses after about 1915. Western Pacific Heights, on the other hand, remains mostly single-family dwellings, though many large buildings here have more than one unit. In eastern Pacific Heights, two great city houses now open to the public, the Haas-Lilienthal House and the Whittier Mansion, let the explorer glimpse preserved interiors from the city of the late nineteenth-century *haute bourgeoisie*. Two other adapted great houses, one the grandest ever built in San Francisco, the Convent and Schools of the Sacred Heart and the Hamlin School, are occasionally accessible to the public.

Even when these were only barren hills in the late 1860s, it was clear that

Fashion would come to rest here once transit linked it with the downtown. In the first division of these blocks, the lots in Pacific Heights were deliberately larger than in the other city neighborhoods so that they could accommodate much bigger houses. While other neighborhoods have seen ups and downs in lots and real estate, Pacific Heights lots, in particular, have always held their value.

Hill-conquering cable cars turned the Victorian city inside out. In the beginning of settlement, the very best streets were the most central ones. Horsecars and ferries began to change that immemorial pattern, drawing the wealthy away from the increasingly congested and polluted center. The cable cars completed the revolution by drawing people to the edge of the city, fringes previously sprinkled with the shanties and shacks of the poor. Bankers, shippers, wholesalers, and lawyers clustered along Stockton moved out to the edge of the city. The elite Protestant churches and the Roman Catholic cathedral followed their powerhouse congregations west.

By the early 1880s, the blocks near Lafayette Park and Alta Plaza were the best streets to live on and luxurious houses clustered on their heights. The *Real Estate Circular* reported in 1882 that "Nine-tenths of the demand for property for fine residences or cheaper homesteads during the past year has been in the Western Addition. That portion of it between Van Ness, Pierce, California and Pacific streets has been by far the most favored section, for large residence sites on the one hand and for the best medium class homesteads on the other."

The Social Manual of San Francisco described the social ordering of San Francisco's neighborhoods in 1884:

... a greater uniformity in reception days prevails from year to year. The rule is as follows: Mondays, the hotels, Tuesday, Nob Hill and Taylor Street to the north, Wednesday, Rincon Hill, South Park and the streets near the Mission, Thursday most of Pine, Bush,

Copyright 1989 William Walters

The high Victorian and Edwardian mansion group on the northwest corner of California and Franklin streets. Left to right: 1834 California (1876 and 1895), 1818 California (1876), 1701 Franklin (1895), and 1735 Franklin (1904).

Sutter, and parallel streets, and the greater part of Van Ness Avenue, Fridays, Pacific Avenue and adjacent streets as far as the Presidio.

San Francisco had been a relatively open economy and society after the Gold Rush 1850s. But the depressed 1870s saw social mobility in San Francisco slow (though it never stopped) and social distinctions harden. It was from the visiting lists of the residents of the grand houses of the Victorian city that the *Social Register* was later compiled. San Francisco's first Society list was published in 1880 and was in two parts: Christians, then Hebrews. According to it, Jews accounted for 20 percent of San Francisco society. (The Christian list, interestingly, included two Jews.) Very soon, San Francisco's social register ran but one religiously integrated alphabetical list. German Jewish merchants, in particular, after flirting with the streets near the Panhandle in the early 1880s,

bought, if they could, in Pacific Heights. Some wealthy Roman Catholic Irish and others built large showy houses with gardens in the sunny Mission District in the 1870s, but by the next decade, Pacific Heights had triumphed.

Because all of the Victorian houses, and some of the later houses, employed servants, more races and classes mingled, or were "layered," in Pacific Heights than elsewhere in the city. In the late Victorian era, Irish-American girls were often the parlor maids and occasionally cooks. German women were most often cooks, and as such, the rulers of the servant roost with the best room in the attic. Chinese men were widely employed as laundrymen and had separate basement rooms. In the first decade of this century, some house servants were young Japanese-American men. Some few truly grand houses had European butlers and chauffeurs.

Some of the palatial mansions in

Pacific Heights ended up being mainly *for* the servants. The baronial turn-of-the-century rich preferred to live on fog-free country estates on the San Mateo Peninsula. In the 1890s the *Real Estate Circular* decried the closed-up mansions on California Street as "palaces of ease" for their servants.

Harriet Lane Levy, in her classic memoir, *920 O'Farrell Street*, listed the many nations and races that served an upper-middle-class household in San Francisco. The baker was German; the fish man, Italian; the grocer, a Jew; the butcher, Irish; the steam laundryman, a New Englander. The vegetable vendor and the regular laundryman who came to the house were Chinese. Levy left one sharp snapshot of Maggie, the lively Irish-American cook in a Polish-Jewish household as remembered by a perceptive little girl:

The kitchen offered the social potentialities of a ballroom, and Maggie missed none of them. Twice a day the tradesmen or his emissary knocked at the kitchen door. In the morning he took the order, in the afternoon he delivered it. The grocer, the baker, the steam laundryman, the fish man, the chicken man, the butcher boy, came twice a day proffering a salty bit of conversation or a flashing glance of fire. Bent over the sink, Maggie Doyle aimed a shaft of repartee over her left shoulder in invitation, or she buried her scorn in a bowl of dough, or she leaned lightly against the jamb of the door in coquettish intimacy with the man who pleased her.

The scarcity of household servants after World War I, and more important, the much simpler tastes among new generations of the already-established rich, led to a quick evaporation of the more cumbersome of society's rituals, especially the "at homes" and their attendant calls. In the 1920s the rich emancipated themselves from the time-consuming socializing of their grandparents and took up tennis and golf instead. At the same time, the gargantuan endless-course feasts of the Victorians were sup-

planted by less elaborate dinners. The very rich stopped building freestanding palaces in the city and erected more "modest" residences or took floors or large apartments in anonymous swank apartment buildings with more security and privacy.

Eastern Pacific Heights' great Victorian piles were one by one torn down for apartments as the modern rich inherited too-large and, to them gloomy, old houses they had no wish to live in. The good views, good transit links with the Financial District, and good name of the district led to the replacement of many "obsolete" Victorian mansions with apartment buildings starting perhaps about 1910 and cresting in the 1920s. A few fine Art Deco apartment buildings went up here even during the depressed 1930s. More apartments were built after the revival of building in the 1950s, with very bulky, often less attractive highrise buildings in the 1960s and 1970s.

While the architecture in Pacific Heights is described in guides because it is visible from the street, the finest aspect of Pacific Heights is the special gardening tradition that flourishes here, marked by plants in containers, ivy trained against trellises, and mostly always green, easily maintained plantings. The invisible back gardens and landscaped decks are the jewels of Pacific Heights. Ruby-throated hummingbirds dart among their flowers, a few of which are in bloom nearly every month of the year. Frederick Law Olmsted's sharp eye for landscape noted this San Franciscan tradition as early as 1866.

Strangers, on their arrival in San Francisco, are usually much attracted by the beauty of certain small gardens, house courts, and porches, and, if they have any knowledge of horticulture, they perceive that this beauty is of a novel character. It is dependent on elements which require to be seen somewhat closely.... It is found in the highest degree in some of the smallest gardens in the more closely built and densely populated parts of the town, in situations where park trees would dwindle for want of light and air.

There is a lot of privacy in Pacific Heights, as in most elite neighborhoods, even though its population density is quite substantial and its buildings cheek-by-jowl. There is only one day of the year when Pacific Heights is "open," Halloween after dinner and to about 8 P.M. Then pumpkins glow in the windows (or, more tastefully, are heaped uncut with corn stalks near the front door) and parents take their small children trick-or-treating door to door. Lighted doorways to lighted parlors open and close, candies are handed to children, and pleasantries are exchanged with neighbors rarely seen. Otherwise, Pacific Heights' inhabited mansions are best seen in the evening when one blind is cocked and you can catch a glimpse of slivers of rooms richly paneled in warm woods and decorated with antique statues and pots of orchids.

VAN NESS AVENUE / HIGHWAY 101 **[1]**

Van Ness Avenue, the terminus of the California Street cable car line, was laid out as part of the Western Addition in 1854, not as a highway but as a spacious, quiet boulevard for mansions. (At 125 feet, it is the widest street in the city.) The lots along it were large, the corner ones especially so. Prestigious Protestant congregations and the Roman Catholic cathedral located along Van Ness Avenue, following their elite congregations west. By 1892 Van Ness was described as "our one show street, purely a residence section." Van Ness Avenue was well served by east-west cable lines, but no noisy transit line disturbed the elegant street itself with its solid blocks of gingerbread mansions. A proposal by a syndicate to construct a trolley line down Van Ness in 1892 by "men rich enough to be honest," as the press put it, united the property owners here in opposition to the transit invasion.

But Van Ness Avenue was slowly infiltrated by commerce in the 1890s with some hotel-boardinghouses, doctors, dressmakers, and hairdressers operating on the street.

When the 1906 earthquake struck and the downtown caught fire, city and Army engineers decided to use Van Ness Avenue as a firebreak. They dynamited all the grand houses on the east side of the street. Though the fire did jump over the break to Franklin Street along some blocks, the line was generally held here. Had this not been done, the entire city could have been consumed. Immediately after the fire, Van Ness Avenue shifted to commerce. At the edge of the surviving residential districts, large and small retailers leased the lots and the few surviving big houses on the west side of the avenue and built temporary stores, which during the rebuilding did a great deal of business.

When the new department stores and retail district around Union Square was ready for occupancy about 1909–1910, retail skipped back downtown. Van Ness Avenue's large corner lots became ideal sites for luxury automobile showrooms with repair shops attached. During the 1920s, when automobiles were still luxuries, a stately row of elaborate landmark-quality auto showrooms was built along Van Ness. The beige, multistory, cube-like, former Don Lee Cadillac building at **1000 Van Ness** at O'Farrell built in 1921 and designed by Weeks & Day is the most interesting. More popular is the former Earl C. Anthony Packard temple at **901 Van Ness** at Ellis, designed by Bernard Maybeck in 1928.

While car servicing and repair continues in smaller garages the side streets between Van Ness and Polk (some are the sites of old livery stables), much car buying has moved off the boulevard. Van Ness Avenue has been designated by the city as a site for multistory housing and several large projects have been built. It is a good location for large apartment and condo buildings, and the reintroduction of residential uses on the street is making Van Ness ever more attractive to pedestrians. With the pedestrians come movie theaters, electronics and furniture stores, and restaurants and cafés. Of the latter, two of the best are **Harris' Steak House** (673-1888), 2100 Van Ness Avenue at Pacific, a fine skylighted Edwardian space and probably the best steak place in town. The **Hard Rock Café** (885-1699) at 1699 Van Ness Avenue at Sacramento draws a young crowd to this immensely popular rock-and-roll-themed hamburger joint.

Perhaps the hidden jewel of the avenue is the **interior of St. Luke's Episcopal Church** on the southeast corner of Van Ness and Clay. Completed in 1910, this white, Gothic Revival church has a splendid interior surrounded on four sides by glowing stained-glass windows, many of them of angels.

1700 California Street [1]
1986, Jorge De Quesada/Kaplan, MacLaughlin & Diaz

This ambitious, eleven-story contemporary building combines parking, ground floor commercial spaces, five stories of offices, and atop that, five stories of luxury condominiums. Its exterior is clad in lightweight panels that look like, but are not, concrete aggregate. They reflect the San Francisco light. Green-tinted windows are set in dark green metal frames, and urn finials give a postmodern touch.

CALIFORNIA AND FRANKLIN VICTORIAN AND EDWARDIAN MANSION GROUP [2]

It is best to walk up the south side of California Street to the Franklin and California Victorian mansion group. This group of great houses and rare gardens is best studied first from across the busy intersection. (Be careful here; Franklin is a one-way speedway north to the Golden Gate Bridge.)

Edward Coleman House
1701 California, corner of Franklin
1895, W. H. Lillie

This 1895 house is a high point in San Francisco architecture and building. Designed by W. H. Lillie in what is now called the Queen Anne-style, it is late Victorian domestic perfection and one of the most beautiful old buildings in San Francisco. Its great round corner tower with curved glass windows accommodates very large bays attached to the principal rooms. In its massing and the arrangement of its component parts, the house shows how Victorian architects turned the corner of an important block, giving the intersection of two important streets a sense of definition and the inhabitants splendid views of their surroundings.

The fine, expansive, corner mansion was finished inside with choice woods. Edward Coleman, who built this house, owned the Idaho Gold Mine in Grass Valley, California and made another fortune in timber. The adjacent lot on Franklin Street was bought for a garden. The house survived the years of active hatred of "Victorian monstrosities" because it was bought by the owners of 1735 Franklin, the red brick townhouse immediately to its north, in order to preserve that house's sunlight and view.

Over the years, 1701 Franklin became a pleasant boardinghouse and later a card club. In 1975 it was restored and converted into law offices. At that time the original gray color of the house was changed to contemporary colors that accentuate the wreath and garland plaster scratchwork bands decorating the house. The conical roof of the round corner tower is capped by an elaborate finial so that the outline of the building comes to a fine flourish on the skyline. The high front porch facing Franklin is light and elegant and incorporates subtle curves. A graceful curve in the coping of the retaining wall flows down the hill and around the corner.

178

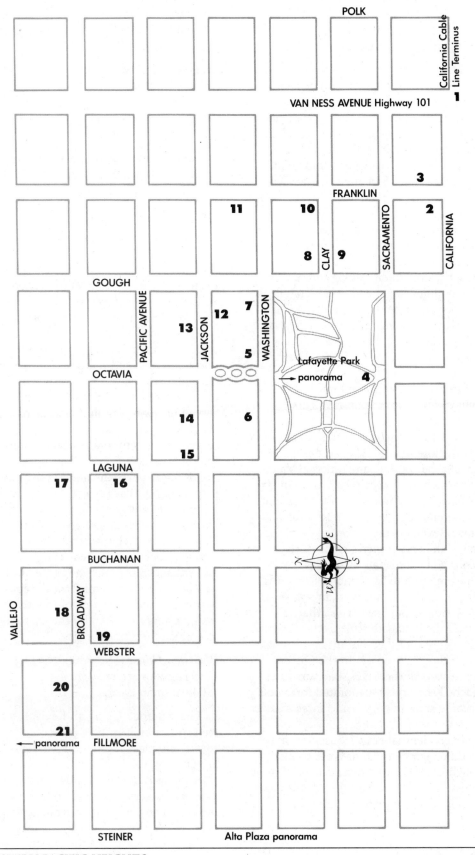

POLK

California Cable Line Terminus

1

VAN NESS AVENUE Highway 101

3

FRANKLIN

11   **10**

2

SACRAMENTO

CALIFORNIA

8 CLAY **9**

GOUGH

PACIFIC AVENUE

7

12

13

JACKSON

WASHINGTON

5

Lafayette Park

→ panorama

4

OCTAVIA

14   **6**

15

LAGUNA

17   **16**

BUCHANAN

BROADWAY

VALLEJO

18

19

WEBSTER

20

21

← panorama   FILLMORE

STEINER   Alta Plaza panorama

EASTERN PACIFIC HEIGHTS

Lilienthal-Pratt House
1818 California Street
1876, architect unknown

The Lilienthal-Pratt House sits atop a graded lot with a high retaining wall capped by a black iron fence (garages were inserted in 1988). The front stairs march straight up to the front door. The building has a flat roof with a very impressive cornice along its top. (Flat roofs evolved in San Francisco because the climate is so mild here with no snow or heavy rains.)

The richly ornamented façade is enlivened with redwood ornament. The general aim was to imitate stone buildings, thus the quoins along the corners. The building is not a simple rectangle in its floor plan; there is a slightly projecting set back "wing" along the right-hand side of the house. In completed rows of such houses, this "slot" allowed ventilation of the rooms in the middle of the house and also permitted reflected sunlight to filter into the house's dark midsection.

This 1876 Italianate Victorian house is worth close attention because it is the "ideal type" of the San Francisco Victorian row house slightly blown up in size.

This style of house is called Italianate in San Francisco because of the Renaissance Revival details adopted from the Pall Mall London men's clubs of the 1840s. (The Italianate style was sometimes referred to as "London Roman.") Slant-sided windows were in vogue. In the Eastlake and Stick styles that followed the Italianate style in the 1880s, the bay was pushed out into a rectangle to capture more space. In the Queen Anne style of the 1890s, bay windows reached their most elaborated form and became smooth curves and three-quarter circles.

The Lilienthal-Pratt House was a wedding gift from Louis Sloss to his daughter Hanna and her husband, Ernest Lilienthal. Sloss formed the Alaska Commercial Company and secured the concession to harvest seal skins off the Aleutian Islands. This became the foundation of a great fortune.

Wormser-Coleman House
1834 California
1876, architect unknown; 1895, additions and remodel by Percy & Hamilton

Standing in unusual isolation on its double lot, this great house is an amalgam of an 1876 Italianate style house (the right-hand side), greatly expanded and partly remodeled in 1895 with a Queen Anne round corner tower by Percy & Hamilton. The 1876 house was built by Isaac Wormser, a pioneer merchant and the "W" in S&W Fine Foods. In 1895 the house was bought by John C. Coleman, a gold miner and utilities investor and the brother of the man who built the corner Queen Anne. Active in telephone, gas, and railroad companies, Coleman was also a director of the California Street Cable Railroad which served his mansion. In the wake of the 1906 earthquake and fire, this house served as the temporary headquarters of the cable line.

For many years the quiet house was preserved by Miss Persis Coleman with its original light gray color scheme, with black window sash and green shades. New owners have freshened up the stately house with agreeable, light colors and enhanced the garden with a lattice gazebo. The great symmetrical tree is a mature Norfolk pine, one of the many exotic plants imported by the Victorians to enliven their treeless city.

Bransten House
1735 Franklin Street
1904, Herman Barth

The red brick Georgian Revival Bransten House built in 1904 presents a severe and plain façade to Franklin Street.

A modern house, in 1904 the Bransten House was very different from the Victorians all around it. It was much simpler looking, calmer, even introspective. This long, narrow house was designed to face the south side of its lot and the garden of the neighboring Coleman House. Many turn-of-the-century San Francisco houses pushed the front door back to the middle of the house, creating more space for a grand parlor facing the street. Centered in the façade is a framed window with Ionic columns and a segmented arch pediment.

Having designed their house to take advantage of the garden next door, the Branstens eventually bought the neighboring mansions at 1701 Franklin and 1818 California to prevent their demolition for apartment buildings, thus protecting their own sunlight and garden view.

The Bransten House was a wedding gift from the William Haases of 2007 Franklin Street when their daughter Florine married Edward Bransten in 1904. Edward Bransten's company was MJB Coffee. Florine continued to live here as a widow from 1948 to 1973, three blocks away from her sister, Alice Haas Lilienthal.

First Church of Christ, Scientist [3]
Franklin and California Streets
1911, Edgar A. Matthews

On this prominent corner at the edge of the burned district, the Christian Scientists built this fine church, notable for its subtle and sophisticated use of color. The exterior of the sober Tuscan Revival church with its corner tower is clad in tapestry brick of a generally light yellowish color. Set into the brickwork is fine polychrome terra cotta. The roof is clad in green glazed tiles. Green copper eaves and soffits circle the church. Over the front doors are inset windows of streaked art glass rich with color. Inscriptions over the doors read: "God is Spirit," "God is Light," "God is Truth," "God is Love."

The fine square tower of the First Church of Christ, Scientist converses with the round tower of the Coleman House across Franklin Street making a gateway to Pacific Heights for the stream of traffic pouring up Franklin Street.

Franklin Street Apartment Buildings [3]
1745 Franklin Street, 1925,
Marian Realty Co.
1755 Franklin Street 1923,
Marian Realty Co.
1740 Franklin Street 1912, architect unknown

Between 1906 and the 1930s upscale apartment buildings replaced the Victorian houses of eastern Pacific Heights.

The floor plans of these units are almost always intelligently laid out. Commodious rooms and "ancillary" amenities such as foyers, glass interior doors, walk-in storage rooms, and built-in storage furniture in kitchens and baths produced a civilized standard of urban accommodation, particularly for singles and couples. These buildings are the real stuff of eastern Pacific Heights. Viewed from across the Bay on the Sausalito ferry, they are the countless facets of white, cubist San Francisco.

Lafayette Park [4]
Sacramento, Washington, Gough, and Laguna streets
1855, John T. Hoff, city surveyor; 1890s, paths and retaining walls

Twin palms announce the entrance to Lafayette Park at the crest of Octavia and Sacramento streets. (The 1 California trolley-bus stops here in both directions.) Four-block square Lafayette Park crowns the highest point in Pacific Heights at 378 feet above sea level. It enjoys fine views, both of Twin Peaks to the southwest and of the Bay to the north. This 12.7-acre hilltop park was one of a series of large parks reserved in the Western Addition when the city expanded west in 1855. The pattern of large, mostly four-block parks between Larkin and Divisadero streets north of Market was probably the best balance of buildings to park space San Francisco has seen in her history. The hilltop parks—Lafayette

181

Park, Alamo Square and Alta Plaza—occupy commanding sites with sweeping panoramas of the Bay or the city. They are also related to one another visually: you can stand in one and look out to the green of the others. The squares placed in the valleys have had a more complex history than the hilltop parks. Eventually east-west streets were run through them and houses, schools, and recreational facilities were built over parts of some of them. But they too have become part of a larger design, attracting sports facilities and active recreation, while the hilltop parks have evolved into places of contemplation.

The Western Addition survey commission exceeded its mandate, resulting in decades of litigation, by ignoring the ordinance that expressly limited parks to one block "corresponding in size to the adjoining block." In December 1864 Samuel W. Holladay, a former City Attorney, began legal action against the city when he claimed the summit of Lafayette Park, the highest, choicest spot in the entire Western Addition. In December of 1867, the court found in Holladay's favor and he began the construction of a large white house, Holladay's Heights, which became a mecca for local and literary society. In what was to be a crucial error, the city failed to appeal this decision to a higher court.

The anomaly of a private mansion in the center of a public park attracted notice. In the 1870s an action of ejectment was brought by the city against Holladay. By this time, he had built his house, planted gardens, and constructed fences on the summit. This time the issue went all the way to the Supreme Court in Washington, which found in favor of Holladay and barred the city from further litigation. A compromise with later claimants to property within the park resulted in the construction of 1925 Gough, the Beaux Arts apartment building on the east side of the park. Holladay's intrusive house was not torn down until 1936.

Though the city litigated over the park, it did not do much to improve it in the Victorian period. In 1890 Lafayette Park was described as "mostly an unimproved sand hill." In the late 1890s the city began to grade and plant the park. It was landscaped in the English style with large lawns falling away from a wooded peak. (The hollow area surrounded by trees at the summit is the site of Holladay's mansion.)

Spreckles Mansion [5]
2080 Washington Street
1912, MacDonald and Applegarth

The palatial reinforced-concrete, white Utah limestone-faced mansion at Washington and Octavia streets was built in 1912 for Adolph and Alma de Bretteville Spreckels. It occupies almost half a block and is distinguished by paired columns, French windows, and balconies with richly scrolled metal balustrades. *Putti* uphold escutcheons over the windows and under the balconies.

Adolph Spreckels was one of the many sons of German-born sugar magnate Claus Spreckels, who came to control all the sugar refineries in San Francisco. Claus developed a vast sugarbeet operation in the Salinas Valley and moved on to finance a Hawaiian sugar kingdom and to control much of its cane production and shipping. His son Adolph followed him into the sugar business.

In 1908, at age fifty, Adolph married twenty-four year-old San Francisco–born Alma de Bretteville. (Young Alma had studied nights at the old Mark Hopkins Institute of Art, and one of her instructors, Robert Aitken, selected her as the model for the figure of Victory that tops the Dewey Monument in Union Square.) Together Alma and Adolph had this grand house built before the opening of the 1915 Panama-Pacific International Exposition. The great fair could be seen on the bayfront below from the mansion's north windows.

When the lots were accumulated for the grand house, Mrs. Spreckels insisted on saving and moving six Victorian houses that sat on Jackson, and two facing Washington Street. In 1924 the Spreckels gave the California Palace of the Legion of Honor in Lincoln Park, also designed by *École des Beaux Arts*-trained George A. Applegarth, to San Francisco; Mrs. Spreckels also gave the museum its fine collection of Rodin sculptures. (*See Tour 13*)

WASHINGTON STREET HOUSES
AND PHELAN MANSION [6]

This block on the view ridge across from Lafayette Park, served by the Washington-Jackson cable line until 1956, was very early one of the finest addresses in Pacific Heights as fashion moved westward. At the corner of Washington and Octavia streets is **2100 Washington Street**, a fine white, French-style city mansion. Its Octavia Street side is especially impressive and makes a fine pair with the French-influenced Spreckels Mansion. Its front yard has been walled-in and an attractive pergola introduced at its entrance.

Next door to the west is **2108 Washington Street**, a house with a complex history. It seems to have been built between 1875 and 1885 for Frank Griffen and stood near the Spreckels wall. In 1921 it was moved to this site and in 1925 was completely remodeled by architect Louis Hobart and faced in red brick. Today it is a Georgian Revival building. The fine first-floor bow "window" solarium that stretches across the front was added in 1988. This house has also walled in its front yard for privacy.

2120 Washington Street is a Classical Revival Box built in 1908 for the president of a lumber company. It banished bay windows from its façade, though one appears on the west side of the house facing the Phelan Mansion.

The Mary Phelan Mansion [6]
2150 Washington Street
1915, Charles Peter Weeks

James Duvall Phelan, scion of a wealthy Irish Catholic banking family, built this *palazzo* for his sister Mary after the fire of 1906 destroyed the family home at Seventeenth and Valencia streets. It was designed by Charles Peter Weeks and completed in 1915 in time for the great Exposition. The buff brick Renaissance Revival mansion was the scene of elaborate receptions. The glassed-in loggia was a later improvement. Neither Senator Phelan nor his sister ever married; James had his own suite in the house. James Phelan served as a reform mayor of San Francisco from 1894 to 1902 and as U.S. Senator from California from 1915 to 1921. He was principal benefactor in the construction of St. Ignatius Church adjoining the campus of the Jesuit University of San Francisco, his *alma mater*. Phelan built an elaborate estate south of San Francisco in Saratoga, Villa Montalvo.

Washington Tower [6]
2190 Washington
1960, Heiada & Muir

On the corner of Washington and Laguna, behind a glitzy sidewalk, is highrise Washington Tower, a Miami-modern import of 1960 on the site of the lost Irwin mansion. It makes no effort to relate to its surroundings.

BEAUX ARTS APARTMENT BUILDINGS [7]

Immediately east of the Spreckels Mansion is the elegant, ten-story, salmon-colored apartment building at **2006 Washington Street**. Designed by C. A. Meussdorffer in 1925, this concrete building is one of the finest, if not *the* finest, "community" apartment house ever constructed in San Francisco. Each floor is a separate unit as large as a sizable house. The building is designed to face not the street but the low-rise Spreckels

Mansion and the Golden Gate to the west. Between it and the Spreckels Mansion there is a large garden with a curving, brick-paved ramp leading to an underground garage. Figures of Pan playing his pipes decorate the garage approach. As with many of San Francisco's most sophisticated traditional buildings, it is painted all one color, with no emphasis given to its decorative elements. The building's salmon color has a warm glow at sunset.

Adjoining is **2000 Washington**, on the corner of Gough, built in 1922 and also designed by C. A. Meussdorffer. While less showy, this fine seven-story, seven-unit, Beaux Arts apartment building is another luxurious building with fine views to the north out over the Bay. It, too, is painted in one color—only its metalwork is painted black.

GOUGH STREET VICTORIANS [8]

Leave Lafayette Park, circumnavigating its summit and exiting by the path downhill, past the tennis courts, to Gough and Clay streets. Built into the edge of the park is **1925 Gough Street**, the St. Regis Apartments, a midrise Beaux Arts luxury apartment house built about 1925 and designed by C. A. Meussdorffer. It is surrounded on three sides by park land and enjoys a unique location. It is the heir to the many claims made to a string of lots within the park. The city, in a compromise, permitted the construction of this building in order to secure the rest of the properties for incorporation into the park.

At **2000 Gough Street**, on the northeast corner of Clay, stands a fine Eastlake-Queen Anne house built in 1886. The old house has been sensitively expanded to the rear with decks and added rooms. Next door is the Belden-Buck House at **2004–10 Gough Street**, a large Queen Anne built in 1889 and designed by T. C. Matthew and Son. This very fine frame house is a great example of a late Victorian San Francisco

upper-class residence. The design features a central chimney that rises through the center of the façade with a two-story cylindrical bay to the right and a one-story round bay to the left. The whole design is an essay in asymmetrical disposition of building elements. Between the first and second floor is a large carved masklike face set in carved foliage. A large stained-glass window depicting the Bay is set in the west side of the house next to the present parking area. Art glass windows were used on the sides of houses to let in light but to obscure the view of neighboring side walls.

Beyond the two Victorians is a pair of townhouses, **2030 Gough Street**, a Tudor Revival stucco design, and **2040 Gough Street**, a red brick Georgian Revival house. These early twentieth-century houses fill out more of their lot than Victorians did and were built with ample garages underneath them. The two dissimilarly styled houses share a similar form and unite to create a U-shape. Of the 1960s apartment building on the southeast corner of Gough and Washington, the less said the better. Such bleak designs will probably experience facelifts in the future, since their location is so superior to their architecture.

CLAY STREET MODERN FLATS [9]

The steep block of Clay between Gough and Franklin streets enjoys fine views of Nob Hill's highrises and the tops of the Financial District's contemporary highrises on the other side of the hill. On the south side of Clay is a group of three three-flat apartment houses built about 1938: numbers **1963–65–67**, **1969–71–73**, and **1977–79–80 Clay Street** designed by Martin Rist. These fine stucco flats are set back from the sidewalk in a staggered pattern with attractively landscaped planter-gardens set in front of them. They are determinedly modern and are among the best designs from an often-uninspired period.

They do not have bay windows; instead they sport International Style wrap-around corner windows, with shallow, false balconies set beneath them. At their garage bases, the buildings have steel columns and curved walls with glass blocks. Portholes decorate the set-back garage doors.

Across Clay is the green canvas canopy of **1950 Clay Street**, a highrise concrete apartment building in the Art Deco style built in 1930 and designed by Baumann & Jose. This swank design features a splashy Art Deco lobby with a metal grille and plate glass door, bay windows, and an Art Deco roofline with jazzy ornament. Even during the depressed 1930s, some construction continued in Pacific Heights and on Russian Hill, oftentimes the best residential highrise construction the city was ever to see.

Golden Gate Spiritualist Church [10]
1901 Franklin Street, at Clay
c. 1900
Services conducted Sunday 6:30 P.M. and Wednesday 7:30 P.M.; they are open to all.

On the corner of Franklin and Clay streets, with its entrance on prestigious Franklin Street, is the restrained, white Classical Revival house built at the turn-of-the-century for one of the Crockers. Edwardian reticence and the reaction against the late Queen Annes resulted in restrained designs such as this archetypical example.

The gumdrop shrubbery around the building and the unadorned lawns on the graded embankments are traditional. The wood house is intended to look like stone, as is the cement-stuccoed brick retaining wall around the high lot. A few minimal alterations were made when the house was converted into a church. Note the way this lowrise mansion sets off the Art Deco wall of highrise 1950 Clay to its west.

The founder of this Spiritualist church was the Rev. Florence S. Becker, a medium who organized a congregation in 1924. Spiritualists affirm that "communication with the so-called dead is a fact, scientifically proven by the phenomena of Spiritualism."

Haas-Lilienthal House Museum / The Foundation for San Francisco's Architectural Heritage [11]
2007 Franklin Street
1886, Peter R. Schmidt; 1927, Gardner Dailey, compatible wing
Open to the public with guided tours Wednesday and Sunday, 12:30–4:30 P.M.; small fee; 441-3004. Heritage also conducts walks and other programs.

Tours of the interior of the turreted Haas-Lilienthal House afford a glimpse of a Pacific Heights Victorian as it was lived in by one San Franciscan family from 1886 to 1972. Alice Haas Lilienthal, born a year before her parents built this house, lived here until her death in 1972. She preserved her family house on the once-fashionable street as all the buildings around were demolished for apartment buildings.

Architect Peter R. Schmidt's 1886 design takes the standardized floor plan of the typical San Francisco row house and increases it in all dimensions to fit this larger, upper-middle-class lot.

The house has evolved over time. The front parlor was remodeled in the 1890s with a warm, yellow Sienna marble fireplace. The middle parlor is paneled in wide boards of fine redwood and has a red Numidian marble-faced hearth. The dining room is late 1880s in feel, with golden oak wainscotting and embossed wallpaper walls. The kitchen has an old sinkboard, servants' call box, and original simple plaster walls and wood cabinets and wainscotting. The stove dates from the 1920s, when many appliances were modernized and an elevator was installed.

In 1974 Alice Haas Lilienthal's heirs donated the old house to The Foundation for San Francisco's Architectural Heritage, founded in 1971 and a member-supported, nonprofit organization dedicated to the preservation of buildings and places important to San Francisco's architectural and historic character. Heritage operates the Haas-Lilienthal house as its headquarters and opens the principal rooms of the landmark to the public for guided tours.

The best view of the Haas-Lilienthal House is from across Franklin Street, at the northeast corner of Clay, looking northwest. From there the long south wall can be seen, along with the building's four gables. The manipulated gables make it appear that the building has a pitched roof; it actually has a flat roof. The corner turret with its framed windows is strictly decorative; its windows are some ten feet off the unfinished tower floor. If you walk north up Franklin to look at the façade frontally, a curious thing happens: The house seems to fold up into a tense, compressed design. Viewed from this angle, the façade becomes an ascending series of three triangles; the porch gable, the false central gable, and the conical roof of the turret with its triangular-pedimented window. The houses of this period—1886–1889—were the most wildly manipulated residential designs California ever saw. They used all the basic geometric forms: rectangles, cylinders, and triangles combined in boldly interpenetrating combinations.

Greenlee Terrace Apartments [12]
1925-55 Jackson Street
1913, Arthur J. Laib

From about 1909 through the 1920s, "courtyard" complexes were built in San Francisco and Los Angeles in prestigious neighborhoods. Almost pueblolike, these flats step up the hill. Stucco and theater produce a most agreeable regional architectural "set" combining Mission Revival and Craftsman imagery. Designed as cells within the city, the building creates a strong sense of place and apartness. The stairs are private and not part of the public sidewalk; the design can be amply

enjoyed visually without entering it. The landscaping here adds much to the islandlike feeling of this complex.

Matson-Roth Houses / West German Consulate [13]
1950 and 1960 Jackson Street
1918, Walter Bliss

This sophisticated pair of townhouses was built for the widow of Swedish-born shipping magnate William Matson. Matson forged a great shipping company, Matson Navigation Co. After his death in 1917, Mrs. Matson built 1950 Jackson Street, the smaller house to the right of the court, for herself. For her daughter and son-in-law, Mr. and Mrs. William P. Roth, she built 1960 Jackson Street. Passageways linked the two houses. After Mrs. Matson's death and the Roths' purchase of Filoli, the William Bourn estate on the San Mateo Peninsula, the twin houses were sold. For some time they were most appropriately the Swedish consulate; in 1987 they were bought, restored, and adapted for the West German consulate. They enjoy fine views of the entrance to the harbor.

2000 BLOCK OF JACKSON STREET [14]

The 2000 block of Jackson Street, between Octavia and Laguna, has an eclectic array of houses, apartments, and condominiums from the Victorian to the modern period. The second house in, **2010 Jackson Street**, is a two-story Neoclassical contemporary house with two statues and a pergola on its second story. It is built around a private central court and was designed by Ted Moulton in 1960; the upper floor was added in 1988. In front of the reticent house is a very fine white granite and black iron low front fence preserved from the Victorian house that once stood here.

The Classic Revival yellow brick mansion at **2020 Jackson Street** was built for I. W. Hellman, the founder of the Union Trust Company and principal owner of Wells Fargo Bank. It dates from about 1902 and was designed by Reid Brothers. Here again Edwardian self-control dominates. A formal Ionic colonnade lines the side entranceway. The front door has a fine iron grille. Immediately after the earthquake and fire in 1906, this house became the temporary headquarters of the Wells Fargo Bank.

2030 and 2040 Jackson Street, a pair of Mediterranean-style houses, form another U shape. Decorated bays, grille work balconies, and emphatically molded ornament create idealized architectural images of California as reinvented in the late teens and booming 1920s.

Across the street, behind the classical balustrade of the back of the 1915 Phelan Mansion, a pair of new condominium buildings at **2045 Jackson Street** was completed in 1988 to designs by Hornberger, Worstell & Associates. These grand condominiums with lofty ceilings present an air of classical formality. A rusticated stucco base links the symmetrical pair. Though they look like stone or concrete buildings, they are conventional frame and stucco. Copper-crowned chimneys and two oval windows make a picturesque, postmodern skyline. This is a sophisticated design that does not attract too much attention to itself. Glimpsed between the pair is the back of the buff brick Phelan Mansion with its loggia and horizontal picture window.

Whittier Mansion Museum / California Historical Society [15]

2090 Jackson Street, at Laguna
1896, Edward R. Swain
Open for house tours at 1:30 P.M. and 3 P.M. on Saturdays and Sundays; changing upstairs galleries open Tuesday–Sunday, 1–4 P.M.; small fee; 567-1848. The 83 Pacific bus stops at Jackson and Laguna in front of the Whittier Mansion.

The red Arizona sandstone-clad Whittier Mansion was designed by Edward R. Swain in 1896 for William Frank Whittier, partner in a large paint and glass company. Whittier was a Maine man who came to San Francisco in 1854 at twenty-two. He became a director of what is today Pacific Gas & Electric Company. Whittier's house is unusual in San Francisco for its steel-reinforced brick walls and red stone facing. Swain designed a house that incorporated all the latest mechanical equipment. There was an electric converter to change city streetcar power to house current, an Otis hydraulic elevator, combination gas and electric lighting fixtures, a central heating system, and a large attic water-storage tank. The house rode out the 1906 earthquake, suffering only toppled chimneys.

The principal rooms on the first floor of the mansion are paneled in oak, mahogany, birch, and other fine woods. The principal parlor is a dark, rich, masculine room with a very fine mahogany and red marble mantlepiece. The view bay in the northeast corner, with good ventilation, has the cozy, intricately decorated Turkish smoking room with its built-in cigar keeper. The original furnishings were scattered, though photographs exist of the opulent original decor. The furnishings in the house today are an eclectic but appropriate mix of late nineteenth-century American furniture.

The outstanding treasure here is the Louis Sloss collection of early California scenes. Examples of the work of William Keith, Thomas Hill, William Hahn, Edwin Deakin, Raymond Yelland, and Grace Hudson capture views of California's unspoiled natural wonders and early Yankee settlements. The second-floor bedrooms have been converted into a series of small galleries that mount interesting changing exhibits on aspects of California history.

The California Historical Society acquired the house in 1956 for its headquarters. The California Historical Society was founded in 1870, revived in 1886, and reactivated in 1922. A privately funded statewide nonprofit educational institution designated by the

California Legislature as the state historical society, the California Historical Society's mission is to collect, preserve, and interpret information about the history of California. There are regional centers in San Francisco, Los Angeles, and San Marino.

Ottilie R. Schubert Hall [15]
2099 Pacific Avenue
1904, Reid Brothers
Open Tuesday–Saturday 10 A.M. to 4 P.M.; small reader's fee

Downhill from the Whittier Mansion is Ottilie R. Schubert Hall, the California Historical Society's important research library, which is housed in this Classical Revival house built for John D. Spreckels, Jr. in 1904 and designed by the Reid Brothers. The California Historical Society bought the house in 1961 to house its rich and diverse research collection whose seed was the collection of Californiana assembled by C. Templeton Crocker between 1915 and the early 1920s when he had the market almost to himself. In 1923 he deposited the books with the California Historical Society and eventually donated them.

Today the library preserves 45,000 books, 350,000 historic photographs, and 8,000 manuscript collections. It also houses the Kemble Collections on Western Printing and Publishing and the post-1906 San Francisco *Chronicle's* clipping archive.

2535 Laguna [16]
c. 1904, Ernest A. Coxhead

Walking down the steep slope of Laguna Street, you can catch a glimpse of Mt. Tamalpais across the Golden Gate. Sandwiched between two large corner lots, now the sites of apartment buildings, 2535 Laguna is a brown shingled townhouse designed by Ernest A. Coxhead about 1904. It is one of the earliest row houses to accommodate the newly introduced automobile. The entrance has been placed on the side of the lot to permit a large, bay-windowed parlor to face the street and catch a side view of the Bay. The house has black-painted, Georgian-inspired trim and an attractive green composition shingle roof which complements the boxwood mini-hedge. The most interesting feature of the house is an element almost never elaborated by architects: the paneled, black wood and clear glass double garage doors with a long transom surmounted by a broken pediment with a central cartouche. It is rare indeed to find such elegant and domestic garage entrances.

This was one of four houses that the English-born Coxhead designed for Mrs. Florence Ward between 1898 and 1904. Presidio Heights, west of Pacific Heights, which experienced a burst of house building by the well-to-do after the fire of 1906, is the area with the most such sophisticated houses. The 3200 and 3300 blocks of Pacific Avenue have outstanding clusters of shingle townhouses with understated black trim and polished brass hardware.

2000 Broadway [17]
1973, Backen, Arrigoni & Ross

The brutal twelve-story highrise at 2000 Broadway at the corner of Laguna introduced a new style to Pacific Heights: 1970s Concrete Brutalism. The base of its Laguna Street side and its Broadway-facing bays display a remarkable arrogance and gracelessness. The rectangular projecting bays along elegant Broadway have stingy little slit windows and present mostly concrete to the street. If the façade almost looks like the back of an industrial building, that is because the west side of the tower, facing the Golden Gate, is the "front" of the complex with metal sash floor-to-ceiling windows looking to the view. The central court that cuts through the dense stack of units is more like a light well than a courtyard. The freestanding concrete entrance canopy with the proud address "2000 Broadway" has all the subtlety of a child's block set. Unpainted gray concrete is a particularly offensive material in San Francisco; it ages unattractively and is dull and depressing in fog or rain.

2040 Broadway [17]
1987, Frizell Hill Moorehouse

The blockbuster towers of the 1960s and 1970s have been outlawed by recent zoning. Today, a kind of "contexturalist" zoning requires recent buildings to fit into their environment—buildings in Pacific Heights tend to be the average height of their neighbors; if the neighbors are set back from the street, so will the new building. 2040 Broadway was built in 1987 to designs by Frizell Hill Moorehouse and has twelve units. The four-story building might be described as being in the postmodern French mansard style. A gas lamp burns over the entrance and the cornice is garnished with heroic-sized grape clusters.

The Hamlin School / James Leary Flood Mansion [18]
2120 Broadway
1901, Julius Krafft

The James Leary Flood mansion is one of San Francisco's great Edwardian mansions. Its lines are quiet, expansive, dignified. Built of wood, it is designed to look like a stone palazzo. It sits behind extraordinarily fine monolithic white granite entrance pillars and a now-green bronze fence. The front stairs and landings are made from single large pieces of the finest granite. Seen from the foot of the steps, the façade of the classically detailed house creates a stacked-up pyramid of forms: the porch, loggia, and the horizontal third-floor window pile one atop the other. The twin gray marble lions guarding the steps are nicknamed Leo and Leona. A peek through the elaborate grille over the front door reveals the golden oak and red brocade paneled central hall.

The most remarkable interior is the red lacquer-paneled, bamboo-ceilinged Chinese Room with green silk-lined walls. An elaborate Chinese-style mantlepiece here has sea-green marble. There were once many of these Chinese-style rooms in San Francisco's mansions; this is one of the last original interiors of its kind to survive. A *porte cochere* stands at the west end of the house, and a path here leads to the playground installed behind the mansion. From there the mosaic-tiled solarium, which projects from the back of the house, can be seen. The view from here is splendid.

Today the building, now called Stanwood Hall, houses offices and classrooms of the Hamlin School. Directly below are the rooftop playgrounds of the new Hamlin school building, McKinney Hall, at **2129 Vallejo Street**, designed by Wurster, Bernardi & Emmons in 1967 in a simple, pure Bay Region version of the International Style. In 1970 Walker and Moody designed a science building, Jennie Mae Hooker Laboratory, which is tucked behind the Vallejo Street building.

Mr. and Mrs. James Flood, and his sister Cora Jane—"Miss Jennie"—moved into the house in 1906 after the earthquake and fire gutted the brownstone Flood mansion atop Nob Hill (today the Pacific-Union Club). Eleven years later, James Leary Flood built another mansion a block west at 2222 Broadway. He and his wife moved there in 1913 and gave this house to Miss Jennie. She retired to the Fairmont Hotel in 1924 and in 1928 Mrs. Edward B. Stanwood, head of the Sarah Dix Hamlin School, bought the mansion from the Regents of the University of California, converting its principal rooms into classrooms and the third-floor servants' quarters into rooms for boarders. Founded in 1863 as the Van Ness Seminary, the school is the oldest nonsectarian independent school for girls west of the Mississippi. It became a nonprofit educational institution in 1955 and is today an independent day school for some three hundred girls.

Bourn Mansion [19]
2550 Webster Street
1896, Willis Polk

The imposing, dark clinker brick

townhouse built for William Bowers Bourn in 1896 at 2550 Webster Street, near Broadway, is one of the most forceful house designs in San Francisco. The façade has at its center one large, ornately framed window. The entrance is a "tunnel" set under this overpowering focal point. While conventionally described as "Georgian Revival," it is perhaps better called Manipulated Georgian. From Broadway, the baronial house presents double gables and a formidable array of towering chimneys. Inside the rusticated ground floor were two waiting rooms, one light and airy and French for ladies, another dark and masculine in the Craftsman style for gentlemen. Beyond the central hall an imposing staircase rises to the second floor, the *piano nobile*. Beyond a reception area embellished with Bruce Porter peacock murals was Bourn's stately reception room with a monumental marble mantlepiece and a great bay window at the north end of the room with a view of the Golden Gate.

Willis Polk designed several monumental buildings for Bourn: this house, the Empire Cottage at the Empire Gold Mine in Grass Valley in 1897–1898, the Jessie Street Substation for PG&E off Mission Street near Moscone Center in 1905–1909, and the great Georgian Revival estate of Filoli in the San Mateo watershed lands in 1916. (*See Tour 14*)

Bourn inherited a gold rush mining fortune and eventually controlled the Spring Valley Water Company (which provided San Francisco with all its water, at a high price) and became president of the San Francisco Gas Company. In 1888 he built the largest stone winery in Napa Valley, today the Christian Brothers Greystone Cellars, in St. Helena. Bourn's princely taste also resulted in PG&E's elegant substations tucked away in alleys throughout the city.

James Leary Flood Mansion / Convent of the Sacred Heart High School
2222 Broadway
1912, Bliss and Faville; 1940, Timothy Pfleuger, conversion into convent and girls' high school

Joseph Donohoe Grant Mansion / School of the Sacred Heart
2200 Broadway, at Webster Street
1910, Hiss and Weekes; 1948, conversion into girls' elementary school

Andrew Hammond Mansion / Stuart Hall for Boys
2252 Broadway
1905, architect unknown; 1956, conversion into boys' elementary school

Probably the greatest single private conserver of great San Francisco architecture is the Convent and Schools of the Sacred Heart. The three great mansions at Broadway and Webster Street are an outstanding architectural grouping: two large red brick mansions frame the set back pink Tennessee marble Italian Renaissance *palazzo* built by James Leary Flood in 1913, the stateliest house ever erected in San Francisco. Designed by Bliss and Faville and built with a budget that knew no bounds, the Flood Mansion (now the Convent of the Sacred Heart High School) was the equivalent of a great hotel in its equipment and scale. The façade of the steel-frame building is clad in the finest stonework in San Francisco. The carefully matched blocks of Tennessee marble form a smooth background for the delicate carving that surrounds the entrance and the great windows. Two spiraled Corinthian columns frame the metal and plate-glass front door. A peek through the superb wrought-iron grille allows a view down the immense, 140-foot-long entrance hall paved with Rosato Vicenza marble, ending in a bay window overlooking the Golden Gate.

A side gate near the children's playground to the right is usually open and you may turn the corner and view the great *cortile*. This magnificent space originally had a large reflecting pool and a fountain. The tree ferns here came from the Australian pavilion at the 1915 Exposition. When the house was unobtrusively converted into a school by master architect Timothy Pfleuger in 1940, the elaborate arcaded bay of the drawing room was filled in with stained-glass windows.

To the right of the Flood Mansion, at 2200 Broadway, is the red brick and limestone Joseph Donohoe Grant mansion designed in 1910 by Hiss and Weekes for the heir to a dry goods fortune. In 1920 Grant helped found the Save-the-Redwoods League; there is a J. D. Grant Redwood Grove in Del Norte State Park named in his honor. In 1948 the mansion was added to the School of the Sacred Heart; it serves today as the girl's elementary school.

To the left of the white Flood Mansion, at 2252 Broadway, is the Andrew Hammond Mansion, an Edwardian red brick townhouse built about 1905 for a lumber and railroad magnate. In 1956 it was converted into Stuart Hall School for Boys.

VIEW OF THE PALACE OF FINE ARTS AND THE GOLDEN GATE [21]

About halfway down the steep block of Fillmore between Broadway and Vallejo, a sweeping panorama of the north Bay and the Golden Gate opens before you. This area was known as Harbor View in the nineteenth century. Today's white, lowrise Marina District at the base of the hill was a tidal marsh filled in for the Panama-Pacific International Exposition of 1915. The great ocher dome of Maybeck's Palace of Fine Arts floats over the west end of the Marina. Green forests blanket the Army Presidio. There is a good profile view of the Art Deco Golden Gate Bridge from here.

Japantown to Cathedral Hill

FROM NIHONJINMACHI
TO NIHONMACHI

What This Tour Covers

[1] Buddhist Church of San Francisco / Buddhist Churches of America

[2] Binet-Montessori School / Former Morning Star School

[3] St. Francis Xavier Roman Catholic Mission for the Japanese

[4] 1800 Block of Laguna Street Victorian Group

[5] Old Bush Street Synagogue Cultural Center / Judah L. Magnes Western Jewish History Center

[6] Konko Church of San Francisco

[7] Christ United Presbyterian Church

[8] Soto Zen Mission Sokoji

[9] Nichi Bei Kai Cultural Center

[10] Japanese American Citizens League

[11] Western Addition YWCA

[12] Japanese Cultural and Community Center of Northern California / CFB-Japanese American History Room

[13] 1825 Sutter Street

[14] Vollmer House: Victorian High Point

[15] Stanyan House

[16] Nihonmachi Mall

[17] Japan Center

[18] Geary Expressway

[19] Fillmore Auditorium

[20] Fillmore Center

[21] Consulate General of the People's Republic of China

[22] St. Francis Square

[23] The Sequoias

[24] St. Mary's Roman Catholic Cathedral of the Assumption

[25] First Unitarian Church

Preliminaries

Best Times To Do This Tour

Sunday at 10 A.M. is the most convenient time to see the fine interiors of Japantown's temples. Start with the second-floor sanctuary of the stupa-capped Buddhist Church at 1881 Pine Street, at Octavia. The traditional recessed altar here is modeled on one in Kyoto and is remarkably beautiful. The Soto Zen Mission Sokoji at 1691 Laguna Street opens at 1 P.M.

Each August, a weekend Nihonmachi Street Fair is held in the Japan Center and the Buchanan Street Mall. First held in 1973, the fair gathers a large multiracial but predominantly young Asian-American audience to listen to a diverse program performed by Asian, black, brown, and white artists doing rock, soul, salsa, and Polynesian music. Over forty nonprofit community organizations, many from the Western Addition as well as Japantown, and many performing arts groups, singers, musicians, and dancers, including the Chinatown Lion Dance company, perform.

Parking

A large city parking garage is located under Japan Center and can be entered from Geary Expressway headed west, between Laguna and Webster, and from

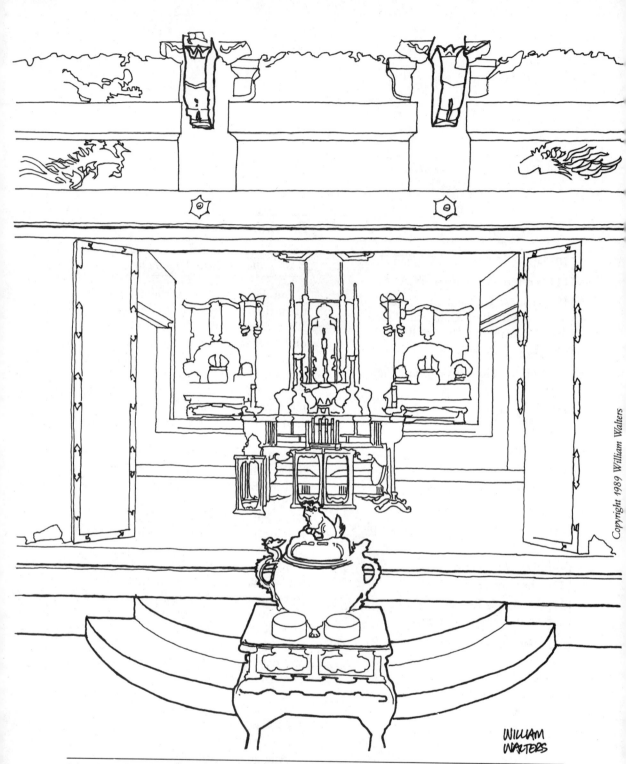

Copyright 1989 William Walters

WILLIAM
WALTERS

The altar of the Buddhist Church of America, on the second floor at 1881 Pine Street, at Octavia, dedicated in 1938 and designed by Gentoko Shimamato, is perhaps the most beautiful room in Japantown.

Fillmore Street between Geary and Post. Parking here puts you at the end of the tour. St. Mary's Cathedral has a large free sunken parking lot entered from Gough Street headed south, at Geary.

Transportation

From Union Square, take the 3 Jackson electric trolley-bus west on Sutter Street and alight at Sutter and Octavia, in front of the Queen Anne Hotel, and walk two easy uphill blocks north to Octavia and Pine and the Buddhist Church entrance around the corner on Pine. At the end of the walk the 38 Geary bus stops in front of St. Mary's cathedral and returns east to Union Square and Market Street.

Restaurants

Isobune, 1737 Post Street, between Buchanan and Webster in Japantown; 563-1030. Lunch and dinner daily; moderate. Sushi and other Japanese dishes.

Yoshida-Ya, 2909 Webster Street, off Union Street; 346-3431. Dinner daily; moderate. A traditional menu including sushi, temoura, teriyaki, sashimi, and yakitori.

Yamato, 717 California Street, near Grant Avenue and Chinatown; 397-3456. Lunch Tuesday to Saturday, dinner Tuesday to Sunday; moderate. Traditional menu and a sushi bar; bamboo mat floor or table setting.

Kabuto Sushi Restaurant, 5116 Geary Boulevard, near Fifteenth Avenue in the Richmond District; 752-5652. Dinner Wednesday to Saturday to 2 A.M., Sunday to 11 P.M.; moderate.

Shopping

A few Japantown shops are mentioned at the end of the tour. Two shops outside Japantown are:

Cando K. Hoshino, 1541 Clement Street, near Seventeenth Avenue, in the Richmond District. Open only Tuesdays and Saturdays from 9 A.M. to 5 P.M. Japanese papers and art supplies.

Jeanne's Bonsai, 2477 Lombard Street, between Scott and Divisadero in the Marina District; 567-7535. Open since 1972; has a large selection of tree varieties; will ship.

Entertainment

Theater of Yugen, 1840 Sutter Street, suite 200; 922-7870. Founded in 1978 by Yuriko Doi; specializes in Noh and Kyogen Japanese theater but performs contemporary non-Japanese theater as well.

Asian American Theater Center, 405 Arguello; 751-2600. Founded in 1973, this company presents contemporary plays, often about the multiracial and generational experiences of young Asian-Americans.

Asian American Dance Collective, 1519 Mission Street; 552-8980. Organized in 1974 and both performs and teaches dance.

Introduction: From Nihonjinmachi to Nihonmachi

Japantown is a small piece of the 1850s Western Addition, a shallow, sandy valley developed between the 1870s and the 1890s as the city's population grew by more than a hundred thousand. It was the first major middle-class expansion beyond the congested, accidentally built-up, mostly jerry-built downtown. Developers built one to perhaps six row houses in groups along street-car routes according to standard plans, sometimes with extra features added. Both native-born Americans and newly successful immigrants bought houses here. There was a notable infusion of Germans,

Christian and Jewish, and of Irish Catholics. After about 1909, a zone along Post and Sutter streets, from Franklin to Fillmore streets, became the spine of San Francisco's Japantown.

Like a historical yin and yang, the evolution of San Francisco's Chinatown and Japantown seem an almost too neat set of opposites. Chinatown is old, rooted, expansive, *ad hoc*, busy, and "exotic;" Japantown is new, diffused, smaller than it once was, planned, quiet, and actually quite American. Although both Chinese and Japanese immigrants suffered discrimination in the past and are successful today, their histories as communities in San Francisco have been remarkably divergent.

Some of these differences are rooted in the histories of China and Japan themselves. While China was a disintegrating empire in the nineteenth century, Japan was a strong and rising power. The weak and disorganized Chinese imperial government exercised little real control over emigration while the Japanese state was highly organized and, until the Meiji revolution of 1868, forbade its citizens to leave the country. Once Chinese went overseas, they were more or less on their own; Japanese emigrants, on the other hand, were long the object of concern of the mother country. Then too, Chinese emigration was quite large, continuing from the 1850s until exclusion in the 1880s; the Japanese migration was smaller and briefer in its first phase. (A striking feature of the Japanese migration is the careful distinctions made within Japanese-American society among the different generations. Every immigrant group to America, of course, knows the tensions inherent in the second, American-born, generation that looks back at the "old country" parents and outward to the larger society. Among the Japanese-Americans these distinctions were refined: the *issei* were the first generation immigrants; the *nisei*, the second generation; the *sansei*, the third generation; the *yonsei*, the fourth

generation; and today, the *shin issei*, the post-1965 migration.)

When Japan dropped her policy of isolation in 1868, a small migration to the United States began that included some political exiles and students seeking modern skills and educations. American cotton and rice were traded for Japanese silks. In 1870 the Japanese government established a consulate in San Francisco, America's chief port on the Pacific. Seven years later the *Fukuin-Kai*, the Japanese Gospel Society, was established in Chinatown by the Chinese Methodist Mission. Many of the earliest westernizing Japanese students embraced Christianity as part of their individual modernization. But this migration was only a trickle, though important.

The first substantial Japanese migrations were to Hawaii, where the newly developed, American-owned sugar plantations were starved for labor. Most immigrants were young male agricultural workers under contract who intended to return to Japan after accumulating some savings. Some stayed on the Islands, eventually becoming the single largest ethnic group there. Their descendants account for a bit less than a third of modern Hawaii's population.

From Hawaii some Japanese moved on to California to work in the fields. The impetus for a substantial migration to California came only after the Chinese Exclusion Act took effect in 1884; by 1890 two thousand Japanese had migrated to the United States. Most worked in agriculture and horticulture where they achieved reputations as skillful workers. A few bought or leased land and became growers themselves, employing their fellow countrymen; others organized wholesale and retail produce outlets. As the Chinese communities in California shrank, the Japanese migration grew fivefold between 1900 and 1930. The peak of migration occurred between 1901 and 1908, yet even at the time of their highest incidence in the population, Japanese immigrants and native-born comprised only 2.1 percent of the population of California. In San Francisco in 1910 there were but 4,518 Japanese, less than 2 percent of the city's population.

Before the earthquake of 1906, two clusters of Japanese settlement existed in San Francisco. The one most noticed by outsiders was adjacent to and mixed in with Chinatown along Grant Avenue from Sutter to Sacramento streets. This settlement was characterized by small art goods shops and restaurants, with the proprietor's family often living over the store. The market in San Francisco for silks and Asian art gave this colony its financial base. A second and larger Japanese cluster was located in the working-class South of Market area along narrow Stevenson and Jessie streets, from Fourth to Seventh streets, and on Sixth Street from Stevenson to Bryant. Here were workers' hotels, restaurants, shops, Japanese baths, missions, and all the usual services found in immigrant ghettos. Boardinghouse owners there often doubled as small-scale agricultural labor contractors. The third, nonresidential, focus of the Japanese community was in the Financial District, east of Sansome Street, where Japanese banks, shipping companies, and the larger import-export firms located to facilitate trans-Pacific trade. A leader in this sector was the Yokohama Specie Bank which opened an agency in San Francisco in 1886 (the parent of today's Union Bank; *see Tour 2A*).

The great earthquake and fire completely destroyed both the Chinatown and South of Market Japanese-American districts. The Chinatown cluster, because of the unchanged focus of the tourist trade and art goods business there, reestablished itself in its former location and by 1941 there were some forty Japanese-American-owned shops in the southern end of Chinatown. The South of Market neighborhood did not come back; that district became increasingly devoted to warehouse and light industrial uses. A small cluster of Japanese hotels, boardinghouses, and service businesses located around South Park South of Market, in the block between Second, Third, Bryant, and Brannan streets. This pocket flourished between 1907 and 1930 because of its proximity to the piers, where immigrants debarked.

The largest Japanese-American concentration, however, settled in the old Victorian Western Addition between Van Ness Avenue and Fillmore Street, today's Japantown. It was here that the *Nihonjinmachi*, "Japanese people's town," took root and flowered, covering thirty blocks by 1940. The Victorian Western Addition had escaped the great fire and enjoyed a great boom from 1906 to about 1909, becoming one of the busiest shopping strips in the city as San Franciscans restocked their wardrobes and new homes. Rents soared in the temporarily overcrowded neighborhood. But as the city quickly rebuilt east of Van Ness Avenue—and as middle-class districts expanded in the Outer Mission and elite housing was built in Presidio Heights— the Western Addition decongested and the real estate market there dropped. As the Japanese-language newspaper *Shin-Sekai (The New World)* editorialized in May 1906, only a month after the fire:

The Japanese here in San Francisco are not financially able to lease new structures which will be built on the fire-wracked sites. They will therefore have little choice but to seek rentals such as those in the Fillmore District that survived the earthquake and fire. Rents, however, in the Fillmore District are still extremely high as they are on [Upper] Market Street. But as new buildings are completed and become available in the city, rents in the Fillmore District will be forced down, and the Japanese will gradually occupy the buildings in that area.

This prediction proved accurate. Old houses were adapted with shops and restaurants inserted at the ground floor and apartments above. Italianate Victorian houses sprouted Japanese shop signs in Roman lettering. Residences, some with rear gardens, boardinghouses, churches, temples, schools, clubs, businesses, restaurants, newspapers, and all the other support services of an almost complete community filled the fancy old Victorians. By 1910 the Western Addition was the center of Japanese-American social life and in 1922 a Nihonjinmachi Improvement Association was organized by the area's businessmen.

Even though the citizens and government of Japan had been the largest foreign contributors to earthquake relief in San Francisco in 1906—more than all other nations combined—an irrational wave of virulent racism swept over San Francisco as Japanese-Americans inherited the brunt of anti-Chinese sentiment. A furor over Japanese-American boys sharing classrooms with young white girls erupted. Hooligans began stoning Japanese-American San Franciscans. In 1905, the Asiatic Exclusion League was formed. In 1906 the San Francisco School Board expelled Japanese students from the public schools; Japanese-American parents refused to enroll their children in the segregated Chinese public school. The Japanese government protested and an international incident erupted. In a compromise, the Japanese government struck its famous "Gentlemen's Agreement" with President Theodore Roosevelt. Under this originally secret agreement, the Japanese government shut off the immigration of laborers, in return, young Japanese-American children were allowed to attend the "white" public schools.

California continued to press Washington for further measures against the Japanese. In 1913 the Alien Land Law was passed in California, depriving Japanese-Americans of the right to buy farm land. This was done despite, or perhaps because of, their great reputation as agriculturists. As the San Francisco *Chronicle*

noted in 1918, "The Japanese farmer in California has always been a great developer and improver." *Issei* farmers, barred from naturalization, circumvented the iniquitous law by vesting title to their land in their *nisei*, American-citizen children. From 1924 to 1952 Japanese immigration was banned by the United States.

As time went on the *nisei* were caught in a double bind. Urged by their education-revering parents to excel in their studies and to attend college, they found when they graduated that no matter how skilled they were, racist barriers prevented them from the jobs they were trained for. Many were forced back to work in family-owned shops and small businesses.

With the Japanese attack on Pearl Harbor in 1941, anti-Japanese hysteria overwhelmed California. On Monday, December 8, every *issei* bank account in America was frozen. Overnight, 1,500 *issei*, the leaders of their communities, were interned by the F.B.I. Under pressure from the U.S. Army commanding general in California, and with the urging of Governor Earl Warren, President Franklin Roosevelt signed Executive Order 9066 which forcibly uprooted 112,000 Japanese-Americans, *aliens and citizens alike*, from the West Coast's cities and shipped them to hastily built detention camps deep in the western deserts of California, Utah, and Idaho. (Many San Franciscans were sent to Topaz Relocation Center in Utah.) Two-thirds of those interned were American citizens. They had committed no crime nor engaged in treasonable activities or espionage.

San Francisco's Japantown was completely emptied in the spring of 1942. Businesses and homes were sold in haste at bargain prices. The neighborhood did not stay empty long; war workers flooded the city in 1942 looking for housing. For the first time, a significant number of these migrants to San Francisco were black. Henry Kaiser's shipyards brought one to three trainloads of new workers to the Bay Area every day for six months. Black workers were recruited in Texas, Louisiana, Arkansas, and the western South. In 1940 there were but 4,846 black San Franciscans, a bare .8 percent of the population; by 1950 there were 43,460, making up 5.6 percent of the city's inhabitants. Fillmore Street became the commercial and cultural spine of San Francisco's first sizable black neighborhood. While that era's jazz clubs are long gone, some of the black Protestant churches organized then (and earlier) continue today.

Upon their release in 1945, Japanese-Americans found their former neighborhood already occupied. Some picked up the threads of their interrupted lives and reopened Japanese restaurants and shops in old Japantown. But most scattered and moved into the Richmond District (now the San Francisco district with the most Americans of Japanese descent), the Sunset, and the suburbs of the East Bay and Peninsula. Japantown's forty blocks shrank to a half dozen. California's panicky forced exile of Japanese-Americans ironically served to accelerate their integration into American society by dispersing the ghetto. Today Japantown has many businesses, churches, clubs, and housing for the elderly, but it is not the population center of the postwar Japanese-Americans; diffuse suburbia is.

The United States-Japan peace treaty signed on September 8, 1951 in San Francisco's Opera House officially ended the "Great Pacific War." A new nonracist Immigration and Naturalization Act was passed the following year. By the early 1970s, Asians constituted nearly one fifth of all immigrants to the United States. In 1987 there were some 12,000 San Franciscans of Japanese ancestry.

"Blighted" Victorian Japantown felt the brunt of a massive Urban Renewal program in the 1950s and 1960s. A master plan by Vernon DeMars called for the bulldozing of the Geary Street Expressway from Franklin to Fillmore and the wiping away of twenty-two blocks of "substandard" Victorian buildings. The drastic A-1 Urban Renewal Project sliced through the black slum and isolated Japantown north of Geary Boulevard.

The A-1 project displaced 4,000 households and carved a mid-twentieth-century automotive city through the "obsolete platting" of the Victorian city grid. North-south Western Addition streets were in many places closed for parks or were assembled by the block into super parcels for gargantuan new development.

Where once there were blocks lined with bay-windowed Victorian houses and shops, St. Mary's Cathedral, Japan Center, and the Geary Expressway together act as a great concrete wall running down the center of the old multiracial Western Addition. The Redevelopment Agency's projects replaced low-income communities of blacks, Japanese-Americans, and Filipino-Americans with racially integrated but middle-class renters, shifting the black poor from the central Western Addition to new developments at Hunters Point, the city's most remote corner.

Though it is rarely noted, urban renewal worked to the great benefit of San Francisco's churches. The state used its power of eminent domain to forcibly buy up private properties, demolish buildings, consolidate small lots into large parcels, and then sell them at low cost to private developers and community organizations, including many churches.

A second wave of Urban Renewal in Japantown fifteen years later destroyed most of the remaining Victorian buildings north of Post Street facing the Japan Center. When they were demolished, and their small businesses and affordable housing displaced, modern Japanese-style buildings were erected. Continuing urban renewal's war on the "outmoded" nineteenth-century street grid and its side-

199

walks, a pedestrian Nihonmachi Mall was built on the block of Buchanan between Post and Sutter. This was filled with unmaintained planters and unwalkable cobbles, some fine Ruth Asawa benches and now dry CorTen steel fountains. Thus redeveloped Japantown has a "center" with a "plaza" and a "mall," all on vacated public streets, the three worst things that can happen to San Francisco's historic urban fabric.

Many of the new buildings are of cheap stucco trimmed with "Japanesque" wood trim and are aging all too rapidly. There are, alas, precious few gardens to distract from the mediocre architecture.

Concurrent with all this upheaval, dislocation, and massive public and private reinvestment in the heart of the old Western Addition, the surviving Victorians all along its edge rose in value. Working couples, straight and gay, bought the abused asbestos shingle-covered Victorians along Japantown's north fringes and restored them. The blocks climbing up toward California Street and Pacific Heights became completely gentrified as fine old redwood houses were restored and meticulously landscaped.

Buddhist Church of San Francisco [1]
1881 Pine Street, at Octavia
1938, Gentoko Shimamato
English service Sundays at 10 A.M.;
Japanese service at 1 P.M.

This plain, Roman Baroque, light-colored corner building designed by *nisei* architect Gentoko Shimamato has stage set broken pediments applied to its façade and gives little hint of the rich temple within. This is despite the small *stupa* (dome and finial) that caps the blocklike multiuse building. Little noticed by the stream of auto traffic that pours west out Pine Street, the *stupa* contains what are said to be relics of the Buddha given to the Buddhist Church in America in 1935 by the King of Siam.

Up a broad staircase is the second-floor *hondo*, or worship hall. This superb room with its recessed gilded altar

flanked by painted screens of peacocks is modeled on that of the mother church in Kyoto. The plain, unornamented timbers are inset with intricate gilded ornamented panels carved in Kyoto. It is a sumptuous yet calm room, one of the most beautiful in San Francisco.

This church's congregation became multiracial as other San Franciscans were attracted to Buddhism. When the Japanese and Japanese-American congregation members were banished to Topaz Relocation Center in Utah's harsh desert, white members continued the corporate life of the congregation and maintained the building, inside of which Japanese-American members deposited important possessions. Upon their release, the building served as a hostel for returning Japanese and Japanese-Americans.

Buddhist Churches of America [1]
1710 Octavia Street
1971, Miles Suda

This blank stucco building has mounted on its façade a copper wheel of life with eight spokes. The Buddhist Bookstore (776-7877) on the second floor is open Monday–Saturday, 9 A.M.–5 P.M.

Binet-Montessori School / Former Morning Star School [2]
1715 Octavia Street
1929, architect unknown

This handsome school building designed in 1929 is from the golden years of school construction in California. It should be looked at from across Octavia Street to fully appreciate its unique façade. This light beige three-story building with brown window frames is styled in Japanese dress with green tile roofs with upturned eaves, an arched entrance treated like a gate, and, at the very top, a colossal green copper "cloud" finial. A green copper madonna and child with Japanese features stands in an ornate white niche in the center of

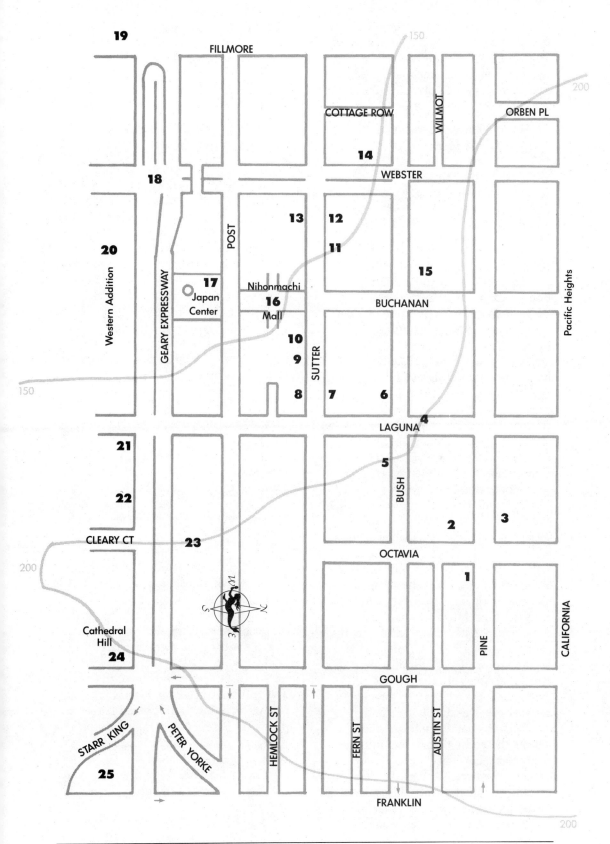

FILLMORE

19

18

COTTAGE ROW

WILMOT

ORBEN PL

14

WEBSTER

POST

20

Western Addition

GEARY EXPRESSWAY

13   **12**

11

15

17
Japan
Center

Nihonmachi

16
Mall

BUCHANAN

10

9

SUTTER

8   **7**   **6**

4

LAGUNA

5

BUSH

21

22

2   **3**

CLEARY CT   **23**

OCTAVIA

1

Cathedral
Hill

PINE

CALIFORNIA

24

GOUGH

HEMLOCK ST

FERN ST

AUSTIN ST

STARR KING

PETER YORKE

25

FRANKLIN

JAPANTOWN TO CATHEDRAL HILL

the façade, making the entire building a pagoda/shrine. Inside is a large ground-floor gymnasium with two floors of classroom above; an ideal size for a school. The school's playground is at the southwest corner of Pine and Octavia.

St. Francis Xavier Roman Catholic Mission for the Japanese [3]
1801 Octavia Street, at Pine
1932–1939, H. A. Minton
English mass Sundays at 10 A.M.;
Japanese mass the third Sunday of each month at 11 A.M.

This modest California Mission-style stucco church with understated Japanese elements serves Japanese-American Roman Catholics from all over the Bay Area. The white stucco frame building has a green tile roof with turned up eaves and a richly decorated dark green Japanese style gatelike entrance porch. Its square tower with restrained pagoda roof capped by a wrought-iron cross converses with the *stupa* across the intersection. This 1930s church preserved and reuses the granite front steps and the retaining wall with its black iron fence surrounding the Victorian house that once stood here.

The building is a combination church and rectory built over a ground-floor social hall and offices. Its small sanctuary is simple and calm. Richly colored stained-glass clerestory windows depict St. Francis Xavier and other Roman Catholic missionaries to Asia. The 1930s liturgical furnishings are spare and handsome. Despite its Jesuit saint name, the church was built by the Order of the Divine Word, a German missionary society. In keeping with the name of the order, the shell-like painted wooden *baldacchino* over the simple freestanding altar acts as a sounding board and reflects the priest's words out into the intimate chapel. The church's most important feature is the garden that surrounds it on three sides. This is perhaps the best California garden in Japantown. It is very much a low-maintenance gar-

den, but with its artistically trimmed shrubbery and one pine tree it recalls the way that Japanese migrants to California took to its botanic possibilities as gardeners and growers.

1800 BLOCK OF LAGUNA STREET VICTORIAN GROUP [4]

The 1800 block of Laguna slopes gently downward and, after the modern buildings at Pine and Laguna's southeast corner, is lined on both sides by restored bay-windowed Victorian houses. This is a unique cluster even in the Victoriana-rich Western Addition. On the west side of the street at numbers **1801–65 Laguna Street** are eleven Eastlake or Stick Style houses built in 1889 by William Hinkel. Gables and turrets pierce the western skyline. Most have been restored after a long decline; a couple still have the asbestos shingle "improvements" of the 1930s and 1940s. Note the different ways the first-floor bay window was designed with various mullion patterns and edgings of colored "flash glass." Shingles enrich the upper stories of some houses. The corner house at the southern end of the complete row has an elaborate two-story bay window capped by a fancy projecting gable facing Bush Street.

Facing them, on the east side of the block, at numbers **1800–32 Laguna Street** are six Italianate row houses with slant-sided bay windows built in 1877 by The Real Estate Associates. In an earlier, more chaste style, the Italianates here face the more decorated later Eastlake or Stick Style row. Most of these houses have had garages tucked beneath them. The trimmed street trees blend with the many small front gardens and potted plants. This street landscaping is a relatively recent achievement concurrent with the gentrification of this block starting in the 1960s—the Victorian city had a bare appearance and very few street trees.

The Real Estate Associates first sold

unimproved lots in the 1860s and then began building row houses in the 1870s. Eventually they built about one thousand houses, mostly in the Western Addition and the Mission. Down payments on these houses ranged from 25 to 50 percent of the average $7,000 cost, with the rest paid in one to twelve years in monthly installments. Architectural historian Anne Bloomfield calculated that the cost of the building broke down roughly at about one-third for wages, one-third for lumber (fir, pine, and redwood), one-eighth for millwork (windows, doors, stairs, and ornament), and one-fifth for plumbing, paint, glass, brick, tile, marble, and hardware. Only especially elaborate houses were individually architect-designed.

Old Bush Street Synagogue Cultural Center / Judah L. Magnes Western Jewish History Center [5]
1881 Bush Street, near Laguna
1895, Moses J. Lyon; 1989, Felix M. Warburg, restoration

The Venetian-Moorish redwood gingerbread façade of the former conservative synagogue of congregation Ohabai Shalome (Lovers of Peace) is well worth seeking out. Designed by Moses J. Lyon in 1895, this is a unique survivor in post-1906 San Francisco. Behind the lacy façade with its Romanesque portal, tracery of Venetian columns, and two square Moorish towers is a vaguely Romanesque sanctuary with a U-shaped gallery. The carved and gilded wood setting for the ark survives; in the apse over the ark is a choir loft. The sanctuary has an especially lofty ornamented plaster ceiling curved to enhance the hall's acoustics. Originally, men sat in the pews on the main floor facing the ark and women sat in the U-shaped gallery facing one another.

The old synagogue has had a varied, quintessentially San Franciscan history and is something of a "Rosetta stone" of San Francisco's distinctive east-west, multiracial and multicultural religious

history. The little wood building with delusions of Venetian stone grandeur was built by fifty European conservative Jews who seceded from congregation Emanu-El in 1863. After meeting in a synagogue on Mason Street a block west of Union Square, the congregation built this new synagogue in 1895. Following its congregation west, in 1934 the synagogue moved a third time to the Richmond District. The old synagogue was sold to a Japanese Buddhist sect known as Soto Shu, followers of the Zen priest Teraro Kasuga. In the 1940s it briefly served a Christian congregation.

After the return of some Japanese-Americans to the neighborhood in 1944, the Sokoji Zen Temple was established here. (It moved to a new temple in 1984; *see entry for Soto Zen Mission Sokoji later in this tour.*) Buddhist priests sat facing each other on the raised stage leading sonorous, trance-inducing chants punctuated by occasional gongs. The San Francisco Zen Center evolved from a group of young white residents of the Western Addition who met here to study *zazen* meditation under Shunryu Suzuki. In 1973 the San Francisco Redevelopment Agency bought the run-down building and leased part of it to the Go Club.

In 1988 the Redevelopment Agency committed the dilapidated, but intact, landmark to the Western Jewish History Center of the Judah L. Magnes Museum and plans were announced for a fund drive to restore this architectural gem to house artifacts, changing exhibits, and various cultural programs relating to Jewish life in California and the West.

Konko Church of San Francisco [6]
1909 Bush Street, at Laguna
1973, Van Bourg/Nakamura
Services in Japanese Monday–Saturday, 7:15 A.M., 10:30 A.M.; service in English Sundays at 10 A.M. On the third Sunday of May the grand ceremony for the Principal Parent of the Universe is held; on the third Sunday of November is the

ceremony honoring founder Konko-Daijin.

This modern Japanese-style temple is a two-story steel-frame, wood and stucco building, designed in 1973 by Van Bourg, Nakamura, Katsura, and Karney. It uses the post-and-lintel form of traditional Shinto architecture; a dramatic Japanese roof with projecting timbers is modeled on the Grand Shrine at Ise, Japan. Social rooms, a kitchen, and a tea ceremony room occupy the ground floor under the sanctuary. The temple itself is an austere room with a beautiful pale wood altar on which offerings of food, flowers, sprigs of greenery, and bottles of rice wine are symmetrically placed. There is a separate ash vault. The light-colored polished wood altar is perhaps the best piece of new design in Japantown and is sparsely decorated with fine bamboo curtains with great silk tassels. Over the altar alcove is a golden disk, the *yatsu-nami*, the Konko symbol of divine light. Tucked over the front entrance is a balcony room used for martial arts.

The Konko religion was founded in 1859 by Ikigami Konko-Daijin, a forty-two-year-old farmer who recovered from a serious illness. (Konko translates as "the teaching of the golden light.") It uses the prayers, rituals, and robes of Shintoism.

After the bland stucco boxes inflicted on the city from the 1950s to the 1970s, architects have returned to the Edwardian flats building, modified this time round by ground-floor garages. The traditionally bay-windowed and ornamented building at **1740 Laguna Street** is brand new but would be taken by most to be a turn-of-the-century building. Next door is a structure built seventy years earlier when the optimal three-story, bay-windowed San Francisco building was first perfected.

Christ United Presbyterian Church [7]
1700 Sutter, at Laguna
1972, Wayne Osaki

Sunday services in English at 10 A.M. and Japanese at 11:15 A.M.; 567-3988

The American Presbyterian Church was among the most active in missionary work in Japan, Korea, and China in the late nineteenth and early twentieth centuries. Many of the ambitious young men who migrated to California in the early twentieth century, especially those who came as students at the great California universities, were Japanese Christians—Presbyterians at that. Though the church's interior is pleasing and refined, its exterior is reticent to the point of dullness. The brown wood trim, thin square tower, and large diagonal skylight hardly counter the blandness of the white stucco building.

Soto Zen Mission Sokoji [8]
1691 Laguna Street, at Sutter
1984, VBN Corporation
Zazen meditation daily from 6:30–8:00 A.M. and 6:30–8:00 P.M. Sunday services at 11 A.M. or 1 P.M.; closed August; 346-7540.

This modern Japanese-style Buddhist temple with projecting roof timbers forming an X was designed by the VBN Corporation and completed in 1984. It is built of cinnamon-stained wood and light yellow stucco. Under the exposed wood eaves over the entrance is a thin wood tablet with fine calligraphy in white and light seafoam green, perhaps the most artistic sign in Japantown. The spare interior was designed for *zazen* meditation and is furnished with black and white cushions.

Nichi Bei Kai Cultural Center [9]
1759 Sutter Street
1972, Mitsuru Tada & Associates

One of the most Japanese of the urban renewal Japantown designs is this set-back, three-story, stucco and wood "traditional" frame building with shingle trim tucked into a Victorian block. Designed by Mitsuru Tada & Associates, it features a small Japanese garden with a stone lantern behind a rustic fence. The chronically neglected garden has the potential of being the best garden in Japantown. It is particularly disappointing in the new and "better" urban renewed Japantown to find so very few gardens, and even fewer constantly manicured and maintained ones. Very much like the rest of San Francisco, the strategy in Japantown is plant it and forget it, thrive or die.

Japanese American Citizens League [10]
1765 Sutter Street
1973, Van Bourg, Nakamura, Katsura, Karney

This new building fuses traditional San Francisco frame architecture with contemporary Japanese elements such as the circular second-floor window. While less literally "Japanese" than most of the post-urban renewal Japantown designs, it is one of the more successful. It was designed by Van Bourg, Nakamura, Katsura, Karney in 1973.

The Japanese American Citizens League (JACL) emerged as a civil rights organization in 1930 from local and regional organizations of *nisei*. It worked for rapid Americanization and assimilation into mainstream American society. Its creed was "better Americans in a greater America." The top leadership of the JACL removed to Salt Lake City before the government instituted the travel freeze that preceded relocation to camps in the interior. The JACL urged Secretary of War Henry Stimson to form the volunteer Japanese-American combat units that subsequently distinguished themselves in World War II. During the immediate postwar years, the JACL emerged as the most important Japanese-American civil rights organization.

Western Addition YWCA [11]
1830 Sutter Street
1912, Julia Morgan

Sutter Street was Japantown's important institutional street during the period between the earthquake and World War II, analogous to Chinatown's Stockton Street. Architect Julia Morgan's 1912 Japanese Branch YWCA at 1830 Sutter Street is actually an eclectic frame and stucco building somewhat Craftsman, or perhaps Tudor, in flavor. The interestingly walled-in structure has a high tile-capped wall and tile roof with upturned eaves. It is one of the earliest examples of "Japanese style" design. The light greenish color mottled roof is quite fine. The walled forecourt shelters a typical San Francisco side entrance and front stairs.

The original interior is substantially intact. In the 1930s this was known as the Japanese branch of the YWCA and along with all the usual activities of a Y taught traditional Japanese dance and ceremonies, martial arts, and flower arranging. During the war, the building served war workers who flooded San Francisco's crowded Western Addition. With the release of the Japanese-Americans from detention, the Y and the neighborhood's churches and temples served as hostels and relocation facilities.

Japanese Cultural and Community Center of Northern California / CFB-Japanese American History Room [12]
1840 Sutter Street
1987, Wayne Osaki

The CFB-Japanese American History Room, a fine historical archive, is open by appointment, 921-1485; for center programs, call 567-5505.

Next door to the YWCA is one of the best and latest Japantown designs, Wayne Osaki's Japanese Cultural and Community Center of Northern California built on a Redevelopment Agency-cleared site. Owned and operated by a consortium of community groups, its purpose is "to preserve and transmit to future generations the Nikkei community's unique history and heritage." The center is constructed of brown timbers with white stucco panels over a cracked-pattern granite base. A fine modern three-part Japanese roof clad in flat brown tiles with a copper ridgepole caps the building. Various community service organizations and activities are housed here and serve neighborhood residents and Japanese-Americans from all over the Bay Area. The ground floor with the easiest access is reserved for the senior center; upstairs are offices and a large meeting room where space is rented to various cultural, artistic, educational, recreational, physical fitness, and social service organizations. The center plans to expand to the rear with a community hall/gymnasium with bleachers. The donor wall in the lobby is distinctive.

1825 Sutter Street
1878, Italianate Row House

At 1825 Sutter Street is a characteristic two-story, bay-windowed San Francisco Italianate row house built in 1878. Captain and Mrs. John Cavarly were its first owners. The house was first restored in the 1960s and then was restored again with invisible additions to the rear. It was imaginatively landscaped in 1983. The oak white (slightly eggshell) monochromatic color scheme elegantly displays the house's restrained redwood ornament. The green boxwood grid of a front garden sets off a black steel abstract sculpture entitled "Streetlight," by James Nestor, again a rare gesture to the city. There are several fine surviving 1870s Victorian row houses and sets of flats on this side of Sutter Street, all carefully restored since the late 1960s.

With a modern garage door unobtrusively tucked in beneath it on the uphill side and a basement flat tucked under it on the downhill side, three-unit **1717–19 Webster Street** is a sober and handsome example of early Victorian house building of the 1860s and 1870s. The flat-front Italianate building has fine cornice and window moldings. The tiny garden with the baby tears groundcover and small-leafed plantings is a subtle contemporary San Francisco garden.

Vollmer House: Victorian High Point [14]
1735–37 Webster Street
1885, Samuel and Joseph Cather Newsom

The ornate, steeple-capped Eastlake row house at 1735–37 Webster Street is one of the most elaborate surviving Victorian architectural works in San Francisco. Architects Samuel and Joseph Cather Newsom here took the basic San Francisco row house box with its standard interior and applied to it one of the richest redwood gingerbread façades ever confected in San Francisco. Like their Carson Mansion of 1884–1885 in Eureka, California, the architectural ornament here projects far from the wall plane of the building giving it a pronounced three-dimensional effect. The right-angled bay window and all the other windows are framed by pipe-stem colonnettes. The entrance porch is capped by elaborate spindle work and a carved basket of flowers. The projecting ornamental gable with its sunburst ornament sports an inventive pyramidal steeple with a round ball finial.

In the mid-1970s, the Redevelopment Agency shifted gears and turned to restoring rather than demolishing the Victorians left along the fringes of its vast swath of cleared Western Addition blocks. The newly founded Foundation for San Francisco's Architectural Heritage worked to find buyers to restore the houses and the Redevelopment Agency moved them.

This landmark building has had a peripatetic history. It was built as a single-family dwelling in 1885 at 773 Turk Street, near Franklin and was one block from the edge of the 1906 fire. Over the years it was converted into a rooming-house with about two dozen inexpensive units and a manager's office/flat inserted where the basement flat is today. When its "blighted" block was condemned in 1975 by the Redevelopment Agency in order to build Opera

Plaza on Van Ness Avenue, this old house and eleven others were jacked up, put on wheels, and towed by night twelve blocks west to the other side of the A-2 Western Addition redevelopment area.

It was a tight fit squeezing this house between its neighbors—part of the left bay had to be shaved off. Despite its extraordinary façade, the house as originally built was plain inside with only a fancy spindlework archway in the main hall. (This is a private residence and should be left undisturbed.)

The corner building at Webster and Bush streets, **2101–01 1/2 Bush Street**, is a two-story Italianate clapboard building with a corner shop and a five-sided corner bay window that projects out over the public sidewalk at the second floor. Visible in side view is the extension to the building. The steplike profile of these three Victorians is typical of the way the Victorian city's individually built frame buildings fit together to form whole blocks. Corner lots were usually larger and more expensive and saw the construction of either grander, more expensive houses (many of which have since been torn down) or a combination of shops and residences, many of which survive. This shopfront was handsomely faced with maroon and black tiles with a thin yellow band, probably in the 1940s.

The Stanyan House [15]
2006 Bush Street
c. 1852

One of the oldest houses in San Francisco, this house dates from the immediate post-Gold Rush city and shows how simple the first wave of Victorian house building was. It makes a dramatic contrast with the Newsom brothers' Vollmer House of 1885. It was owned by the family of San Francisco supervisor Charles Stanyan who had a hand in the creation of Golden Gate Park and the Haight-Ashbury, where a street was named for him. This house originally sat in a large corner garden. It is typical of

the gable roofed, open-porch, clapboard houses, many built with imported lumber, that New Englanders and other Easterners built in sandy San Francisco in the early 1850s. Its steeply pitched roof proved to be unnecessary in a climate where it rarely rains and never snows.

Flanking the Stanyan House at **2000–12 Bush Street**, near Buchanan, are two two-story, bay-windowed Eastlake or Stick Style flats buildings developed by the Stanyans about 1885 as income property. They exhibit the classic San Francisco row house form: flat rooflines, bay windows rather than open porches, and machine-carved ornamental redwood trim.

Nihonmachi Mall [16]
1700 Block of Buchanan Street, between Sutter and Post
1971–1980, Okamoto-Liskamm with Van Bourg/Nakamura & Associates, Japantown master plan; 1976, Okamoto & Murata/Van Bourg Nakamura, mall design; Ruth Asawa, fountains

Post Street is the dividing line between the A-1 Western Addition redevelopment area to the south and the A-2 Western Addition redevelopment area, of which the Nihonmachi Mall is a part, to the north. In the first wave of urban renewal, total demolition consolidated blocks into huge parcels on which monumental concrete buildings could be built. Reaction against this drastic approach resulted in a second wave of downscaled projects.

The Nihonmachi, or Buchanan Street, Mall wiped away many vintage Victorians that had been adapted over time to Japanese shops and restaurants. These small businesses were displaced by demolition and then the construction of this modern "Japanese village" arrangement with a central paved mall. A stark modern concrete-and-timber Japanese gate faces Sutter Street at the north end of the mall and a tall square tower faces Post Street at the south end of the vacated block. Rough granite paving blocks are laid to create a "river" where the street once was. Ruth Asawa's two fine CorTen steel fountains, which look like folded steel flowers, are usually dry, but are among the best new public art in the city. (She and schoolchildren also made the lively ornamented sidepanels of the benches here by casting dough figures in concrete.) As malls go, this one probably has potential, though real streets and sidewalks are always superior for San Francisco shopping districts. The modern wood-and-stucco Japanese-style buildings grouped here have a human scale and agreeable intricacy but do not seem to be aging well. The center of the mall seems unfinished: "arms" where Hemlock Alley should continue resolve instead into clusters of unsightly dumpsters.

The modern square tower building is the former Kokusai Theater (since converted to fast food) designed by Rai Okamoto & Associates in 1971. Facing it at **1698 Post Street** at Buchanan is the well-stocked **Soko Hardware** Company designed by Van Bourg/Nakamura in 1980. (*Soko* is the Japanese word for *San Francisco*.) The finest shop in the mall is treasure-filled **Genji Kimonos and Antiques** at 1731 Buchanan; the wood chests in the back of the shop are noteworthy.

Japan Center [17]
Three blocks bounded by Post, Sutter, Laguna, and Fillmore streets
1968, Minoru Yamasaki and Van Bourg/ Nakamura & Associates. Yoshiro Taniguchi with T. Y. Lin, Kulka, Yang & Associates, engineers, Peace Pagoda

This five-acre complex houses a large parking garage, a sixteen-story hotel, and lowrise shops, restaurants, art galleries, a major bookstore, professional offices, travel agencies, a Japanese bath, a cineplex, and originally the Japanese Consulate. It is a period piece of sterile 1960s mall design, a monument to the bad city planning and worse architecture of 1960s urban renewal. Eminent domain

was used to clear the three blocks; revenue bonds financed an 800-car city-operated parking garage on the ground level. The air rights over the garage were sold to Honolulu insurance magnate Masayuki Tokioka who formed a joint venture with Nippon Railway Co. and a theater company.

Japan Center's one accent is the Peace Pagoda, a gift from the people of Japan. Its twelve rectangular pillars support five copper-clad roofs. Above the topmost roof is a *karin*, a nine-ringed spire, supporting a *hoshu*, flaming golden ball. The pagoda's design is adapted from that of the 1,200-year-old Pagoda of Eternal Peace in Nara, Japan. Unfortunately, the reflecting pool has long been dry.

Some of the best shops in the Japan Center include **Ginza Discount Imports** (922-2475) in the East Building, which is trinket city. In the Kintetsu Building, the **Ikenobo Ikebana Society** (567-1011), immediately to the left before the floor rises for the Webster Street bridge, carries books on flower arranging, implements, and containers. They also display fine flower arrangements in their show windows; open Tuesday through Saturday, 9:30 A.M.–5 P.M. **The International Art Guild Society** (567-4390), a hole-in-the-wall art gallery on the right-hand side of the Webster Street bridge has nineteenth-century and contemporary Japanese prints, some quite fine. **Kinokuniya Bookstore** (567-7625) in the West Building, second floor, has a large stock of Japanese and English language books, excellent art books and guides to Japan, as well as some inks, brushes, and paper; open daily 10 A.M.– 7 P.M. except the first Tuesday of each month. Downstairs, on the first floor of the West Building, in front of the castle model, is **Asakichi Japanese Antiques and Art** (921-2147), open daily, Monday–Saturday, 10 A.M.–6 P.M. and Sunday, 11 A.M.–6 P.M. The **Kabuki Hot Springs**, located in the West Building, is a recently remodeled Japanese-Style bathhouse with private and communal

baths. Open Monday–Friday, 10 A.M.–
10 P.M., Saturday and Sunday, 9 A.M.–
10 P.M. Shiatsu massage weekdays after
2 P.M. and after 11 A.M. on weekends.
Costs from $8 for the communal bath
and sauna to $60 for a private room and
a one-hour massage. The entrance to the
hot springs is located at 1750 Geary Boulevard, outside the Japan Center.

Geary Expressway [18]
Geary Boulevard from Franklin to
Broderick streets
1950s, San Francisco Redevelopment
Agency; master plan by Vernon DeMars

The Japan Center turns its back to the
Geary Expressway, which cleared a wide
swath from east to west, linking the
downtown with the middle-class Richmond District to the west. The expressway project, built to Vernon DeMars'
master plan, included the demolition and
redevelopment of all the flanking blocks
of Geary from Franklin to Broderick
streets. A narrow pedestrian bridge was
flung across the busy expressway at
Geary and Webster streets and a two-
block underpass for automobiles constructed at Geary and Fillmore streets.
On the underpass walls are four brightly
colored metal graphics installed in 1986.
The two designs on the south wall, a
West African cow and a Ghanan *gye
nyame*, or spirit symbol, face two Japanese *mon*, or family crests, one with a
yin-yang design and the other a crab.
Wisteria and bougainvillea were also
planted by landscape architect William
Carney but have not taken.

Fillmore Auditorium [19]
1807 Geary Boulevard, at Fillmore
1912, Reid Brothers
Call 567-2060 for programs and
information

Fillmore and Geary was once a very
lively crossroads. On the southwest corner stands a blocklike, three-story, yellow brick building with all its original
upper-floor windows intact. There are
shops on the building's ground floor; the

Fillmore Auditorium is upstairs. Over the
years, the Fillmore Auditorium has been
the venue for a great many events. Promoter Bill Graham leased the hall in
1967 and staged the first of his six-days-
a-week "Summer of Love" rock concerts.
On June 20, 1967 Graham debuted with
the Jefferson Airplane, Gabor Szabo, and
Jimi Hendrix here. This first rush of the
psychedelic San Francisco sound was
accompanied by novel light shows projected on the walls. Recently, after many
years, Bill Graham has again begun pre-
senting programs in the mellow, historic
hall.

Fillmore Center [20]
Three blocks bounded by Fillmore,
Steiner, O'Farrell, and Turk streets
1988–1989, Daniel, Mann, Johnson &
Mendenhall; Lifescapes, Inc., landscape
architect

The somewhat round, peak-roofed
towers visible south of Geary Expressway, east of Fillmore Street, are part of
Fillmore Center, a nine-acre residential
and commercial complex consisting of
1,113 rental units in five-story apartment
buildings and four sixteen-story towers;
there are also 1,260 covered parking
spaces. These sandy blocks composed
one of the city's principal black neighborhoods until the forces of eminent
domain and the Redevelopment Agency
combined and razed them in the 1960s.
The design promises "extensively landscaped and waterscaped gardens" in the
center of each block, which, if actually
filled with water and maintained, will be
unique. (There are those who believe in
the miraculous, chief among them the
American city planners who put fountains in their dreary plans).

Consulate General of the People's
Republic of China [21]
1450 Laguna, at Geary Boulevard

The anonymous white stucco complex at the southeast corner of Geary
and Laguna was built for the Salvation
Army but has since been bought by the

People's Republic of China for its consulate general. The red flag with yellow stars flies here in neutral nondescript territory, far from Chinatown with its predominantly Nationalist sympathies.

St. Francis Square [22]
Geary Boulevard, from Webster to Laguna streets
1962, Marquis & Stoller; Lawrence Halprin and Associates, landscape architect

210   From the 38 Geary bus, on the right, or south side of Geary Boulevard, are the cypress trees bordering the parking lots of St. Francis Square, a co-operative housing project developed by the Pacific Maritime Association and the International Longshoremen's and Warehousemen's Union. St. Francis Square's brave-new-world design took San Francisco's evolved residential pattern and turned it inside out. Parking lots create a no-man's-land on the Geary Boulevard perimeter, while freestanding rows of housing designed by Marquis & Stoller face away from the public street and sidewalk and into the landscaped interior of the block.

The Sequoias [23]
1400 Geary Boulevard, between Gough and Laguna
1969, Stone, Marraccini & Patterson

The elegantly designed white concrete tower standing on a horizontal base dominating the north side of Geary Boulevard is The Sequoias, a large retirement and hospital facility built by Northern California Presbyterian Homes. Designed in 1969 by Stone, Marraccini & Patterson, it must have made a beautiful architectural model. The residential tower with views and a "floating" hospital base are artistically fused. The design is a modern sculpture blown up to gargantuan size, one of the best architectural designs of its day. Standing alone on a mountain slope it would be splendid but built as a two-block concrete wall, artistic as it is, it sterilizes its

adjoining blocks. The Sequoias is best appreciated from a helicopter or driving east on the Geary Expressway, not from the human-scaled housing across the street from it.

St. Mary's Roman Catholic Cathedral of The Assumption [24]
1111 Gough Street, at Geary
1971, Pietro Belluschi, Pier Luigi Nervi, McSweeney, Ryan & Lee; John Staley, landscape architect; Gyorgy Kepes, stained glass; Richard Lippold, baldachino
Open 6:30 A.M.–5 P.M. Sunday masses at 7:30, 9, 10:30 A.M. and 12:15 and 5 P.M. The 10:30 A.M. mass is sung.

San Francisco has had three Roman Catholic cathedrals: Old St. Mary's at California and Grant between the Financial District and Chinatown, which still stands; a great red brick "plant" of impressive proportions built on Van Ness Avenue between 1887 and 1891, which burned in 1962; and today's novel monument at Geary and Gough, completed in 1971 atop Cathedral Hill.

Its travertine-clad form rises from a square base to become an equal-armed Greek cross surmounted by a thin silver cross. The four "seams" in the reinforced concrete cupola are filled with abstract stained-glass windows representing fire to the west, sky to the north, water to the east, and earth to the south. Because the cathedral was placed on a vacated block of O'Farrell Street when the Redevelopment Agency assembled this two-block superblock, the gleaming white cathedral is visible from the very heart of downtown.

The splendor of the building and its importance for our time lie in its interior. The great cupola imagined by Pietro Belluschi and engineered by master Italian engineer Pier Luigi Nervi joins four hyperbolic paraboloids in a triangular coffered dome that soars upward 190 feet. The entire structure rests on four gracefully formed freestanding piers. Bands of glass around the perimeter of the square plan "open up" the church and bring views of the city to the congregation. You should perambulate the vast space examining it slowly from various angles. If there are no services, walk directly under the cupola and look up and all around. The concrete pedestal for the organ is poured concrete become art. Walk the perimeter of the cathedral with its view of the finely detailed great green copper dome of Bakewell and Brown's opulent City Hall to the southeast.

This was the first Roman Catholic cathedral built after the liturgical reforms of the Second Vatican Council in 1962. The priest celebrating the mass faces the congregation across a simplified but luxurious stone altar. The austere altar has a raised stone platform devoid of ornament backed by a fine dark wood screen that makes the robed celebrants stand out. A gold cross hangs above the altar. Over that the cathedral's glory, Richard Lippold's *baldachino*, a silver rain of thin glinting rods falls like a shower of light on the altar.

The St. Mary's complex includes more than its 2,500-seat sanctuary. Directly under the cathedral is a 1,200-seat auditorium and a ring of meeting rooms and offices. Built into the sloping two-block site on the downhill side facing Ellis Street is Cathedral High School, a rectory, and a convent.

First Unitarian Church [25]
1187 Franklin Street, at Starr King Way
1887–1889, George W. Percy; 1967–1968, Callister, Payne & Rosse; landscape architect, John Carmak
Services Sunday at 11 A.M.; for other programs phone 776-4580.

This old stone Romanesque church is tucked artfully into what is essentially a large triangular traffic island. A brilliant addition was designed by Callister, Payne and Rosse and built between 1967 and 1968. While the old church at the corner of Franklin and Geary is routine, if venerable, the modern addition is both inventive and deliberately regional. The

contemporary concrete with redwood trim complex has two human-scaled courtyards, one courtyard surrounded by a new chapel, parish offices, comfortable meeting rooms, an auditorium, and a kitchen, and the second the focal point of a two-story elementary school. One of the best contemporary designs in San Francisco, this building represents the humane, nature-oriented qualities of the best Bay Area design. The Callister, Payne & Rosse design is important for visitors who wish to see distinctively Bay Area modern architecture.

The First Unitarian Church in San Francisco has been at the forefront of religious, cultural, political, economic, and social reform since its organization in the wake of the Gold Rush. The first Unitarian service was preached in San Francisco on October 20, 1850, and the Unitarian society was organized in 1852. In the 1860s, under its famous minister Thomas Starr King, the First Unitarian Church was the first to open its pulpit to all faiths. King is buried under the white marble tomb facing Franklin Street, under the corner palm. Over the years First Unitarian's pulpit has been distinguished by Ralph Waldo Emerson, Julia Ward Howe, Edward Everett Hale, Charles Eliot, David Starr Jordan, and many others. Ecumenical efforts in San Francisco have always been strongly supported here and this congregation and reform Temple Emanu-El hold a joint Thanksgiving Day service.

Mission Dolores and The Mission District

THE REVOLVING DOOR INTO
AMERICAN SOCIETY

What This Tour Covers

[1] Sixteenth Street: The Mission's
Oldest Street / Basilica of San Francisco

[2] Mission Dolores Chapel / Museum
and Old Cemetery

[3] Old Notre Dame School / Site of
Costanoan Ranchería / Original Mission
Chapel Site / Camp and Albion streets

[4] Chula Lane and Abbey Street
Victorian Cottages

[5] 3639–41 Seventeenth Street

[6] Dolores Street Palms and
Landscaping

[7] Mission High School

[8] Mission Dolores Park / Downtown
Panorama

[9] Dolores Street from Cumberland to Liberty

[10] 100 Block of Liberty Street

[11] 827 Guerrero Street

[12] Valencia Street: Feminist Epicenter

[13] Lexington Street Victorian Enclave

[14] Plaza de la Raza/Parking Garage

[15] Twenty-second Street and San Jose Avenue / Forgotten Historic Trail

[16] Twenty-second Street / Mission Street Marquees

[17] St. John's Lutheran Church Victorian Group

[18] Mission District Mural

[19] Capp Street Victorian Row

[20] Mission United Church

[21] Twenty-fourth Street Latino Shopping Strip / Balmy Alley Murals / "Raza History" Mural

[22] BART Station / BART Mural

Preliminaries

Best Times To Do This Tour

Weekdays at 7:30 A.M. mass is said in the old mission; the Saturday 5 P.M. mass is also celebrated there. Sunday services are in the less interesting adjoining basilica; the noon mass is sung in Spanish. The old mission is open daily 9 A.M. to 4 P.M.; small donation requested. Sunday mornings are good times to explore the neighborhood; churches are open, families are on their way to worship, the neighborhood is relaxed and happy, and no trucks rumble through the streets.

On one October weekend each year some of the painters, photographers, sculptors, weavers, and other artists with studios in the upper two floors of the former Sears Building, 3435 Army Street near Mission, hold open studios. Write to Open Studio/SF, 1800 Market Street, Suite 252, San Francisco, CA 94102 for dates.

Parking

Street Parking on Sixteenth Street, between Valencia and Guerrero, BART back to car at end of walk.

Copyright 1989 William Walters

Mission Dolores, built of adobe to the designs of Father Francisco Palou and dedicated in 1791, has withstood two great earthquakes. In the earthen plaza in front of this church the Native American peoples once performed their dances.

Transportation

J Church Streetcar to Church and Sixteenth streets, walk one block east on Sixteenth to Mission Dolores. Or take BART to Sixteenth Street station and walk three blocks west to the mission.

Restaurants, Cafés, and Bars

Café La Boheme (285-4122), 3318 Twenty-fourth near Mission, is open from 7 A.M. to 11 P.M. **Artemis Café** (821-0232), 1199 Valencia near Twenty-first, a woman's café welcoming all; has live entertainment on weekends. **Café-Babar** (282-6789), 994 Guerrero between Twenty-first and Twenty-second, has the spirit of the North Beach cafés of the 1950s.

Interesting restaurants continue to pop up along Guerrero and Valencia streets. These are not high-class restaurants: their plastic-tablecloth decor is both "south of the border" in feeling and thoroughly working class in reality. **Alejandro's** (668-1184), 1840 Clement near Twentieth Avenue in the distant Richmond District, housed in San Francisco's only Spanish-Peruvian Edwardian, serves Spanish, Peruvian, and Mexican food. In the North Mission is the **Rite Spot Café** (552-6066), 2099 Folsom near Seventeenth, a hang-out for local artists.

Shopping

Left-wing, feminist and lesbian, children's, Latin-American, and labor-oriented books and newspapers are what the Mission offers uniquely in a zone along Guerrero and Valencia streets, and here and there on Twenty-fourth as well. **Discoteca Habana**, on Twenty-fourth and Harrison, has Caribbean and samba records. **Discolandia**, 2964 Twenty-fourth near Alabama, is good for salsa and Central American rhythms.

Shops along Twenty-fourth street offer the best regional selection of Central American tropical produce, spices, and condiments. **La Palma Mexicatessen**, 2884 Twenty-fourth at Florida, has handmade tortillas and a fine assortment of dried chiles. The open-fronted **Casa Lucas Market**, 2934 Twenty-fourth near Alabama, imports a dozen different kinds of bananas. Alas, the Mexican bakeries along Twenty-fourth are ordinary. **Lucca Ravioli**, 1100 Valencia at Twenty-second, has its own pasta manufactory visible through a sidewalk window. **Rainbow Grocery**, 1899 Mission at Fifteenth, is the ultimate synthesis of

progressive politics, expanded consciousness, and organic food.

Ben Davis work clothes, the homeboys' favorite, and other excellent work and outdoor clothes are best bought at **Lightstone's Menswear**, 1696 Valencia at Mission, near Army. Mission Street lost most of its big furniture stores to the freeways; along Valencia and Guerrero there are some secondhand stores. **Past Tense**, 665 Valencia near Sixteenth, has 1930s–1960s collectibles. **Groger's Western Wear** at 1445 Valencia at Twenty-fifth carries pointy-toed cowboy boots, Stetson hats, bolo ties, boot tips, and traditional, brand-name Western wear.

Galería de la Raza/Studio 24, 2857 Twenty-fourth at Bryant, displays Latino art and Central American folk art, books, and cards.

Entertainment

Women's Building/Edificio de Mujeres, 3543 Eighteenth north of Valencia; 431-1180. Women and men; variety of progressive and peace programs in funky Dovre Hall. San Francisco's cutting edge.

Theater Artaud, 450 Florida at Seventeenth, 621-7797. New theater, dance, and music in a converted industrial building.

Theater Rhinoceros, 2926 Sixteenth near South Van Ness; 861-5079. Gay theater in the basement of the San Francisco Labor Temple.

New Performance Gallery, 3153 Seventeenth near Shotwell; 863-9834. Modern dance and theater.

Intersection Art Center, 766 Valencia, near Sixteenth; 626-2787. *Avant garde* theater, performance art, and readings.

Mission Cultural Center, 2868 Mission near Twenty-fifth; 821-1155. Various Latino exhibits and programs.

York Movie Theater, 2789 Twenty-fourth near York; 282-0316. One of SF's best repertory movie theaters, a vanishing breed.

Introduction: The Revolving Door into American Society

The Mission and the Presidio are the two oldest Spanish foundations in what became the city of San Francisco. The original mission site at today's Camp and Albion streets was selected by Lieutenant José Joaquin Moraga on June 28, 1776. It was the sixth of the twenty-one missions established in Spanish Alta California. Father Font's diary records that:

Passing through wooded hills and flats with good lands, in which we encountered two lagoons and some springs of good water, with plentiful grass, fennel, and other useful herbs, we arrived at a beautiful arroyo which, because it was Friday of Sorrows [the Friday before Palm Sunday], we called the Arroyo de los Dolores. On its banks we found much and very fragrant manzanita and other plants, and many wild violets. Near it the lieutenant planted a little maize and chickpeas to test the soil, which to us appeared very good....

The Mission period of California history, from the 1770s to the mid-1830s, is very difficult to uncover, buried as it is under a distorting, pious romanticism that began in the 1880s. The coming of the gray-clothed Franciscan friars from the convent of San Fernando in Mexico City was not the salvation but rather the utter obliteration of the native peoples. Absolute cultural contempt was accompanied by smallpox and other "new" diseases that wiped away virtually the entire race of native peoples in a couple of generations. For them, the Christians' God of Love accompanied extinction.

The tribe that the Spanish cavalry and Franciscan friars gathered at Mission Dolores were known as the Ramaytush, one of the people who the Spanish called the Costanoan, or coast people. They ranged over the San Francisco peninsula, the East Bay, and as far south as Big Sur. Most early explorers were struck by the great variation of tribes in the Bay Area, which was an intricate patchwork of different language groups. The San Francisco mission embraced eighteen recognized tribes by 1816. Before the coming of the Europeans, these peoples had a relatively simple material culture. Their houses and rafts were made of tule rushes, and their diet was based on acorns, salmon, and shellfish. They were forced by the Spanish soldiers to abandon their favorite sunny places around the Bay and to cluster in *rancherías,* European-dominated villages near the mission churches. Here they saddened, sickened, and died. Louis Choris observed in 1816 that "After several months spent in the mission, they usually grow fretful and thin, and they constantly gaze with sadness at the mountains which they can see in the distance." By 1850 a United States Indian Agent found but one survivor, Pedro Alcantara, who lamented, "I am all that is left of my people—I am alone."

The Mission District is a revolving door into American society. The history of the succession of its peoples is in microcosm the history of the city, and to a degree, that of the state of California. Native American tribes, Spanish explorers and colonists, Mexican settlers, and Yankee squatters have all lived here. Following the Yankees in the 1860s came a substantial wave of German and Scandinavian immigrants who were in turn followed by the Irish and Italians, especially after 1906 when the South of Market and North Beach districts burned. "The Mish" developed its own accent, said to be something like that of Brooklyn. Between 1950 and 1970, the Spanish-speaking, or Latino, population in the low-rent Mission doubled every ten years, going from 11 percent in 1950 to 45 percent by 1970. Unlike all other California *barrios,* the Mission is not predominately Mexican but has a multinational population of Mexican, Guatemalan, Salvadorian, Costa Rican, Nicaraguan, Colombian, and other Latin American peoples. The turmoil in Cen-

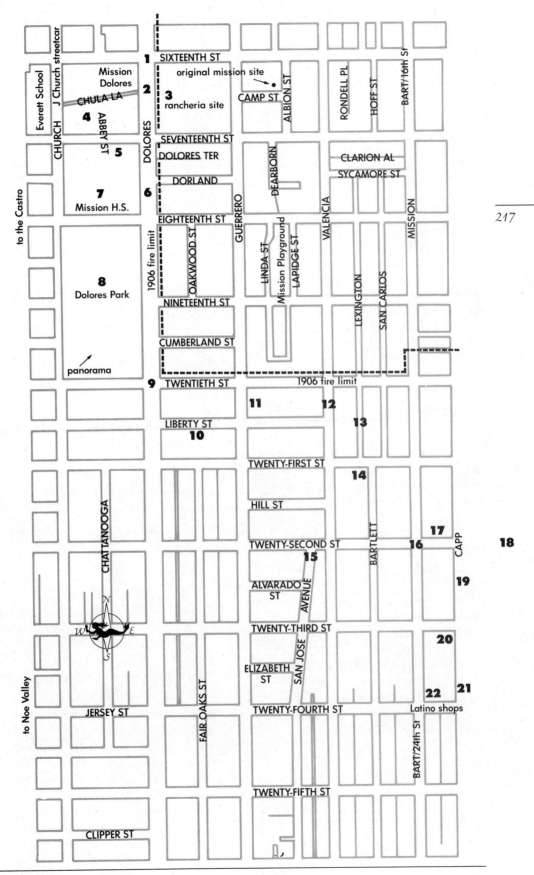

1 SIXTEENTH ST

original mission site

Mission Dolores

2 **3** rancheria site

CAMP ST

CHULA LA

4

ABBEY ST

Everett School

CHURCH

J Church streetcar

to the Castro

5 SEVENTEENTH ST

DOLORES TER

DOLORES

7

Mission H.S.

6 DORLAND

EIGHTEENTH ST

1906 fire limit

OAKWOOD ST

GUERRERO

DEARBORN

LINDA ST

Mission Playground

LAPIDGE ST

VALENCIA

CLARION AL

SYCAMORE ST

LEXINGTON

SAN CARLOS

MISSION

ALBION ST

RONDELL PL

HOFF ST

BART/16th St

8

Dolores Park

panorama

NINETEENTH ST

CUMBERLAND ST

1906 fire limit

9 TWENTIETH ST

11 **12**

13

LIBERTY ST

10

TWENTY-FIRST ST

14

HILL ST

17

16 CAPP

18

TWENTY-SECOND ST

BARTLETT

15

19

ALVARADO ST

AVENUE

TWENTY-THIRD ST

20

ELIZABETH ST

SAN JOSE

22 **21**

Latino shops

CHATTANOOGA

N W E S

FAIR OAKS ST

JERSEY ST

to Noe Valley

TWENTY-FOURTH ST

BART/24th St

TWENTY-FIFTH ST

CLIPPER ST

THE MISSION DISTRICT

tral America has continued to add to this flow in the 1980s.

SIXTEENTH STREET: THE MISSION'S OLDEST STREET [1]

Sixteenth Street at the corner of Dolores was the site of the old adobe mission quadrangle begun in 1782. Old surveys show that the complex extended out into what is now Sixteenth Street. The *convento*, or priests' quarters, adjoined the mission chapel and connected with a storehouse. Behind the quadrangle were gardens, orchards, and a vineyard. During the mission era, a string of adobe houses sprang up along what is now Sixteenth street, from Dolores to Guerrero, on the trail to the port at Yerba Buena (today's downtown). After the priests abandoned the mission in the 1830s, this small Mexican settlement continued to grow slowly. Records indicate that as late as 1844, some Native Americans continued to live in a community, with a *mayordomo*, or administrator, at the former mission. In that year the Mexican inhabitants here unsuccessfully petitioned the governor at Monterey to declare the settlement a pueblo and to grant house lots. Among the petitioners were Francisco de Haro, Francisco Sanchez, Francisco Guerrero, Jesús Noe, Cand'llo Valencia, and José Bernal, all of whom eventually had their names given to Mission streets. The governor refused; instead, over time, the former mission lands were granted as ranchos, many to former soldiers.

In the late 1840s, Yankee squatters turned the mission complex into a hotel, gambling den, and small brewery. Far from the settlement at Yerba Buena, the "over the line" Mission attracted duelists, bear bating, bull fights, and horse racing. The Catholic Church did not regain the old mission and two plots containing the former mission gardens and orchards until 1857. In 1861, after the mission had been returned to the church, the *convento* had a second story added and became a

seminary. In 1876 the convento was demolished for the opening of Sixteenth Street and the erection of a now lost red brick Gothic church that was dedicated on the mission's centennial.

Basilica of San Francisco [1]
1913; 1926
Sixteenth and Dolores
Sunday masses held at 8, 10 (sung) A.M. and 12 P.M. (sung in Spanish).

On the southwest corner of Sixteenth and Dolores streets stands the ornate Churrigueresque Revival Basilica of San Francisco begun in 1913 and remodeled with fanciful towers in 1926 for the sesquicentennial of the founding of the mission. (The title "basilica" is an honor conferred by the pope. Pius XII conferred this dignity in 1952, and a pontifical red and gold umbrella and papal coat of arms flank the altar.) The basilica is not really worth entering, but it is worth looking at from the outside and comparing it with its venerable neighbor, Mission Dolores. As a whole, with its strong diagonal from the top of the tallest basilica tower to the small wall shrine to the Virgin in front of the old cemetery, this is one of the most beautiful block-fronts in San Francisco.

Mission Dolores / Museum and Old Cemetery [2]
320 Dolores Street
1791; Francisco Palou
Open daily 9 A.M.–4 P.M.; small fee. Masses held in old mission weekdays at 7:30 A.M. and Saturday at 5 P.M. Sunday masses held in basilica at 8 and 10 A.M. (sung) and at 12 P.M. (sung in Spanish).

The old mission, officially the Mission San Francisco de Asis, is one of the great historical and architectural treasures in San Francisco. It was begun in 1782 and completed in 1791, and survived both abandonment in the 1840s and 1850s and the earthquakes of 1868 and 1906. It has seen sensitive preservation, including a restoration by Willis Polk in 1918.

The mission was designed by Father

Francisco Palou, who is buried near its south wall in the adjoining cemetery. The chapel is built of adobe, a building technique introduced to California by the Spanish. The soft contours and powdery surface of the adobe have been covered with a hard cement stucco coating to preserve the building from rain. Paired, engaged columns decorate the façade, making this a Baroque design. The three original bronze bells carried overland from Mexico in the 1820s still hang in their niches. A narrow wooden balcony runs across the front of the church and a deep overhang shelters the church façade. In front of the chapel, where Dolores Street runs today, was an earthen plaza with a large cross.

Enter the old mission by a door to the left. Inside, the cool mission, 22 feet wide and 114 feet long, with walls 4 feet thick, feels as ancient as it is. When the eye travels down to the end of the dim church, it is dazzled by the painted and gilded altar and its *reredos* (background), a piece of Baroque Spanish art strained through distant Mexico. Old statues and paintings fill the room; an old Mexican statue of Saint Francis occupies a prominent place to the left. The church is now only infrequently used for mass, but it still serves as the baptistry for the parish, and there is a fine Victorian marble font to the side. The hand-wrought altar rail and the ironwork around the font are probably from the mission workshops. The door of the tabernacle with its picture of Christ came from Spanish workshops in Manila, another part of the vast Spanish empire linked to Acapulco, Mexico by the famous Manila galleons. Lieutenant José Joaquin Moraga, the leader of the June 1776 colonizing expedition, is buried within the church.

The most interesting artistic feature of the mission is the ceiling. It is patterned after Costanoan basket designs and is the most beautiful in the city. It employs earth tones in a chevronlike design painted over the beams and the flat ceiling. The design appears different when seen straight up, or when looked at in perspective. It is the only monument to the arts of the extinct Costanoan peoples.

Leave the chapel through the door to the right of the altar. Outside is a modern Mission-style veranda with an interesting series of pictures of what the mission looked like at various stages in its history. In the small museum tucked behind the chapel is a glass window in the left-hand wall that allows a glimpse of the adobe construction underneath the modern white stucco. Mounted high on the wall is a model of how the struts and the ridge-joints of the rafters were originally bound with rawhide thongs. (In the restoration of 1918, they were augmented with steel supports.) Mementos of the old mission are housed here. Alas, thieves stole the original silver chalices and monstrance of the Franciscan missionaries. Behind the museum is a well-designed courtyard with a fountain and restrooms installed in 1978.

The old cemetery adjoins the mission to the south; originally it covered a larger area. Here are buried some 5,500 Costanoans and many pioneers: Spanish, Mexican, and Yankee. After 1857 the parish was a heavily Irish-American one, and many of the tombstones here record that migration. The highrise marble obelisks of the rich face Dolores Street, while humbler tombs, most unmarked, are in the back of the plot. Burial next to the wall of the church was reserved for priests and governors; Captain Luis Antonio Arguello, the first Mexican governor of Alta California, and Francisco de Haro, the first *alcalde* (mayor) of San Francisco, are buried here, as well as Father Palou.

At some time in the present century an unattractive grid of concrete paths was laid over the cemetery. Recent "improvement" of the plantings has been naïve, though the fragrant roses are welcome. The most interesting monument in the cemetery is in the far corner toward the front: a large brown sandstone Victorian extravaganza decorated with firemen's helmets and upside-down torches. Here lies Charles Cora, an Irishman, who, it was said, hanged himself while awaiting trial by the Vigilance Committee of 1856. James P. Casey and James "Yankee" Sullivan, two other victims of the vigilantes, are also buried here. The dazzling white wall of the mission is often the foil to the clinging bougainvillaea, which bursts in magenta sprays.

Old Notre Dame School / Site of Costanoan Rancheria [3]
347 Dolores Street
1907, Theodore W. Lenzen

At 347 Dolores Street, across from the mission, is the former Notre Dame High School and Convent of the Sisters of Notre Dame de Namur, which closed in 1981. Founded in 1868, it was the first girls' school in San Francisco. That building was dynamited in 1906 to save the old mission across the street from the fire. In 1907 the present mansard-roofed building was designed by Theodore W. Lenzen and constructed on the old foundations.

The block on which this old school stands was one of the two parcels flanking Dolores Street granted by the United States government to the Catholic Church and Bishop Alemany in 1857. Between here and Valencia Street was the rancheria established by the Spanish authorities to "civilize" the wandering Native American tribes, members of the Penutian language family who originally ranged over the San Francisco peninsula, the East Bay, and as far south as Big Sur and Soledad. Their prehistoric population has been estimated at seven thousand; by 1910 they were extinct. No signs, of course, remain from their primitive settlement, but this is a potentially important archeological zone in San Francisco and merits identification and protection.

Original Mission Chapel Site [3]
Camp and Albion streets
The first mission chapel was a temporary log-and-thatch structure alongside a stream near the present-day intersection of Camp and Albion streets, a block and a half to the east of the mission. It faced a long-since filled-in lagoon fed by the Arroyo de los Dolores, the Stream of Sorrows. The ground here proved too soft and the mission chapel was pulled back to its present site at Dolores and Sixteenth streets in 1782.

CHULA LANE AND ABBEY STREET VICTORIAN COTTAGES [4]

Past the shrine to the Virgin Mary in the cemetery wall and to the right is Chula Lane. Walk up Chula Lane to Abbey Street, a quiet cul-de-sac of modest Victorian houses. Cars slow to a crawl here and children play in the streets. To its residents the Mission is a honeycomb of out-of-the-way back streets such as these. Up Chula Lane the houses are set at a sawtooth angle to the sidewalk. The lots and house placement reflect the ad hoc subdivisions that survive here and there within the regular, square-block grid extended into the Mission Addition in the early 1850s.

From Abbey Street the tile-clad dome of the tower of Mission High School can be seen in the distance. Number **37 Abbey Street** is a simple, one-story, flat-front Italianate. Facing it, at Numbers **40−42 Abbey Street**, is a plain three-story frame building of a type known locally as Romeo flats because of the open stairway's balcony at the second floor.

Beyond the nearby parking lot at **445 Church Street** is the back of the modest white stucco headquarters of the Roman Catholic archdiocese of San Francisco built in 1955. Historically Irish and Italian, today half of San Francisco's population of 165,000 church-going Roman Catholics are Spanish-speaking. It is also interesting to note that about half the parishoners of Mission Dolores in the late 1980s are gay.

3639–41 Seventeenth Street [5]
1874, Italiante House

Number 3639–41 Seventeenth Street is a classic two-story, bay-windowed Italianate house built in 1874. It has a small front garden softened with ferns, fuchsia, and jade plants. Its side wall is visible from the sidewalk. This is the house type which has, in the last twenty years, again become the architectural trademark of San Francisco.

DOLORES STREET PALMS
AND LANDSCAPING [6]

In 1904 the Outdoor Art League, a pioneer city beautification group that was part of the reformist, progressive wave that swept San Francisco during the first decade of this century, urged the "improvement and adornment" of barren Dolores Street. The handsome date palms were planted by Golden Gate Park's John McLaren about 1910. The Dolores Street palms make elegant a street solidly lined with houses, flats, and apartment houses, and sprinkled with churches. In the landscaped median is a cast-iron replica of a mission bell on a pole that looks like a shepherd's crook. In the earliest days of leisurely motor touring, the California Women's Club marked El Camino Real with these emblems. Each marker originally had a sign posting the number of miles to the next mission. The bay-windowed, three-story frame flats and apartments that line this part of Dolores Street were mostly built between 1907 and 1929 in the area burned in 1906. It is a most agreeable street to walk or drive along. The buildings preserve the old Victorian house lot sizes, which give the blocks a human-scale of twenty-five-foot building fronts.

Mission High School [7]
3750 Eighteenth Street
1926, John Reid, Jr.

On Eighteenth Street facing Mission Dolores Park is this large, red tile-roofed high school with a lofty and richly ornamented tower. It was designed by John Reid, Jr., the architect responsible for many of San Francisco's finest school designs. (That he was Mayor James Rolph's brother-in-law does not seem to have hurt his career.) Plain walls and rich ornament concentrated at the entrance and tower make a stark, effective contrast. Here the simple white-walled, arcaded, red tile-roofed imagery of the early California missions was adapted for a modern structure—the imagery of adobe in modern reinforced concrete and factory-cast terra cotta ornament. The school was completely reconstructed and its ornament more securely fastened in 1978 as part of the seismic upgrading of all the public schools in California.

In the prosperous 1920s, Mission-style architecture became immensely popular in California. The early colonial days provided a unifying architectural image of white stucco walls and red tile roofs. Many then-unfashionable Victorian houses had their gingerbread stripped away and were coated in stucco. With red tile fringes attached to their cornices, they became weirdly vertical "adobe" buildings. The Mission style has been the region's favorite style, judging simply by the number of attempts at it. Fortunately, mediocre Mission is always better than mediocre anything else. And, embowered in semitropical vegetation, the total effect is almost always pleasing.

Mission Dolores Park / Downtown Panorama [8]
Between Dolores, Church, Eighteenth, and Twentieth streets
1861, Jewish cemeteries; 1905, city park

These two blocks were originally purchased in 1861 for the cemeteries of Temples Emanu-El and Sherith Israel.

221

Cemeteries occupied much of the high ground to the west of the nineteenth-century city and formed a barrier to the city's expansion by the turn of the century. (Cemeteries and some fenced-in amusement grounds and beer gardens were the best landscaped parts of the sandy Victorian city.) After a long political struggle, the city refused to permit new burials within its limits, forcing the cemeteries to relocate to a valley in Colma south of the city line. Most of the remains in Dolores Park were transferred to the new burial grounds.

In 1905 a park was laid out here to serve the populous Mission District.

Today, Mission Dolores Park is the largest park in the Mission. The landscape plan is agreeable and open with groups of palms in the corners and an axial path along the line of Nineteenth Street. Unfortunately, an ugly little park building mars the very center of the park. Also more a blight than an ornament, a massive concrete monument with a replica of Mexico's "liberty bell" was installed at Dolores and Nineteenth in 1962. The bell itself might have been attractive in the park, but the completely useless concrete plaza is stunning in its ugliness and provides more concrete where there should be grass. The ridiculous plaza was built to make an impressive stage for the monument's dedication and has since served mainly as a target for beer bottles.

Up the slope, on the west side of the park, is an indifferent bronze statue of Miguel Hidalgo y Castilla, the priest who is considered the George Washington of Mexico. A streetcar line is hidden in a depression along the western edge of the park. From the far corner at Twentieth and Church streets, there is an impressive panorama over the downtown to the northeast and Bay beyond. Dolores Heights, with its agreeable mixture of small houses and rich vegetation, rises to the southwest (*see Tour 10*).

DOLORES STREET, FROM CUMBERLAND TO LIBERTY [9]

Walk up Dolores Street to Cumberland Street opposite the south side of the park. On the corner at 655 Dolores Street is the competent Beaux Arts **Second Church of Christ, Scientist,** designed by William H. Crim, Jr. in 1915. It makes a nice contrast with its red-brick Gothic Revival neighbor, **Golden Gate Lutheran Church** at 601 Dolores Street. The two churches show the change from Victorian to Beaux Arts taste: from medieval to classical models, and from red brick to white stone or stucco.

Continue up Dolores to Liberty. From the crest there is a sweeping view north down palm-lined Dolores Street. The fortresslike, streamlined Moderne **United States Mint** visible in the distance was designed by Los Angeles architect Gilbert Stanley Underwood and built atop Blue Mountain in 1937. American and Filipino coins were struck here; today this mint produces only proof sets for collectors and is not open to the public.

100 BLOCK OF LIBERTY STREET [10]

The eighteen blocks between Dolores to Mission and Twentieth to Twenty-third streets comprise the **Liberty Hill Historic District**, established by the city in 1987. Owners of buildings must secure Certificates of Appropriateness to alter exteriors visible from the public streets. All the houses on Liberty Street are worth looking at; it is one of the Mission's architecturally richest streets. Number **159 Liberty Street**, a large Italianate house atop a high retaining wall, was built by Judge Daniel Murphy in 1878 during the brief period when some thought the Mission's "warm belt" might develop into a suburban luxury district. But the conquest of the steeper hills by the cable car in the 1870s turned the tide of fashion north, and Pacific Heights with its marine views became the poshest residential district. The Murphy house is one of the largest houses in the Mission and is noted for the visit to it made in 1896 by Susan B. Anthony, an early leader of the woman-suffrage movement. It has since been subdivided into many units.

The row of houses downhill from number 159 displays several of the styles once popular in San Francisco. **Number 151–53**, the house immediately to the east, was probably built around 1917 on what had been the side yard of number 159. Built in an aggressive Craftsman style, it is typical of the housing built after World War I in the East Bay and in the western districts of the city, especially the Inner Richmond.

Next down the hill, **123 Liberty Street** is a good example of the Queen Anne style of the 1890s, with scratchwork plaster ornament and a round corner tower. **Numbers 121–21A, 117–19, and 111–15 Liberty Street** are three Stick-style houses of the 1880s. Last in the row, **109 Liberty Street**, is a flat-fronted Italianate built in 1870 with elegant window moldings and a side garden.

The south side of the block, with its view of the city, attracted the fancier houses, while more modest houses were built on the north side. At the turn of the century, flats and apartment houses were built on the corners of the main streets in the Mission such as the one at **850–52 Guerrero Street**. They define the side streets by enclosing them, creating a roomlike effect within each side street. Number **110 Liberty Street** is a late Queen Anne-Tudoresque house from the 1890s with a gable roof.

827 Guerrero Street [11]
1881, architect unknown; 1890, remodeled Moorish Queen Anne

The dramatic house at 827 Guerrero Street with the Moorish or Moon Gate entrance with new wrought-iron roof cresting was built in 1881 and then much expanded and remodeled in 1890. It has a round bay, stage-set balconies, fine art glass windows, and a vaguely *Arabian Nights* air. Note the rich texture of the walls; virtually every surface, and originally the roof as well, was treated as an opportunity for pattern and ornament. While the architect of this *tour de force* is unknown, this entrance arch is much like the main hall arches in Samuel and J. Cather Newsom's great Carson Mansion of 1884–1885 in Eureka, California, the greatest surviving Victorian mansion in the state.

VALENCIA STREET: FEMINIST EPICENTER [12]

Heavy through-traffic along Valencia and Guerrero streets has created relatively unattractive and therefore low-rent commercial strips, attracting chronically low-profit progressive bookstores, peace groups, left-wing political organizations, and evangelical churches. **Modern Times Bookstore**, 968 Valencia Street near Liberty, carries new international—especially Latin American—literature and progressive books. It is an island of calm with comfortable chairs and a mother lode of free newspapers and flyers reflecting what's happening in radical circles in the Mission. A sort of Christian Science Reading Room for the left, Modern Times sponsors lectures and readings. **Casa El Salvador** at 988 Valencia Street is only one of several peace groups in the neighborhood.

Radical politics has deep roots in the Mission District. Not only the traditionally conservative craft unions such as the carpenters are based here but radical workers groups as well. Today the **Henry George School of Social Science** is at 3410 Nineteenth off Valencia. George's *Progress and Poverty*, published in 1879, was the one book written in San Francisco in the nineteenth century that was read around the world. George set out to explain the phenomenon of deepening poverty amid advancing wealth in modern society and found his single cause in the monopoly of land by a few corporations.

Valencia Street, sandwiched between the gay male Castro and the low-rent Mission, has emerged as the epicenter of the women's movement. **Old Wives Tales**, 1009 Valencia Street near Twenty-first, opened in 1977 and is a nerve center for "womens visions and books" and for children's books. Guides and information can be secured here on Valencia's feminist and lesbian businesses, activities, and restaurants. Low-key **Artemis Café**, 1199 Valencia Street at Twenty-third, opened in 1977 as the Artemis Society, a women's private club. Sexual politics over admitting the eight-year-old son of one of the women working in the club induced Sara Lewinstein, the owner, to eschew separatism and to open the place to all in 1980.

One-half block off Valencia, at 3543 Eighteenth Street, is the **Women's Building/Edificio de Mujeres** (431-1180) in Dovre Hall, originally built as the Norwegian meeting hall. The building supports many women's, gay and lesbian, peace, and progressive groups and is the setting for meetings, lectures, films, and other programs. A mural painted across the second story depicts progressive women: Katherine Smith, Dolores Huerta, Louise Nevelson, Marva Collins, and Polly Bemis. From the beats of the 1950s to the cultural, sexual, and health care politics of the 1980s, San Francisco has harbored within herself the active yeast of contemporary world culture.

The **900 block of Valencia**, between Twentieth and Twenty-first streets, harbors a string of six two-story, bay-windowed Italianate houses all built between 1875 and 1877 by the Real Estate Associates, mid-nineteenth-century San Francisco's largest developer and house builder. They are surviving elements from the largest piece of town planning and building the Real Estate Associates achieved. In 1875 the Real Estate Associates, essentially William

Hollis and partners, bought the block bounded by Mission, Valencia, Twentieth, and Twenty-first streets and cut two narrow streets, today Stevenson and San Carlos streets, through it. They subdivided the parcel into 120 house lots. On Mission and Valencia streets, the Real Estate Associates surveyed large lots and built Italianate villas which sold for about $7,400. All have been demolished. On Valencia Street standard middle-class two-story, bay-windowed Italianate row houses were built which sold for about $5,800. This row survives. Lots and houses on Twentieth and Twenty-first streets were slightly smaller and cheaper; those on the narrow interior streets were smaller still. These houses sold typically to craftsmen, small proprietors, and teachers for about $3,700 on San Carlos Street (closer to Mission) and $3,350 on Lexington Street. Corner lots, the largest and most expensive of all, were developed with mixed commercial-residential buildings for grocers who lived over their shops. They averaged a high $9,990.

At 970 Valencia, over the entrance to an unnoticed bay-windowed Edwardian apartment building, is the small white and blue sign of Mother Teresa's **Missionaries of Charity Queen of Peace Convent** quietly established here in 1985. These Roman Catholic nuns are dedicated to serving the poorest of the poor and the dying.

LEXINGTON STREET VICTORIAN ENCLAVE [13]

The contrast between palm- and residence-lined Dolores Street and stark Valencia with its auto shops is dramatic. East of Valencia, heading downhill, the character of the streets changes from what was originally professional and middle-class housing on the high ground to lower middle-class and working-class housing on the flat land.

Lexington Street can be seen as California's first tract housing. The small-scale, speculator-subdivided side streets in the Mission, blessedly free of through traffic, harbor architecturally coherent and socially diverse residential enclaves. Side streets like Lexington, which is only three-and-a-half blocks long, have a strong sense of visual definition and an intimate sense of place. The closed-in vistas of the narrow streets define a cell with the larger neighborhood. Most of the two-story, flat-front Italianate houses here were built between 1876 and 1877. Though built as single-family houses, they were easily and neatly subdivided into upstairs and downstairs flats when buildings became absentee-owned investment properties. Among the first owners here were a bookkeeper, a master mariner, a theatrical and musical manager, a waiter, and a plasterer.

Plaza de la Raza / Parking Garage [14]
50 Bartlett Street
1987, Conrad & Associates

Here fifty-one units of state-financed, low-income housing were built over a three-level, two-hundred-stall city parking garage. Public housing *has* evolved— even though construction of it has dwindled to almost nothing. At least the central "open space" of this compound is gated. (It is debatable, however, whether housing should be built over concentrated auto exhaust.) The building's chief urban design fault is not its featureless windows, or the cheap appliquéd mock Victorian sunrise designs in the gables, or even the brutality of the block-long Bartlett Street side of the garage; it is the unforgivable interruption of the continuous shopping strip along Twenty-second Street on the other side of the block.

On the corner of Twenty-first and Bartlett is a remarkable Eastlake house at **3243–45 Twenty-first Street**, which has settled unevenly into the soft ground. It was built in 1883 for $4,000 for George Pattison. The lathe-turned redwood ornament on this house is emphatic and strong. Robust designs and durable materials—redwood rather than

cheaper cast plaster and sheet metal— marked the best buildings of the booming 1880s. This house represents the high-water mark of Victorian house design in San Francisco.

TWENTY-SECOND STREET AND SAN JOSE AVENUE / FORGOTTEN HISTORIC TRAIL [15]

If you look at a map of the Mission, you will notice that San Jose Avenue angles idiosyncratically through the regular grid. Once part of the San Jose Road, *El Camino Real* was established by the Spanish military along animal and Native American trails to the south.

Much of the historic San Jose Road, later grandly rechristened San Jose Avenue, survives south of Twenty-third in southern San Francisco. There are many old buildings along this vestigial path. On the southwest corner of Twenty-second and San Jose Avenue, at **3315 Twenty-second Street**, is a three-story building with a corner store seen in perfect profile. Everything that could happen to a building has happened here. Probably built in the mid-1870s, the building had additions made to its rear and over time was chopped into many units. In the twentieth century, its redwood gingerbread was stripped off and the building coated in thin stucco to make it look modern. Cheap metal-sash windows completed the "improvements."

TWENTY-SECOND STREET / MISSION STREET MARQUEES [16]

Looking north up Mission Street from Twenty-second you'll see San Francisco's best surviving cluster of old neon and electric signs, attached to a string of movie theaters and furniture stores. They create steeplelike vertical accents down the long commercial strip. The moderne "New Mission," the "Cine Latino" with its knight's helmet, the old-fashioned "El Capitan" (whose auditorium has been demolished for a parking lot), and "Starlight Furniture" boast rare old illuminated signs. Looking to the south, down Mission, you can see the streamline Moderne "Grand Theater." Great neon signs were beacons of attraction on pre-1950 main streets.

Mission Street from Twentieth Street south to the San Mateo County line is (along with Columbus Avenue) one of San Francisco's "sleepers." Because Mission Street did not burn in 1906, layers of San Francisco history can be seen along this oldest land route into the city. Mission Street is San Francisco's working-class "main street".

ST. JOHN'S LUTHERAN CHURCH VICTORIAN GROUP [17]

Across busy Mission Street and down Twenty-second are the lacy Gothic spires of St. John's Lutheran Church at 3126 Twenty-second Street, the centerpiece of a remarkable Victorian cluster. The cornerstone of the church is engraved "1900: Ev. Luth. St. Johannes Kirche," though in style the conservative church belongs to the nineteenth century. It is a pleasing piece of nineteenth-century carpentry with convincing ornament: a stone cathedral translated into redwood for a German-speaking congregation. Alas, its rose window has been lost, but that can be reversed some day.

On the corner to the left of the church is **3144–46 Twenty-second Street**, an L-shaped, three-story, Eastlake-style building with a typical corner storefront with 1930s tile splash panels. To the right of the church is **3126 Twenty-second Street**, the parsonage, a fine two-story, bay-windowed Italianate house with a parish office built over its front lawn that brings the church out to the sidewalk. Behind a white picket fence next door is **3122 Twenty-second Street**, a charming one-story, flat-front Italianate cottage with a uniquely ornamented parapet. It is perched atop a garage inserted in the 1920s. The old cottage has been beauti-

fully restored and adapted into two units. The simple pergola-ed "carport" alongside leads to an iron gate through which can be glimpsed a delightful oasis of a garden with a carriage-house cottage at its back.

Mission District Mural [18]
"Inspire to Aspire: Tribute to Carlos Santana"
1987; Michael Rios, Carlos Gonzalez, Johnny Mayorga

Exploding in vivid colors on the southeast corner of Twenty-second Street and South Van Ness Avenue facing a corner parking lot is a vibrant "neo-Aztec" mural entitled "Inspire to Aspire: Tribute to Carlos Santana" painted by Michael Rios, Carlos Gonzalez, and Johnny Mayorga in 1987. It depicts Latino musicians, Mexican *mariachis*, plumed serpents, a mandala, and an Aztec pyramid set before the San Francisco skyline with the Transamerica Pyramid. Chicano murals first emerged in the *barrios* of East Los Angeles in the late 1960s. From there the idea spread to the East Bay where militantly political and revolutionary themes dominated. In San Francisco, which has seen murals come and go in black, hippie, Latino, Chinese, and Filipino neighborhoods, the murals have had sunnier themes, in particular music and dancing. This is one of the best of what is by its nature an ephemeral art and was funded by the city.

CAPP STREET VICTORIAN ROW [19]

The most extensive row of identical Stick-Eastlake houses is on the east side of Capp between Twenty-second and Twenty-third streets. All were built between 1889 and 1894 by Australian-born architect T. J. Welch for developer Mary E. von Schroeder. Of the fifteen houses, ten are substantially intact. The row is very beautiful, its mass-produced woodwork lacy and fanciful. The "flash glass"—small colored squares surrounding the main window pane—survives on many of them. One house has been shingled, three "improved" with asbestos shingles, and one stuccoed and fringed with red tiles, probably in the 1920s. Capp Street is fortunate to retain its handsome 1920s streetlights.

Mission United Church [20]
Twenty-third and Capp streets
1891, Percy and Hamilton

At Twenty-third and Capp is the Mission United Presbyterian Church designed by Percy and Hamilton in 1891. It is an excellent example of the Romanesque shingle style and boasts a fine tower, recently restored. Organized in 1868, this was the first "suburban" Presbyterian congregation in San Francisco. The church flourished during the second half of the nineteenth century, attracting many well-to-do members. After 1900, factories and warehouses expanded into the area and middle-class families began to drift toward the suburbs down the Peninsula or across the Bay in Oakland. The fire of 1906, which destroyed adjoining parts of the Mission and all of the heavily working-class South of Market, accelerated the change. Surviving houses were profitably subdivided and the old mixture of middle class and working class in the district tipped toward being solidly working class. The restoration of Mission United Church is a heroic achievement and marks a turning point for the Mission District.

To the east of Capp Street on filled-in Mission Bay was San Francisco's—and the West Coast's—first large industrial zone. Iron works, breweries, sugar refineries, lumber mills, and factories of all kinds grew along the bayshore and the railroad tracks. Many of the Mission's immigrant residents walked to jobs in those factories.

TWENTY-FOURTH STREET LATINO SHOPPING STRIP [21]

The commercial strip of Twenty-fourth Street from Mission east to about Bryant Street is the axis of Latino shopping and restaurants in San Francisco. Twenty-fourth Street's Nicaraguan, Salvadoran, Costa Rican, and other Latin-American restaurants and shops reflect the West's most complex Latino community. War and disruption in Central America has steadily fed migration to the Bay Area. Many exiles have opened small businesses and employ fellow Latinos. Here are old ladies with the immemorial faces of peasant Central America, an abundance of exotic tropical fruits and vegetables, and a full spectrum of Spanish-speaking businesses and services. It's a street where the restaurants have plastic tablecloths, artificial flowers, and mementos of home.

At the southeast corner of Twenty-fourth and South Van Ness is a fine mural entitled **"Golden Dream of the New World"** showing Latin dancers with a background of cleverly painted Victorian houses. It was executed by Daniel Galvez in 1984.

BALMY ALLEY MURALS [21]

Balmy Alley, a service alley lined with board fences, garage doors, and a few small tenements, is always choked with cars. Hidden here is a series of murals begun in 1973 on the political agony of contemporary Central America. They are the work of *Placa*, Chicano slang for graffiti, a group of some forty artists and community workers. The murals are quite varied and repay individual examination; some, unfortunately, have attracted spray-can graffiti, the Mission's environmental curse.

Balmy Alley ends across the street from cheerless **Garfield Square** with its 1950s indoor swimming pool. Garfield Square, far south down Mission valley, was the only park reservation in the Victorian Mission. Set aside as part of the Outside Lands in 1863, by the early 1880s it was an important recreation ground with one of the earliest baseball diamonds, which drew people from all over the city to this sunny spot. Today the park is dreary and abused; the only valiant fragment of its old landscaping is a mature cypress. Putting buildings in the Mission's scarce green space was an error (even if that building is a much-needed public swimming pool).

Back on Twenty-fourth Street at the southeast corner of Bryant Street is the **Galería de la Raza**, a showcase for contemporary Latino artists. They can provide you with a pamphlet listing the Mission's many fine murals. Next door is **Studio 24** with Mexican and Central American folk art and Latin-American literature, the best place for souvenirs.

"Raza History" Mural [21]
2701 Mission Street
1974, Chuy Campesino, Luis Cortázar, and Michael Ríos

Inside a branch of the Bank of America at Mission and Twenty-third streets is a fine 1974 mural by Chuy Campesino, Luis Cortázar, and Michael Ríos entitled "Raza History," depicting the present-day Latino population of the Mission. In the tradition of Mexican muralists, it is a people-crowded didactic work: a swirling exhortation to work, struggle, and study.

BART Station [22]
Mission at Twenty-fourth Street
1973, Hertz and Knowles

BART Mural [22]
Mission and Twenty-fourth streets
1975, Michael Rios, Tony Machado, and Ricardo Montez

Both the Sixteenth and Twenty-fourth Street BART stations were designed by Hertzka and Knowles in 1973. Aboveground they are equally unattractive: sterile brick-paved holes in the ground. The Twenty-fourth Street station has the more successful underground of the two. Its barrel-vaulted ceiling is tiled in colors somewhat reminiscent of the painted ceiling of old Mission Dolores.

The aboveground mural at the Twenty-fourth Street station, now increasingly masked by trees, was painted in 1975 by Michael Rios, Tony Machado, and Ricardo Montez. In a biting allusion to the .5 percent sales tax used to finance BART, a sleek silver BART train is shown resting on the backs of the people. BART, originally intended to "improve" the Mission by introducing the construction of highrises like the disruptive Bay View Federal Savings highrise at Mission and Twenty-second, instead galvanized the Mission to thwart the demolition and displacement of Urban Renewal. In 1968 the Mission Coalition Organization brought together some two hundred neighborhood groups and local interests to pressure for city policies that would preserve the small businesses and affordable housing characteristic of the district. With conservationist city building controls, BART now serves the Mission rather than the Mission serving BART.

Continuation

From here either turn back to the BART station or catch the 48 Quintara bus on the north side of the street to Noe Valley to the west. At Twenty-fourth and Castro, transfer to the 24 Divisadero bus to get to Castro and Market streets and MUNI Metro.

The **Mexican Museum** (441-0404) at Fort Mason, Building D, mounts exhibits on Mexican themes from the pre-Hispanic to modern periods. Open Wednesday–Sunday, 12–5 P.M.; small donation, free on Wednesday. (*See Tour 4B*)

The Castro and Noe Valley

OLD BOTTLES, NEW WINES

What This Tour Covers

[1] Market and Castro Streets / Muni Metro Station

[2] Castro Common Condominiums

[3] 2300 Block of Market Street Shops

[4] 400 Block of Castro Street / The Castro Theater

[5] Castro and Eighteenth Streets: Castro Village

[6] 700 Block of Castro Street Victorians

[7] 500 Block of Liberty Street / Liberty Street Steps

[8] Downtown Panorama

[9] Panorama of Victorian Neighborhoods

[10] Noe Valley Ministry

[11] Twenty-fourth Street Commercial Strip

[12] Noe Valley Branch Library

Preliminaries

Best Times To Do This Tour

Daytime Sundays from about 11 A.M. to 3 P.M. are when the people are out—and this should be a tour of people as much as buildings. To get beneath the street life of the district, attend one of the gay churches active here. The Metropolitan Community Church conducts Protestant services Sunday at 10:30 A.M. and 7 P.M. at 150 Eureka Street, near Nineteenth, 863-4434. Most Holy Redeemer Roman Catholic church at 100 Diamond, near Eighteenth, has many gay parishioners. Dignity, a gay Catholic organization, holds masses at Dolores Baptist Church at Fifteenth Street and Dolores Sunday at 5:30 P.M. Two sexually progressive Jewish congregations meet in the Castro: Congregation Ahavat Shalom (621-1020) has *shabbat* services Fridays at 8:15 P.M. at 150 Eureka Street, near Nineteenth, and Sha'ar Zahav (861-6932), which means "Golden Gate," has its synagogue at 220 Danvers Street, near Nineteenth Street. All these congregations welcome visitors.

Parking

There are city-owned, metered, mini-parking lots near the Castro Theater on Castro between Seventeenth and Eighteenth, and around the corner on Eighteenth between Castro and Collingwood.

Transportation

During the summer season and into the fall historic trolleys run up Market Street terminating at Castro and Market, (*see Tour 1*). At other times take the fine MUNI Metro L, M, or K cars to the modern Castro Station; this is how the locals get to work downtown.

Restaurants, Cafés, and Bars

The Castro has many inexpensive cafés and restaurants, several with window tables so you can watch the passersby. The **Café San Marcos** (861-3846) at 2367-69 Market near Castro is a very modern upstairs bar with views down onto the street. The **Village Deli Cafe** at 495 Castro, near Eighteenth Street, has refreshments and good window seats. In Noe Valley the choices are more restricted. **A Taste of Honey** (285-7979) at 751 Diamond at Twenty-fourth is a "natural" bakery (no sugar or white flour) and juice bar that serves vegetarian meals. The **Meat Market Coffeehouse** (285-5598) at 4123 Twenty-fourth is a favorite hangout for newspaper-reading Noe Valley locals.

Shopping

The most interesting shops are on the 2300 block of Market, south side, between Sixteenth and Seventeenth streets. The very latest in clothing, accessories, furniture, and flowers cluster here. Castro and Eighteenth streets have a half-dozen interesting modern men's clothing shops. Clever card shops abound here, too.

Twenty-fourth Street in Noe Valley also makes good browsing. **Out of Hand** at 1303 Castro, near Twenty-fourth, has contemporary crafts. The **Philosophers Stone Bookstore** at 3814 Twenty-fourth has "New Age" books. **Star Magic** at 4026A Twenty-fourth Street sells astral accoutrements and "celestial music."

Introduction: Old Bottles, New Wines

Change is the only constant in life and few parts of San Francisco have seen as great a change as Eureka and Noe valleys. Here fine old buildings have been lovingly restored and given new life. Along with Twin Peaks, these valleys were originally part of the 4,000-acre Rancho San Miguel granted to Mexican San Francisco's last *alcalde*, or mayor, José de Jesús Noe in 1845. With the arrival of the Yankees came a wave of land speculation. In 1854 John M. Horner bought most of the virtually undeveloped ranch for $90,000 and platted out Horner's Addition, a grid of blocks from Castro to Valencia and from about Eighteenth to Thirtieth streets. The rest of the San Miguel Ranch became the property of two French speculators, Pioche and Bazerque, and their American partner, Parsons. Twin Peaks was absorbed into the vast real estate empire of Adolph Sutro by 1880.

The main north-south streets in Horner's Addition were named after early Mexican ranchers: Castro, Noe, Sanchez, Guerrero, and Valencia. This subdivision was slow to develop since it was far from the downtown and hard of access, while there were still many empty lots much closer to downtown. Small dairy ranches, truck gardens, and a few brickyards and sanatoriums were built here. In 1864 the Eureka Homestead Association was formed and four years later the Noe Garden Homestead Association incorporated. These cooperative associations bought blocks of property which they then subdivided into house lots and sold to members or to contractor-builders who erected wooden Victorian houses. Comfortable Victorian houses began to appear, first in the valleys, then on the slopes. In 1868 the *Real Estate Circular* reported:

An active demand has been noticeable for lots lying within the bounds of Eighteenth, Twenty-Sixth, Valencia and Castro streets. This locality is occupied with rolling hills and tableland, and heretofore has not been in favor with purchasers.... But the perfect nature of its title, the fine view which is obtained from most of the land, and the good drainage which it will have, have lately operated favorably in elevating its prices.

The real boom in house building followed the opening of the Castro Street segment of the Market Street Cable Railway in 1887. This line linked the Ferry Building at the foot of Market with Twenty-sixth Street in Noe Valley. The Castro Street line had some of the steepest grades of any cable line with an 18.4 percent grade between Twenty-second and Twenty-third streets.

With a transit system in place, lower-middle-class families flocked to these sunny valleys. The relatively high rates of San Francisco workers' pay were reflected in these comfortable dwellings. German, Scandinavian, and later more and more Irish-American families clustered here. Many were Roman Catholic and the local churches became important neighborhood institutions, as were the many corner groceries and saloons.

The area has never suffered real neglect, and, with every year, the gardens behind these houses and the twentieth-century pruned street trees along the sidewalks soften more of these precipitous streets. Because of San Francisco's justifiably famous marine views, the "inland" cityscapes are frequently overlooked. In these valleys, where Victorian houses lie draped over the furrowed slopes of Twin Peaks, remarkable views of nothing but nineteenth-century houses with twentieth-century gardens are memorable to all who look for them.

After the boom of the 1920s, during which new banks and a fancy movie theater were built on Castro Street, the neighborhood saw little improvement. Like all American inner-city neighborhoods, Eureka and Noe valleys went into a relative decline after World War II. FHA-backed mortgages and the spread of the automobile drew many of the children raised in cities to the expanding suburbs. Irish-Americans continued their historic southwestward drift across the

A row of Queen Anne–style cottages designed by John Anderson and built in 1897 on the south side of the 500 block of Liberty Street, between Castro and Noe streets.

Copyright 1989 William Walters

city and out to Daly City and Pacifica. Eureka and Noe valleys began to fade.

All this changed in the early 1970s as downtown San Francisco's highrise boom took off. From a commercial and industrial city with many ethnic blue-collar workers, San Francisco began a rapid transformation into a post-industrial city marked by a shift from manufacturing and an explosion in white-collar office work and service industries. The factories left for techno-logical and cost reasons: new one-story plants could only be built on cheap land beyond the suburbs. But as industry and jobs left, skyscrapers and office work increased.

These economic and employment shifts were accompanied by dramatic social and cultural changes. The spread of college education, in particular, uprooted young people from their birth-places and took them to schools often quite far from home. Upon graduation few returned home; most looked for skilled jobs in the cities. The suburban-bred singles' migration back into the heart of the old, culturally attractive cit-ies accelerated. Because of its small size, this migration has been most noticeable in San Francisco. As the total population of the city drifted downward by 5 per-cent between 1970 and 1980, the number of people between twenty-five and thirty-four exploded by more than 25 percent. Many were highly educated, energetic, and ambitious, and they revitalized San Francisco with the most important of all forms of capital: human capital.

This new migration had a curious quality: while relentlessly modern, it had a real appreciation of old architecture, especially Victorian houses. In fact, the new migrants loved these buildings more than many natives, who saw them as obsolete. In the 1970s a wave of restoration swept San Francisco. The new migrants refurbished old houses and made them resplendent. Between 1973 and 1976, vintage houses in San Francisco quintupled in value.

But there was more to it than real estate, important as that religion remains. Gays in particular, feeling the social liberation of the 1970s—in 1973, the American Psychiatric Association dropped homosexuality from its list of mental disorders—registered to vote and formed active political clubs, changing the face of politics in what had been an old-fashioned, ethnic-based political system. In 1972 San Francisco was the first American city to pass an ordinance forbidding discrimination in employment and housing on the basis of sexual orientation. Harvey Milk, a New York-born camera-store owner from the Castro, became the first openly gay man elected to public office in 1977. While real numbers do not exist, by the late 1980s perhaps one of every five adults, and one out of every four voters in San Francisco was gay.

History, however, is the unexpected, quite often the brutally unexpected. With the eruption of acquired-immune-deficiency syndrome (AIDS) in 1981, a deep seachange began in the Castro and in San Francisco generally. The party-hardy seventies have been succeeded by the sober eighties. But groups, unlike individuals, endure. Gay culture has evolved. A remarkable proliferation of social service agencies has emerged,

many in the Castro, but in other parts of San Francisco as well. Hospices for the dying, home care for the ill, public education on hygiene for the living, and counseling for the anxious have sprung up to face the crisis. While one must always mistrust tricks with language—without clear language, there can be no clear thinking—the Castro can be said not to be dying from AIDS, but living compassionately with it.

The social changes in Noe Valley, over the Castro Street hill, have been less attention-getting but just as profound as those in the Castro. New vigor has come to this old part of town. Babies are back in vogue, and many professional families with young children live here. This is a discernibly committed-to-the-city population, including many artists and writers. They contribute to one of the most agreeable neighborhoods in San Francisco. By 1987 writers Cyra McFadden, Warren Hinckle, and Armistead Maupin had settled in Noe Valley. As McFadden notes, "Busy little fingers are typing all over the place." Fortunately the noise is not too loud and the side streets on the southern slope of the hill remain quiet, serene, and well worth random exploration.

MARKET AND CASTRO STREETS [1]

At Castro Street, Market Street is deflected from its course by the base of the Twin Peaks hills that rise at the center of the San Francisco peninsula. The Castro Street cable car turntable once stood near here. The foot of Market, at the eastern end, is marked by the tower of the 1896 Ferry Building. At the western end is the Sutro television tower built in 1973, a handsome piece of utilitarian design.

MUNI Metro Station [1]
Castro and Upper Market Streets
1974, Reid and Tarics

Under this busy intersection is the MUNI Metro station designed by Reid

233

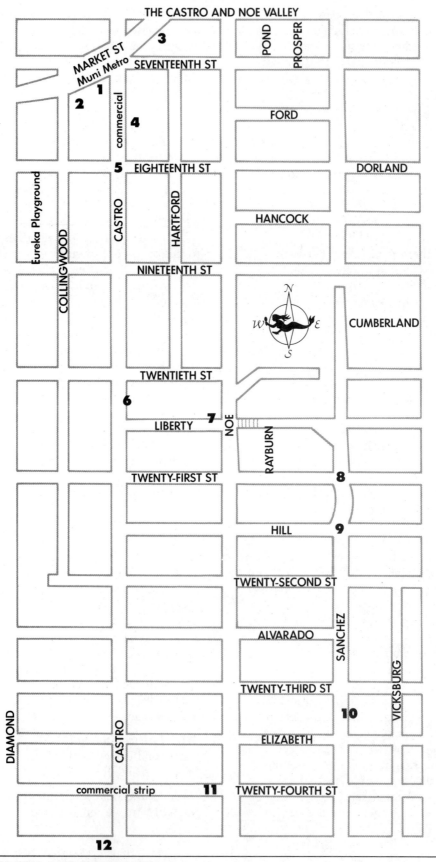

MARKET ST
Muni Metro

SEVENTEENTH ST

POND

PROSPER

1

2

3

commercial

4

FORD

CASTRO

HARTFORD

DORLAND

5 EIGHTEENTH ST

Eureka Playground

COLLINGWOOD

HANCOCK

NINETEENTH ST

N

W E

S

CUMBERLAND

TWENTIETH ST

6

7 NOE

LIBERTY

RAYBURN

TWENTY-FIRST ST

8

HILL

9

TWENTY-SECOND ST

ALVARADO

SANCHEZ

TWENTY-THIRD ST

VICKSBURG

10

DIAMOND

CASTRO

ELIZABETH

commercial strip

11 TWENTY-FOURTH ST

12

234

and Tarics in 1974, the cheeriest underground transit station in San Francisco, far lighter in feeling than the ponderous BART stations built about the same time. It is, however, as devoid of life as any American transit station. The orange brick and inventive graphics look better than they sound. The landscaped stairway-entrance to the station is known as **Harvey Milk Plaza** and is marked by an unattractive bronze plaque in honor of the assassinated city supervisor.

Castro Common Condominiums [2]
2425 Market Street
1982, Daniel Solomon and Associates

Immediately west of the Metro entrance, down a brick-paved pedestrian bridge, is the transparent white grid fence of Castro Common, unusually handsome condominiums designed by Daniel Solomon and Associates in 1982. Solomon, a professor of architecture at the University of California at Berkeley, is one of the best of the new designers active in the 1980s. When this roughly T-shaped parcel was developed, the mature symmetrical Norfolk pine was preserved, adding much to the appeal of the project. The grid fence continues the street wall and makes an interesting counterpoint to the square grids employed in the building itself. The building is broken up into three separate sections linked by a courtyard and set upon a parking garage.

Castro Common is worth looking at from various angles. It is the best architectural play on the curious fascination with square grids that overtook graphic design in the early 1980s. Built of common materials and painted the color of every architect's office interior—flat white—this building is a model of how architecture can be wholly new yet mesh smoothly with San Francisco's established character. It is instructive to compare this piece of high art with the vernacular building backs and sides visible next door.

2300 BLOCK OF MARKET STREET SHOPS [3]

The south side of Market Street, between Sixteenth and Seventeenth, houses the most interesting of the Castro shops. Costly and ferociously up-to-the-nanosecond, they display both men's and women's clothing, furnishings, electronic goods, and flowers-become-art. Here the latest trends are showcased in old shopfronts (a few with "design statement" interiors) making this one of the most interesting window shopping strips in Northern California. (The north side of Market is much less interesting.) The **Café San Marcos** (861-3846) here is an aggressively modern bar upstairs with a balcony that lets you look down on the busy pedestrian whirlpool at Market and Castro. It's a good place to come back to once this exploration is over.

400 BLOCK OF CASTRO STREET [4]

At the southwest corner of Castro and Market streets, at **400 Castro Street**, is a branch of the Bank of America designed by Edward T. Foulkes in 1921. Originally this was a more ornate building with elaborate terra cotta ornament. It was stripped at some point to make the building look more modern.

On the opposite, southeast, corner stands the **Twin Peaks Bar** with its projecting sheet-metal sign showing the profile of the hills. While not an architectural monument, it is a sociological one. It was the first openly gay bar with floor-to-ceiling plate glass windows looking out on the world.

Halfway down the block at 444 Castro Street is the grandiosely named Empire of America Federal Savings designed in 1985 by Neeley Lofrano. This was built for Atlas Savings, the first and short-lived, gay-founded bank. The building is a parody of a typical bay-windowed Edwardian and has a white-painted steel open-work front standing before a glass and mirror façade. It has two second-story "bay windows" and an open-work pedimented gable with a mirrored gable behind. Trick façades with mirrors seem particularly inappropriate for financial institutions, though in this case it turned out to be ominously prescient.

Next door to the transparent bank is a standard bay-windowed Edwardian that was stripped of this classicizing ornament and covered with stucco in a moderne mode. It is a not unpleasing face-lift.

The Castro Theater [4]
429 Castro Street
1924, Timothy Pflueger

Fantasy *is* appropriate for movie palaces, and Timothy Pflueger's Castro Theater is one of the best such efforts in the Bay Area. Built as the flagship theater of the pioneer movie-exhibitor Nasser family, this Spanish Renaissance extravaganza is marked by a giant blind window flanked by elaborate ornament and surmounted by an empty niche. Its splendid neon-trimmed marquee and giant vertical sign have become something of an icon for the reborn neighborhood. The Castro has an elaborate, intact interior; the plaster ceiling has been made to look like the inside of a tent with swags, ropes, and tassels. The theater hosts imaginative screenings and is one of the venues of the San Francisco Film Festival.

Architecture, however, is not likely to be what attracts most of the attention here. It's the street life that makes the Castro special, a lively street scene of mostly gay young men shopping, doing errands, chatting, bar-hopping, milling about. More gay women are visible on Castro Street in the 1980s, though the population here is still mostly male and mostly young. Styles are casual, often athletic. These are great blocks for people-watching.

CASTRO AND EIGHTEENTH STREETS: CASTRO VILLAGE [5]

The Castro is sometimes referred to as Castro Village, no doubt after Greenwich Village in New York City. The intersection of Castro and Eighteenth is its Times Square. In its urban form, if not in population, Eureka Valley is a microcosm of the typical nineteenth-century California town, consisting of a grid of residential streets, with one, Castro Street, as a transit and commercial strip. One block behind this commercial strip is the local church and grammar school with its ballfield. All else is housing. The Castro hill is crowned with charming peak-roofed cottages built in rows in the 1890s. The hill's silhouette looks as if it was cut with pinking shears. Now painted a variety of colors, this is one of the most distinctive views in San Francisco.

On the southwest corner of Castro and Eighteenth streets, with the Elephant Walk bar in its corner space, is a commercial-residential building designed by John Davis Hatch in 1912. It is mildly Secessionist in its upstairs architectural treatment. Facing it across the street was a Hibernia Bank branch at **501 Castro Street**, a reminder of the originally dominant population in the neighborhood, with a Neoclassical corner building built in 1929 and a modern glass addition designed in 1979 by Robert Sarnoff. The new wing is cut back at a 45 degree angle, the design signature of the late 1970s. In this space the Castro erects its neighborhood Christmas tree—the Christmas lights here are some of the best in the city. This corner is often the site of ironing board-equipped petitioners circulating the latest political broadsides in this politically energized neighborhood.

The flanking blocks of Eighteenth Street have many small shops and inexpensive eating places. The **Midnight Sun**, a bar at 4067 Eighteenth Street, has a high-tech-Deco interior behind its assertively anonymous gray sheetmetal façade.

At **527–33 Castro Street**, beyond the bank are the semicircular bay windows of the three-story Komsthoeft Building built early in this century. It was originally a bakery and the old brick ovens remain in the back; since then the ground floor has been converted into a minimall of boutiques, and a restaurant with an outdoor eating area has been inserted in the back. From the restaurant garden, the visitor can see the back of this typical building and the inside of its block. The once-utilitarian space has been inexpensively transformed with wooden decks and lavish plantings. Here is an archetypical example of the way new life has been infused in old buildings using imagination and plants.

At **580 Castro**, on the northwest corner of Nineteenth Street is a Stick-style commercial and residential building designed by the prolific Fernando Nelson in 1887. More of his houses are up the hill. Up the block to the west, at 4143 Nineteenth Street near Collingwood, tucked in an old storefront is **Isak Lindenauer Antiques** (552-6436), a veritable museum of Craftsman and Arts and Crafts oak furniture (known in California as Mission style), art pottery, and hammered-copper artifacts.

700 BLOCK OF CASTRO STREET VICTORIANS [6]

If you who don't wish to climb steep hills, catch the 24 Divisadero bus going uphill and alight at Liberty Street. Between Twentieth and Liberty, on the east side of Castro, is a group of Victorian houses designed by Fernando Nelson. Born in New York in 1860, Nelson built some four thousand Victorian houses in the city. He reduced house-building to a formula, going so far as to call his two house types "A" and "B." On the southeast corner of Castro and Twentieth is **701 Castro Street**, a whimsical one-story Queen Anne cottage with a round corner tower built by Nelson for himself in 1897. It was originally in the back of the lot and had a stable underneath it for Nelson's work horse. A later owner moved the house to the corner and built brick garages underneath.

Immediately up the hill at **711–733 Castro Street** is a row of five houses, one a Queen Anne and the others Stick Style, all built by Nelson in 1897. Some boast Nelson's "deluxe $5 front door." The curiously shaped donut capitals of the porch columns were Nelson's signature. These houses all sport modern color schemes that pick out their gingerbread. Their dramatic false gables with sunburst ornaments emphasize verticality and create an animated profile. At **757 Castro Street** is a Queen Anne house built about 1897, and at **787 Castro Street** is another Queen Anne built about 1891.

500 BLOCK OF LIBERTY STREET / LIBERTY STREET STEPS [7]

Unlike the twentieth century, when quiet side streets are preferred to busy through streets, in the Victorian era cable car-served streets were preferred to lateral pedestrian streets. Liberty Street contains the peak-roofed cottages seen from Castro and Eighteenth streets. A decade after the main streets were built up with multistory houses, less costly one-story cottages filled the side streets. These cottages were built by developers for speculative sale to prosperous "mechanics." John Anderson built the four peak-roofed Queen Anne cottages at **563–77 Liberty Street** in 1897. Another row of five cottages at **541–59 Liberty Street** was built by Carlson and Anderson in the same year. The seven cottages with the gingerbread drips and donut capitals were built by the ubiquitous Fernando Nelson in 1897.

At Liberty and Noe streets is a good view of a white Moderne flats complex at **741 Liberty Street** built about 1940.

The simply white stucco boxes step up the hillside quite agreeably. It is one of the most ambitious Moderne developments in any San Francisco neighborhood. Climb the steps and look back. Spread out before you is a panorama few visitors get to appreciate: San Francisco's overlooked "inland" cityscape. Pale houses and dark green trees cover the steep amphitheater of hills. The red rock mass of Corona Heights is to the north and the grassy slopes of Twin Peaks are due west. Houses of every period, style, color, and shape merge; at night the lights in the houses make these hills look like heaps of diamonds. From the top of the Liberty steps, San Francisco Bay and the Contra Costa hills appear to the east.

Also at the top of the steps is Rayburn Street, lined with garages and very simple houses. Follow it to Twenty-first Street and walk up the slight incline to Sanchez Street.

DOWNTOWN PANORAMA [8]

At the corner of Twenty-first and Sanchez there is a startling view of the new downtown highrises. The dark Bank of America and the white Transamerica Pyramid make a perfect contrasting pair from this high vantage point. The white peaked-hat structure is St. Mary's Cathedral. A red tile-roofed church with a dome and twin towers rises in the valley below next to a long, low, rectangular structure with a tile roof; this is Mission Dolores (*see Tour 9*). The great green dome in the middle distance caps Bakewell and Brown's City Hall of 1915 in the Beaux Arts Civic Center. To the far left are the slender residential highrises of Pacific Heights with always-changing San Francisco Bay beyond.

On the northeast corner of Sanchez and Twenty-first, at **3690 Twenty-first Street** is the Casa Ciele, a Tudor cottage nestled under old pine trees. It was built in 1930 by Mayor "Sunny Jim" Rolph, who served as mayor from 1911 to 1930

and then as Republican governor of California. Rolph built the splendid City Hall below and many of San Francisco's finest public buildings and schools during his long reign.

From the fire-alarm box on the southeast corner of the intersection is a fine view of historic Mission Valley below, Potrero Hill with its peak-roofed cottages, the calm Bay, Oakland, the Contra Costa ridge, and Mt. Diablo, the highest peak in the region.

PANORAMA OF VICTORIAN NEIGHBORHOODS [9]

A century ago this rocky hill was used for grazing sheep and goats. It has had more than its share of names: Dolores Heights, Sanchez Street Hill, Noe Hill, Liberty Hill, Mineral Springs Hill, and Nanny Goat Hill. At **849 Sanchez Street**, on the northeast corner of appropriately named Hill Street, is a two-story streamlined Moderne stucco house with porthole windows built in 1938. It has been enlivened with a modern abstract stained-glass window.

Catercorner from this house is a fine panorama to the south of the densely built Mission District. The two tall needlelike steeples rise from St. Paul's Roman Catholic Church at Twenty-ninth and Church streets built in 1890. Its bells can be heard pealing out over the quiet valley. The wind, and an occasional distant truck or bus shifting gears, are the only other sounds heard atop this "peak in the wind" set in the center of the busy city. Hilltop parks, some forested, some open hills, frame the horizon.

Noe Valley Ministry [10]
1021 Sanchez Street
1888, Charles Geddes

Down the hill is the steeple of the Noe Valley Ministry, a Stick Style church with a Gothic-style porch designed by Charles Geddes and dedicated in 1889. It cost $3,880 to build. The congregation was first known as the Noe Valley Presbyterian Church but changed its name to the Lebanon Presbyterian Church shortly thereafter. Geddes was born in Halifax, Nova Scotia and came to California in the 1850s. He evolved from a carpenter to a builder to an architect. Though its woodwork may seem rich to us, this is a plain building for its period. The church's gable has three different shingle patterns. After 1906 the church was jacked up, enlarged, and a ground floor with meeting rooms added. The church was restored in the late 1970s and painted a pleasing pearl gray and white. Today the revitalized church serves as Noe Valley's informal community center and is used for worship, lectures, a co-op nursery school, senior programs, dance and exercise classes, local merchants' meetings, and is the home of the neighborhood newspaper, *The Noe Valley Voice*.

The wide, quiet streets and sidewalks lined with small, light-colored houses have a pleasing serenity that is the quintessential "feel" of so many of San Francisco's clean, tucked-away neighborhoods. Behind these vintage houses are carefully tended gardens even more peaceful and remote. Hummingbirds and typewriters are the loudest sounds.

TWENTY-FOURTH STREET COMMERCIAL STRIP [11]

José de Jesús Noe built his adobe ranch house in the mid-1840s near the intersection of Twenty-fourth and Noe streets. With the coming of the Castro Street cable car in 1887, Twenty-fourth Street became the shopping strip for the valley. Today Noe Valley is a post-hippie, post-Vietnam, post-sexual-revolution, post-mellow zone with organic food, spiritual books, charts of the heavens, and imported gourmet foods. Young families and strollers enliven the street. The shopping strip includes a small supermarket, shops, local services, bookstores, restaurants and cafes. The **Meat Market Coffeehouse** at 4123

Twenty-fourth, in a former butcher's shop, is a local hangout.

The pressures on a street like Twenty-fourth are more intense than casual visitors imagine. A great concern in San Francisco is the preservation of moderate-rent housing such as the apartments on the upper floors of mixed commercial-residential buildings. The City Planning Commission does not permit the conversion of upstairs residential units to higher-income retail or office use. There are also limits on new bars and restaurants lest those more profitable uses drive out all the other community-serving businesses. Both the local merchants and the surrounding residents have active organizations that zealously monitor changes on the fragile street. What looks so "natural" to the visitor is not that way at all; "success" can spoil a street as fast as poverty. San Francisco's neighborhood commercial strips are a continual balancing act between change and continuity.

Noe Valley Branch Library [12]
451 Jersey Street
1916, John Reid, Jr.

One block south of Twenty-fourth and Castro is the Noe Valley Branch Library, dedicated in 1916. It is a little gem, a model of the appropriate scale for neighborhood facilities. The building is the result of steel magnate Andrew Carnegie's farseeing philanthropy. Carnegie was the one robber baron who was a secularist at heart; rather than endow churches, he decided to elevate the intellectual level of his adopted country. He launched a program that spread free public libraries, both great and small, across the United States and in his native Scotland as well. He paid for elegant buildings if communities would agree to fill them with books and keep them open. In this way he enticed local involvement and created what is very often still the finest architectural work in many small American towns.

The Noe Valley Branch Library is

handsomely ornamented in brick and terra cotta and has four engaged columns across its façade framing large windows. Swags and garlands with open books between them enrich the façade. Inside, along with the usual departments, is a special women's collection, imprints from Bay Area small presses, and the Noe Valley Community Archives. The work of some of Noe Valley's many artists is sometimes displayed here. Evening lectures make it "the people's university."

Over the entrance to the library is an open book and the San Francisco Public Library's stern motto: "Life without literature is death."

Continuation

From Twenty-fourth Street you can return via the 24 Divisadero bus to Market and Castro and continue to Pacific Heights (*Tour 7*). Or you can board the 48 Quintara bus heading east on Twenty-fourth Street to the Twenty-fourth Street BART station and the Mission District (*Tour 9*).

The Haight-Ashbury

ANTHROPOLOGICAL
WILDLIFE REFUGE

What This Tour Covers

[1] Spencer House Bed and Breakfast Inn

[2] 1100 Block of Haight Street

[3] Buena Vista Park

[4] Buena Vista Avenue West

[5] Java Street, Masonic Avenue, and Waller Street / Victorian Rows

[6] Haight Street Commercial Strip

[7] Haight and Ashbury Streets

[8] Golden Gate Park Panhandle

[9] 1700 Block of Oak / 400 Block of Clayton

[10] 500 Block of Cole Street

[11] Park Branch Public Library and Mural

[12] Page and Shrader Streets

CONTINUATION

Some Haight Street Landmarks

Preliminaries

Best Times To Do This Tour

The fog over the Haight burns off late and comes back early; midday between 11 A.M. and 3 P.M. is the sunniest time here. Saturday is when the shoppers are loose, and cafés and stores then are a *tableau vivant* of post-punk urban culture.

The Haight is most alive during the summer when many Americans and foreigners come here looking for hippies. The Haight-Ashbury Street Fair every summer is always worth checking out for new forms of urban life as well as old standbys like Deadheads and bikers.

Parking

There is a free parking lot in the Golden Gate Park Panhandle; enter from Masonic Avenue headed south. Parking is easiest on weekdays. You will see some people park their cars across the pedestrian crosswalks; please do not emulate them.

Transportation

MUNI's 6 Parnassus, 7 Haight, and 71 Haight-Noriega bus lines all link Haight Street with Market Street downtown. The N Judah bus (not streetcar) runs every 30 minutes down Haight to Market Street from midnight to 6 A.M.

Restaurants, Cafés and Bars

At 1419 Haight near Masonic, **Hunan on Haight** (621-0580) has a big, airy interior, large plate glass windows that make the passing parade look like life in an aquarium, and acceptable Chinese food. **Dish**, at 1398 Haight at Masonic (431-3434), is popular especialy for Sunday brunch.

There are many coffee places and ice cream and cookie vendors along Haight. A neighborhood retreat is the **Tassajara Bakery and Café** (664-8947) away from hectic Haight at 1000 Cole, corner of Parnassus. They also operate the renowned Greens Restaurant at Fort Mason, (*see Tour 4B*). Also in the Carl and Cole commercial pocket at 901 Cole Street is the **Ironwood Café** (664-0224) in a fine Edwardian shop interior. On the opposite corner is **The Other Café** (681-0748), a small comedy club at 100 Carl Street. The N Judah MUNI Metro streetcar links this hidden, agreeable valley with Market Street and the downtown.

Haight Street's nightlife draws today's bohemians. The **I-Beam** (668-6006) at 1748 Haight, near Cole, in the second-floor space built for the Park Masonic Lodge, is one of California's best modern music dance clubs with live bands weekly as well as DJs; they play R&B, funk, soul, and progressive rock. A post-punk art set gathers at **Nightbreak** (221-9008) at 1821 Haight with live bands on weekends; contemporary underground rock. The **Full Moon Saloon** (668-6190), a sports bar at 1725 Haight, also has an adjoining room for live rock, world beat, R&B, blues, and other programs. **Rockin' Robins** (221-1960), at 1840 Haight Street is another dance club at the park end of Haight Street. All draw young, black-clad crowds mostly in their twenties. The **Achilles Heel**, a pleasant new Old Victorian pub at the corner of Haight and Clayton, has comfortable seats and tables with views of the street scene.

Shopping

Haight Street, with some 180 small, individual shops and only a few chain store outlets, preserves the Edwardian module of long, narrow, ground-floor shops with plate-glass windows that face the sidewalk. This is ideal retail space both as individual shops and as a sequence of varied, changing businesses that pulls the walker down the sidewalk.

The "head shops" on Haight today are fakes conjured up over the past few years to cater to the tourist demand for things hippie. Two shops for tarot cards, crystals, oils, and related ritualistic paraphernalia are **Touch Stone** (621-2782); at 1601 Page, corner of Clayton, and **Uma's Occult Shop** (668-3132) at 1915 Page, near Shrader, both on the walk between Haight and the Panhandle.

Haight Street is a museum of American fashion and has many clothing shops, with both new and vintage garments. You will see a lot of black. Some of the fresh, pastel-colored Southern California surfing styles with their overscaled logos popular with skateboarders can also be found here. If you have a teenager on your gift list, you could do worse than to get him or her something "rad."

The small record shops on and off Haight, such as **Reckless Records** (431-3434), 1401 Haight at Masonic, cater to the local Bay Area teen and college market and sell music that is loud, hard, fast, and short. Most of the labels sold here will probably not cross over into the mainstream. (What the Haight is listening to is aired over KUSF radio, 90.3 FM, college radio broadcasting from the nearby University of San Francisco.)

Comix rule on Haight, OK? Perhaps we can look at them as art. For literate San Franciscans, the happiest trend on Haight is the proliferation of good book shops, both new and used. At 1369 Haight, near Masonic, is the **Bound Together Anarchist Collective Bookstore** organized in 1976; check here for events flyers and free newspapers.

Introduction: Anthropological Wildlife Refuge

The Haight gave its name to an epoch. The 1960s lastingly altered the social composition and political consciousness of this Victorian district. The Haight today is the most left-wing of San Francisco's neighborhoods, just as the west of Twin Peaks districts are its most conservative. Nothing in its nineteenth-century history pointed in this direction. A provocative description of the Haight-Ashbury—or at least of the youthful street scene along Haight Street—is that of community organizer Calvin Welch, who has described his neighborhood as "an urban lifestyle archaeological dig in which you can find all the urban social movements of the last forty years.... There are punks, hippies, remnants of the beats, antiwar health faddists, prowar joggers, skinhead skateboarders ... name it." The Haight also has gays, anarchists, real estate agents, blacks, teenagers, French tourists, bikers, English expatriates, hobos, and yuppies. It is San Francisco's most culturally diverse neighborhood, more an anthropological wildlife refuge than a "dig."

The Haight-Ashbury, as its hyphenated name implies, consists of two distinct areas: the Haight itself, located along the commercial strip of Haight Street and the flats along the Golden Gate Park Panhandle; and Ashbury Heights, a fancier district south of Haight Street that climbs the slopes of Buena Vista Heights. All of this land was originally part of the municipally owned Outside Lands west of Divisadero Street, but was claimed by squatters. In 1865 the Supreme Court ruled that the City of San Francisco was the legal successor to the Mexican pueblo of Yerba Buena and that as such it was the rightful heir to the 17,000 acres of the pueblo's Outside Lands. In 1866 Congress affirmed municipal title to the sand dunes north of

Mixed shops, hotels, and apartments were built along the streetcar lines in the nineteenth century; at the southeast corner of Haight and Masonic stands 1200 Masonic Avenue designed in 1896 by William H. Lillie. In 1895–1896, Cranston and Keenan designed the row of Queen Anne houses that marches south up Masonic Avenue.

today's Wawona Street from Divisadero to the Pacific Ocean.

But court rulings and congressional confirmation only put the vexed question of the ownership of the land west of the built-up city in the hands of the city's politicians. All the Outside Lands were claimed by somebody—in many cases several somebodies, since all could see that the city would have to expand westward and that great profits would be made when sand dunes became city lots. The squatters who claimed this land were not a ragtag bunch of small holders; many were substantial citizens active in state and municipal politics who hired men to build shacks and fences in order to claim ownership. The state legislature had to approve any disposition that the city made of these lands, and the big land speculators had a firm grip on the state legislature in Sacramento.

Frank McCoppin was the supervisor who represented the eleventh ward, which included the Outside Lands, from 1859 to 1866. He was one of the earliest

advocates of the creation of a major "pleasure ground" in the park-starved city. In 1866 he was elected mayor and decided to secure a park through the settlement of the Outside Lands question. He brought the principal land claimants together in a secret meeting to hammer out a deal, asking the "squatters" how much land they would give up to the city in return for clear title to the rest of the tract. The smallest amount they were willing to surrender was 10 percent; John B. Felton was willing to give up 25 percent. In the final deal 10.75 percent of the Outside Lands was reserved to the city, chiefly for the creation of Golden Gate Park, Buena Vista Park, a handful of other parks, and school and firehouse lots. Ninety percent was turned over to the squatters. Some ended up with parcels of twenty, fifty, or as many as one hundred blocks. The city had to go even further to get the consent of the politically well-wired speculators; it had to agree to compensate those who claimed what became the public reservations. To do this a one-time assessment of 10.75 percent of the appraised value of the land was made on the 90 percent to pay off the "dispossessed" 10 percent. This left the municipality with no profit, only the costly obligation to develop its sandy tenth into a grand park. Clearing title touched off wild speculation in Outside Land lots that raged for about eighteen months before collapsing in 1869.

A dispute arose over the shape of the 10 percent reserved by the city for Golden Gate Park. Supervisors Monroe Ashbury and Charles Clayton wanted the great city park to begin at Divisadero and to cut straight west to the Ocean Beach. But the valley between Divisadero and what became Stanyan Street was closest to the city and had the best soil. Supervisors Charles H. Stanyan, A. J. Shrader, and R. Beverly Cole managed to whittle down the eastern end of the park into a one-block-wide Panhandle and to push the eastern edge of the main park ten blocks west to Stanyan Street. This benefited politically well-connected land speculators. Governor Henry Huntly Haight signed the necessary state legislation confirming the oddly shaped park. Both the heroes and villains in the piece had streets named after themselves in what became the Haight-Ashbury.

In 1870 work began on landscaping the Panhandle and the eastern end of Golden Gate Park. In 1883 the Haight Street cable car line built by Southern Pacific Railroad opened. It terminated at Haight and Stanyan; nearby was the depot of the Park and Ocean Railroad that went out along the southern edge of the park to Ocean Beach. A private baseball field was laid out at Stanyan and Waller in 1887, and an amusement park called The Chutes was built on Haight between Clayton and Cole in the 1890s. All these attractions brought people out to the western edge of town and led to the construction of a cluster of hotels, restaurants, and bars at this transfer point. (The Stanyan Park Hotel at Stanyan and Waller, built in 1904 and handsomely restored in 1983, dates from this era.) Thus, the park end of the Haight evolved as an amusement zone.

In the 1880s, houses began to be built along the Panhandle, Victorian high society's favorite carriage drive, and on Ashbury Heights. The late 1880s and early 1890s were the heyday of the Queen Anne style and roughly three-quarters of the 1,160 Victorian houses in the neighborhood are Queen Annes. They are characterized by gable roofs, round towers and turrets, and elaborate redwood gingerbread and plaster ornament.

The earliest residents of the Haight-Ashbury were a cosmopolitan mix of Americans and successful immigrants. There was a noticeably Jewish flavor to the Panhandle area in the 1880s, when that was an *arriviste* neighborhood. The census of 1900 recorded American-born and German, Irish, Swedish, Scottish, Swiss, Australian, and French homeowners with some black, Japanese, and Chinese live-in domestics in the largest houses. The devastation of the downtown districts in 1906 touched off a building boom in the undamaged Haight. The neighborhood was filled with the sounds of the sawing of wood and the pounding of nails. More flats and small apartments appeared along Haight between 1906 and 1915 over groundfloor shops. Haight Street itself finally filled in with more than a hundred businesses. Anita Day Hubbard wrote in 1924 that "there is a comfortable maturity about the compact little city that San Francisco knows as Haight-Ashbury.... [A] nice upholstered, fuchsia garden sort of grown-up-ness, just weathered enough to be nice, and new enough to be looking ahead to the future instead of sighing futilely over the past."

Then during the Depression of the 1930s the neighborhood began to decline as maintenance was deferred and buildings faded. From an upper-middle-class suburban fringe in the 1880s, the area changed into a working-class inner-city district by the 1930s. By 1939 only 10 percent of the Haight's houses were still single-family dwellings; most properties were owned by absentee landlords. During the World War II boom, when the city's factories were working at capacity but housing stopped being built, many of the Haight's roomy old Victorians were subdivided.

When the city Redevelopment Authority began wholesale demolition of the Victorian Western Addition slums, poor black families began to move into the Panhandle area, the next neighborhood over. In 1950 the black population between Oak and Waller and Stanyan and Baker was 3 percent; in 1960, 17 percent; and in 1970, 50 percent. Rents in the Haight stagnated and it became a relatively cheap place to live. Meanwhile, on the other side of the city, in North Beach, the tourist boom began to drive up commercial rents and to displace the beatniks. Some drifted to the Panhandle area. A small "post-beat" subculture emerged in the flats and slowly spread up the slopes toward Ashbury Heights. By 1962 a significant but unpublicized bohemian subculture was suffused through the Haight, though, of course, they were never the majority. The first hip business was the Blue Unicorn Café at 1927 Hayes, north of the Panhandle, which opened in 1965.

Things came to a head, so to speak, in January 1966 when Ken Kesey hosted a Trips Festival at Longshoreman's Hall near Fisherman's Wharf. Thousands attended, dropped acid and spaced-out on rock music. The word *hippie* was born. Through a new kind of music, psychedelic rock, the pacific hippie message spread around the country and the world. The "San Francisco Sound" emerged and people wore flowers in their hair and passed them out to San Franciscans on their way to work downtown. On January 14, 1967 the Human e-In/Gathering of the Tribes was celebrated at Golden Gate Park's old Polo Field and the new bohemia got its first media attention.

In the Haight, Victoriana came back in decor and dress. Lithographs of Hindu icons, dancing elephants with many heads, served as signs of some half-perceived cultural confusion. Rock posters took turn-of-the-century Viennese lettering and clashing color combinations to make vibrant posters for bands with names like The Charlatans, The Chocolate Watch Band, Quicksilver Messenger Service, the Electric Flag, Big Brother and the Holding Company, Blue Cheer, Jefferson Airplane, and the enduring Grateful Dead. Drugs, music, polymorphous sex, vivid art, and visionary poetry swirled in a multisensory mix.

Some of the Haight's Victorians were painted in strong colors: red, yellow, green, brown, black, purple, violet, dark blue, with every different architectural feature painted to stand out. Façades and interiors were painted with the strong coloring of masks. It was the first time the colors of San Francisco's old houses had been changed from their traditional light-reflecting pale colors.

In 1967 *Time* magazine announced that the Haight was the "vibrant epicenter of America's hippie movement" and publicity turned the attention of America's footloose youth to this beautiful Victorian neighborhood with its mature parks and foggy summer weather. An avalanche—the police claimed 75,000—of young people descended on the fragile scene. During the spring of 1967, the Gray Line began taking tourists in sealed buses on the "Hippie Hop: the only foreign tour within the continental limits of the United States." Hippies trotted alongside the buses, which were crawling their way through the traffic jam of gawkers, holding mirrors up to the bus windows.

As Charles Perry, the best historian of the "Summer of Love," wrote in *Rolling Stone,*

The actual composition of the Haight was diverse. Among the things that brought people were traditional bohemian impulses of artistic

*self-assertion and the romantic search for
mystery and authentic experience; the search
for non-violent social forms; curiosity about the
meaning of psychedelics; the lure of the drug
marketplace, for both customer and dealer;
rejection of a comfortable social upbringing;
loneliness and rejection in other communities;
uncertainty about goals; desire to evangelize,
organize or bust the people already in the
Haight; and the sheer momentum of the
phenomenon.*

Along with the day-trippers and "plastic hippies" came violent individuals, drug dealers, and the mentally deranged. The hippie pastoral dream became a nightmare. A quick downward spiral of drug abuse devastated the hippie subculture as drug users became addicts. Many OD'd. On October 6, 1967, the Diggers staged a "Death of Hippie" march. What was left of the Haight was wiped out by a flood of cheap heroin in 1970–1971.

By the early 1970s Haight Street looked like skid row. All the beauty was gone, only the bumbling burnouts remained. About a third of the shopfronts were empty. City health inspectors began closing down the unsanitary communes. Police busted the dealers. The city instituted a Rehabilitation Assistance Program in 1973 whereby city inspectors examined buildings in the Ashbury Heights area, tallied up deficiencies, and then offered property owners subsidized loans to bring their buildings up to code. The city also rezoned large parts of the neighborhood to reduce the number of units permitted in new construction. This made restoration of vintage buildings economically attractive. Along Haight Street the unnatural commercial depression induced speculators to pick up buildings and to "flip" them. The wild house inflation of the mid-1970s that raged citywide rescued the Haight from decay. Between 1973 and 1978 real estate prices increased from 100 to 500 percent.

Two streams of new residents revitalized the Haight, young urban professionals and gays. Grocery stores and taverns are the surest barometers of a neighborhood; by 1979 gay bars outnumbered straight ones five to three along Haight Street. Owner-occupancy increased from 14 percent to 54 percent between 1970 and 1977. Neighborhood organizations were revitalized by these new homeowners. The spiraling rents also made the Haight a center of agitation for citywide rent control which was adopted in 1979.

House colors all over the Haight have become very sophisticated. Pleasing combinations of pale colors—with a lot of white used for windows and trim—reflect warm-colored light onto the streets and into the apartments. The near-universality of using white for windows and trim produces a Wedgwood-like effect of white raised ornament over varying light background colors.

In the early 1980s the Haight saw a brief moment when some thought that the street would shift to luxury boutiques and tony restaurants and become another Union Street. But the more ambitious restaurants failed to draw a city-wide clientele and the neighborhood would not support pricey *nouvelle cuisine*. By the mid-1980s the Haight street commercial strip settled down to a lively, viable mixture of radical (or nostalgic) clothing stores, inexpensive restaurants, and many new and used book stores and record shops.

Spencer House Bed and Breakfast Inn [1]
1080 Haight Street
1895, Frederick P. Rabin
Call 626-9205 for reservations and information.

On the northeast corner of Haight Street at Baker is the three-story corner turret of the elegant Spencer House built in 1895. This imposing Queen Anne-style house was designed by German-born Frederick P. Rabin for Dr. John C. Spencer, a local philanthropist; it is one of the most opulent houses built in this

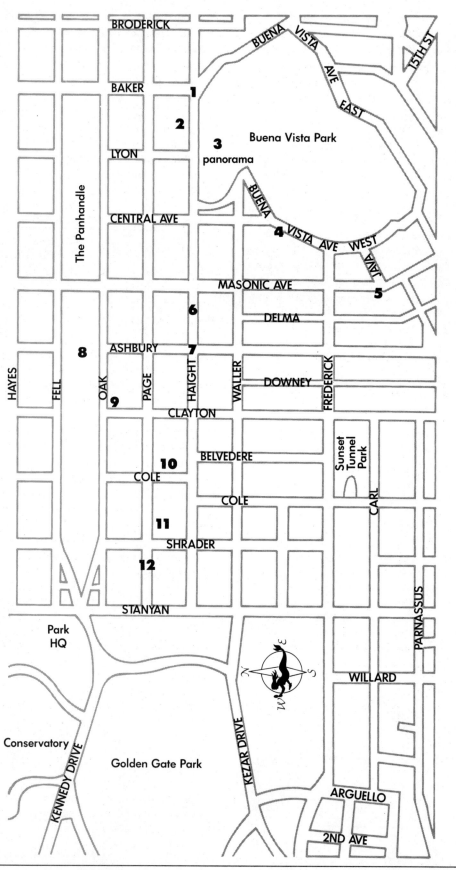

THE HAIGHT-ASHBURY

part of the city. It is unusual for its triple-sized corner lot and for being freestanding and ornamented on all four sides. Its corner tower is squared at its base, octagonal at the second and third floors, and capped by a faceted, conical roof. The stained-glass transoms in the first-floor Palladian windows with their soft canary-yellow glass and transparent faceted "jewels" glitter invitingly at night. The front porch is sheltered by triple Richardsonian-Romanesque arches. A white marble stoop leads to a mosaic entryway and wood-grained front doors.

The house is now a bed-and-breakfast inn, and passersby can sometimes peek into the golden-oak paneled vestibule with its crazy-pattern parquet floors. The interior of the mansion has been perfectly restored and furnished with antiques. Luxuriant palms flourish in the narrow side garden to the east. It is worth walking half a block down Baker and looking back at the Spencer House to admire the manipulation of its roof forms and its very fine side bay.

Across Haight, on the triangular lot formed by Buena Vista East, is **1081 Haight/1-3 Buena Vista East**, a flatiron with a corner turret built in 1894 and designed by John J. Clark. The black iron fence here is a rare original survivor. This intersection, with its four turrets, serves as a dramatic gateway to the Haight-Ashbury.

Across Baker at **One Baker Street** on the northwest corner of Haight is a recent twenty-two unit contemporary building built around a courtyard. It is in a mock Victorian style and is, unfortunately, cheaply built. (If you look closely, you can see where the carpenters pounded the nails into the boards. Victorian builders, and clients, would not have accepted such slapdash work.) Down Baker on this side is a row of Stick Eastlake houses. Numbers **15, 17, 19, and 21 Baker Street** were designed by Hugh Keenan and built in 1890. This fine row has curious porch columns with silhouette flower patterns. Number 21

was restored in 1977; number 19 awaits the eventual restoration that rising real estate values will no doubt some day induce.

THE 1100 BLOCK OF HAIGHT STREET [2]

The flat block of Haight between Baker and Lyon streets facing Buena Vista Park was prime real estate in the Victorian era and attracted fine architecture. At **1128 Haight Street** is a Queen Anne house built in 1891. Now apartments, it has a fine, decorated cylindrical corner tower. Number **1132–34–36 Haight Street** is a three-flat Edwardian built about 1910 with semicircular bay windows. At **1144–46 Haight Street** is a pair of Queen Anne flats with another corner tower. A complex grid pattern is worked out through the porch hood, front doors, transoms, porch paneling, and in the design of the top lights of its double-hung windows. This is an outstanding example of how important window design was to Victorian architects.

Return to Haight and Baker and the corner staircase entrance to Buena Vista Park. Looking east there is a view over the city to the Bay, Oakland, and the Contra Costa mountains.

BUENA VISTA PARK [3]

Enter Buena Vista Park from the stairs at Haight and Baker and take the path to the right. As you climb, there is a superb view to the left: the white Transamerica Pyramid, Lafayette Park's treetops, the slate-covered dome of Temple Sherith Israel of 1905, the green terraces of Alta Plaza with forested Angel Island behind it, the twin piers of the Golden Gate Bridge against the high hills of Marin County, and the trees and H. A. Minton's 1932 Gothic tower of Lone Mountain College (now part of the University of San Francisco). Keep walking uphill and to the right to the small children's play area built in 1975. The grand twin-towered church in the distance with the dome and square campanile is Jesuit St. Ignatius on the campus of the University of San Francisco, designed by Charles J. I. Devlin and built in 1914. Immediately below the park, on Haight Street, is the warm yellow brick and red tile roofed Tuscan Revival façade of the Third Church of Christ, Scientist designed by Edgar A. Matthews in 1918. The church is enriched with terra cotta ornament. The band of trees between the two churches is Golden Gate Park's Panhandle.

Buena Vista Park was originally known as Hill Park and was reserved by the city in 1867 as a part of the Outside Lands. Its summit is 569 feet above sea-level and the park covers 36.5 acres. The city paid $88,250 to squatters with claims to the hilltop in the state legislation that established Golden Gate Park. Originally treeless, the summit of the park was one of the chief visitors' overlooks of the nineteenth-century city. Forestation, including the preservation of a grove of native oaks, began about 1880. The name Buena Vista Park was adopted in 1894. About 1910 park neighbors organized an improvement club to pressure the city into improving the park and the road around it and in 1913 the handsome new staircases, paths, and tennis courts were dedicated.

Though it looks wild, Buena Vista is essentially man-made. John McLaren oversaw the park's forestation. Some of the trees were planted by school children on Arbor Day with seedlings provided by Adolph Sutro. Monterey cypress, Monterey pines, several kinds of eucalyptus, redwoods, acacia, and Australian tea trees flourish here. There are also some madrone, toyon, deodar cedars, Torrey pines, Italian stone pines and Japanese black pines.

From the play area with its sweeping view, walk down the path out of the park to its perimeter sidewalk. You pass a grove of native California oaks to one side and an eclectic array of houses and apartments across Buena Vista Avenue West.

BUENA VISTA AVENUE WEST [4]

Richard Spreckels Mansion Bed and Breakfast
737 Buena Vista Avenue West
1897, Edward J. Vogel
Call 861-3008 for information and reservations.

Another of the grand houses built facing the park is the Richard Spreckels house of 1897 designed by Edward J. Vogel in the Colonial Revival style for Richard Spreckels, the nephew of sugar magnate Claus Spreckels. The house has a columned semicircular porch, marble stoop, and a tall iron gate to its right. The side wall of the house has two curious round stained-glass windows framed by leaves and angels' heads. The side bay window has a fine art glass window with fish and an urn. Today the garishly painted grand old house has been converted into a posh bed-and-breakfast inn. Immediately next door is **731 Buena Vista West**, an annex to the Spreckels bed and breakfast inn. It is notable for its elaborate front porch protective iron grille executed by E. A. Chase in 1979.

Buena Vista Avenue West, developed a decade later than the blocks down the hill, is notable for the great variety of its architecture. At **639 Buena Vista West** at Frederick Street is a classic stucco box with an elegant entrance probably built about 1915. At **635 Buena Vista West** is another stucco house with elegant French windows and a fine cornice from the same period. Number **615 Buena Vista West** is a shingled Tudor house with an elaborate central bay.

At **601 Buena Vista West** is a Queen Anne house with a tower built in 1895 by William H. Armitage. Note the smooth curve where the tower meets the front wall. This house is now several units. Between it and its neighbor is a curious view of the seemingly free-floating shingled onion dome and odd copper chimneys added to the top of 1450 Masonic Avenue. At **595–97 Buena Vista Avenue West**, on the southeast corner of Java, is a modern, two-flat building designed about 1950 by Henry Hill, one of the Bay Area's modernist designers. Originally of unpainted wood, that "natural" finish did not weather well and the building has been painted. At narrow Java Street, turn right to busy Masonic Avenue.

JAVA STREET, MASONIC AVENUE AND WALLER STREET / VICTORIAN ROWS [5]

Java Street is a short one-block connector to Masonic Avenue. It has a good view of the planted eucalyptus forests of Mt. Sutro, once part of Adolph Sutro's vast real estate holdings. Masonic Avenue is a busy street lined with fine houses with lush greenery and many flowering plants in pots and in the small plots in front of the houses. At **1482 Masonic Avenue**, at the corner of Java is a large shingled house with a projecting third floor. The house incorporates hints of the Mission Revival in its welcoming porch. Down the hill on the same side of the street is **1450 Masonic Avenue**, a Queen Anne house with a tower designed in 1891 by A. J. Barnett. Modern copperwork panels have replaced the plaster scratchwork at the cornice, and contemporary stained-glass windows have been added to the tower at the second floor. A contemporary sculpture-house number stands in the yard. This is the house whose onion dome and copper chimneys were visible from Buena Vista West. The building seems an amalgam of Victoriana and vaguely hippie artwork. Number **1430 Masonic Avenue** almost hidden under its trees, is a fine turn-of-the-century house with a clinker brick base and classical detailing.

The 1300 block of Masonic sports a row of six Stick-Eastlake row houses at

1322–1342 Masonic Avenue built in 1891 and identical in form, though now painted in a variety of color schemes. They were designed by Robert Dickie Cranston for developer J. A. Whelan in a somewhat *retardaire* style. The houses are set on high bases that emphasize their verticality. They originally had false gables and cast-iron cresting on their roofs. Note the applied ornamental "sticks" that seem to rise from the base straight to the cornice. In the 1920s, when the Haight-Ashbury was comfortable but a bit faded, such houses were described as sitting "with their poker faces like close-mouthed Yankees refusing to divulge any secrets."

At Waller and Masonic are several choice rows. The corner house at **1301–03 Waller Street** sits on a dramatic base and has curved glass. It and its neighbor, **1307–09 Waller Street**, were built in 1901. A row of house—**1315, 1321–23, 1327–29, and 1333–35 Waller Street**—were all constructed in 1896, again for developer J. A. Whelan. All the houses here, varying from single-family residences to flats, are set on high bases, have gable roofs, and a lush embroidery ornament. Note the central medallion at the second floor of 1315 Waller. These houses represent the highwater mark of ornament in San Francisco architecture. Number 1321–23 was "improved" with stucco when Victoriana was unfashionable; number 1333–35, the last in the row, was restored in 1988. When the misimprovements of the façade were removed, the "ghosts" of the original ornament were revealed and new ornament was custom-made.

Facing the Waller Street row, on the northwest corner of Masonic and Waller where Masonic Avenue widens, stands **1265–67 Masonic Avenue**, a suave corner house on a yellow brick base with a three-quarter round bay window at the corner. The bay has curved glass, a design motif picked up in the semicircular porch opening. A very fine small stained-glass window with a semicircular hood is placed on the smooth first floor façade facing Masonic. The double-hung windows here are more horizontal than vertical and make the house more restful than its exaggeratedly vertical neighbors. Along its Waller Street side march four semicircular bays in an even rhythm. The house dates from the late 1890s when San Francisco architects were striving to design houses with more elegant, restrained ornament.

One of the most spectacular rows of Queen Anne houses marches down the **1200 block of Masonic Avenue** from Waller to Haight. There prime lots on the sunny side of prestigious Masonic Avenue were developed by Robert Dickie Cranston and his partner Hugh Keenan in 1895–1896; number 1244–46 Masonic Avenue was designed in the same year by Martens and Coffey. Note the swirling leaf design in the peak of the gables. The row is distinguished by "witch's cap" turrets, some round, some faceted. The lingering fancy for somewhat garish paint schemes in the Haight survives here.

HAIGHT STREET COMMERCIAL STRIP [6]

On the southeast corner of Masonic and Haight stands turreted **1200 Masonic Avenue** (see illustration), a mixed commercial and residential building erected for a Mrs. Borgart, a cashier at the San Francisco *Examiner*. A dentist's parlors occupied the second-story corner bay. This Queen Anne was designed by William H. Lillie in 1896. Facing it across Masonic are much plainer brick commercial buildings on the southwest and northwest corners of Haight and Masonic designed by Meyers and Ward for the Goldberg Bowen Company in 1904–1905. A peculiarity in the development of the Haight was that the John H. Baird Estate owned a blocks-long swath along both sides of Haight Street which it did not sell to developers until the early 1900s. The result is that today's neighborhood is a sandwich consisting

of plainer Edwardian commercial-residential buildings built between 1900 and 1915 along Haight Street, flanked by 1880s–1890s housing along the streets to either side.

On the fourth, northeast corner of Haight and Masonic stands a mixed commercial residential building at **1398 Haight Street**. For many years it was a corner drugstore and many of the original fittings survive in the restaurant. In 1967 this became the site of the Drogstore café, a celebrated hippie hang-out. It's said that the café wanted to keep the name "Drugstore" along with its apothecary-jar decor, but that the police insisted on an alteration in the name, hence "Drogstore." Today **Dish** (431-3534) is one of the better eating places in the Haight, and a popular place for brunch. It has preserved the original turn-of-the-century interior, decorating it with different dishes, thus the name of the new business.

HAIGHT AND ASHBURY STREETS [7]

A block west is the famous intersection of Haight and Ashbury, the coordinates that gave this neighborhood its name and which was adopted to refer to the hippie bohemia that blossomed here. Those with a particular interest in the shrines of the hippie era will want to make a detour one block uphill on Ashbury Street, past Waller, to **710 Ashbury Street**, the former Grateful Dead house. This very fine Queen Anne row from **704 to 714 Ashbury Street** was built about 1890 and designed by the active Robert Dickie Cranston. While similar in design, each façade has its particular variations. Number 710 has original doors and the number "710" in stained glass in its transom. The Dead were busted here on October 2, 1967. (This is a private residence, so please do not disturb the occupants.) Across the street, conveniently enough, was the Haight-Ashbury Legal Organization at **715 Ashbury**. Both sides of this block are lined with three-flat buildings marked by bay windows held up by decorative brackets.

At Haight, continue down Ashbury past **525–501 Ashbury Street**, a solid row of three-story, three-flat, gable-roofed Queen Anne buildings designed by Daniel Einstein about 1900. These multifamily dwellings were made to look like large single-family houses.

At the northeast corner of Ashbury and Page is a row of five houses at **1550–42 Page Street**. These Queen Annes were designed in 1891 by the ubiquitous Cranston and Keenan and sport their "trademark," the sun faces on the second story. The corner house is particularly fine, with a wood-grained entry with squat Romanesque columns, elegant hardware, and a shallow, bow-shaped second-floor porch. The side wall facing Ashbury has a decorated chimney, decorative panels, and projecting bays with textured plaster work on their undersides.

Number **461 Ashbury Street**, at the northwest corner of Page is distinguished by a lovely oval corner bay window with curved glass. Next door is **459 Ashbury Street** with two overly ornamented "Victorian" garages. Above them rises a splendid Queen Anne building of 1893 by Cranston and Keenan with a bulging second-floor porch with a semicircular arch. The whale weathervane is an inauthentic modern addition. (Such houses often had wood or iron finials, but not weathervanes.) The cottage on a raised basement has a square bay and interesting "outrigger" porch brackets. Next to it is **429 Ashbury Street**, a three-story, gable-roofed Eastlake house designed in 1891 by the Shipman Brothers. The original owner was a deputy superintendent of streets for the city. This lacy façade has a beautiful porch hood and eye-catching spindle work and columns on its second floor.

At the foot of Ashbury is the Golden Gate Park Panhandle, lined with mature eucalyptus trees. The Panhandle was one of the first parts of the park to be landscaped in 1870 and was originally enclosed by a fence that was locked at 9 P.M. The Panhandle was laid out with a now-lost carriage drive with three small "islands" of plantings. Here San Francisco's High Society went for afternoon carriage drives to see and to be seen. San Francisco's swells thronged the Panhandle to see the ladies and show off their mounts. One gossipy description of the scene from the 1882 *San Francisco News Letter* ran:

> A closed carriage [passed], carrying Mrs. C. and Miss C.C., of Sutter street, both robed in exquisite costumes fresh from New York. M., the lawyer, he of the flowing locks, was their attendant cavalier. S.W.'s family in an open carriage, driven by his son R., Mrs. R. expanding more and more daily, in comfort and happiness. R.L. on horseback. Judge H. and family in a carryall. Gov. S[tanford]'s beautiful turn-out—gold-mounted harness and perfectly appointed servants making it a feature of the crowd; Mrs. S., dressed in mourning, was accompanied by Miss G., of Sacramento.

In 1906, immediately after the earthquake and fire, the Panhandle and park became a refuge for fleeing families. Eleven babies were born here the first night. Tents and later wood cottages eventually housed thirty thousand refugees. During the hippie period, the Panhandle was the scene of outdoor rock concerts that caused heavy wear-and-tear on the fragile landscape. Today the Panhandle is somewhat seedy. Vagabonds in buses and beat-up cars are drawn here as one of the last vestiges of 1960s-style folk wanderings; the homeless are also drawn to the park. From the very rich to the very poor, the Panhandle has experienced a complete revolution of Fortune's wheel.

253

The block of Oak Street facing the Panhandle between Ashbury and Clayton streets harbors a cluster of fine Victorians. Number **1705 Oak Street** was designed by Maxwell G. Bugbee in 1893. Number **1709 Oak Street** is a superb shingled house with a streamlined first floor and a brick arched entrance; the two-story upper section juts out with a second-story bay window and a third-story, look-out-style gable window. It was designed by the zappy Joseph Cather Newsom in 1890; note the fancy shingle work. Number **1711 Oak Street** is by M. J. Walsh and dates from 1887; **1751 Oak Street** is a delightful one-story Queen Anne cottage on a raised basement built by Adolph Lutgens in 1896, a late date for such a small building on a prime street. Numbers **1759 and 1763 Oak Street** are looming, three-story buildings with swallow's nest stucco work in their gables; they were designed by architect William H. Lillie in 1891.

On the southeast corner of Oak and Clayton is **400 Clayton Street**, the McFarlane House, designed by Coxhead and Coxhead in 1895 and built for $7,261. Engaged Corinthian columns and an off-center entrance create a formal yet quirky Mannerist façade. Over the small front door is a broken pediment with an oval window and a rich garland ornament. The double-hung windows in the "wings" of the façade are stretched out to create a horizontal effect. Coxhead often used conventional ornament in unconventional ways, and this house is an individualistic essay in tortured architectural formality.

Up the 400 block of Clayton are more architectural treasures. On the southwest corner stands **401–07 Clayton Street** a group of four Eastlake designs by J. B. Hall built in 1894–1895. Note their varied stoops and porches. These four houses cost a total of $4,900. Numbers

409 and 411 Clayton Street are by Soule and Hoadley and date from 1893. Number 409 is a wild Queen Anne with balconies; it was once called 409 House, with reading and meditation rooms on its first floor, psychiatric counseling on the second floor, and the offices of *The Journal of Psychedelic Drugs* in the attic. Number 411 Clayton has an oval spindlework screen and a basket of carved flowers and exuberant foliage in its gable. This row of fine vintage houses is terminated by **1700 Page Street**, an egregious thirteen-unit apartment building with exposed parking on the northwest corner of Clayton and Page. Peek through its entrance grate for what can only be called punk architecture. Such "higher and better" uses threatened much of the Haight in the 1960s until zoning rules were rewritten in the 1970s to prevent such disruptive development.

Another instructive contrast is offered by **1727 and 1726 Page Street**, on opposite sides of the street. Number 1727 is a robustly ornamented Eastlake cottage on a raised basement built for M. Wiegman in 1889. It has a beautiful front door with incised wood panels and colored flash glass, also with incised ornament. Facing it is 1726 Page with sandpaper stucco panels, ugly yellow glass windows, and a heavy metal fire escape characteristic of the early 1960s. Also in this block of vintage buildings is **1768 Page Street**, a modern building with two-story, generously proportioned bay windows but too much bleak cement at the ground level and too large a garage door. Designing in-fill buildings in Victorian districts is difficult. While it is desirable to accommodate parking on the ground floor, such overlarge garage doors are visually disruptive.

Number **1762 Page Street** was designed by Edward Swain in 1895. Here fake "colonial style" mullions have been added to the double-hung windows in a most inappropriate "East Coast antique" manner. Number **1767 Page Street**, set between larger flats buildings, is a fine

Edwardian house with a round corner tower and a smooth curve where the tower meets the flat façade. Narrow ship-lap clapboard is set flush. A generous porch and suave detailing complete the design. Number **1777 Page Street** was built in 1894 by the prolific Cranston and Keenan as Robert D. Cranston's own home. It is distinguished by decorative plaster work and owls' heads.

500 BLOCK OF COLE STREET [10]

On the southeast corner of Page and Cole streets stands **500–06 Cole Street**, designed by Cranston and Keenan in 1899. This almost wildly expressive Queen Anne does a clever job of tucking four upper flats and two ground-floor flats onto a corner lot, making the result look like a single mansion. The U-shaped front stairs lead to the porch with its Richardsonian columns and redwood ornament. The third floor is marked by an unusual turret set between two gables. Delicate ribbons and garlands decorate the tower. Facing it across Cole is **503–07 Cole Street**, also by Cranston and dating from 1899 as well.

Up the block toward Haight Street is yet another Cranston and Keenan row, **508, 510, 512, and 516 Cole Street**, built in 1899. The last house in the cluster, 516, boasts a particularly lacy façade with fine bay windows and a handsome porch. Elaborate mullions decorate the upper windows, while the lower pane is plain for unobstructed views of the street. Notice what an astonishingly large proportion of the façade is devoted to windows.

Park Branch Public Library and Mural [11]
1833 Page Street
1909, McDougall Brothers

Return to Page Street and walk west toward Golden Gate Park. At 1833 Page Street, tucked away inconspicuously, is Public Library Branch No. 5, the Park Branch, an elegantly proportioned, light yellow brick library with a terra cotta-framed entrance and oak and glass doors designed by the McDougall Brothers in 1909. Inside is a large reading room with windows on all four sides. These plain windows are handsomely proportioned. In the raised basement are community meeting rooms. The vivid mural on the neighboring building, one of the finest ever done in the Haight, was painted by Selma Brown and Ruby Newman in 1975–1976. Dancers, masks, and musicians are set against an idyllic California landscape with a rainbow. All races, ages, and cultures blend in the design. Inscribed in the corner of the mural is a most hippie motto: "Come together each in your own perceiving of your self."

PAGE AND SHRADER STREETS [12]

At the northwest corner of Page and Shrader Streets stands **1900–02 Page Street**, a nine-unit building with both flats and apartments. This three-story building has a corner tower and turret. The first-floor windows and the two side entrances and side bay are distinguished by semicircular designs. The rusticated clapboard siding, so called because of the narrow, accentuated grooves, sets off the fancy millwork. The cornice has a band of wreaths and swags. It is, all in all, a very San Francisco Victorian painted an appropriate white. The facing Salfield flats at **1890 Shrader Street**, on the northeast corner of Page were designed by Samuel Newsom in 1889. There is fine ornament between the second and third floors, intricate shingle work, and swallow's nest stucco work.

On the southwest corner of Page and Shrader is **1901 Page Street**, a Queen Anne/Colonial Revival house designed by Edward J. Vogel in 1896. It is unusual in being set off by small front and side yards and still has its original iron fence. Note the odd placement of the porthole windows on the side wall. Author Kathleen Thompson Norris lived here in the 1920s before moving to New York, where she wrote her best-selling novels. Later a workshop here made embroidered church vestments.

At **510 Shrader Street**, tucked between two larger neighbors, is an elaborate Eastlake cottage on a raised basement built as late as 1891. Its transoms have very fine stained-glass windows.

Continuation

From here you may either walk up Haight into Golden Gate Park and McLaren Lodge (*Tour 12*), where you may obtain a map of the vast park, or continue on Haight Street, browsing in its shops, restaurants, and enjoying the funky street scene.

SOME HAIGHT STREET LANDMARKS

The former Masonic Lodge at **1748 Haight Street**, with shops on its ground floor, is a large, plain three-story building with a cavernous space upstairs. Masonic Lodge No. 449 was organized in 1914 and had its peak membership right before the stock market crash of 1929. After a second boom in the post-World War II period, the lodge withered and sold off its building. For a decade it has housed the I-Beam, a popular rock club.

Number **1779–83 Haight Street**, near Shrader, consists of two flats and a small ground-floor shop and was built in 1893 by the Brooklyn Planning Mill. It is the oldest intact building on the strip. Neda's Flowers at **1677–81 Haight Street** is a Parisian style building designed by South-of-Market born architect James F. Dunn. The interior of this 1904 flower shop is close to original. These two blocks, bounded by Haight, Waller, Cole, and Clayton streets were the site of The Chutes amusement park. There a three-hundred-foot inclined plane descended from a seventy-foot height to a small artificial lake. Gondolas were released from the top to rush down the incline and splash in the lake. The Chutes also had a merry-go-round, shooting gallery, bandstand, and a circular "Darwinian Temple" where evolution was popularized. The park closed and the blocks were developed after 1902.

Number **1775 Haight Street** was once the Diggers' free crash pad. At **1736 Haight Street** was the I-Thou Coffee Shop. This block also once housed the Mouse Studios/Pacific Ocean Trading company, where many psychedelic posters originated. The corner commercial-residential building at **1701–05 Haight Street at Cole** was designed by Charles J. Rousseau for Maurice Rosenthal. The initials MR are worked into the pediment of the corner bay window. On the Cole Street side of the building is Joana Zegri's mural of 1969, **"Evolution Rainbow,"** restored in 1981 and 1983.

On the southwest corner of Haight and Belvedere at **1635 Haight Street** is the First Interstate Bank, built for the German Savings Bank. It is a Neoclassical temple with fine marble counters and wainscotting in a warm, brown-veined marble. A series of old photographs of Golden Gate Park decorate its interior.

Across the street at **1660 Haight Street** is the façade of the old Superba Theater built as a nickelodeon in 1911 for J. Van Husen. It has a richly ornamented Beaux Arts façade like a proscenium arch. After serving as a food market, it has been adapted as a toy store.

Golden Gate Park to Lands End

FROM THE CITY TO THE SEA

What This Tour Covers

[1] McLaren Lodge / Park Headquarters

[2] Fuchsia Garden

[3] The Conservatory of Flowers

[4] Tree Ferns

[5] John McLaren Memorial Rhododendron Dell

[6] Music Concourse and Pavilion (California Academy of Sciences / M.H. de Young Memorial Museum / Asian Art Museum / View of Sutro Television Tower)

[7] Japanese Tea Garden

[8] Strybing Arboretum and Botanical Gardens

[9] Stow Lake / Strawberry Hill

[10] Rainbow Falls / Prayerbook Cross

[11] Lloyd Lake / The Portals of the Past

[12] Old Speedway / Lindley Meadow

[13] Spreckels Lake

[14] Buffalo Paddock

[15] The Chain of Lakes

[16] The Dutch Windmill / Wilhelmina Tulip Garden

[17] Beach Chalet / Lucien Labaudt Murals

[18] The Great Highway / Ocean Beach

[19] The Cliff House / Seal Rocks

[20] Sutro Heights Park

[21] Lands End / The Golden Gate

Preliminaries

Best Times To Do This Tour

The eastern end of the park fills up with distracting automobiles and roller-skaters with boomboxes on weekends; weekdays are best. The park is sunniest from about 10 A.M. to 3 P.M.; it chills quickly when the fog rolls in. But the fog transforms the park into a landscape of smokelike trees and meadows people with only occasional figures. It is also quite special by car on a lightly rainy day when it becomes your vast, private garden. The park is safe at night and is quite different viewed in the moonlight. The soothing quality of this romantic landscape awaits the explorer unconventional enough to savor it when others don't.

How To Tour Golden Gate Park

The best way to see Golden Gate Park is by bicycle. Bikes can be rented at **Lincoln Cyclery** (221-2415) at 772 Stanyan and **Avenue Cyclery** (387-3155) at 756 Stanyan. Bring your own lock and chain if you wish to go inside the Conservatory or the park's museums. Please stay on the designated bike paths.

Those who wish to just sample the park and Ocean Beach should see the Conservatory and the eastern end of the park, and perhaps the Asian Art Museum and Japanese Tea Garden. Then walk north out of the park to Fulton Street and catch the 5 Fulton trolley bus which passes along the northern edge of the park to La Playa, one short block from Ocean Beach (there is a supermarket here). The 18 Forty-sixth Avenue bus travels north on La Playa up to the Cliff House, Sutro Heights, and Lands End. At the end of your tour at Forty-eighth Avenue and Geary is the terminus of the 38 Geary bus, which brings you directly back downtown. You can alight from the 38 Geary at about Twentieth Avenue and walk one block north to Clement Street with its many inexpensive restaurants, including many Asian places.

Transportation

The quickest way to the park by public transit is to take the 38 Geary bus to Sixth Avenue and transfer to the southbound 44 O'Shaughnessy bus, which passes through the Music Concourse. The 21 Hayes trolley-bus turns north at Hayes and Stanyan, one block from McLaren Lodge where this tour begins. The 7 Haight and the 71 Haight-Noriega pass up Haight Street to Stanyan at the east end of the park.

Maps

McLaren Lodge, the bookshops of the de Young Museum and the Academy of Sciences, and the Strybing Arboretum have maps of Golden Gate Park. The free GGNRA map is useful for Lands End and is available at the Visitor Center underneath and behind the Cliff House.

Restaurants, Cafés, and Bars

The few concessions in the park are minimal. There is a good cafeteria-style restaurant in the de Young Museum. It's best to bring your own picnic hamper. There is a supermarket on Stanyan Street at Haight.

Introduction: From The City To The Sea

The real, the only reason why a great park should be made, is to bring the country into the town, and make it possible for the inhabitants of crowded cities to enjoy the calm and

The Victorian Conservatory of Flowers in Golden Gate Park was erected in 1878 and stands in an artistically graded garden designed by William Bond Prichard.

Copyright 1989 William Walters

restfulness which only the rural landscape and rural surroundings can give ... all other objects must, in a great park, be subordinated to the one central, controlling idea of rural repose, which space alone can give.
—Charles Sprague Sargent, 1888

Golden Gate Park is a 1,023.16-acre Eden, one of the premier works of Victorian landscape design in North America. In the 1860s this rectangle stretching from the edge of the city to the Pacific was described as "a mass of white, trackless, moving sands, without vegetation, and not pleasing to the senses." What few trees grew here were described as "stunted growths, seemingly ashamed to claim membership in the tree family."

The land transformed into this verdant oasis was originally a fraction of the Outside Lands. Squatters, some in the pay of well-connected land speculators, threw up fences and shacks claiming the city fringes. In 1864, 89.71 percent of the land was deeded to the squatters in exchange for the 10.29 percent reserved for public use, out of which Golden Gate Park was eventually carved.

The early prognosis for Golden Gate Park was not encouraging. The public's tenth had the most sand and the least water: the press dubbed it "The Great Sand Park." When Frederick Law Olmsted, America's foremost landscape architect and the designer with Calvert Vaux of New York City's Central Park, was shown the site and asked his opinion in 1866, he declared it impossible to create a park. "It would not be wise nor safe to undertake to form a park upon any plan which assumed as a certainty that trees which would delight the eye can be made to grow [in] San Francisco," he said.

Nonetheless, Mayor Frank McCoppin and Governor Haight persisted. (Some claim that McCoppin, the principal stockholder in San Francisco Grading Company, then engaged in carting fill from Lone Mountain to the Mission District's swamps, pushed the "impossible" park project in expectation of securing the lucrative contract to grade it dead level.) On April 4, 1870 the California legislature passed "An Act to Provide for the Improvement of Public Parks in the City of San Francisco." The governor appointed the first Park Commission and the project was launched. The commission put the topographical survey out to bid and awarded it to twenty-four-year-old surveyor William Hammond Hall, who came in with the lowest bid, $4,860. Hall produced a detailed topographic survey and a preliminary park plan in only six months. The commissioners were so pleased that they appointed him the first superintendent of Golden Gate Park in 1871.

William Hammond Hall is the man chiefly responsible for the park's superb landscape design, something he had never done before. He was born in Maryland in 1846 and raised in Stockton, California. He studied surveying and in 1865 joined the Board of Military Engineers. Later, with City Surveyor William P. Humphreys, he worked on the Outside Lands survey and tramped over the entire western fringe of the city. He served as park superintendent from 1871 to 1876. Through a "leak" to influential General Alexander, Hall frustrated McCoppin's plan to flatten the site. McCoppin never forgot. In 1876 Hall resigned after being wrongly accused by a legislative investigating committee of appropriating park property. Hall went on to a brilliant career as an engineer and worked in Nevada, England, central California, South Africa, the Russian Transcaucasus, Panama, and Turkey. He became California's first State Engineer and made a handsome profit on land he bought which he foresaw would be needed for San Francisco's Hetch-Hetchy water system. He was roasted in the press for this. He died at eighty-eight in 1934.

Hall's immediate problem was holding down the shifting sand in "The Great Sand Park." United States Army General Barton S. Alexander gathered information on European dune reclamation techniques. The first beach grass, *Ammophila arenaria*, was imported from Paris in 1873 and planted on the shifting beach dunes. For most of the park, barley and lupine were sown together on the sand. The quick-sprouting barley held the sand down while the lupine took root.

In 1874 a now-lost Casino with a dining hall and private rooms upstairs was built near what is today Conservatory Drive West. Operated by a concessionaire, it became a notorious rendezvous. The *San Francisco News Letter* complained in 1886,

[Private concessions have] desecrated the park by providing fast men and women with an enlarged edition of Marchand's. French dinners, high-priced wines, private bedrooms, fast scenes and night orgies are not the aesthetic influences expected to be cultivated by an institution maintained at the public expense, and which, instead of catering to the low, the vulgar and degrading, was expected to, and is well capable of administering to all that is purifying, elevating and ennobling in man's nature.

In 1873 Hall completed the Main— now Kennedy—Drive all the way to Ocean Beach. But after Hall's resignation, the park was neglected and between 1876 and 1886 money and greenery dried up. In 1886 Governor Stoneman fired all the Park Commissioners and called Hall back as consulting engineer. Hall agreed, but only for a year and only in order to hand-pick his successor. He chose a Scottish-born gardener, John McLaren, whose fame eventually overshadowed Hall's critical original role.

John McLaren was born in Scotland in 1846 and worked on estates there and at the Royal Botanical Gardens in Edinburgh. He came to America and by 1872 was employed as a gardener on several San Mateo County estates. McLaren dedicated his life to filling out the park plan, planting trees, and outfoxing politicians. In so doing he earned the undying affection of San Franciscans. In 1917, when "Uncle John" reached the city's mandatory retirement age of seventy, an ordinance was passed exempting the Superintendent of Parks from this rule. His pension was cancelled and his salary doubled.

McLaren continued as ruler of the city's expanding park system for twenty-six more cycles of the seasons. He died in 1943, at ninety-six, in the Lodge inside the park he loved so well and was laid in state in the City Hall Rotunda for two days of official mourning. He nurtured his beloved park for fifty-six years, defying all the canons of modern "managerial science." He was autocratic, swore at his men (who swore right back), liked his nip of Scotch, lived where he worked, loved what he did, and outlasted all political trends and fads. Stories about the cagey old man with the thick Scottish burr continue to grow like the trees he planted. Of him it can truly be said, "If you seek his monument, look about you."

Golden Gate Park has not stood still in time. The passive contemplation of pastoral scenery has been augmented by active recreational uses. Every special interest wants its own piece of the park. Baseball, polo, tennis, golf, archery, soccer, model yachts, flycasting, professional sports, lawn bowling, kite flying, roller skating, skateboarding, off-road bicycles, model airplanes with noisy motors, and massive rock concerts have invaded the park. The municipality itself is another despoiler: the park has a former police academy and present-day police stables, a senior center, a large stadium with parking, and an odiferous sewage treatment plant inside it. In the 1950s, the Department of Highways wanted the entire Panhandle and chunks of the rest of the park for a "landscaped" freeway. (The infamous Trafficways Plan of 1951 drafted by the State of California's Department of Highways proposing the Panhandle and parts of Golden Gate Park as the convenient site for a massive freeway. This brutal proposal helped spark the famous "Freeway Revolt" in San Francisco, the first time any American city thwarted the bulldozing of a superhighway through its mature districts.) Museums, fine as they are in themselves, are another invasion, as blockbuster art exhibits flood the fragile park with thousands of automobiles. Every ethnic group wants a highly visible statue to their hero. Every historical interest wants just one more commemorative plaque. Every assassinated president must have a depressing memorial. Today, many (some say hundreds) homeless people camp in the park, threatening its future.

Hall's plan for a "natural" park involved massive, but undulating, grading of virtually the entire site, section by section. He devised a plan that eventually turned the moving dunes into a stable honeycomb of valleys and low hills to create meadows walled in by windbreaking stands of trees. Each meadow acquired a different designated use, from baseball to polo. Like a grand hotel with many rooms, Golden Gate Park accommodates many, many different activities. But since each is screened by bands of trees, a visually restful landscape is the result.

Golden Gate Park slopes gently from east to west. It can be divided into two parts, with Stow Lake and Strawberry Hill at the center. The eastern end of the park is the oldest and houses the more exotic plants, and also cultural institutions. The western half of the park has more open space, a relaxed landscape, simpler horticulture, and physical activities that need space like horseback riding and archery.

Once the land was graded and planted with lupine, trees were set out. Some hundred species of conifers were planted, ranging from the hardy Monterey pine and cypress to Torrey pines and pines from New Zealand. Evergreen conifers were selected because they absorb the moisture in the foggy winds. Many varieties of Australian eucalyptus were also planted. Flowering and deciduous trees were only infrequently used. Carrying on a worldwide correspondence with botanical gardens, McLaren oversaw a steady exchange of information, seeds, cuttings, and plants. Specimens came from the Mediterranean, South Africa, China, Japan, and in particular, Australia and New Zealand.

If you have limited time, the best way to sample Golden Gate Park is to follow Kennedy Drive. As you travel along the wide, winding drive, the romantic theater of nineteenth-century landscaping unfolds. The sequence of views is as thought out as an extended piece of music. Each passage has its mood: from the exotic to the "natural," from the complex to the simple, from the cultural to the recreational, from the dense to the spacious, from the city to the sea.

McLaren Lodge / Park Headquarters [1]

Fell and Stanyan streets
1896, Edward R. Swain

At Fell and Stanyan streets, immediately inside the park, is the handsome sandstone, red tile-roofed headquarters of the San Francisco Recreation and Park Commission built in 1896 to designs by Edward R. Swain. It is considered one of the earliest Mission Style buildings. Originally built to house John McLaren and his family to the left and the Park Commission to the right, the Lodge is notable for its restful horizontal lines, porch, loggia, and fine interior.

Enter through the handsome oak door to the counter in the foyer; you can obtain a map of the park here. Ask if you may see the Park Commission's meeting room, a handsome Craftsman interior lined with pigskin and presided over by a large oil portrait of John McLaren. The chairs around the large oak table are especially fine. In 1949 the Playground Commission was merged

with the Park Commission to form the Recreation and Park Commission. In 1950 McLaren Lodge Annex was built behind the old Lodge. From here San Francisco's superb system of over 215 parks and playgrounds is administered. In front of the Lodge is a lofty Monterey cypress affectionately known as "Uncle John McLaren's Christmas Tree." It is strung with colored lights every December. In 1943, as McLaren lay dying, he requested that, despite the war-time blackout, the tree be decorated. It was, and he saw it lit for one last time.

Across John F. Kennedy Drive (originally Main Drive) at the intersection of Kezar Drive is a glimpse down a long meadow framed by tall trees. Here is your introduction to the completely artificial, English-style landscape designed by William Hammond Hall. As you proceed west down Kennedy Drive, an artfully planned sequence of such long vistas opens before you and closes as you move on. The great success of this consummate work of landscape art is that most people think all this just happened.

FUCHSIA GARDEN [2]

Just beyond the Lodge to the right is Conservatory Drive East, which leads to the **Camellia Gardens** planted about 1920. They bloom January through March. North of the camellias is the Fuchsia Garden begun about 1940; more than 350 varieties grow under the shade of a tall canopy of trees. The vivid fuchsias bloom from July to August and continue blossoming until October. They are a plant particularly well adapted to San Francisco's cool climate. Gnarled, old fuchsia bushes can be found in the backyards of all the Victorian districts of the city. Their pendant, lanternlike buds explode to display wildly clashing colors: red, pink, white, purple—even fuchsia. This corner of the park was one of the first sections to be landscaped. Rustic picnic shelters built out of tree trunks

Inner Sunset
District

LINCOLN WAY

BOWLING GREEN DRIVE

MIDDLE DRIVE EAST

Nursery

4 Tree Ferns

CONSERVATORY DRIVE

FULTON

Inner Richmond
District

ARGUELLO

Lawn Bowling

Tennis Courts

JOHN F. KENNEDY DRIVE

3 Conservatory

CONSERVATORY DRIVE WEST

ARGUELLO

263

KEZAR DRIVE

Carrousel

Children's Playground

2 Fuchsia Garden

Camelia Garden

CONSERVATORY DRIVE EAST

Sharon Meadow

Kezar Stadium

KEZAR DRIVE

FREDERICK

Kezar Pavilion

Alvord Lake

McLaren Lodge
1 Park HQ

STANYAN

WALLER

HAIGHT

Haight-Ashbury

N
S
E
W

OAK

FELL

MASONIC AVE

The Panhandle

BAKER

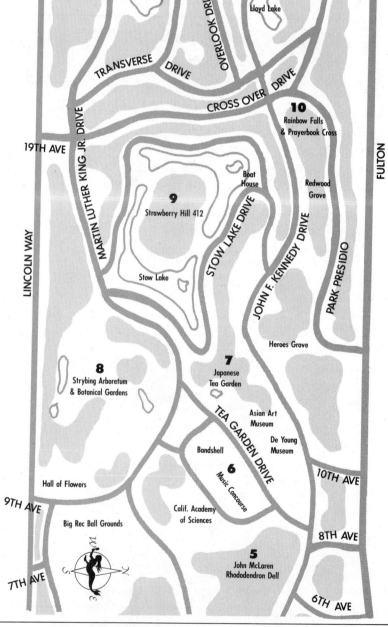

Outer Sunset District

Mallard Lake

MIDDLE DRIVE WEST

25TH AVE

Elk Glan Lake

OVERLOOK DRIVE

JOHN F. KENNEDY DRIVE

12
Old Speedway Meadow

MARX MEADOW DRIVE

Marx Meadow

11
Portals of the Past

25TH AVE

Lloyd Lake

Outer Richmond District

FULTON

TRANSVERSE DRIVE

CROSS OVER DRIVE

10
Rainbow Falls & Prayerbook Cross

19TH AVE

MARTIN LUTHER KING JR. DRIVE

Boat House

Redwood Grove

9
Strawberry Hill 412

STOW LAKE DRIVE

JOHN F. KENNEDY DRIVE

PARK PRESIDIO

LINCOLN WAY

Stow Lake

Heroes Grove

8
Strybing Arboretum & Botanical Gardens

7
Japanese Tea Garden

TEA GARDEN DRIVE

Asian Art Museum

De Young Museum

Bandshell

6
Music Concourse

10TH AVE

Hall of Flowers

Calif. Academy of Sciences

9TH AVE

Big Rec Ball Grounds

8TH AVE

7TH AVE

5
John McLaren Rhododendron Dell

6TH AVE

CENTRAL GOLDEN GATE PARK

Pacific Ocean

Ocean Beach

THE GREAT HIGHWAY

Esplanade

18 to the Cliff House →

Beach Chalet (murals)
17

16

Dutch Windmill

Soccer Pitches

Murphy
Windmill

JOHN F. KENNEDY DRIVE

47TH AVE

Sewage Plant

Children's
Playground

Archery Field

Pitch & Putt
Golf Course

MARTIN LUTHER KING, JR. DRIVE

CHAIN OF LAKES DRIVE WEST

CHAIN OF LAKES

15

Chain of Lakes

North Lake

CHAIN OF LAKES DRIVE EAST

Bercut Equitation Field

South Lake

LINCOLN WAY

Middle Lake

JOHN F. KENNEDY DRIVE

14

Buffalo
Paddock

FULTON

Fly Casting Pool

Senior Center

36TH AVE

Riding Academy

Polo Field

Stadium

13

Spreckels Lake

MARTIN LUTHER KING, JR. DRIVE

MIDDLE DRIVE WEST

JOHN F. KENNEDY DRIVE

SPRECKELS LAKE DRIVE

Metson
Lake

30TH AVE

WESTERN GOLDEN GATE PARK

and twisted branches originally graced this part of the park.

The Conservatory of Flowers [3]
1876, William Bond Prichard, grading plan; 1878, conservatory probably designed by J. P. Gaynor; 1883, John Gash, central dome

Golden Gate Park's Conservatory of Flowers is the crown jewel of Victorian architecture in Victoriana-rich San Francisco. This white bauble floats behind large flower beds laid out before it like oriental carpets. The trees around the Conservatory create perhaps the best arboreal composition in the park. A fascinating view of the glass house can be had from the beautifully designed pedestrian tunnel under Kennedy Drive. Approached from there, the Conservatory appears suddenly like a mirage.

The Conservatory was ordered in 1875 by California real estate magnate James Lick, probably from the Hammersmith works in Dublin, Ireland. Lick owned property all over the city and the state, and left bequests to many cultural and educational institutions. He died in 1876 before he could erect the great glass house on his San Jose estate as he had planned. A consortium of wealthy men headed by Leland Stanford (who at the time was seeking permission to build the Park and Ocean Railroad through the southeast corner of the park) donated the prefabricated glass house to the new park. A fire in 1883 destroyed the central dome and its exotic plants; a new, higher dome with insets of colored glass was designed by John Gash. The wood-frame structure rode out the earthquake of 1906 unscathed.

Enter the grand building trying your best to ignore the cacophony of trinkets and souvenir junk that now mars the once-elegant vestibule, formerly graced not with a cash register but with a large carved jardiniere from the Italian cloister of the Panama-Pacific International Exposition. The great central dome protects enormous palm trees and other tropical plants. A band of brilliant flash glass lends just a touch of color, the way a flower brightens a plant. There is an orchid collection here. Walk to the right. The east wing houses fantastic greenery; the pavilion at its far end contains the water lily pond, now, unfortunately, without the *Victoria regia* water lily. In the murky pond, fat Japanese carp glitter in the half-light.

Walk back to the central dome and toward the west wing and its end pavilion, where seasonal flowers are displayed at the peak of their bloom. The cycle includes cyclamen, cinerarias, Easter lilies, calceolaria, schizanthus, begonias, chrysanthemums, and poinsettias. An unfortunate "restoration" in the 1970s tore out the intimate, old concrete paths here and installed modern interlocking pavers, an act akin to flooring a landmark Victorian with Astroturf. Some day this too should be removed and the appropriate pavement reinstalled.

Behind the Conservatory are greenhouses and forcing beds off limits to the casual visitor. In front of the Conservatory, great flower beds, and the city's floral "welcome mat" display small colored plants arranged to make pictures, a most Victorian custom. Immediately to the east of the Conservatory are the remains of what was once a splendid Arizona cactus garden, a park feature that should be accurately restored.

TREE FERNS [4]

Across Kennedy Drive from the Conservatory is a small, seemingly primeval glade of prehistoric-looking **tree ferns**, acanthus, and banana trees. It is a delightful Amazonian-looking minijungle; you almost expect to see dinosaurs foraging here.

JOHN McLAREN MEMORIAL
RHODODENDRON DELL [5]

Further west on Kennedy Drive is the John McLaren Memorial Rhododendron

Dell, twenty acres devoted to the Scottish plantsman's favorite flower. McLaren hated statues and spent most of his life fighting the introduction of "stookies," as he called them. His method was to accept them under duress and then to plant low shrubs around them which would eventually envelop them. When he died, a statue was erected in his memory. It is a very fine piece of work by M. Earl Cummings and dates from 1944. The stocky Scotsman stands in his tweed, vested suit, with bow tie and goatee. Behind him is the stump of a tree fern that touches the back of the figure; in his hand he holds a pine cone which he contemplates. As a concession to the subject's well-known hatred of statuary, the green bronze statue stands directly on the ground, not on a pedestal.

Up the drive, nearly hidden in its McLaren-designed setting, is a statue of the Scottish poet, Robert Burns, atop an eight-foot high pedestal. It is also by M. Earl Cummings, a gift of the Scots of San Francisco, and was placed here in 1908. Another well-hidden statue lurks in the bushes at the corner leading to the Music Concourse. It was modeled by Daniel Chester French in 1892 and memorializes Thomas Starr King, 1824–1864, a Unitarian minister from Boston who vigorously championed the Union cause and who was the first San Francisco clergyman to open his pulpit to all faiths. The eight-foot-high, heroic-size bronze stands atop a pink granite base with one hand on a fasces, symbolic of the Union, and the other holding a book.

MUSIC CONCOURSE AND PAVILION [6]

The formally landscaped low depression that is today the Music Concourse was designed by engineer M. M. O'Shaughnessy for the California Midwinter Fair of 1894, held to stimulate the city's economy in the wake of the Depression of 1893. Several large, eclectic pavilions were built around the concourse and a tall steel tower was erected in the center. Two relics survive from the fair on the north side of the Music Concourse, the bronze **Apple Press monument** of 1892 from the French exhibit, and Guillaume Geefs' "pompier" **Roman Gladiator** dressed in a cloak and helmet brandishing an upraised sword, cast in 1881. The pair of concrete sphinxes across the road replaced the bronze sphinxes sculpted in 1903 by Arthur Putnam. They once stood before the Egyptian-style art museum inherited from the Midwinter Fair that sat behind the palm grove here.

267

The oldest structure here is the classically styled **Music Pavilion of 1899** at the western end of the central space built of Colusa sandstone and designed by James and Merritt Reid, with trumpet-blowing nudes by Robert I. Aitken. It was the gift of sugar magnate Claus Spreckels. Music is often presented here on Sunday afternoons at 2 P.M. At the opposite end of the concourse is a memorial to Francis Scott Key, the lyricist—if that's the word—of our national anthem. It was originally erected in 1887 as part of the James Lick bequest.

The Music Concourse, with its pollarded English plane trees, three fountains, and gravel floor contains the only noticed deciduous trees in evergreen Golden Gate Park. Its formal French axial design is completely different in spirit from the (equally man-made) "natural" English, or romantic, landscaped park in which it is embedded. It gives the park a center, a destination of music, art, and science.

California Academy of Sciences
Open daily 10 A.M.–5 P.M.; call 750-7145 for current attractions.

The oldest scientific institution on the West Coast, founded in 1853, the Academy of Sciences includes a natural history museum, the Steinhart Aquarium, the Morrison Planetarium, a library, and a research institute. The Whale Fountain in the courtyard is by Robert B. Howard and was made for the 1939 Fair on Treasure Island.

M. H. de Young Memorial Museum
Open Wednesday–Sunday 10 A.M.–5 P.M.; call 750-3600 for information

The de Young Museum, opened in 1919 to designs by Louis Christian Mullgardt replicating his Court of the Ages at the Panama-Pacific International Exposition of 1915. Its elaborate terra cotta ornament was later stripped off. Michael Harry de Young joined his older brother Charles to edit the *Daily Dramatic Chronicle*, founded in 1865 as a four-page theater program with a news supplement. In 1868, it became the *Daily Morning and Evening Chronicle*, the ancestor of today's San Francisco *Chronicle*. The de Young brothers' newspaper vigorously promoted the Midwinter Fair, and the profits from that fair created a permanent art museum for the city. In front of the museum is the 1917 Pool of Enchantment by M. Earl Cummings depicting a Native American boy on an island piping to two listening mountain lions.

The de Young has many treasures. Pictures from the Kress and Mr. and Mrs. Laurence Rockefeller collections stand out in the de Young's galleries.

Asian Art Museum
Open Tuesday–Sunday, 10 A.M.–5 P.M.; call 668-8921 for information.

The Asian Art Museum of San Francisco is located in a wing of the de Young Museum designed by Dailey and Associates in 1965. Built around the core collection of Chicago insurance man Avery Brundage, this is San Francisco's Asian treasure house. Nearly half of Brundage's collection was of Chinese origin; the Chinese scroll paintings displayed are always very fine. The Magnin Jade Room is extraordinary.

VIEW OF SUTRO TELEVISION TOWER

Visible to the south of the Concourse is the 980-foot-tall Sutro Television Tower, the tallest structure in San Francisco, erected in 1973 by a consortium of television stations. Called a candelabra configuration, the $12 million steel tripod was designed by Albert C. Martin and Associates in Los Angeles and fabricated in Columbia, South Carolina. On a clear day it is visible for fifty miles. While a generally unloved structure, its Empire-waisted design is a fine piece of engineering much more pleasing than the pseudo-Seattle space needle that the City Planning Commission actually approved.

Japanese Tea Garden [7]
1894, George Turner Marsh/Makoto Hagiwara
Open daily from 9 A.M. to 6:30 P.M.; the teahouse closes at 5:30 P.M.; fee.

Beyond the de Young Museum is the famous Japanese Tea Garden, operated by Australian-born George Turner Marsh during the 1894 Midwinter Fair. Marsh spent his teenage years in Japan and came to San Francisco in 1875, becoming one of the first dealers in Asian art. He built his house in the wild sand dunes at Twelfth Avenue and Clement and named it after his birthplace, Richmond, a suburb of Melbourne, hence the name of today's polyglot Richmond District north of Golden Gate Park.

Marsh is usually credited with laying out the Japanese Tea Garden as part of his Japanese Village, though others credit Makoto Hagiwara, born in Japan in 1854, with the design. When the Midwinter Fair closed, the popular Japanese garden was retained. In 1895 Makoto Hagiwara received the concession to operate the teahouse and the garden, which he did until 1925—with a brief *hiatus* between 1900 and 1908 when anti-Japanese sentiment was rampant in San Francisco.

The five-acre garden has a surprisingly complex horticultural and architectural history which this guide can only outline. The eastern half of the garden dates from the 1894 fair, and the western section was completed in 1916. The two-story Main Gate (closest to the museum) is called a *roman* and was part of Marsh's Japanese Village. It was originally built by a Japanese carpenter for Marsh's summer house in Mill Valley, Marin County. The simpler South Gate was part of the Japanese exhibit at the Panama-Pacific International Exposition of 1915. The lake in front of the Tea House survives from the 1894 Village. At the Tea House, Jasmine and green teas are served by kimono-clad women.

The ten-and-a-half-foot bronze Buddha with the halo was cast in Tajima, Japan in 1790 and was the gift of S. & G. Gump & Co. in 1949. It represents the *Amazarashi-No-Hotoke*, "the Buddha who sits through sunny and rainy weather without shelter."

The plants make the Japanese Tea Garden special. Most are from Japan and some are natives of China, though the Monterey pines overhead are California natives pruned to blend with the Japanese garden. In the garden are Japanese maples; Chinese magnolia and wisteria; deodar cedars; flowering cherry; Japanese black, white, and red pine; Japanese flowering quince; Japanese wistaria; timber bamboo; and redwood; gincko trees; Korean pines; mock orange; and many other rare exotics, along with several California natives. From March to May the azaleas are in bloom; the garden is at its peak in March and April, when the cherry blossoms float over it like small white-pink clouds. Crowds spoil the garden's mood; in fact, one of the best times to visit is during the fog or rain when the garden is empty and its borders seem to vanish in the mist.

Strybing Arboretum and Botanical Gardens [8]

Open 8 A.M.–4:30 P.M. weekdays; 10 A.M.–5 P.M. on weekends and holidays; free tour daily at 1:30 P.M.; call 558-3622 for information. The Information Kiosk sells a complete guide to this living library of plants and also has maps of Golden Gate Park.

The main entrance to the seventy-acre Strybing Arboretum and Botanical Gardens is off South Drive near the Ninth Avenue entrance to the park. The Arboretum was begun with the bequest of Helen Strybing and built in 1937 with WPA funds. The current landscape was designed by Robert Tetlow of the University of California Department of Landscape Architecture between 1959 and 1966. Other landscape architects have designed subsections within the Arboretum. Among the special gardens here are the **garden of fragrance** with labels in braille (the mellow weathered limestone walls were built with stones from a medieval Spanish monastery bought by William Randolph Hearst but never assembled), a collection of **California native plants**, a **redwood trail**, a fine **succulent garden**, a **Biblical garden**, and **demonstration gardens**, among others. Also located here is the **Hall of Flowers**, an exhibit hall and the scene of San Francisco's annual August flower show. The congenial **Helen Crocker Russell Library of Horticulture** was designed by Gardner A. Dailey and Associates in 1967. The **gazebo** of the demonstration gardens was designed by Thomas Church using naturally weathered redwood.

STOW LAKE / STRAWBERRY HILL [9]

Stow Lake, built in 1895, is at the center of the park and serves as its principal reservoir. A scenic drive circles the lake and leads to the **boathouse**, where small boats can be rented and refreshments secured. W. W. Stow was a lawyer and president of the Park Commission and persuaded Collis P. Huntington, one of the Big Four, to donate the funds to construct this 15-million-gallon reservoir. (Golden Gate Park requires over 4 million gallons of water every day to keep it green.) In the middle of the lake is Strawberry Hill, a man-made mountain 428 feet high. The bridge garnished with cyclopean boulders on the south side of

the lake was designed by Ernest Coxhead in the 1890s. A gentle dirt roadway
corkscrews its way to the top of Strawberry Hill. On the east side of the hill is
Huntington Falls, which cascades from a
smaller reservoir atop the hill into the
lake, one of two artificial waterfalls in
Golden Gate Park. Strawberry Hill is
thickly wooded with cypress, eucalyptus, and long-leafed acacia. Through the
trees are tantalizing glimpses of the
white city spread all around the verdant
park. To the northwest you can glimpse
the twin red piers of the Golden Gate
Bridge with Mt. Tamalpias in the distance. Descending Strawberry Hill, you
get a distant view of the golden onion
domes of the Russian Orthodox Cathedral of the Holy Virgin on Geary Boulevard in the Richmond District.

RAINBOW FALLS / PRAYERBOOK CROSS [10]

On Kennedy Drive north of Stow
Lake is Rainbow Falls, an artificial waterfall built in the 1930s. John McLaren
once noted that he often went on walks
in the countryside, and when he found a
striking effect in nature such as a "bon-
nie brook," he would attempt to dupli-
cate it in the park. Atop the bluff behind
the falls is a fifty-seven-foot tall Celtic
cross carved from Colusa sandstone and
designed by Ernest Coxhead. It was dedicated at the opening of the Midwinter
Fair of 1894 and commemorates the first
Anglican service held by Sir Francis
Drake's chaplain, Francis Fletcher, perhaps at Drake's Bay north of San Francisco, in June 1579.

LLOYD LAKE / THE PORTALS OF THE PAST [11]

Cross Over Drive, built in 1936, cuts
the park in half. On its other side, on the
north side of Kennedy Drive, is Lloyd
Lake, named for a former park commissioner. Reflected on its tranquil surface
are the six Ionic columns known as the

Portals of the Past. They once framed
the entrance to the A. N. Towne residence atop Nob Hill (*see Tour 6*). That
elegant house was consumed in the
flames after the earthquake of 1906. A
photographer took a picture of the city's
ruins through the surviving columns and
entitled it "The Portals of the Past." In
1909 the portico was reerected here to
create this dreamy and romantic set
piece. It is San Francisco's only architectural monument to the catastrophe of
1906.

OLD SPEEDWAY / LINDLEY MEADOW [12]

The large meadow across Kennedy
Drive from Lloyd Lake is called Old
Speedway Meadow, surely an oxymo-
ron. The bicycle path that runs through
it follows the alignment of the old
Speedway, a racetrack built for horses
and carriages that was immensely popular with speed demons in the Victorian
period. The Speedway was the first
instance of a private interest group—the
owners of racehorses—securing a piece
of the park for their exclusive use. It
leads to the Golden Gate Park Stadium,
originally the Polo Field, another aristocratic usurpation. The Polo Field was
carved out of the park in 1906. There, in
1911, President William Howard Taft cer-
emoniously broke ground for the Panama-Pacific International Exposition.
After vigorous protests, the great Exposition was built on bayfill in the Marina
District rather than inside fragile Golden
Gate Park. The Human Be-In/Gathering
of the Tribes was held here on January
14, 1967, the first event to attract massive media attention to the Haight-Ashbury hippies.

Next up Kennedy Drive is Lindley
Meadow. The curving, flowing drive and
the relaxed, informal placement of the
stands of sheltering eucalyptus and
cypress trees knit the park's sections into
a harmonious whole. A casual traveler
through the vast park might think it
nothing but trees and lawns, so well-hid-

den are its many and varied uses. Across Lindley Meadow rises a totemic sculpture, **The Goddess of the Forest**, carved in 1939 for the Treasure Island fair by Dudley C. Carter. It was carved out of a single redwood log as an example of art-in-action. The goddess is represented as a crouching nude female figure supporting a bear in her lap (California's emblem), and holding an owl in her hands; an eagle protects the back of her head. The unvarnished redwood has achieved the soft, grayish-green patina characteristic of the way wood weathers in Northern California's climate. Like some enormous fetish, the goddess is accumulating the paired initials of lovers all around her base. She seems contented with the view.

SPRECKELS LAKE [13]

Further west along Kennedy Drive is Spreckels Lake, the model-yacht pond, completed in 1904 and named after park commissioner Adolph Bernard Spreckels, who later with his wife donated the Palace of the Legion of Honor in Lincoln Park. The lake is held up like a shimmering, reflecting platter with views of the stuccoed Richmond District visible through a thin screen of cypress trees. At the intersection with Thirty-sixth Avenue is the **Model Yacht Club House** erected by the WPA in 1938, an agreeable period piece.

Not visible from here, facing Fulton Street at the head of Thirty-seventh Avenue, is the **Senior Center**, originally the San Francisco Police Academy, an elegant little jewel of a building designed by John Reid, Jr. in the Beaux Arts manner favored under Mayor James Rolph's nineteen-year-long administration. Would that all civic buildings were as fine. John McLaren, who resisted putting nonpark buildings in his preserve, put the building here to keep the city from cutting a road across the park.

BUFFALO PADDOCK [14]

Next to Spreckels Lake and to the right is the Buffalo Paddock. Here stands a small herd of buffalo, an institution in the park since 1892. The buffalo are large, shaggy, unwieldy-looking creatures that stand motionless. Their sudden apparition, especially if you come across them in the fog, is altogether surreal. Before the opening of the Fleischhacker Zoo in the 1930s, Golden Gate Park was something of a menagerie with an aviary, goats, moose, elk, deer, kangaroos, bears, seals, elephants, and sheep. Only the nearly catatonic buffalo remain. As the park's forests have matured, however, skunks, raccoons and other small mammals have moved in and now flourish here.

THE CHAIN OF LAKES [15]

The Chain of Lakes, three artistically landscaped reservoirs, was completed in 1909 to John McLaren's designs. The six islands in the North Lake were originally each differently landscaped. The tiny islets are disposed with all the art of a few rocks in a Japanese garden. Swamp cypress indigenous to Florida's Everglades grow here in the water. Beyond North Lake the trees are planted along Kennedy Drive in straight rows, the only reminder that all of this is the work of human hands. To the north is the **pitch-and-putt golf course**. At the intersection with South Drive turn right, passing the large **Soccer Field** which attracts an international gathering on weekends. Before the development of the park, there was a large tidal lake where the Soccer Field is today.

THE DUTCH WINDMILL / WILHELMINA TULIP GARDEN [16]

At the northwestern corner of the park stands the Dutch Windmill designed by Alpheus Bull and erected in 1902. Because the park consumes large amounts of water, and because the monopolistic Spring Valley Water Company charged high rates, the park commissioners sought their own water supply. As it happens, an underground river runs under parts of the park; in 1902 this windmill was constructed to tap this source. The Dutch Windmill was designed as a utilitarian yet picturesque addition to the park. It was one of the largest sail windmills in the world with sails 114 feet across; it pumped thirty thousand gallons of water an hour. It was so successful that a second windmill was donated to the park by Samuel G. Murphy and built in 1905. After the city bought the water company in 1929, the mills fell into disuse and eventually lost their blades. In 1981 the Dutch Windmill was restored, though, alas, it is strictly decorative and no longer pumps water. The Murphy Windmill to the south remains bladeless. The Dutch Bulb Growers Association sends hundreds of tulip bulbs each year to stock the Queen Wilhelmina Tulip Garden, which is at its peak in April.

BEACH CHALET / LUCIEN LABAUDT MURALS [17]

Facing the Great Highway, at the west end of Golden Gate Park, is the Beach Chalet, designed by Willis Polk in 1921. Inside this two-story, red-tile-roofed, white pillared structure is some of the finest public art in the city, a series of frescoes executed by Lucien Labaudt in 1936–1937. They cover all four walls of the ground floor bar and make a complete tour of the city. Their theme is play and recreation and they complement the Coit Tower frescoes devoted to the working life of California (see Tour 4A).

Over the inside of the front door is a phrase from a poem of Bret Harte's, "Serene, indifferent of fate thou sittest at the Golden Gate." The scene surrounding the front entrance shows a man feeding pigeons and a woman knitting a sweater in Union Square. Step to the

left. The next figure, an architect standing between the two windows, shows Arthur Brown, Jr., San Francisco's master builder. He holds the plans for Coit Tower, another public embellishment of the 1930s. Behind him rises the Beaux Arts Civic Center and his magnificent City Hall, fittingly the finest building in the city. A Corinthian capital is at his feet and steelwork rises behind him.

Next, in the southwest corner, are boaters at the St. Francis Yacht Harbor. The quotation here from Joaquin Miller reads, "Sails are furled from furthest corners of the world." To the left are sightseers at Lands End looking out at the Golden Gate. A ship lies wrecked on the rocks below. On the headlands rises the Moderne, vaguely Mayan, Veterans' Hospital built in 1933. Also visible is Baker Beach and the Presidio.

On the wall over the righthand side of the bar is a large fresco depicting recreation in Golden Gate Park. From left to right in the background are visible the Portals of the Past, the Conservatory, the de Young Museum, and the Japanese Tea Garden. In the foreground, among all the users of the park, is a man in a green plaid tweed suit who appears to be blessing and accepting a new seedling. It is "Uncle John" McLaren. In the center of this wall, over the bar, is a quote from Ina Coolbrith, "Fair city of my love and my desire." At bar level is a small painted-in plaque that reads, "Federal Art Project, 1936–1937, Lucien Labaudt." The left side of the bar represents picnickers at Lands End with the Marin hills in the distance and a single pier of the unfinished Art Deco Golden Gate Bridge, completed in 1937. In the corner of the north wall is a scene showing the catching and selling of crabs at Fisherman's Wharf. The quotation is from George Sterling and reads, "At the end of our streets, the stars." In the corner of the left is a scene at the waterfront at Pier 26 with docks, sailors, and fishermen. The man pushing the cart was the then-controversial head of the Long-

272

shoremen's Union, leftist, Australian-born Harry Bridges (later a Port Commissioner). Completing the cycle is a view with Chinatown in the background and a policeman and a florist in the foreground. It is a thought-provoking pairing representing perhaps the tough and the gentle, the full spectrum of life in the big city.

THE GREAT HIGHWAY / OCEAN BEACH [18]

The 18 Forty-sixth Avenue bus runs along the Great Highway from the western edge of Golden Gate Park, up to the Cliff House, and then down Point Lobos Avenue to the Legion of Honor art museum in Lincoln Park. Or you can walk the approximately four blocks to the Cliff House and Seal Rocks.

Tawny Ocean Beach is a favorite place of release and relaxation for San Franciscans. Many bus lines end near it, bringing people of all ages to this, the edge of the continent. The water is cold and the undertow here very dangerous, but the air is brisk and clean and the waves soothing, their rhythm relaxing. Brown pelicans can be spotted diving for fish. Dogs romp in the surf. Lovers walk by the edge of the sea.

The city reserved Ocean Beach in 1868 as public land and fought private encroachments. When the Park and Ocean Railroad which ran along Lincoln Way was completed in December of 1883, Ocean Beach suddenly became accessible for ten cents. Previous to that, expensive carriage rides were the only way out here—many poor people lived and died in San Francisco without ever having seen the Pacific. The Great Highway was named in 1874 and stretches from the Cliff House to the north to the San Francisco Zoo to the south.

THE CLIFF HOUSE / SEAL ROCKS [19]

The current Cliff House is, unfortunately, a drab building. It is the fifth building on this site; the first was erected in 1858. Alas, it is nothing like the bold French-château-on-a-rock that Adolph Sutro erected here in 1896 and that burned in a spectacular fire in 1907. That confection, designed by C. J. Colley and F. S. Lemme, is the one lost architectural work that lives on in the city's collective memory and in countless postcards that still sell well. A seven-story gingerbread pile perched so improbably on its high rock, it summed up the daring act of building on the barren, isolated, arid San Francisco peninsula. The late Victorians knew flamboyance, and *this* was flamboyant. It was hallucinatory by day and glittered like a beacon at night. Would that some philanthropist would give it back to San Francisco just the way it was! The GGNRA operates a Visitor Center tucked away in the base of the building, near the Camera Obscura, where you can get the fine GGNRA map and other informative brochures on the wildlife offshore here.

The splendid site remains as dramatic as ever. The surf boils among the jagged rocks below. Four hundred feet offshore are the **Seal Rocks**, a favorite rendezvous for Steller sea lions and marine birds. The lusty barking of the gregarious, polygamous seals is a happy sound; like the cable cars and the fog horns, they are passages in San Francisco's unique music. The Seal Rocks were the apple of Adolph Sutro's eye and he kept people from hunting the fur-bearing sea lions. Deeded by Congress to the city in 1887, the rocks were placed under the protection of the Park Commission.

Visible to the north is the magnificent sweep of the mountainous, untouched shore of Marin County, all part of the GGNRA. On clear days the **Farallon Islands**, seven rocky points thirty-two miles offshore, can be spied on the horizon. A U.S. Light Station was established atop Beacon Rock there in 1855. Murre eggs were gathered on the Farallones until the federal government

273

banned all egg gathering in 1897. President Theodore Roosevelt made them a Federal Bird Reserve in 1907.

Immediately north of the Cliff House, between it and rocky Point Lobos, lie the concrete ruins of the pools of **Sutro Baths**. Also built by Adolph Sutro and opened in 1896, the baths covered three acres and boasted the world's largest indoor pools of both fresh and salt water. Inside the baths were terraces with parterres planted with rare flowers and shrubs. This resort closed in 1952 and burned in 1966. An artistic, ultramodern, glass-enclosed swimming pool should be built here. The ruins are unsightly, the location incomparable.

SUTRO HEIGHTS PARK [20]

Across the Great Highway from the Cliff House is a parking lot and bus shelter, and beyond them a path into Sutro Heights Park, today another unit of the GGNRA. On the grounds are a delightful Victorian kiosk and a terraced overlook on the summit. On the wind-sheltered south side of the peak is a rock garden filled with blooming plants.

Adolph Sutro was one of the most remarkable men of nineteenth-century San Francisco, a man of vision, determination, achievement, and lasting good works. Born to a wealthy Jewish textile manufacturer in Aix-la-Chapelle (Aachen, Prussia) in 1830, he studied mineralogy in his native city. In the reactionary wake of the revolutions of 1848, the entire Sutro family migrated to Baltimore, then a great German magnet. Adolph moved further west to San Francisco, arriving in 1850. He ran a tobacco store, something of a German specialty, and then went to Nevada when the Comstock silver bonanza was discovered. There he saw the chronic flooding and the foul air of the early mines and set about to devise the better system. He conceived of a tunnel that would run under the separate mines to drain and ventilate them and formed The Tunnel

Company, incorporated in Nevada in 1865. After many reversals and battles, the great engineering feat was completed in 1869 and a ten-foot-high, twelve-foot-wide, three-mile-long tunnel (with two miles of lateral branches) was installed, improving conditions for the miners. The Tunnel Company exacted a royalty of from $1 to $2 per ton of ore mined and made Sutro rich.

In 1879 Sutro sold his shares in the Sutro Tunnel and invested his "colossal fortune" in San Francisco real estate. He bought undeveloped, sandy wastes which he spent the rest of his life developing and planting with trees. From the French Bank he bought all this property at Point Lobos where potatoes had been cultivated in the 1840s. Sutro eventually owned one-twelfth of all the land in San Francisco, including the great San Miguel Rancho which encompassed Twin Peaks and all the city's central hills.

Here at Sutro Heights, in the remote northwest corner of the city, he engineered a waterworks, built a now-lost mansion, planted gardens (crowded with atrocious statuary), assembled a great scientific library (parts of which survive as the Sutro Library near San Francisco State University) and art collection, and then threw the lavish grounds open to the public. He served as a reform Populist mayor in 1894–1896. In 1898, sadly, he was declared incompetent and died at sixty-eight. Sutro was a freethinker, a voracious reader, a man with a scientific bent, a creative businessman, and a great philanthropist. He was the child of an age that believed in Progress.

LANDS END / THE GOLDEN GATE [21]

Off the Great Highway, north of the Cliff House and Sutro Heights Park, is Merrie Way, now a gravel parking lot with a spectacular view that offers a good place to watch the sunset and afterglow. Paths beyond the parking lot lead to the disused roadbed of the Ferries & Cliff House Railway, which circumna-

274

vigated these precipitous cliffs. Point
Lobos, the westernmost tip of the San
Francisco peninsula, was named by the
Spanish for the sea lions that once
thrived here.

Lands End, today part of the
GGNRA, is a wild and broken shore,
especially interesting in the winter when
the rains cause the tiny wildflowers that
grow here to blossom. This scenic corner
of the city has a fine view of the Golden
Gate and the Marin shore. Steep paths
lead down to the water where great
rocks break the pounding surf. Many
ships have foundered here; at low tide,
the periscope of an unlucky submarine
can be spotted. The trails lead to Lincoln
Park with its public golf course and the
Legion of Honor Museum (*see Tour 13*).

The Presidio and Along the Golden Gate

A SCENIC DRIVE

What This Tour Covers

[1] Marina Boulevard / Marina Green

[2] The Palace of Fine Arts / Memories of the 1915 Fair / The Exploratorium

[3] The Presidio of San Francisco: Red White, and Green / Lombard Street Gate and Trophies

[4] U.S. Army Presidio Museum / Refugee Cottages

[5] Funston Avenue Victorian Officers' Quarters: American Architectural Benchmarks

[6] Pershing Hall

[7] Old Protestant Chapel / Roman Catholic Chapel of Our Lady / Site of Spanish and Mexican Presidio

[8] Officers' Open Mess / Old Comandancia

[9] Pershing Square: Flag and Focal Point

[10] Montgomery Street Enlisted Men's Barracks: Brick Row

[11] Parade Ground / Centennial and Bicentennial Trees

[12] Post Chapel / WPA Murals

[13] San Francisco National Military Cemetery

[14] Fort Point / The Seawall

[15] The Golden Gate Bridge: Art Deco Masterpiece / Golden Gate Bridge Vista Points

[16] Lincoln Boulevard to Baker Beach / Battery Chamberlin Disappearing Gun

[17] El Camino del Mar / Sea Cliff / China Beach

[18] Lincoln Park / California Palace of the Legion of Honor

[19] Hiking Trail to Lands End and the Cliff House / Roadbed of the Ferries and Cliff House Railway

Preliminaries

Transportation

BY PUBLIC TRANSIT

The heart of the Presidio can be seen by foot and reached by public transit. Take the 45 Greenwich electric trolley bus on Sutter Street a block north of Union Square to its terminus at Lyon and Greenwich; from there transfer to the 45 shuttle bus and ask the driver to let you off at Lincoln Boulevard and Funston Avenue across the street from the U.S. Army Museum. The 29 Sunset bus also stops at Lincoln Boulevard and Funston Avenue and proceeds to the Golden Gate Bridge Toll Plaza, where you can alight near the view area. The bus continues along the scenic bluffs on the Pacific coast side of the huge post, across the Richmond District along Twenty-fifth Avenue, and into the middle of Golden Gate Park near Stow Lake.

BY CAR

A leisurely automotive exploration with a good map along the Presidio's winding scenic roads and past its many buildings and fortifications is the best way to see the spacious Presidio. Allow frequent stops to inspect sites and enjoy panoramas. Virtually all the grounds are open to the public twenty-four hours a day. Enter through the Lombard Street Gate with its sandstone carvings of Liberty and Victory and flanked by antique Spanish bronze cannons. Pass the modern Letterman Army Medical Center to the white clapboard Army Museum at Lincoln Boulevard and Funston Avenue. Park here and at the museum. Ask the museum guard where you can secure a map of the post. Then walk up Funston Avenue to the intersection with Presidio Boulevard to examine the two exemplary groups of Victorian officers' quarters that line the maturely landscaped street. Return to your car to continue up Funston to the original site of the Mexican presidio. See Fort Point and then drive along Lincoln Boulevard. There is a fine view point along the road's shoulder near Battery Dynamite.

MARINA BOULEVARD / MARINA GREEN [1]

Marina Boulevard is the bayward edge of a vast tract of tidal marsh filled in for the 1915 Panama-Pacific International Exposition, part of which became Marina Green, a favorite sunbathing spot popular on sunny weekends. That great one-year-long fair, the most elaborate San Francisco ever saw or ever will see, officially celebrated the opening of the Panama Canal, but actually celebrated the rapid and booming rebuilding of the city between 1906 and 1915.

For the exposition, vast wood-and-plaster palaces were built, classically decorated on the outside, plain timber sheds on the inside. These were the Palace of Fine Arts, of which a replica survives, the Palace of Horticulture, the Great Palace of Machinery, the Palace of Education and Social Economy, the Palace of Liberal Arts, the Palace of Manufacture and Varied Industries, the Palace of Transportation, the Palace of Agriculture, and the Palace of Mines and Metallurgy. Extensive landscaped courts and colonnades linked the huge palaces. The fair was a dream of Inevitable Progress, a dream that had died the year before with the outbreak of World War I.

Along Marina Boulevard, with its lots looking over the Marina Green to the Bay, grand houses and flats have been built from the 1920s to the present, many in stucco. In the Marina District, stucco predominates as the exterior building material. It is less expensive than wood and is easily patched and maintained. Painted light colors, stucco reflects the light and the skies.

The Palace of Fine Arts / Memories of the 1915 Fair [2]
Baker and Beach streets
1915, Bernard Maybeck, original building and landscaping; 1962–1975, William G. Merchant and others, replication in concrete

Floating like a dream across a pond dotted with exotic ducks is the huge, freestanding rotunda and colonnade of Bernard Maybeck's Palace of Fine Arts of 1915. This Beaux Arts hallucination was built for the Panama-Pacific International Exposition and outlasted the temporary materials it was originally made of. It was replicated—and simplified—in reinforced concrete between 1962 and 1975. It took a philanthropist, Walter S. Johnson, who lived across the street and loved the building, a 1959 city bond issue, and matching funds from the State of California to raise the money to preserve this architectural extravagance for San Francisco.

Park and walk along the giant colonnade to the lofty, open rotunda. Imagine an endless-seeming series of such triumphal spaces from here to Fort Mason. That was the Panama-Pacific International Exposition of 1915. The elevated planter boxes with the draped female figures looking downcast were sculpted by Ulric Ellerhusen and represent "the melancholy of life without art." The boxes were intended to hold trees and vines, enfolding the Palace in plants. Around the exterior of the dome are rectangular panels showing a nude woman, representing Art, being defended by nude men (Idealists) battling centaurs

Fort Point, built between 1853 and 1861 to designs by the U.S. Army Corps of Engineers, originally mounted 149 cannon in four tiers. Joseph B. Strauss, the chief engineer of the Art Deco Golden Gate Bridge, built between 1933 and 1937, designed a great steel arch to preserve the landmark fort.

(Materialists). The Panama-Pacific International Exposition provided an endless stream of such didactic art; guidebooks explained their recondite and intricate symbolism to the public. As relief from all this uplift, The Zone, an amusement park of "a necessary garishness," as the fair directors put it, was carefully designed at the east end of the fairgrounds. The Zone had six thousand feet of commercial footage along a Midway lined with attractions.

Exploratorium [2]
3601 Lyon Street, at Bay, behind the Palace of Fine Arts
Wednesday 1–9:30 P.M., Thursday and Friday 1–5 P.M., Saturday and Sunday, 10 A.M.–5 P.M., closed Monday and Tuesday. Adults $5, children 6 to 17, $1; 563-3200.

Behind the rotunda and colonnade is the semicircular, great shedlike pavilion originally used to display academic paintings and sculpture. Today it houses the Exploratorium, a science museum organized around the theme of human perception. It is especially enjoyable for families with children.

THE PRESIDIO OF SAN FRANCISCO: RED, WHITE, AND GREEN [3]

The Presidio of San Francisco, a spacious 1,540-acre reserve with seventy-five miles of scenic roads set on the heights commanding the Golden Gate, is a mini-garden city set in its own buffering forest. The Army created a model installation on this enormous reserve at the most scenic spot of the Bay Area.

The Presidio embodies the power of the state and prominence of the military in the creation and sustenance of San Francisco. The Presidio of San Francisco is a great treasure for the student of American history, landscape design, architecture, and military industrial technology. Every period of American building from the 1850s on is preserved somewhere here.

Once principally a fortification, the Presidio evolved into an administrative headquarters and a medical center with an important hospital and adjoining scientific research institute. Today it is the headquarters of the Sixth Army and has a commissary, Officers' Club, and golf course for active and retired military. It employs about three thousand military and about the same number of civilians.

On September 17, 1776, José Joaquin Moraga established a *presidio*, or fort, here; it was the third of four in Alta California (San Diego's fort was established in 1769; Monterey in 1770; San Francisco in 1776; and Santa Barbara in 1782). Presidios were frontier outposts of the Spanish Empire centered in Madrid. The Presidio was placed here in a global imperial chess game: Spain garrisoned this distant peninsula to keep Russia or Britain from gaining a foothold on San Francisco Bay. From here four missions, two *pueblos* (towns with their own government), a rancho, and an *asistencia* (outlying branch of a mission but without a resident priest) were founded.

The presidio garrisons forced wandering Native American bands into mission *rancherías*, or settlements, next to the missions. There Franciscan priests Christianized them and taught them subsistence agriculture and herding. The adobe quadrangle at the presidio of San Francisco had its own chapel separate from that of Mission Dolores at approximately the site of today's Roman Catholic chapel on Moraga Avenue near the head of Funston Avenue.

In 1822, by accession, this fort became the northernmost outpost of the new Mexican Republic. Spanish imperial regulations required that ships visiting San Francisco Bay anchor near the Presidio, in an area of what is now landfill near today's Beach and Divisadero streets, in the Marina District. In December 1824 strong ebb tides resulting from unusually heavy freshets made this anchorage dangerous. Visiting ships, mostly British and Yankee whalers, shifted to Richardson Bay off Sausalito or to Yerba Buena Cove (today's Financial District). Mexico became more concerned with routes of overland migration than seaports when Yankee pioneer wagon trains suddenly began to appear on this side of the Sierras. In 1835 Mexico abandoned the Presidio at San Francisco and shifted its frontier garrison northward to Sonoma (now Sonoma State Historic Park). The unmaintained adobe cluster at the Presidio of San Francisco washed into ruins.

In March 1847, during war with Mexico, two companies of the U.S. Army's New York Volunteers occupied the derelict Presidio and rebuilt its adobe buildings, adding cleaner roofs with wood shakes, better windows, and wood floors. But by August 1848 the Presidio lay abandoned again, not to be reoccupied for several years. On November 6, 1850, President Fillmore set aside for harbor defenses a vast tract of the northwest tip of the San Francisco peninsula, from what is now Aquatic Park to approximately the ocean end of Golden Gate Park—plus Alcatraz, Angel, and Yerba Buena islands in the Bay. San Franciscans protested the tremendous size of the new military reserve and on December 15, 1851, Fillmore cut back the Presidio and Fort Mason to their present boundaries.

The Army built a few frame buildings for a new post in the late 1850s, replacing the inherited adobes (the last fell in the 1906 earthquake). Most of the budget of the 1850s, however, went into constructing massive, red-brick, granite, and iron Fort Point, a French-style fort.

Little was done at the Presidio itself until 1862–1863 when Army engineers, using the old Mexican quadrangle as its southeast corner, laid out a parade ground oriented from the southwest to the northeast, looking down the sheltered valley to San Francisco Bay. That vast rectangle of space is one of the Bay Area's most magnificent pieces of landscape design and remains the core of the Army post. To the east of the parade ground, a row of plain frame or Greek Revival duplex Officers' Quarters was built in 1862. The officers' quarters on the east side of the parade ground, commodious barracks on the west side, and ceremonial buildings and a flagpole at the head of the parade ground completed the expansion.

Immediately after the Civil War in 1865, the Army turned its attention to Indian subjugation in the West. During the Indian Wars, conducted from 1865 to 1890, the Army's Department of the Pacific moved its headquarters from downtown San Francisco to the Presidio. Troops billeted at the Presidio for the Modoc War in 1870 and the campaigns against the Apaches in the Southwest. In the 1870s, the Army opened the Presidio grounds to the public and it soon functioned as an unofficial auxiliary to the city's parks, in particular for wealthy neighboring Pacific and Presidio Heights. (The city's Julius Kahn Playground at Pacific Avenue and Spruce Street, inside the Presidio wall, still serves as the playground for the city's wealthiest neighborhood.)

In March of 1883, Major W. A. Jones of the Army Corps of Engineers initiated a massive program of forestation with his landscape plan for the treeless, wind-swept, sandy Presidio. As a work of landscape design—here truly "environmental design"—Major Jones' plan ranks with that of Golden Gate Park for beauty and utility. Jones' plan called for planting the ridges of the hills with pine, cypress, acacia, and eucalyptus to create the illusion of a continuous forest larger than it is—and it is large. His dark forests provided the yin for the yang of the open parade ground. The headlands were threaded with view drives, today's scenic Lincoln Boulevard with its panoramic view of the Golden Gate.

In 1884, the Army designated the Presidio burial ground on the hill overlooking the parade ground a National Military cemetery. Originally ten acres, the San Francisco National Military Cemetery now covers 28.3 acres within its precise rectangular encampment.

Between 1890 and 1914, the Presidio was rebuilt and improved. Many frame buildings gave way to permanent brick, stone, and concrete structures. The outstanding row of red brick barracks with white trim on Montgomery Street along the western edge of the Parade Ground was built between 1895 and 1897. In the mid-1890s, the Army began the construction of modern reinforced concrete and earthwork batteries mounting giant guns to replace obsolete Fort Point. Experimental Battery Dynamite, which shot charges of explosives, was constructed in 1894–1895. The Presidio's batteries were only part of a much larger system of seacoast and harbor fortifications armed with breech-loading rifled artillery. These defenses preempted vast tracts of land and expanded greatly in the 1890s. Without their guns, the batteries—the third wave of fortification of San Francisco Bay—are historical sites today and have been incorporated into the GGNRA.

In 1899 the Presidio Army General Hospital was established for sick and wounded American soldiers infected during the subjugation of the U.S. colony in the Philippines, which America took from Spain. That early hospital, designed by San Francisco architect W. H. Wilcox and built between 1899 and 1902, was a model of modern hospital design with natural ventilation, sunlight, and gardens woven into its pavilion design. Most of it was thoughtlessly demolished in 1975. A fragment of the hospital with its agreeable lowrise wings and courts survives along General Kennedy Avenue west of the new midrise Letterman hospital built in 1969. Adjoining Letterman Army Medical Center is the 1979 concrete bunker of the Letterman Army Institute of Research.

An extensive golf course lies between the scattered Officers' Quarters in the eastern portions of the post and the clustered Enlisted Family Housing at the far west end of the reservation. Entered from Arguello Street in Presidio Heights, this scenic golf course was established by the civilian San Francisco Golf Club in 1895 with nine holes. Not until 1955–1956 did the military take over complete management of the course, permitting the civilian club members to continue using the course. Over time it has been irrigated, and in the 1930s the WPA planted fifteen thousand young trees here.

In 1908 Fort Winfield Scott, functionally almost a separate fort, was built on the high ridge west of the old post to man the great new earthwork batteries. It has its own central parade ground ringed by enlisted men's barracks. These new buildings are built of modern concrete and stucco and were styled in a Spanish or Mission style with curvilinear gables and red tile roofs. This rare, well-preserved Mission Revival cluster was the first step in "Hispanicizing" the Presidio, a design process that is being continued after a brief and disastrous hiatus in the 1960s and 1970s. The Spanish or Mission color scheme of white walls and red tile roofs unified virtually all the post's buildings, from commandant's quarters to barracks, from warehouses to guardshacks. In the 1930s Georgian Revival duplex brick Officers' Quarters were constructed in strings along the ridges in the Presidio. Their East Coast "Colonial Revival" façades meld with the Mission, or Spanish Colonial Revival buildings.

The Presidio is important for its well-preserved array of utilitarian buildings.

The red brick stables of 1913–1914 west of the National Cemetery, and the 1917–1919 "temporary" frame warehouses with their great shed roofs glimpsed from the entrance to the road to the Golden Gate Bridge are outstanding examples of American industrial design. The cluster of maintenance shops near the Coast Guard Station preserves the rare Crissy Army Airfield hangers of the early 1920s. Utilitarian buildings like these, lost everywhere else because of the pressures of real estate taxes and the need to continually reuse all the building sites in the cramped city, are a rare barometer of American building and technological history. The "least important," that is everyday, structures are the most important here in this outdoor museum of American architecture.

During World War II, the Presidio's dormant harbor defenses were reactivated and the post was closed to the public. A new underground control point for the harbor's defenses was built at Fort Winfield Scott, while nearby Fort Mason became the Pacific Port of Embarcation for the war with Japan between 1942–1945. After World War II, the Army expanded housing on the post when its role as a fortification ceased, but its administrative and medical functions continued. The Presidio saw its last armaments in the 1950s when a Nike missile group was stationed here as part of the network of Bay Area missile defenses. Today, it is a favored last post for Army brass about to retire.

The Presidio was designated a National Historic Landmark in 1960. In 1965 its choice Funston Avenue Victorians were given new concrete foundations. In the mid-1970s there were several large demolition projects at the Presidio, like a delayed-action Urban Renewal campaign. The historic hospital was mostly demolished, leaving only a fragment. A series of disruptive—not white and red—new buildings erupted including the Letterman Army Medical Center and Institute of Research and the

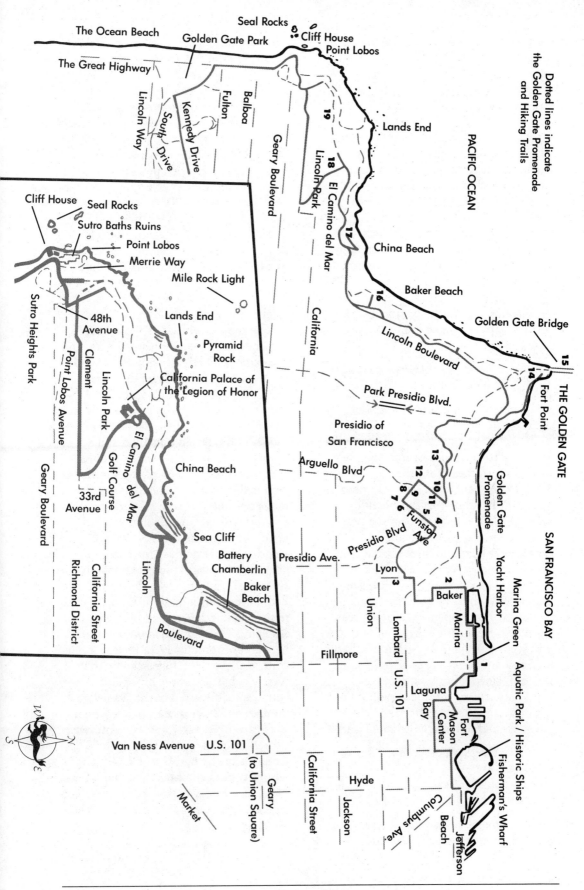

THE PRESIDIO AND ALONG THE GOLDEN GATE

yellowish Enlisted Women's Barracks on the site of the old hospital. Just as in the city as a whole, context was ignored—or fought—in new designs, so the Presidio lost sight of its architectural tradition.

In 1971 the Golden Gate National Recreation Area was formed under the National Park Service. Massive Fort Point, the historic earthwork batteries, and the beaches and shoreline were turned over to the new national park. The horticultural riches of the reservation include 210,000 pine, cypress, and eucalyptus trees, 70,000 of which were planted in the 1880s by post commander Irwin McDowell. The Army continues to occupy the heart of the post, but has an agreement with the National Park Service to turn over to it any surplus land.

Lombard Street Gate and Trophies [3]
1894, J. B. Whittlemore

The Presidio and Ferries Railroad opened in 1880 with a combination of cable, as far west as Steiner Street, and a steam railroad connector into the post; cable was extended into the Presidio in 1892. In 1894 architect J. B. Whittlemore designed the stone Presidio boundary wall which was erected over the next three years. The pylons at the Main Entrance at Lombard Street include figures of Liberty and Victory, and the castlelike emblem of the Army Corps of Engineers with its motto: "Essayons." The two bronze Spanish cannons were cast in Seville, Spain in 1783 and are engraved with the monogram of Charles III. Lombard Street's extension into the Presidio, Lincoln Boulevard, curves gently into the government reservation, disconnecting the post from the city's relentless and differently oriented grid.

U.S. Army Presidio Museum / Refugee Cottages [4]
Lincoln Boulevard and Funston Avenue
Tuesday–Sunday, 10 A.M.–4 P.M.; free.

This handsome two-story white clapboard and brick hospital was built in 1864 and originally faced west to the parade ground. In 1878 it and the row of officers' quarters on Funston Avenue were reoriented toward the east. In 1897, as medicine became more scientific, a separate, two-story octagonal wing was added to the north side of the building for a laboratory. It is a conservative building, and its open porches with their square white timber columns give a hint of what post-Gold Rush San Francisco downtown hotels looked like in the late 1850s. It is the only example of this once-important type of architecture left in San Francisco. Over time the third-floor porch was glassed in, the fate of almost all open porches and balconies in bright but windy San Francisco.

The museum inside is most interesting; there are layers of history here, and the exhibits clearly separate and explain them. Several models and dioramas from the Golden Gate International Exposition of 1939 held on Treasure Island are on view here including a model of the Presidio in 1806 and a model of Mission Dolores' U-shaped compound. A diorama of the summit of Nob Hill depicts the great Victorian mansions and the new Fairmont Hotel on April 18, 1906 as the flames of the great fire consume the downtown. Another elaborate diorama shows the great Panama-Pacific International Exposition of 1915 in today's Marina District. Behind the museum are two earthquake refugee cottages designed by General Adolphus Greeley which were moved here and restored in 1986. Photos in one cottage show the refugee camps that were established in the city parks. The cottages were rented out to homeless families at $2 per month in a lease/purchase arrangement. The last camp was cleared from the parks in June, 1908. Cottages to the number of 5,343 were removed from the camps, all but a few to be used as dwellings. The second cottage is furnished as it might have been in 1906.

Funston Avenue is named after General Frederick Funston the man who captured Aguinaldo, the Philippine rebel, and who was in command at the Presidio when the earthquake struck in 1906. He made the decision to dynamite firebreaks at Van Ness Avenue and along other streets to prevent the entire city from being consumed in the three days of fire that followed the quake.

To the student of American architecture, the Funston Avenue row of some dozen Victorian frame houses is a prize specimen, a historical model of the evolution of the basic American frame house and its utilities from 1862 to the present. These freestanding buildings on large lots—without the obscuring fences and walls that exist between individual privately owned properties—can be seen from all sides. They were built for officers of the 9th Infantry Regiment in 1862. The split columns of the front porches and the porch's simple railings are classic examples of American carpentry. Here, continually maintained and uninterruptedly lived in is a row of classic, all-American frame houses. Plumbing was added in 1883–1884, electricity in 1912; around 1947 the single-family houses were unobtrusively converted into duplexes; and carports were added in 1951. In 1965, new reinforced concrete foundations were inconspicuously built under the antique houses to preserve them.

At Presidio Boulevard and Funston Avenue is another cluster of four two-story-with-attic houses built in 1885. Very conservative designs for 1885, they were designed by Captain Daniel D. Wheeler of the Presidio Quartermaster's Office. They are strikingly handsome, straightforward Stick Style houses with hospitable, old-fashioned porches. They, too, are classically American.

Pershing Hall [6]
Moraga Avenue at Funston Avenue
1903, James Campbell

At the head of Funston Avenue is three-story, red brick Pershing Hall with its fine white porches looking down the Victorian officers' row. It, too, is a most American design. Built in 1903 as a Bachelor Officers' Quarters, it was constructed by James Campbell. The symmetrical T-plan building is a classic American congregate housing type seen most often in schools and colleges.

285

Old Protestant Chapel / Roman Catholic Chapel of Our Lady/Site of Spanish and Mexican Presidio [7]
1864, architect unknown; 1952, remodeled by Hewlitt Wells

Up Moraga Avenue, named for José Joaquín Moraga, who founded the Presidio in 1776, is the old post chapel. This is approximately the site of the long-lost Mexican adobe presidio. The 1864 frame chapel was a simple single-story, New England-style gabled building with a square bell tower. By 1902 vines planted around it had engulfed the façade leaving the bell tower peeping through a clipped mound of greenery. In 1952 the chapel was thoroughly reworked by Hewlitt Wells keeping only parts of the old building. The result is an interesting "California" frame building that has opened itself to a walled garden linking inside and out.

Officers' Open Mess / Old Comandancia [8]
Moraga Avenue
1821–1830, architect unknown; 1934, Barney Meeden; 1973, Robert B. Wong

Beyond the old chapel and a small Victorian building is the entrance to the Officers' Open Mess with its canvas canopy and antique green bronze cannons. The adobe Mexican-era *comandancia* of 1821–1830 was located here. In 1847 occupying Army troops rebuilt the crumbling adobe and built a two-story plaster and wood addition. In 1934, to the designs of Quartermaster Barney Meeden, the entire complex was expanded, coated in lath and plaster, and roofed with red tiles to create a Spanish Colonial Revival building. This was a WPA project. In 1973 Robert B. Wong designed a large addition with a square tower and terraces carefully placed behind the old relic. The new building has slots in its red tile roof to allow light onto its view terraces. It is a model of the respectful integration of much larger new structures in historic landscapes by carefully respecting sightlines.

PERSHING SQUARE: FLAG AND FOCAL POINT [9]

The post's standard and the cannon fired at 6 A.M. and 5 P.M. stand in Pershing Square, the center of the post. Historic artillery is mounted here; some are war trophies. There is a fine view down the parade ground. The squat stone structure with the pyramidal red tile roof at the corner of Sheridan and Anza Avenues to the north is the old **U.S. Army magazine** built of local stone in 1863. The tile roof was added in 1940.

Montgomery Street Enlisted Men's Barracks: Brick Row [10]
Montgomery Street
1895–1897, U.S. Army Corps of Engineers

One of the finest architectural formations on the post is the solid row of red brick barracks with white porches that marches down Montgomery Street. These five, two-story-with-attic barracks fronting the parade ground were constructed between 1895 and 1897 and have recently been upgraded and restored. This, too, is a most American group.

PARADE GROUND / CENTENNIAL AND BICENTENNIAL TREES [11]

On the east side of the main parade ground is the centennial eucalyptus planted in 1876, now tall and stately, and the bicentennial cypress planted in 1976. These two trees are living benchmarks of American history.

The large white buildings along the east side of the parade ground are the headquarters of the Sixth U.S. Army. After seeing the heart of the post, drive to and walk through the San Francisco National Military Cemetery on the forested hill to the west. At the foot of the parade ground across Lincoln Boulevard is the bus stop for the 29 Sunset bus.

Post Chapel and WPA Murals [12]
Fisher Loop, near cemetery
1932, U.S. Army Corps of Engineers

During the 1930s, federal programs like the Works Progress Administration worked on improving the Presidio, building a new movie theater and a new post chapel. The 1932 hilltop chapel on Fisher Loop near the National Cemetery is in Spanish Colonial Revival style and has 1935 murals on the "Peacetime Activities of the Army" by Victor Arnautoff.

San Francisco National Military Cemetery [13]
Sheridan Avenue and Lincoln Boulevard
1884, U.S. Army Corps of Engineers

The San Francisco National Military Cemetery is today enfolded in an evergreen curtain of forests. This orderly rectangle of the dead with its occasional obelisks and Victorian monuments is set on the bluff above the parade ground. It is instructive to walk through this beautiful cemetery, with its commanding panorama of the Bay, and to read the names and dates of the soldiers, the names of the places where they fell, and the dates of wars they fought. America's reach west across a continent, and further west across the Pacific Ocean to Asia, is recorded in these markers. Beginning with the Indian Wars in the wild West, and reaching out to Alaska, Hawaii, the Philippines, Guam, China, Japan, Korea, and Vietnam, the pulses of American expansion are recorded here.

Fort Point / The Seawall [14]
At head of Marine Drive
Open daily 10 A.M.–5 P.M.; free.

Fort Point, constructed between 1853 and 1861, is operated by the National Park Service. It is the first and only brick coast artillery fortress built west of the Mississippi River and is similar in plan to Fort Sumter, outside Charleston, South Carolina. The massive fort is built of locally manufactured red brick, granite, and iron. Its accurately restored courtyard has elegant cast-iron balconies along one side. Antique artillery is displayed and the fort is well labeled. The view from the top of the fort, directly under the bridge, looking across the Golden Gate between the X-braces of the two piers is memorable. Joseph Strauss admired the solidity of Fort Point. The elevated approach to the Golden Gate Bridge makes a great steel arch over the fort, preserving it. The fort was technologically obsolete within a year of its completion because shells and rifled cannons developed during the Civil War achieved the ability to pierce brick fortifications.

When the waters are rough, great waves splash up against the granite seawall and leap high into the air. The wall, with its interlocking granite blocks, is an impressive piece of solid construction and dates from the early 1850s. San Francisco began at this commanding site, the rock-bound portal to the Golden State.

The Golden Gate Bridge: Art Deco Masterpiece [15]
1937, Joseph P. Strauss, chief engineer; Irving F. Morrow, consulting architect

The Golden Gate Bridge is one of the few things in life that does not disappoint. It is a magnificent, impressive,

artistic structure spanning a submerged cleft in the Coastal Mountain Range, the Golden Gate. Through this rocky gate the waters of California have carved a channel to the sea. The name Golden Gate was given to this strait by Captain John C. Fremont in 1848.

The great "international orange" (more a terra cotta red) bridge is the joint work of chief engineer Joseph P. Strauss and consulting architect Irving F. Morrow. The bridge was locally planned and financed by San Francisco and the five coastal counties to the north. It took only fifty-two months to design and construct the Golden Gate Bridge, which opened in 1937.

The Golden Gate Bridge is as much architecture as engineering. Irving F. Morrow's assertive use of Art Deco decoration makes the bridge what it is, an elegant, faceted, soaring design. The bridge's "arches" as you drive across it toward San Francisco look like the proscenium arch in a theater with the city like a painted backdrop. Morrow wanted no X-braces marring the top of the bridge (they do exist, underneath the roadbed, bracing the bases of the two piers). In the resulting design the telescoped piers, which become thinner as they rise, and the horizontal struts create a "ladder" with four differently sized openings.

The concrete abutments and anchorings of the bridge are the most artistic concrete construction in the region and were the first use of more durable high-silica cement. The span between the two towers is 4,200 feet and was the longest in the world until 1959. The clearance between the roadbed and mean low water is 220 feet, a height set by the military. The two towers are 746 feet tall. The cables are 7,650 feet long from anchorage to anchorage. The maximum side sway of the roadway in high winds at center span is 27.7 feet. As handsome as the bridge is, even more memorable is the way the fogs pour in and out of the gate, dissolving this massive bridge in white mist.

The new toll booths were designed by Donald MacDonald in 1980–1982 after an architectural competition and relate well to the landmark bridge while still being designs of our own time.

GOLDEN GATE BRIDGE VISTA POINTS [15]

Two major vista points offer free parking lots, one on the San Francisco side and one in Marin County. Enter the south, or San Francisco vista point from Lincoln Boulevard, right before the toll plaza underpass, or from the extreme right-hand lane of Highway 101 just before the toll booths. There is a statue of engineer and promoter Joseph P. Strauss. Near the pedestrian entrance to the bridge is a fine low circular stucco and glass pavilion designed in 1937 by Irving F. Morrow. A visitor center with maps and souvenir shop are in the pavilion. Enter the Marin vista point from the right lane of Highway 101 at the north end of the bridge. There are restrooms here and an overlook of San Francisco like that from a choice box seat. This is a beautiful view on a clear night. The spacious Bay is ever changing colors. There are sidewalks on both sides of the bridge, but the constant roar of the traffic right beside you makes the walk unpleasant.

There is another spectacular viewpoint from the ridge of the Marin hills along Conzelman Road. From there sparkling San Francisco is seen framed by the red steel harp of the bridge. Take the Alexander Avenue exit immediately north of the Marin vista point, turn left at the first intersection onto Battery Road, and pass through the tunnel. Beyond a small patch of military housing, turn left and travel south on McCullough Road; at the first intersection turn left onto Conzelman Road; which here is one-way. Who can say which is the best view of San Francisco? Certainly a contender for the prize is this vista on a clear moon-lit night, with silvery fog gliding through the Golden Gate and suspending the bridge and eventually dissolving the glittering lighted city—all to the musical accompaniment of fog horns with their melancholy warnings. The panorama changes at times so quickly that real time seems a time-lapse film.

The underside of the bridge is best seen from the San Francisco side from the seawall in front of red brick Fort Point.

Lincoln Boulevard to Baker Beach / Battery Chamberlin Disappearing Gun [16]

Beach open 7 A.M. to dusk, park rangers man the disappearing gun on the first weekend of each month, phone 751-2519 for information.

Lincoln Boulevard passes along the crest of the bluff at the western edge of the Presidio and enjoys commanding views of the Pacific. A string of great fortifications was built here at the turn of the century and today preserved as historic sites. There is parking and a vista point near Battery Dynamite. Further south is the turn off to Baker Beach and Battery Chamberlin. This sandy beach enjoys a splendid view of the Golden Gate and the bridge. North of the parking lot, behind the ice-plant covered sand dunes, is Battery Chamberlin with its disappearing gun carriage. This 1904, 95,000-pound cannon from the Smithsonian's collection can still be raised from behind the battery to its firing position. At the opposite, or south, end of the beach is a good view of the Mediterranean style houses that stand on the edge of the rocky cliff along Seacliff Avenue, a picturesque assemblage of pale stucco cubes capped by red tile roofs. The steep cliff beyond, capped by evergreens, is Lands End. Point Bonita across the Golden Gate has a white lighthouse at its tip. Beyond the red brick building at the south end of the beach is a short trail up a bluff to the foot of Twenty-fifth Avenue North (gate locked at 10 P.M.). This *cul de sac* is a corner of Sea Cliff Gardens, a luxurious subdivision begun in 1904. Views from the top floors of the houses here have resulted in elaborate sun porches, viewing areas, and view-focussed windows.

El Camino del Mar / Sea Cliff / China Beach [17]

Lincoln Boulevard leads to El Camino Del Mar and Sea Cliff, an immaculate residential district with well-tended gardens. To see Sea Cliff it is best to drive directly to China Beach and its parking area and then walk along Seacliff Avenue. Walk on the high, or southern sidewalk. Visible between the free-standing houses built in the 1920s are slices of the dramatic panorama of the Golden Gate with the red Marin headlands across the water. Sea Cliff is the only San Francisco neighborhood that touches the ocean; all the rest of the ocean shoreline is public parks. The northeast corner of the district, the east end of Seacliff Avenue and the area near Twenty-fifth Avenue North, was laid out in 1904 by the John Brickell Company which organized a homeowner association here and named the tract Sea Cliff Gardens. In 1916 a larger parcel to the west bounded approximately by California Street to the south, Twenty-eighth Avenue to the east, and Thirtieth Avenue to the west was developed by H. B. and Lawrence D. Allen and called Sea Cliff. Most of the houses here were built between 1920 and the Crash of 1929 in the then-popular Mediterranean style. The gardens here are lush and boast meticulously pruned, vivid green shrubbery, some displaying fantastic forms. Where the road descends to China Beach stands 330 Seacliff Avenue, a 1920s Mediterranean style, L-shaped house with a red tile roof and a picturesque, wind-swept pine tree.

China Beach, named after the Chinese fishermen's shacks that once huddled here, is a pocket beach set in a dramatic cove. Above the cove, in a bowl-like amphitheater, are ranged terraces of large stucco houses whose windows face the Golden Gate. This beach is also known as Phelan Beach after James Duval Phelan, a banker who served as a reform mayor in San Francisco between 1897 and 1901 and who emphasized urban beautification and the expansion of the city's park system. He urged the preservation of this scenic cove. The concrete beach house here was built in the early 1950s and is a typical, if over-looked, piece of California public beach architecture of the period. Lifeguards are on duty here in the summer months from 10 A.M. to 5 P.M. for those hardy enough to brave these chilly waters. The rocky cliffs of Lands End visible from China Beach are colored gray, green, and maroon. The waves dash against the offshore rocks. On clear days the white cliffs of Point Reyes appear on the horizon to the north. The highest point visible is Mt. Tamalpias. At the east end of the beach is a submerged mass of rectangular granite paving stones dumped here after the earthquake and fire of 1906 and now polished smooth by the ceaseless sea. The rumbling stones make a death rattle clatter as they roll back down the slope when the waves move out.

LINCOLN PARK [18]

Around the shoulder of the rocky peninsula is Lincoln Park, originally reserved in 1868 as part of the Outside Lands for the Golden Gate Cemetery, the city's paupers' cemetery. The first burials here occurred in 1870 when pioneer remains were disinterred from Yerba Buena Cemetery so that it could be used for the new city hall (today the site of the Civic Center Public Library). Many Chinese were buried here before their bones were disinterred for shipment back to their native villages. Nearby landowners objected to the unkempt, depressing potter's field—indeed to all the cemeteries within the city. After a bitter fight the city prohibited burials within the city limits after 1901 and a chain of new cemeteries was opened in Colma, over the line in San Mateo County. This commanding site was relandscaped by John McLaren as Lincoln Park, and a golf course was opened here in 1909. A Victorian Chinese funerary monument survives today in the middle of the Lincoln Park golf course.

California Palace of the Legion of Honor [18]
Lincoln Park
1920, George Applegarth
Open Wednesday–Sunday, 10 A.M.–5 P.M.; fee; 221-4811; organ recitals held here Sunday afternoon.

In 1920 the splendid California Palace of the Legion of Honor was completed to plans by George Applegarth, modeled on the Legion of Honor in Paris. It was the gift of Adolph Bernard and Alma de Bretteville Spreckels in memory of California's World War I dead. Few art museums have as beautiful a situation as this one. Inside the limestone palace is a collection of French art, opulent period rooms, and a sizable collection of Rodin sculptures assembled by the Spreckels. The superb **Achenbach Foundation** downstairs holds an outstanding collection of prints. One of the finest Rodin bronzes, The Shades, stands across the parking lot from the museum. The view of the park-laced city from here is very fine.

Hiking Trail to Lands End and the Cliff House / Roadbed of the Ferries and Cliff House Railway [19]
El Camino Del Mar dead ends just north of the California Palace of the Legion of Honor near the Lincoln Park Golf Course. There is parking here and the head of a trail that skirts the rocky edge of Lands End and leads to Merrie Way, a parking lot near the Cliff House and the Sutro Baths ruins. This was once the roadbed of the Ferries & Cliff

House Railway, a narrow gauge steam railroad that ran out California Street and operated here from 1888 to 1906. This scenic trail offers splendid views of the Golden Gate and forests of twisted cypress trees. The wild, broken shore, the booming surf, and the sense of remoteness from the city make this one of the best nature walks in San Francisco. Stay on the trails for the cliffs here are unstable and dangerous. The Park Service has planted California poppies along part of the trail which becomes a shining, golden road in the spring. The #18 46th Avenue bus terminates at the Legion of Honor near the head of the trail; the #38 Geary bus has its terminus at Geary and Forty-eighth Avenue, about two blocks from the other end of the trail.

Day Trips

San Francisco Bay Islands

Angel Island State Park /
Old Immigration Station

Treasure Island

Marin County

Coastal Highway 1

Sausalito

Mill Valley

Muir Woods National Monument:
Primeval Redwood Grove

Marin County Civic Center: Frank Lloyd
Wright Masterpiece

Point Reyes National Seashore

Napa Valley

Trefethen Vineyards

Yountville

Domaine Chandon

Robert Mondavi Winery

Skalli-Atkinson Vineyards and Winery

Inglenook Winery

Rutherford

St. Helena: Main Street Jewel

Beringer Vineyards

Christian Brothers Greystone Winery

Napa Valley, continued

Bothe-Napa Valley State Park
Clos Pegase
Calistoga / Silverado Trail
Mt. St. Helena / Robert Louis Stevenson
State Park

The East Bay

The Oakland Museum: The Museum of
California
The University of California, Berkeley:
The Athens of the West
John Muir National Historic Site
Tao House / Eugene O'Neill National
Historic Site

San Mateo Peninsula

Stanford University: A Pinnacle of
Regional Environmental Design
Filoli: Great Estate and Garden

Monterey Bay and Peninsula

Santa Cruz: Turn-of-the-Century Seaside
Resort
The City of Monterey: California's First
Capital
    Larkin House
    Allen Knight Maritime Museum
    Annual Adobe House Tour
    Colton Hall Museum
    Casa de la Torre Viewing Garden
    Casa Amesti
    Robert Louis Stevenson (Gonzales)
    House
    San Carlos de Borromeo de Monterey
    Cathedral / Old Royal Presidio Chapel
    Alvarado Street: Old Main Stem
    Fisherman's Wharf
    Cannery Row
    Monterey Bay Aquarium
The City of Pacific Grove: Victorian
Chatauqua
Del Monte Forest / The Seventeen-Mile
Drive
    Pebble Beach
Carmel-by the-Sea
    Ocean Avenue Shops
    Mission San Carlos Borromeo del Rio
    Carmelo / Father Junipero Serra's
    Tomb
    Robinson Jeffers' Tor House
Monastery Beach
Point Lobos State Reserve

292

Preliminaries

It cannot be emphasized too strongly that weekdays are the best times for sightseeing outside the city. Saturdays and Sundays, when city people rush to the beaches and clog the back roads, are often overcrowded and congested. Sausalito, Muir Woods, the Napa Valley, and the Monterey Bay Aquarium are at capacity on weekends, especially in the summer. Try to make your visit bridge a weekend and some weekdays to see both the city and its richly scenic surroundings.

It is not always easy, or possible, to get to the region's attractions without an automobile. Recent transit cutbacks have left important places like Muir Woods National Monument without public transit access.

San Francisco Bay Islands

Alcatraz Prison Tour
Red & White Fleet
Pier 41, near the foot of Powell
$7 round trip for adults; $4.50 for children.
Tickets are limited and are best bought in advance during the summer season at Pier 41 or through any Ticketron outlet; 546-2653. Schedules vary with the seasons. You may stay on the island as long as you wish; however, be sure to note the time of the last return trip. The Golden Gate National Park Association publishes an excellent map and guide to Alcatraz. Park Rangers offer hourly tours of the island. Dress warmly.

Located in San Francisco Bay, rocky, fog-shrouded Alcatraz has been successively a roost for pelicans, hence its Spanish name; a harbor fortification; a military prison; and from 1934 to 1963, a federal prison for incorrigibles. A lighthouse has functioned here since 1854, the first on the West Coast. Alcatraz was reserved by the U.S. Army in 1850 and a brick fort was constructed here in the early 1850s. In the 1860s the island was used to hold Civil War prisoners, and from 1870 to 1890, Indian prisoners. The Cellhouse of 1911, built by prisoners, was one of the largest reinforced concrete structures in the world at its completion.

Since 1972 the island has been a national park and is preserved as a bleak, peeling, stabilized ruin. Visitors may see the prison's ruinous interior: "Broadway," "Times Square," the solitary confinement cells, and the Recreation Yard familiar from Hollywood gangster movies. Among the prisoners incarcerated here were Al Capone and "Machine Gun" Kelly. Robert Stroud, the "Birdman of Alcatraz," was never allowed to keep birds when he was transferred here for killing a guard at Fort Leavenworth Prison. While the island is ugly architecturally, the views back to San Francisco are splendid.

While Alcatraz is quite popular (children especially seem to like it), visitors with only a couple of days in San Francisco can do better things with their time than spend half a day visiting a ruined prison. The ferry to Sausalito passes quite near Alcatraz and gives a good enough view of it. A day trip to see the towering redwoods in Muir Woods National Monument north of San Francisco makes a much better outing.

Angel Island State Park / Old Immigration Station
Red & White Fleet
Pier 43 at Fisherman's Wharf
$6.60 round trip
Ferries also leave Tiburon, in Marin County; $4 round trip. Schedules vary with the seasons; call 546-2896 for hours.
Angel Island is a California State Park and camp sites are available; phone (916) 323-3988 for information and reservations. For park rangers, phone 435-1915.

North of the Golden Gate Bridge, off Highway 101, is Frank Lloyd Wright's Marin County Civic Center designed in 1957 and built in stages. The boomerang-shaped building bridges two valleys and is a classic of 1950s futuristic design.

Forested Angel Island is one of San Francisco Bay's least crowded, most pleasurable "secrets." The mile-wide, triangular island is threaded with hiking trails and bicycle paths. No automobiles are permitted. From the 776-foot summit of Mt. Livermore there is a stunning panorama of the north Bay and gleaming San Francisco.

The island was discovered in 1765 by Gaspar de Portola; in 1775 Lieutenant Juan de Ayala anchored here while charting San Francisco Bay. The island became part of the harbor fortifications in 1863 with the establishment of Camp Reynolds. From 1910 to 1940 part of the island served as an Immigration Station; some 175,000 Chinese immigrants passed through here. While being held in the two-story detention barracks, some of these immigrants carved poems on the walls recording their anguish and their hope. Once scheduled for demolition, the barracks has been preserved as a museum and the poems found on its walls have been published by the Chinese Culture Foundation. The island with its historic military post and old immigration station became a California state park in 1956.

Treasure Island
Treasure Island Museum,
Treasure Island, Building 1; 765-6182.
Daily, 10 A.M.–3:30 P.M. Navy, Marine Corps, Coast Guard museum.

Marin County

Marin County has a hard time of it from critical intellectuals. It *does* seem to be lotus land, where the sun always shines and everyone drifts by in a laid-back, tranquilized state of mind. An affluent suburban area with beautiful and varied geography, Mellow Marin harbors a beautiful and mostly monochromatic white-collar population. The clean environment, the houses with generous gardens, the tidy, high-style, lowrise office complexes and shopping centers stocked with upscale goods, and the almost litter-free roadsides give the driver exploring Marin for the first time the feeling that he is passing through a life-sized scale model we could call Modern America.

Marin County was once cattle country. Portuguese-American cowboys worked the herds on these high coastal hills. Later ferries from San Francisco and electric railroads running inland up the picturesque valleys led to development of summer colonies for San Franciscans. San Rafael, the county seat, became the largest town. Sausalito and Tiburon served as railheads linking the railroads with the ferries to San Francisco. The Golden Gate Bridge broke the county's isolation, and the county suburbanized in the 1950s.

Along with the suburban boom, Marin became an automotive Utopia. Only those who could afford a car and a new home came to Marin, creating a well-educated, well-paid population of professionals who demanded strict building controls. No highrise construction was permitted in Marin and high land values have justified high-style, state-of-the-art designs in houses, condominiums, and lowrise office and shopping center construction. In addition to all this good fortune, about half of Marin County is protected watershed or park land. Virtually the entire ocean side of the scenic, mountainous county is forever green and open.

Coastal Highway 1

The California Coastal Commission's *California Coastal Resource Guide* is the indispensable guide for those who want to know the coast. For weather conditions on the north coast, phone the Stinson Beach weather report at (415) 868-1922.

The only practical way to see the coast is with an automobile. Public transportation to the coastal highway north of San Francisco is scarce. One Golden Gate Transit bus leaves San Francisco for Point Reyes at 8 A.M. on weekends and holidays. On the south coast, SamTrans (San Mateo County Transit) runs buses on the coastal highway; the problem is getting from the city to those bus lines. Those driving the coastal highway for the first time will want to be off it and back on Highway 101 before dark; though well marked with white reflectors along the center of the road, it is a difficult road to drive in the dark.

A Park Service map of the GGNRA shows parking areas and trails in coastal Marin. Walk to the top of some hill or bluff to look down on the coast spread out before you. Even overcast days have their own moody beauty on the north coast. The sea turns shades of slate gray, with burning silver patches where the sun breaks through the close cloud cover.

The California coast immediately north and south of San Francisco is unpeopled, unspoiled, rocky, wild, tonic. Both Marin County and Point Reyes to the north and the Monterey Peninsula and Bay to the south are among the great scenic treasures of North America. Most of the coast is protected in county or state shoreline parks and has been made accessible through very well designed roads, view spots, parking lots, and picnic spots. Highway 1, which winds along the coast, is designed for pleasure driving only—no trucks travel it. Many wide shoulders along the view side of the road offer travelers the opportunity to stop briefly to survey the panorama.

To the north is open, rocky coast, redwood forests, and the Audubon Canyon Ranch Bird Sanctuary at Bolinas Lagoon. Point Reyes, a little farther north is a vast, windswept, moorlike landscape. To the south of San Francisco, off Point Lobos State Park, near Monterey and Carmel, is one of the richest undersea biological zones on the 1,264-mile California coast. Off this verdant, rocky point, great beds of giant kelp grow and sea life flourishes. The delicate red seaweeds strewn on the gravel beach at Lovers' Point in Pacific Grove are as impressive in their miniaturized delicacy as the redwoods are in their great size.

Sausalito

BEST DAYS AND TIMES

The climate is pleasant, if windy, all year round. Summer weekends are very crowded and parking is impossible. Weekdays are always more relaxed and rewarding.

TRANSPORTATION

Golden Gate Transit's clean buses provide excellent service from San Francisco to Marin County. Phone (415) 332-6600 for information. Sit opposite the driver's side for a memorable view when crossing the Golden Gate Bridge.

Unless you are driving further north, it is not advisable to drive to Sausalito on weekends, since the town is small and trying to park is frustrating. The town of Sausalito collects more from parking fees and fines than from property taxes. Take the ferry. If you do drive, take the Alexander Avenue exit off Highway 101 immediately after crossing the Golden Gate Bridge and enter Sausalito from the south. From the road you will see houses clinging to the steep cliffs, with parking areas atop the buildings.

The Golden Gate Ferry speeds passengers (no cars) from the Ferry Building at the foot of Market Street in San Francisco to the foot of El Portal in Sausalito. Phone (415) 332-6600 for schedule and fees; be careful to inquire when the last ferry back leaves (usually about 8 P.M.). It is a bracing ride and on the way there are views of Alcatraz and through the Golden Gate. The view back to San Francisco is also splendid and displays the port city as it is best seen, from the water.

What is now the posh, cliff-clinging town of Sausalito was part of the Rancho Saucelito, 19,571 acres granted to London-born William A. Richardson in 1838 by Mexican governor José Figueroa. Legend has it that the name *Saucelito* means willow grove and refers to a bank of willows that grew near this steep shore. Richardson, who had converted to Catholicism three years earlier and married the daughter of the presidio *comandante*, had been named captain of the port at Yerba Buena where he was expected to collect duties and enforce Mexico's trade bans. British and Yankee captains gravitated to Whaler's Cove because water that would keep could be found there, and firewood could be cut at nearby Angel Island. Richardson sought to lock up San Francisco Bay by administering the Mexican customs at the legal port at Yerba Buena Cove and conducting smuggling operations at Whaler's Cove, now Richardson Bay, off his Rancho Saucelito.

Modern Sausalito began when twenty San Francisco businessmen organized the Sausalito Land & Ferry company in 1869. They bought three miles of water front property, the southern portion of Captain Richardson's old Rancho Saucelito, and subdivided it for San Franciscans seeking "a quiet rural home in a lovely place." By 1880 there was a small town here with two yacht clubs. Each lot buyer was given a pass for the company-run ferry to San Francisco. By 1885 Sausalito had about 1,500 residents and eight hotels. Eventually rail lines—at first steam, but electrified by 1905—reached up from Sausalito into bucolic Marin County. Wealthy San Franciscans began the colonization of the scenic county. In 1920 a frustrated San Francisco commuter, Harry E. Speas, incorporated the Golden Gate Ferry Company to provide modern auto ferries to the city. The art deco span of the Golden Gate Bridge ended that era and Speas' fleet was dispersed, some ships going north to Puget Sound and one going as far as the Río de la Plata in Argentina.

Commercial Sausalito has evolved

into two parts. South of the ferry slip at El Portal, **Bridgeway**, the scenic street along the water's edge with fine views of San Francisco has become a tourist strip with generally upscale restaurants and shops. North of the ferry slip, beyond the yacht harbor and across Bridgeway, is a small grid centered on Caledonia Street. This is **New town**—its shops and restaurants serve the local residents. El Portal is a one-block-long street flanked by **Viña del Mar Plaza**, a small park named after Sausalito's sister city in Chile. The fine fountain and improbable elephant light standards were designed by local architect W. A. Faville and are relics from San Francisco's famous Panama-Pacific International Exposition of 1915. Viña del Mar Plaza, with its lordly palms, is a landscape jewel. It has had to be closed to foot traffic and converted into a viewing-only oasis. On the corner of El Portal and Bridgeway, facing the park, is a delightful piece of naïve California Mission design—the **Sausalito Inn**, with its red tile-capped bay windows and impossible curvilinear Mission style parapet with cutouts. Built in 1915, its exaggerated parapets look like a child's paper crown. The **Sausalito City Hall** at Caledonia and Litho Streets in off-the-beaten-track New Town has a small historical museum open Monday, Wednesday, and Saturday from 10 A.M. to 4 P.M.

Most visitors turn left at the fountain and spend their visit exploring Bridgeway and its shops. A more interesting alternative is to turn right at the fountain, cross the public parking lots, and wander up and down the wooden piers among the immaculate white sailboats that fill the spacious Sausalito **Yacht Harbor**. The best indication of the wealth in Marin is this bobbing, tinkling, sparkling flotilla of white hulls and blue canvas coverings.

At the end of one pier is a pleasure barge that looks like a white gingerbread Taj Mahal.

Leave the yacht harbor and follow the asphalt bike path heading north. During World War II this area boomed as the Kaiser shipyards, with 17,500 workers who built ninety-three ships. When the war ended, squatters moved in and built houseboats here out of salvaged materials. Near Gate 5, just outside the Sausalito city limits, is a funky assortment of occupier-built houseboats, constructed atop everything from abandoned ferries slowly sinking into the mud to old barges and small ships. Marin County has waged a running war with this tenacious bohemian colony, mainly over sewage and sanitation problems.

As is so often the case, the bohemian pioneers have been followed by more conventional (and legal) imitators. At Gate B, further to the north of Richardson's Bay, is a neater, more orderly, and less romantic houseboat colony, looking much like a floating suburb of shingled, skylighted, architect-designed houseboats all carefully arranged.

Even if you follow the usual path down Bridgeway, you can taste the residents' Sausalito by climbing up one of the steep staircases on the west side of the street. Just a few yards up, even on the busiest weekend, the paths and streets here are quiet and serene. When originally ferry-centered Sausalito was laid out, public easements were reserved for staircases that cascade down the slope, making pedestrian connectors between the terraced streets. One or two flights up any Sausalito staircase brings you to a quiet, tree-embowered world of patrolling house cats and residential serenity. The best architectural designs in Sausalito are these contemporary houses with sweeping views of the Bay and distant San Francisco. They do not show much of themselves from the twisting hillside streets, however, as they turn their faces out to the view. At **100 Bulkley Avenue** is the shingle-clad First Presbyterian Church, designed by Ernest Coxhead in 1909—a fine example of the rustic imagery so dear to Northern Californians. There is also a good view down the hill to Viña del Mar Plaza.

Mill Valley

Perhaps the most characteristic town in Marin County worth exploring is nontourist Mill Valley. The Golden Gate Transit District (call 415-332-6600 for schedules and fares) serves the town from both San Francisco and Sausalito. This narrow valley was once also a part of the Rancho Saucelito; a sawmill was built here in 1834 by Juan Read, an Irish-born sailor. The area was subdivided in 1891, and a town was founded. Built at the head of a narrow, redwood-filled valley, the town began developing when the electric interurban rail line opened, linking this sheltered, sunny valley with Sausalito and the San Francisco ferries. The depot at the head of the valley was the single node around which the town grew. San Franciscans began building small, uninsulated, rustic cottages under the trees within climbing distance of the depot. Immediately after the earthquake of 1906, many city people came to live here year round, insulating and expanding their summer cottages.

Today Mill Valley is a favorite residence for San Francisco architects, who appreciate the unpretentiousness of the local houses. Weathered, shingled houses stand nestled among the whispering trees along one-lane roads. Timber-reinforced stair paths lead up many of the steep slopes. The settlement has accommodated growth without spoiling its rustic charms. The downtown is still highly walkable and has a few shops featuring the works of local artists and artisans—prints and glass in particular. **Fireworks**, at 4 El Paseo, features fine ceramics and glass.

Architect Bernard Maybeck's **Mill Valley Art and Garden Club**, a few paces away from the old depot at the corner of Buena Vista and Blythedale Avenue, sums up the architectural tradition of early Marin and North Side Berkeley. This ingratiating clubhouse, set in a simple garden with redwoods and oaks, was built in 1904 and has been perfectly preserved. The club was founded with the express purpose of preserving the natural qualities of the town. The building's unusual roof-truss system pops through the roof.

When you have finished your exploration you can retire to the old depot, now a café and bookstore. A new, small, brick-paved plaza in front of the depot occupies the area where tracks once were. Here the town's life comes to a public focal point. Sitting here you get an accurate picture of the valley's youth, old folks, and middle-aged inhabitants. It is a very Californian spot.

Muir Woods National Monument: Primeval Redwood Grove

No public transit goes directly to Muir Woods. Call (415) 388-2595 for information.

Visitor center with pamphlets, books, and refreshments; no picnicking or camping permitted.

Open from 8 A.M. to sunset. The park has six miles of trails; the main path is wheelchair accessible. It is cool in these dense, shady groves; a warm jacket is good to have along.

This majestic grove, the closest virgin stand of redwoods to San Francisco, is named after California's most famous conservationist, Scotland-born John Muir, one of the founders of the Sierra Club in 1892 and a tireless writer and campaigner for natural preservation in the United States. But the people who actually saved this lordly grove were Marin Congressman William Kent and his wife Elizabeth Thatcher Kent. Alarmed by a water company's proposal to flood Redwood Canyon for a reservoir, Kent bought the central 295 acres of the present park and then donated them to the federal government. President Theodore Roosevelt used the Antiquities Act of 1906, written to protect the Southwest's ancient sites, to proclaim the grove a national monument.

Today Muir Woods embraces 550

acres of towering redwoods, some of which reach 240 feet into the sky. The *Sequoia sempervirens* grow only in a coastal belt reaching from south of Monterey to the southwestern corner of Oregon. Their usual life span is from 400 to 800 years, though a few are upwards of 2,000 years old. The redwoods depend on the constant mist from coastal fogs for moisture. Their thick bark helps protect them from forest fires. Walking among these trees, you learn the meaning of the word awesome. Their straight trunks seem to reach up to heaven itself. Their cool shade creates open forest floors carpeted with lacy swordferns.

Muir Woods is a popular place, and its main trail is sometimes congested on weekends. But if you secure a map at the Visitor Center you can explore less-crowded paths deeper in the park. Please stay on the marked trails, since trampling the earth here compacts the soil and damages the plants.

Marin County Civic Center: Frank Lloyd Wright Masterpiece

North of San Rafael, off Highway 101 For information about hours and free docent tours, phone 499-6104. Call 332-6600 for Golden Gate Transit information.

On this undulating site of grassy, oak-dotted hills, so typical of all that is most beautiful in the California landscape, Frank Lloyd Wright designed one of California's great buildings, a work of visionary art. It is a futuristic vision curiously both dated and timeless. "Big Pink," as county workers call it, is one of Wright's last works. It was designed in 1957 and built in phases beginning in 1960. Wright and the Taliesin Associated Architects, with Aaron Green, associate architect, created a master plan calling for a low-lying boomerang-shaped building spanning the crowns of three hills. Roads pass under bridge-like buildings leading to the front gates and escalators. Inside, long skylights cut

through all the levels of the Administration Building, resulting in hallway balconies that look down on a linear garden. The building's great metal roof is painted blue like the sky. A small, freestanding Post Office east of the main building is the only U.S. government commission Wright ever received.

After Wright's death in 1959, William Wesley Peters and Taliesin Associated Architects completed the landscape plan with its fairgrounds and lagoon and designed the circular Marin Veterans Memorial Auditorium of 1972 and an Exhibit Hall. The 160-acre site is most festive on the Fourth of July when Marin County holds its annual county fair here and fireworks burst over Wright's great building. Wright's theme here is the one he adopted in his last works, the circle. The circle, the globe, the dome, and the arch are all embroidered into the site's and the building's design in decorative grilles, finials, pavements, and furnishings. Wright's courtrooms in the Hall of Justice are round, with spectators sitting in curved rows. The gold, needlelike, triangular spire (actually an antenna) serves as a counterpoint to all the curved forms. The small, sheltered terrace garden near the spire, with its circular pool and planters, is the complex's hidden oasis.

Point Reyes National Seashore

Call 663-1092 for park information. A map of the park is available at park headquarters.
Point Reyes National Seashore can be reached by Golden Gate Transit (415-332-6600) only on Saturday, Sunday, and holidays via the 80 bus which leaves Seventh and Market streets in downtown San Francisco at 8:06 A.M., with pickups along Van Ness Avenue at Geary, Sutter, Clay, and Union streets. At Fourth and Hetherton streets in San Rafael, underneath the elevated freeway, transfer to the 65 bus to Point Reyes. Inquire about the bus back for your return. For weather conditions on the

north coast, phone the Stinson Beach weather report at (415) 868-1922.

Beyond the Bolinas Lagoon, Highway 1 travels right over the San Andreas Fault to the small hamlet of Olema and the Point Reyes National Seashore Headquarters beyond. The San Andreas Fault, some 650 miles long and extending from Point Arena in Mendocino County in the north to Baja California in the south, is the great "strike-slip" fracture between the Pacific plate and the North American plate, two of the six great pieces of the earth's crust. It is California's longest and best-known earthquake zone, where the two plates grind past each other at the rate of about three inches a year. The sudden movement of about sixteen-and-one-half feet here in 1906 caused the devastating San Francisco earthquake.

Point Reyes was named by the explorer Sebastián Vizcaíno in 1603 after the Feast of the Three Kings, or Epiphany. An estuary here is named Drake's Bay and is presumed by many to be the place where the English adventurer Francis Drake beached his ship, the *Golden Hind*, in 1579 while on a privateering expedition that took him around the globe. While on the Northern California coast, either here or in some other protected spot, he was crowned by the local (probably coast Miwok) Indians and claimed the land for Queen Elizabeth I, naming it Nova Albion. He then sailed westward across the Pacific, returning to London where he was knighted by the Queen.

Point Reyes is the foggiest spot on the California coast. A lighthouse was built here to guide coastal shipping. The surf and tides here are treacherous and not recommended for swimming. Heavy fogs and its remoteness kept the peninsula from development until the American era, when dairy and cattle ranches were eventually established. In 1962 the unspoiled peninsula was made a National Seashore with an added

agreement that existing ranching could continue. In 1972 Point Reyes became part of the Golden Gate National Recreation Area, which extends from here to the southern edge of San Francisco. North of Point Reyes Station is the long slit of Tomales Bay, also a part of the San Andreas Fault. The local specialty is giant Pacific oysters grown in the bay from Japanese stock. Oyster beds can be seen near Millerton Point and other spots. The southern end of Tomales Bay is a refuge for countless migrating waterfowl. Point Reyes is famous as a whale-watching spot. On New Year's Day, avid fans of the California gray whale jam the roads and bluffs seeking glimpses of these huge creatures on their southern migration.

Napa Valley

Best Days and Times

September and October are harvest time, and the wineries are in full operation then. See Mondavi and Krug in the winery listing for summer concert series.

Transportation

The best way to see the wine country is by car. Cross the Golden Gate Bridge and travel north on Highway 101 to Highway 37. Follow Highway 37 east to Highway 12/121. Highway 12/121 continues east through beautiful rolling country to Highway 29, the Mt. St. Helena Highway, which passes up the Napa Valley and past the wineries.

The select list of wineries in this chapter follows this south-to-north pattern.

Greyhound runs buses about six times daily from San Francisco, Vallejo, and Napa and then up the valley to Yountville, Oakville, Rutherford, St. Hel-

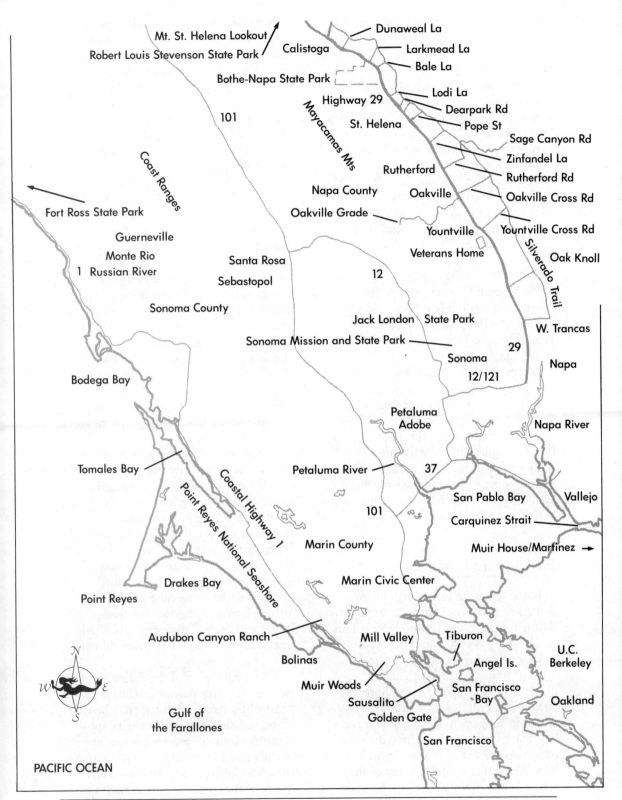

NORTH OF SAN FRANCISCO: MARIN COUNTY AND THE NAPA VALLEY

ena, and Calistoga. St. Helena is probably the best place to get off. There is no bus service in the valley itself; you will have to walk.

Many tour companies offer one-day bus excursions from San Francisco's Union Square area to Napa Valley. They are far less agreeable than being on your own, however. Shop around for the best prices and tours.

Picnics: The Oakville Grocery, 7856 St. Helena Highway, Oakville, CA 94562, (707) 944-2011, is a gourmet's delight, a museum of food and wine.

Information: The Napa Chamber of Commerce, P.O. Box 636, Napa, CA 94559, (707) 226-7455, can provide a list of lodgings and coming events. The Wine Institute, 165 Post Street, San Francisco, CA 94108, (415) 986-0878, provides a list of all the wineries in California.

Notes: Many wineries are closed on major legal and religious holidays. Phone ahead to be certain the one you want to visit is open.

Be aware that the California Highway Patrol is vigilant here: designate a non-drinking driver for safety's sake. Already-opened wine bottles can be legally transported in the trunk but not in the passenger area of the car.

Islands on the Land

Napa Valley, an hour north of San Francisco, is the most famous wine-producing region in the United States. This gentle valley is only about thirty-five miles long and from one to five miles wide. It trends north-south and is drained by the Napa River, a short tidal stream that empties into San Pablo Bay, which in turn opens onto San Francisco Bay. State Highway 29, "the wine road," passes up the valley framed by rolling hills. Along this road are many of the state's best-known wineries. The valley is defined by the Mayacamas Range on the west, with Sonoma County on the

other side, and the lower Howell Range to the east. These low mountains form barriers against the cool ocean fogs to one side and the summer heat of the interior valley on the other. At the northern end of Napa Valley are 4,343-foot-high Mt. St. Helena and the sulfurous spas clustered around Calistoga, the source of California's best-known bottled mineral water.

Both soil and climate in the Napa Valley are perfect for grape growing. Orderly rows of pruned vines staked out on wire trellises blanket the flat valley bottom and billow over the lower foothills. As with all California agricultural landscapes, there is an underlying mathematical rigor to the marching rows. The colors of the valley change with the seasons: in the winter months the landscape here is a deep emerald green; in the spring the new growth on the vines is light green or yellow; in the summer the vines are dark green; and in the fall, at harvest time, the vines turn gold and scarlet and are hung with purple or green clusters of ripe fruit.

While the valley enjoys a moderate climate, with a yearly mean temperature of 57.7°F (14°C), occasional frosts do descend and can decimate the vineyards. Hence the mysterious propellers connected to warming devices that dot the landscape. In mid-April, when chills fall, they serve as giant fans to temper the air. In the newest vineyards, sprinkler systems spray a fine mist that freezes in a thin glazing of ice over the tender leaves and buds. This protective shield insulates the vines from lower, destructive temperatures.

The central part of the valley north of the fog-blocking Yountville Hills is the heart of the great wine region. The climate, soil structure, and varied exposures to sunlight here are most congenial to the prized Chardonnay and the rich, complex Cabernet Sauvignon grapes. Many of the most famous wineries in America cluster here and, in good years, produce world-class vintages. The clear

302

skies, moderately warm temperatures, and gravelly soils of the Napa River flood plain nurture privileged vines and produce noble wines. The Rutherford Bench, the gravelly benchlands west of Highway 29 between Yountville and St. Helena, boasts many famous American wineries, including Robert Mondavi, Beaulieu, Heitz, Oakville, and Inglenook.

Traditionally, wineries were set in dense "islands" of shade trees and palms. Often a pair or row of palms, or some other tall windbreak, announced the entrance to each ranch. Some wineries sit on the floor of the valley nestled in sun-shading trees; others are set back on the low foothills. Wire trellises begin abruptly at right angles to the roadside and stretch back to the hills in taut rows.

The completion of the railroad led to a boom in vineyards and winery construction. The valley is studded with fine old Victorian houses, wineries, warehouses, and excavated hillside caves from the first era of expansion. San Francisco architects of note designed many of these buildings.

A Brief History of Wine Making in California

The Franciscan missionaries were the first to make wine in California. They imported the black grapes now known as "Mission grapes," which produced a heavy wine. In Carpinteria, south of Santa Barbara, *la viña grande*, a mammoth vine planted in mission days, still stands. In the post-Gold Rush period European immigrants from many lands planted vines and produced homemade wines. The key figure, however, in the history of commercial wine making in the state was a Hungarian, Agoston Haraszthy, who persuaded the governor of California to commission him to scour Europe for vines and information in 1861. When Haraszthy returned from his expedition, he brought back with him 150,000 cuttings and the latest

French and German technology. His official report launched scientific viticulture in California. These experimental vines were planted in Sonoma County at Haraszthy's Buena Vista winery.

It took time for Californians to discover the best areas for grape growing. Robert Louis Stevenson noted in 1883 that wine making in California was still in the experimental stage. "The beginning of vine planting is like the beginning of mining for the precious metals," he observed. "The wine-grower also 'prospects.' One corner of land after another is tried with one kind of grape after another. This is a failure; that is better; a third is best. So, bit by bit, they grope about for their Clos Vougeot and Lafitte." In due time viticulture flourished, and when phylloxera devastated the vineyards of Europe in the 1870s and 1880s, cuttings of the pest-resistant American roots were shipped there to be grafted onto European vines.

A different kind of blight attacked California's vineyards fifty years later: the Volstead Act of 1919, which ushered in thirteen years of Prohibition in the United States. This remains one of the strangest chapters in the puritanical history of American manners and morals. Only "medicinal" and sacramental wines could be sold during this time. Many of Napa Valley's vineyards were converted to orchards or cattle ranches. The vital thread of continuity in wine making was snapped. The vineyards that survived grafted over to grapes suitable for shipment to home wine makers. In those years an average of 50,000 carloads of wine grapes were shipped from California, mostly to Italian-American communities in the big Eastern cities. Interestingly, this was enough to produce 375 million bottles of wine, more than the amount produced by the 700 wineries that existed in 1920.

It took about a generation for the art of wine making to revive after the repeal of Prohibition. When it did, it did so with a new technology, including stainless-steel fermentation tanks and many other innovations. The University of California at Davis became the disseminating center for the reborn industry. Today—in everything from planting to tending to picking to crushing—the wine making process is highly automated.

By 1960 the contemporary wine boom was on, and prices for choice land in the valley echoed the boom. In 1970 an acre of prime Napa soil cost $1,000; by 1980—if you could find it—an acre here cost $25,000. In 1971 there were fewer than thirty wineries in the valley; by 1988 there were 240 federally bonded wineries. So-called "boutique wineries" proliferated; Californians who made their fortunes in other places came to Napa Valley to be gentlemen wine makers. Individuals were followed by corporations such as Getty Oil, Atlantic Richfield Oil, Superior Oil, R. J. Reynolds tobacco, the Tejon Ranch, Coca-Cola, Pepsi-Cola, and even a division of the Hughes Corporation went into the grape-growing business. By 1986, California produced about 366 million gallons of wine, about 86 percent of the national wine market.

The City of Napa

Napa Chamber of Commerce, 1900 Jefferson Street, at Hayes, Napa, CA 94558, (707) 226-7455. Open Monday–Friday, 9 A.M.–5 P.M.; and Saturday and Sunday, 10 A.M.–3 P.M.

Of the first, wooden, Napa River-oriented city nothing remains. However, many solid brick and stone railroad-era buildings survive downtown. With the automobile, Napa's commercial activity shifted to large modern shopping centers built north and west of the city near Highway 29, which is a full-scale California freeway with three interchanges west of the city of Napa. The city has

always been the county seat for prosperous Napa County.

Downtown Napa today is a Victorian sampler of California nineteenth-century architecture and twentieth-century urban planning. The **Napa County Historical Society** at 219 First Street has its research library and changing exhibits in the native stone 1902 Goodman Library, a gift from banker George E. Goodman and designed by architect L. M. Turton. It is open Tuesday and Thursday from noon to 4 P.M.; call (707) 224-1739 for information about changing exhibits. Napa's close-in, tree-lined, leafy residential streets are rarely visited and rich in perfectly perserved Victorian houses. The blocks south of Division Street and the Victorian Gothic First Presbyterian Church of 1874 are well worth careful exploration.

Trefethen Vineyards

Three miles north of Napa at 1160 Oak Knoll Avenue, Napa, CA 94558; (707) 255-7700. By appointment; no public tours or tastings but vineyards and production facilities can be seen. The 1886 winery barn is a classic utilitarian California farm building.

Yountville

Tiny Yountville takes its name from George Calvert Yount, a North Carolina-born trapper who entered California in 1831, became a naturalized Mexican citizen, and obtained a land grant to 11,000-acre Rancho Caymus here in the Napa Valley. The town is canted slightly off the highway. The old brick Groezinger winery built in the 1870s has been converted into a tourist boutique complex called **Vintage 1870** (closed Monday). The town gem is **Mustards Grill**, 7399 St. Helena Highway; call (707) 944-2424 for reservations. Mustards serves lunch and dinner daily and has an excellent, moderately priced seasonal menu of "new American" dishes. It boasts a mesquite grill, woodburning oven, and a stylish modern interior.

Domaine Chandon

California Drive, at Yountville off Highway 29, Veterans Home exit, P.O. Box 2470, Yountville, CA 94599. Open Wednesday–Sunday, 11 A.M.–5:30 P.M.; tours; tastings; retail sales; (707) 944-2280 for information and restaurant reservations. Fine French-classic and nouvelle-cuisine restaurant serves lunch and dinner; reservations advised two weeks ahead of time. Sparkling wine, never called "champagne" here, is produced at this modern winery by the traditional *méthode champenoise*. Begun in 1973 by France's Moët-Hennessy, the contemporary winery was designed by San Francisco architects ROMA. The informative tour explains the making of sparkling wine.

Robert Mondavi Winery

7801 St. Helena Highway 29, P.O. Box 106, Oakville, CA 94562. Open daily 10 A.M.–4:30 P.M.; tours; tastings; retail sales; (707) 963-9611. The Robert Mondavi Summer Festival presents Sunday evening jazz concerts in July. Robert Mondavi established this winery in 1966. A great arch and tower distinguish this contemporary California Mission-style stucco building designed by Cliff May. Mondavi and Château Mouton-Rothschild have begun making a Bordeaux-style wine from the Napa Valley's Cabernet Sauvignon and Cabernet Franc grapes.

Skalli-Atkinson Vineyards and Winery

8440 St. Helena Highway, P.O. Box 38, Rutherford, CA 94573. Tours 10 A.M.–4:30 P.M.; (707) 963-4507. This state-of-the-art winery was built by a French vintner with the Italian-sounding name of Skalli. The brand-new winery was built in 1988 behind the Queen Anne-style Atkinson house of 1881. Gordon Ashby designed the informative exhibits.

Inglenook Winery

In Rutherford on Highway 29; P.O. Box 19, Rutherford, CA 94573. Open daily 10 A.M.–5 P.M.; (707) 963-7184. Established in 1879 and a property of Heublein, Inc. since 1964, this winery is set in a mature "island" of landscaping. A modern winery is tucked behind the fine large Victorian building designed by William Mooser in 1879.

Rutherford

The small town of Rutherford grew up around the railroad station located here. The acclaimed, and expensive, **Auberge du Soleil** prepares French cuisine with a California touch. This restaurant-hotel serves lunch and a *prix fixe* dinner daily. A terraced dining room has views of the valley. Located at 180 Rutherford Hill Road, Rutherford; call (707) 963-1211 for reservations.

St. Helena: Main Street Jewel

The St. Helena Chamber of Commerce, 1080 Main Street, Highway 29, P.O. Box 124, St. Helena, CA 94574 is located in an appropriately inconspicuous building on the right-hand side of the road on the way north from San Francisco. Good selection of brochures and information.

The jewel of St. Helena's main street is the brick and timber Richie Building at **1331 Main Street**, designed by the Corlett Brothers of Napa in 1892 and highly ornamented with spindle work and fancy trimmings. Shops occupy the ground floor; the Masons met in the auditorium upstairs. Across the street is the less elaborate but still fine pressed-brick **Odd Fellows Building** of 1885. It was a common pattern in small California agricultural towns for the town merchants' Masonic hall to be paired with the less fancy Odd Fellows' hall in the center of town. The farmers' simpler

Grange Hall was usually on a cheaper plot on a county road outside the towns.

Prosperity, as evidenced in the high-quality shops that pepper Main Street, has permitted St. Helena to preserve her small town form. No large shopping center on the edge of town turns this nineteenth-century main street into a retail desert. Picnickers will want to stop at **The Model Bakery**, 1357 Main Street, to buy bread with herbs; some is baked with fragrant rosemary. The best art gallery in town is **Henry Evans, Printmaker**, at 1124 Pine Street, P.O. Box 640, St. Helena, CA 94574, (707) 963-2126; gallery hours are 12 to 5 P.M. Saturday and Sunday. Evans' botanical prints of California flora are contemporary classics and make artistic and evocative reminders of your trip. Literary buffs may want to see the **Silverado Museum**, 1490 Library Lane, P.O. Box 409, St. Helena, CA 94574, (707) 963-3757, which is open 12 to 4 P.M. daily, except Monday and holidays. Housed in its own wing of the St. Helena Public Library Center built in 1979, this specialized museum is devoted to the works of Robert Louis Stevenson. A block east off Main Street at Railroad Avenue near Hunt Avenue is the **Miramonte Restaurant** serving French country-style cooking; dinner only; Wednesday through Sunday; patio; expensive; (707) 963-3970. **Tra Vigne Restaurant**, at 1050 Charter Oak Avenue immediately off Highway 29 just south of downtown has outside as well as indoor lunch and dinner daily. They serve fine northern Italian cuisine and memorable house-baked bread. Prices are moderate, call (707) 963-4444 for reservations.

Beringer Vineyards

2000 Main Street, St. Helena, CA 94574; (707) 963-7115. The Beringer Winery dates from 1876, and has its wine tasting and retail in the old Beringer house built in 1883 and designed by William M. Mooser, Sr. This "Rhine castle" is built of stone and half-timbering. A tour includes cool caverns where wines are stored. Chinese-American laborers excavated these caves a century ago.

Christian Brothers Greystone Winery

2555 Main Street, P.O. Box 311, St. Helena, CA 94574. Open daily 10:30 A.M.–4:30 P.M.; tours; tastings; retail sales; (707) 963-2719.

Built for William Bowers Bourn in 1888 and designed by Percy & Hamilton, this imposing stone winery is the largest masonry structure erected in the Napa Valley. The Christian Brothers, a teaching order of Roman Catholic Church, produce both table and sacramental wines here.

Bothe-Napa Valley State Park

Four miles north of St. Helena at 3801 St. Helena Highway North/Highway 29; (707) 942-4575. For campsite reservations between April and October phone Mistix at 1 (800) 444-7275 in California; out of state, call (619) 452-1950: $3/car, campsites $10/day; swimming pool open mid-June through Labor Day.

This nearly 2,000-acre state park features a water-powered gristmill with a large overshot wheel built in 1846 and recently restored by the State of California. It is a picturesque monument to early agricultural technology. The only public campground in the Napa Valley, the state park is booked solid in the summertime.

Clos Pegase

1060 Dunaweal Lane, one mile south of Calistoga, P.O. Box 305, Calistoga, CA 94515 (look for the Stonegate Winery sign south of Calistoga). Tastings daily from 10:30 A.M. to 4:30 P.M.; (707) 942-4981.

Opened in 1987, this new winery is the result of an architectural competition juried at the San Francisco Museum of Modern Art and won by Michael Graves Architects, with painter Edward Schmidt. In Greek mythology, Pegasus, the winged horse from heaven, touched his hoof on Mount Helikon and broke open the spring of the Muses. Here Michael Graves, a professor of architecture at Princeton, has set an "archaic," almost Minoan orange monument against a green, oak-clad volcanic knoll that juts out of the narrow valley floor here. This is a great work of contemporary architecture, worthy of the valley it crowns.

Calistoga / Silverado Trail

Underground at the head of the Napa Valley is a superheated pool of 250-degree mineral water that erupts in hot springs and can be tapped by wells. These medicinal hot springs were frequented by the Native Americans. Calistoga's motels and low-key spas offer mud baths, hot mineral water Jacuzzis, saunas, massages, and blanket wraps. The mud baths are small, square, tile tubs filled with a dark, bubbling goo made of Canadian peat and Calistoga volcanic ash infused with hot mineral water. When submerged to your neck, you feel a sense of weightlessness. Most spas have separate baths for men and women. Prices range from about $40 to $130, depending on treatments, massages, and such extras as facials. The Calistoga Bookstore at 1343 Lincoln Avenue, is good for local maps, guides, and books on wine. Otherwise the shopping and restaurants here are not noteworthy. French-owned Source Perrier today owns the bottling plant for California's best-known mineral water. It is just outside the town near the head of the Silverado Trail (no tours).

Just outside Calistoga, at the east end of Lincoln Avenue, is the beginning of the Silverado Trail, a scenic, less-traveled road that skirts the base of the hills on the east side of Napa Valley and ends at Trancas Street, just north of Napa. It and Highway 29, together with several cross roads, form a ladderlike pattern in the valley.

Mt. St. Helena / Robert Louis Stevenson State Park

Mt. St. Helena rises 4,343 feet from the Mayacamas Range to dominate the Napa Valley. Russian explorers named it in the early nineteenth century in honor of their empress. Silver and quicksilver were mined here in the mid-nineteenth century. Robert Louis Stevenson honeymooned in an abandoned silver mine seven miles north of Calistoga in what is now Robert Louis Stevenson State Park, which he modeled Spyglass Hill in *Treasure Island* after. The five-mile Robert Louis Stevenson Memorial Trail climbs to the summit of Mt. St. Helena; the state park claims 3,670 acres. On a clear day the view stretches from the formidable Sierra Nevada to distant San Francisco. The verdant Napa Valley spreads out at your feet and in the fall the vines are tinged with scarlet. Call (707) 942-4575 for park information.

The East Bay

The Oakland Museum: The Museum of California

The Oakland Museum's second name, "the Museum of California," is more accurate than its formal name. Located at 1000 Oak Street, Oakland, CA 94607, one block east of the Lake Merritt BART station and five blocks east of the Nimitz Freeway. Open Wednesday–Saturday 10 A.M.–5 P.M., Sunday 12–7 P.M.; (415) 273-3401. Inexpensive parking under the museum.

The Oakland Museum is the outstanding regional museum and presents all California in microcosm in three sections devoted to the art, history, and ecology of the state. Opened in 1969 and designed by Kevin Roche, John Dinkeloo and Associates, with Dan Kiley, landscape architect, this outstanding contemporary building, with its courtyard and landscaped terraces, is a modern Hanging Gardens of Babylon. Much of the building is underground, tucked into its gently sloping four-block site, with lavish plantings atop it. The art gallery presents select Californian works, from the earliest artist-explorers to the latest trendsetters, with an important display of early twentieth-century paintings and Craftsman artifacts. The history gallery displays pieces from the largest collection of Californiana in existence—everything from Indian pictographs to the recent past presented in chronological sequence. The natural history section is arranged to take you on an imaginary walk across the eight different environmental zones of the state, from the Pacific shore to the Sierra crest and the Great Basin. This last section is particularly handsome, with meticulous models showing the geology, botany, and animal life of California. The museum's bookshop is good for California art books and natural history guides.

The University of California, Berkeley: The Athens of the West

BART links San Francisco's Market Street with downtown Berkeley; the campus is a few blocks east of the Berkeley BART stop. A more scenic return to San Francisco is offered by the AC Transit F bus, which passes south down Shattuck Avenue in downtown Berkeley, across the San Francisco-Oakland Bay Bridge, to the TransBay Terminal in Downtown San Francisco.

The Visitor Center in the lobby of the Student Union, near Telegraph Avenue and Bancroft Way, can provide you with a map and walking tour booklet about the 1,232-acre campus with its more than 320 buildings. The information desk here can also tell you about the day's events.

California included a state university in its first state constitution and, along with Michigan and Wisconsin, was among the first states to realize the tremendous economic and cultural benefits a great public university could bring. The University of California at Berkeley, familiarly known as Cal, has its origins in the Contra Costa Academy, founded in Oakland in 1853 and directed by Congregationalist minister Henry Durant. This high school became the College of California in 1855. In 1860 a new site was dedicated at what is now Founders' Rock in Berkeley. Absorbed and chartered by the state in 1868, the college moved to Berkeley in 1873, the same year that it graduated its first class of twelve men. Today Berkeley is the flagship campus of the nine-branch University of California system.

The University of California at Berkeley is situated directly east of the Golden Gate. Frederick Law Olmsted and Calvert Vaux produced the first campus plan in 1865, with an axis (now Campanile Way) pointed toward this dramatic feature. But the most important moment in the campus' history occurred when Mrs. Phoebe Apperson Hearst decided to found a school of mining here in memory of her mine-owning husband, Senator George Hearst. Guided by Bernard Maybeck, she was induced to sponsor an international competition for a new campus plan that was juried in 1899. A Paris architect, Emile Henri Bénard, won with a grand, if not grandiose, plan reflecting the monumental ideals of the École des Beaux Arts. But Bénard refused to leave Paris to execute the plan and the university Regents selected École des Beaux Arts-trained New York architect John Galen Howard, a member of the fourth place team, to adapt the Bénard plan to reality and to carry out the building of the new campus.

Howard became University Architect, revised the plan, designed many of the university's best buildings, and founded the Department of Architecture. He set his formal "Athens of the West" between the tree-lined banks of the north and south branches of Strawberry Creek.

University House, the president's house, is a Renaissance villa in a walled garden; Low Library could house the pope; and the Women's Gymnasium of 1925 is a Hollywood Roman Empire hallucination. Also notable is the Howard-designed Greek Theater of 1903, modeled on the theater at Epidaurus and donated by William Randolph Hearst. Around this monumental white-granite core, Howard also designed many less-costly but equally artistic brown-shingled frame buildings, a few of which survive. Unfortunately the explosive growth of the campus after World War II ignored Howard's fine plan and crowded the campus with indifferent, if not positively unsightly, structures you cannot fail to notice. The lush campus landscaping distracts the eye from some, though not all, of these later behemoths.

The open spaces surrounding the Student Union, Sproul Hall, and, one level down, Zellerbach Auditorium exemplify the best of mid-1960s design. Designed in 1965 by DeMars & Reayl/Hardison, with Lawrence Halprin Associates as landscape designers, this is one of the few California "plazas" that actually functions like a plaza. Here is the social center of the campus, the best spot to sit and watch the ebb and flow of the back-pack-toting students and the activities of the expositors of the social, political, or religious trends of the moment.

Beyond Sproul Plaza is John Galen Howard's beautiful **Sather Gate**, the ceremonial entrance to the campus, completed in 1910. The bronzework of this gateless gate is especially handsome. The pedestrian bridge here spans Strawberry Creek, the chief natural feature of the central campus. Beyond the gate are the academic buildings. Walk straight ahead between Wheeler and Durant Halls, both by Howard, to Campanile Way. Walk up this handsome axis to the lofty campanile.

The symbolic center of the campus is the 307-foot-high, steel-frame, white-granite-clad campanile, **Sather Tower**,

modeled on the bell tower of St. Mark in Venice and dedicated in 1914. An elevator takes you to the observation loggia at the top, open daily from 10 A.M.–4:15 P.M. except university holidays; small fee. A twelve-bell carillon is played here three times a day. The soaring tower is John Galen Howard's masterpiece and is one of the most beautiful architectural embellishments in California. It is capped by a bronze light that makes real the university's motto, "Fiat Lux"—Let there be a light.

From the Campanile Esplanade there is a superb view down Campanile Way, across the Bay, to the Golden Gate and its great bridge. The white building to the right houses the Bancroft Library, with its famous collection of Western Americana, and the Doe Library. The red brick Victorian structure to the left is South Hall, built in 1878 (the oldest building on the campus). Beyond the looming concrete bulk of Evans Hall is Mining Circle and the handsome granite-clad **Hearst Mining Building**, completed by Howard in 1907. Its Memorial Vestibule, with its steel-lattice trusses and tile vaults with skylit domes, is reminiscent of Labrouste's Reading Room at the Bibliothèque Nationale in Paris.

Across Bancroft Way is the modernistic **University Art Museum**, open Wednesday–Sunday from 11 A.M.–5 P.M.; small fee; (415) 642-0808. Designed by Mario Ciampi and opened in 1970, within this concrete ziggurat is a great space and a series of cantilevered ramps and galleries with both permanent and changing exhibits. The art displayed here tends toward the unconventional and large-scale. A permanent collection of Hans Hofmann works occupies the uppermost gallery. On the ground floor is the outstanding **Pacific Film Archive**; its intimate theater screens both historic and avant-garde works. Pacific Film Archive information can be obtained by calling (415) 642-1124. There is a small cafe here as well. The **Lowie Museum of Anthropology** located in Kroeber

Hall, is open weekdays, 10 A.M.–4:30 P.M.; Saturday–Sunday, 12–4:30 P.M.; small fee. The museum mounts small but select changing exhibits from one of the finest anthropological collections. **Lawrence Hall of Science**, a science museum and planetarium, sits on the ridge above the campus. Open 10 A.M.–4:30 on weekdays and until 9 P.M. on Thursday; open 10 A.M.–5 P.M. on weekends; small fee; phone 642-5132 for planetarium schedule. The **Botanical Garden** nearby, located in Strawberry Canyon is open from 9 A.M.–4:45 P.M. daily; free. Among many other features, it boasts a fine cactus collection.

Berkeley might have the best collection of bookstores in the nation. University Press Books at 2430 Bancroft Way, near Telegraph, across the street from the campus, is a unique resource for serious books in all fields, 548-0585; cafe attached. Cody's Books at 2454 Telegraph Avenue, at Haste, is a superb general bookstore and has a postmodern cafe attached, 845-7852. Several other interesting bookshops are located nearby along Telegraph Avenue. Black Oak Books, 1491 Shattuck Avenue, off Vine, is a literary landmark and presents readings on occasion, 486-0698. Athletic clothing is the other Berkeley shopping specialty.

Berkeley's and the Bay Area's gastronomic monument is Alice Waters's Chez Panisse at 1517 Shattuck Avenue, between Cedar and Vine, 548-5049, worth the trip as the French would say. Reservations are essential; closed Sunday; expensive but memorable.

If you have a special interest in Northern California's distinctive regional architectural flowering of the early twentieth century, you should explore the North Side Berkeley hills beyond the campus' North Gate at Hearst and Euclid. The tangle of streets and paths east of Euclid Avenue and north of Cedar Street— including Rose Walk, Buena Vista Way, La Loma Avenue, and several *cul-de-sacs* in this hilly terrain—contains a concentration of deliberately rustic, brown-shingled houses designed by Bernard Maybeck, John Galen Howard and many other gifted architectural designers on the University of California School of Architecture faculty. Those influenced by the Arts and Crafts Movement sought "honest" houses simply furnished and integrated with their settings.

Under the influence of the Hillside Club, the originally grass-covered hills, with their fine view of the Bay far below, were laid out with contoured streets threaded together by pedestrian paths. Over time the houses here have been overgrown by a jungle of trees and vines, making the architecture somewhat hard to see and fulfilling, perhaps all too well, the original intention of blending with nature. The intellectual and stylistic roots of Northern California's environmentalist mentality are here in this bosky enclave. If you are driving, you should park and explore the area on foot, since that is the only way fully to experience this unique neighborhood. Individual houses are not as important as the total effect achieved by this seemingly unplanned, planned environment.

John Muir National Historic Site
4202 Alhambra Valley Road, Martinez, CA 94553
Open daily 10 A.M. to 4:30 P.M. except Thanksgiving, Christmas, and New Year; small fee; (415) 228-8860

Take Highway 4 to Martinez and the Alhambra Valley Road exit, turn left under the freeway and park in the lot for the John Muir National Historic Site. By public transit, take the BART Concord line to Walnut Creek; transfer to the 116 County Connection bus (676-7500), which runs Monday to Saturday, between 10:30 A.M. and 3:30 P.M., and which stops at the Muir House.

John Muir, author of some of America's finest nature writing, the great champion of wilderness and its conservation, and first president of the Sierra

Club, was born in Scotland in 1838, studied geology and botany at the University of Wisconsin, and explored on foot the Midwest, Gulf Coast, Alaska, and the Sierra. In his forties he married Louise Strentzel, the daughter of an Alhambra Valley fruit rancher. Here between 1881 and 1891 he managed his and his father-in-law's fruit ranches. When his father-in-law died, Muir and his wife moved into this great square 1882 Italianate house. (The Martinez adobe of 1849 is also on the property.) From here Muir wrote and conducted his campaigns to save wilderness areas from destruction. He agitated for the preservation of Yosemite, which was made a National Park in 1890. He also persuaded the Cleveland and Theodore Roosevelt administrations to create the first federal forest reservations.

The National Park Service has furnished the house in period; Muir's own desk is in the recreated study upstairs. A fine brief film on Muir's life is shown and a shop here carries some of Muir's undying books. *The Wilderness World of John Muir*, edited by Edwin Way Teale, is the best compendium and makes a fine companion to Yosemite and California's great natural wonders. Maps can be secured here for Muir's grave, which lies about a mile to the south in a small private burial ground that can be glimpsed in the fields behind 5031 Alhambra Valley Road.

Tao House / Eugene O'Neill National Historic Site
P.O. Box 402, Danville, CA 94526. The two-hour National Park Service tour and the van ride to Tao House are free, but reservations are required; phone (415) 838-0249. The van departs Wednesday through Sunday at 10 A.M. and 1:30 P.M. from Danville's Clock Tower parking lot on Hartz Avenue. By public transit, take BART's Concord line to the Walnut Creek station, transfer to the 121 County Connection bus (676-7500), which runs to Danville

approximately every 30 minutes except Sundays and holidays.

When playwright Eugene O'Neill won the Nobel prize, he had built for himself and his wife, actress Carlotta Monterey, this spacious house on fifteen acres on Las Trampas Ridge in Contra Costa's scenic San Ramon Valley. The house enjoys a sweeping view of the Bay Area's tallest peak, 3,849-foot Mt. Diablo. O'Neill named his dwelling Tao House after the Chinese philosophy he practiced. The house blends California's white-walled Mission Style with a black-glazed Chinese-looking tile roof. Inside, two carved teak Foo dogs guard the stairs to the study. In this study, between 1937 and 1944, behind three closed doors, O'Neill wrote his last five plays including "The Ice Man Cometh" and "Long Day's Journey into Night." O'Neill gave his manuscripts and books to Yale University, but a National Park Service exhibit here recounts his life from his birth in New York City in 1888 to his death in Boston in 1953.

San Mateo Peninsula

Originally cattle country, the fine climate on the San Mateo Peninsula attracted fruit orchards, especially apricot orchards, by the turn of the century. Today it is California's premier high-technology industrial zone, known as Silicon Valley, where smokestackless laboratories and factories produce microchips, the fingernail-size silicon wafers that govern computers, modern weapons, and electronic games. This is one of the places that puts California in the forefront of the modern world. The suburbscape here consists of pale, one-story industrial park buildings that are set back from the road behind landscaped parking lots and sport tasteful, low-to-the-ground signs bearing utterly uncommunicative high-tech names or inscrutable initials.

Professor Frederick Terman of Stanford University is generally credited with being the father of Silicon Valley. In 1937 he persuaded two of his brightest students, William Hewlett and David Packard, to found their own company locally rather than go east in search of employment. With $500 and a rented garage in Palo Alto, the two young engineers founded Hewlett-Packard, which by 1976 had passed $1 billion per year in sales of computers and electronic instruments. With the invention of the transistor by Schockley, Bardeen, and Brattain in 1957 and of the microelectric integrated circuit by Noyce and Kilby, also in 1957, the groundwork was laid for the development of the modern computer.

Stanford University: A Pinnacle of Regional Environmental Design

Guide and Visitor Service: Stanford University, Stanford, CA 94305. Tours: (415) 497-2862. Daily Events: (415) 497-0336. Excellent map available in Hoover Tower lobby.
By car from San Francisco: A half-hour drive south on I-280 or Highway 101 in Palo Alto.
Bus from San Francisco: SamTrans 7F from TransBay Terminal. For information call (415) 965-3100.
Train from San Francisco: Southern Pacific Depot, 4th and Townsend streets; stops at Palo Alto railroad station.
Campus Transit: Free shuttle bus on weekdays from the Stanford Shopping Center, the "Marguerite," from 11:30 A.M. to 1:30 P.M.

New York-born Leland Stanford amassed one of the largest fortunes in the West as one of the four founders of the Central (later Southern) Pacific Railroad, the first transcontinental railroad and the utility that made the United States a continental market. The railroad was built with generous federal subsidies and given a baron's portion of the public lands in California. Stanford

and his wife, Jane, had one child, Leland Stanford, Jr., who was raised like the crown prince of California in his parents' Nob Hill mansion. But in 1884 the boy died of typhoid fever at fifteen while on a trip to Italy with his parents. The Stanfords were disconsolate. The Episcopalian minister who traveled back home with the Stanfords and their son's casket introduced the couple to spiritualism. Through séances they felt they achieved contact with the lost Leland, Jr. The Stanfords determined to preserve the memory of their son by founding a university and naming it after him.

The Stanfords gave the new institution, founded in 1885, 83,000 acres of what were described at the time as "the most valuable estates in California," consisting of three great ranches. The Palo Alto Farm became the university campus; hence Stanford's nickname: The Farm. It consisted of 7,200 choice, sunny acres—the finest horse country in California and a classic stretch of California landscape. Today the campus embraces 8,200 acres. Part is leased to the Stanford Shopping Center, and other sections are leased to the Stanford Industrial Park.

In 1888 Leland Stanford engaged Frederick Law Olmsted to do the landscape plan, and Shepley, Rutan and Coolidge to design the original buildings. All were Boston-area designers. The strong hand of the client ruled in both landscape and architecture. The result is one of the most forceful, coherent, and successful architectural and landscape designs from the late 1880s in the nation. Charles Allerton Coolidge was a *protégé* of the great Henry Hobson Richardson, and in Stanford's Old Quad he fused Richardsonian massing, arches, and decorative detail with Mission-style red tile roofs and "southwestern" landscaping to create one of the region's earliest and best Mission-style designs. Emphatic yellow sandstone arches link the old campus buildings into a whole around a central court with islands of semitropical landscaping.

Stanford had clear political purposes in mind when he formulated his grant of endowment. Fundamental principles of American government were to be taught so that "agrarianism and communism can have only an ephemeral existence." Another purpose of the new university was to provide "complete protection against the monopoly of the rich"—a curious end for a fortune extracted by a railroad commonly known as "the Octopus."

Two features of Stanford's donation were novel and progressive. The first was the prohibition of "sectarian teaching" and the desire for an ecumenical atmosphere—basically Protestant, but with a consistent interest in Far Eastern religious thought. The second progressive feature was the specific inclusion of women students.

Stanford has become one of the great American universities. Its buildings and grounds are the finest extensive architectural and landscape monuments of the booming 1880s in the West. The visitor who lingers even briefly in its arcaded quadrangles will immediately know why this institution commands such fierce loyalty among its sons and daughters. The bright blue skies, the warm, yellow sandstone cloisters, the vast and immaculate grounds, and the serene air of this unhurried, insulated world leave an unforgettable impression.

The approach to Stanford University up **Palm Drive** provides a sense of space, power, wealth, and ease. Traveling almost due south you pass through a large, unbuilt reserve that separates the university from the outside world.

At the head of Palm Drive is the sunken **Oval** and the north face of the **Outer Quad**. There is visitor parking here. (There is also visitor parking in front of the University Museum where this walk ends.) The best procedure is to park here and walk to the lobby of Hoover Tower and secure the excellent

bird's-eye-view map of the campus, then return to the broad stairs and the front terrace.

Hoover Tower, designed by Bakewell and Brown, looms over the campus in a vaguely Moderne style. A thirty-five-bell Belgian carillon, cast for the New York World's Fair of 1939, was installed in the tower at its completion in 1941. The carillon is played at noon and 5 P.M.

Take the elevator to the observation platform atop the 285-foot-tall tower; from here there is a fine view of the ordered sea of red-tile roofs of the old buildings and the surrounding later ones. South of the Quads are the untouched, oak-dotted hills that billow back to the Coast Range.

To the east, on the flat industrial bayshore, is the enormous gray Moffett Field dirigible Hanger No. 1, built by the Navy in 1933. Today the Ames Research Center occupies part of this base. There, it has been reported, is Illiac 4, a system of sixty-four massive computers connected to hydrophones planted in the world's seabed. They monitor the ocean for the sounds of Soviet submarines. Beyond Moffett Field is the flat, blue sheet of San Francisco Bay and on its other side the Contra Costa range.

Leaving the Tower, you can visit paired rooms in its base with mementos of both Herbert and Lou Henry Hoover.

A triple-arched gate at the far end of Memorial Court leads to the **Inner Quad**, the heart of the university. This rectangular quadrangle runs east-west and creates a minor axis crossing the major north-south axis of Palm Drive. This change of direction makes the three-acre Inner Quad the crossroads, or center, of the campus. It is completely surrounded by arcades with semicircular arches. Behind these arcades are twelve one-story buildings.

Integrated into the center of the far side of the quad is the façade of the **Memorial Church**, originally constructed in 1903 and then rebuilt with a steel skeleton in 1913 after the earthquake. The base of the opulent church has the most exuberant stone carving of any Stanford building. Originally San Francisco architect Clinton Day modeled the design on Richardson's famous Trinity Church in Boston. But in 1906, when the eighty-foot-high central tower fell, the church was rebuilt and provided with a humdrum dome in place of the daring tower. The interior has some fine mosaic work and beautiful stained glass windows.

Beginning at the front door of the church and running west under the arcade are numbered plaques, underneath which each senior class has deposited its memorabilia. Note the seemingly infinite regression of the arches ahead and the strong patterns of the window frames with their sunken windows. Continue around the Inner Quad, passing Memorial Court where you entered, turn right at the corner to the east entrance gate. Leave the Quad and walk toward the round fountain.

Beyond the fountain is the **Green Library** of 1919, designed by San Francisco architects Bakewell and Brown. Nearby is the Thomas Welton Stanford Art Gallery with changing exhibits. From the fountain walk under the row of oaks toward the antlerlike fountain by Aristides Demetrios in White Plaza. The Stanford University Bookstore is near the fountain and is a good place for books and souvenirs. Beyond and to the right is **Tresidder Memorial Union**, where you can buy something to eat and sit on the terrace under the trees among the students.

Walk to the Oval and down its center. One block down Palm Drive to the left is Museum Way, which leads to the **Leland Stanford Junior Museum**, an amalgam of fine art and Stanford-family memorabilia. Though architecturally dull, it was designed by Ernest Ransome in 1892 using a then-revolutionary material: reinforced concrete. The Asian art and the Rodin collection are

particularly notable. The famous gold spike driven by Stanford in 1869 to mark the completion of the transcontinental railroad is here, along with photographs by Eadweard Muybridge of horses in motion that were forerunners of the motion picture.

An appropriate conclusion to your visit is the gray-granite, templelike **Stanford Mausoleum**, set in the spacious **University Arboretum**. Four marble sphinxes guard the tomb—two male sphinxes in front and two female sphinxes to the rear. Here lie father, mother, and son next to a truly magnificent ancient oak.

Near the Mausoleum is a smaller circular path that contains the fascinating living ruins of the Stanfords' cactus garden. It is a quiet, abandoned spot where the century-old plants have gone wild, creating a botanical tangle with its own curious charm. Cactus gardens were very popular in Victorian California, and this was once one of the most extensive.

To see the exterior of the **Hanna House**, designed by Frank Lloyd Wright in 1937, walk up Mayfield Avenue and turn right at Frenchman's Road. At number 737 is one of Wright's first hexagonal grid houses. Even its beds were originally hexagonal. Not surprisingly, this turned out to be impractical. The red brick and stained-wood horizontal house is set between old oaks in perfect harmony with its hilltop site. All along Mayfield Avenue you will see a varied array of modern California houses built for Stanford's faculty.

The **Lou Henry Hoover House** was built in 1919 on Cabrillo Avenue at the head of Santa Ynez Street. (A closer view of the back of the house is possible from Mirada Avenue.) This fascinating, stucco-covered, concrete-and-hollow-tile house was designed by Mrs. Hoover, who had unconventional ideas. Its flat roofs were used for terraces connected by outside stairways. In style it is almost pueblolike, or cubist. While its exterior is fresh and innovative, its interior is finished with Tudor-style woodwork. It was here that Herbert Hoover received news in 1928 that he had been elected president. Today the house serves Stanford's presidents.

In the hills behind the Old Quad, and extending underneath Interstate 280, is the two-mile-long **Linear Accelerator** operated by Stanford for the U.S. Department of Energy. Used in particle physics research, this is the most powerful electron accelerator yet built. Tours are available; call (415) 854-3300 for hours; free.

Filoli: Great Estate and Garden
Filoli is on Cañada Road twenty-five miles south of San Francisco near the Edgewood Road exit off scenic I-280. Reservations can be made in advance by writing to Garden Tours, Filoli Center, Cañada Road, Woodside, CA 94062. There are tours Tuesday through Friday and on Saturday morning; admission charge; or phone (415) 364-2880.

This great Georgian Revival estate designed in 1916 by Willis Polk for utility baron William Bowers Bourn has some of the finest gardens in America. Bourn was the heir to a Gold Rush mining fortune (see Tour 7) and a utility magnate who headed the San Francisco Gas Company and San Francisco's Spring Valley Water Company. On the choicest part of the huge, ancient-oak-dotted Spring Valley watershed, Bourn built this mansion and began its extensive gardens. The name Filoli is derived from his motto: "Fight, Love, Live." The original gardens were designed by Bruce Porter and Isabella Worn and lavishly loved by Mrs. William P. Roth, the subsequent owner of the estate who donated it to the National Trust for Historic Preservation. The sixteen acres of gardens are laid out as a succession of distinct areas leading from the formal Walled Garden to Yew Alley. April and May are the peak months for floral displays.

Monterey Bay and Peninsula

Santa Cruz: Turn-of-the-Century Seaside Resort

Best Days and Times: The Santa Cruz Boardwalk is open from Memorial Day to Labor Day and on weekends the rest of the year. The town offers varied accommodations, including motels and hotels.

Information: The Convention and Visitors Bureau, P.O. Box 1476, Santa Cruz, CA 95061, (408) 423-6927, provides walking-tour maps of Victorian neighborhoods.

Santa Cruz sits on the northern edge of Monterey Bay, opposite the city of Monterey. The coastal mountains, with redwoods in their canyons, rise behind it. A mission was founded here on August 28, 1791, near the San Lorenzo River, and named *Mission La Exaltacion de la Santa Cruz*, the mission of the Exaltation of the Sacred Cross. This mission was abandoned and vanished. The present building outside town is a replica and is not noteworthy.

Modern Santa Cruz began when a public bathhouse was built near the beach in 1865. Redwood logging and some manufacturing gave economic life to the city. In 1904 a huge casino-dance hall was built and day-trippers from San Francisco were lured to the town. A boardwalk (now paved with asphalt) was begun in 1903 by the Santa Cruz Beach, Cottage, and Tent City Corporation. It became the democratic resort for the northern half of the state. While nearly all of California's turn-of-the-century seaside resorts have sadly been demolished—San Diego's Belmont Park, the Long Beach Pike, and San Francisco's Playland—Santa Cruz's **Boardwalk** is still going strong. The 1907 Casino has gone through many alterations but is still here. The 1910 carousel, with its fine horses carved by Charles I. D. Looff, has been restored. The Giant Dipper roller coaster, designed by Arthur Looff and built in 1924, dominates the Boardwalk like some huge sculpture and is especially beautiful at night when illuminated by its 3,150 light bulbs. Painted white with a red track, the huge timber rollercoaster is one of the last and the best of its kind. It and the carousel are both on the National Register of Historic Places. There is an agreeable, nostalgic quality to an afternoon in this fun zone where you can walk about eating french-fried artichokes and looking at the rides and their riders, a tangy blend of innocence and sleaze and unself-consciousness lacking in the overproduced and too-expensive "theme parks" of the present. Second and Third streets on Beach Hill behind the north end of the Boardwalk have many fine Victorian houses, including some impressive examples of the Shingle style of the 1890s.

The local population of the town of Santa Cruz are zealous guardians of the town's appearance. Many fine Victorian, Craftsman, and even a few Moderne stucco buildings in Santa Cruz make a day of random exploration of side streets a delight. The welcoming, courtyarded, Monterey Revival-style Santa Cruz City Hall designed by C. J. Rylan in 1937–1938 and built by the WPA says a lot about the city's self-respect. The tactful wing added in 1967 and designed by Robert Stevens Associates says even more.

Located in the hills northwest of town, the campus of the **University of California at Santa Cruz** consists of 2,000 acres of rolling meadows and redwood forests overlooking Monterey Bay. It was once the Henry Cowell Ranch, site of a lime quarry and cement factory and later of a cattle ranch. In 1961 the Regents of the University of California purchased the handsome site and engaged John Carl Warnecke and Thomas D.

Church to prepare the campus plan. Their idea was to keep the rolling meadows open and to build the college buildings in small clusters beneath the hillside redwoods. While the recent buildings on other major UC campuses are banal, the aim here from the first was to produce an architectural showplace, and in this the regents have succeeded. Taken together these structures, designed by a variety of outstanding architects, are the best collection of designs from the 1960s and 1970s in California.

At the entrance to the campus, several of the old ranch and lime-processing structures have been carefully preserved. This is one of the very few places in the state where you can see preserved examples of typical vernacular structures from a century ago. Included in this grouping are a granary, a cooperage, lime kilns, a blacksmith's shop, a bull barn, a slaughterhouse, a powder house, a cookhouse, workers' cabins, and a horse barn. Most have been converted to new uses, though a few are maintained as stabilized ruins. At the red-painted, wood-and-stone Cook House, you can secure a guide map and also inquire about student-led tours; or call (408) 429-4008 for information.

The City of Monterey: California's First Capital

Information: The Visitor Center for Monterey State Historic Park (behind the Conference Center) is at 210 Oliver Street, Monterey, CA 93940; (408) 649-2836. Good maps are available of state historic sites. The Monterey Chamber of Commerce, P.O. Box 1770, is located at 380 Alvarado Street, Monterey, CA 93940, and can provide its *Hotel and Motel Guide* and its *Restaurant Guide*; call (408) 649-3200. The best map is the AAA "Tour Map of Monterey," which has a detailed map of downtown Monterey.

Best Time to Visit: Summer can be very congested, especially in quaint Carmel. Plan your visit for early autumn through late May, instead. The famous three-day **Monterey Jazz Festival** is held each September at the Monterey County Fairgrounds. Contact the Chamber of Commerce for dates and information. The **Adobe Tour**, held by the Monterey History and Art Association each April is the single best day to visit Monterey. Write the Association at 550 Calle Principal, P.O. Box 805, Monterey, CA 93940, or call (408) 372-2608 for information.

Monterey is a somewhat open harbor sheltered to the south by a rocky, forested peninsula. The Bay of Monterey was discovered in 1542 by the Spanish explorer Juan Rodríguez Cabrillo, who named it La Bahia de los Piños (The Bay of the Pines). In 1602 Sebastián Vizcaíno, sailing under orders from the Viceroy of Mexico, Gaspar de Zúniga, landed near the mouth of the Carmel River. Vizcaíno named the best anchorage he discovered on his exploration—he missed San Francisco Bay—after Viceroy Zúniga, the Count of Monterey. A settlement was established here in June, 1770, and in 1775 it was made the capital of Alta California. The bay provided the chief reason for settling here.

On June 3, 1770, an expedition led by Gaspar de Portolá and accompanied by Father Junípero Serra established a presidio, or fort, here (today the U.S. Army Presidio outside town) and soon thereafter a mission at nearby Carmel. Under Spanish rule between 1770 and 1820, Monterey consisted of a walled stockade within which the inhabitants lived. The British explorer Vancouver visited the place in 1792, and in 1796 the first American ship, the *Otter* from Boston, dropped anchor in the open bay. In 1822 the remote outpost became part of the new Mexican Republic after its break with Spain. During this period adobe houses sprang up outside the walled stockade and the fort evolved into a town. By the 1830s traders from Boston and other United States ports began frequenting the port.

Some Americans stayed, converted to Catholicism, and married into the local Mexican elite. This brief cultural fusion had a marked influence on the architecture of the town. Yankee house builders took Mexican adobe construction and married it with Yankee woodwork in the form of doors, windows, hipped roofs, and, especially, second-floor balconies. Thus was born the Monterey style, California's first local architectural creation.

Property and influence were in the hands of the Californios during the early period, but that quickly changed. With the United States' occupation on July 7, 1846—and United States law—political power, land, and influence passed to the Protestant Yankees. Yankee-imposed county taxes required cash from Californio landowners who had little cash. When their land had to be auctioned off for failure to pay these taxes, wealthy Yankee investors and partnerships snapped it up.

Monterey's early American period was marked by a classic example of barely legal land grabbing. The city of Monterey, as the successor to the Mexican pueblo, held thousands of acres of surrounding property. Delos Ashley, a young lawyer, secured the job of investigating the title of these lands for the city and presented the town with a bill for $991.50. The city treasury was empty, and at Ashley's prompting the city's politicians quietly passed an act to sell the municipal lands to pay the city debt. An obscure notice was published in an out-of-town paper, and a public auction was held on the steps of Colton Hall on February 9, 1859. The only bid was made by Ashley's partner, Scotland-born David Jacks, who offered $1002.50 for 30,000 acres of choice Monterey Peninsula land. Ashley billed the city $11 for drawing up the transfer papers, thus the city ended up with precisely nothing

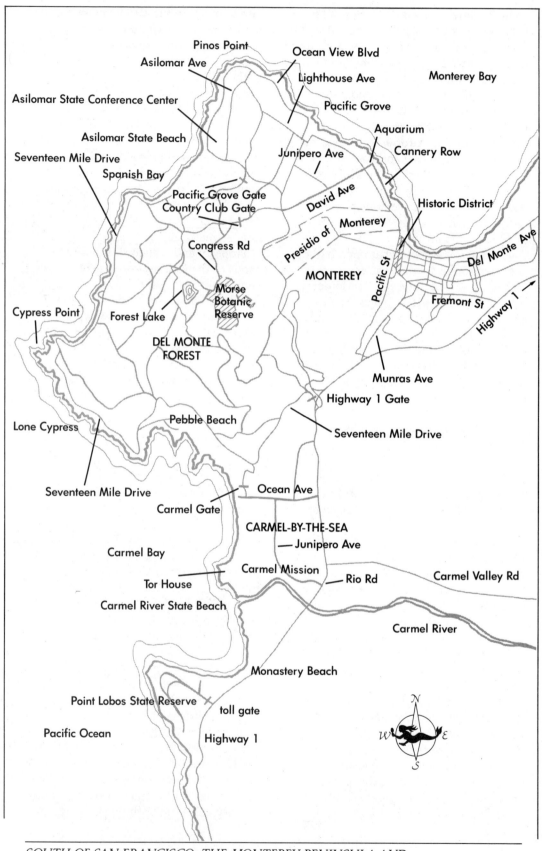

SOUTH OF SAN FRANCISCO: THE MONTEREY PENINSULA AND HISTORIC MONTEREY

from the auction. Eventually Jacks bought out Ashley for $500 and ended as the largest landowner on the peninsula.

By the late nineteenth century, San Franciscans in particular had discovered the charms of the sleepy fishing village. Small hotels opened, and the third phase of Monterey's history began. Because one of the first things the Americans did upon taking California in 1846 was to move the capital from Monterey, some of the old Monterey-style buildings in the town survived unchanged when it became a backwater. Poverty preserved these early examples of specifically Californian design. Some of the very earliest efforts at architectural preservation in the West were here in the old colonial capital. Individuals, patriotic organizations, the city of Monterey, and finally the State of California all contributed to rescuing this unique historic town.

In 1882 Father Angelo Cassanova, the resident priest in Monterey, had the roofless sanctuary of the ruined Carmel mission cleaned in order to examine the tomb of Father Junípero Serra, which was found to be intact. In 1884, he raised the funds to put a roof over the decayed church to mark the centenary of Serra's death. In 1900 the Native Sons of the Golden West leased the adobe Custom House from the Treasury Department and three years later persuaded the State of California to take the lease and promise its restoration (the building did not open to the public until 1929). In 1938 the Custom House became part of the then cutting-edge State of California park system.

Today the beautifully designed Monterey State Historic Park consists of two loose clusters of about two dozen adobes and other historic buildings. Travelers from San Francisco should enter Monterey on Fremont Street. At Fremont and Camino el Estero, across the street from the lagoon of El Estero Park, at 699 Fremont, is G. T. Marsh & Company, (408) 372-3547, the oldest

Asian art importer and antique dealer in California, established in 1876. The elaborate concrete Chinese-style building was constructed in 1927 and designed by Orrin Jenkins. It has an interesting interior filled with Asian art goods and antiques, enclosed gardens, and a suite of Japanese rooms.

Drive first to the Larkin House, and sign-up for a house tour, and secure a Monterey State Historic Park map. (If it is a weekend between 2 and 4 P.M. you may want to see the interior of the Casa Amesti a block away at 516 Polk Street. It does not appear on the state park's map.) If there is time before the tours, walk all around the block on which the Larkin House sits: Calle Principal, Madison, Pacific, and Jefferson. This is the heart of the most interesting of the two surviving clusters of Monterey Style adobes. It is a unique environment of antique buildings and colonial street patterns.

Larkin House
Corner of Jefferson Street and Calle Principal
Tours daily at 10 A.M., 11 A.M., 1 P.M., 2 P.M., 3 P.M., (and at 4 P.M. March through October); closed Tuesday; $1; (408) 649-7118.

The brightest jewel in Monterey is the interior of the Larkin House, the first two-story house built in Monterey. This 1835 Monterey-style adobe originally housed American Consul Thomas O. Larkin's store and merchandise on the ground floor and living quarters for his family upstairs. The historic house was bought in 1922 by Alice Larkin Toulmin, Larkin's granddaughter. She filled both floors of the house with her collection of antique furniture, including a few original Larkin items such as his Boston-made desk, and commissioned interior decorator Frances Elkins to brighten up the interior with well-chosen colors. In 1957 Alice Larkin Toulman gave the Larkin House, its furnishings, and an endowment for its maintenance to the

State of California. This is one of the finest house museums in California with an outstanding collection of antique English, American, and some Chinese furniture and furnishings put together in a way that makes a most comfortable home, so rarely the feeling house museums give. The State of California guides give a superior tour.

Allen Knight Maritime Museum

550 Calle Principal, P.O. Box 805, Monterey, CA 93940.
Open daily except Mondays and national holidays; 10 A.M.–4 P.M. weekdays and 2 P.M.–4 P.M. weekends. From 15 September to 15 June, weekday hours are 1 P.M. to 4 P.M.; free; (408) 375-2553.

A shrine to the ship, this collection of models and nautical mementos was begun by a former mayor of Carmel. Included is a scale model of the U.S. Navy sailing frigate *Savannah*, Commodore John Drake Sloat's flagship when he took Monterey in 1846.

Annual Adobe House Tour

Monterey History and Art Association
550 Calle Principal, P.O. Box 805, Monterey, CA 93940; (408) 372-2608

Headquartered in the same building as the maritime museum is the Monterey History and Art Association, founded in 1931 and one of the key institutions in the conservation of Monterey and the preservation of its significant gardens, buildings, and artifacts from Spanish, Mexican, and early American California. The informative, old-fashioned historic markers on metal poles in front of many historic buildings are some of the History and Art Association's work. The booklets published by the Association are available at the Knight Maritime Museum. Each year, usually the last weekend in April, the Association holds its fund-raising Adobe Tour. This is the single best day to visit Monterey. Write for information and reservations.

Colton Hall Museum

West side of Pacific Street, between Jefferson and Madison
1847-1849, Walter Colton; 1872, portico; 1949, restoration
Open daily 10 A.M.–noon and 1–5 P.M.; free.

Colton Hall was erected in 1847–1849 by Monterey's first American mayor, the Rev. Walter Colton, who came to California as chaplain on one of Commodore Sloat's frigates. It is the oldest American building in California and was patterned after New England academy buildings. The ground floor of the two-story structure housed school rooms, and the upstairs served as the town hall. The building is a taut and sober New England design built of an easily worked, light yellowish-white local limestone. The building probably had a second-story wooden porch along its principal façade instead of the small porch and two exterior staircases that were added in 1872. From September to November 1849, forty-eight delegates elected from ten districts met in the second floor hall to write California's first constitution. That charter was written in both English and Spanish, though it was modeled on those of New York and Iowa. After serving the county, and then the city of Monterey for many years in many capacities (the ground floor still houses city offices), the unique building was restored in 1949 and the second-floor assembly hall made into a museum maintained by the city of Monterey.

Adjoining Colton Hall is the **old jail** built of hard Monterey granite in 1854 with iron work provided by San Francisco foundries. It contained six cells, a debtors room, and a large room for the jailer and served as a jail until 1959.

Casa de la Torre Viewing Garden / Fremont Bank Mortgage Office

502 Pierce Street, southwest corner of Jefferson

A short block north of Colton Hall is

this one-story adobe built by Francisco Pino in 1852 and today embowered in trees. Here is the most carefully tended Monterey garden that the public can see. Looking over the low fence at the side garden here offers a peek into the hidden garden treasures that exist secluded on the picturesque Monterey Peninsula.

Casa Amesti
516 Polk Street, between Hartnell and Alvarado streets
1833–1850s; 1918, Frances Elkins, restoration and gardens
Open Saturdays and Sundays, except Christmas, from 2 P.M.–4 P.M.; tours conducted by the Monterey History and Art Association; small admission fee; (408) 372-2608.

The curiously pruned and sculpted cypress trees in front of Casa Amesti are startling. This lot was granted to José Amesti, a Spanish Basque immigrant, in 1833. He began the construction of a one-story adobe house, which he later added on to in the 1850s. This is a classic Monterey-style adobe with a wood porch and slightly pitched shingle roof. José Amesti became *alcalde*, or mayor, of Monterey. He gave his large house to his daughter Carmen when she married James (Santiago) McKinley, a Scottish sailor who became a Mexican citizen. In the late nineteenth century the big adobe became a boardinghouse. Some credit a Frenchwoman who ran the boardinghouse with planting flowers in front of her building and forcing Polk Street to bend around her garden.

In 1918, Frances Elkins, a noted interior decorator, bought the historic house and decorated and furnished it. She planted a formal Italian boxwood garden in the back which is only now at splendid maturity. Frances Elkins left the house to the National Trust for Historic Preservation upon her death in 1953. The Old Capital Club, established in 1955, leases and maintains the house and opens it to the public on Saturday and Sunday afternoons. A functioning city club, the house is not a house museum. The second-floor gallery or, living room, best retains the Elkins atmosphere. In that room Chinese pieces meld with European furniture in a worldly whole. Be sure to walk through the boxwood garden behind the house after the tour.

Robert Louis Stevenson (Gonzales) House
530 Houston Street
Open daily; tours at 9, 10, and 11 A.M. and at 1, 2, 3, and 4 P.M.; small fee. Part of Monterey State Historic Park.

This two-story adobe was begun in the 1830s by Rafael Gonzales, a customs official. A Swiss-born merchant, Jean Girardin, bought it in 1856 and added to the house on the Houston Street side. (This street was known as merchants' row in the early days.) Later it became the French Hotel. Robert Louis Stevenson stayed here in the fall and winter of 1879 while pursuing Fanny Van de Grift Osbourne, who was summering at the Bonifacio Adobe. He wrote "The Old Pacific Capital," a sketch of Monterey in the 1870s, while here. At Christmas a penniless Stevenson moved to San Francisco. The historic adobe with its literary associations was bought in 1937 by Edith C. van Antwerp and Mrs. C. Tobin Clark to save it from destruction. They give it to the State of California, which has installed a small museum of Stevensoniana in the house. A children's room displays period clothing and fancy antique toys. Behind the house is a large garden.

San Carlos de Borromeo de Monterey Cathedral / Old Royal Presidio Chapel
Church Street, opposite Figueroa
1795, master mason Manuel Ruiz; 1858, expansion; 1942 restoration by Harry Downie
Open daily; masses at usual times.

The church built on this site in 1775 was damaged by a fire in 1789. In 1795 the present stone and adobe building was dedicated. The design for it was drawn by the Academy of San Carlos in Mexico and the original drawings survive in the National Archives in Mexico City. It has a severe neoclassical façade surmounted by a scalloped gable and a square bell tower with a pyramidal roof and is built of sandstone quarried near Carmel. The Native American laborers worked under Mexican master mason Manuel Ruiz. Ruiz probably carved the chalkrock Virgin of Guadalupe over the front door, the oldest piece of "European" art in California. In 1850, the chapel became the first cathedral in California; in 1858 the interior of the church was enlarged, leaving the original façade intact. Probably at that time the fine exterior transept doorframes on the side of the church were added. Some experts think the stone portals were originally side altars at Carmel Mission transferred here in 1858. The interior of the chapel was provided with a wood floor and a carved *reredos* behind the alter in the Victorian period. In 1942 Harry Downie "restored" the chapel, reinstalling a tile floor and simplifying the interior. The large crucifix installed behind the altar is from Barcelona and dates from 1880. The statue of Mary of the Immaculate Conception in the niche to the left of the crucifix dates from the eighteenth century and may have been brought from Mexico by Father Serra.

ALVARADO STREET: OLD MAIN STREET

Though adobes and gardens attract people to Monterey, the rest of the tidy town is also worth examining. Alvarado Street is a classy version of the typical California main street with interesting vintage buildings studding it. The **Old Monterey Book Co.'s** (408-372-3111) interior is the downtown's hidden treasure at 136 Bonifacio Place, off Alvarado. Open Monday to Saturday, 11 A.M. to 5:30 P.M. Old and rare books, first editions, and prints fill this nostalgic bookshop. An artful mural on one wall depicts characters emerging from books.

The **Monterey Hotel** of 1904 at 406 Alvarado Street has a splendid façade with fine bays and elaborate windows.

At the end of Alvarado Street, across Del Monte Avenue, is the new Monterey shaped by urban renewal. Historically, this beach zone was devoted to maritime and railroad needs. In 1964 a forty-five acre redevelopment area was cleared here leaving a few historic buildings including the **Custom House** and the **Pacific House** adobes. The master plan was by Harold Wise, with architects Wurster, Bernardi and Emmons and Milton Schwartz and Associates, with Lawrence Halprin, landscape architect. Lighthouse Avenue was tunneled under **Custom House Plaza**, a walled-in, theaterlike space with an attractive modern Mission-style central fountain. The walled Memory Garden behind Pacific House (where the **State Park Information Center** is), begun in 1927, is the most appealing part of the new Custom House Plaza design. The new convention center is comfortable, but forgettable architecture.

FISHERMAN'S WHARF

Monterey's Fisherman's Wharf, a pier that juts out into Monterey Bay, is solidly and cozily lined with small seafood restaurants, outdoor food vendors, and gift shops. It is a perfect tourist mecca, more fun than brand-new, ersatz Cannery Row, and has the happy air of an old-fashioned California amusement pier. The French-fried squid here are tempting and tasty. This agreeable honky-tonk has escaped the deadening hand of planners.

To the east, beyond the parking lots, is **Municipal Wharf No. 2**, built in 1926 and today's working fish pier. The wholesale fish warehouses at its end specialize in squid that is shipped worldwide. There are good views from here. Between Fisherman's Wharf and Wharf No. 2 is the **Monterey Marina** with its flock of sparkling white pleasure boats.

Once an important fishing port, Monterey harvested the silvery sardines that teemed along the California coast. F. E. Booth opened the first large fish cannery in 1895 with vast outdoor drying racks giving off a pungent odor. In 1906 the ramshackle Chinese fishing village clinging to the rocks on China Point burned to the ground. The site was redeveloped with a string of large sardine canneries. New Monterey, the streets up the hill from Cannery Row, then called Ocean View Avenue, filled up with fisherfolk and cannery workers. Honky-tonks, restaurants, cheap hotels, and whorehouses sat across the street from the bustling canneries. By the 1940s thirty sardine and fish canneries worked round the clock along this strip fed by a fleet of one hundred fishing boats. In this milieu John Steinbeck created the characters for his novels *Cannery Row* and *Sweet Thursday*. With its "tin and iron and rust and splintered wood, chipped pavement and weedy lots and junk heaps" Cannery Row for him became "a poem, a stink, a grating noise, a quality of light, a tone, a habit, a nostalgia, a dream."

In the 1940s the sardines inexplicably vanished from coastal waters and the canneries fell silent. The last one closed in 1973. Derelict oil-soaked canneries burned or were torn down leaving a bleak no-man's-land. But the power of the name Cannery Row led to the marketing and rebuilding of the former industrial zone with hotels, large complexes of tourist shops, restaurants, bars, and clubs. All of this sprouted since the mid-1970s—Steinbeck wouldn't know the place.

Monterey Bay Aquarium
886 Cannery Row
1977-1984, Esherick, Homsey, Dodge & Davis
Open 10 A.M.–6 P.M. daily, closed Christmas; admission fee; phone (408) 375-3333. Fine bookshop with local guides and nature books.

The most popular attraction on redeveloped Cannery Row is the Monterey Bay Aquarium, dedicated to the interpretation of the marine riches of the Monterey Bay. It is least crowded early in the morning and on weekdays. Focusing on the Bay, with its rich abundance of sea life, both plant and animal, this modern educational institution brings the hidden ocean depths up to the land. Terraces face the bay and step down to the water to embrace tidal pools. This outstanding aquarium was designed by Esherick Homsey, Dodge & Davis between 1977 and 1984. It is the munificent gift of industrialist David Packard, one of the founders of Silicon Valley's Hewlett-Packard, and undertakes research on the marine environment as well as public exhibits. The aquarium is built on the site of the Hovden Cannery and portions of the old cannery have been incorporated in the new building. This is one of the best new museum buildings in California, a building that understands its site and is a stimulating place to learn about the biological riches of the California coast.

323

The City of Pacific Grove: Victorian Chautauqua

Pacific Grove Chamber of Commerce
Forest and Central streets, P.O. Box 167, Pacific Grove, CA 93950; (408) 373-3304.

Pacific Grove Museum
Forest and Central streets
Local natural history including the Monarch butterfly migrations and local seaweed; (408) 372-4212.

The city of Pacific Grove, located at the northern tip of the Monterey peninsula, is a complex quilt of grids, parks, and subdivisions. The city's shoreline from Lovers' Point around Point Piños and south to Asilomar State Beach and Conference Grounds is all part of a public park of intricate beauty. Pacific Grove was founded as a dry Methodist summer tent city and chautauqua. The first chautauqua in the West was held here in 1879. (Chautauquas were camp meetings or summer family vacations of sermons, psalm-singing, uplifting lectures, and simple living.) The small-scale grid of streets between Lighthouse Avenue and Ocean View Boulevard, lined with miniature Victorian cottages with elaborate and lovingly cared-for landscapes of plants in containers set out in front of them, is a national treasure. This is probably the finest modest seaside Victorian cottage cluster on the West Coast.

Post-Darwinian science came to this Methodist Eden in 1892 when Timothy Hopkins, the adopted son of Mark Hopkins, endowed the Hopkins Marine Laboratory of Stanford University in Pacific Grove. It studies the rich offshore marine life here. Off the coast at Pacific Grove is the undersea Marine Gardens Park, a protected sanctuary for plants and sea life.

Del Monte Forest / The Seventeen-Mile Drive

The scenic Seventeen-Mile Drive is a private toll road through Del Monte Forest, now owned by 20th Century-Fox. Enter at the Pacific Grove Gate at Sunset Drive, pay the $5 fee, and secure the map. Most travelers simply follow the red line along the coast and out the Carmel Gate. You may, however, wander about all the roads in this vast, privately policed forest. Smoking and fires are prohibited. Off Congress Road (not on the map provided at the gate) is the **S. F. B. Morse Botanical Reserve**, hidden in the heart of the forest.

This superb landscape was originally the Rancho el Pescadero, which sold for $500 in 1846. David Jacks, a Scotsman, purchased it for 12¢ an acre in 1858 and then made a handsome profit when he sold it to railroad baron Charles Crocker's Pacific Improvement Company

for $5 an acre. On part of his 7,000-acre barony, Crocker erected the ornate Del Monte Hotel in 1887 (burned in 1924), which became *the* resort for San Francisco society. A private scenic drive circled out from the grand hotel and back.

In 1915 Samuel F. B. Morse, grandnephew of the inventor of the telegraph and the 1906 captain of the Yale football team, became manager of the Pacific Improvement Company. At that point the sand mine on the property was its most profitable asset. Morse began major improvements, building The Lodge at Pebble Beach and laying out what became the world-famous Pebble Beach Golf Course in 1916.

During the opulent 1920s, Seventeen-Mile Drive was paved, bridle paths were threaded through the pine and cypress forests, and lots were sold to the wealthy for the construction of palatial seaside mansions. The style imposed on all construction was Spanish or Mediterranean, and Morse engaged the well-known Santa Barbara architect George Washington Smith to design the Cypress Point Clubhouse. Smith also designed the most prominent building visible as you enter the Carmel gate, the Crocker Marble Palace, begun in 1926. Built for Mrs. Templeton Crocker of the railroad and banking fortune, this mansion is encrusted with Italian marble. Such was its opulence that its private beach was heated with underground pipes! Today many of the luxurious establishments here are owned by large corporations that use them for executive seminars and meetings.

Pebble Beach

This wealthy residential enclave is surrounded by three of the finest golf courses anywhere. The golf courses skirt the sea and are of an unbelievably brilliant emerald green. The California coast is especially beautiful and pristine here.

The low rocky shore is a filigree of eroded granite with scattered pockets of pure white sand. Unique Monterey pines and wind-sculpted Monterey cypresses cling to the rocks and blanket many slopes in great evergreen forests laced with quiet private roads.

The three golf courses that frame Pebble Beach are: the Pebble Beach Golf Links, the Spyglass Hill Golf Club, and the Cypress Point Club. **Golf Central** handles reservations for Spyglass Hill, for the Old Del Monte course, and for Pebble Beach. Call (408) 624-6611 or 624-3811, extension 239 for information. Master sheets show what days groups are booked; try to avoid them unless you can be placed well ahead of the field. Remember to reconfirm your tee time twenty-four hours before play.

The Lodge at Pebble Beach

Write the Lodge at Pebble Beach, Pebble Beach, CA 93953 or call (408) 624-3811 for information and reservations.

The Lodge at Pebble Beach was at first a rustic pine log lodge built in 1908 on the vast parklike property of the great Del Monte Hotel. The Del Monte Hotel in the City of Monterey opened in 1880 and, with its companion 7,000-acre Del Monte Forest, was developed by Charles Crocker's Pacific Improvement Company and linked to San Francisco by the Southern Pacific Railroad. The great gingerbread pile of the "Del" became *the* high society hotel for San Francisco's elite until it burned down in 1924. To this great railroad-accessible resort wealthy families transported mountains of luggage, servants, and horses and carriages for the season.

In 1919 the Pebble Beach Golf Links opened here when golf first became popular among the elite. The Pebble Beach course at the Lodge was designed by Jack Neville and Douglas Grant (players, not golf course architects) for Samuel Finley Breeze Morse, the manager of the Pacific Improvement Company.

On the third Sunday of August, the Concours d'Elegance is staged here. The velvet lawns are then briefly invaded by green and white striped tents and a string of long, low, luxurious Duesenbergs, Bugattis, Rolls Royces, and other Great Gatsby-like conveyances.

Beyond Pebble Beach is the much-photographed **Lone Cypress**, sculpted by the constant winds (and held together by wires). The Monterey cypress and Monterey pine grow only in this small region. The cypress is a rare survivor from the Pleistocene era. Crocker Grove preserves a stand of these trees.

If you leave the Del Monte Forest by the Carmel Gate, you will emerge in (almost too!) picturesque Carmel, near Ocean Avenue's string of posh shops.

Carmel-by-the-Sea

Carmel is a unique community in California. It began as a seaside colony for professors from Stanford and Berekely and for writers, artists, musicians, and others seeking peace, quiet, and natural beauty. The mile-square village is chiefly known for its setting and for what it does *not* have. Restrictive zoning passed in the 1920s preserves the residential character of the village of 5,000 and strictly controls all commercial development. There are no neon signs, no tall buildings, and no paved sidewalks or streetlights in the residential areas. Houses here have no numbers; mail is picked up at the post office, which serves as the nerve center of the village. So zealous is the village about preserving its character that a few years ago it passed an ordinance forbidding outdoor plastic plants! What abides are quaint, flower-bordered cottages nestled under the twisted pines. Today Carmel is too expensive for most writers, but in the past it was the home of Jack London, Sinclair Lewis, Upton Sinclair, and poet Robinson Jeffers. The Harrison Memorial Library of 1927 at Ocean and Lincoln, designed by Bernard Maybeck, testifies to the strong literary interests of the inhabitants. The Carmel Art Association on Lincoln Avenue sometimes exhibits local work.

OCEAN AVENUE SHOPS

Carmel has since attracted one of the greatest concentrations of upscale boutiques in the nation. All along Ocean Avenue and overflowing into the side streets of the quaint, one-story town, are posh shops selling luxury goods. On weekends the congestion approaches pedestrian gridlock; weekdays are the best time to visit. Carmel's stringent controls prohibit walk-away food, including ice cream cones. The most famous shop might be Talbot Ties with two shops on Ocean Avenue, one at Dolores and another at Monte Verde. At the foot of Ocean Avenue is Carmel Beach, one of the prettiest in California. Its white sand makes a perfect spot to sunbathe or picnic, but swimming isn't safe here.

MISSION SAN CARLOS BORROMEO DEL RIO CARMELO / FATHER JUNÍPERO SERRA'S TOMB

A few blocks from Ocean Avenue's shopping frenzy is the quadrangle at the Mission of San Carlos Borromeo del Rio Carmelo. This mission, built between 1793 and 1797, is one of California's chief beauty spots. The sunshine, space, and flowers within the quadrangle etch themselves onto one's memory. The yellow stone chapel is the quintessential California mission. This was Father Serra's favorite mission of the nine he himself founded, and he made it the headquarters of the mission chain.

Born in 1713 on the island of Majorca, Father Serra became a Franciscan priest and studied at the Lullian University in Palma de Majorca. There he taught philosophy for fifteen years before becoming the religious leader of the Sacred Expedition sent from Spanish Imperial Mexico City to colonize and evangelize Alta California. When he died here in 1784 he was buried at the foot of the main altar.

The present stone church was begun in 1793 under Father Lasuen and dedicated in 1797. The church is one of the loveliest buildings in California. It has a Baroque façade with a star-shaped central window and a bell tower capped by a Moorish dome. The church formed part of an irregular, arcaded quadrangle with the priests' quarters, a kitchen, soldiers' quarters, a smithy, a carpenter shop, and girls' quarters arranged around a fountained court. Indian families lived in a village nearby. Under Father Lasuen, the mission reached a peak population of 927 and 1794. In 1833 the mission was closed down by the Mexican government, and by 1840 nothing remained but ruins.

Restoration began in 1882, when Father Angelo Cassanova, the parish priest at Monterey, had the site cleared and the tombs of Serra, Crespi, and Lasuen identified and examined. In 1884 the mission was inexpertly "restored," with an incongruous peaked roof replacing the original catenary arches. In 1924 Father Ramón Mestres began an accurate restoration of the mission church. In that year a Mortuary Chapel was built next to the old church to house an elaborate California marble sarcophagus, by sculptor Jo Mora, with bronze figures of Fathers Serra and Crespi. Also in this chapel is a statue of the Virgin that Father Serra brought with him to the founding of Mission San Diego (the first mission) and then later to Monterey. The peaked roof was replaced with the appropriate arched roof, and excavations in the surrounding bean fields uncovered the outline of the adobe compound. The *reredos* was adapted from the antique *raredos* at Mission Dolores in San Francisco and completed in 1957. The humble quarters of Father Serra have been reproduced.

There are two interesting museums at the mission, and some of the most romantic gardens in the state surround the mellow old church.

Robinson Jeffers' Tor House
3870 Ocean Avenue and Stewart Way
At Ocean Avenue turn left onto Scenic Road and continue south to Stewart Way. There turn left, go one block, and turn left again onto Ocean View Road. Watch for the granite boulder tower a little down the road.
Open from 1–4 P.M. on Friday and 10 A.M.–4 P.M. on Saturday; call (408) 624-1813 to be sure the house is open.

One of California's greatest, and darkest, poets was Robinson Jeffers, who came to Carmel in 1914 seeking isolation from the world's madness. Here he communed with this granite coast and its people and wrote poems decrying the folly of mankind and proclaiming the eternal solace of the earth and sea. On a cliff overlooking the ocean he built, with his own hands, a granite house for himself and his wife Una, which he named Tor House after the rocky eminence it crowns. From Hawk Tower he scanned the horizon for the swift birds he loved. A copy of Jeffers' *Selected Poems* remains the best companion to this elemental coast.

MONASTERY BEACH

South of Carmel, right before reaching Point Lobos State Reserve, immediately off Highway 1 with free parking along the road, is Monastery Beach, or San Jose Creek Beach, the southern end of the Carmel River State Beach Park. The coarse-grained decomposed granite beach descends steeply from here to the Carmel Submarine Canyon, an underwater canyon more than ten thousand feet deep. Upwelling water here brings the nutrients that feed the exceptionally rich marine life of Carmel Bay. The brown "seaweed" visible just offshore is the top of a stand of kelp. Off this beach is the Carmel Bay Ecological Reserve established in 1960, the nation's first underwater marine wilderness reserve. Though divers may explore here, they may not disturb the rich marine life.

This blustery, windy beach has its own glory. The sea here is a vivid aquamarine color that shades off to deep blue edged with white breakers crashing on granite shores.

POINT LOBOS STATE RESERVE

State nature reserve open daily from 9 A.M.; no admittance after 6:30 P.M.; park closes at 7 P.M.; $3.50 per car. No smoking, dogs, fishing, specimen collecting, or feeding the animals; picnicking in designated areas only, diving by permit only; free guided nature walks. Information station and pamphlet and book stall at the main parking lot inside the reserve; call (408) 624-4909 for information.

Point Lobos State Reserve, one of the jewels of the California State Park System, consists of both the 554-acre peninsular reserve south of Carmel Bay and the adjoining 750-acre underwater Ecological Reserve. This dramatic wave-dashed rocky headland is crowned by a great grove of Monterey cypress and fringed by scattered offshore rocks. The point derives its name, la Punta de los Lobos Marinos (the point of the sea-wolves), from the California and Steller sea lions, whose lusty barking echos among these rocks. Sea lions, sea otters, pelicans, migrating birds, and gray whales also flourish here.

In 1933 the Save-the-Redwoods League acquired this almost primeval area and gave it to the State of California for a state park. It and Pebble Beach on the other side of Carmel Bay, are the only places in the world where Monterey cypress grows naturally.

The park is laid out with a minimum of roads, and the best way to experience its scenic splendor is on foot. The park closes at night to leave its wild denizens free to feed.

About the Author

Randolph Delehanty was born in 1944 in Memphis, Tennessee, and raised in Englewood and Tenafly, New Jersey. He holds degrees in history from Georgetown University, University of Chicago, and Harvard, where he was a University Prize Fellow. In 1970 he moved to Berkeley and began researching California history at the Bancroft Library on the University of California campus. From 1973 to 1978 he was the first historian for The Foundation for San Francisco's Architectural Heritage. In 1983 he returned to Harvard for two years to study American social history. Randolph Delehanty has also written *San Francisco: Walks and Tours in the Golden Gate City*, and *California: A Guidebook*. With photographer E. Andrew McKinney he wrote *Preserving the West*, a survey of the current state of landscape and architectural preservation in the seven far western states for the National Trust for Historic Preservation. He lives in San Francisco and is a city-planning and architectural consultant and convention speaker.

About the Artists

William Walters was born in 1953 in Gainesville, Florida. He studied architecture at the University of Florida and graduated in 1974. In that year he came to San Francisco. He founded William Walters Architectural Consulting in San Francisco in 1983.

John Tomlinson is an artist and cartographer and lives in Portland, Oregon. He was born in 1946 in Portland. He studied geography at Portland State University and graduated in 1972. His bird's-eye views began with postage-stamp size sketches of each building and block as seen by the walker. He then assembles, manipulates, and redraws these sketches as a single view.

Index

AAA, *See* California State
    Automobile Association
Abbey Street, 220–21
    —37, 220
    —40–42, 220
Abrahamsen Building, 36
Academy of Art College Gallery,
    31
A. Cavalli & Co., 114
Ace Café, 22
Achenbach Foundation, 290
Achilles Heel, 242
A Clean Well-Lighted Place for
    Books, 31
Adobe House Tour, Monterey,
    317, 319
African-American Historical and
    Cultural Society, 23
AIDS, 233
Airporter bus, 6
Airports
    Oakland, 7
    San Francisco, 6–7
Aitken, Robert I., 33, 267
Alaska Commercial Building, 50–
    51, 64
Alaska Commercial Company,
    180
Albro, Maxine, 120
Alcatraz, 2, 133
    Prison Tour, 293
Alcoa Building, 69
Alejandro's, 215
Alemany, Joseph Sadoc, 102, 115,
    220
Alexis, 160
Alfred Dunhill of London, Inc., 30
Alice Marble Tennis Courts, 136,
    147
Alien Land Law, 198
Alioto's Restaurant, 108
Allen Knight Maritime Museum,
    320
Alma, 129
Alta California, 60
Alta California, 87–88, 216, 218–
    20, 280
Alta Plaza, 174
Alvarado Street, Monterey, 322
American Express, 6

American Youth Hostels, 21
Amesti, José, 321
Amundsen, Roald, 66
"Andrea," 131
Andrew, Charles E., 154
Andrew Hammond Mansion,
    190, 191
Angel Island State Park, 94, 293–
    94
    ferry, 8
Anna Giselman Building, 101
Anthony, Susan B., 223
Antiquities Act of 1906, 298
Anton Borel Bank, 61
A-1 Urban Renewal Project, 199
A. P. Giannini Plaza, 67
Applegarth, George, 290
Apple Press monument, 267
Aquatic Park, 130
Aquatic Park Casino, 130
Argonaut Book Shop, 31
Arguello, Antonio, 219
Arnatoff, Victor, 120, 286
Artemis Café, 214–15, 224
Arts and Crafts Movement, 137
"Arts, The," 75
A. Sabella's Restaurant, 108
Asakichi Japanese Antiques, 208
Asawa, Ruth, 131, 200, 207–08
Ashbury, Monroe, 245
Ashbury Street
    —429, 253
    —459, 253
    —461, 253
    —525–01, 252
    —704–14, 252
    —710, 252
    —715, 252–53
Ashe, Elizabeth, 117
Ashley, Delos, 317–19
Asian American Dance
    Collective, 195
Asian American Theater Center,
    195
Asian Art Museum, 23, 268
Asiatic Exclusion League, 198
Associations
    Chinatown, 81–86, 94, 95,
        101
    neighborhood, 93, 117

A. Sulka & Co., 30
Atkinson House, 146
Auberge de Soliel, 305
Audubon Canyon Ranch Bird
    Sanctuary, 295
Avenue Cyclery, 258
Avery Brundage Collection, 268

Backen, Arrigoni & Ross, 188–89
Baker Beach, 288–89
Baker Street
    —1, 249
    —15–21, 249
Bakewell and Brown, 36, 103,
    148, 313, 314
Balance Street, 54
Balboa Cafe, 174
Balclutha, 94, 129
Banana Republic Outlet, 43
Bank of America, 6, 48, 50, 58,
    66–68, 114
Bank of California, 48, 62–63
Bank of Canton, 60–61, 90
Bank of Italy, 58
Bank of Lucas, Turner and Co., 56
Bank of San Francisco, 60
Barbary Coast, 54
Barons
    railroad, 156, 157, 164–65,
        166
    silver, 160–61
BART, 7, 46, 69, 240
    mural, 228
Bartlett, Washington A., 88
Basilica of San Francisco, 218
Batteries, 132
    Battery Chamberlain
        Disappearing Gun, 288–89
    Battery Dynamite, 288
Bay Bridge, 154–56
B. Dalton Book Shop, 31
"Beach Blanket Babylon," 114
Beach Chalet murals, 121, 272–73
Beatniks, 32–33, 110, 118
Becker, Rev. Florence S., 185
Belli Annex, 55
Belli Building, 55
Belli, Melvin, 55
Belluschi, Pietro, 67, 210
Bemiss Building, 36
Bénard, Emile Henri, 308
Bennett, Edward, 49
Beringer Vineyards, 306
Bernal, José, 218
Bicentennial tree, 286
Bicycle rentals, 258
Big Four, 154, 156, 164–65, 166
Big Four Restaurant and Bar, 150,
    165
Billy Blue, 30
Binet-Montessori School, 200–02
Bing Kong Tong, 99
Biordi Art Imports, 115
Bix Restaurant and Lounge, 46–47
Black Cat Bar, 55
Black Oak Books, 310
Black Point, 132

Bliss and Faville, 36, 40, 63, 103,
    154, 156, 190–91
Bliss, Walter, 186
Boardwalk, Santa Cruz, 315–16
Bohemian Club, The, 41–42
Bohemian Grove, 41
Bohemians, 55, 57, 109–11, 246,
    297
Bolinas Lagoon, 295
Born, Ernest, 11
Botanical Garden, University of
    California, Berkeley, 310
Bothe-Napa Valley State Park, 306
Bound Together Anarchist
    Collective Bookstore, 243
Bourn Mansion, 189–90
Bourn, William Bowers, 36, 186,
    190, 306, 315
Boynton, Ray, 119
Brannan, Samuel, 88
Brannan Street
    —275, 43
Bransten, Edward, 181
Bransten House, 180–81
Brick Row Book Shop, 31
Bridgeway, Sausalito, 297
Britex Fabrics, 30
Broadway, 111–13, 146
    —1020, 146
    —2000, 188
    —2040, 189
Broadway's Rock, 113
Broadway Tunnel, 111–13
Brocklebank Apartments, 163
Brown, A. Page, 61, 137
Brown, Arthur Jr., 118, 119
Brown, Selma, 255
Brundage, Avery, 268
    Collection, 268
Buddha's Universal Church, 90
Buddhist Churches of America,
    200
Buddhist Church of San
    Francisco, 200
Buddhist temples
    Chinatown, 78, 87, 90, 94,
        98–99, 101
    Japantown, 200, 203–04
Buena Vista Café, 130
Buena Vista East
    —1–3, 249
Buena Vista Park, 249–50
Buena Vista West
    —595–97, 251
    —601, 250–51
    —615, 250
    —635, 250
    —639, 250
    —731, 250
Bufano, Beniamino, 102
Buffalo Paddock, 271
Bull, Alpheus, 271
Bullock & Jones, 30
Burgee, John, 37, 68
Burgren, A. W., 103
Burnham and Root, 49, 70
Burnham Plan, 49
Burnham, Daniel, 49

Burton, Philip, 133
Bush Street
    —1, 71–72
    —130, 72
    —2000–12, 207
    —2101–01 1/2, 207
    —530, 104
    —540, 104

Cable Car Clothiers—Robert Kirk
    Ltd., 30
Cable cars, 2, 7, 8–13, 102, 109,
    152–53, 154, 168, 174
    lines: California Street, 12,
        138, 152, 154
    lines: Clay Street Hill, 9, 168
    lines: Haight Street, 245
    lines: Hyde Street, 138
    lines: Market Street, 73, 231
    lines: Powell-Hyde, 13, 154
    lines: Powell-Mason, 12–13,
        154
    lines: to Fisherman's Wharf,
        106–08
    Powerhouse and Museum, 9,
        11–12
Cable Car Theater, 39
Cabrillo, Juan Rodríguez, 317
Cadenasso, Guiseppe, 143
Café-Babar, 215
Café La Boheme, 214
Caffè Esprit, 43
Caffè Roma, 46, 108
Café San Marcos, 230, 235
Caffè Trieste, 108
Calder, A. Stirling, 73
California Academy of Sciences,
    24, 267–68
California Coastal Resource Guide,
    295
California Crafts Museum, 23
California Culinary Academy,
    171
California Fruit Canners
    Association, 125
California Hall, 171
California Historical Society, 187–
    88
California Masonic Memorial
    Temple, 165
California Palace of the Legion of
    Honor, 22–23, 183, 290
California Star, 88
California State Automobile
    Association, 2–4
California Street, 48, 63–68
    cable line, 12, 46
    Cable Railroad, 138, 152
    —101, 72
    —345, 50
    —464, 62
    —580, 68
    —1021, 160
    —1700, 178
California Women's Club, 221
Calistoga Bookstore, 307
Calistoga, CA, 307

Calle de la Fundacion, 90
Calvary Presbyterian Church, 33
Camellia Gardens, 262
Camera Obscura, 273
Campesino, Chuy, 228
Campgrounds, in San Francisco, 21
Campton Place Bar and Restaurant, 28
Cando K. Hoshino, 195
Candy Jar, The, 29
Canessa Building, 55
Cannery Row, Monterey, 323
Cannery, The, 125, 129
Cannons, Seville, 284
Cantin, A. A., 76, 97
Capital Co., 66, 114
Capp Street, 226–27
Carlsen, Emil, 144
Carmel Bay, 327
Carmel-by-the-Sea, CA, 325–27
Carnegie, Andrew, 239
Carnelian Room, 48, 66, 68
Carousel Museum, 24
Carter, Dudley C., 271
Cartier Jewelers, 29
Casa Amesti, 321
Casa Coloniale Italiana, 114
Casa de la Torre Viewing Garden, 320–21
Casa El Salvador, 223
Casa Lucas Market, 215
Cassady, Carolyn, 138
Cassady, Neal, 138
Cassanova, Father Angelo, 319, 326
Castanis, Muriel, 68
Castro Common Condominiums, 235
Castro Street
    —400, 235
    —444, 235–36
    —501, 236
    —580, 237
    —701, 237
    —711–33, 237
    —757, 237
    —787, 237
Castro Theater, 231, 236
Castro Village, 236–37
Castro, The, 229–40
C. A. Thayer, 94, 129
Cavalli Building, 114
Cemeteries
    Chinese, 289–90
    Jewish, 221–22
    military, 281, 282, 286–87
Centennial tree, 286
Central Pacific Railroad, 156, 166
CFB-Japanese American History Room, 205–06
Chain of Lakes, 271
Chambord Apartments, 169
Chan, Woo, Yuen Family Association, 97
Charlotte Newbegin's Bookshop, 31

Chart House Bar and Restaurant, 129
Chautauquas, 324
Chee Kung Tong, 93
Chevron/Standard Oil of California, 71
Chevron's World of Oil Museum, 24
Chez Panisse, 310
Chiang Kai Shek, 95
China Beach, 289
China Books and Periodicals, 81
China, Nationalist, 93–94, 95
Chin and Hensolt Engineers, Inc., 11
Chinatown, 77–104, 196, 197
    Gate, 87, 104
    YMCA, 100
Chin, Clement, 88
Chinese American Citizens Alliance (CACA), 96
Chinese Central High School, 95
Chinese Chamber of Commerce, 78, 101
Chinese Consolidated Benevolent Association, 95
Chinese Culinary Walk and Luncheon, 78–80
Chinese Culture Foundation, 78–80, 294
    Gallery, 88
Chinese Exclusion Act of 1882, 81, 96, 196–97
Chinese Free Press, The, 93
Chinese Heritage Walk, 78–80
Chinese Historical Society of America Museum, 78, 92
Chinese Immigration Station, 294
Chinese Masonic Temple, 99
Chinese Methodist Episcopal Church, 96
Chinese New Year, 78
    Parade, 78
Chinese, overseas, 81–84
Chinese Six Companies, 85, 94, 95, 100
Chinese Telephone Exchange, Old, 87, 90
Ching Chong Dong Building, 98
Chinoiserie, 86–87
"Christ at the Mount of Olives," 104
Christian Brothers Greystone Cellars, 190, 306
Christ United Presbyterian Church, 204
Chronicle Building, 49
Church of the New Jerusalem, 137
Church, Thomas D., 130, 316
Chutes, The, 245, 256
Ciampi, Mario, 73, 309
Circle Gallery, 31, 37
Circolo Restaurant and Champagneria, 75
Cirque Bar, 152
Citibank, 6
Citicorp Center, 50, 73–74

Citicorp Savings, 6, 90–91
Citizens Committee to Save the Cable Cars, 11
City Box Office, 29
City Lights Books, 110, 113
City of Paris
    department store, 36
    rotunda, 37
City of Shanghai, 30
Civil Rights Act of 1965, 86
Clarion Music Center, 81
Clay Street
    Hill Railroad, 9, 168
    —1083, 163
    —1950, 185
    —1963–65–67, 184–85
    —1969–71–73, 184–85
    —1977–79–80, 184–85
Clayton, Charles, 245
Clayton Street
    —401–07, 254
    —409–11, 254
Cliff House, The, 273, 290
Climate, San Francisco, 4
Clos Pegase, 306–07
Clothing stores, 30, 43
Clubland, 40–42
Cody's Books, 310
Coffee Gallery, 118
Cogswell, H. D., 115–16
Coins, historic, 63
Coit, Lillie Hitchcock, 115, 118–19
Coit Tower, 110, 118–21, 122, 139, 147, 272
    murals, 119–21
Cole, R. Beverly, 245
Cole Street
    —500–06, 255
    —503–07, 255
    —508–16, 255
Coleman, Edward, 178
Coleman, John C., 180
Colley, C. J., 273
Colma, CA, 222, 290
Colton, David, 164–65
Colton Hall Museum, 320
Colton Mansion, 164–65
Colton, Rev. Walter, 320
Columbus Avenue, 57, 111, 116
Columbus Cutlery, 115
Columbus Savings Bank, 55
Columbus Tower, 111
Comme Des Garçons, 30
Commercial Street, 61, 100–01
    —569, 61
Commonwealth Club of California, 42
Compound, The, 122
Comstock Apartments, 169
Comstock lode, 63, 160, 161, 274
Concours d'Elegance, 325
Connick, Charles Jay, 166
Conservatory of Flowers, 266
Consolidated Chinese Benevolent Association, 85
Consolidated Virginia mine, 160

331

Consulate General of the People's Republic of China, 209–10
Contra Costa Academy, 308
Convent and Schools of the Sacred Heart, 174, 190–91
Convention & Visitors Bureau, San Francisco, 2, 5
Cookbook Corner, 31
Coolidge, Charles Allerton, 312
Coppola, Francis Ford, 111
Cora, Charles, 220
Coronado Apartments, 170–71
Corona Heights, 238
Cortázar, Luis, 228
Costanoan
    Indians, 216, 219, 220
    ranchería, 220
Cottages, refugee, 284
Coulter Marine Paintings, 65–66
Coulter, William A., 65–66
Coxhead, Ernest A., 142, 188, 269, 270, 297, 254
C. P. Shades Outlet, 43
Craft & Folk Art Museum of San Francisco, 23
Cram, Ralph Adams, 166
Cranston, Robert Dickie, 251, 252
Crissy Army Airfield, 282
Crocker Bank, 50
Crocker, Charles, 153, 154, 166, 167, 324
Crocker, C. Templeton, 188
Crocker Galleria, 74–75
Crocker Mansion, 166
Crocker, William H., 166
Crookedest street, 147–48
Crown Point Press, 43
Crown-Zellerbach Building, 71–72
Cummings, M. Earl, 267, 268
Curran Theater, 39
Custom House, 322
    Plaza, 322

Dailey, Gardner, 118
Daily Herald, 60
Daroux, Frank, 40
Davies, Louise S., 139
Davis, Jacob W., 124
Day trips, 291–328
de Ayala, Juan, 294
de Bretteville, Alma, 182, 183
de Haro, Francisco, 87, 218, 219
de Portolá, Gaspar, 294, 317
De Soto, 7
de Young, Charles, 268
de Young Memorial Museum, M. H., 23, 268
de Young, Michael Harry, 268
Deak International, 6
Dean, Mallette, 120
Del Monte Forest, 324–25
Del Monte Hotel, 324
Del Norte State Park, 191
DeMars, Vernon, 199, 209
DeRosen, John H., 167
Dewey Monument, 33, 182

Dharma Realm Buddhist Association, 101
Dick-Young Apartments, 100
Diggers, 247, 256
Discolandia, 215
Discoteca Habana, 215
Dish, 242, 252
DNA Lounge, 22
Dolores Street, 221
Domaine Chandon, 305
Donatello, 28
Don Soker Gallery, 43
Doubleday Book Shop, 31
Downtown Center Box Office, 29
Drake's Bay, 300
Drake, Sir Francis, 300
Drogstore, 252
Drumm, John S., 162
Dubois Building, 100–01
Dunn, James F., 169, 170, 256
Dupont Street (Grant), 91, 101
Durant, Henry, 308
Dutch Windmill, 271–72

Earthquake, 1906, 36, 41, 49, 54, 56, 62, 65, 66, 95, 153, 162, 165, 177, 187, 189, 196, 245, 253, 280, 284
East Bay, 307–11
Eastern Newsstand, 31
Eastlake style, 180
Eastwind Books & Arts, 81
"Eclipse," 69
Eddie Bauer, 30
Ed Hardy, Inc., 31
Edificio de Mujeres, 215, 224
Ed's, 28
Edward Coleman House, 178, 181
Eichler, Joseph, 142
871 Fine Arts, 43
El Camino del Mar, 289, 290
El Camino Real, 7, 221, 225
Ellerhusen, Ulric, 278–79
Emanu-El, 33, 203, 221–22
Embarcadero Center, 50, 61, 68–70
Embarcadero Freeway, 112–13
Emperor Herbal Restaurant, 92
Emporium-Capwell, 32, 38
Eng Family Benevolent Association, 99
Erika Meyerovich, 31
Ernie's, 46
Esherick, Homsey, Dodge & Davis, 139, 144, 323
Esprit Factory Outlet, 43
Eugene O'Neill National Historic Site, 311
Eureka, 129
Eureka Homestead Association, 231
"Evolution Rainbow," 256
Exchange, foreign, 6
Executive Order 9066, 198
Experimental Battery Dynamite, 281
Exploratorium, 24–25, 279

Fair, James Graham, 62, 153, 161–63
Fairmont Hotel, 154, 161–63
    Pharmacy, 162
Fair, Theresa Alice, 161–62
Family Club, The, 40
Fantoni, Charles, 116
Fan, Victor Q., 100
F.A.O. Schwartz, 31
Farallon Islands, 273–74
Far East Café, 80
Far East Fine Arts, 32
Far East Restaurant, 101–02
Fargo, William George, 62
Fault, San Andreas, 300
Federal Reserve Bank, Old, 70
Felton, John B., 244
Ferlinghetti, Lawrence, 110, 113
Ferries
    Alcatraz, 293
    Angel Island, 8, 293–94
    Golden Gate, 296
    Larkspur, 8
    Sausalito, 8, 128
    Tiburon, 8
Ferries & Cliff House Railway, 12, 136, 274–75, 290
Ferry Building, 128, 296
Feusier Octagon House, 139–42
Fields Book Store, 171
Figoni Hardware, 115
Figueroa, José, 87, 296
Filbert Street
    Steps, 122–23
    —222, 123
    —224, 123
    —228, 122–23
Fillmore Auditorium, 209
Fillmore Center, 209
Fillmore, Millard, 132, 280
Filoli, 2, 315
Financial District, 44–76
Finocchio Club, 113
Fior d'Italia Restaurant, 116
Fire, 1906, 49, 103, 111, 139, 148, 161, 162, 177, 183, 197, 227, 245, 285
Fireworks, 298
First Bay Regional Tradition, 170
First California Bank, 50
First Chinese Baptist Church, 99–100
First Church of Christ, Scientist, 181
First Congregational Church, 33
First Interstate Center, 64
First Presbyterian Church, 96
First Presbyterian Church, Sausalito, 297
First Unitarian Church, 33, 211
Fisherman's Grotto, 108
Fisherman's Wharf, 106–08, 124–33
Fisherman's Wharf, Monterey, 322–23
Fishing Fleet, Historic, 128
Fleischhacker Zoo, 271
Fleur de Lys, 28

Flood, James Clair, *160–61*
Flood, James Leary, *189, 190–91*
Flood Mansion, *153, 154, 160–61*
Florence Street, *146*
—37, *146*
—40, *146*
Fog, *1, 3, 300*
Fog City Diner, *124*
Folsom
—871, *43*
Fook Yum Tong, *101*
Foreign Exchange, Ltd., *6*
Forgotten Woman, The, *30*
Fort Mason Center, *132–33*
Fort Mason Foundation, *133*
Fort Point, *133, 281, 284, 287*
Fort Winfield Scott, *282*
Foundation for San Francisco's
Architectural Heritage, The,
185–86
"Four Districts" Association, *84*
Fournou's Ovens, *157*
Francisca Club, The, *40*
Franklin, Benjamin, statue of, *115*
Franklin Street Apartment
Buildings, *181*
Franciscan Restaurant, *108*
Freed, Teller, and Freed, *171*
Freeman, J. E., *98–99, 101*
Freeway Revolt, *261*
Fremont Bank Mortgage Office,
320–21
French Bank Building, former, *74*
French Consulate, *104*
Frenchman's Hill, *104*
Fresh Market Restaurant, *37*
Fuduin-Kai, *196*
Fugazi Bank, *57–58*
Fugazi Hall, *114*
Full Moon Saloon, *242*
Fuller-Goldeen, *31*
Funston Avenue, *285*
Funston, Frederick, *162, 285*

Galería de la Raza, *215, 228*
Galleries, Art Institute, *148*
Galvez, Daniel, *227*
Garages *See* Parking
Garfield Grammar School, *139*
Garfield Square, *227–28*
Geary Expressway, *199, 209*
Geary Street, *33*
Geary Theater, *39*
Gee Family Association, *99*
Geefs, Guillaume, *267*
Genji Kimonos and Antiques, *208*
George, Henry, *223–24*
Geothermal springs, *307*
Ghirardelli Chocolate Company,
125
Ghirardelli Company, *56*
Ghirardelli, Domingo, *56, 131*
Ghirardelli Ice Cream Parlor, *131*
Ghirardelli Square, *123, 131–32*
Giannini, A. P., *57, 58–60, 67–68,
101, 114*
Gibb Warehouses, *123*

Gibson, Rev. Otis, *96*
Ginsberg, Allen, *110*
Ginza Discount Imports, *208*
Glass Key, The, 170
Goddess of the Forest, The, *271*
Goethe Institute, *104*
Gold Central, *325*
Golden Court, *170*
Golden Dragon Restaurant, *97*
"Golden Dream of the New
World," *227*
Golden Era, *55*
Building, *55*
Golden Gate Bridge, *191, 287–88,
296*
road to, *282*
vista points, *288, 289*
Golden Gate Ferry, *296*
Golden Gate Lutheran Church,
222
Golden Gate National Recreation
Area (GGNRA), *128, 130, 132–
33, 284, 295, 300*
map of, *4*
Visitor Center, *273*
Golden Gate Park, *244, 245, 250,
257–75*
Golden Gate Promenade, *133*
Golden Gate Spiritualist Church,
185
Golden Gate, the, *275, 276, 287*
Golden Gate Theater, *39*
Golden Hind, 300
Goldfield's Original Tattoo
Studios, *113*
Gold Mountain Sagely
Monastery, *101*
Gold Rush, *48, 61–62, 81, 88, 118,
123, 124, 157, 161, 175, 178,
190, 315*
Gonzalez, Carlos, *226*
Gonzales House, *321*
Gough Street
—2000, *184*
—2004–10, *184*
—2030, *184*
—2040, *184*
—2645, *142*
Grace Cathedral, *154*
Grace Episcopal Cathedral and
Close, *166–67*
Graham, Bill, *209*
Grain Exchange Hall, *65*
Grant Antiques, *117*
Grant Avenue, *90, 100, 103–04,
117–18*
—400, *104*
—445, *104*
—450–64, *103*
—500, *103*
—631, *101–02*
—654–70, *101*
Grant, James Donohoe, *191*
Great Highway, *273*
Greeley, Adolphus, *284*
Greenlee Terrace Apartments,
186
Green Library, *314*

Greenpeace Shop, *132*
Greens Restaurant, *133*
Green Street
—1011, *142*
—1030, *142*
—1039–43, *142*
—1040, *142*
—1050, *142*
—1055, *142*
—1101, *139*
—1111–33, *139*
Greenwich Steps, *121–22*
Griffith, Alice, *117*
Grip, cable car, *138*
Grogan-Lent-Atherton Building,
56
Groger's Western Wear, *215*
G. T. Marsh & Company, *319*
Guaymas, *8*
Guerin, Jules, *70*
Guerrero, Francisco, *218*
Guerrero Street
—827, *223*
—850–52, *223*
Guillermina, *80*
Guinness Museum of World
Records, *24*
Gump's, *31–32, 80*

Haas-Lilienthal House and
Museum, *174, 185–86*
Haas, William, *181*
Hagerup, Nils, *65, 66*
Haight Ashbury, The, *241–56*
Haight, Gov. Henry Huntly, *245,
259*
Haight Street
cable line, *245*
—1081, *249*
—1128, *249*
—1132–34–36, *249*
—1144–46, *249*
—1398, *252*
—1635, *256*
—1660, *256*
—1677–81, *256*
—1701–05, *256*
—1736, *256*
—1748, *256*
—1775, *256*
—1779–83, *256*
Hale Brothers Department Store,
39
Halleck, Henry W., *55, 60*
Hallidie, Andrew Smith, *9, 74,
152, 168*
Hallidie Building, *74*
Hallidie, Sir Andrew, *9*
Hall, William Hammond, *260,
261*
Halprin, Lawrence, *71, 73, 123–24*
Hamburger Mary's, *22*
Hamlin School, *189*
Hammarkerg and Herman, *169*
Hammett, Dashiell, *170*
Hang Ah Tea Room, *80*
Hanna House, *314*

333

Haraszthy, Agoston, 303
Harcourt's Gallery, 40
Hard Rock Café, 178
Harris, George, 120
Harrison Memorial Library, 325–26
Harris' Steak House, 178
Harte, Bret, 55
Harvey Milk Plaza, 235
Haslett Warehouse, 130
Hayes Street Grill, 125
Healy, Clyde, 147
Hearst Mining Building, 309
Hearst, Phoebe Apperson, 308
Hearst, George, 152, 168, 308
Hearst, William Randolph, 129, 308, 309
Heil, Dr. Walter, 119
Helen Crocker Russell Library of Horticulture, 269
Hellman, Isaias W., 62, 186
Hellmuth, Obata & Kassabaum, 38, 42, 123
Henry Cowell Ranch, 316
Henry Evans, Printmaker, 306
Henry George School of Social Science, 223–24
Hercules, 129
Heritage, See Foundation for San Francisco's Architectural Heritage, The
Hermitage, The, 144
Hertzka and Knowles, 71, 228
Hesthal, William, 121
H. G. Walters Warehouse, 123
Hidalgo y Castilla, Miguel, statue of, 222
Highway 1, 295–96, 300
Hiler, Hilaire, 130
Hillside Club, 310
Hip Sen Tong, 97
Hiss and Weekes, 191
Hobart, Lewis P., 38, 41, 70–71, 142, 166
Holbrook Building, 51
Holiday Inn Financial District, 88
Holladay, Samuel W., 182
Hollis, William, 224
Holmes, Howard C., 12
Hong Kong Tea House, 80
Hoover, Herbert, 313, 315
Hoover Tower, 313
Hopkins Mansion, 157–60
Hopkins Marine Laboratory, 324
Hopkins, Mark, 92, 153, 154, 157–60
Hopkins, Mary, 157
Hop Sing Tong, 97
Horner's Addition, 231
Hostels, 21
Hotaling Annex, 57
Hotaling, Anson Parsons, 56–57
Hotels, directory of, 13–21
Hotel St. Francis, 32, 36
Hotel St. Francis Theater Ticket Agency, 29
Hound, 30
House of Shields, 48, 75

Howard, John Galen, 61, 308, 309, 310
Howard, John Langley, 121
"Howl," 110
Huagiao, 81–84
Humphreys, William P., 260
Hunan on Haight, 242
Hunan Restaurant, 80
Hunan Shaolin, 152
Hunter-Dulin Builidng, 74
Hunter's Bargain Bookstore, 31
Huntington, Collis P., 154, 164, 269
Huntington Hotel, 165
Huntington Park, 164–65
Hyatt Regency Hotel, 69
Hyde Street
    cable line, 138
    Pier, 128–29
    —2238, 147

I-Beam, 242
Idaho Gold Mine, 178
Ikenobo Ikebana Society, 208
Il Cenacolo, 109
Il Fornaio, 124
I. Magnin, 36–37
Improvisation, 39
Ina Coolbrith Park, 136
Inglenook Winery, 305
International Art Guild Society, 208
Internment, of Japanese-Americans, 198, 199, 200
Intersection Art Center, 215
Ironwood Café, 242
Isak Lindenauer Antiques, 237
Isobune, 195
Issei, 196, 198
Italian-American Bank, 61
Italianate style, 180
Italian French Baking Co. of San Francisco, 115
Italian Swiss Colony wine warehouse, 124

Jackson Square Historic District, 48, 49, 54–57, 109, 131
Jackson Street
    —400, 56
    —407, 56
    —408, 56
    —415–31, 56
    —432, 56
    —440, 56
    —440–44, 56
    —441, 56
    —445, 56–57
    —451, 56–57
    —463–73, 56–57
    —472, 56, 57
    —2010, 186
    —2020, 186–87
    —2030, 187
    —2040, 187
    —2045, 187

Jack's Restaurant, 46
James Leary Flood Mansion, 189, 190–91
Janot's, 28
Japan, 196, 198
Japan Center, 199, 208
Japanese American Citizens League (JACL), 205
Japanese Cultural and Community Center of Northern California, 205–06
Japanese Gospel Society, 196
Japanese Tea Garden, 268–69
Japantown, 192–211
Japonesque, 74
Java Street, 251
Jazz, 110, 113
Jazz Workshop, 113
Jeanne's Bonsai, 195
Jefferson Street, 126–27
Jeffers, Robinson, 325, 327
Jenkins, Orrin, 319
Jeremy Norman & Co., 31
Jessica McClintock Boutique, 30
Jewelry stores, 29–30, 92–93
Jewish Community Museum, 23
J. Harold Dollar Building, 64
Jim Mate's Pipe Shop, 30
J. M. Lang Antiques, 29
Jogging, 2
John Berggruen Gallery, 31
John C. Portman Jr. and Associates, 69, 70
John F. Kennedy Drive, 262
John McLaren Memorial Rhododendron Dell, 266–67
John Muir National Historic Site, 310–11
John Pence Gallery, The, 31
John Scopazzi, Bookseller, 31
Johnson, Philip, 37, 68
Johnson, Sargent, 130
Johnson, Walter S., 278
John Walker & Co., 29
Jones Street
    —1250, 169
    —1740, 143
    —1742, 143
    —1950, 143
Jones, W. A., 281
Joseph Donohoe Grant Mansion, 190, 191
Joseph D. Randall Junior Museum, 23
Joss houses, 98
Judah L. Magnes Museum, 23
Judah L. Magnes Western Jewish History Center, 203
Julius Castle Restaurant, 122

Kabuki Hot Springs, 208–09
Kabuto Sushi Restaurant, 195
Kagiwara, Makoto, 268–69
Kaiser, Henry, 198–99
Kaplan, McLaughlin & Diaz, 70, 74, 178

Kaplan's Surplus & Sporting
   Goods, 30
Kasuga, Teraro, 203
Kaufman, Ron, 69–70
Kearney, Denis, 167
Kelham, George, 66, 70, 71, 72,
   73, 75, 160
Kemble Collection, 188
Kent, William, 298
Kepes, Gyorgy, 210
Kerouac, Jack, 138
Kesey, Ken, 246
King, Thomas Starr, 211, 267
Kinokuniya Bookstore, 208
Klussman, Frieda, 11
"Knife Edge Figure," 69
Kohl Building, 66
Komsthoeft Building, 237
Kong Chow
   association, 85
   temple, 87, 94
Konko Church of San Francisco,
   203–04
Kortum, Karl, 130
Krafft, Julius, 189
Kris Kelly, 30
Kuo Ming Tang Headquarters, 95
Kyogen theater, 195

Labaudt, Lucien, 121, 272–73
Lafayette Park, 174, 181–82
Laguna Street
   —1740, 204
   —1800–32, 202
   —1801–65, 202
   —2535, 188
Laib, Arthur J., 168–69, 186
"La Madre del Lume," 116
Lands End, 274–75, 288, 290
Langdon, Gordon, 119
La Palma Mexicatessen, 215
Larkin House, 319–20
Larkspur ferry, 8
La Quiche, 28
Lascaux Bar and Rotisserie, 28
Laura Ashley, 30
Laver, Augustus, 160–61
La Vita Italiana, 122
Law, Hartland, 162
Law, Herbert E., 162, 169
Lawrence Hall of Science, 24, 310
Lawrence Halprin and Associates,
   71, 131, 210, 309
Leavenworth Street
   —1155, 170
   —1201–09, 170
   —1202–06, 170
Le Club, 152, 169
Le Corbusier, 71
Lee, Clayton, 87, 104
Lee Family Association, 98–99
Lee, Stephen, 95, 97
Leland Stanford Junior Museum,
   314
Lemme, F. S., 273
Lentelli, Leo, 73
Le Petit Café, 136

Leroy Place, 170
Les Jeunes, 146
L'Etoile Restaurant, 152, 165
Letterman Army Medical Center,
   282–84
Levi's Plaza, 123–24, 125
Levi Strauss & Co., 123–24
Levy, Harriet Lane, 175–76
Lexington Street, 224–25
Liberty Hill Historic District, 222
Liberty Street
   —109, 223
   —110, 223
   —111–15, 223
   —117–19, 223
   —121–21A, 223
   —123, 223
   —151–53, 223
   —159, 222–23
   —541–59, 237
   —563–77, 237
   —741, 237–38
Lick, James, 266
Lightstone's Menswear, 215
Lilienthal, Alice Haas, 181, 185–
   86
Lilienthal-Pratt House, 180
Lillie, William H., 178, 252, 254
Lincoln Boulevard, 288–89
Lincoln Cyclery, 258
Lincoln Park, 289–90
Lindley Meadow, 270–71
Linear Accelerator, 315
Lin, T. Y., 42, 208
Li Po-Tai, 92–93
Lippold, Richard, 210, 211
Livermore, Horatio P., 137, 144,
   146
Lloyd Lake, 165, 270
Locke, CA, 104
Lodge at Pebble Beach, The, 324,
   325
Lombard Street
   crooked block, 147–48
   Gate, 284
   —1100, 148
Lone Cypress, Monterey
   Peninsula, 325
Looff, Charles I. D., 316
Look Tin Eli, 103
Lorraine Hansberry Theater, 39
Lost & Found Saloon, 117–18
Lou Henry Hoover House, 314–
   15
Louis Vuitton, 29
Lowie Museum of Anthropology,
   24, 309–10
Lowry Estate Building, 101
Lucca Ravioli, 215
Lun On Shop, 80
Luxor Cab, 7
Lyon Street
   —2107, 137

MacAdam, M. V. B., 163
MacDonald and Applegarth, 74,
   182

MacDonald, Donald, 163, 288
Machado, Tony, 228
Macondray Lane, 143
   —68, 143
Macy's California, 6, 38
Magic Theater, 133
Maiden Lane, 37
Malloch Apartment Building, 122
Malm Luggage, 29
Maltese Falcon, The, 170
Mandarin Hotel, 64
Mandarin Restaurant, 131–32
Manora's Thai Restaurant, 22
Maps, 2–4, 258
Marina District, 278
Marin County, 294–300
Marin County Civic Center, 299
Marine's Memorial Theater, 39
Marine View Apartments, 146–47
Mario's Bohemian Cigar Store,
   108
Maritime Book Store, 4, 128
Maritime Museum, 129, 130
Mark Cross, 29
Market Street, 72–73
   Cable Railway, 73, 231
   —388, 72
Mark Hopkins Hotel, 148, 157–60
Marshall, John, 88
Marshall's, 39
Marsh, George Turner, 268–69
Martens and Coffey, 168, 252
Martin, Leonard V., 129
Mary Phelan Mansion, 183
Masa's, 28
Masonic Avenue
   —1200, 252
   —1265–67, 251–52
   —1322–42, 251
   —1430, 251
   —1450, 251
   —1485, 251
Masonic Museum, 165
Mason Street Theater, 39
Mason Street Townhouse, 160
Mason Street Wine Bar, 28
Mastropasqua, Louis, 122, 143
Mathews, Arthur F., 75
Matson Building, 103
Matson Navigation Co., 186
Matson-Roth Houses, 186
Matson, William, 186
Maupin, Armistead, 143, 233
Max's Diner, 29
Maybeck, Bernard, 116–17, 177,
   191, 278, 298, 308, 310, 325–26
Mayorga, Johnny, 226
McDowell, Irwin, 284
McCoppin, Frank, 244, 259–60
McKinney Hall, 189
McLaren, John, 164, 221, 250,
   260–61, 267, 270, 271, 290
McLaren Lodge, 258, 262
Meat Market Coffeehouse, 230,
   239
Mechanics Institute Library, 75
Meiggs, Harry, 124
Memorial Church, 313–14

Mercantile Library Assocation, 75
Merchant's Exchange Building, 65
Mestres, Father Ramón, 326
Metropolitan Club, The, 40
Metropolitan Transportation
  Commission, 4
Meussdorffer, C. A., 40, 183, 184
Mexican Museum, 228
Mexican War, 88
Michael Graves Architects, 306–
  07
Midnight Sun, 236–37
Milk, Harvey, 233
Miller and Pfleuger, 50, 76, 171
Mills Building, 49, 70–72
Mills, Darius Odgen, 63, 71
Mill Valley, 298
Mill Valley Art and Garden Club,
  298
Miramonte Restaurant, 306
Missionaries of Charity Queen of
  Peace Convent, 224
Mission Bay Project, 43
Mission Chapel, Original, 220
Mission Cultural Center, 215
Mission District, 212–28
Mission Dolores, 212, 216, 218–
  20, 280
Mission Dolores Park, 221–22
Mission High School, 221
Mission San Carlos Borromeo del
  Rio Carmelo, 326
Mission San Carlos Borromeo de
  Monterey Cathedral, 321–22
Mission United Presbyterian
  Church, 227
Mitsubishi Bank, 63
Model Bakery, 306
Model Yacht Club House, 271
Modern Times Bookstore, 223
Modoc Wars, 281
Molinari's Delicatessen, 113
Monastery Beach, 327
Monterey Bay Aquarium, 323
Monterey, CA, 316–23
Monterey Hotel, 322
Monterey Jazz Festival, 317
Monterey Marina, 322
Monterey Peninsula, 315–27
Monterey State Historic Park, 319
Montez, Ricardo, 228
Montgomery Block, 54, 60
Montgomery Gallery, 48
Montgomery, John B., 88
Montgomery Street, 54, 122
  Enlisted Men's Barracks, 286
  —456, 61
  —708, 55
  —722, 55
  —728–30, 55
  —732, 55
  —804, 56
Moore, Henry, 69
Moore, Joseph, 38
Mooser, William M., Jr., 130
Mooser, William M., Sr., 129,
  130, 131, 305, 306
Mora, J. J., 41, 326

Moraga, José Joaquin, 216, 280,
  285
Morgan, Julia, 65, 142, 162, 205
Morphy, Edward A., 144
Morrow, Irving F., 287–88
Morrow's Nut House, 29
Morsehead Apartments, 160
Morse, Samuel F. B., 324
Moscone Convention Center, 42
Mt. St. Helena, 307
Mt. Sutro, 251
Mud baths, 307
Muir, John, 298, 310–11
Muir Woods National
  Monument, 2, 293, 298–99
Mullgardt, Louis Christian, 268
Muni, 13
  map, 4
  Metro Station, 233–35
Municipal Pier, 130–31
Murals, 70, 130, 148, 165, 255,
  256
  Beach Chalet, 121, 272–73
  Chinatown, 92, 94, 100, 101–
    02
  Coit Tower, 110, 118, 119–
    21
  Grace Cathedral, 167
  Mission District, 226, 227–28
  Presidio, 286
Musée Mechanique, 24
Museum of Conceptual Art, 24
Museum of Modern Art, San
  Francisco, 23
Museum of Modern Mythology,
  24
Museum of Russian Culture, 24
Museum of the Money of the
  American West, 23, 62, 63
Music Concourse, 267
Music Pavilion, 267
Mustards Grill, 304–05
Muybridge, Eadweard, 156–57

Nagare, Masayuki, 67
Nam Kue Chinese School, 101
Napa, CA, 304
Napa County Historical Society,
  304
Napa Valley, 300–07
Napier Lane, 122, 123
  —10, 123
  —21, 123
Native Sons of the Golden State,
  96
Navy ships, 125–26
Neiman-Marcus, 32, 37
Nervi, Pier Luigi, 210–11
Nestor, James, 206
Nevelson, Louise, 69
Newman, Ruby, 255
New Montgomery Street, 75
New Performance Gallery, 215
New Year
  Chinese, 78
  Financial District, 46

Newsom, Joseph Cather, 142,
  206–07, 254
Newsom, Samuel, 142, 206–07,
  255
Nichi Bei Kai Cultural Center,
  204–05
Nightbreak, 242
Nihonjinmachi, 195, 197
Nihonjinmachi Improvement
  Association, 197
Nihonmachi, 195
Nihonmachi Mall, 207–08
992 O'Farrell Street, 176
Ning Yung Benevolent
  Association, 85, 99
Nisei, 196, 198, 205
Nob Hill, 136, 136–37, 149–71
Nob Hill Community
  Apartments, 163–64
Noe Garden Homestead
  Association, 231
Noe, José de Jesús, 218, 231, 239
Noe Valley, 229–40
Noe Valley Branch Library, 239–
  40
Noe Valley Ministry, 238–39
Noh theater, 195
Nordstrom, 32, 38
Norfold Alley, 22
Norras Temple, 78, 98–99
Norris, Frank, 110
Norris, Kathleen Thompson, 255
North Beach, 106, 108, 109–24
North Beach Museum, 114
North Point Gallery, 132
North Point Street
  —872–80, 132
Notre Dame des Victoires, 104
Notre Dame School, Old, 220
Nuestra Señora de Guadalupe,
  163

Oakland Museum, 307–08
Oak Street
  —1705, 254
  —1709, 254
  —1711, 254
  —1751, 254
  —1759–63, 254
Oak Tin Benevolent Association,
  97
Obiko, 30
O'Brien Brothers, 97, 98, 99, 104
O'Brien House, 142
Ocean Avenue, Carmel, 326
Ocean Beach, 273
Octagon houses, 24, 139–42
Odd Fellows Building, St. Helena,
  305–06
O'Farrell, Jasper O., 33, 72–73,
  115, 136, 171
Officers Club, 132
Officers' Open Mess, 285–86
Okamoto-Liskamm, 207–08
Old Bush Street Synagogue
  Cultural Center, 203
Old Comandancia, 285–86

Old Mint Museum, 24
Old Monterey Book Co., 322
Old Royal Presidio Chapel, 321–22
Old Speedway Meadows, 270–71
Old Wives Tales, 224
Olmsted, Frederick Law, 176, 308, 312
Olympic Club, The, 41
Omi-Lang, 123–24
O'Neill, Eugene, 311
Opium dens, 91
Orientations, 31
O'Shaughnessy, Michael M., 96, 267
Other Café, The, 242
Ottilie R. Schubert Hall, 188
Outdoor Art League, 221
Outlets, clothing, 43
Out of Hand, 230
Outside Lands, 227–28, 243–45, 259, 260
Oyster farms, 300
Oz, 28

Pacific Film Archives, 23, 309
Pacific Gas & Electric, 187
    old, 103
    substations, 104, 190
Pacific Grove, CA, 323–24
Pacific Grove Museum, 323
Pacific Heights, Eastern, 172–91
Pacific Heritage Museum, 60–61, 101
Pacific House, 322
Pacific Improvement Company, 324, 325
Pacific Street, 54
Pacific Telephone and Telegraph Company, 76
Pacific Telephone Exchange, 87, 90
Pacific Telephone Headquarters, 51
Pacific Telesis Tower, 74–75
Pacific-Union Club, 154, 160–61
Packard, David, 323
Paff and Baur, 41
Page Street
    —1550–42, 253
    —1700, 254
    —1726–27, 254
    —1762, 254
    —1767, 254–55
    —1768, 254
    —1777, 255
    —1900–02, 255
    —1901, 255–56
Palace Hotel, 63, 75 See also Sheraton-Palace Hotel
Palace of Fine Arts, 191, 278–79
Palace of the Legion of Honor, 22–23, 183, 290
Palm Drive, 313
Palou, Francisco, 218–19
Panama Canal Ravioli Factory, 115

Panama-Pacific International Exposition, 63, 65, 96, 102, 191, 278
Panelli Bros. Delicatessen, 114
Panhandle, 245, 246, 253–54, 261
Parade, Chinese New Year, 78
Parade Ground, Presidio, 286
Paradise Lounge, 22
Park and Ocean Railroad, 245, 266, 273
Park Branch Public Library, 255
Parking
    Castro, 230
    Chinatown, 80
    Financial District, 46
    Fisherman's Wharf, 106
    Haight Ashbury, 242
    Japantown, 193–95
    Mission District, 213
    Nob Hill, 150
    Pacific Heights, 173
    Russian Hill, 135
    Union Square, 27
Partridge, John, 103
Pasquale Iannetti, 31
Past Tense, 215
Patigian, Haig, 41, 115–16
Peace Pagoda, 208
Pearl Harbor, attack on, 198
Pebble Beach, CA, 324–25
Pebble Beach Golf Course, 324
Percy & Hamilton, 180, 227, 306
Perry, Charles O., 69
Pershing Hall, 285
Pershing Square, 286
Peters, William Wesley, 299
Pfleuger and Pfleuger, 36–37
Pfleuger, Timothy, 33, 160, 162, 236
Phelan, James D., 49, 183, 289
Philosophers Stone Bookstore, 230
Phylloxera, 303
Piers
    Fort Mason, 132–33
    Municipal, 130–31
    —39, 127–28
    —45, 125–26
Pierre Deux Original Fabrics, 30
Pine Street
    —900–08, 160
Pioneer Park, 118
Pioneer Woolen Mill, 131
Piper, George, 88
Pissis, Albert, 38, 61, 73
Placa, 227
Plaza de la Raza, 225
Pleasant Street
    —75, 168
Point Bonita lighthouse, 288
Point Lobos State Reserve, 295, 327–28
Point Reyes National Seashore, 299–300
Polk & Polk, 144–46
Polk Street, 171
    —1214, 171
    —1326, 171

Polk, Willis, 65, 66, 70–71, 73, 74, 110, 143, 144–46, 160, 161, 189–90, 272
Polo Field, 270
Polo—Ralph Lauren Shop, 30
Pompei's Grotto, 108
"Portals of the Past, The," 165, 270
Porter, Bruce, 88, 146, 315
Portman, John C., Jr., 40–41, 68, 69, 70
Portman San Francisco Hotel, The, 40–41
Portsmouth Square, 48, 87–90
Portsmouth Square Garage, 88
Postermat, 115
Post Street
    —1698, 208
Powell-Hyde cable line, 13
Powell-Mason cable line, 12–13
Prayerbook Cross, 270
Presidio & Ferries Railroad, 136
Presidio of San Francisco, 132, 276–87
Prichard, William Bond, 266
Prohibition, in California, 303–04
Protestant Chapel, Old, 285
Public Works of Art Project (PWAP), 119–21
Purcell, Charles H., 154
Putnam, Arthur, 73, 267

Quantity Postcards, 117
Quant Sang Chong & Co., 91
Queen Anne style, 180

Railroad barons, 152–54, 156, 157, 164–65, 166
Rainbeau Factory Store, 43
Rainbow Falls, 270
Rainbow Grocery, 215
Ralston, William, 63, 75
Ramaytush Indians, 216
Rancho Caymus, 304
Rancho el Pescadero, 324
Rancho San Miguel, 231
Rancho Saucelito, 296, 298
Randall & Windall, 31
Rand McNally Map Store, 4
"Raza History," 228
Read, Juan, 298
Real Estate Associates, 202–03, 224
Reckless Records, 243
Recreation and Park Commission, 262
Red & White Fleet, 293
Redevelopment Agency, 199, 203, 206–07, 209, 246
Redwood Park, 58
Redwoods, 298–99
Regional Transit Guide/Map, 4
Rehabilitation Assistance Program, 247
Reid and Tarics, 233–35

337

Reid Brothers, *39, 161, 187, 188, 209, 267*
Reid, John Jr., *221, 239–40, 271*
Rent control, *51*
Residence clubs, *21*
Restaurant at Saks, The, *38*
Restaurants, *21–22, 28, 46–48, 80, 108, 136, 152, 174, 195, 214–15, 230, 242*
Restrooms, downtown, *32*
R. Iacopi & Co. Meat Market and Deli, *115*
Richardson Bay, *296*
Richardson, William A., *87, 296*
  site of trading post, *100*
Richard Spreckels Mansion Bed and Breakfast, *250–51*
Richie Building, St. Helena, *305*
Righetti & Kuhl, *100–01, 103*
Rings Fine Seasonal Cuisine, *22*
Ríos, Michael, *226, 228*
Ripley's Believe It Or Not Museum, *24*
Rite Spot Café, *215*
Rivera, Diego, *148*
Rivera Gallery, *148*
Robert Dollar Building, *64*
Robert Louis Stevenson House, *321*
Robert Louis Stevenson Monument, *88*
Robert Louis Stevenson State Park, *307*
Robert Mondavi Winery, *305*
Rockin' Robins, *242*
Rodgers, Charles E. J., *96, 101*
Roller, Albert F., *50*
Rolph, James "Sunny Jim," *96, 238, 271*
Roman Catholic archdiocese, *220–21*
Roosevelt, Franklin D., *121, 198*
Roosevelt, Theodore, *33, 119, 198, 298*
"Roseleaf parties," *144*
Ross Alley
  —14, *93*
  —23, *93*
Ross Alley Improvement Association, *93*
Ross, T. Patterson, *103*
Roth, William M., *131*
Rotunda Restaurant, The, *37*
Rousseau, Charles M., *90, 93, 256*
Royal Exchange, *48, 69–70*
Royal Theater, *171*
Ruiz, Manuel, *321, 322*
Russ Building, *70*
Russell Place
  —29, *138*
Russian Hill, *134–48*
Russian Hill Place, *143–44*
Rutherford, CA, *305*
Ryan, W. D'Arcy, *90*

Sabella & La Torre, *108*
Sacramento Rail Road, *56*

Sacramento Street, *101*
  —728–30, *101*
  —755–65, *101*
  —1150, *163*
  —1172, *164*
  —1190, *164*
  —1230, *168–69*
  —1242, *168–69*
Saks Fifth Avenue, *32, 38*
Saloon, The, *117*
Sam Bo Trading Company, *93*
SamTrans, *6*
Sam Yup Association, *84, 85, 101*
San Andreas fault, *300*
Sanchez, Francisco, *218*
Sanchez Street
  —849, *238*
San Francisco Archives for the Performing Arts, *24*
San Francisco Art Institute, *23, 135, 144, 148*
San Francisco Centre, *38–39*
San Francisco Fire Department Museum, *24*
San Francisco Gas Company, *190*
San Francisco Golf Club, *282*
San Francisco Health Food Store, *29*
San Francisco History Room and Archives, *24*
San Francisco International Toy Center and Museum, *24*
San Francisco Lodging Guide, *14*
San Francisco Maritime Museum, *129*
San Francisco-Oakland Bay Bridge, *154–56*
San Francisco Sugar Refinery, *63*
San Francisco Zen Center, *203*
San Francisco Zoo, *24*
San Francisco
  AIDS, *233*
  bars in, *21–22*
  best time to visit, *1*
  black migration to, *198–99*
  bohemians in, *57, 109–11*
  building booms in, *32, 48–50, 51, 231–33*
  cable cars, *2, 7, 8–13, 102, 106–08, 109, 138, 152–53, 154, 168, 174, 231, 245*
  campgrounds in, *21*
  Catholic Church in, *102, 216, 218–20*
  Chinese migration to, *81–86, 92, 196–97, 294*
  City Beautiful movement, *36, 96*
  city grid, *72–73, 111, 117, 136, 168, 171, 199–200*
  climate, *1, 4–5*
  conventions in, *42–43*
  day trips from, *291–328*
  driving in, *7*
  Edwardian city, *49–50, 87, 111, 117, 169, 170*
  French migration to, *104*
  gay migration to, *233*

  gentrification in, *122, 232–33*
  hostels, *21*
  hotels, *13–21*
  Italian migration to, *92, 109*
  Japanese migration to, *196–97*
  maps of, *2–4*
  mission period, *216, 218–20, 225, 243, 280, 285–86*
  museums, *9, 11–12, 22–25, 29–30, 60–61, 62, 63, 76, 78, 92, 101, 114, 129, 130, 157, 165, 174, 185–86, 187–88, 228, 268, 279, 284, 306, 307–08, 309–10, 314, 320, 323*
  original site, *87–90*
  parking in, *7–8*
  parks in, *115–16, 118, 136, 181–82, 221–22, 244–45, 249–50, 257–75*
  prostitution in, *91, 96–97, 111*
  public art in, *65–66, 70, 119–21, 272–73*
  public transit, *4, 8–13, 46, 80, 106–08, 135–36, 150–52, 173–74, 195, 214, 230, 242, 258, 277–78*
  racism in, *86, 92, 93, 198, 199*
  rent control in, *51*
  restaurants, *21–22, 28, 46–48, 80, 108, 136, 152, 174, 195, 214–15, 230, 242*
  shipping in, *65–66, 123, 124–25, 128–29*
  skyscraper sampler, *70–76*
  social status in, *175–76*
  statistics, *xi*
  tipping in, *5*
  tourism in, *124, 125*
  urban renewal in, *69, 88, 199–200*
  Victorian city, *48–49, 91, 174, 175–76, 178, 180, 202–03, 206–07*
  Vietnamese migration to, *86*
  views of, *2, 68, 94, 102, 119, 129, 135, 139, 154–56, 191, 238, 249–50, 270, 275, 288*
  during World War II, *132–33, 282*
Sang Wo Company building, *90*
San Jose Road, *225*
San Mateo Peninsula, *311–15*
Sansei, *196*
Santa Cruz, CA, *315–16*
  mission, *315*
Sather Gate, *309*
Sather Tower, *309*
Sausalito, CA, *296–97*
Sausalito City Hall, *297*
Sausalito ferry, *8*
Sausalito Inn, *297*
Sausalito Land & Ferry co., *296*
Sausalito Yacht Harbor, *297*
Save-the-Redwoods League, *191, 327*

338

Savoy-Tivoli, *108*
Sawyer, Tom, *60*
Scheuer Linens, *30*
Scheuer, Suzanne, *120*
Schmidt, Peter R., *185*
School of the Sacred Heart, *190–91*
Schrader Street
    —1890, *255*
Scoma's Fisherman's Wharf, *108*
Scotch House—Sweaters from Scotland, Ltd., *30*
Scott's Seafood Grill & Bar, *125*
Sea Cliff, *289*
Seal Rocks, *273*
Searles, Edward, *148, 157*
Second Church of Christ, Scientist, *222*
Security Pacific Bank, *66*
Sequoias, The, *210*
Serra, Father Junípero, *317, 326*
Seventeen-Mile Drive, *324*
Seventeenth Street
    —3639–41, *221*
S. F. B. Morse Botanical Reserve, *324*
Shaklee Terraces, *72*
Sharon Building, *75*
Shell Building, *72*
Sheply, Rutan and Coolidge, *312*
Sheraton-Palace Hotel, *75*
Sherman, William Tecumseh, *54, 56*
Shin issei, 196
Ships
    Gold Rush, *123*
    historic, *128–29*
    Navy, *125–26*
Shorenstein, Walter H., *67*
Showplace Square, *54*
Shrader, A. J., *245*
Shrader Street
    —510, *256*
Shreve & Co., *29*
Shreve Building, *32*
Sierra Club, *71*
Silicon Valley, *311, 312*
Silverado Museum, *306*
Silverado Trail, *307*
Silver barons, *152–54, 160–61*
Sing Chong Building, *103*
Sing Fat Building, *103*
Six Sixty Center, *43*
Sixteenth Street, *218*
Skalli-Atkinson Vineyards and Winery, *305*
Skidmore, Owings and Merrill, *50, 60, 64, 66, 67, 69, 71, 72, 74–75, 102*
Skyscrapers, *49–50, 70–76*
"Sky Tree," *69*
Slesinger, Bruce, *43*
Slim's Nightclub, *22*
Sloss, Louis, *187*
Smith, Andrew *See* Hallidie, Andrew Smith
Soccer Field, *271*

Society for the Improvement and Adornment of SF, *49*
Society of California Pioneers, *24*
    Museum, *29–30*
Soko Hardware, *208*
Sokoji Zen Temple, *203*
Solari Building East, *56*
Solari Building West, *56*
Soma Caffe, *22*
Soo Yuen Benevolent Association, *100*
Sotomayor, Antonio, *167*
Soto Shu Zen sect, *203*
Soto Zen Mission Sokoji, *204*
Southern Pacific Railroad, *164*
    headquarters, *154*
South of Market, *42–43, 73, 75, 197*
Southside, *22*
Speas, Harry E., *296*
Spencer House Bed and Breakfast Inn, *247–49*
Spiritualists, *185*
Spofford Street
    —33, *94*
    —36, *93*
Spreckels, Adolph Bernard, *182, 183, 271, 290*
Spreckels, Claus, *182, 250, 267*
Spreckels Lake, *271*
Spreckels Mansion, *182–83*
Spreckels, Richard, *250*
Spring Valley Water Company, *36, 136, 190, 272, 315*
S.S. *Jeremiah O'Brien, 132–33*
Stackpole, Ralph, *110, 120, 121*
Stained-glass windows, Grace Cathedral, *167*
Standard Oil of California, *71*
Stanford Court Hotel, *156–57*
Stanford, Leland, *92, 152, 154, 156–57, 266*
Stanford, Leland Jr., *157, 312, 312–13*
Stanford Mansion, *156–57*
Stanford Mausoleum, *314*
Stanford University, *156–57, 312–15*
    Museum, *23, 157*
Stanyan, Charles H., *207, 245*
Stanyan House, *207*
Stanyan Park Hotel, *245*
"Star Figure," *73*
Starlight Roof, *29*
Star Magic, *230*
Star of Alaska, 129
STBS, *29*
Steepest paved street, *147*
Steinbeck, John, *322*
Stephen Wirtz Gallery, *31*
Stern, David, *124*
Stevenson, Robert Louis, *88, 153, 306, 307, 321*
St. Francis of Assisi Roman Catholic Church, *115*
St. Francis Square, *210*
St. Francis Xavier Roman Catholic Mission for the Japanese, *202*

St. Helena, CA, *305–06*
Stick style, *180*
St. John's Lutheran Church, *226*
St. Luke's Episcopal Church, *178*
St. Mary's Cathedral, *195, 199, 210–11*
St. Mary's Church and Rectory, Old, *102, 115*
St. Mary's Square, *102*
Stockton Street, *94–96, 116*
    Tunnel, *96, 104*
Stone, The, *113*
Stow Lake, *269–70*
Stow, W. W., *269*
Strauss, Joseph P., *287–88*
Strauss, Levi, *124*
Strawberry Hill, *269–70*
Street lamps
    Grant Avenue, *90*
    Market Street, *73*
"Streetlight," *206*
St. Regis Apartments, *184*
Strybing Arboretum and Botanical Gardens, *269*
Strybing, Helen, *269*
Sts. Peter and Paul Roman Catholic Church, *116*
Stuart Hall for Boys, *190–91*
Stud, *22*
Studio 24, *215, 228*
Subtreasury, *60–61*
Sue, Ed, *87, 90, 94*
Sue Hing Benevolent Association, *98*
Sullivan, John, *102*
"Summer of Love," *246–47*
Summit Apartments, *142–43*
Sun On Company, *84*
Sun Yat-Sen, *93, 95*
    statue of, *102*
SuperShuttle, *6*
Sutro, Adolph, *231, 251, 273–74*
Sutro Baths, *274, 290*
Sutro Heights Park, *274*
Sutro Library, *24, 274*
Sutro Tower, *268*
Sutro Tunnel, *274*
Sutter Street, *33–36*
    —1825, *206*
Swaine Adeney Brigg and Sons, Ltd., *29*
Swain, Edward R., *187, 262*
Swan Oyster Bar, *152*
Swig, Benjamin H., *162*
Sze Yup Association, *84, 101*

Tadich Grill, *46, 64–65*
Taft, William Howard, *270*
Tai Chong Company Building, *103*
Tales of the City, 143
Taliesin Associated Architects, *299*
Taniguchi, Yoshiro, *208*
Tao House, *2, 311*
Tarantino's Restaurant, *108*
Tassajara Bakery and Café, *242*

339

Tassajara Bread Bakery, *133*
Taste of Honey, A, *230*
Tattoo Art Museum, *24*
Taxi Café, *22*
Taxis, *7*
Taylor Street, *167–68*
  —1124–32, *168*
  —1135–41, *168*
  —1153–57, *168*
  —1234, *168*
  —1255–57, *168*
  —1629, *146*
Telecommunication Museum, *76*
Telegraph Hill, *109, 110, 111,*
  116–24
Telegraph Hill Dwellers
  Association Clinic, Old, *116–17*
Temples
  Chinatown, *78, 87, 90, 94,*
    98–99, 101
  Emanu-El, Waller Street
    Masonic Memorial, *165*
  Japantown, *200, 203–04*
Terman, Frederick, *312*
Tessie Wall's Townhouse, *40*
Tetlow, Robert, *269*
Tharp, Newton J., *33, 139*
Theater Artaud, *215*
Theater of Yugen, *195*
Theater on the Square, *40*
Theater Rhinoceros, *215*
Theaters
  alternative, *195, 215*
  downtown, *39, 40*
Therien & Co., Inc., *31*
Thomas Brothers Maps, *4*
"Three Districts" Company, *84*
Tiburon ferry, *8*
Ticketron, *29*
Tickets, theater, *29*
Tiffany & Co., *29*
Tin How Temple, *78, 98*
Tipping, *5*
Tobacco stores, *30*
Tokyo Sukiyaki, *108*
Tongs, Chinatown, *81–86, 94, 95*
Topaz Relocation Center, *198,*
  200
Topless craze, *113*
Top of the Mark, *152*
Tor House, *327*
Touch Stone, *243*
Towaway zones, *8*
Tower Records, *135*
Traction Railway Company, *9*
Trader Vic's, *28*
Trafficways Plan, *261*
Transamerica Building, Old, *57–*
  58
Transamerica Corporation, *58*
Transamerica Flatiron, *55, 58*
Transamerica Pyramid, *50, 58–60*
  Observation Room, *58*
Transportation
  from airport, *6–7*
  city transit, *4, 8–13, 46, 80,*
    106–08, 135–36, 150–52,

173–74, 195, 214, 230, 242,
  258, 277–78
maps, *2–4, 258*
Tra Vigne, *306*
Treasure Island, *294*
  Museum, *24*
Trefethen Vineyards, *304*
Tresidder Memorial Union, *314*
Trinity Espiscopal Church, *33*
Twain, Mark, *55, 60*
Twenty-first Street
  —3243–45, *225*
  —3690, *238*
Twenty-second Street
  —3122, *226*
  —3126, *226*
  —3144–46, *226*
  —3315, *225*
Twin Peaks, *238*
Twin Peaks Bar, *235*

Uma's Occult Shop, *243*
Union Bank, *64*
Union Ferry Depot, *61*
Union Square, *26–40*
United Nations charter, *162*
United States Mint, *222*
United States v. Wong, 96
Universal Cafe, *97*
University Arboretum, *314*
University Art Museum, *23, 309*
University Club, *156*
University of California, Berkeley
  308–10
University of California, Santa
  Cruz, *316*
University Press Books, *310*
U.S. Army, *132, 279–87*
  magazine, *286*
U.S. Army Corps of Engineers,
  60, 280, 281, 284, 286
U.S. Army Presidio Museum, *284*
U.S. Post Office, Chinatown, *94*
U.S.S. *Pampanito, 125–26*
U.S.S. *Portsmouth, 88*

Valencia Street, *223–24*
Valencia, Cand'llo, *218*
Vallejo Street
  improvements, *143*
  —1071, *146*
  —1085, *143*
Van Bourg/Nakamura &
  Associates, *203–04, 205, 207–08*
Vanessi's, *152*
Van Heusen Outlet, *43*
Van Ness Avenue, *177–78*
  —901, *177*
  —1000, *177*
Vaux, Calvert, *308*
Venetian Room, *152, 162*
Vesuvio Cafe, *110, 113*
Veteran's Cab, *7*
Victorian Park, *130*
Victoria Pastry, *114*

Victor's Daughter's Restaurant,
  152
Vidar, Frede, *120*
Vienna Coffee House, *152*
Village Deli Cafe, *230*
Ville Contemporain, *71*
Ville Radieuse, *71*
Vintage 1870, *304*
Viña del Mar Plaza, Sausalito, *297*
Vioget, Jean Jacques, *87–88*
Visitor Information Center, *2*
Vizcaíno, Sebastián, *300, 317*
Vollmer House, *206–07*
Volstead Act of 1919, *303*

Walker and Moody, *127–28, 189*
Walks
  Chinatown, *78–80*
  Heritage, *185*

  —1301–03, *251*
  —1307–09, *251*
  —1315–35, *251*
Wall, Tessie, *40*
Wapama, 129
Warfield Theater, *40*
Warnecke, John Carl, *50, 88, 73,*
  316
Warren, Earl, *198*
Washington Montgomery Tower,
  54
Washington Square, *115–16*
  —2000, *184*
  —2006, *183–84*
  —2100, *183*
  —2108, *183*
  —2120, *183*
  —733, *90*
  —737–39, *90*
Washington Tower, *183*
Waverly Place, *96–100*
  —151–55, *97*
Wax Museum, *24*
Webster Street
  —1717–19, *206*
Weeks and Day, *157, 165, 177*
Weeks, Charles Peter, *183*
Wells Fargo Bank, *62, 186–87*
  History Room, *61–62*
Wells, Henry, *62*
Western Addition, *182, 195, 197–*
  200, 207–08, 246
  YWCA, *205*
West German consulate, *186*
Whaler's Cove, *296*
Whale-watching, *300*
Whisler-Patri, *38*
Whittier Mansion, *174*
  Museum, *187–88*
Whittier, William Frank, *187*
Whittlemore, J. B., *284*
Wilhemina Tulip Garden, *271–72*
William Pereira and Associates,
  36, 58, 73
William Stout's Architectural
  Books, *54, 56*
Williams, Dora Norton, *144*

Williams-Polk House, *144–46*
Williams-Sonoma, *30*
Williams, Virgil, *144*
Wine country, *300–07*
Wineries, *See* Wine country
Wok Shop, The, *100*
Women's Building, *215, 224*
Wong Family Benevolent
    Association, *99*
Wong Gow Building, *97*
Woodruff, Glenn B., *154*
Worcester, Rev. Joseph, *137*
Works Progress Administration
    (WPA), *102, 119–21, 286*
Wormser-Coleman House, *180*
Wormser, Isaac, *180*
Wright, Clifford, *119–20*
Wright, Frank Lloyd, *37, 299, 314*
Wurster, Bernardi and Emmons,
    66, 67, 131, 189

Yamasaki, Minoru, *208*
Yamato, *195*
Yan Wo Company, *84*
Yee Fung Toy Family Association,
    97–98
Yellin, Samuel, *167*
Yellow Cab, *7*
Yeon Building, *56*
Yerba Buena, *243*
Yerba Buena Books, *31*
Yerba Buena Cemetery, *289–90*
Yerba Buena Cove, *54, 87, 100,
    218, 296*
Yick Keung Benevolent
    Association, *97*
Ying On Merchant and Labor
    Association, *100*
YMCA, Chinatown, *100*
Yokohama Specie Bank, *64, 197*
Yonsei, 196
York Movie Theater, *215*
Yoshida-Ya, *195*
Young China Daily, 95
Young Wo Company, *84, 85*
Yount, George Calvert, *304*
Yountville, CA, *304–05*
Yung, Nicholas, *153, 167*

Zakheim, Bernard B., *119, 120*
Zanolini, Italo, *57–58, 114*
Zúniga, Gaspar, *317*